X-Wing Collector's CD-ROM:

The Official Strategy Guide

Now Available from Prima

Computer Game Books

The 7th Guest: The Official Strategy Guide
Aces Over Europe: The Official Strategy Guide
Alone in the Dark: The Official Strategy Guide
Betrayal at Krondor: The Official Strategy Guide
CD-ROM Games Secrets, Volume 1
Computer Adventure Games Secrets
DOOM Battlebook
DOOM II: The Official Strategy Guide
Dracula Unleashed: The Official Strategy Guide & Novel
Front Page Sports Baseball '94: The Official Playbook
Harpoon II: The Official Strategy Guide
Lemmings: The Official Companion (with disk)
Lode Runner: The Legend Returns - The Official Guide to the Evil Empire
Master of Orion: The Official Strategy Guide
Microsoft Flight Simulator: The Official Strategy Guide
Microsoft Space Simulator: The Official Strategy Guide
Might and Magic Compendium: The Authorized Strategy Guide for Games I, II, III, and IV
Myst: The Official Strategy Guide
Outpost: The Official Strategy Guide
Pagan: Ultima VIII—The Ultimate Strategy Guide
Prince of Persia: The Official Strategy Guide
Quest for Glory: The Authorized Strategy Guide
Rebel Assault: The Official Insider's Guide
Return to Zork Adventurer's Guide
Shadow of the Comet: The Official Strategy Guide
Sherlock Holmes, Consulting Detective: The Unauthorized Strategy Guide
Sid Meier's Civilization, or Rome on 640K a Day
SimCity 2000: Power, Politics, and Planning
SimEarth: The Official Strategy Guide
SimFarm Almanac: The Official Guide to SimFarm
SimLife: The Official Strategy Guide
SSN-21 Seawolf: The Official Strategy Guide
Strike Commander: The Official Strategy Guide and Flight School
Stunt Island: The Official Strategy Guide
SubWar 2050: The Official Strategy Guide (with disk)
TIE Fighter: The Official Strategy Guide
Ultima: The Avatar Adventures
Ultima VII and Underworld: More Avatar Adventures
Under a Killing Moon: The Official Strategy Guide
Wing Commander I and II: The Ultimate Strategy Guide
X-COM UFO Defense: The Official Strategy Guide

How to Order:
Individual orders and quantity discounts are available from the publisher, Prima Publishing, P.O. Box 1260BK, Rocklin, CA 95677-1260; (916) 632-4400. For quantity orders, include information on your letterhead concerning the intended use of the books and the number of books you wish to purchase.

X-Wing Collector's CD-ROM:

The Official Strategy Guide

Rusel DeMaria

David Wessman, David Maxwell

Prima Publishing
P.O. Box 1260BK
Rocklin, CA 95677
(916) 632-4400

Secrets of the Games is a trademark of Prima Publishing, a Division of Prima Communications, Inc., Rocklin, California 95677. Prima and Prima Publishing are trademarks of Prima Communications, Inc.

Copyright © 1995 by Lucasfilm Ltd. All rights reserved. No part of this book may be reproduced or transmitted in any form or by any means, electronic or mechanical, including photocopying, recording, or by any information storage or retrieval system without written permission from Prima Publishing, except for the inclusion of brief quotations in a review.

Star Wars, is a registered trademark of Lucasfilm Ltd. All rights reserved. Used under authorization. X-Wing Collector's CD-ROM is the ™ and © 1994 LucasArts Entertainment Company. LucasArts is a trademark of LucasArts Entertainment Company. All other products and characters mentioned in this book are trademarks of their respective companies.

Publisher: Roger Stewart
Managing Editor: Paula Munier Lee
Senior Acquisitions Editor: Hartley Lesser
Project Editor: Kip Ward
Creative Director, Secrets of the Games: Rusel DeMaria
Cover Production Coordinator: Anne Flemke
Copyeditor: Becky Whitney, Rick Barba
Book Design: Rusel DeMaria
Layouts: Marian Hartsough Associates, Rusel DeMaria, Shawn Morningstar
Adaptation to Cover: Dunlavey Studio

Important:
Prima Publishing, Inc., has made every effort to determine that the information contained in this book is accurate. However, the publisher makes no warranty, either express or implied, as to the accuracy, effectiveness, or completeness of the material in this book; nor does the publisher assume liability for damages, either incidental or consequential, that may result from using the information in this book. The publisher cannot provide information regarding game play, hints and strategies, or problems with hardware or software. Questions should be directed to the support numbers provided by the game and device manufacturers in their documentation. Some game tricks require precise timing and may require repeated attempts before the desired result is achieved.

ISBN: 1-55958-785-7
Library of Congress Card Number: 94-069108
Printed in the United States of America
95 96 97 98 BRG 10 9 8 7 6 5 4 3 2 1

Contents

PART IV ORIGINAL TOURS OF DUTY 149

PART V X-WING CD MISSIONS 319

Acknowledgments

I have a lot of people to thank and acknowledge, and not much space to do it in.

First, I have to thank Larry Holland. Larry got me involved in writing *The Farlander Papers*, which led directly to my writing this book. I also want to thank Larry for the years of dedication he's put into providing us all with such great products.

Next, I have to thank the two Daves—"Wotan" and "Max." In fact, this book was largely written by them. As lead testers and mission builders for X-Wing, David Maxwell and David Wessman were in a perfect position to help produce this book quickly and accurately. They devised almost all of the strategies, and wrote the mission strategies and the general strategies and tactics. You'll see some of "Wotan's" military studies coming out in the Situational Awareness sections.

"Max" and "Wotan" also took most of the screen images. They deserve as much credit as I can give them, not only for helping design such a great game, but for their efforts beyond the call of duty to make this the best strategy book possible.

I also want to thank Ed Kilham for his graciousness under fire, and "Bucky" for helping us get the 3D images you see throughout this book.

Thanks to Mary Bihr at LucasArts for her friendship and help in getting this project (and several others) underway, and for her constant availability to handle crises of all kinds. Thanks also to Lucy Wilson for helping get this project moving.

And then there's Kalani Streicher and Khris Brown, whom I'd like to thank for their help in securing various materials, and Sean Casey and Kerry Nordquist at ILM for their help in getting certain obscure images.

Closer to home, I want to thank Ocean Quigley for his constant enthusiasm for *Star Wars* imagery, as well as his unexpected skills as a starfighter pilot. Ocean always creates fantastic artwork for my books, but this time he also destroyed the Death Star several times, and helped save the Alliance and preserve freedom everywhere.

Thanks also to Jeronimo Barrera for taking other duties off my shoulders and for getting that "Nice shot!" message a lot; Marian Hartsough for helping me get this thing laid out; and to Prima Publishing, for the support that made this book possible.

Also, thanks to West End Books for their wonderful series of *Star Wars* guides. To keep consistent, we often referred to them.

Finally, thanks to George Lucas for *Star Wars*, and Theodore Sturgeon, my Obi-Wan.

Introduction

The Farlander Papers was a small, limited edition book/manual I wrote for LucasArts to include in the X-Wing game package. You'll find most (but not all) of that book between these pages as well. Why? Because The Farlander Papers is a collector's edition, but we all felt that the information contained in that book is a necessary part of the X-Wing experience. If you already have The Farlander Papers, don't worry. You haven't wasted your money with this book. There's a lot more in here that we believe you'll find very valuable (see the Road Map on the following page).

X-Wing Collector's CD-ROM: The Official Strategy Guide is divided into discrete parts. Some of the book is just a story tying together the missions and X-Wing experience through the eyes of Keyan Farlander, a recent Alliance recruit. I've made every attempt to create an entertaining and (mostly) consistent story for your enjoyment. However, it should not be necessary to read any of the story elements to gain mastery of the game. All the important strategy information is given in clearly differentiated pages of the book. Story elements begin with the following icon (except at the beginnings of chapters):

You can skip these sections if you want. Mission descriptions always start like this:

OP 1: DESTROY IMPERIAL CONVOY

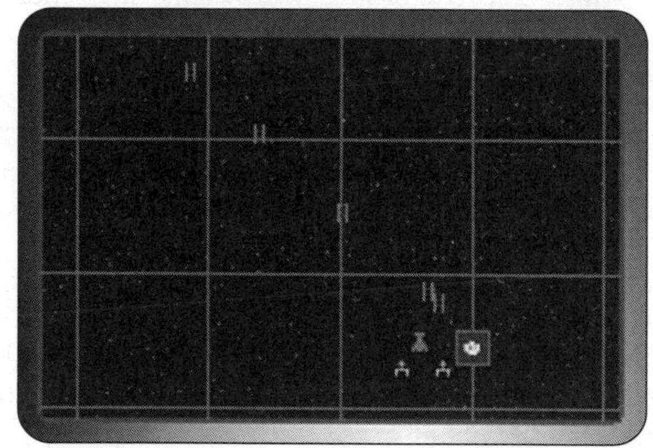

The text in the mission strategy sections also looks different. To find the page number for each mission strategy, look in the table of contents.

You may discover some discrepancies in the fiction. In some cases, it is difficult to organize all the information you will want to know and keep the timeline of the fiction intact. For instance, in the *Starfighter Pilot's Handbook*, the TIE Advanced fighter is described, even though Keyan is reading this document before the appearance of the TIE Advanced (or its prototype, at any rate) during the Battle of Yavin. We don't mention the B-wing or the Interdictor there, but both spacecraft appear in the technical section (Appendix C).

Even more important, some of the information about the game simply doesn't fit into the fiction at all. This applies especially to the **Mission Notes** which give you information you could not possibly have when flying the mission in the "real" world (galaxy). I've included this information in special shaded areas at the end of the mission, when applicable.

Road Map

- **Part One** of this book is nice if you want some background on the *Star Wars* fiction and storyline. It is essentially reprinted from the Farlander Papers.
- **Part Two** is loaded with strategies and tactics. The Starfighter Pilot's Handbook has been expanded significantly, and you'll find a lot of very useful information here.
- **Part Three** provides specific strategies for each historical mission.
- **Part Four** provides specific strategies for the original tour of duty missions.
- **Part Five** provides specific strategies for tours four and five, as well as bonus and B-wing historical missions.
- **Appendix A** covers the scoring system used in the game. You'll find that very interesting. It also deals a little with enemy artificial intelligence.
- **Appendix B** is a brief guide to using the Film Room (or as Keyan calls it, the Holo Film Room).
- **Appendix C** is an expanded version of the Imperial technical document Keyan recovers in his historical mission (X-wing #6). We've added the TIE Advanced, the B-wing Starfighter, and the Interdictor Cruiser to these pages.
- **Appendix D** is a good one. It contains pages and pages of mission statistics gleaned directly from the X-wing developers. You'll find the information in this section fascinating.
- **Appendix E** contains brief biographies, and an interview with Larry Holland and Ed Kilham.

One thing nobody can do is make somebody else a better pilot, of course. You'll need a steady hand and a lot of concentration to get though some of these missions, even with this strategy guide. I wish you lots of good luck, and happy spacing.

Foreword

In 1977, the movie *Star Wars: A New Hope* appeared in cinemas around the world, and a new phenomenon was born. With its masterful blend of classic storytelling, unforgettable characters and revolutionary special effects, the *Star Wars* movie trilogy left a permanent impact on its audience. The vivid images of the space battles, the resonating sounds of Darth Vader's ominous breathing . . . the fierce roar of a TIE fighter's attack, all combined to create an experience that few of us have forgotten.

The great (and unanticipated) achievement of the *Star Wars* movies is that they created a completely captivating, richly detailed and believable fantasy world; a world of characters, places and futuristic technology that has transcended the original films. I think the most powerful reason for claiming the *Star Wars* trilogy a classic of American film, and of storytelling, is the ease with which its world has continued to find new expression in novels, comic books, and computer games. What a rich world George Lucas gave us!

The computer entertainment industry has often looked to films for inspiration, and to the *Star Wars* trilogy in particular. The creating of "interactive movies" that combine compelling storytelling with a powerful and intense visual experience has long been the holy grail of computer game software. A year ago, we realized that home computers had become sufficiently powerful to allow an experience that would do justice to George Lucas' *Star Wars* vision, and, more importantly, to the indelible impression it had left in all of us. So X-Wing was born, an ode to all those moviegoers, who like ourselves, longed to jump into the cockpit of an X-wing and take up the fight of the Rebel Alliance.

Rusel DeMaria was part of the X-Wing project from the earliest days as author of *The Farlander Papers*. In that book, he introduced Keyan Farlander and told the exciting story of his initial mission as a Rebel starfighter pilot. With this latest book, he has provided a detailed strategy guide while continuing to contribute to the ever-growing pool of exciting *Star Wars*-based fiction.

Rusel's work has great value for two reasons: First, he has added a rich installment to the *Star Wars* lore by creating new insights into the workings of the Rebel Alliance, building a wonderful foundation for understanding the life of a Rebel pilot. Second, he has built a powerful and thorough resource for game players wishing to improve their skills as X-Wing starfighter pilots and understand more about the game itself. *X-Wing Collector's CD-ROM: The Official Strategy Guide* is a wonderfully organized reference book of practical strategies for mission success, filled with extras like Ocean Quigley's action-packed 3D graphics, as well as delightful tidbits of information about the game and the *Star Wars* universe. Rusel has admirably carried on the *Star Wars* legacy and provided a "must-have" book for all *Star Wars* and X-Wing fans.

—Lawrence Holland
Edward Kilham

X-Wing Collector's CD-ROM: The Official Strategy Guide

Part I

PART ONE

KEYAN FARLANDER'S STORY

You have taken your first step into a larger world.

— Obi-Wan Kenobi

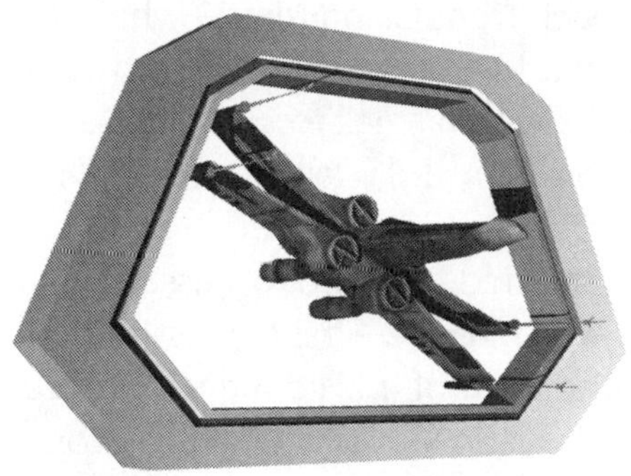

Keyan Farlander's Story

The Sentence

There was no trial, no hope of appeal, just the blaring voice of the Imperial commander reading our sentence:

"People of Tondatha, on the planet of Agamar, in the Lahara sector . . . You have been found guilty of sedition against the Empire, and of plotting against the great Emperor Palpatine. Your punishment will be imposed without delay."

This was followed by the immediate scream of concussion missiles launched from orbit, then explosive detonations that shook the ground with staccato convulsions, and finally the heavy blaster fire, ripping through roofs, burning our families and friends. . . .

I try not to think about the day my town was obliterated—the day everything I believed about humanity and the order of the galaxy was turned upside down. My parents died that day, and I became, at heart, a Rebel.

Were my parents truly Alliance collaborators, and somehow deserving of their fate? Was anybody in our small, backwater town guilty of the crimes we were accused of, and then punished for without mercy? I knew I wasn't. Not yet, anyway.

I was on my way back from Calna Muun, what we used to call the "Big City," on that fateful day. I had just run an errand for my father, and was taking a short detour through a small forest of binka trees. I liked to use the trees as obstacles, pushing my T-16 landspeeder to the limit as I zigzagged through the grove.

From a distance, I spotted the Empire's assault vehicle dropping into the upper atmosphere. It was massive—the biggest thing I'd ever seen in the skies above Agamar—and the sight of it filled me with foreboding. I pushed my 'speeder to the brink of overload, racing towards home.

The Imperial craft seemed to parallel my course, moving slowly but steadily toward Tondatha. My stomach flip-flopped and my head pounded. A visitation by an Imperial assault craft . . . It didn't seem like that could possibly have positive connotations.

I considered myself a loyal subject of the Empire—if any young man on a faraway planet in a distant arm of the galaxy can be said to be loyal. At least I wasn't completely indifferent. In fact, I had never questioned the status quo, simply accepting that the Empire was the Empire. The fact that the Emperor ruled our galaxy had little to do with me or my daily life.

Everything political happened in the Hub—among the dense, populated planetary systems. Here on the Rim, we were farmers, merchants, and craftspeople. Rarely, if ever, did we see a government official, much less receive a visit from Imperial forces.

I remember once, when I was about five or six, a small flotilla of Imperial warships had come to our sector, and a few landing vehicles had flown over Tondotha. I looked at them with awe and wonder, and my friends and I chattered for weeks about becoming pilots for the Imperial Navy, flying off to strange and faraway worlds.

So why was it that I viewed this assault vehicle with such dread?

By the time I arrived at Tondatha, the huge ship was directly overhead. I slewed my 'speeder through the streets toward home. It was unnaturally dark, as the Imperial ship blotted out the sun. Dust kicked up behind me in spreading clouds and small whirlwinds as I pushed my landspeeder past its previously tested limits through the deserted streets.

I arrived at my home in time to hear the sound of the Imperial commander's voice pronouncing sentence, and then the distinctive and unmistakable crackling of heavy blasters, mingled with the deafening concussion of the missiles as they impacted. I burst through my front door, calling out for my parents and my sister.

There was no response, nor was there time for one, as a searing blaster bolt incinerated the kitchen, and the roof of the house collapsed in a storm of heat and debris.

I was thrown to the floor, nearly blinded, coughing as my lungs filled with smoke and dust. I crawled through the rising flames, still calling for my family. Something heavy fell, and I was certain I was dead.

THE AFTERMATH

Three months later, Tondatha still lay in ruins. The death toll had been too high, the destruction too thorough, to attempt rebuilding.

Incredibly, I had survived with only minor burns and a mild concussion. The wounds of my spirit, however, were much deeper than those of the flesh.

Both my parents were dead. My sister, Kitha, had been badly burned, and I had resolved to send her to Oorn Tchis, where we had relatives and where she might receive treatment. I feared that she would never recover.

I stayed behind. I had no idea what I would do on Agamar, but I think even then that I was considering the Rebellion. I needed a new home, but more than that, I needed a focus for what was left of my life.

More than anything else, I craved revenge.

I had already suffered my punishment, now, I reasoned, I would commit the crime.

I moved to Calna Muun, and lived by doing odd jobs. I kept to myself, but I also kept my ears open. Several months passed.

I sought out places where the talk, in Imperial terms, was treasonous. People spoke with conviction of the Rebellion, and, when they heard my story, they accepted me without much hesitation. And though they trusted my sincerity, they also respected my grief, and sensed correctly that I was not yet ready to commit my life to the Alliance.

That was about to change, completely and forever.

One evening, deep in discussion with other friends of the Resistance, the word was passed that the time for decisive action was at hand, and that an important Rebel leader would soon arrive to address the groundswell of Alliance support on Agamar.

Until that time, our clandestine meetings were filled with talk, but often in the abstract. Concepts such as truth, justice, and freedom from tyranny were easy rallying points, but what, we wondered, could Rebels on Agamar do to bring down the mighty Empire? The rhetoric served to keep people interested, but it had grown tiring. Now, perhaps, a time for action was finally at hand.

Somehow I knew that this was what I had been waiting for.

THE GATHERING

The old warehouse was buzzing with low, nervous voices. Each of us had been assigned different arrival times, and small groups of Resistance members had been entering the meeting place for about an hour. As I watched the room fill to capacity, I could feel the tension rising.

There was good reason for the nervousness. This was a big gathering of Resistance members, and would therefore be a perfect target for an Imperial surprise attack. Despite the assurances we had been given, the risks involved seemed considerable.

While the crowd waited for the meeting to come to order, I took the opportunity to strike up several brief conversations, learning some interesting bits of information in the process. Speaking in hushed tones, I discovered:

- That the Old Republic was indeed a democratic union of worlds, governed by a duly elected Senate, and that it represented the needs of all beings, regardless of their race, species or home sector.
- That Emperor Palpatine was a Senator himself, before seizing power and beginning a tyrannical rule. Under Palpatine, much personal freedom had been subjugated, and all but a small faction of dissent crushed.
- That currently the Empire was in the process of enslaving or destroying all the nonhuman races.
- And that, despite the seemingly invincible might of the Empire, many in the audience held out hope for the Rebel Alliance.

The background noise evaporated abruptly as a woman stepped onto the makeshift dais at the front of the room. I heard whispers of "Mon Mothma," and I realized that this was the founder of the Alliance herself. The entire room tensed in preparation for her first words. A few scattered whispers were the only sounds.

Mon Mothma's Speech

Mon Mothma wasted no time. Her voice rang out, filling the small warehouse.

"Beings of the galaxy unite!" she cried. "Together, we will shed the yoke of Imperial oppression!"

Now, even the whispers stopped, and when she continued, Mon Mothma's voice was softer, almost conversational.

"Thank you all for coming tonight, at the risk of your own safety. I wish that I felt truly free to enjoy the beautiful planet of Agamar.

"First, I want you to know that this area has been blanketed by our forces. Our battle cruiser orbits above us, and picket droids have been deployed along the perimeter. There is no chance of the Imperials surprising us. For the moment, we are safe to speak the truth.

"I have come here tonight, my friends, to tell you more than you might wish to know about the greatest threat our galaxy has ever faced.

"There is hope for our survival, but only if we stand together. And it is crucial not only that the Rebellion gains your support, but also that you understand why you should fight for the Alliance.

"The Empire has been built on the basest of human emotions and motivations. Greed! Corruption! Deceit! Oppression! And hate! These are the forces that drive the Empire towards its sinister goals."

As she spoke, the Alliance leader's voice grew more forceful with each successive indictment, until finally she paused. When she continued, her speech was more controlled, but just as penetrating: The voice of a storyteller, filled with the conviction of truth.

Behind her, brutal images of Imperial oppression occasionally appeared on a simple flat screen, and all who heard Mon Mothma's words found themselves transported back to another time. A time far, far away, but not so long ago. . . .

A History of the Empire

"It wasn't always this way. The galaxy knew peace following the Clone Wars. Guided by the Jedi Knights and the government of the Republic, a war-weary citizenry rebuilt lives and restored worlds. The central authority of the Republic insisted on freedom for all, and prosperity naturally followed.

"But the galaxy is vast, and with a thousand thousand worlds to govern, a handful of greedy Senators found that they could abuse their power. At first, this abuse manifested itself in small ways, but it grew steadily and insidiously.

"Slowly, corruption infected the Republic.

"More and more Senators, seduced by power and wealth, allied themselves with special interests. Many worlds suffered, and eventually the Republic began to crumble.

"Into this situation came a young Senator named Palpatine. Now, he is called 'Emperor,' but I remember him as a very ordinary man.

"Even then, he was surely devising the cruel master plan that would lead to his ascension, though at the time he did nothing that would have attracted attention. Palpatine waited, and plotted, and when the proper time came, when the Republic was most vulnerable, he carried out his plan to perfection.

"The authority of the Senate had weakened at an alarming pace. Crime was on the increase across the galaxy, and many worlds threatened to secede. Other planets simply did as they wished while pretending loyalty.

"A solution was needed, and that is what Palpatine offered. Through a combination of political maneuvering, half-truths masquerading as promises, and sometimes out-and-out fraud, Palpatine got himself elected head of the Senatorial Council: President of the Republic.

"Many of the most honest and ethical Senators backed Palpatine for President because he promised unity, and he had carefully concealed his own corruption. At the same time, the worst members of the Senate expected a weak, controllable President; a figurehead that would represent justice to the populace even as the Senators continued to serve their own self-interests.

"I was senior Senator during Palpatine's rise to power, and though it was obvious to myself and a handful of others that a monster was about to be unleashed, the voices of dissent were drowned out by those who sought a quick solution to a galaxy of problems.

"Still, no one could have guessed at the transformation that would take place following the election. With the power of the Presidency secured, Palpatine suddenly emerged as a dynamic and increasingly ruthless leader, often playing Senators against one another on crucial issues, bogging the government down in bouts of petty bickering.

"Little by little, Palpatine assumed complete control, as the Senate consumed itself in increasingly bitter inner rivalries.

"Once the reins of power were firmly in his grasp, and he was entirely confident of success, Palpatine declared himself Emperor. He announced a New Order, and filled the Senators' heads with grand rhetoric, promising to lead the Republic into a glorious golden age, akin to the Kitel Phard Dynasty of old.

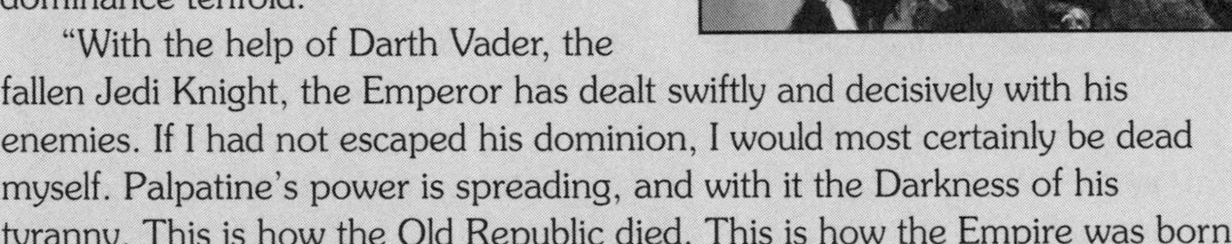

"It is Palpatine's New Order that now crushes your freedom with an iron fist.

"Some tried to defy him, but to no avail. We are now fugitives, and Palpatine has allied himself with the dark side of the Force, increasing his dominance tenfold.

"With the help of Darth Vader, the fallen Jedi Knight, the Emperor has dealt swiftly and decisively with his enemies. If I had not escaped his dominion, I would most certainly be dead myself. Palpatine's power is spreading, and with it the Darkness of his tyranny. This is how the Old Republic died. This is how the Empire was born.

THE RESISTANCE GROWS

"As I mentioned, before the Emperor disbanded the Senate, some of us had dared to take an active role against him. Chief among my allies was Senator Bail Organa of Alderaan, and, though we seldom agreed on the Senate floor, we both came to understand the danger inherent in Palpatine's rise to power.

"Even as Senator Palpatine outmaneuvered and defrauded the Senate, Bail Organa and I plotted secretly, meeting repeatedly at Chatham House, Organa's home in Imperial City.

"At first, Organa had resisted my call for a general revolution, horrified at the thought of abandoning the government to which he had devoted much of his life. Then came the massacre at Ghorman, a small planet in the Sern sector, just outside the Hub Worlds.

"Following the incident at Ghorman, Bail Organa agreed to assist in the diversion of weapons and funds to the growing Resistance effort. Perhaps even more importantly, Organa helped the Rebel Alliance gain classified information that was integral to our early survival.

"In fact, when I was eventually discovered as a Rebel leader, well-placed operatives allowed me to flee the capital only moments before I would have been apprehended.

"The stated goal of the Rebellion has been to create an Alliance of planets, as was first accomplished in the Corellian System. Under the guidelines discussed during the Chatham House meetings, the three major Corellian Resistance groups were convinced to join together. Under a system of centralized leadership, the Corellians enjoyed the benefits of increased communication, and greater access to much needed funds, supplies and weaponry.

"The Corellian Treaty was the true beginning of the Alliance, and remains a shining example that there is enough strength in Rebel unity to combat even the Empire.

"Since the signing of the Corellian Treaty, I have traveled from world to world, and been welcomed by beings of conscience, independent thinkers, and victims of Imperial atrocities. They have joined the Alliance, as I hope you good beings will also join. I have come as a messenger of hope, offering fellowship in a growing galactic movement.

It was then that B'ante Hatcher, the leader of the Resistance on Agamar, stepped forward, and addressed Mon Mothma with mock skepticism.

"But what does the Alliance have to offer us?" said Hatcher, doing his best to affect a whining lament. "Why should we join you?"

A nervous buzz swept across the crowd, but Mon Mothma hardly seemed caught off guard. As the chatter subsided, she continued her address.

"That's a fair question," Mon Mothma replied. "I'm glad you asked."

"Let's suppose that Imperial warships were headed for your planet, intent on causing complete destruction. You have perhaps a dozen obsolete Headhunter starfighters, and maybe five of them are battleworthy. Furthermore, you wouldn't even know that the Imperial ships were on their way until they opened fire, because you have no tactical communication outside of Imperial channels.

"But suppose that Agamar were linked to a sector-wide network, with surveillance droids watching the Imperial fleet, and secret communiqués from Allied worlds able to warn you well in advance of any threat. Neighboring

systems would also be part of the network, ready to assist in your defense with men, weapons and starfighters.

"The benefits are obvious. How many lives might have been saved at Tondotha with advance warning?

"The Alliance offers experienced leadership, coordination of information, and logistical support for every world that truly desires freedom.

"And you needn't worry about trading one Empire for another. I am the Alliance Chief of State, and Supreme Commander of the Rebel Forces, but, unlike the Emperor, my job is temporary. Every two years, the Advisory Council calls a vote, and at any time they can replace the Chief of State. And, as soon as the Emperor is deposed, all the worlds in the Alliance will participate in forming a New Republic, and organizing a new governing body.

"Let me read to you an excerpt from our formal Declaration of Rebellion, which was addressed directly to the Emperor himself.

"'We, the Rebel Alliance, in the name of and under authority from the free beings of the galaxy, solemnly declare our intentions:

- We will fight and oppose the Empire and its forces, by any and all means at our disposal.
- We will refuse to enforce any Imperial law deemed contrary to the rights of free beings.
- The Rebellion will continue until such time as the Emperor is dead, and the Empire dismantled and destroyed.'

"I have pledged my life to this cause, and I implore you to do the same.

"Also consider, for a moment, what I call the Empire's Great Lie. Palpatine has continued the pretense that he will end social injustice and corruption, but his true goal has always been the subjugation of worlds and the enslavement of citizens. He rules by fear, rather than by consent. He preaches that all beings are equal, even while he conducts ruthless campaigns of genocide.

"The Empire seems unstoppable. Often has that been said. But hear the words of Palpatine's own Grand Moff Tarkin, and consider them well:

> "'Even the excellent pace with which Your Majesty is strengthening his fleets cannot provide security for the Empire, should a significant number of planets begin to defy your will,' noted Tarkin recently. 'We are many years away from a force vast enough to secure every system simultaneously.
>
> "'I would advise His Majesty to rule through the *fear* of force, rather than through force itself. If we use our strength wisely, we shall cow thousands of worlds which might otherwise consider rebellion.'"

Mon Mothma paused, allowing the words of Grand Moff Tarkin to be thought upon deeply before concluding her speech.

"Friends, the Empire is evil, guided by an evil creature in alliance with the dark side of the Force. You *must* find the courage within yourself to resist.

"They cannot subdue us all! They have admitted it! Only fear keeps them in power, and if we act now, together, we can cast off their oppression, and dispel this horrible Darkness. For the sake of all who cherish freedom, not only *can* the Empire be defeated, it *must* be!

"As we gather here tonight, other beings from all quadrants of the galaxy are rising up against the Empire's injustices, bravely defying the Imperial overlords in a life-or-death struggle. They need your help!

"The Resistance is not insignificant. Moff Tarkin himself has conceded that.

"The Alliance offers the peace and unity that all beings deserve, but this can only be achieved through total Rebellion. Only by working together, by coordinating efforts with other planets and systems, can the will of the Emperor be defied. It is my urgent plea to you who have gathered here tonight: Join the growing Rebel Alliance. Separate, we shall fail, but together, we shall prevail!"

Afterward

The speech and the subsequent cheering were long since over, and most of the Agamar locals had departed. There had been some additional discussion of Mon Mothma's proposal, and it seemed almost certain that the Agamar Resistance would join the Alliance. Regardless, I had already made *my* decision.

As I stood listening to the others talk, a pretty young woman approached me. Her smile was dazzling, but her eyes were very serious. She was one of the Alliance team who had accompanied Mon Mothma, and she handed me a small synth-paper pamphlet, saying; "Read this. It will help you understand more."

As she walked away, she turned, and added; "Be sure to return that to me, or destroy it before you leave. To be caught with it by the Imperials means certain, painful death."

I took the small pamphlet, and began to read. . . .

A Call to Reason

In the spirit of galactic peace and cooperation

A Call to Reason

If you care about freedom and your future . . . join the Rebellion! Resist oppression, and help us form a New Republic based on equality and freedom for all beings!

This is your chance. Don't wait. **Do it now!**

In these pages, you will read about our galaxy, learn tolerance, and begin to understand what we fight for. Who are your friends? Who are your enemies? Learn the truth, and then join us!

Your Friends . . . And Foes.

Mon Mothma was once a young and idealistic Senator of the Republic. Hailing from Chandrila, she was practically born into government service. Her father was Arbiter-General of the Republic and her mother was a Governor of Chandrila. Next to Leia Organa, Mon Mothma was the youngest member to serve on the Senate. Despite her age, Mon Mothma rose to the esteemed position of Senior Senator before the abolition of the Senate. Now she is the Chief of State of the Rebel Alliance and works tirelessly to overthrow the Emperor.

Viceroy Bail Organa of Alderaan was one of the heroes of the Clone Wars, fighting alongside the famous general, Obi-Wan Kenobi. When the wars ended, Organa returned to his home planet to lead them into an age of peace and freedom. All weapons were banned on Alderaan. Soon after Palpatine declared himself Emperor, Bail Organa left the Senate and returned to Alderaan. He helped create the Alliance, making Alderaan a center for dissent and resistance. (Photo unavailable.)

Admiral Ackbar was one of the first of the Mon Calamari to be taken as a slave by the Empire. A great leader before his capture, he was instrumental in convincing the Mon Calamari to help the Alliance by providing ships. After his capture, he became the servant of Grand Moff Tarkin, where he was able to learn about the enemy firsthand. Though he had learned of a great secret weapon, he was unable to discover what it was. In a dramatic encounter, Ackbar was rescued when Tarkin's shuttle was attacked by Rebel forces and the Admiral was left behind. Due to his great abilities and his knowledge of the enemy, he was recently named Admiral of the Rebel Fleet.

General Crix Madine was an officer in the Imperial Army with high prospects for advancement. Amid some considerable mystery, Madine defected from the Empire and joined the Alliance. Such a defection would normally have aroused suspicion . . . was he a double agent? But whatever the circumstances, Madine was obviously trustworthy. Among those backing Madine was General Rieekan, one of Mon Mothma's most trusted officers. On his recommendation, Madine was put in charge of the Rebel Army. His knowledge of Imperial strategy and tactics has proved invaluable in planning operations against them. (Photo unavailable.)

Obi-Wan Kenobi was one of the great leaders of the Clone Wars. A Jedi Knight, he dropped out of sight shortly after peace was restored. It is feared that he, like all the other Jedi, has been killed by the Emperor's minion, Darth Vader, or one of his many assassins. Still, hope remains that he, or one like him, will re-emerge to join the fight against evil.

Emperor Palpatine was once an uninspiring bureaucrat who, through deceit and political maneuvering, became first the President of the Republic and later, the Emperor. Little is known about Palpatine. Many suspect that he has great powers in the dark side of the Force, but how he acquired power is completely unknown. He was never trained by any Jedi Knight that we know of, yet much of his success is unexplainable if some larger Force is not taken into account.

Crimes of the Emperor (a partial list)

Emperor Palpatine has:

- disbanded the Senate, stifling any participation by citizens in the government;
- begun a policy of genocide against nonhuman races;
- removed the rightful leaders of planets and systems, placing his own lackeys as Moffs and Governors;
- arbitrarily raised taxes;
- murdered and imprisoned millions without trial or justice;
- stolen land and property from its rightful owners;
- created a military force whose sole purpose is tyranny!

— paraphrased from the Formal Declaration of Rebellion

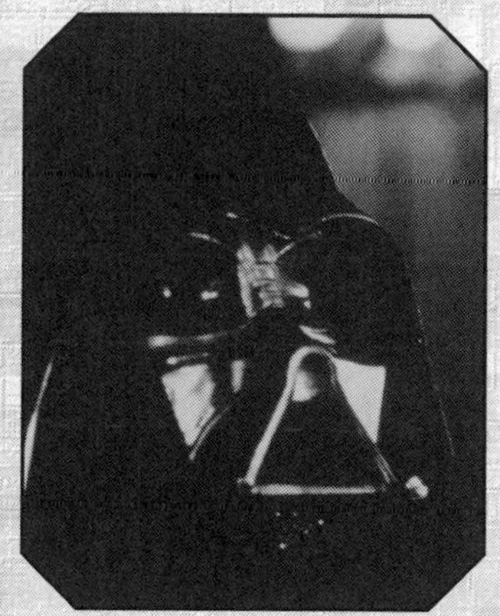

Darth Vader was once a pupil of Obi-Wan Kenobi. A promising Jedi Knight, Vader was seduced by the "easy" road of the dark side. He challenged his master and was left for dead when he failed, but though severely disfigured, Vader survived. His startling outfit keeps him alive, and also instills fear in his enemies. It is rumored that he has grown very strong in the dark side of the Force, and that he is the Emperor's main hatchet man.

Next to the Emperor himself, Vader is the most feared being in the Galaxy. Even his own men are terrified of him, as he is quick to anger, and his wrath is deadly.

Grand Moff Tarkin began as a warship captain, but after the incident at Ghorman, his rise was rapid. He is generally given credit for engineering the Empire's policy of "rule by fear," and is also rumored to be leading a project for the construction of a new super weapon.

Jabba the Hutt is one of the kingpins of galactic crime. Huge is a word often used to describe his empire of crime, not to mention his own unbelievably corpulent self.

Boba Fett is a notorious bounty hunter and assassin. A veteran of the Clone Wars, Boba Fett is feared throughout the Galaxy. Nobody knows the source of his considerable power, but he carries a formidable arsenal of weapons. Few have met him, and of those, even fewer are alive to tell the tale. Boba Fett is known to work on occasion for Jabba the Hutt, and it is suspected that he also performs missions for Darth Vader.

List of Key Worlds

Alderaan was one of the planets practically decimated by the violence that swept through the Galaxy during the Clone Wars. Its leader, Viceroy Bail Organa, returned from the Wars to promote a peaceful transition to citizenship in the Republic. Advocating non-violence and the abolition of weapons, he soon turned Alderaan into a model for restoration, peace, and freedom. Now Alderaan is the symbol of the Rebellion against the tyrannical Empire.

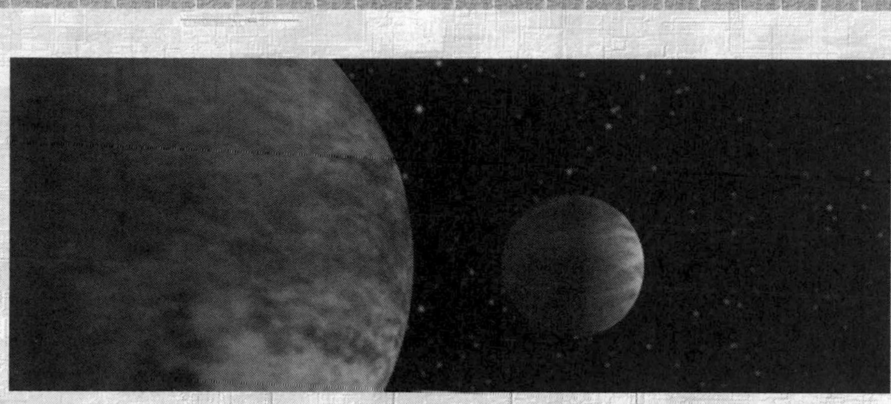

Mantooine is a system located in the Outer Rim of the Galaxy. Sharing Atrivis Sector with the Fest System, Mantooine was the site of a massacre as Mantooine's "Liberators" took on an overwhelming Imperial force. It was their defeat that helped identify the need for the Alliance proposed by Mon Mothma. Had the Liberators been allied with their neighbors in the Fest System, they would have known of the Imperial strike fleet orbiting nearby moons. Forewarned, they might have retreated into the impenetrable forests of Mantooine instead of taking up residence in a captured Imperial base.

The Corellian System was the site of the famous Corellian Treaty, which bound several rival contingents of the Rebellion into a unified force. Under Mon Mothma's skilled leadership, this treaty has formed the basis for the growing Rebel Alliance.

Ghorman was the scene of an early massacre, portent of the future of the Empire. A peaceful demonstration against rising taxes turned to tragedy and horror as the Republic warship sent to collect the taxes landed despite the protesters, killing or injuring hundreds. And the warship's commander? Was he punished? To the contrary, Captain Tarkin was promoted to Moff and later to Grand Moff.

Calamari is the watery world of the Mon Calamari and the Quarren. This tectonically stable planet has few land masses, almost no mountains, and very little readily available metal. Despite that, the Mon Calamari and the Quarren, working together, have created a peaceful, technologically advanced culture with huge floating cities and a thriving economy.

The Calamarians have long viewed the stars as islands in a galactic sea. With this somewhat poetic view of space, it is no wonder that they have become great travelers.

End Racism—We're All in It Together

Many of you may have been approached by members of COMPNOR (Commission for the Preservation of the New Order). Beware. Though it started out as a well-intentioned and idealistic social club, COMPNOR is now another of the many propaganda organs of the Emperor. Though their message may sound reasonable on the surface, COMPNOR is run by the Select Committee, who are vassals of the Emperor.

What is the Emperor's purpose? From our analysis, COMPNOR's main goal is to spread a subtle philosophy of racism. Their goal is to turn Human against Wookiee, Mon Calamari against Quarren, Sullustan against Twi'lek.

Don't let this happen. We are all equal citizens of the galactic community. Don't let the Emperor's doctrine of hatred and racism turn you against your fellow beings.

Know Your Allies

The Galaxy is vast, and there are many beings who belong among the citizens of the worlds. Some have traveled throughout the galaxy, while others have stayed close to their home worlds. Here are a few of those you may come to know.

Gamorrean

Description: Gamorreans stand approximately 1.8 meters tall when full grown and weigh about 100 kilos. Their green-skinned bodies are squat and powerful, and their hands and feet are large for their overall body size. Their facial features are distinctly porcine, with large tusks dominating their mouths and horns atop their heads. Their eyes are small and their noses are more like snouts.

Gamorrean

The Gamorreans of Gamorr are intelligent as well as physically impressive. However, their culture has evolved along a distinctly violent path. Only female Gamorreans actually do productive work. The males spend all their time engaged in fighting, training to fight, and engaged in more fighting.

Gamorrean males delight in conditions that would repel most beings, and have found their way into space as mercenaries. Some have become laborers (contrary to their cultural heritage) and if the labor is particularly unpleasant, they may find it to their liking. If fighting or mistreatment of others is involved, Gamorreans can get the job done.

Many Gamorreans are in the service of the Empire, and have no idea how mistreated they are. Few are known to work in the service of the Rebellion, partially because they have no concept of the ideals involved, and partially because they tend to shoot first and not bother to ask any questions later. We are doing our best to win them over to our side, and teach them to respect their own freedom.

Ithorian

Description: Ithorians are known as "Hammerheads" by many galactic citizens. This name is derived from the shape of their heads, which are flat and ribbonlike, and feature two eyes at the top and two mouths, one on each side of the "face."

Ithorians are natives of the lush planet Ithor in the Ottega System. They are peaceful creatures who hold the sanctity of life and the beauty of nature above all else. Many young Ithorians aspire to become ecological priests of "Mother Jungle."

The Ithorians' language uses their twin mouths in a stereo effect that is impossible for most beings to duplicate without complex apparatus. However, some protocol droids can approximate Ithorian. The Hammerheads themselves speak common Basic quite well.

Ithorian

The Ithorian way of life involves what they call "herds," but which are really hovering cities. They have taken this concept into space, following an ingrained curiosity about life. Ithorian merchant "herds" are welcome through-out the Galaxy, particularly in the Outer Rim Territories, where they often bring news and rare goods. They are not very offensive-minded, but carry strong defensive capabilities, which protect them from pirates and the other dangers of space.

Mon Calamari

Description: The Mon Calamari are bipedal, salmon-colored beings with webbed hands and feet, high dome-shaped heads, large eyes and vestigial external gills. With special lenses in their wide-set eyes, they have a 270 degree field of vision.

Calamarian

The Mon Calamari are intelligent beings whose skills in spacecraft design are famous throughout the galaxy. Originating on the water world of Calamari, the Calamarians live on shore, but retain a love of the ocean. They have established a long history of peace and cooperation with their ocean-dwelling neighbors, the Quarren.

Despite this peace, the Calamarians were drawn into the war with the Empire when Imperial ships invaded Calamari and began enslaving its population and looting their property. When the Calamari resisted, the Empire blasted three large floating cities, staining the oceans red with Calamarian blood. Now the Calamari are among the most steadfast friends of the Alliance, using their considerable skills to refit their space freighters into war cruisers for the Rebellion. Calamarian spacecraft are known for their individuality. Each is a work of art, handcrafted as much for esthetic considerations as for functionality. Like anything so lovingly produced, Calamarian craft are exceptionally durable and well constructed.

Admiral Ackbar is the most famous of the Mon Calamari. Once a leader of his people, he was taken by the Empire and made a slave to Grand Moff Tarkin. He was rescued by Rebel forces when they intercepted a shuttle carrying Tarkin on his way to inspect a military installation.

Quarren

Description: The Quarren are most recognizable by their triangular-shaped heads, tentacled mouths, and small, turquoise eyes, which are most comfortable in low light. Quarren are bipedal with leathery skin that can change colors (though this ability is usually only demonstrated during mating rituals).

The Quarren share the water planet of the Mon Calamari. They have long sustained a peaceful, but sometimes controversial, symbiosis with the Calamarians. Originally living deep in the oceans, the Quarren have mined the riches of the ocean bottom and provided them to the Calamarians. The "Mon Cal" have reciprocated by using their ingenuity to develop a technology that the two races share. The Quarren now live deep in the floating cities built by the Mon Cal.

Quarren

Some among the Quarren think they have gotten the short end of the deal, and there is an undercurrent of unrest among them. Nevertheless, the Quarren have accompanied the Mon Calamarians into space and can be found living in the deeper recesses of Calamarian ships.

It was a Quarren who originally betrayed Calamari by disabling the planet's defense systems, thereby allowing the Imperial warships to destroy three cities in one of the worst atrocities of modern times. However, the end result has been to unite the Mon Calamari and the Quarren with the Rebel Alliance against the Empire.

One somewhat notorious Quarren is Tessek. Consumed with a lust for power, he is one of Jabba the Hutt's Chief Lieutenants. Little is known about Tessek, but he is certainly a remarkable example of his species, building a reputation on intelligence and ruthlessness.

Sullustan

Description: Sullustans stand between 1 and 1.5 meters tall. These humanoids feature large, luminous eyes; large ears; masklike facial features; and bald, domed heads.

Throughout their evolution, the Sullustan have lived in tunnels and warrens beneath the surface of their volcanic world. Their innate sense of location has taken them to the stars as pilots and navigators, where their skills are in high demand. Their high-pitched chattering language is hard for others to duplicate, and it is suspected that they have a rudimentary sense of echo-location, perhaps an evolutionary holdover.

Sullustan

Despite their subterranean origins, most Sullustans display a sunny disposition, with a remarkable sense of humor. Many a starship bridge has been temporarily disrupted when the Sullustan navigator tells the one about the Twi'lek and the Ithorian. "What do you mean, that's not your pseudopod?" is one of many punchlines.

The main economy of Sullust, the Sullustans' home world, is the huge mining enterprise, the SoroSuub Corporation. Though many Sullustan citizens have joined the Rebellion, Sullust is officially allied with the Empire. We suspect that a poll taken on Sullust would show a high degree of unrest, but for now, Sullust is controlled by the Emperor.

Twi'lek

Description: Twi'leks are tall, thin, hairless humanoids with large, bony supra-orbital projections. The most remarkable feature of a Twi'lek is the pair of twin tentacular appendages that extend from the backs of their heads. These large, fleshy prehensile growths, called tchun-tchin in the Twi'lek language, are a source of Twi'lek pride. They are also integral to their society.

The Twi'lek language uses the tchun-tchin to expand the meaning of words, making Twi'leki one of the most difficult languages for outworlders to attempt.

Twi'lek

Fortunately, Twi'leks are adept at languages, and can learn most of the languages in common use.

Twi'leks actually view each appendage separately. The one on the left is called *tchun* and the one on the right is the *tchin.* Little is known of the specific functions of each, but they are used as adornments and in mating rituals.

The Twi'leks' home world is located in the Ryloth Star System in the Outer Rim. Without an axial rotation, Ryloth is a world of extremes. One side bakes in the sun while the other is constantly in darkness. Atmospheric phenomena called "heat storms" rage across the planet regularly. Although these destructive storms are a danger to the Twi'leks, they also serve to regulate the overall temperature of the planet, warming the dark side and cooling the light side.

Twi'leks are not warlike, but prefer subtlety and cunning to fighting. Their native technology is somewhat crude by galactic standards — relying largely on wind generation for energy — and much of their development has been underground to escape the extremes of the surface. Little is known of the Twi'leks' home world, as few outworlders have visited there.

Many Twi'leks have been taken into slavery by the Empire. Of particular value are Twi'leki dancing girls whose movements of body and tchun-tchin are considered seductive by humans and several other species. Needless to say, few Twi'leks have reason to love the Empire.

Wookiee

Description: Wookiees are tall (over two meters), fur-covered, bipedal beings of high intelligence and a long life span. Their vaguely canine faces are highly expressive, with piercing blue eyes. However, when a Wookiee smiles, many beings are prone to run, as they display huge canine teeth and a fierce expression.

Wookiee

Wookiees hail from Kashyyyk, a jungle planet famous for its giant, multi-level rain forests. Wookiees live in arboreal cities where life is relatively safe. Lower in the canopy, life becomes increasingly dangerous, to the point that even Wookiees must watch their step at the lowest levels.

Wookiee cities are remarkably complex, and the Wookiees' technological ability is well known. They handle all weapons with a natural skill and deadly effectiveness, and are adept at repairs. The Wookiee weapon of choice, however, is the bowcaster—a combination of ancient craftsmanship and modern weapons technology. The bowcaster is a hand-made crossbowlike device that fires a high-energy explosive projectile. Few beings can operate a bowcaster, as it takes the famed strength of a Wookiee to ready one.

Wookiees are among the strongest beings known in the galaxy. When angered, Wookiees have been known to tear their enemies literally limb from limb. And Wookiees have quick tempers.

On the other hand, Wookiees are intensely loyal and can form life bonds with others, even nonWookiees. For instance, Wookiees often see their closest friends and colleagues as "honor families," and their loyalty to an honor family is without equal. If you should find yourself in the unique position of having saved a Wookiee's life, you'll find yourself with a Wookiee companion who would gladly sacrifice his or her life for you. Such a "life-bond" will last until the Wookiee decides the debt has been repaid, and sometimes even beyond that.

Wookiees, though immensely strong, cannot defeat a whole battalion of stormtroopers, and many Wookiees have been enslaved. One well-known Wookiee is known as Chewbacca. Having formed a life-bond with the notorious smuggler, Han Solo, Chewbacca is now a wanted criminal as well. He is the copilot on Solo's equally infamous ship, the *Millennium Falcon.*

The Problem of Droid Abuse

The Empire's campaign of prejudice and hate shows no favoritism. All are equally to be reviled, ridiculed, enslaved, and murdered. This is no less true of the many non-human races than it is of the nonliving. Most of us depend on droids, whether we know it or not. And yet the Imperial attitude toward these highly sensitive, intelligent, and, yes, potentially sentient beings is to smash them, to exile them, and to use them without proper care.

A droid is more than a machine. A repulsorlift is a machine. A tractor beam generator is a machine. A droid is an entity. Admittedly, some droids are more advanced than others, but they are all highly sophisticated. There is no reason to shun them, to mistreat them, or to fear them.

Look at the many ways droids serve us:

- **Astromech droids**, such as the sturdy and versatile R2 units from Industrial Automaton, help maintain and repair starships. They can plug directly into the central computer to help analyze and solve problems. Astromechs also function as outboard computer/operator pilot enhancement modules in many single-seat starfighters such as the X-wing. They can also be programmed for up to 10 hyperspace jumps.

Some R2 units may be equipped with a veritable arsenal of tools and extra capabilities. Some have holo recorder/ projectors built in. They may also carry such diverse systems as welding units, electro-shock prods, saws and laser cutters, spotlights, and special grabbers.

Astromechs are more than just machines, however. They often show a remarkable degree of personality and loyalty, especially when they are not subjected to regular memory wipes. Whether these traits are considered positive or negative is a matter of conjecture, but if treated respectfully, astromechs tend to develop a helpful personality. If mistreated, they may go rogue, to the regret of their owners.

An R2 Unit being loaded onto a starfighter

A Protocol Droid

• We're the first to admit that some **protocol droids** can be more than a little irritating, but their capabilities can be extensive. If properly programmed, they can speak and translate instantly up to 7 million languages. They can be fitted with a variety of added modules, but are generally unsuited for tasks other than general protocol and communications.

Even more than astromechs, protocol droids can develop extensive personalities when their memories are left intact for a long period. Some demonstrate startling insights and begin to offer very definite opinions not contained in their original programming. There are scientists who sincerely believe that these droids are capable of full sentience and that regular mind wiping is a criminal act.

• Many a patient has been thankful for the quick, efficient treatment he, she, or it has received from highly sophisticated **medical droids**. There are many kinds of medical droids, varying from simple diagnostic models, like the MD-0, to the MD-4 microsurgery models. Most medical droids have their specialties, but the MD-5 is a general practitioner that can serve in places where specialists are not available.

Another popular droid is Geentech's Too-Onebee (2-1B), a highly versatile model, somewhat older than the MD series, but still found throughout the Galaxy.

Medical droids do not seem to develop many personality traits, though some may begin to display a sense of pride in their work, while others require periodic "vacations" to recharge their circuits and function at full efficiency.

A Too-Onebee model

Probot planetside

• Some people have the mistaken impression that **probe droids** are among the least sophisticated droids. In fact, it would be a mistake to think that the more modern probots do not respond to proper treatment. A probe droid will always carry out its mission, whether that be surveillance, exploration, search, rescue, or early warning; but probots have certain latitude. For instance, there is the example of probe droid D-127X whose self-sacrifice and immediate response may have saved Mantooine from a terrible Imperial surprise attack. There is no proof that D-127X would have done any different if mistreated, but would you want to trust your star system to a resentful droid?

• **Assassin droids** are dangerous. Period. Even though they have been outlawed for several decades, these single-minded killing machines still exist. Many of them have lost their primary targets, but all are still dangerous and unpredictable. Unlike other droids, assassin droids are incapable of developing positive personality traits. If you think you've seen one, notify the authorities and make tracks. Do not engage an assassin droid in conversation or trade with one. However, if an assassin droid does demand something of you, cooperate. Chances are it won't kill you. If it had wanted to kill you, you'd already be dead. Only a fully trained Jedi Knight stands a chance against an assassin droid in single combat, and, depending on the model, the droid may still win as much as half the time.

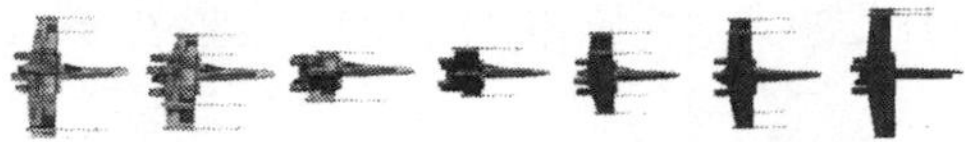

When I had finished reading, I turned the pamphlet over, and perused the back cover. It read:

Are you ready to fight for your freedom? Are you prepared to lay down your life, if need be, to save your homeworld? Seek out the Rebel Alliance, and fight at our side. We will defend one another, and together, we will destroy the Empire.

I studied it a moment more, and then looked for the woman who had given it to me. She was nearby, working with the others to remove any evidence of the meeting that had taken place. I caught her eye, and she moved towards me. I handed her the pamphlet.

"I want to be a starfighter pilot," I said, and her eyes sparkled . . . with amusement?

Suddenly, I saw myself as she must have: Some backwater rube with dreams of glory. I started to take offense, and then realized that I fit the description perfectly. What did it matter? I didn't mind having something to prove.

"Where do I sign up?" I asked.

"You're sure that this is what you want?" she said, her expression changing to one of genuine concern. "It might be a long time before you can return to Agamar if you leave with us now."

"I'm sure," I told her, although I think that my voice wavered a little. "Anyway, there's nothing to keep me here."

"Well then, my name is Lynia," she said, extending her hand in greeting. "I'll introduce you to someone. . . ."

✘ ✘ ✘

PART TWO

PART TWO

EARLY TRAINING

Strategy & Tactics

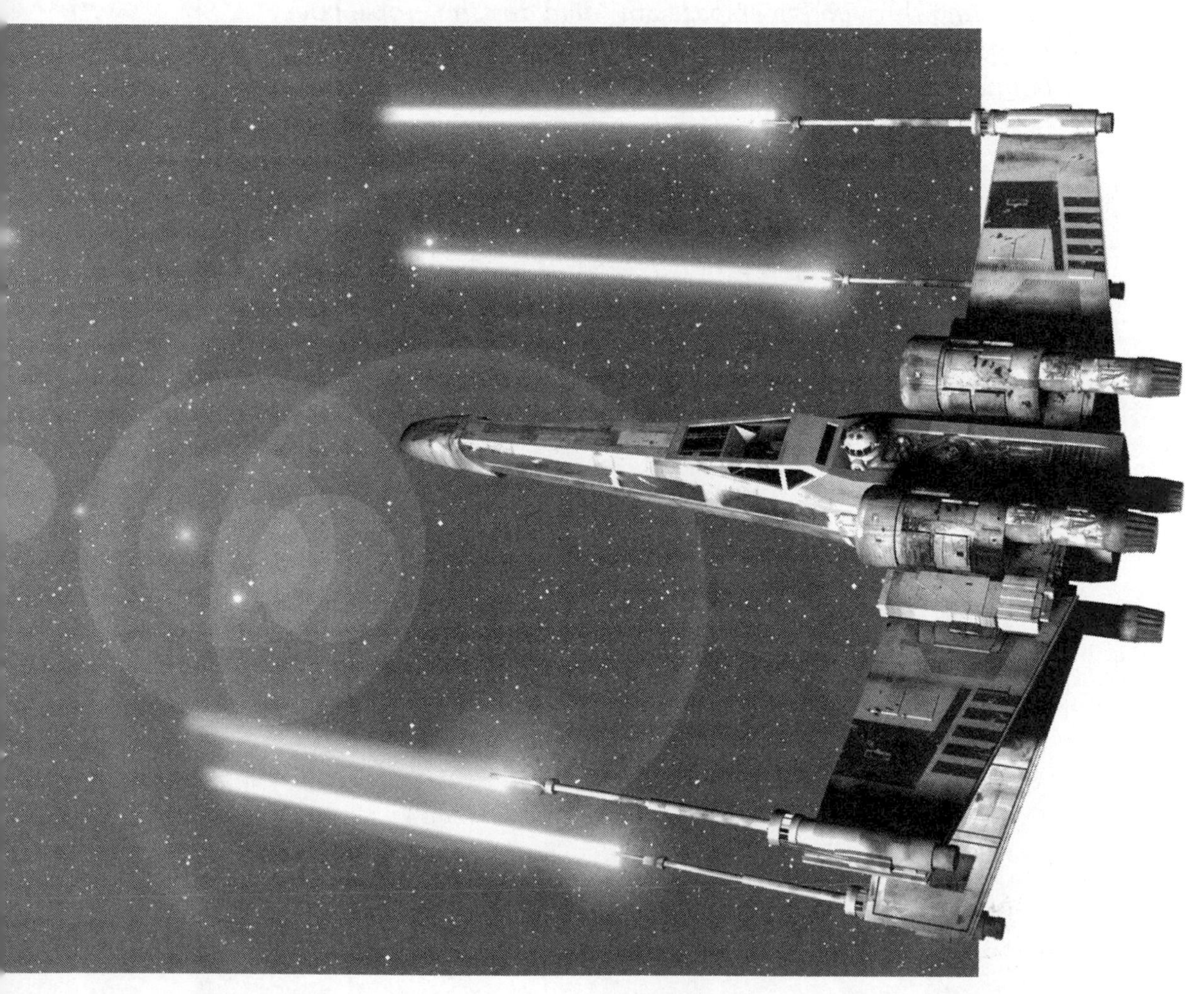

Traveling through hyperspace ain't like dusting crops, boy. Without precise calculations we'd fly right through a star or bounce too close to a supernova, and that'd end your trip real quick, wouldn't it?

— Han Solo

Early Training

My life ended on Agamar and began again on the Rebel flagship *Independence*. I came up on a crowded shuttle soon after Mon Mothma delivered the speech that had so inspired me. Mon Mothma had already gone up in a different shuttle, but there were several members of the ship's crew as well as three other new recruits from Agamar. Lynia was there, sitting next to me. I suppose that I looked nervous.

"Don't worry," she said. "You'll be fine."

I turned and met her lavender eyes as steadily as I could. It was my first time off-planet, my first time in a starship, and my first time making a big decision in my life without my family to advise me.

"I'm not worried at all," I lied. "I just can't wait to get my hands on the controls of a starfighter."

She laughed, clearly seeing through my bravado, and then turned more serious. "There's no other task you think you could perform for the Alliance?" she asked. "Nothing other than flying one of those death traps?"

Death traps? What kind of talk was that? Feeling mocked and underestimated, I told her, "You wouldn't understand." My tone was surly.

"Wouldn't I?" she bristled, her expression momentarily stricken. "If you're still around in a few weeks, come ask me about my brother."

I felt like a real fool. What I had thought was mockery was probably real concern. She obviously knew something more than I about starfighters and starfighter pilots. Still, I could not let her shake me. There was one, and only one, goal before me.

"I'm sorry," I told her. "I didn't mean to snap. But I know what I'm here for."

She looked at me with a half smile that told me I was forgiven, but that she still harbored doubts. We sank into silence again.

I had never seen anything like it. The Mon Calamari vessel was huge. Our tiny shuttle floated next to it like a bitz bug next to a bantha. The strange organic shapes of the hull turned into elongated hemispheres when seen from this close. Here and there I saw long streaks of black—battle scars, I guessed.

I nearly missed my first sight of an X-wing. It flashed by our shuttle, and I caught just a glimpse of it through the viewport. How can I describe that moment? For a boy whose ideas of power and speed had been embodied in a maxed-out landspeeder, this was pure poetry. The X-wing moved like a bird of prey, its S-foil wings glinting in the burning light of the sun, cleaving the emptiness of space silently and with deadly grace. Then it was gone, and I spent the rest of the shuttle ride searching for another.

I saw no more X-wings that day, but I had plenty to occupy my attention. The shuttle docked in a huge airlock near the rear of the Calamarian vessel. At least I assumed that it was the rear. The Calamarian design was unlike anything I had seen, but I think that I spotted the engine housings just before we entered the lock.

As we disembarked, Lynia hesitated and then said, "Good luck. I'll look you up in a few days. Just to see how you're doing." Before I could think of anything else to say, she was gone.

We were in a shuttle bay, and dozens of shuttles of different sizes were there. I looked hopefully for another glimpse of a starfighter, but there were none.

"New recruits from Agamar," boomed a basso voice. "Please report to me. Gart! Poussan! Jan-lo! Farlander!"

I jumped at the sound of my name. Somehow, hearing it spoken in this strange place made the reality, and finality, of my decision solidify in my mind. This wasn't a dream. I was really here!

The source of the voice turned out to be a short alien creature with large, nocturnal eyes, gray-green skin, and a puzzled-looking expression seemingly indigenous to its face. It was dressed in a military uniform and blinked every few seconds. After the creature had assured itself that we were all present, it set out briskly toward a far wall. I followed with the other new recruits as we trekked through the gigantic hangar. There were luminous arrows in the floor, and we seemed to be following them.

A crosshatch of structural beams arched overhead, layer on layer of flattened ribbon-like constructions that formed the outer shell of the *Independence*. I had never seen anything built like this and had no idea even what the building material was. Nothing was square or at right angles. It was a little disorienting. It looked incredibly strong, though.

The luminous arrows led us to an iris that opened when we approached. On the other side was a long, well-lit hallway, wide enough to accommodate at least five people abreast. Iris doors lined the hallway, and unfamiliar devices studded the walls, but our guide continued without allowing us time to examine these Calamarian wonders.

There was plenty of activity around us, and I guessed that we were in one of the main routes through this part of the ship. I saw many humans, of course, but I also spotted a variety of nonhumans and droids—most of them completely unfamiliar to me. The hallway was anything but straight, curving first to the right for a while and then back again to the left. I judged that we were taking a serpentine route toward the center of the cruiser.

After about ten minutes of nonstop marching, we came upon a smaller hallway, a tributary to this main stream. After another minute or two, we were delivered into a small room containing nothing but a table, ten chairs, and a couple of plaques on one wall. Our guide said, "Wait here," and left us.

"What do you think will happen now?" asked one of the others. He was a tall, thin young man with reddish hair and small, slit-like eyes. He had fidgeted on the shuttle and was obviously having trouble staying calm. His name was 'Ndranth Poussan, I think. I had spoken to him once before, on Agamar, but I hardly knew him.

"We wait," answered another of the Agamarians. Sunnar Jan-lo was a strong, committed member of the Resistance. Solidly built, decisive and energetic, Jan-lo had always been a leader on Agamar. She had said nothing during the long shuttle ride. Now her comment was characteristically short and to the point. She sat at the table and motioned for Poussan and Breth Gart, the other recruit, to sit also.

I had wandered over to examine the plaques on the far wall. One listed the crimes of the Emperor. It was the same list I had seen in the booklet *A Call To Reason*. The other plaque was a laser-paper version of the Formal Declaration of Rebellion. It read much like Mon Mothma's speech, and I wondered whether she had been its author.

I was just finishing reading when I heard the hiss of a door opening. I turned in time to see an odd quartet of Rebel officers enter the room. Two were human; the other two were like nothing I had ever seen. One was a salmon-colored creature with a high, domed head featuring large eyes set to either side. I was to learn later that he was a Calamarian—a member of the race who had built this starship. The other officer was even stranger to my unaccustomed eyes. His face looked much like some aquatic creature from my home world. The image that came to mind, in fact, was of a creature with a squid for a head. Ironically, I was to learn later that these creatures, called Quarren, were sometimes referred to as Squid Heads. After I had come to know them, however, I found that appellation distasteful.

The Quarren officer called my name in a sibilant voice. "Follow me, please," he said in strongly accented Basic. Hesitantly, I fell in behind him.

We walked down another hallway and into an elevator of some kind. As we rode down to the lower decks, I kept sneaking glances at this strange specimen beside me.

Finally, we emerged from the elevator into a dark, narrow hallway. The lighting was distinctly more dim than that of the upper decks, but my guide seemed right at home. I later learned that Quarrens evolved from deep in the seas of Mon Calamari, and that they preferred low light. The section of the ship I had been assigned to was a still-unmodified Quarren area.

The Quarren stopped before a doorway and gestured in a very humanlike way.

"This is cabin 11489, your new home, Flight Cadet Farlander," he said. I didn't respond immediately, but stood there, a little frozen by the implications of his statement, still fascinated with his alien looks, and, I'm afraid, staring foolishly at him.

"First time off-planet?" he half asked, half stated. "Imagine what your face looks like to me." The sound he made was something like a drainpipe backing up, and I found myself hoping that it was his species' version of a chuckle. If that was the case, I wanted to avoid being so amusing as to provoke a full-on belly laugh.

"I . . . I'm so . . . " I tried to apologize, hoping to salvage some dignity.

"Here," he interrupted. "Take this holo disk and study it." The Quarren reached out a suckered limb and proffered a standard holo. I reached for it. The sucker released it as my hand closed on the small disk. "If you're to be a starfighter pilot, you need to learn the ropes. If you have any questions, your liaison will be Lt. Hamo Blastwell. Don't worry. He's a human."

The sound of a gurgling drainpipe echoed down the small hallway as the Quarren turned and walked away. I stood a moment, chagrined and afraid that I had made a bad first impression; then, with a sigh of resignation, I retreated into the small room that was to be my temporary home.

x x x

It wasn't much: a small desk and chair with an antiquated personal holo deck; a tiny holo wall with a limited selection of topics; a tiny privy (apparently set up for human needs, with a few extra nozzles and buttons I didn't dare touch); a simple cot that came out of the wall at the touch of a button. That was all.

I had brought very little with me on this journey. Most of my possessions had been destroyed during the Imperial attack, so I carried only a few clothes and personal items. I had nothing much to do and didn't dare leave my cabin, fearing that I would get lost among the tunnels and hallways of this huge ship. I popped the holo disk into the deck and started my education as a starfighter pilot.

The Starfighter Pilot's Handbook

An Introduction to the Alliance Fleet

What is the Rebel Alliance?

The Rebel Alliance is an association of freedom fighters from many worlds throughout the galaxy. Our goal is to defeat the Dark Forces of the Empire and its leader, Emperor Palpatine. In the short run, the young Alliance has pledged its military forces to the protection of the people and planets that have joined the struggle for freedom. It is also the aim of the military to seize equipment and resources needed in the long struggle ahead, and to disrupt the smooth functioning of the Imperial oppressors.

Though the task is immense, and the Empire's power vast, every one of us—every soldier, officer, tactician, mechanic, pilot, and even our civilian liaisons—have pledged their lives to this cause.

Get to Know the Alliance

Before you go any further, familiarize yourself with the chain of command. The Alliance military was created for flexibility and unity. Under the Alliance High Command, which consists of all the group commanders, are two distinct divisions—the Alliance Forces and the Sector Forces. Alliance Forces are independent of any specific galactic sector, while the Sector Forces are responsible for keeping order and conducting operations locally. Both groups are under the direct control of the Alliance High Command.

The civilian Head of State of the Alliance is also the supreme Commander-in-Chief of all military forces. Currently this title is held by Mon Mothma, who, with former Senator Bail Organa, crafted the structure of the Alliance. Mon Mothma exercises final authority over the Alliance war machine.

Commander-in-Chief:	Mon Mothma
Fleet Commander:	Admiral Ackbar
Spec Forces Commander:	General Madine
Starfighter Commander:	General Dodonna

The Alliance military is divided into seven main operational commands:

Fleet Command

Admiral Ackbar in conference.

The Alliance Fleet represents the single most important division of the Allied Forces. Under the command of Admiral Ackbar himself, the Fleet Command directs and coordinates all Fleet operations, maneuvers, and missions. While the other commands are considered equal in rank to the Fleet Commander, deference is paid to Admiral Ackbar, both because of the extreme importance of the Fleet to the Alliance's efforts, and also because of the admiral's demonstrated strategic skills.

The Fleet Commander controls the operation of all capital ships and support vessels, ranging from assault craft to the massive Mon Calamari cruisers. Only starfighters are controlled under a separate command.

Briefly, there are five main categories of ships:

Capital ships such as the Mon Calamari MC80 cruiser are used in major campaigns and as bases for training and maneuvers.

Close support vessels such as the Nebulon-B Frigate are used to defend the capital ships and to carry out smaller operations.

Transport and supply ships such as the Corellian corvette are primarily used for moving people and critical supplies, although they may see action in certain missions, especially where the target is small or the Alliance needs every available ship.

Starfighters are under the command of Starfighter Command. Their role is in escort and attack missions.

Support vessels such as boarding craft and other small specialized combat craft also serve specific purposes.

Starfighter Command

Under General Dodonna, Starfighter Command has general and specific responsibility for the deployment of starfighters, the training and deployment of starfighter pilots, and the operation of starfighters in special missions. Starfighter Command determines where specific squadrons will be assigned. For instance, some squadrons are assigned to the Fleet, while others are placed in specific sectors, where they come under the control of local Sector Command operations. Some of the most prestigious divisions are the so-called "rogue" squadrons, which are not attached to a specific sector or Fleet division, but are moved as needed for special operations or to back up other squadrons that have gotten into trouble.

The starfighter fleet is divided into wings, squadrons, flights, and elements. A wing consists of three squadrons. A squadron consists of three flights of four starfighters. An element consists of two starfighters—a leader and a wingman. As a new recruit, you will start out as the wingman for a more experienced pilot. In time, if you distinguish yourself, you may be promoted to an element or flight leader or beyond.

The main goals of the Starfighter Command are to disrupt the functioning of the Empire, to secure needed information and materials, and to deny the Empire uncontested control of space. To accomplish these goals, starfighter squadrons are posted aboard Frigates and cruisers, on outpost worlds and sectors, and in special free-flying units capable of responding as needed.

Although there are many specific strategies and tactics in use, they can be summarized in three words: Attack, Defense, and Reconnaissance.

Attack missions are usually lightning strikes on specific targets. Using split-second timing and the all-important hyperspace abilities of the Alliance starfighters, special missions move in quickly, accomplish their objectives, and then hyperspace out again. Often, Starfighter Command is called upon to supply protective cover for larger missions involving the capital ships of Fleet Command; therefore, there are very strong links between the two commands.

Defense, in the most absolute sense, is impossible. The Empire can always muster far more firepower than we can. We must pick our battles carefully. However, there are times when the Alliance forces must defend against Imperial attacks. In such cases, the best defense is a delaying tactic to allow as many Alliance personnel and equipment as possible to evacuate. Once the Empire discovers an Alliance base, it is lost. All that can be done is to salvage as much as possible before it is overrun.

Reconnaissance missions are generally passive observation missions in which a starfighter may shadow a known Imperial location, monitoring traffic, estimating strength, and relaying information to its base. If discovered, the pilot will do his best to escape. In no case should the pilot allow himself to be captured. Recon missions are not considered cakewalks.

Special Forces Command

Special Forces (or Spec Forces) Command controls the elite of the Alliance's ground forces. Under the guidance of General Madine, these forces range from special assault troops used in seizure and capture missions to solo operatives engaged in assassination, courier missions, and counter-intelligence. Spec Forces is highly involved in the communications network of the High Command, and it is often from General Madine that the commanders first hear about Imperial plans.

Sector Command

Sector Command is the local operation of the military in an individual part of the galaxy. The operation of ground and space units is under the control of individual sector commanders, although there are times when one individual sector may "borrow" ships or troops from another, or from the Fleet. Such requests are always routed through High Command, however, to keep Alliance operations consistent and coordinated.

Fleet Intelligence

Fleet Intelligence has two main duties. First, it must interpret information supplied from other High Command intelligence sources. Second, it must operate and monitor the deep picket line of droids. This picket line spreads over many thousands of kilometers and warns the Alliance of the approach of any unexpected ships. With adequate warning, the Fleet can respond to any Imperial incursions—either by marshalling an attack or a retreat, as circumstances warrant.

Ordnance and Supply

Ordnance and Supply carries out the immense and challenging task of keeping the Fleet and Special Forces supplied with food, arms, fuel, and other essentials. Sector operations are expected to be independent, so Ordnance and Supply concentrates its efforts on the Alliance Forces. Some of Ordnance and Supply's modest budget also goes to research and development of better weapons and ships.

Support Services

Support Services controls the movement and operation of the Alliance's transports, including freighters and specialized vessels such as medical ships and mobile repair docks. Naturally, there is a symbiotic relationship between Support Services and Ordnance and Supply.

Important:

All starfighter applicants must read the information contained in *Qualifying as a Starfighter Pilot.*

Qualifying as a Starfighter Pilot

So you want to be a starfighter pilot?

True, the Alliance is in desperate need of starfighter pilots, but we won't take just anyone. You have to prove you've got the right combination of reflexes, poise, and judgement to pilot the fastest, deadliest fighters ever developed.

Step One: The Pilot's Proving Ground

Before any pilot is allowed behind the controls of a starfighter, he or she must train. To earn your wings, you will be sent to a top secret Rebel pilot training site. There you will demonstrate to our leadership that you are worthy of further training, and the expense it will require to bring you to battle readiness.

The Pilot's Proving Ground (also known as the "Maze") consists of a specialized obstacle course in which your ability to maneuver and your aptitude for weapons will be assessed. You will be trained on X-wings, Y-wings and A-wings, and some of you will get to try out the new B-wings. You can never tell what craft will be assigned to you in the heat of battle.

Your score will be based on your shooting accuracy, your maneuvering skills, and the time it takes you to complete the course. As you progress through the course, new obstacles and challenges will present themselves. Although it will all seem quite authentic to you, you will be in no real danger. Therefore, it will be to your advantage to push yourself as hard as you can. Be the best starship pilot you can. If you stand up to the challenges, you will be honored with the opportunity to defend the free beings of the galaxy from the evil of the Empire.

You can return to the Proving Ground at any time to increase your skills. If you perform especially well, you will be listed on the Pilots' Honor Roll.

Step Two: Combat Simulation Training

The second important step in your training as a starfighter pilot is the historical simulator. Here you will find yourself in a life or death struggle against real Imperial enemies recreated from actual missions. You will re-enact the roles of some of the Alliance's greatest pilots and learn their tactics and skills, adding to your training and preparing yourself for the real thing. Make no mistake. Next to actual combat, these simulations are the best preparation you can get. Don't pass them up.

There are six historical missions for each type of starfighter, and if you can survive them all, you will certainly be ready for your first Tour of Duty.

Combat Ranks

You start out as a flight cadet, but if you do well in training, and later in actual missions, you can look forward to some promotion. In progressive order, your distinguished service may earn you the rank of flight officer, lieutenant, captain, commander and general.

Medals and Awards

The Alliance appreciates the sacrifice of its brave pilots, and has instituted a system of awards to recognize their service. The first award you will earn is your Flight Badge upon earning your wings in the Proving Ground. There is one Flight Badge for each vehicle course you complete. The ultimate award is the Kalidor Crescent, which is earned only by extraordinary service to the Alliance.

Flight Badges

You will earn a Flight Badge the first time you complete one of the starfighter courses in the Pilot's Proving Ground for a particular craft. At this time, patches are offered for the X-wing, Y-wing, A-wing, and B-wing starfighters.

Battle Patches

You will earn a Battle Patch for each historical simulation you successfully complete. These and the Flight Badges are worn on the sash of your uniform.

Tour Ribbons

Note that a complete Tour of Duty ribbon includes 12 segments, regardless of the number of missions in the tour.

Combat Awards

Combat awards are presented for Tour of Duty missions, as well as specific acts of heroism and bravery.

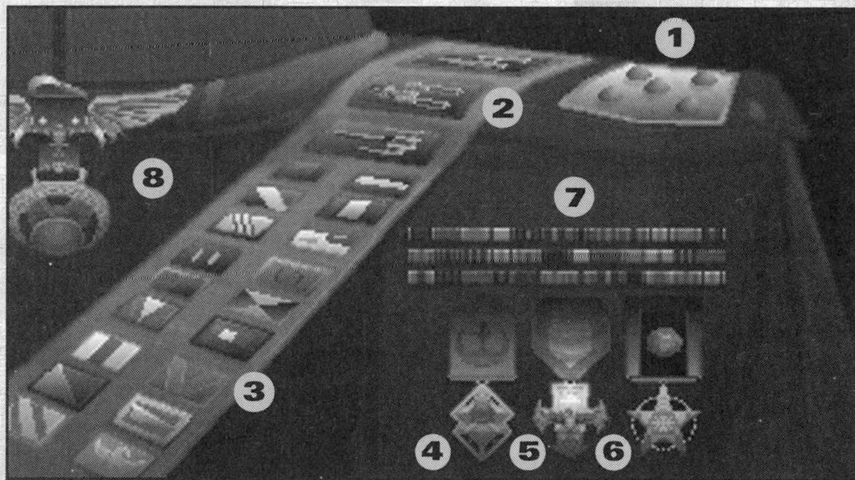

Your uniform accomodates these awards

1. Insignia of Rank
2. Flight Badges
3. Battle Patches
4. The Mantooine Medallion
5. The Corellian Cross
6. The Star of Alderaan
7. TOD Mission Ribbons
8. The Kalidor Crescent

Medals case

In your medals case are kept the ribbons for Tours of Duty four and five (at top right), the Flight Badge and Battle Patches for the B-wing (at left), and The Talons of Hoth (left medal) and The Shield of Yavin (right medal).

First Tour: The Corellian Cross

This award commemorates the signing of the Corellian Treaty, which marks the effective birth of the Alliance. By unifying three independent resistance groups under this treaty, our leader, Mon Mothma, forged the initial structure of the Alliance.

Second Tour: The Mantooine Medallion

This award commemorates the courage of the resistance and freedom fighters on the planet Mantooine. Their bold attack on an Imperial outpost set an example for many other resistance groups. Subsequently decimated at the hands of the Empire, they were instrumental in convincing other resistance leaders to pool their forces and join the Alliance.

Third Tour: The Star of Alderaan

This award commemorates the role played by the peace-loving planet Alderaan and its leader, Bail Organa, in creating the structure of our Rebel Alliance. Even while a Senator, Organa risked his life to plot rebellion with Mon Mothma. His contribution cannot be overemphasized. Neither can the example set by the once warlike citizens of Alderaan, who have rebuilt their society based on peace and equality of all races.

The Kalidor Crescent

Named for the famed winged predator from the planet Davnar, this award commemorates the unparalleled grace and power of the Kalidor. No more perfect flying creature has been found within the galaxy. Its spectacular aerial maneuvers and unerring accuracy symbolize our aspirations as starfighter pilots.

The Kalidor Crescent is awarded to pilots for heroic and extraordinary achievements during their Tours of Duty. It rewards exceptional feats of bravery and skill, and is the most prestigious award given to pilots in the Rebel Alliance. Recipients of this medal are looked upon with great respect, and are universally granted celebrity status among their peers. There are five upgraded classes of this medal for those who continue to distinguish themselves beyond the call of duty.

Kalidor Crescent Upgraded Awards

- **Bronze Cluster**
- **Silver Talons**
- **Silver Scimitar**
- **Golden Wings**
- **Diamond Eyes**

To date, no one has earned the Diamond Eyes.

For more information about medals and scoring in X-Wing, see Appendix A.

Starfighter Systems and Basic Tactics

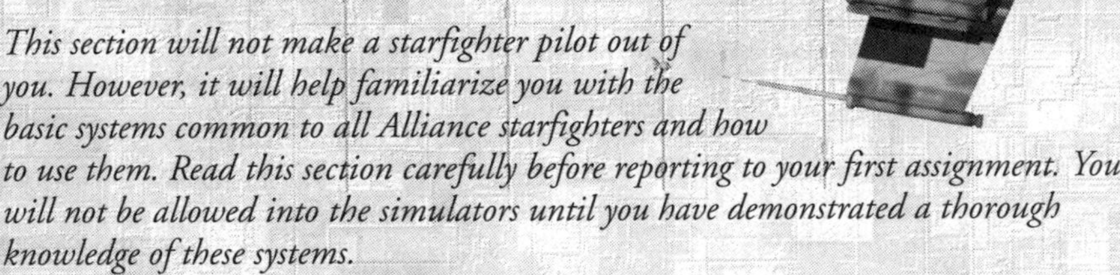

This section will not make a starfighter pilot out of you. However, it will help familiarize you with the basic systems common to all Alliance starfighters and how to use them. Read this section carefully before reporting to your first assignment. You will not be allowed into the simulators until you have demonstrated a thorough knowledge of these systems.

Introduction

Modern starfighters are, kilo for kilo, the most powerful and the most destructive weapons platforms ever developed. When you take the controls of a starfighter, you must master power, speed, and maneuverability unlike anything you've experienced before. Those of you who have flown the T-16 Skyhopper at high speeds will have some advantages, as the controls are similar on some of our models, but that is all. Flying a T-16 cannot prepare you for the sheer thrust and momentum you will have to contend with. You will learn a new language, a new way of thinking, or you will soon be dead. Pay attention to your instructors. The information they pass on to you may be your only hope of survival.

Power Systems

A starfighter's main generator system provides the necessary energy to drive the forward propulsion engines, the flight control thrustor jets, the deflector shields, the onboard computer systems, and the weapon systems. Some starfighters carry backup generators, but these will only maintain life support and other systems at reduced power. A pilot must choose the proper mix of power distribution. For instance, power can be diverted from the engines to maximize shield strength or to increase power to the weapon systems. However, such a decision results in slower speed and reduced performance. On the other hand, in a tight spot a pilot may choose to divert all power to the engines. This often results in a turbo effect which boosts speed beyond ordinary limits. However, shields are then minimized, and remember: You can't outrun a laser!

Flight Control

In addition to the main propulsion engines that provide the starfighter's forward thrust, there are a number of small thrustor jets that are linked to provide fluid and versatile maneuvering whether in space or in atmospheric flight. There are three main systems of flight control:

1. The **repulsorlift generators** are used when docking or during planetside takeoffs or landings. However, when operating from large starships and their crowded hangar bays, tractor beams generally move small ships (including starfighters) until they are clear of the launch area. Once a starfighter is safely out in space, the pilot regains complete control of his or her spacecraft.

2. In most other circumstances, maneuvering is controlled through the **main thrustor jets** by means of the cockpit controls. These controls are linked through your nav computer or onboard R2 unit to provide automatic synchronization of directional thrust and stabilizer jets. The result is a smooth turning radius. There are manual overrides, but these are only used if all other systems break down.

Starfighter controls operate very much like the controls of aircraft in atmospheric flight. In part, this is because the X-wing and other starfighters are designed for planetary surface flight, and the designers wanted the flight controls in both environments to be similar. Also, because the early designers and pilots were experienced in atmospheric craft, their concepts and designs carried over.

In a starfighter, pulling back or pushing forward on the flight stick pitches the nose of the 'fighter up or down, while moving side to side causes the craft to turn. This is accomplished by the flight control system, which translates the stick movements into a carefully coordinated series of bursts from the thrustor control jets mounted in the wings and fuselage of the spacecraft.

3. The third control system involves the **axial roll thrustor jets**, which temporarily override the main thrustor control jets and allow a pilot to change the attitude of a starfighter without changing its direction of movement. Axial roll is often needed to orient one spacecraft to another. It is also very important to know how to adjust your axial roll in combat. Often a pilot can turn a potential disaster into a victory by simply rolling to a new attitude and then using main thrustors to come around on an enemy craft. Only practice will teach you this skill.

Sensor Systems

Sensors are devices whose purpose is to detect and analyze environmental phenomena. These may include light, sound, electromagnetic disturbances, motion and vibration, gravitational fluctuations, heat, pressure, trace chemicals, nuclear and magnetic fields, and even other sensors. Technically, anything that allows you to perceive more of what's going on around you could be considered a sensor—even a pair of field glasses! However, when we refer to sensors in starfighters, we are referring to specific, complex arrays of highly sophisticated data-gathering and analysis devices, working in conjunction with your onboard computer systems.

The most powerful sensors are too large to be carried aboard a starfighter, but a highly compact array of complex equipment is provided on Alliance starfighters, primarily to detect and analyze a variety of transmissions and fluctuations in the space around the craft. Fortunately, this information is analyzed and interpreted by your onboard computer or R2 unit, and the results then projected in readable form in the cockpit. On older starfighter models, you may still encounter somewhat glitchy cockpit CRT displays, but the newer models feature the revolutionary new IN-344-B "Sightline" holographic heads–up display recently developed by Incom engineers.

Starfighter sensors fall into two general categories:

1. Long-Range Sensors are grouped into a single unit called the **Phased Tachyon Detection Array.**

- Monitors craft/object locations.
- Monitors craft/object type or identification (limited at long range).

Normal commercial traffic transmits ID codes on normal comm channels. Military craft suppress this transmission, but friendly craft transmit special codes on secure channels. Our sensors can usually identify friendly craft as well as enemy military vehicles and ordinary commercial spacecraft. Some readouts feature a color-coding system to identify friendly, enemy, neutral, or unidentified craft.

2. **Short-Range Sensors** are grouped into the **Primary Threat Analysis Grid.**
   - Monitors craft flight characteristics and telemetry information used by the weapon tracking computer for laser targeting and missile locking. The sensors work together with the targeting computer to calculate trajectories of warhead flight paths.
   - Monitors enemy craft threat status, providing warning if an enemy is using targeting computers to track and/or lock on to your craft.
   - Limited analysis of cargo and/or life forms aboard another craft.

Sensor Identification Chart

Red = Enemy Craft/Unknown
Green = Friendly Craft
Blue = Neutral Craft
Yellow = Missiles
White = Satellites, Mines, etc.

Your sensor readouts are your eyes in space. You must check your sensor readouts frequently. Don't ever forget this. The pilot who sees his enemy first is usually the pilot who survives. Most starfighters carry standard all-directional long-range and short-range sensor units. Forward and aft readouts show all nearby activity unless another ship is jamming the sensors. You must memorize the color chart. Know your position. Know your enemy's position. Be first, or you won't be last.

Weapons

The weapons systems aboard an Alliance starfighter are extremely powerful. No doubt you'll be impressed with their destructive potential. When used in conjunction with the onboard targeting computer, they make a lethal combination. But just so you won't grow overconfident, remember that you may find yourself up against Imperial starships with hundreds of times the power of your tiny craft. Learn to use your weapons effectively, sparingly, and accurately.

There are two classes of weapons:

1. **Line of sight energy weapons and particle beams**
   - **Laser cannons** are the most common starfighter weapons. Their highly focused bursts of energy can inflict great damage. They are fired at very high velocity on a straight path. Laser cannons may be fired in rapid bursts, though a small delay is required to cool the laser beam focusing barrel. This weapon is powered by the ship's main power generator. Continuous firing will drain the laser power cells and your weapons may take some time to recharge. Your laser cannon can be fired singly or fire-linked for maximum spread and power. However, recharge times are greater when weapons are fire-linked. Adjusting more power to the weapon systems will reduce recharging time, but at the cost of either shields or engines, or both.

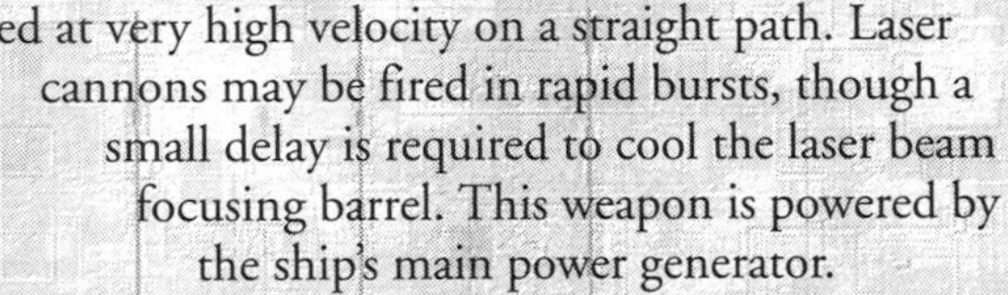

   - **Ion cannons** are specialized weapons requiring a larger power plant than laser cannons. Ion cannons shoot bursts of high-energy ionized particles which do not destroy enemy craft, but disable the electronics and machinery of the target. Ion cannons are useful for missions in which boarding an enemy craft, or capturing it intact, are required. Ion cannons require even more energy than laser cannons, and consequently can drain the power cells even more quickly and may need longer to recharge. Like laser cannons, ion cannons can be fire-linked for more concentrated power. They are rarely fired singly; most often, your ion cannons will be linked in pairs.

2. **Warhead-carrying homing projectiles**
   - **Concussion missiles** are incredibly fast homing projectiles that carry a small warhead. Though not very powerful, they pack enough power to destroy a starfighter and damage a medium-size craft. Their onboard electronic guidance systems are sophisticated enough to track and home in on even the most evasive target, once the targeting lock has been achieved.
   - **Proton torpedoes** are slower-moving and much larger than concussion missiles. They also carry a much more destructive payload. Because they are slower and carry less sophisticated guidance systems, they are usually most effective against ground targets or larger, slower ships.

Targeting Systems

In older starfighter models, pilots were required to target their main cannons by eye with the help of a crude sight. Recent innovations in target acquisition have culminated in the development of the Fabritech ANs-5d "lock track" targeting system. This new system allows our pilots to lock on to one or more targets. It illuminates the target and then "lights up" the gunsight when the correct firing angle is achieved. With the exception of a few "old guard" veterans, our pilots universally praise this new targeting system. However, we do recommend that new pilots spend some of their simulator time with the system turned off. In real combat, you may have only a split second to get a shot off. Developing good deflection shooting instincts can spell the difference between a clean shot and a clean miss.

Your spacecraft may be armed with either proton torpedoes or concussion missiles. A positive lock is required before firing, and you will use your targeting system to determine when to fire. The longer you can keep your target centered in your sights, the more effectively the computer can plot an intercepting path.

After the targeting computer has locked onto the target, it downloads the appropriate electronic emissions signature to the warhead's onboard homing systems. Once the telemetry has been completed, your targeting computer will flash a green lock signal and you may fire as long as the lock remains on. Once fired, the missile or torpedo will follow the electronic signature of its target. In battle, you won't get many chances, so make them count.

Defense Systems

Imperial starfighter pilots are expendable. They fly in huge wings of TIE fighters and overwhelm their enemies with sheer numbers. However, the TIE fighter is vulnerable and one clean hit will destroy it. The Alliance takes a different view. Each of our pilots is important to us. For this reason, each of our starfighters is armored and shielded. We do everything we can to get you back alive.

There are two kinds of shields—particle and ray/energy—and both are required to protect your spacecraft. Particle shields protect against missiles and other physical objects such as small meteorites. Ray/energy shields protect against lasers and other energy beams, and require more energy output than particle shields.

There is very little you can do about the armored hull of your starfighter, but shields are very much your responsibility. You may increase or decrease power to shields as well as adjust them to forward, aft, or overall coverage. Shield direction can be adjusted almost instantly, and there will be times when you will need to protect your ship from heavy front or rear attacks. Remember, rotating shields forward provides double protection from the front, but leaves the rear of the craft unshielded. You must know where the enemy is at all times.

Shields become depleted after repeated hits, but will recharge if given time. In an emergency, you may apply more energy to the shields. This will reduce the time needed to fully recharge them—however, engine performance and weapon recharging rates will suffer.

Navigation

The hyperdrive is one of those scientific miracles that only a few claim to understand, but it has become the mainstay of galactic commerce and transportation. Each point in real space has its equivalent point in hyperspace, and that point's location relative to a real space location can be calculated. Using powerful and efficient fusion generators, the hyperdrive engine hurls a spacecraft into hyperspace to a location calculated by the astrogation computers.

All navigation aboard a starfighter is handled by the on-board nav computer or the socketed R2 unit. Astronavigation is impossible without powerful computing capabilities, and even with an R2 or an advanced nav computer, most systems are put on minimum power while hyperspace calculations are made. Although hyperspace jumping is one way to escape a losing contest, remember that your targeting computer system will be inoperative while astrocalculation is taking place.

Damage Control Systems

Your system readout will contain a holo image of your ship. During battle, you should check frequently for damage, especially if your shields have been depleted. Fortunately our starfighters are extremely durable, and those with R2 units on board are particularly fortunate, as the R2 can effect immediate repairs, reroute systems to keep them functioning, and warn you of imminent failures and other dangers.

Communication

Each starfighter is connected by subspace transmission to the rest of its group. You will hear a lot of crosstalk during operations. Learn to filter out the transmissions that are intended for you, and otherwise keep your lips buttoned. There is no room in combat for extraneous chatter. We know your enthusiasm may occasionally get the better of you, but remember, while you are talking, you aren't listening. And if you don't listen, you may miss a message that could save your life!

Life Support

Alliance starfighters are equipped with full life support systems, which eliminates the need for cumbersome spacesuits. The cockpits of our starfighters are kept comfortable by a combination of compressors, temperature regulators, and special atmospheric scrubbing units which can be adapted for beings of various races. In addition, our starfighters are equipped with Guidenhauser ejection seats which include a limited oxygen supply, wrap-around ceramic armor, and a deployable para-foil for atmospheric ejections. Ejection seats can provide almost instantaneous escape from a doomed starfighter, but the pilot's probability of survival in space is not high unless help is immediately available. In atmospheric ejections, survival odds increase greatly.

Standard Operational Directives of Starfighter Combat

Flying a Rebel starfighter is a demanding task, frought with danger and full of unforseen complications. This section serves to underscore the importance of the many different variables a pilot must be constantly aware of, not only during a confrontation, but also before and after engaging the enemy.

Situational Awareness and Energy Management

A Rebel starfighter pilot needs more than dogfighting skills to defeat the Empire. Situational awareness and energy management are the two keys to developing effective starfighter tactics. **Situational awareness** is knowing where you are, where your enemy is, and what you need to do to accomplish your mission goals. **Energy management** is the process of configuring your ship's power system to achieve maximum efficiency. Proper utilization of these skills depends on your ability to constantly analyze and reassess your situation in the midst of a rapidly changing environment.

Situational Awareness and the Combat Multiview Display (CMD)

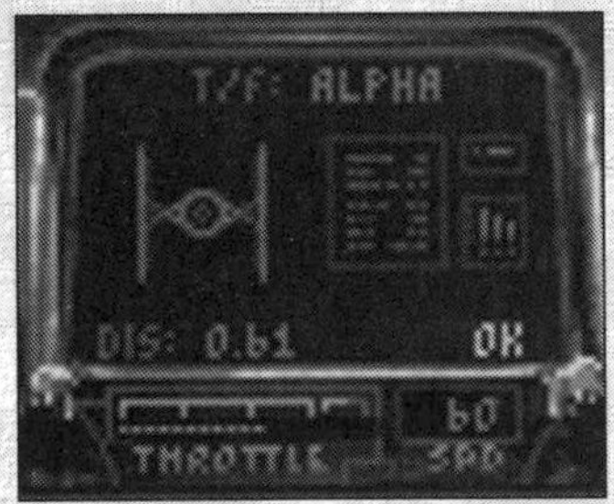

The CMD

The Combat Multiview Display (CMD) is the most important part of your targeting system. The first thing you should do at the beginning of any mission is query the CMD (in ID mode) for the nearest enemy fighter [R]. Note that, although they're armed, shuttles and transports aren't considered "starfighters," and are not selected by the targeting system in this manner. If enemy ships are nearby, you have to decide quickly whether to engage or proceed. **You should consider yourself already under attack if an enemy is less than two clicks away!** Using the targeting system and the CMD, quickly cycle through all the craft displayed on your sensors, noting their type and distance ([T] and [Y]). Pay particular attention to the ships that are most critical to your mission.

As time allows, assign them to the memory locations of the targeting computer for quick reference during the mission (Shift F5 to F8). As new ships enter the area, your R2 or ship's computer alerts you with an appropriate message. Special sound cues alert you when a new message is displayed. Target the new arrivals in the CMD to see how they affect the overall situation. As you do this, you should be building a mental map to help you determine the best method to achieve your mission.

Energy Management and the ELS Display

The ELS display

The primary consideration during any mission is which power configuration will optimize your chances for success. There are three main elements of concern: engines, weapons, and shields. Depending on mission goals and the needs of the moment, energy levels may be optimized for maximum speed, firepower, or defense. Trade-offs always exist, and you have to learn the pros and cons of each one. As the mission proceeds, you may find it necessary to make frequent adjustments. There is no "perfect" configuration. Nevertheless, you should always strive to maintain fully supercharged cannons and full primary and secondary shields.

Here are some tips for managing energy in battle:

- **Shift weapon energy to shields.**

When you begin a mission, your cannons are already at their supercharged levels. Your primary shields are fully charged, but your secondary shields are not charged at all. The cannons recharge more rapidly than the shields do. Experienced pilots have found that they can bypass certain inefficiencies in shield recharge rates by setting the cannon recharge rate at maximum and then transferring that energy to the shields (apostrophe ['] or Shift F10). Quickly build up your secondaries by transferring any accumulated cannon energy directly to the shields.

Lasers on maximum.

- **Use shields to store energy.**

Lasers on minimum.

Shields dissipate energy more slowly than the cannons do. Use shields to store energy like a battery. When you are redirecting as much energy as possible to the engines for greater speed, but still want to maintain your shields, you can keep the shields at their normal recharge rate and redirect all the cannon energy to the engines. Then, when you need to fire your weapons, you can quickly transfer shield energy to the cannons ([;] or [Shift][F9]). Don't forget to reset the recharge rate for the cannons, though!

- **Use cannons to charge shields.**

Another alternative that allows good speed, shield maintenance, and some firepower is to redirect all shield power to the engines and set the cannon recharge rate to one above normal. Then manually transfer cannon energy to the shields every few moments. This technique increases your workload, but in a low-threat environment, in which you're not using the cannons much, this strategy works well. You can build up a full charge for both systems in this way!

Lasers one notch up.

- **Redirect energy to engines for maximum speed.**

Full power to engines.

For maximum possible speed, you have to adjust both cannon and shield energy to be redirected to the engines. As long as you have already maximized your shield strength first, you should have a few minutes before that energy dissipates. Normal recharge rates merely maintain current energy levels. (Firing cannons or taking hits to the shields results, of course, in a loss of energy.)

- **Redirect energy to other systems to slow down.**

This tip is the corollary to the preceding one, but it is sometimes overlooked by novice pilots. When it is necessary to reduce speed (for instance, when you want to keep a slower-moving target within range), you may choose to redirect energy from engines to shields or to weapons rather than cut your throttle. In this way, you achieve the desired speed but also gain additional charging for other important systems. Just don't forget to correct your settings when more speed is required.

Minimum power to engine.

Basic Energy Configurations

Your starfighter is a versatile craft designed to accomplish a variety of tasks. It is an effective weapon, however, only if you understand how to use it. If you've studied the information about energy management in the preceding section, you understand that this is one of the key skills you have to master. The following list of basic configurations is intended only as a guideline. Their use is *completely situational.* In other words, you must determine when to implement any energy strategy.

Normal Maintenance

Cannons: 50 percent
Shields: 50 percent
Throttle: Full

This setting, used to maintain energy levels, is best used in nonthreatening environments. Also, this setting can be used for extra speed in dogfights if shield and cannon levels have been previously charged to maximum. You must remember to reset cannon energy before you run out of laser power. Or, if you are not in danger of being hit, you can transfer energy from shields to cannons.

Normal Maintenance

Speed

Cannons: 0
Shields: 0
Throttle: Full

Use this setting to achieve the highest possible speed your starfighter is capable of attaining. In emergencies, this is the only possible setting, but remember that your shield and cannon energy will slowly drain.

Speed

Normal Attack

Cannons: 100 percent
Shields: 50 percent
Throttle: Full

Use this setting for normal attack situations. Your cannons remain fully charged, even with constant shooting, and your shields remain stable. If your shields are hit, you can transfer energy from cannons to charge them back up.

Normal attack

Speed Attack

Cannons: 100 percent
Shields: 0
Throttle: Full

Use this setting to gain extra speed during an attack while keeping your cannons fully charged. In this setting, it is the pilot's responsibility to keep his shields charged by frequently transferring energy from the cannons.

Speed attack

Slow Down (Non-threat charging)

Cannons: 100 percent
Shields: 100 percent
Throttle: As needed

Slow down

Use this setting to attack slow-moving enemies, such as TIE Bombers. It's more efficient to raise your shield and cannon energy levels than to lower your throttle. You may also have to adjust throttle, but, often, setting cannons and shields to maximum has the desired effect.

This setting is also used in nonthreatening environments for maximum charging effectiveness.

Weapons, Targets, and Firing Configurations

Weapon selection and firing configuration decisions often determine the success or failure of a mission. A few general rules apply to almost every situation.

Homing Projectiles

Homing projectiles, such as concussion missiles and proton torpedoes, are intended to give you some "standoff" attack capability. Because these projectiles are "fire-and-forget" weapons, their rapid deployment can quickly help you shift the odds in your favor.

Torpedoes are designed for attacking larger and slower ships. Torpedoes, although faster than a starfighter, can't turn as well. An alert pilot can always evade one, so avoid using them against starfighters unless the enemy is flying straight and level or in a head-on attack. Also, Imperial doctrine prohibits "wasting" torpedoes on starfighters, so you probably will not find yourself targeted by one. Concussion missiles, on the other hand, are designed for dogfighting. *Because of their great speed, they are also somewhat effective at intercepting torpedoes.*

When you're targeting an enemy ship, you will find that large ships must be within six clicks for a lock-on to be achieved. Against small ships, the distance must be less than two clicks. At extremely long range, you must keep the target absolutely centered in the targeting box. You will discover that Imperial ships are capable of achieving solid lock-ons while you are still "acquiring" your lock. This is one area in which they maintain a slight technological edge.

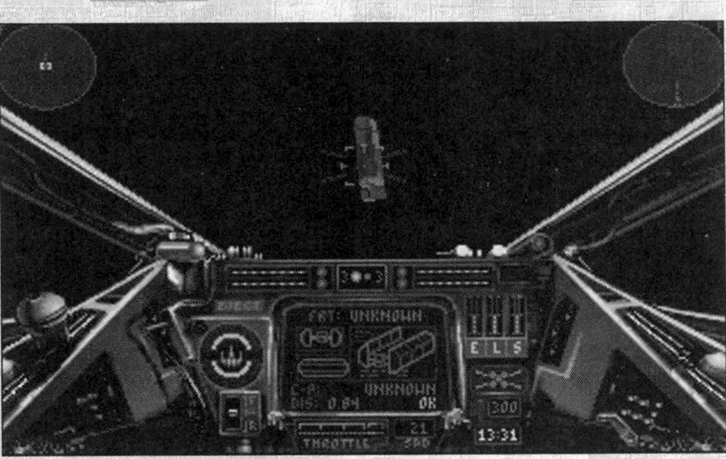

Locking on to a target.

Cannons

For most combat and almost all dogfighting, you rely on your cannons. The dual-fire mode has been shown to be the most effective compromise when you're considering power, targeting opportunities, and firing speed. In the Y-wing, this is especially true, because the cannons are in a twin mounting that places their fire in a very small area. If the target is hit at all, it is hit by both guns, and may as well receive the double shot! In the X-wing, and to a lesser degree the A-wing, dual-fire mode is preferred because the wing-tip mounting of the cannons allows a much larger area to be considered by the targeting system. Although this results in less efficient use of cannon energy (because as many as half the shots may miss), it is offset by the benefit of having more firing opportunities against a small, rapidly maneuvering target, such as a TIE fighter. *In fact, because TIE fighters are smaller than an X-wing's wingspan, they can find safety between the cannons, right in the center of your targeting box!*

Shooting a TIE.

General Notes About Combat

Combat in space is all about position. You want to be in a position to hit the other guy. You also want to avoid being in a position where he can hit you. Best of all is any position that fits both these criteria! In engagements between starfighters, this task is a straightforward one. A starfighter's weapons all face forward, so if you can position yourself on the enemy's tail and stay there, you will defeat him.

- **Finish what you start.**

When you're dogfighting, pick a target and stay with it until you have destroyed it. (See the section relating to hull damage, in this handbook under *The Principles of War*, for an exception to this rule.)

- **Break up a formation.**

When you're breaking up an attack by several enemy ships in formation, your primary task is to keep firing long enough to force a particular ship to break formation. Continue to attack each ship in the formation until all have been forced out of their attack run. After that, destroy at will or continue with mission objectives.

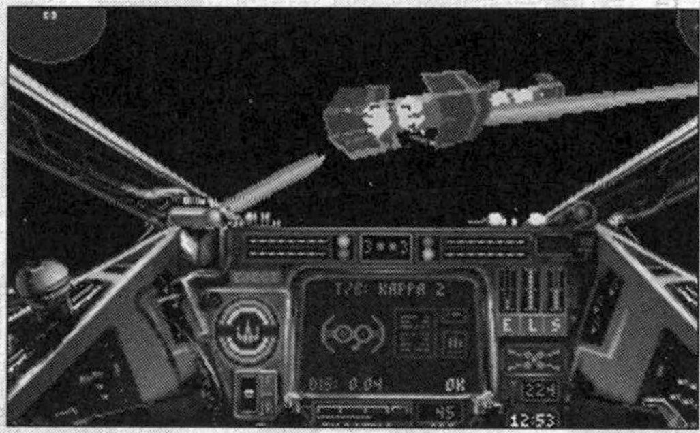

Breaking up a formation.

- **Use missiles on a flight group.**

When you're attacking a multi-ship flight group with missiles or torpedoes, lock and fire as quickly as possible. If a missile or torpedo is evaded at first, don't worry; it continues to track the target. After you have fired at each of the enemy ships, go back through the target list to the earliest one that still survives. Fire another projectile if necessary, but try to take it out with cannons if you can. Remember that there aren't any reloads in a dogfight! Use them wisely.

When you're employing missiles or torpedoes against stationary targets, it is not necessary to get a solid lock. A few seconds of "yellow" is sufficient.

- **Escort duty.**

When you're flying a defensive patrol, stay within a few clicks of the vessel (or vessels) you are protecting. When you move to intercept any attackers, try not to go more than eight to ten clicks away. A second attack on the other side will catch you too far away to get back in time.

Also, when you protect other ships, try to draw off the fire of large enemy ships by flying within range of their guns and popping off a few shots yourself.

- **Suicide attacks.**

In a one-for-one war of attrition, the Empire will win. They know this and do not hesitate to spend their starfighters in suicide attacks against ours. In a head-on attack, never assume that an Imperial pilot will try to avoid colliding with you. His devotion to the Emperor, his honor and bravery are all confirmed when he dies while destroying the forces of the Rebellion. Fortunately for the Alliance, the ruggedness of our starfighters enables them to withstand most collisions with enemy starfighters. This is especially true when all shields are fully charged. However, despite the fact that these collisions usually result in the destruction of the enemy fighter, this is not considered a good tactic!

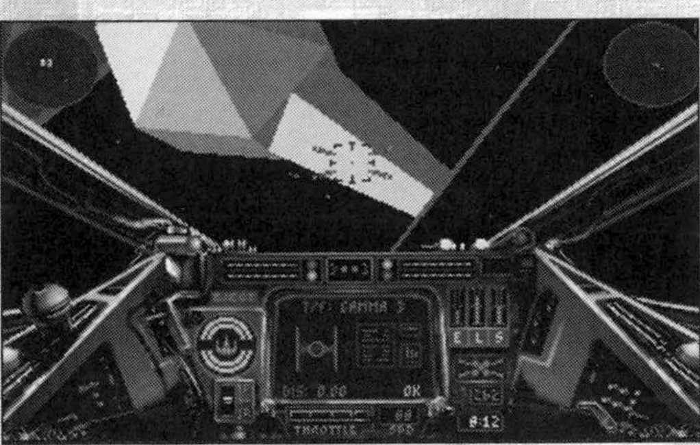

Suicide attack

Note that because of the rate of closure during head-on attacks, you can begin firing at 1.7 to 1.9 clicks. When you're making a head-on attack into heavy fire, you are advised to avoid enemy fire by maneuvering in a "corkscrew" manner until you have closed to dogfighting range. Then, when your target flies past, turn in behind him and attack.

In the case of TIE fighters or any other fighter with hull damage, you can maintain a straight and level head-on attack because the target is destroyed with only a few shots. This strategy is risky, however, because you take several hits to your forward shields.

- **Use the "Wotan Weave."**

Learn to do the Wotan Weave. This spiral, or corkscrew, maneuver enables you to avoid enemy fire while maintaining a particular heading.

Basic Wotan Weave

First target the craft you want to head toward (or away from). With this craft as your reference point, begin turning while simultaneously pulling back (or pushing forward) on the stick. If you are doing this correctly, the targeted craft's blip appears about halfway from the center of the appropriate sensor display. Your stick is approximately halfway toward a corner position but requires constant small adjustments. Generally speaking, when you're avoiding fire from a large ship, use a slow spiral. (The greater the distance, the slower the spiral.) When you want to avoid enemy starfighters (or missiles), a tight, fast spiral is best.

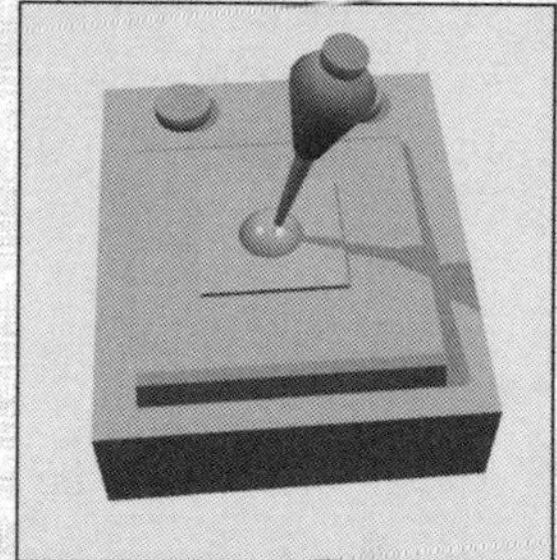

Joystick position

- **Attack large ships.**

When you attack large ships, the Wotan Weave is absolutely essential for making repeated attack runs. The standard method is shown in these steps:

1. Have shields and cannons fully charged, with recharge rates at maximum.
2. "Weave" in and begin firing at 1.6 clicks and maintain fire as you close on the target. You may want to reduce your speed to keep from getting too close. This strategy also serves to maximize your fire on the target.

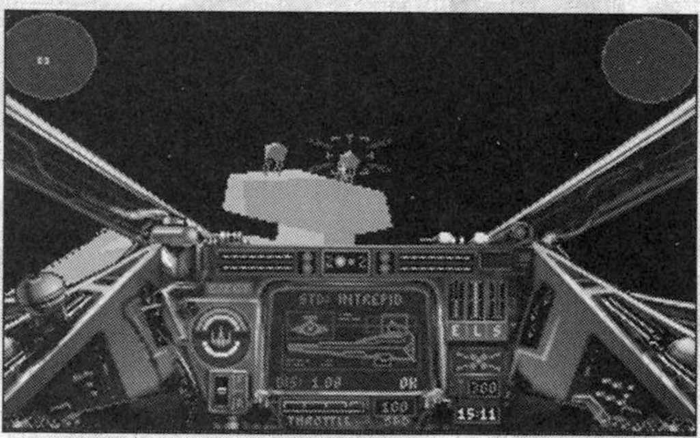

Attacking a large ship

3. When you've taken enough hits to require breaking off, reverse direction and go to full throttle.
4. Transfer all available energy to the rear shields.
5. Begin "weaving" and continue to fly away until you're out of range or ready to make another run.
6. Restore shields to even distribution.

- **Balance shields.**

Whenever you've taken a few hits, be sure to even out your shields. Press [S] three times. This technique is especially important when you are going to transfer energy from the cannons to the shields. The reason is that if, for example, your forward shields are down but your rear shields remain at full power, you won't be able to transfer the energy! (Our engineers are working on this.)

- **Use missile escape maneuvers.**

To avoid a missile, you must have it targeted in the CMD. You must be moving at high speed (generally at least 100). Turn away from the missile, and then, when it is about 0.4 clicks away, turn hard toward it. Assuming that you are successful, keep turning toward it until it self-detonates. Because Y-wings are generally unable to do this, greater reliance must be made on their stronger shields and hull.

- **Keep cannons supercharged.**

Supercharged cannons fire farther as well as hit harder. Need we say more?

- **Know your target.**

Know your target's characteristics, especially speed and armament. When you're closing to "dogfighting" range, less than 0.75 clicks, match speed with your target. This strategy helps you stay on his tail and keeps you from overshooting into a disadvantageous position.

- **Keep checking the message line.**

Because the message line is often overlooked during combat, musical themes have been assigned to particularly important events. These events are the arrival of friendly and enemy ships, the destruction of friendly and enemy ships, and the presence of enemy ships within combat range.

- **Control your energy; control your speed.**

Use ELS configuration adjustments to control speed. In the X-wing and A-wing, each level adjustment to the lasers or shields results in a 12.5 percent change in engine-power level. For the Y-wing, there is a 6.25 percent change. The actual adjustments are rounded up in your favor. For a more complete discussion of speed adjustment, see the section "Energy Management and the ELS Display," earlier in this chapter.

Other Important Factors

- **Hull damage.**

Let ships with hull damage go, unless their complete destruction is part of your mission objective. If other waves or the arrival of other ships depends on their destruction, this strategy helps delay the event. At a certain level of hull damage, a ship automatically heads toward its mother ship or its hyperspace exit point. They don't always make it—and failing to escape prevents entirely the creation of other ships.

Hull damage

- **Pilot skill level.**

When you assign pilots, don't worry about the default skill levels. You can only improve their skill levels. If the pilot you assign is less skilled than the one who was assigned when the mission was built, no change occurs. Of course, you may still lose the pilot in combat!

No cockpit mode

- **Locate distant enemies.**

Turn off the cockpit view momentarily to locate enemies who are just coming into visual range. Press [.] on the numeric keypad to toggle the cockpit on and off. Remember that your radar gives you only an approximation of where other ships are.

- **Nonplayer starfighters.**

Note that nonplayer craft do not fire torpedoes at enemy starfighters, or missiles at other enemy craft that are not starfighters.

- **Highlighted ships.**

The highlighted red part of a ship displayed in the CMD has no meaning except in the case of the Star Destroyer.

- **Brush off your wingmen.**

When you do close fly-bys of other ships, avoid rolls and hard turns if you have wingmen. They try to maintain position and often collide with the craft you're flying by.

The Principles of War

The principle tactics of the Rebellion, as outlined below, should be second nature to all who serve its cause.

- **Maintain the objective**

Choose an objective and stick with it. In warfare, the commander must conduct operations with limited knowledge of what is happening. There is a tendency to attempt to change the objective in response to changes in the situation. This wastes time and energy.

- **Economize forces**

This principle means using the right amount of offensive power for the job. For the Alliance, this principle is especially critical because we simply do not have sufficient resources to accomplish everything we want. Raids are conducted, therefore, with the minimum number of ships and troops required, which enables us to maintain a sizable reserve; also, when required, large forces can be massed.

- **Remain flexible**

This principle is the counterpart to maintaining the objective. It involves leaving options open during the planning and conduct of operations. It requires the commander to anticipate problems and have a response ready.

- **Initiative**

Get there first, with forces prepared to accomplish the objective. By capitalizing on our faster command structure, we force the Empire to respond to our actions.

This strategy complicates and disrupts their own planning, and allows the Alliance to determine the tempo of operations.

- **Maneuverability**

To win, we must outmaneuver the Empire. Combined with initiative, this means that we don't just avoid the Empire's attacks—we make our own when and where they least expect them.

- **Security**

Loose lips blast ships. So seal your lips. We must keep the enemy from discovering our plans. Good security translates directly into saved lives, and is the prerequisite for achieving surprise in combat.

- **Simplicity**

Warfare is chaotic and unpredictable. No plan survives contact with the enemy. Complex and elaborate plans often fail for this reason. Therefore, Rebel operations are typically characterized by their simplicity. This means that there are fewer things that can go wrong.

- **Surprise**

Surprise is the principal weapon of the Rebellion. History has shown surprise to be the most effective force multiplier. Surprise allows a smaller and weaker force to defeat a larger and stronger one.

General Notes About Scoring

- **Conserve your firepower!** You receive a bonus for high accuracy and a penalty for poor accuracy. Don't fire your weapons, especially homing projectile weapons, unless you feel certain of hitting your target.
- **You get points for killing Rebel ships.** Yes, it's true. If you want the highest score possible, kill everything left in the sky after the Mission Complete message appears. To make this score even easier, give your wingman "wait" orders. Remember not to assign pilots you want to keep, though!

* For more information about scoring in X-Wing, see **Appendix A:** ***Scoring and AI***

Mission Start

This section presents a typical mission checkout procedure. You may not always follow these exact steps, but during training, get used to using them. Later on, you can adjust your procedures to fit the situation at hand. You must learn to perform these steps very quickly. You don't generally have time to think about what you're doing. Make it automatic.

1. [C] to start camera. (Remember: a film record is the only way you can analyze the mission later.)
2. [X] to select dual-fire mode.
3. ['] (apostrophe) or [Shift] [F10] as many times as necessary to transfer cannon energy to the shields until the secondary shields are fully charged.
4. [F9] twice to set cannon recharge rate at maximum.
5. [F10] twice to set shield recharge rate at maximum, unless high speed is to be maintained.
6. [Bksp] to go to full throttle, if you're not already there.
7. [R] to locate the nearest enemy fighter. If you have a wingman, you may want to order him to attack this target, depending, of course, on the mission objectives. To do so, press [Shift] [A], and then [T] to locate another target. (Take this one yourself.)
8. After secondary shields are fully charged, press [F10] three more times to set the shield recharge rate to normal.
9. After cannons are fully supercharged, press [F9] three times to set the cannon recharge rate to normal (unless you're currently engaging the enemy).

It is often possible to do two things at one time. The [C] and [X] keys are next to each other, for example, so both keys can be pressed at the same time. Similarly, [F9] and [F10] can be pressed together to save time. Be sure to check your displays to verify what you've done, however.

Communications in Battle

Shift A ("Attack target!") is the most important wingman command. Use it often, especially when the enemy is coming from more than one direction. It is also a good way to get concentrated firepower on a single target, such as a freighter or corvette, when you want to destroy it as quickly as possible.

Shift C ("Cover me!") should be used with caution. The reason is that, if your wingman is already engaged and you order him to come to your aid, he ignores the enemy he was fighting. That enemy then has an easier time getting your wingman! You must be currently targeted by an enemy craft in order to get a response.

Shift I ("Ignore target!") should also be used with caution. It is useful for getting a wingman to break off an attack (if you want to finish his target off yourself), but it may make your wingman a sitting duck! You may notice that, despite acknowledging your order, your wingman might continue pressing the attack.

Shift W ("Wait for additional orders!") should be used with extreme caution. It is more effective for getting a wingman to break off an attack but definitely makes him a sitting duck! Be sure that you don't forget to . . .

. . . Shift G ("Go ahead and engage!") to order "waiting" ships to get going.

Shift H ("Head home!") is useful for pilots who are so skilled that wingmen just get in the way (and prevent you from making *all* the kills!) Be careful, though, because this is another way to make it easy for the Empire to kill one of yours. The reason is that the ship receiving this order has to make it to its hyperspace jump point, which may be some distance away, and is vulnerable until it gets there.

In the heat of battle, discipline is often difficult to maintain. Avoid putting yourself between a wingman and his target, and you will avoid "friendly fire."

Special Characteristics of Alliance Starfighters

Each craft particular to the Alliance has certain characteristics that it would benefit you to know, at least in general.

X-Wing

The X-wing is the most versatile of the Alliance starfighters. Fast and agile, powerfully armed and armored, it represents an almost ideal blend of characteristics. These features make it supremely well-suited to the multiplicity of roles assigned to it.

Unique to the X-wing is the efficiency of its cannons. At full recharge, this efficiency allows continuous fire. When you're dogfighting, keep the cannons in dual-fire mode. There are two exceptions to this general rule. When you engage Assault Gunboats or TIE Advanced Fighters, quad-fire is preferred. The Gunboat is a relatively large target, and you have a high probability of hitting it with all four cannons. When you attack the TIE Advanced, it is difficult to get the quick series of hits necessary to defeat its shields. The increased firepower of quad-fire damages the shields more quickly with each shot, and with the TIE Advanced, you have to make each shot count!

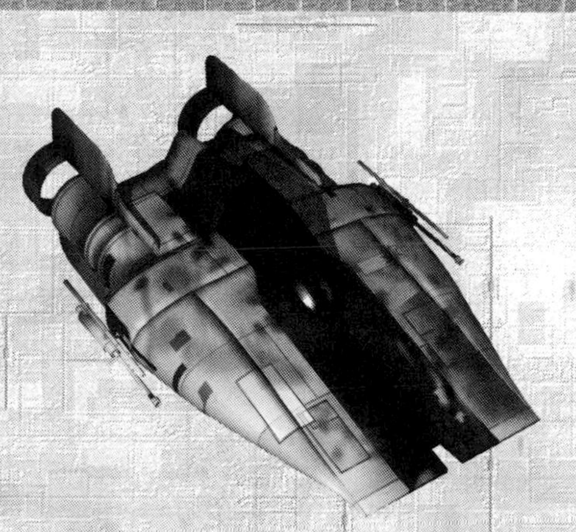

A-WING

The A-wing trades firepower and shielding for sheer speed and maneuverability. Special sensors make it the most effective armed reconnaissance craft in the Rebel arsenal. A dozen concussion missiles make it a formidable high-speed interceptor also.

Y-WING

The Y-wing is the most heavily armed starfighter available. It also boasts the most powerful shields and armor. Unfortunately, this armor results in a craft that is slow compared to other starfighters and not as maneuverable.

Unique to the Y-wing are its ion cannons, which can be used to disable enemy ships without destroying them. This capability is absolutely essential when the objective is to capture another craft. Nonetheless, most missions do not require ion cannons.

To redirect ion cannon energy most efficiently to your laser cannons, transfer it first to the shields and then back to the cannons. It is evenly distributed to both ions and lasers, but at least some of it is now available to the lasers. If the shields are already fully charged, you have to transfer shield energy to cannons first, before following the procedure just discussed.

Special Characteristics of Imperial Starfighters

The characteristics of enemy craft are equally important to the Rebel pilot.

TIE FIGHTER

The most common Imperial starfighter, the TIE is small and highly maneuverable. Like the TIE Bomber and Interceptor, it has no shields and even less armor. Cruising speed is the same as the X-wing. Quite deadly in the hands of a skilled pilot, it is nevertheless completely outclassed by all Rebel fighters.

TIE BOMBER

TIE Bombers are the most heavily armed Imperial fighters. Each TIE Bomber carries lasers, concussion missiles, and proton torpedoes! In some ways, the TIE Bomber is comparable to the Y-wing. They have the same cruising speed and are the "heavies" of their family. Although not as challenging in a dogfight, its missiles make it the most dangerous of all the Empire's starfighters—beware!

TIE INTERCEPTOR

Basically, the TIE Interceptor is a faster TIE fighter with a stronger hull and four cannons rather than two. With a cruising speed equal to that of the A-wing, the TIE Interceptor is much more dangerous than its predecessor. In the hands of a highly skilled pilot, it is tough to beat, especially in a Y-wing.

TIE ADVANCED

The latest in the TIE series of starfighters is the TIE Advanced. Like others in this family, it has no hyperdrive capability, but it does have shield generators. Its shields are not powerful, but they regenerate quickly. Because it is so difficult to hit, there is usually enough time between hits for the shields to recover.

First encountered during the Battle of Yavin, this craft is even faster and more maneuverable than the A-wing! Even in the hands of a mediocre pilot, this craft is an extremely formidable dogfighter. TIE Advanced pilots require considerably more training, however, than do pilots of other craft. Fortunately, the Empire has yet to produce significant numbers of them. Needless to say, it is even tougher to beat than the TIE Interceptor, and almost impossible for a Y-wing.

ASSAULT GUNBOAT

The Assault Gunboat is the first Imperial design to incorporate shields and hyperdrive capability. Its cruising speed lies between that of the Y-wing and the X-wing. This one also carries concussion missiles, making it quite dangerous in combat. Apparently learning from the Alliance, the Empire has begun to employ these Gunboats, using hit-and-fade tactics similar to ours! Operating in small independent groups, they also conduct armed reconnaissance and are often the prelude to major Imperial attacks.

IMPERIAL TROOP TRANSPORT

Though not considered a starfighter, this small spacecraft is nevertheless a heavily armed and dangerous threat. It possesses ion and laser cannons as well as proton torpedo launchers. And, of course, it can carry up to 30 stormtroopers or 10 spacetroopers. Add to this its hyperspace ability and you have a versatile and potent weapon capable of surprise attacks and ambushes. Though slow, it is surprisingly maneuverable, but it's no dogfighter!

IMPERIAL SHUTTLE

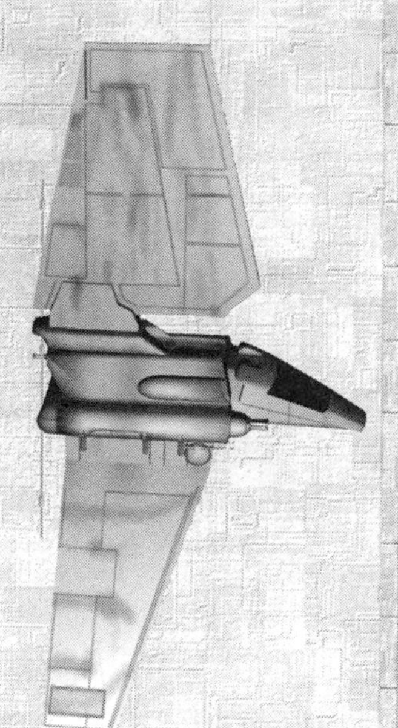

The *Lambda*-class Shuttle is not a starfighter, but nevertheless poses a threat to starfighter operations. Armed only with lasers, it is no match for any Alliance starfighter. Don't be overconfident, though, as a large number of them can overwhelm you if you aren't careful. Large enough to carry up to 14 passengers and crew members, it is only slightly faster than the Imperial Transport. It is also hyperdrive equipped.

SPECIAL CHARACTERISTICS OF VARIOUS STARSHIPS

Rebel forces should also be familiar with other types of spacecraft they might encounter on various missions.

CORELLIAN CORVETTE

The Corellian corvette is a small, fast starship—probably the single most popular starship in the galaxy. A favorite of smugglers and pirates, it is also known as the Blockade Runner. Most are armed with two or three twin-mounted turbolaser gun batteries. Because of the dorsal mounting of these guns, there is a narrow blind spot along both sides and the rear, making the corvette vulnerable to attack from these areas. The gun batteries can be destroyed without destroying the ship.

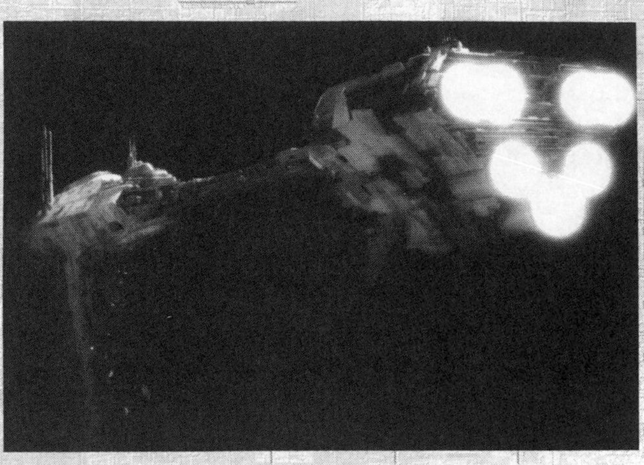

NEBULON-B CLASS FRIGATE

The Nebulon-B Frigate is a versatile ship of medium size. Popular with the Alliance and the Empire, a Nebulon B is capable of deploying two squadrons of starfighters and possesses a devastating arsenal of on-board weapons as well. This formidable warship has no obvious weaknesses on which to capitalize.

MC80 CLASS STAR CRUISER

The Mon Calamari had never created warships until they were called on to aid the Rebellion. A peaceful race who enjoyed space travel for its beauty and diversity, they quickly adapted their fleet of pleasure craft. The MC80 is a converted passenger liner, but, due to the Calamarian engineers' amazing skill, it is a capital warship second only to the Imperial-class Star Destroyer. Capable of deploying three squadrons of starfighters, this ship is the backbone of the Rebel fleet with no obvious weaknesses on which to capitalize.

IMPERIAL CLASS STAR DESTROYER

Long the instrument and the symbol of Imperial power, this huge ship is the means by which the Emperor seeks to control the galaxy. Its awesome firepower usually serves to terrify the Empire's targets of conquest into submission. Those who resist are ruthlessly crushed.

Able to deploy six TIE squadrons, this ship is best avoided, even by Calamari cruisers. One weakness is the vulnerability of its shield generators. Located on top of the main superstructure, these generators can be destroyed by a skilled starfighter attack, bringing down the entire shield system. Recognition of this flaw has increased the role of the ship's starfighter complement in defending against Rebel starfighters.

Speed Chart (all ELS settings at 50%)

X-wing	100	Transport	55
Y-wing	80	Shuttle	65
A-wing	120	Space Tug	11
TIE Fighter	100	Freighter	18
TIE Bomber	80	Corellian Corvette	22
TIE Interceptor	110	Nebulon-B Frigate	18
TIE Advanced	125	Calamari Cruiser	11
Assault Gunboat	90	Imperial Star Destroyer	11

Maximum speeds for X-wing (150), Y-wing (90), A-wing (180).

Hits to Kill Table

Craft	Lasers (Shields Down/Kill)	Missiles (Shields Down/Kill)	Torpedoes (Shields Down/Kill)
X-wing	11/4	2/1	*/1
Y-wing	16/9	3/1	1/1
A-wing	11/3	2/1	*/1
TIE fighter	*/2	*/1	*/1
TIE Bomber	*/6	*/1	*/1
TIE Interceptor	*/4	*/1	*/1
TIE Advanced	12/4	2/1	*/1
Assault Gunboat	21/6	4/1	1/1
Shuttle	21/5	4/1	1/1
Transport	15/10	3/2	1/1
Space Tug	*/1	*/1	*/1
Cargo container	40/8	7/1	2/1
Bulk freighter	97/24	>12	5/1
Corellian corvette	81/40	>12	4/2
Mines and Satellites	*/1	*/1	*/1

The first number is the usual minimum number of blasts necessary to bring down the shields. Shields regenerate, however, so if there is a pause in the attack, more shots are necessary. The second number is the number of additional shots to destroy the target. For example, an Assault Gunboat's shields begin to fail after taking more than 20 hits. They may not completely fail for a few more hits, and then the hull itself can take a few more shots.

These figures are based on continuous fire with supercharged lasers. Concussion missiles are *not* effective against the larger vessels. Furthermore, Frigates and Capital ships are not listed because a single starfighter simply doesn't have the firepower to defeat these types of ships.

How long he had stood in the doorway behind me I don't know, but I was studying the section called "Starfighter Systems and Basic Tactics" for the third time when I felt a distinct tension at the back of my neck. I usually get that feeling when someone is behind me.

"Excuse me. Are you busy?"

He couldn't have been more than a few years older than I, but the guy leaning casually in the doorway to my room was wearing lieutenant's insignia. With his hair a month overgrown and his uniform only partially buttoned up, he looked more like one of my friends back in Tondatha than an Alliance officer.

"Some of the crew around here call me Lieutenant Blastwell. But you can call me Hamo if I can call you Keyan. Deal?" He smiled and held out his hand.

"Aren't I supposed to salute or something?" I asked, extending my hand.

"That'll come later," he said. "I just thought you might like to get a bite to eat," he added.

"Do they serve mugruebe stew?" I asked, hopefully. Mugruebe was one of my favorite Agamarian dishes, and I realized that I was hungry. Very hungry.

Hamo laughed. "You want to be a starfighter pilot, do you? And you can't be more original then mugruebe stew? Come on, Keyan. Live dangerously. Take a chance. You've got to try the Mutandan porf."

"Porf?" I was dubious. "Doesn't sound very good. What's in it?"

"Don't ask." Hamo grinned and gestured for me to follow.

✗ ✗ ✗

Hamo turned out to be from a small planet like Agamar, and we found much to talk about. Too soon, however, Hamo called a halt to our discussion. With a last sip of non-alcoholic Veronian berry wine, I followed Hamo back down the dark passage that led to my cabin.

"Tomorrow you go to the Maze. Best you get some sleep. You have a lot to learn, and tomorrow it begins."

"The Maze?"

"The Pilot's Proving Ground. You have to check out there before you can get on the simulators."

"You don't waste time around here, do you? I thought I'd have to cool my heels for days before I got a crack at anything like real training."

He clapped me on the back. "Hey, Keyan. Get this. The Alliance has no time to waste. No time at all. Besides," he added very seriously, "I've got a good feeling about you. I'm betting you'll ace your training."

"And if I do?"

"Hey! I'll even try some of your mugruebe stew."

"And what if I don't?"

"You get to eat porf," he said with a wicked smile. "But you'll do it, kid. Besides, I need a new wingman."

When we reached the door to my cabin, he stood at attention and saluted, and then he smiled and pressed the stud to open my door.

"I'll see ya at the crack of dawn," he quipped. "Figuratively, that is," he added as he headed down the dark hallway. Not sleepy at all, I entered my room and reopened the *Starfighter Pilot's Handbook*.

THE PILOT PROVING GROUND (THE MAZE)

I was sent to a secret training area the next morning. I have no idea where it was, and I'm sure that it isn't there anymore. Rebel facilities have a way of changing locations frequently, for obvious reasons.

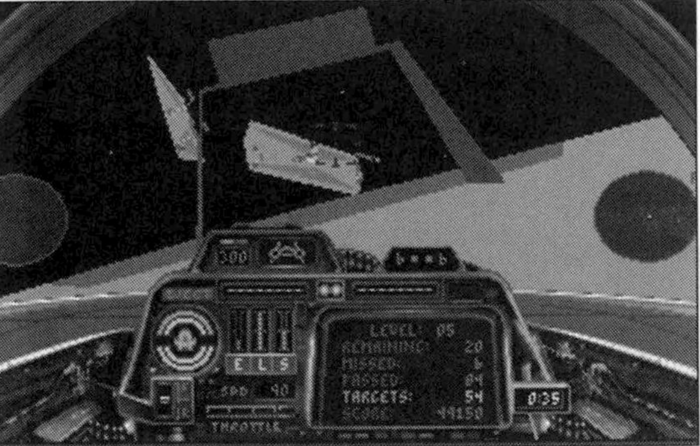

In the Maze.

The Maze was a series of gates and targets designed to familiarize pilots with the basic operation of their craft. I spent two days flying the Maze and learning how to manage different starfighters.

There was no real danger. The Maze is designed so that nothing you do can really hurt you. The damage is simulated. But the effect is real enough. My shoulders ached after the first few hours of concentrated effort. I did pretty well my first run, but Hamo flew up next to me as I ran out of time and told me to keep trying.

Eventually I got the knack of flying the Maze and could keep going all the way past the eight main levels. On the third day of training, we all realized that I couldn't really learn anything more from the Maze. Next stop: the simulators!

Here's some of what I learned in the Maze:

- Different ways of controlling my energy and speed settings. For instance, I learned that I could slow down at times by increasing laser or shield recharge rates instead of changing throttle settings.
- To fly most of the time with full throttle, full power directed to lasers, and shield recharge rates set to normal.
- To look ahead, anticipate the next set of gates, and use my maneuvering thrusters to angle my fighter into position for an easy pass.
- To redirect laser energy to my shields to recharge them when they get low.
- To balance my shield coverage so that I am covered both in front and in back.
- To aim quickly and shoot accurately because each target I hit gains me some time.
- Not to crash into anything, which stops my fighter and loses precious time.

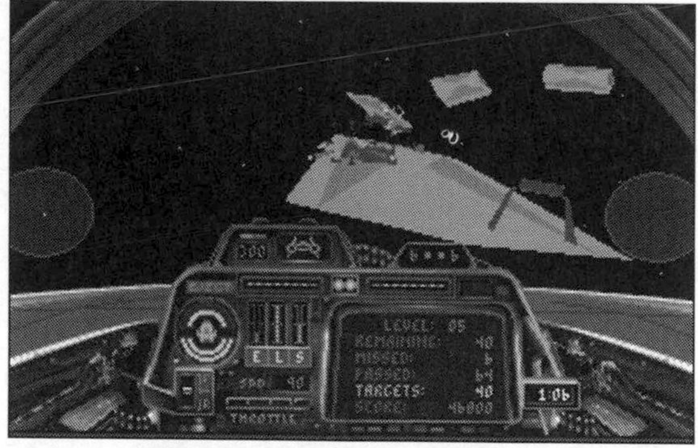

Looking ahead.

More Maze Tips

Here are a few less common tips:

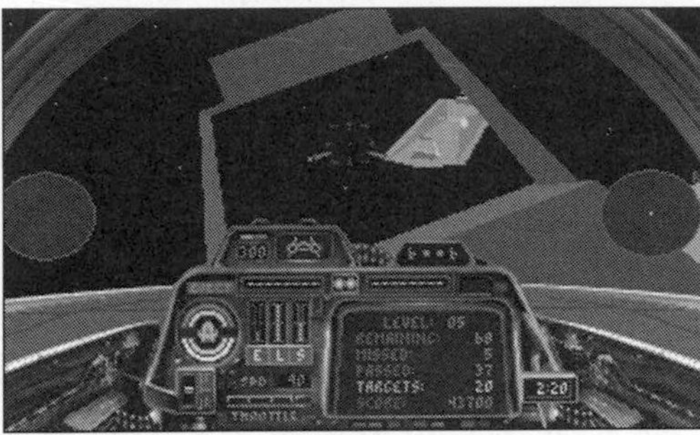

Look ahead. Remember, you don't have to fly through the middle of each gate.

- You don't have to fly through every gate. You can get credit for gates if you just clip them with a wing or any part of your fighter. Knowing that, I was able to take different angles to fly through some gates.
- Sometimes you can slow down and shoot the targets at the next platform before you get there. Control speed and get the targets, and then zoom through the gates.
- If you miss a gate, you can sometimes loop around and go back for it. Some pilots never do this. Others say that they can loop back around faster than the 15 seconds they would lose if they skipped the gate.
- Speed isn't really the key. Accurate shooting and conservation of energy are more important.

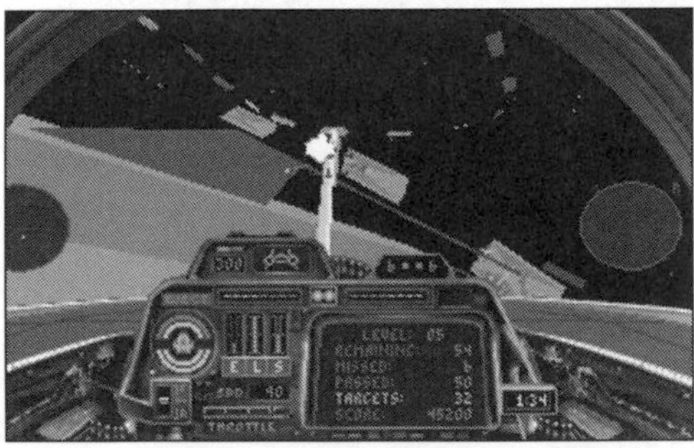

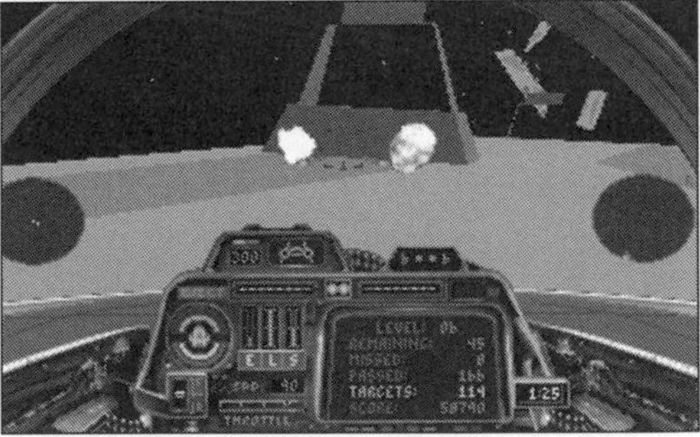

Make your shots from all angles. See if you can hit two targets with one shot.

Completing a level.

- You can shoot targets from odd places. For instance, you can shoot right through raised platforms. You can even shoot targets from underneath the main platform!
- If you get in real trouble in one of the later levels, you can hide under the platforms to recharge your shields and lasers. Although this strategy may take some time, it is still possible to complete the course if you've been able to move quickly through the gates, you hit the targets, and you don't crash into anything.

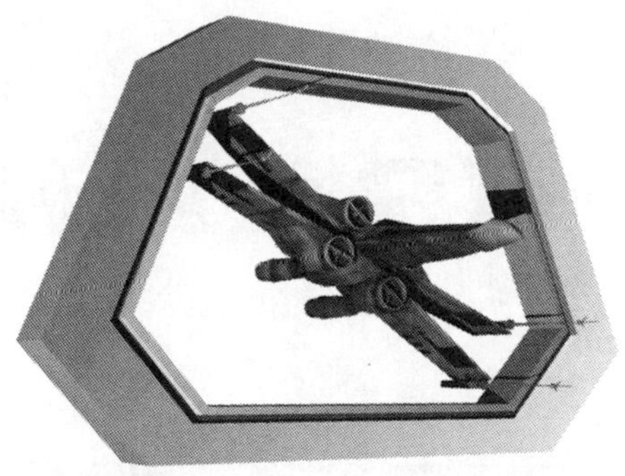

PART THREE

PART THREE

HISTORICAL COMBAT MISSIONS

This is the weapon of a Jedi Knight. Not as clumsy or as random as a blaster. An elegant weapon for a more civilized age. For over a thousand generations the Jedi Knights were the guardians of peace and justice in the Old Republic. Before the dark times, before the Empire.

— Obi-Wan Kenobi

Hokey religions and ancient weapons are no match for a good blaster at your side, kid.

— Han Solo

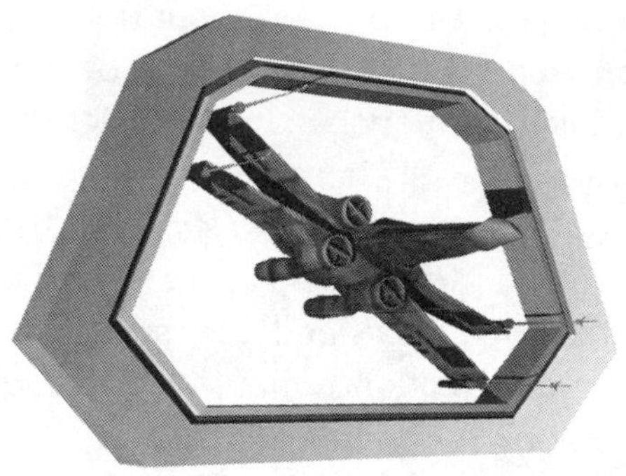

Historical Combat Missions

When I first came onboard the *Independence*, I was anxious to begin my training. There was nothing I wanted more than to get behind the controls of a starfighter and blast away at Imperial ships. By the time I had read the *Starfighter Pilot's Handbook*, that desire had become unbearable.

And after I had mastered the Pilot's Proving Ground, I knew that I was ready. But Hamo was always around, and he never failed to assure me that I had much to learn. Even after I had passed the Maze, in his own words, "with flying colors," he wouldn't authorize me for any real duty.

Instead, he sent me back to the simulators, where I met Commander Wex "TIE-Die" Dafid, tactical training officer. From this tactical master I was to learn the lessons that kept me alive later, when the blasters were real and there were no second chances.

X-Wing Historical Combat Missions

"All right, beings. For some of you, I'm your final hurdle. You've got to get by me to get your hands on a real starfighter. I'm here to make sure you don't leave here as TIE meat. We can't spare the ships."

I think that this was meant to be a joke, but nobody laughed. We were all scared to death. Commander Dafid was the kind of instructor young pilots had nightmares about—a tough, experienced, no-nonsense kind of man who had seen it all and lived (barely) to tell about it.

The tactical training officer paused and surveyed the room, his eyes locking with each of ours in turn. Absently, he rubbed the three-inch scar along his cheek with his good hand, and after staring each of us down, he'd mutter something practically inaudible that sounded vaguely like, "Hmm nnun." My first impression? A genuine nut case.

In the stories floating around the mess, Dafid had ignored practically every rule of combat in his 150 or so sorties and had just about fragged a couple dozen times. That was how he learned the importance of proper tactical flying. But these were just stories. Who knew the truth?

The commander had finished his survey and intimidation drill, or whatever it was, and began to lecture again, pacing the room like a caged rancor and occasionally rubbing the scar on his cheek. He seemed almost to have forgotten about us, but I knew that he hadn't.

"Each mission you fly in the simulator is meant to teach you something. Be sure you learn your lessons. I don't care if you ace through each mission the first time or fail your first ten attempts. Just as long as you get the message. If I can help it, none of you will set foot in a starfighter until you've completed all the historical simulations." Dafid gestured toward the simulator and the big holo screen behind him. "Who wants to be first to demonstrate his skills in battle?" he asked.

There were no volunteers.

Mission Note: For these first missions, you are reminded which keys to press on the keyboard for many of the operations you perform. The keys to press are inside square brackets. To set cannon power, for instance, press the F9 key; it's notated as [F9]. Be aware that the square brackets are, themselves, used during the game. For clarity, curly brackets are used to indicate when you should press the square brackets during the game.

MISSION 1: DEV'S SIDESTEP

File Name: waistem

Mission Briefing
In this mission, you learn to adjust your power configuration system, target the enemy, and destroy unarmed Imperial TIE fighters and stationary cargo ships.

Dafid's Training Objective
"O.K., rookies. Here's your chance to beat up on some helpless opponents. It's not that much of a contest. I expect you to learn how to use your targeting computer, how to shoot straight, and how to move quickly from one target to the next. Master this lesson, and you'll go on to the next."

Tactical Summary
Your ship has "accidentally" hyperspaced into an Imperial Training Area. The enemy ships are mostly stationary or slow-moving, and only two are armed. This is an opportunity, therefore, for you to practice some combat skills in a low-threat environment.

Target the TIE fighter.

As the mission begins, you find the first TIE fighter less than one click ahead. Because no enemies are attacking you, it is not necessary to transfer laser energy to the shields. Also, because the enemy craft are moving slowly or not at all, keep your own speed low so as not to overshoot your targets. Switch to dual mode and destroy the first TIE. Query the CMD for the next target (another stationary TIE fighter), and destroy it, too.

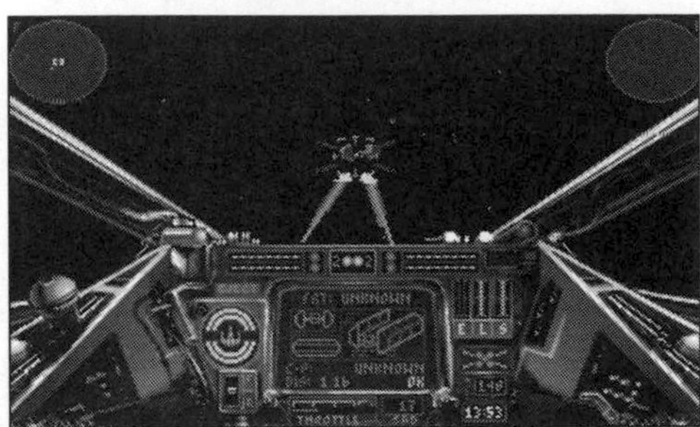
Use torpedoes on the freighter.

Now go after some Bombers.

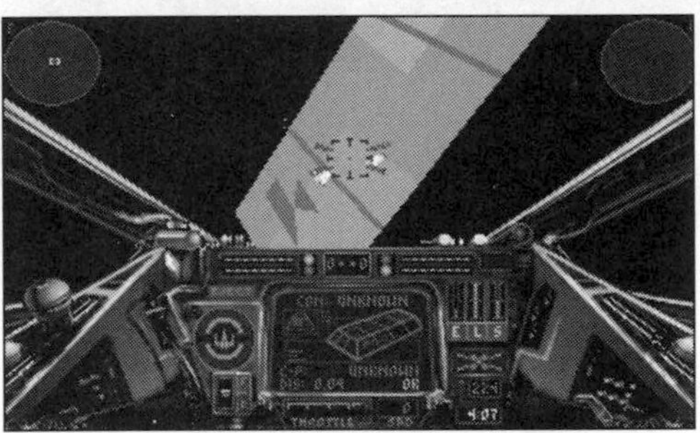
Slow down and blast the container.

The FRT *Rouh* should be your next target. Switch to torpedoes and fire all six in dual mode to blow it up. You don't have to wait for a solid lock because the *Rouh* is not moving. Switch back to lasers and query the CMD for the next target. This is one of a pair of TIE Interceptors moving in a slow circle. Increase speed to two-thirds (]) power and destroy both. Then cycle forward (T) to the next target, the first of three stationary transports. Reduce speed to one-third ([) power while attacking them.

After you have eliminated the transports, query the CMD again to locate a pair of circling TIE Bombers. Increase speed again to two-thirds (]), destroy the Bombers, and then query the CMD again to locate another pair of circling TIE Bombers. Now locate and destroy a stationary group of three TIE fighters.

Next, cycle forward again to locate the first of two empty containers. Destroying these containers causes a pair of TIE fighters to appear with orders to attack you. They are about two clicks away, so you have time to eliminate the group of three TIE Interceptors about .75 click away. Go to full throttle to engage the attacking TIE fighters. Finally, query the CMD once more to locate the last group of enemy ships, a pair of TIE Bombers that attempt to evade you.

Win Conditions

Destruction of *all* enemy craft.

Mission Note: T/F group Zeta hyperspaces into the mission after the *destruction* of CON group Phi. In the original mission design, they were supposed to come out when CON *Phi 2* is *attacked*.

MISSION 2: WINGMEN ARE IMPORTANT

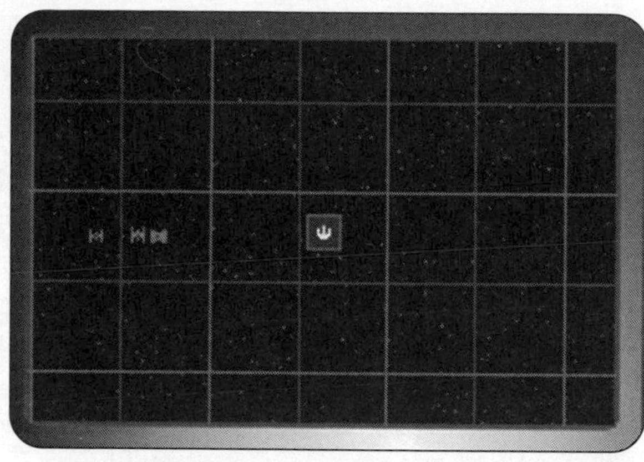

File Name: max4

Mission Briefing

In this mission, you engage Imperial forces for the first time. You learn the value of a wingman and the importance of working as a fighter team.

Dafid's Training Objective

"You're here to learn the wingman's role. Don't underestimate it. Your primary objective comes first: Protect your flight leader. Also in this mission, I expect you to manage your energy output to shields and weapons and to control your speed. Practice targeting enemy fighters and shooting them with a minimum of effort."

Tactical Summary

You and your flight leader face three pairs of TIE fighters. In this very simple and short engagement, you can learn basic dogfighting techniques.

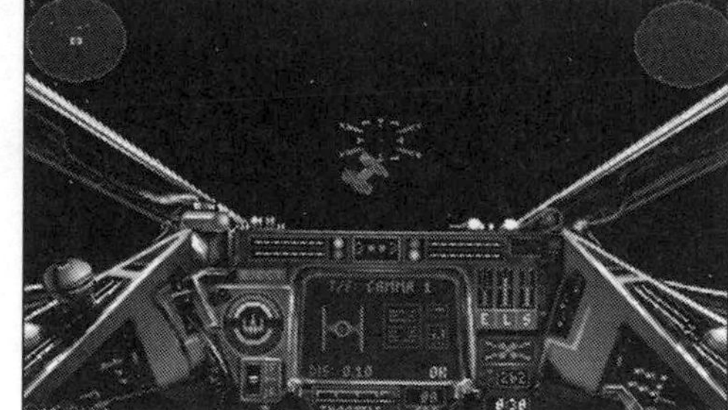

Attack the Gamma Squadron.

After adjusting your power levels, you will notice that your flight leader pulls ahead of you. This is fine. Cycle through the targets to find T/F *Gamma 1* and attack it. After you've killed this one, cycle forward to find T/F *Gamma 2* and go after him. Your flight leader takes care of the others, but feel free to lend a hand! When you are more confident in your skills, try giving your flight leader the Return Home (Shift-H) order at the beginning of the mission, and take on all six enemy ships yourself.

Win Conditions

Destruction of *all* enemy craft.

MISSION 3: SATELLITES NEAR CORUSCANT

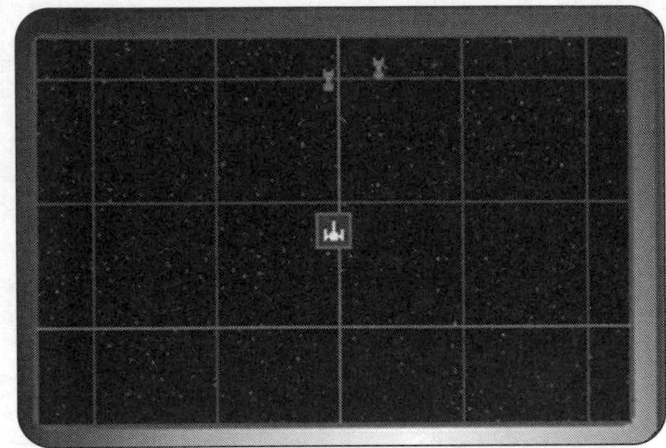

File Name: satlit1

Mission Briefing

This mission teaches you to use your laser guns with precision by targeting and destroying small objects, such as satellites and mines.

Dafid's Training Objective

"Quick targeting under pressure, precise speed control, and navigation in 3-D space. These are the objectives of this mission. Learn to jink to avoid the lasers, and learn to aim and fire without effort. Or don't, and get fragged."

Use torpedoes on the transports.

Tactical Summary

In this mission, you must be quick and efficient in order to eliminate the targets before the Empire's forces can respond (four minutes).

Reduce your speed to zero as you enter the area. There are no enemy fighters to trouble you, and the mines can't chase you. Engage the targeting system ([T]) to locate the first of two transports. Switch to dual-fire torpedoes and eliminate them before proceeding to deal with the minefield. Make sure that you have a solid lock before firing.

Switch back to lasers and select quad-fire. Destroying a mine requires only a single laser blast, but quad-fire greatly improves the chances that the targeting system will find a firing solution for at least one of the guns.

With shields fully charged, throttle up to one-third ([[]) and target the nearest mine. As you close on the minefield, keep an eye on your forward

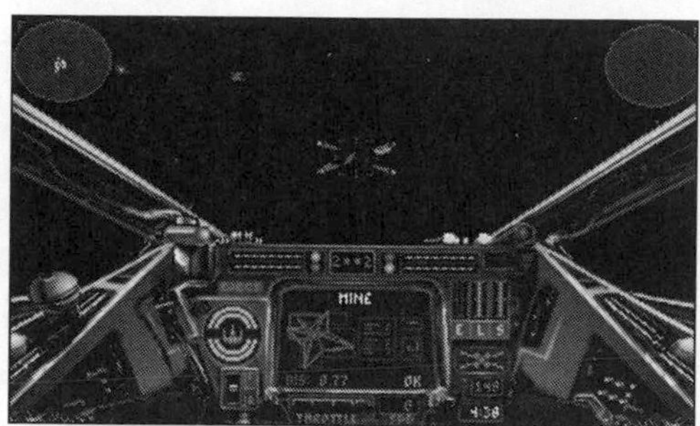

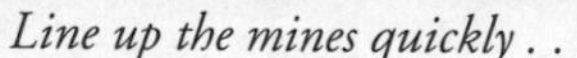
Line up the mines quickly . . .

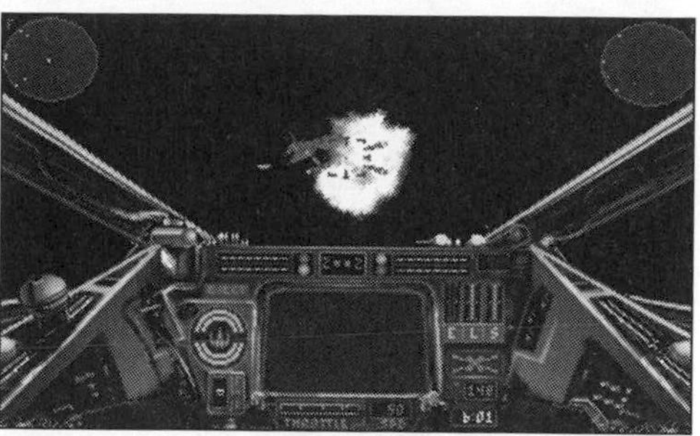
. . . and fire!

shields. When the secondary shield has been brought down, turn away and go to full throttle (Backspace). As you pull away, rebalance your shield energy and transfer laser energy until the shields are fully charged. Now turn back to the mines and reduce speed to one-third ([) again. Repeat this procedure until all the mines are eliminated.

Another way to conserve shields is to transfer energy from your cannons to your shields (Shift-H or [']). Keep your shields balanced (press S three times quickly), and keep hitting the key to transfer energy. This technique works best if you fire cannons in single- or double-fire mode, because you have two drains on the cannon energy. Try going in at full throttle rather than one-third power. Keep weaving to avoid being hit as you approach the mines; then, when you're close enough, shoot them in rapid passes. Practice until you can target and shoot a mine almost in one motion. Efficiency of effort and shield maintenance are the keys here.

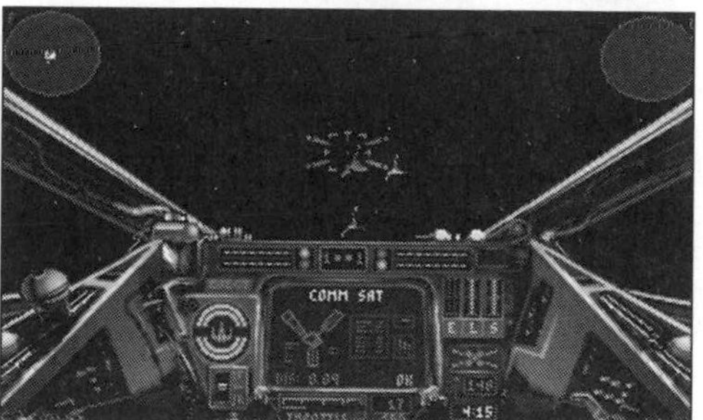

Finally, destroy the comm sat.

When the mines are all gone, you can destroy the satellites unmolested. If you have been quick, the Imperial Frigate *Sentinel* will only now be arriving. If you're feeling cocky, you may want to take on the *Sentinel's* TIEs!

Win Conditions

Destruction of *all* mines and satellites, as well as the two transports.

MISSION 4: BEAT THE ODDS

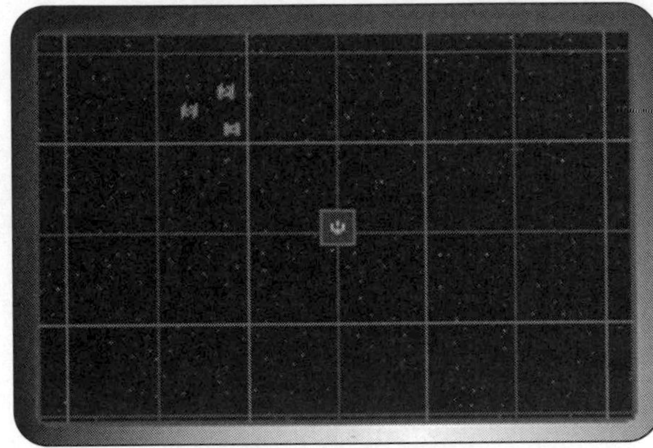

File Name: max5

Mission Briefing

Rebel starfighter pilots almost always fight the Empire outnumbered by at least three to one. This mission teaches you to beat these odds.

Dafid's Training Objective

"Learn to shoot TIE fighters. Don't look for deep philosophy here. Just shoot fast, don't miss, and get out with your skin."

Tactical Summary

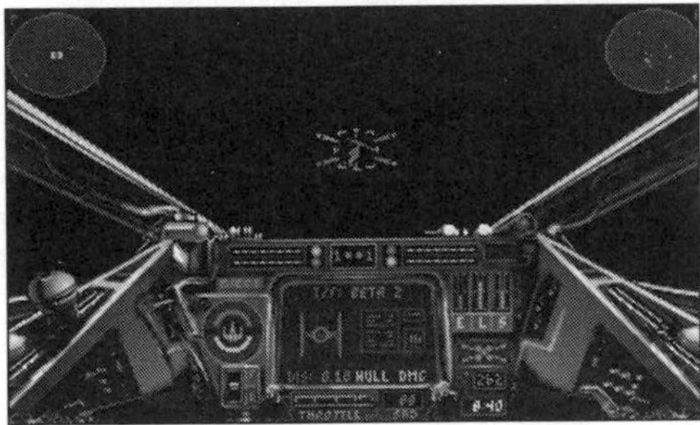

Use a torpedo in a head-on pass.

Your flight group of three X-wings has been sent to test Imperial defenses near Circarpous IV. You encounter three groups of three TIE fighters. As you close in on the nearest enemy 'fighter, switch to torpedoes and fire one in a head-on pass. Switch back to lasers and query the CMD for the next enemy fighter. Proceed in the same manner as you continue the dogfight. You have to be quick to get your share of kills. If you're fully confident in your abilities, send your wingmen home at the beginning of the mission and try your hand at nine-to-one odds!

Win Conditions

Destruction of *all* enemy craft.

MISSION 5: RESCUE AT MON CALAMARI

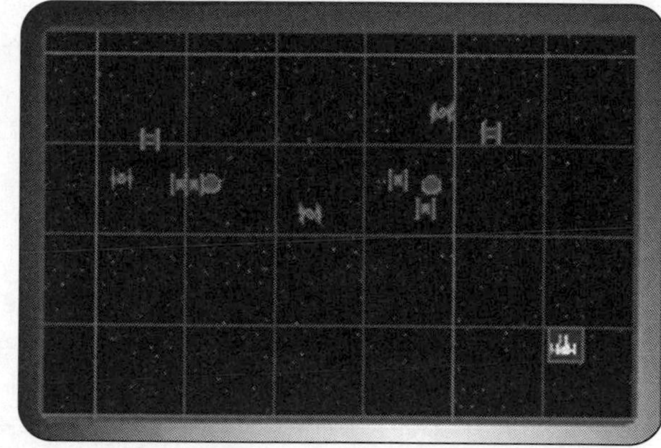

File Name: halley

Mission Briefing

This mission re-creates one of the most spectacular life-or-death rescue missions in history—especially from the view of a particularly daring X-wing pilot: Halley Kadorto.

Dafid's Training Objective

"Destroying the enemy is only part of your job. A starfighter is also a defensive weapon. You must learn to help the Alliance in any way you can. In this mission, you must identify the containers that contain slaves. Do so quickly so that a rescue team can 'space in and rescue the Calamarians. Rescuing the Calamari slaves is the primary purpose of this mission! After you have identified the containers, protect the rescue operation. Finally, destroy any Imperial ships or supplies before you 'space out and return to base.

"Learn to identify unknown vessels and how to provide a protective screen for our noncombatant forces."

Tactical Summary

The Imperial Star Destroyer *Warrior* is about to rendezvous with a supply convoy. Among the convoy's cargo are a number of Calamarian slaves. You play a critical role in their rescue.

At the beginning of the mission, the closer of two Imperial freighters, *Betar,* is about four clicks ahead and slightly to your right. Order your wingman to attack it, and then cycle back (Y) for the other freighter, *Wiggins.* Assign it to the targeting system (Shift-F5). Now you must eliminate the TIE fighter escorts so that the Y-wings will be safe. Query the CMD for the nearest one (*Alpha 1*) and engage it and then its wingman. Proceed in the same manner until all the TIE fighters are eliminated. As soon as the FRT *Betar* is destroyed, begin assigning your wingman to the remaining TIES.

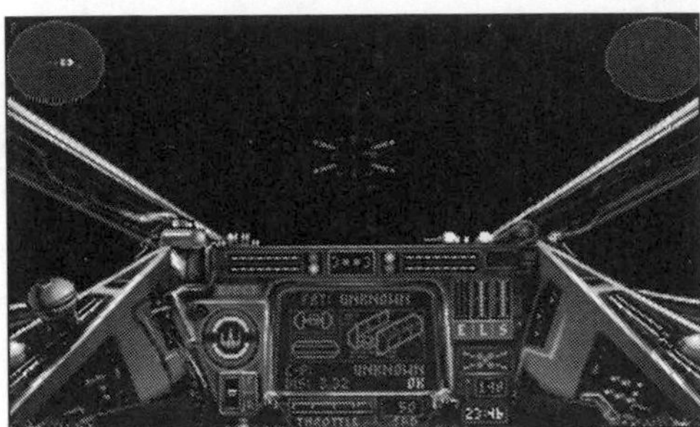

Head for the distant freighters.

When all the TIEs have been destroyed, ID all the containers and, last of all, the other freighter. CON *Xi 1* and FRT *Wiggins* have the Calamarian slaves. The other containers should be destroyed.

The Star Destroyer drops out of hyperspace about ten clicks away, three minutes into the mission. It begins launching attack waves of TIE fighters and Bombers; however, their orders are to attack the slave-holding ships, not you! Nevertheless, you must stop them, because they will likely destroy the friendly rescue freighters, *Citadel 1* and *2*, while trying to kill the slaves.

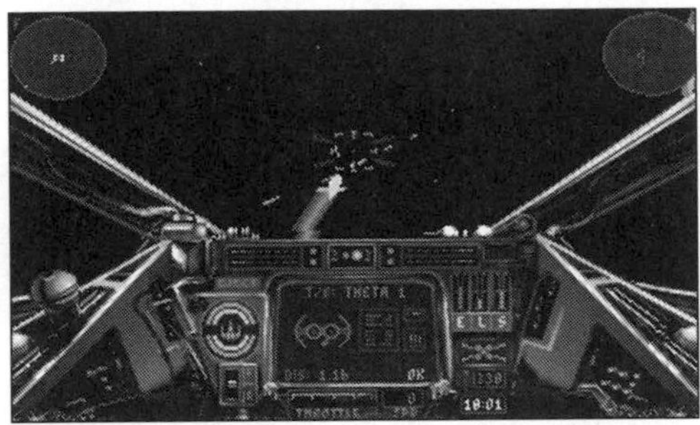

Torpedo the Bombers before they get close.

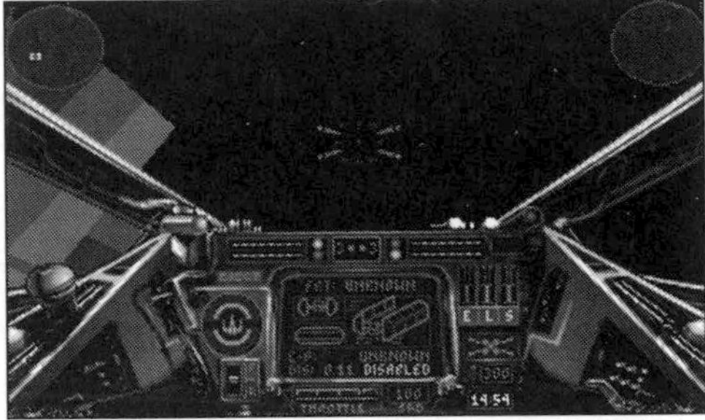

Identifying the freighters

A couple of space tugs are also in the area. They are no threat, but that shouldn't stop you from destroying them!

Win Conditions

Y-wing Gold must disable the FRT *Wiggins* and escape into hyperspace. FRT *Citadel 1* must dock with CON *Xi 1* and escape into hyperspace. FRT *Citadel 2* must dock with FRT *Wiggins* and escape into hyperspace. FRT *Betar* and CON *Psi* must be destroyed.

Mission Note: Enemy ships can not affect each other as intended in this mission. Torpedoes and laser blasts pass through targets with the same affiliation as the shooter. (The Imperial FRTs and CONs should have been "neutral" in order for this mission to work properly.)

Meeting Halley Kadorto

It happened after my first day on the historical simulators. I was in the mess hall. Hamo was away on some mission he couldn't talk about, so I was eating alone. I found a table that was practically empty. I had decided to think about the day's events for a few minutes while I ate.

The only other occupant of the large table was an older man dressed in civilian clothes. At first, I was going to sit at the far end of the table, but something prompted me to sit nearer the old man.

"Starfighter cadet?" he asked as I sat down.

"Yes, sir. Keyan Farlander. Just joined up . . . at Agamar."

"Ahh. Agamar. I was there once. Nice planet," the man said. "Pleased to meet you. I'm Kadorto. Halley Kadorto."

I must have looked like a stunned hoska, because he laughed and nodded his head.

"That's right. I'm the one from the simulators. You flown my mission yet?"

"Yessir. I did it today, as a matter of fact."

"The key, you know, is identifying the containers with the slaves. I was lucky. We knew something was up around Mon Calamari, but we never suspected the Imperial scum would actually try to destroy the slave containers before we could get there. I saw the TIEs zeroing in on the distant containers and took off to see what they were up to. I wasn't following orders. Instinct, maybe. Luck. Doesn't matter much, does it?"

I didn't know what to say, so I just smiled knowingly.

"I've been shot up a lot of times. In the early days, our ships were prone to fail on us. You don't have that in the simulators. They're better these days, but back then . . . I was technically dead three or four times, but the medical droids always brought me back.

"That day, I was sharp. I flew circles around those TIE bastards and shot them all to hell. By the time reinforcements arrived, well . . . there wasn't much left. It was a proud day, young Farlander, but I flew a lot of missions before and after that one, and every one of them was just as important. Remember that. Don't let up for an instant, or you'll be staring into the ugly face of one of those medical droids—if you're lucky!"

I was still sitting with Halley Kadorto when Hamo suddenly appeared in the mess. He seemed to be in a hurry. When he spotted me, he came directly over to the table.

"Come on, Farlander. There's a call for volunteers to fly a very important mission. They need more pilots, and I volunteered you."

✘ ✘ ✘

Many people have already heard the story of my first mission. It became the subject of general conversation on the *Independence* after I returned. Perhaps much has been made of it—it being my first mission and all—but I figure that I was just lucky, in spite of what Mon Mothma told me after my promotion.

Reluctantly I followed Hamo to a briefing room. By this time, I had a better idea about how things worked on board, but I was pretty surprised to see Mon Mothma and Admiral Ackbar heading up the briefing. The admiral began speaking soon after we arrived.

"The Frigate will pop in here." The Calamarian was pointing to a spot in the holo projection. A label indicated that it was a quadrant of the Hadar sector. A Corellian corvette filled the lower corner of the projection. A small world was visible in the background. As the admiral spoke, a Nebulon-B Frigate popped into view in the upper quadrant. Within moments, a stream of TIE fighters appeared and headed directly for the Frigate. Then a squadron of X-wings appeared behind the TIE fighters, catching them in a crossfire between their guns and the Frigate's. The

second X-wing squadron and the Y-wings surrounded the corvette.

"Blue Squadron will flank the enemy fighters, catching them in a crossfire with the Calamarian Frigate *Liberator*. Red Squadron will protect the *Storm Unit* as it attempts to board the corvette *Talon*. The Y-wings of Gold Squadron will use their ion cannons to disable the corvette's weapons and electricals. If Blue Squadron is successful, there should be limited resistance; but Red Squadron, your job is to protect the Y-wings and the *Storm Unit*.

"When the *Storm Unit* successfully boards the *Talon*, the commandos will make their way to the captain's quarters and to the bridge. They will confiscate all available holos and capture any senior ranking officers. In addition, R2 units will scan the corvette's computer system and retrieve anything found there. Are there any questions?"

Captain Charger, one of our senior officers, stood up and asked, "Do we take the corvette when we leave, destroy it, or abandon it?"

The admiral was quick to answer. "Carry out the mission objectives and retreat immediately. We want as few casualties on this mission as possible. And we don't want any complications. Just hit hard, hit fast, and get out!"

When assignments were made, Hamo was assigned to Red Squadron. He volunteered me as his wingman. I kept asking myself what I was doing here. I asked Hamo the same question.

"There are a lot of ops going on right now," he replied later, as we made our way back to our quarters. "They're short on pilots." He grinned and added, "So you're elected."

Ready or not, Empire, here I come. This was what I had joined the Alliance for, after all. I just hoped I made it back.

"Don't worry," Hamo told me, for the hundredth time, it seemed. "You'll be fine."

We had a few days before the mission, and Hamo yanked me from my normal training schedule to drill me in X-wing maneuvers and get me some real flight time. It was perhaps the most exciting time of my life. It would have been fun too, if I could have forgotten what lay ahead. But every time I questioned my abilities, Hamo would reassure me, and slowly I gained confidence in myself.

The X-wing did feel much like a T-16—only better.

The day arrived. We strapped in and did our instrument checkouts. Then the tractor beams floated us from the hangar and into space. It wasn't the first time I had seen the black, infinite canvas of space from inside an X-wing, but it was the first time I was going to hyperspace into battle. My stomach was queasy, and I could hardly maintain my focus on the equipment and the readouts from the console before me.

"You OK, Red Two?" It was Hamo, checking in.

"Fine," I answered, not entirely truthfully. "I'm fine." I struggled to gain control, taking deep breaths and letting them out slowly. Gradually, I put aside all fear of the future and concentrated on handling my starfighter. My starfighter, I thought. I was finally ready for action. "I'm ready," I breathed into my communicator.

"What's that, Red Two?" came Hamo's reply.

"Nothing, Red Leader. Ready when you are," I answered, this time with some conviction.

"Just stick close to me," he replied. "Hyperspace in T-minus 15."

I had been in hyperspace a few times by now, but I never got used to the feeling of losing my reference points. I could feel my body's anchor in the real world literally rip away. I could sense myself receding from my known point in space and heading for another. When I described this feeling to others, they all looked at me blankly or implied that it was just my imagination—except for one Sullustan navigator

who said nothing, but nodded sagely and offered what passed for a smile among Sullustans.

This eerie sensation was all the more intense when it was just me and the X-wing alone in limbo. Fortunately, it didn't last long. We came out a few clicks from a raging battle.

There was a slight pressure change. Faint static played over the comlink. And off in the distance, laser bursts flashed and ships were disintegrating in iridescent blues, greens, and violets against the backdrop of a distant galaxy. In that surreal moment, I think I formed an image of space battle that would forever haunt me: contradictory visions of beauty and death; of graceful, weightless dancing; and awesome, destructive power.

All this in a heartbeat.

I found myself pulling hard on the controls and spinning into an approach position, the enemy corvette filling my view screen. I could see Hamo's X-wing just ahead of me, and I adjusted to match his trajectory. I pushed too hard! Suddenly I lost him, spinning off course as I tried to compensate. In a speeding X-wing, a small miscalculation can really throw you off.

Angry at myself for making this stupid error, I started to come around again when I spotted two TIE fighters speeding in my direction. A quick mental calculation told me that they were headed straight for Hamo's X-wing!

I swung in behind the closer of the two. He had almost lined up with Hamo already. "Watch out, Red Leader," I yelled as I punched the fire button.

My hand wasn't steady, and my aim was off, but one of the quad-linked lasers hit the TIE on the side panel just before his green lasers squirted out at Hamo. I could see the TIE slew sideways, and his shot went wide, a single beam just clipping the back of Hamo's X-wing.

I kept the TIE fighter in my sights and closed in to finish him off. It all happened so fast; I was flying on instinct. I noticed that the TIE seemed to be circling to starboard. Later I realized that his steering was probably damaged, but at the time, I just took an angle inside his turn and fired a couple of dual-linked blasts. The second one hit him amidships, and the small TIE fighter lit up with electrical sparks and careened off course, spinning out of control. A moment later, the ship exploded, sending pieces flying in all directions.

"Good shooting, Red Two." It was Hamo on the comm. "And thanks. But next time, watch out for the wingman. I barely got him off your tail."

The wingman! I had forgotten about him as I concentrated on the TIE in front. If it hadn't been for Hamo acting as my wingman, I would have been dead meat.

"Red Two, come in."

"I'm here, Red Leader. I'm OK, I guess."

"Hey kid, that was good shooting. You'll be all right. But listen. I'm afraid I've been damaged. It's not too severe, but my R2 has been disabled. I won't be able to return to base—no hyperspace, you know—unless I can dock with the *Liberator*. I'm leaving the fight to you, Red Two. I'm joining Blue Squadron. You're on your own. You copy?"

"Sh... shouldn't I stay with you, Red Leader?" I asked. I didn't know whether to be scared, angry, or flattered that Hamo was going to leave me to fend for myself. Angry and scared were top contenders, however.

"Negative. Complete the mission. Hurry now, or you'll miss all the fun." The comm clicked off and then on again. "Good luck, Keyan."

"Thank you, sir. Same to you," I answered dubiously.

"Hey, kid. Don't worry. Just keep your wits about you. You're a natural, you know."

Then Hamo's X-wing banked and flew out of view. I was headed for the *Talon*. Staying on course, I watched the Y-wings firing ion blasts at specific locations, trying to penetrate the corvette's shields. Other X-wings from Red Squadron were helping by targeting the active guns.

I began weaving my way around the laser shots, heading in toward one of the gun emplacements. So far, it wasn't much different from the simulation drills. If you kept moving, the ship's lasers couldn't home in on you. Then a call come over the comm.

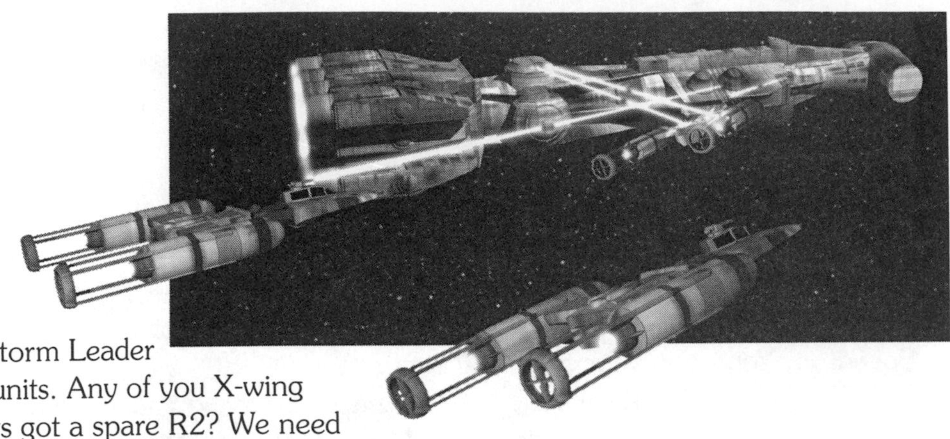

"Storm Leader to all units. Any of you X-wing jockeys got a spare R2? We need help here at the main air lock. Come in . . . ."

"Red Leader to Red Two. You hear that? Go on in, boy. Give the commandos a hand." Hamo was still watching out for me.

"Acknowledged," I called. "Red Two to Storm Leader. Where's the air lock? Come in, Storm Leader."

"This is Storm Leader. Red Two, come in along the belly, aft of amidships. You'll see our boarding craft jamming the hatch. You should be able to squeeze your X-wing around it. We'll meet you in the landing bay."

"I'm on my way, Storm Leader," I told him. I finished my pass at the gun emplacement, squeezing off three or four shots before I veered around the edge of the corvette and circled under it.

The boarding craft was smoking, so it was easy to spot. I pulled up to the air lock, slowing my engines nearly to zero, and drifted past the boarding craft. I could see a gaping hole in the hull, and smoking fumes from burning metal poured out into the vacuum.

As I eased out of the cockpit, assault troopers began removing my R2 unit from its socket in the X-wing. I climbed down and saluted the officers who approached me.

"We've finally got this section secured," one of them told me. "We're trying to jam their gun computers. A few of the others have already gone forward to find the bridge."

"What should I do?" I asked. I hadn't planned on boarding the *Talon*, although I had been briefed on some basics of the ship's layout.

"Take your R2 forward and see if you can help us jam the guns. This section has been cut off from the main defense computers. And while you're there, get anything that looks important and get back here. You've got 15 minutes."

Now I know that if I had thought about it much, I would have been scared to death. I was scared, I'll admit that. But I was also excited. This was an adventure beyond even my own youthful daydreams. I forged ahead, the R2 guiding me with its characteristic beeps, pops, whines, and sproings. I didn't know what any of it meant, but the intent was generally to turn one way or the other at an intersection, and I got the idea quickly enough.

The corridors were mostly empty. Here and there, we passed the bodies of Imperial stormtroopers and Rebel assault commandos where heavy battles had apparently taken place. A few commandos passed, going in the opposite direction or moving down side corridors. We had been told that this ship would be lightly defended, but the evidence suggested otherwise.

The air was filled with an acrid smell. Blaster burn? The sight of the bodies deflated my excitement, but my R2 unit didn't seem to notice. I hurried to keep up.

The stormtrooper was waiting, his blaster pointed directly in my face as I hurried around a corner. Fortunately for me, I think that he was almost as surprised as I was. He probably didn't expect anyone to blunder into him like that. Whatever the reason, he didn't shoot quickly enough, and I slashed upward with my arm, knocking the blaster from his gloved hand. A sharp pain

lanced through my wrist as it contacted the hard ceramic armor, and my own blaster fell from my grip as I instinctively grabbed the painful area. The stormtrooper reached out and took me by the throat.

He pushed me down on my back, my own blaster trapped beneath me, poking uselessly into my spine through the flight suit. I couldn't breathe, and I had no weapon. Fists were pretty useless against ceramic armor, and, although I tried to break his grip on my throat, I could do nothing. My vision was beginning to dim as I ran out of air. I was on the verge of unconsciousness.

Then the stormtrooper shuddered violently, went stiff, and fell off me. His hands released their death grip, and I inhaled a deep, gasping breath. Next to the stormtrooper, who appeared to be dead or unconscious, my R2 unit was retracting a half-meter-long shock probe.

Now I had never heard of a droid attacking a human like that, but I wasn't about to question it just then. All I could think of was that perhaps shocking the trooper wasn't technically harming him, just immobilizing him. Or perhaps someone had tinkered with this one. Or maybe it had been mistreated by stormtroopers. Whatever the reason, it was clear that this apparently simple R2 unit was more than just a navigation droid. It was also a loyal companion.

"Thanks, R2," I said, when I had caught my breath again. The droid beeped a contented sound, or at least that's how I interpreted it. I got to my feet and ran onward.

When I reached the bridge, it was a wreck. I quickly spotted roughly ten dead stormtroopers and at least half that many Rebel commandos. But now the place was deserted. I began to search for anything that might be useful while the R2 linked with the command computer, first shutting down any external guns that were still active and then downloading information from the ship's memory banks.

I found nothing that looked important and was about to give up when I heard the muffled sound of a blaster being fired nearby. It came from behind a wall with no apparent doorway, but it was unmistakably the sound of a blaster. I suspected that there must be a doorway, even if I couldn't see it.

"R2?"

"Beep . . . pop?" it answered. Or something like that.

"I think there's a door or something over on that wall," I said. "Can you open it?"

The droid whistled a few more times, and then the entire wall slid aside, revealing a secret room. Inside, burning holo disks were

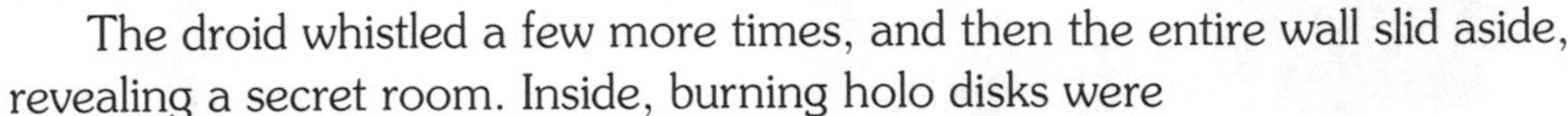

everywhere. An older man in an Imperial officer's uniform stood behind a large desk, his expression that of someone caught in the act. He held a blaster pointed roughly in my direction. When he saw me, he raised the blaster and fired. A heartbeat later, I fired my own blaster, hitting him square in the chest. He crumpled and fell behind the great desk.

It was only after I had fired that I realized two things. First, I was still alive—in fact, I hadn't even been hit. Second, he hadn't been aiming at me. His blaster had been aimed at another pile of holo disks on the desk between him and me.

I ran cautiously over to see what had happened to him. It was immediately obvious that he was dead, his face frozen in a rictus of surprise. I felt weak. I had just killed a man, face to face. And he hadn't even been shooting at me. I felt momentarily dizzy and had to clutch the edge of the desk to keep from falling. I had never killed a man before.

I realized suddenly that this was, in fact, the second man I had killed, the first being the pilot of the TIE fighter I had shot. Was it more noble or acceptable to shoot an enemy pilot, or to shoot an officer in cold blood? I found myself wondering what could be in these disks that he had thought was worth dying for.

I regained my composure and remembered that the commando in the air lock had given me 15 minutes. I didn't have much time left. I gathered all the holos I could find. Some were still undamaged; others were little more than slag, but I took them all and stuffed them into the pockets of my flight suit.

I took a last look at the man I had shot, and, as an afterthought, I took his ID badge. Perhaps it would be useful to know who he had been. I knew that I would never forget him.

"Come on, R2. I think we got what we came for," I said after taking a deep breath. "Let's get out of here."

I ran from the bridge, followed by the R2 unit, who was emitting a solid stream of high-pitched whistles, pops, and sproings. I made my way back to the air lock and took off in my X-wing as soon as it was ready, saluting the commandos who were beginning their own evacuation.

"R2?" I called over the comm. "'Space us out of here. Let's go home."

✘ ✘ ✘

Of course, I didn't know the importance of the holos I had recovered. And I think that Mon Mothma and the other commanders made too much of my exploits. But who could complain? I got a promotion to lieutenant and made many new friends. And I guess that any group of loyalists, outnumbered and outgunned, would try to boost morale by creating heroes. I just didn't really see myself as one.

It was what Mon Mothma told me privately about my having something to do with destiny and the Force that bothered me most. That and the dreams I was starting to have. But that's another story.

MISSION 6: FARLANDER'S FIRST MISSION

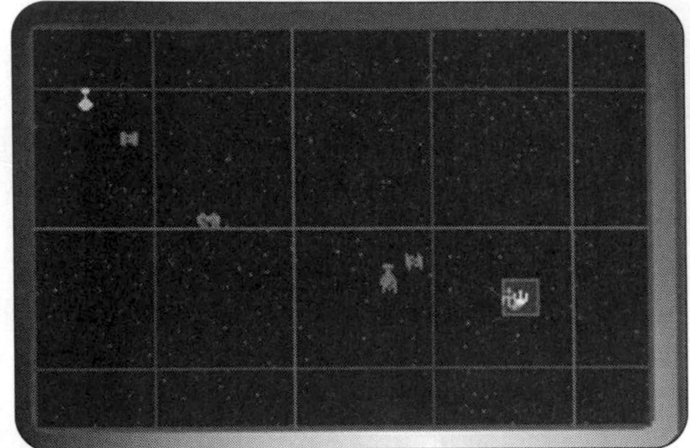

File Name: keyan

Mission Briefing

This mission teaches you the importance of teamwork in a complicated operation to capture secret Imperial documents.

Dafid's Training Objective

"Welcome back, *Lieutenant* Farlander. We've got another surprise for you. Your little adventure has become one of our training missions. And you get to fly it again!

"In this mission, you must realize the value of teamwork. Take care of your responsibilities, and lend a hand to the others whenever possible. You won't be called upon to board the *Talon*, as Farlander was, but you will have an opportunity to reduce our losses, which were considerable on this mission. Try to secure the *Talon* first, and then help out Blue Squadron and protect the *Liberator*."

Tactical Summary

As you begin this mission, a furious battle will already have begun between the Alliance Frigate *Liberator* and the Imperial corvette *Talon's* TIE escorts. Two groups of two TIE fighters will have remained with the *Talon*.

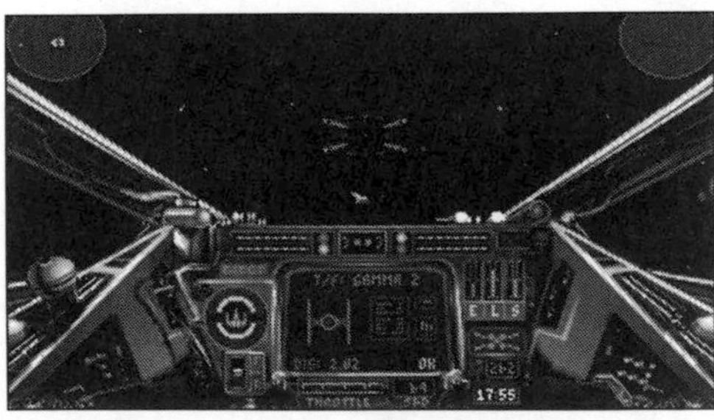

Heading for T/F Gamma 2.

Go to full throttle and query the CMD for the nearest TIE fighter as you head toward the *Talon*. Order your wingman to attack it and select the next one for yourself. Try to eliminate it on the first pass. As soon as possible, fire two or three torpedoes at the *Talon* to help bring down its shields and make the Y-wings' job

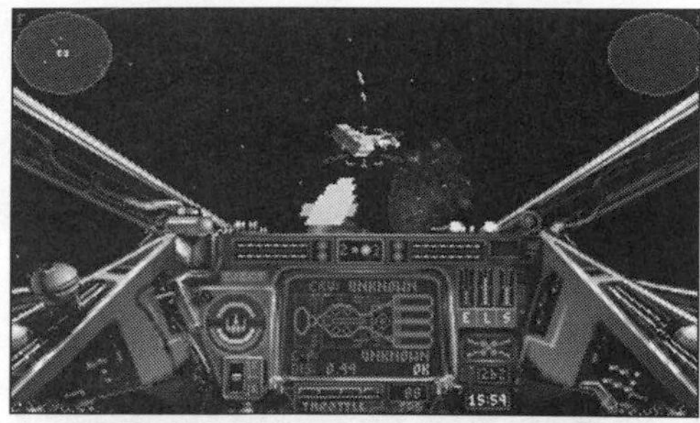

On the way to the Talon.

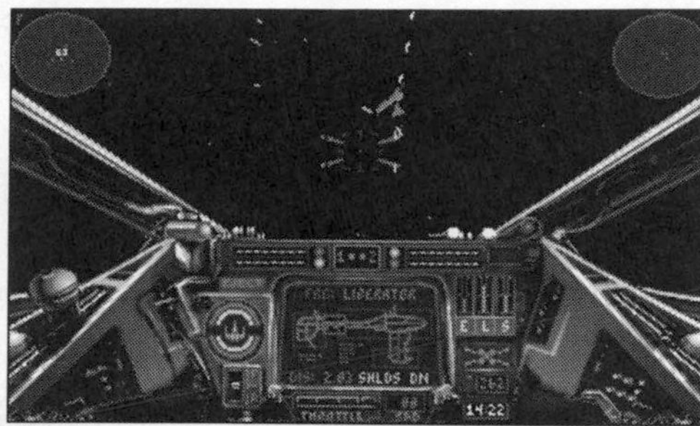

Helping out the Liberator.

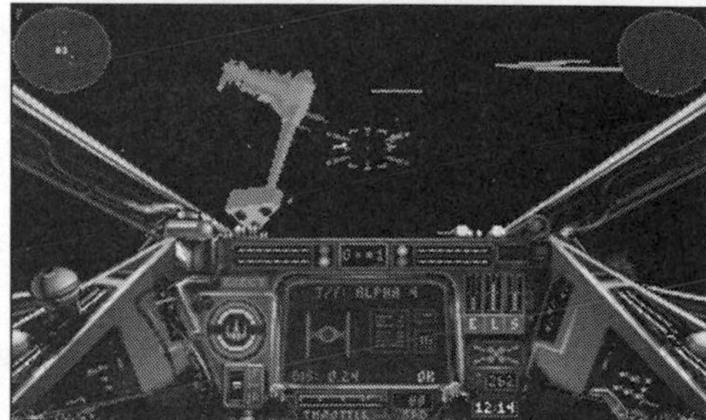

Getting a deflection shot at T/F Alpha 1.

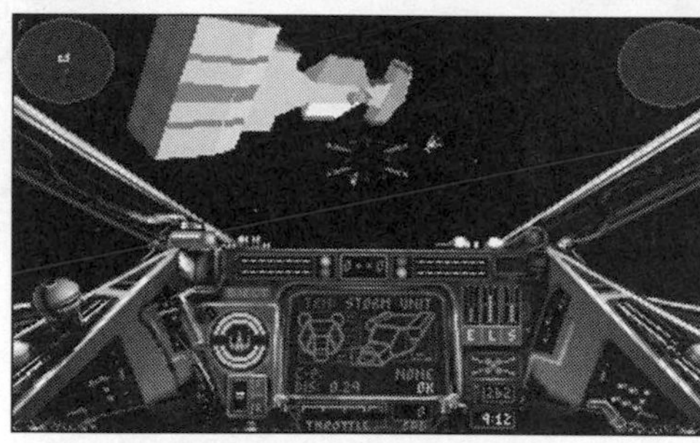

Guarding the Storm Unit.

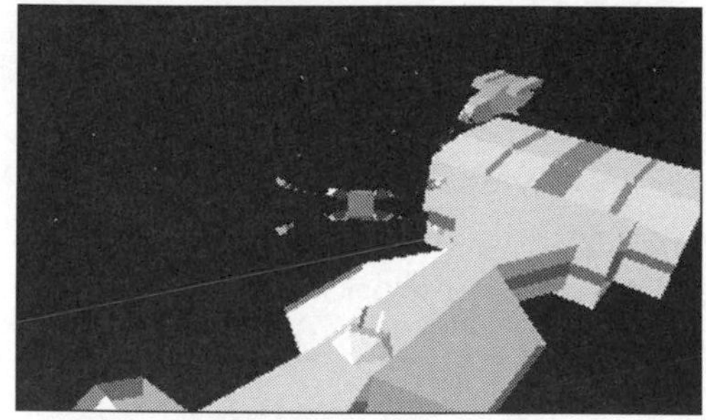

The Storm Unit *is done.*

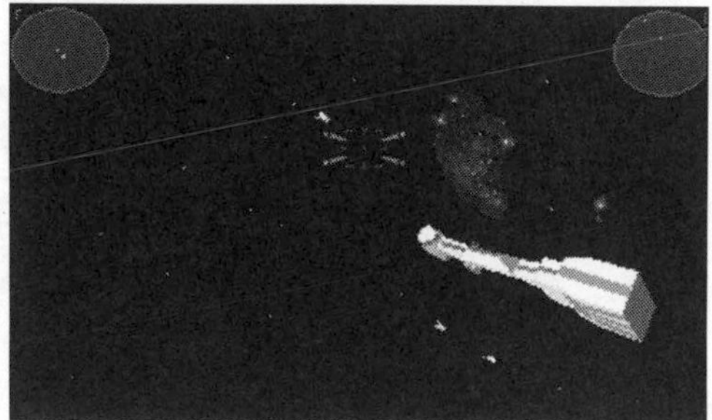

End of the mission.

easier. Be careful not to destroy it! Proceed to eliminate the remaining TIE fighters as quickly as possible. After the corvette has been disabled, make a close fly-by to ID it so that the *Storm Unit* commandos will enter.

If the area around the *Talon* is safe for the boarding party, you may want to go to the assistance of the *Liberator* by engaging the remaining TIE Bombers that are attacking it.

Win Conditions

T/F Gamma and T/F Delta must be destroyed. TRN *Storm Unit* must board CRV *Talon* and then escape into hyperspace.

Y-WING HISTORICAL COMBAT MISSIONS

MISSION 1: COMMERCE RAID

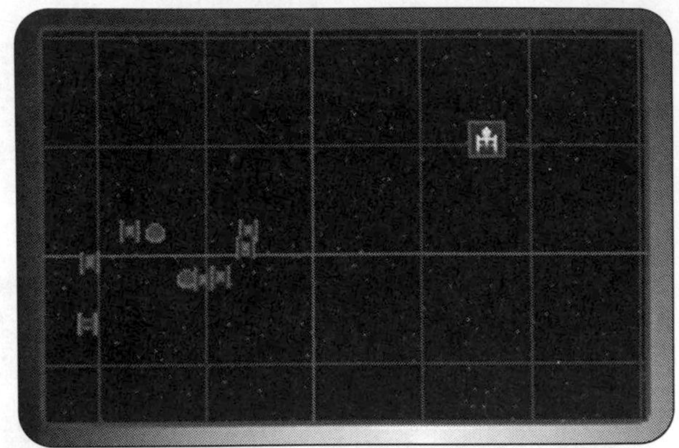

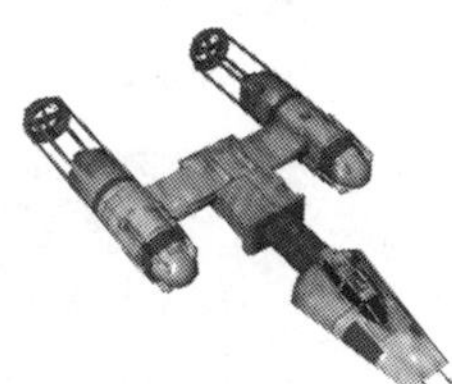

File Name: ywastem

Mission Briefing

In this mission, you learn to track and destroy enemy starfighters. Use all the Y-wing's weapons to destroy as many Imperial craft as you can.

Dafid's Training Objective

"This is your first mission in a Y-wing, so I want you to pay attention to how your systems operate. Learn to use your targeting controls and your weapon systems. Just because you can fly an X-wing doesn't mean that you can just hop into a Y-wing and know everything. Pay attention to your energy configuration, and use it to control speed and firepower."

Tactical Summary

This mission is an easy one because most of the Imperial craft aren't even moving. You learn to assign targets to memory locations in the targeting computer, issue wingman commands, switch between weapon systems, and adjust speed to maximize firepower on a target.

Use the normal mission start sequence. Cycle through the targets until you locate a freighter, and order your wingman to attack it. Also, assign it to a memory location (Shift-F5) and continue cycling to find the other freighter and assign it to a memory location, too (Shift-F6). Freighters should be your first priority—they can escape, while the containers aren't going anywhere!

As always, time is critical, because Imperial reinforcements are triggered by the destruction of the FRT *Banthar*. Switch to torpedoes and fire one at the nearest freighter. Now target containers and fire one torpedo at each, saving at least one torpedo for later. By now you should be within cannon range of the nearest containers, so switch to lasers and reduce speed to one-third ([). As you close on the freighter, try to destroy a few of the containers you've weakened with torpedoes. Now help your wingman finish off the freighter at F5. As soon as you've done this, order him to attack the freighter at F6 while you destroy containers.

When the shuttle arrives, go to full throttle and switch to torpedoes. Fire one at it as soon as you get a lock, and then finish it off with lasers. If you've closed fairly rapidly, you may have to reduce speed back to one-third ([). When the shuttle is gone, increase throttle to full (Backspace), and head back toward whatever targets remain. Reduce throttle to one-third ([) again as you come within cannon range. As new freighters enter the area, order your wingman to attack them.

The Space Tugs aren't part of the mission's win conditions, but they are easy to destroy, requiring only one shot each. Target them if you find them conveniently in your path. The Imperial Frigate should arrive just as you've cleared the area. This is a good time to leave unless you want to engage the many TIE fighters it will launch. For more of a challenge, send your wingman home at the beginning of the mission and take out the first freighter as quickly as you can, using four torpedoes, and then cannons to finish.

Win Conditions

Freighters *Banthar* and *Deddite*, shuttle *Krayt*, and container *Lambda 3* all must be destroyed. Also, at least 50 percent of (each group of) container groups Lambda, Kappa, and Iota must be destroyed.

Note: The names of containers Lambda, Kappa, and Iota should be Chi, Psi, and Pi, respectively.

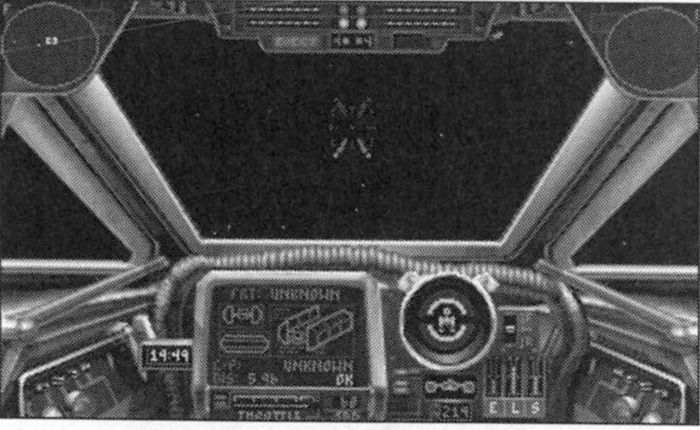

Targeting a freighter.

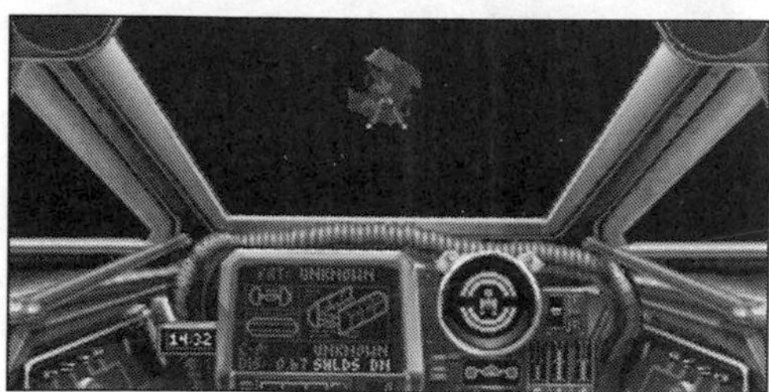

The freighter's shields are down.

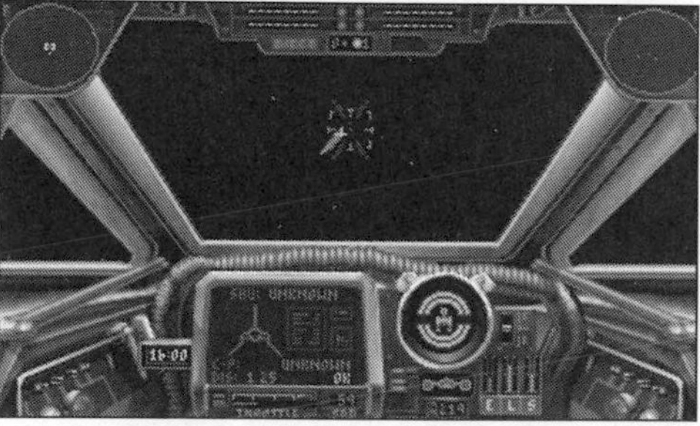

Shoot down the shuttle.

MISSION 2: Y-WING GUNNERY PRACTICE

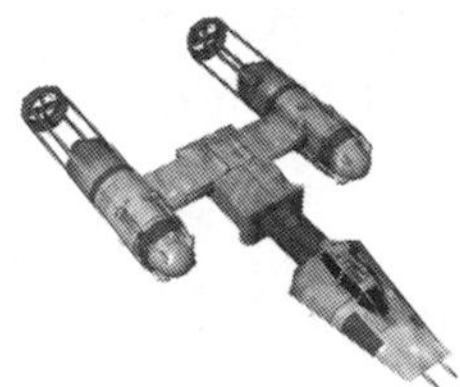

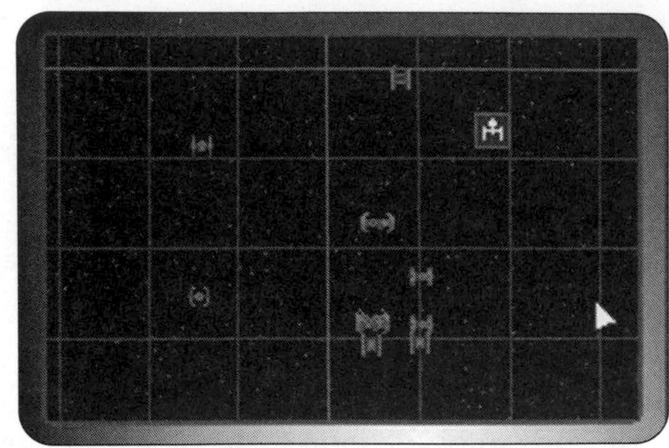

File Name: ywaistem

Mission Briefing

When Wedge Antilles discovered an Imperial testing base, we were able to send in a lone Y-wing to destroy the prototype starfighters there.

Dafid's Training Objective

"In this mission, you learn to track and destroy enemy starfighters. You won't have any torpedoes on this mission, so you have to learn to be efficient with your cannons. Most importantly, you learn to use the targeting system to quickly locate the nearest enemy fighter. Many of the targets are moving, but none is shooting back. You can take advantage of this to practice transferring shield energy to the cannons to keep them fully charged. Be aware when the Imperial reinforcements arrive, because they will come in shooting!"

Tactical Summary

Use the normal mission start sequence with the following exception: Do not transfer any cannon energy to the shields. Query the CMD for the nearest fighter (R) (a TIE Bomber from group Eta), and note that it is over three clicks away. Therefore, turn to the right and attack the freighter you find there. As you close on the target, reduce speed to one-third ([).

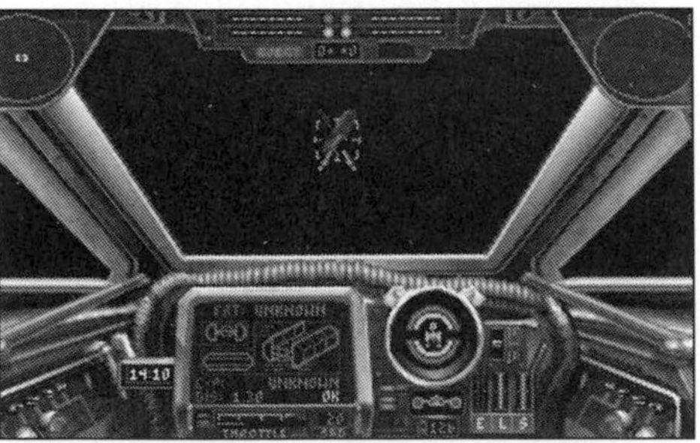

Head for the freighter.

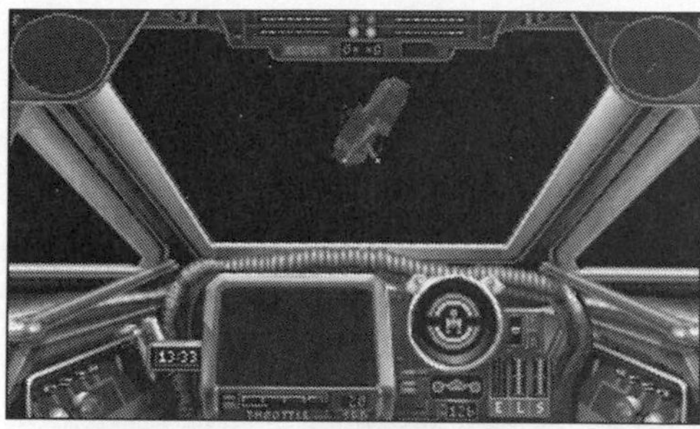

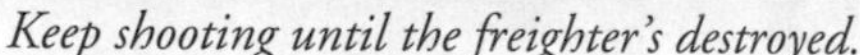
Keep shooting until the freighter's destroyed.

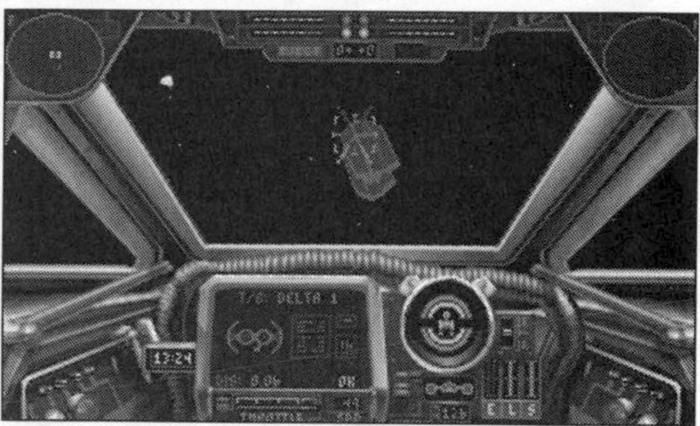
Shoot the slow-moving Bombers.

Keep an eye on the weapon status bar, and be sure to transfer shield energy to the cannons (Shift-F9 or ;) to keep them supercharged.

After the freighter has been destroyed, query the CMD again, and you will find the nearest fighter. Go to full throttle and reduce shield recharge rate to normal in order to redirect power to the engines for more speed. Chase down and eliminate the target, but be careful with your speed as you close in because the fighter will be moving relatively slowly and you risk overshooting or colliding with it. As soon as you've destroyed it, query the CMD again. Now eliminate the moving TIEs that remain from the Zeta, Eta, Theta, and Iota groups. At some point, you should be near the containers, and your query should target one of the stationary TIEs from groups Alpha, Beta, or Gamma. These are easy kills, but don't forget to slow down so that you can get them all in one pass! Finally, you may go back to get the two containers before you hyper home.

As usual, you can always stick around to engage the Imperial reinforcements when they arrive!

Win Conditions

TIE fighter groups Alpha, Gamma, Zeta, and Theta; TIE Bomber groups Beta, Delta, and Eta; and TIE Interceptor group Iota must *all* be destroyed.

MISSION 3: S.O.S. FROM CORVETTE KARINNE

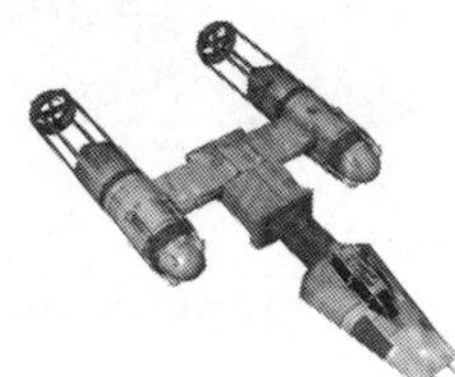

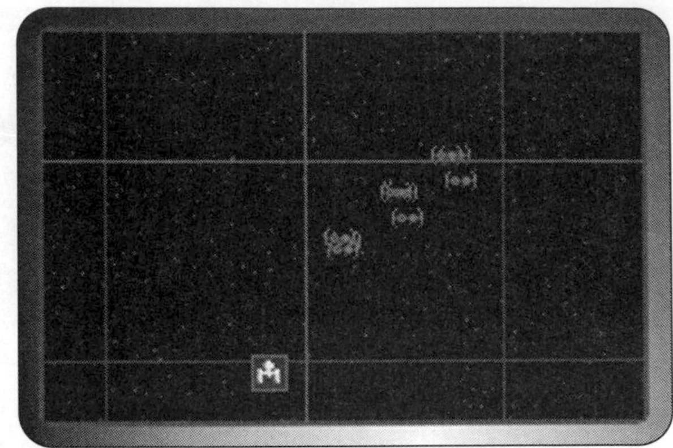

File Name: hello

Mission Briefing

This mission requires you to use your proton torpedoes to stop an Imperial attack against a neutral corvette.

Dafid's Training Objective

"TIE Bombers can cause unbelievable amounts of destruction. You shouldn't even think about going out there where the real action is unless you know how to get the Bombers before they get our ships! Learn to use your torpedoes to take out the Bombers. You'll soon find out that acquiring a solid lock on a small craft such as a starfighter takes a very steady hand."

Tactical Summary

At the beginning of this mission, you drop out of hyperspace right behind an Imperial Star Destroyer! Don't panic, though: It hyperspaces out at once.

Use the normal mission start sequence. You are attacked immediately by T/B groups Gamma and Beta, so begin evasive maneuvers at once! The TIE Bombers fire concussion missiles every chance they get, and even a Y-wing's shields can't take many of those! Try to kill at least two of these TIE Bombers as quickly as possible, and then redirect all cannon energy to the engines and go after T/B group Alpha. These

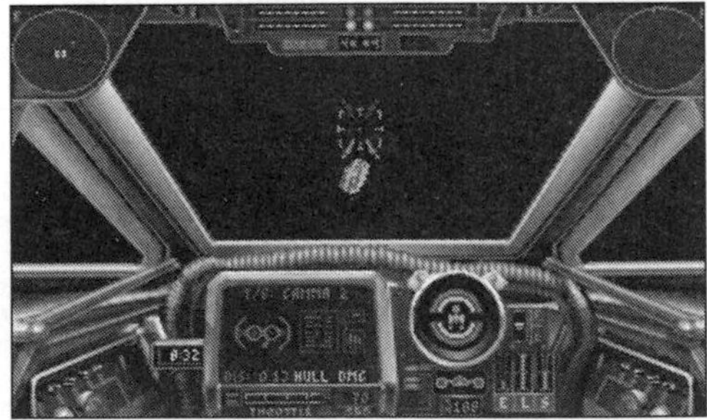

With hull damage, this Bomber's a goner.

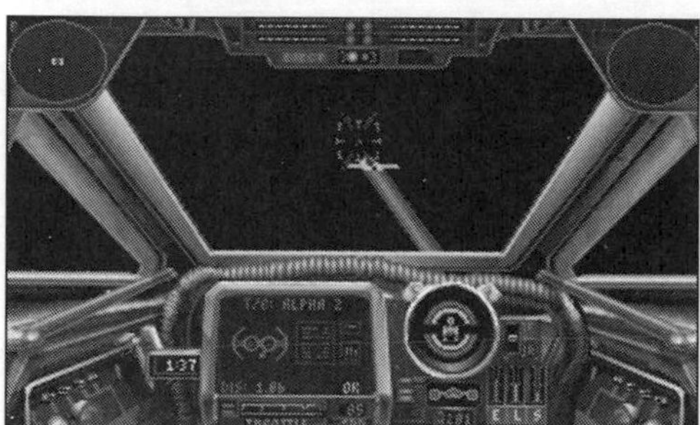

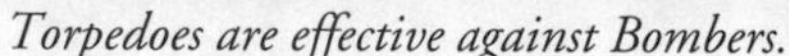

Torpedoes are effective against Bombers.

Bombers are in pursuit of the corvette, and you must destroy them before they get within torpedo range. One salvo from all three and the *Karinne* is doomed. You have to rely on your wingman to keep the others occupied while you chase down Alpha. Switch to torpedoes and fire as soon as you have a lock. (Note that nonplayer craft do not fire torpedoes at enemy starfighters, or missiles at other enemy craft.)

If your dogfighting skills are up to it, you can eliminate all of Beta and Gamma before going after Alpha. You have to be extremely quick, though. When you're done, you have to redirect all cannon and shield energy to the engines for maximum speed in order to catch up to Alpha. This is OK because no one will be shooting at you now; they're all dead! Use torpedoes as just instructed, and then wait for the *Karinne* to hyperspace out.

Win Conditions

TIE Bomber groups Alpha, Beta, and Gamma must all be destroyed. Corvette *Karinne* must survive.

Mission Note: T/B Alpha and Beta's orders should be Attack FRTs, as corvettes are considered the same as freighters for this order. CRV *Karinne*'s order should be Starship Fly Once.

MISSION 4: PRISONERS FROM KESSEL

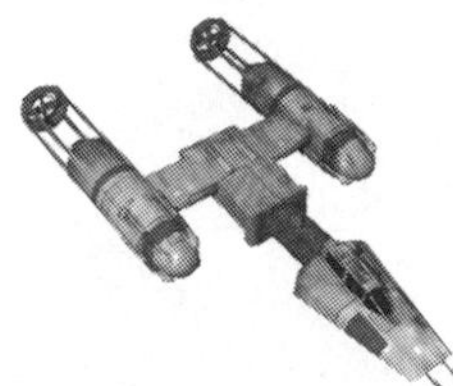

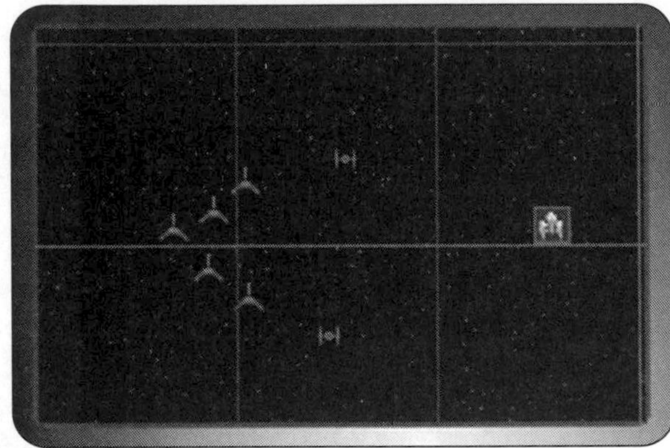

File Name: max7

Mission Briefing

In this mission, you learn to quickly identify and disable enemy craft. Then you defend Allied forces while they board these ships to seize their cargo.

Dafid's Training Objective

"The Alliance often uses Y-wings to disable ships we want to preserve for one reason or another. You may be called upon to use your ion cannons during such a mission. In this mission, you assist in the rescue of Rebel P.O.W.s. Use your ion cannons to disable the Imperial shuttles as quickly as possible. You will learn that ion cannons require quite different gunnery skills than do laser cannons. This is because the ion blasts travel much slower than lasers. Your targeting computer allows for this, but it still takes some practice to get used to it."

Tactical Summary

Use the normal mission start sequence. Your wingman will probably kill the two escorts before you can get to them. If so, proceed after the shuttles. Switch to ion cannons and slow to one-third ([) throttle when you get within half a click, because the shuttles are moving quite slowly. Begin shooting as soon as you have a green target box. Continue until all the shuttles are disabled.

Disable the shuttles.

You should have noticed that a group of three TIE Interceptors were launched from the Star Destroyer shortly after the beginning of the

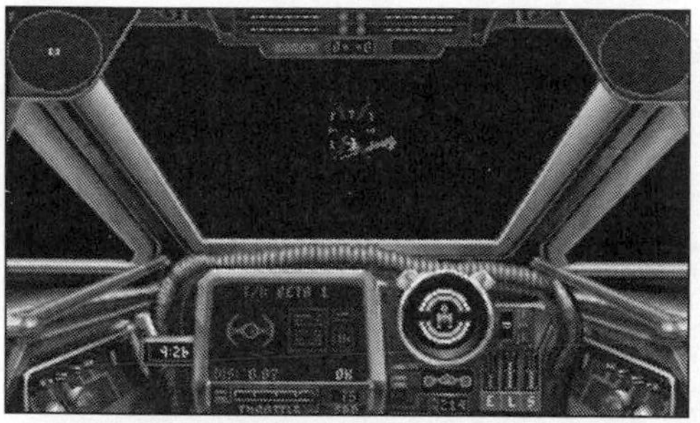
Get to the Interceptors quickly.

mission. You should now proceed at top speed to intercept them. Make sure that you have full shields and cannons, and then set shield and cannon recharge rates to normal. Switch to torpedoes and fire one at the closest approaching TIE. Switch to lasers and engage the others. As soon as you eliminate these TIES, the Star Destroyer launches another wave. Engage and destroy this wave and another that follows. By the time you have done this, the Rescue shuttles should have made it into hyperspace, so you can leave too.

Mission Note: The AI for nonplayer Y-wings doesn't allow for them to switch weapons appropriately. If they have to disable anything, they are "stuck" with ion cannons for the entire mission. Yes, it does look silly to be dogfighting with ion cannons!

Win Conditions

SHU *Rescue 1* must board SHU *249*, SHU *Rescue 2* must board SHU *227*, SHU *Rescue 3* must board SHU *247*, SHU *Rescue 4* must board SHU *224*, and SHU *Rescue 5* must board SHU *213*. All Rescue shuttles must survive.

MISSION 5: ESCAPE FROM MYTUS VII

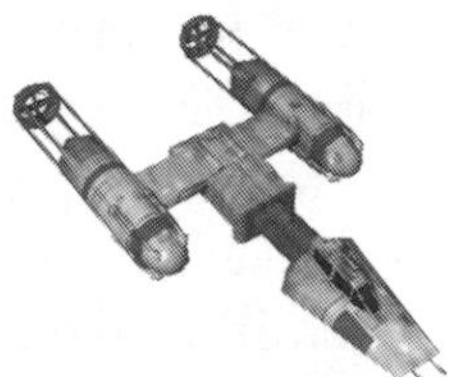

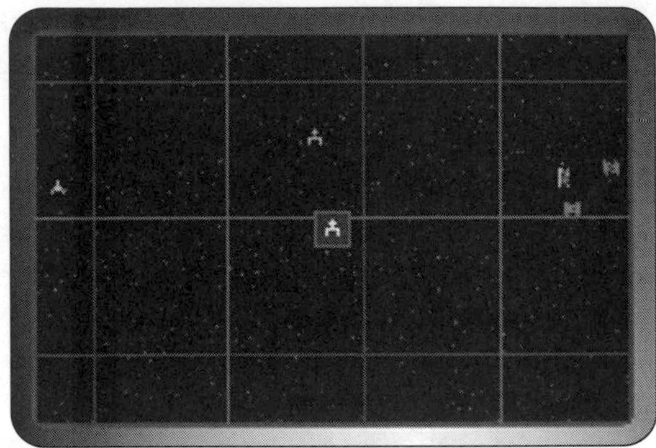

File Name: wyresc2

Mission Briefing

This mission shows why the Y-wing is considered the most versatile starfighter in the galaxy. You learn to escort Alliance ships while engaging Imperial forces.

Dafid's Training Objective

"The Y-wing is well stocked with firepower. Use it, and use it wisely. Get in the habit of switching from torpedoes to cannons as the situation requires. You're on escort duty, so keep those ships protected and alive. Don't let anybody shoot them."

Tactical Summary

Use the normal mission start sequence. Target the transport and switch to torpedoes. Select dual-fire mode; as you close, the targeting computer registers a lock on the target, but don't fire any torpedoes from this angle! Notice that the transport is shielded by the sides of the freighter. The transport needs three minutes to successfully board the freighter, so switch

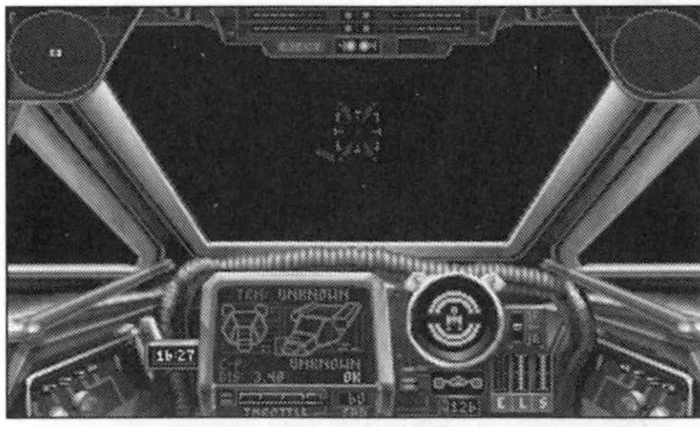

Target the transport, but don't shoot yet.

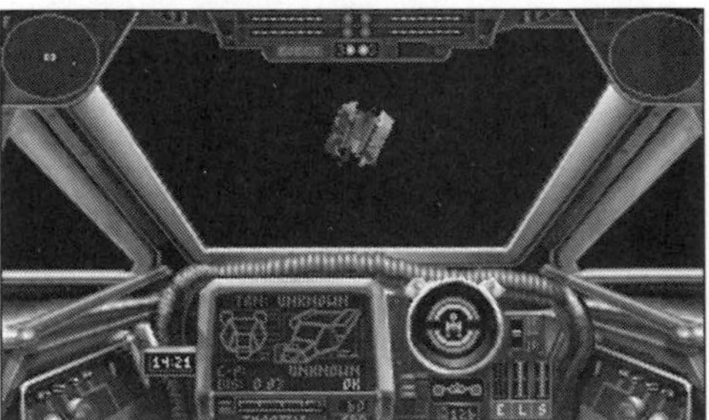

Angle into position to get the transport.

back to lasers and query the CMD for the nearest enemy fighter. Try to kill at least one as you pass by on your way toward the freighter. Switch back to torpedoes and maneuver for a shot at either end of the transport. Note that it is docked and stationary, so you don't have to wait for the red lock-on signal. Instead, just a few seconds of yellow or even a point-blank shot will do the trick. Now get back to the TIE fighters and destroy them all.

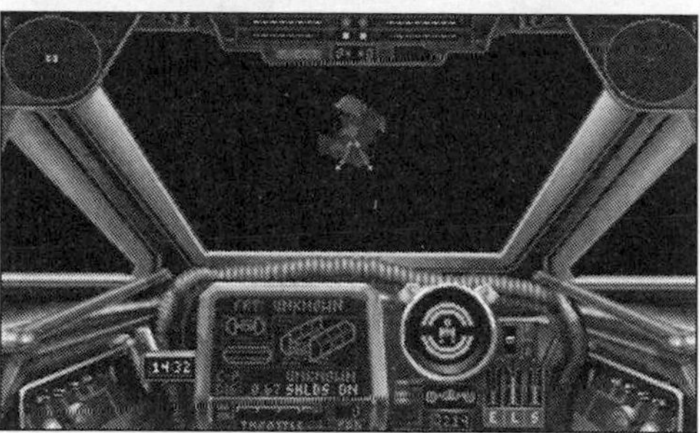
Now guard the freighter.

An Imperial Frigate will appear two minutes after you attack the transport, and begin launching TIE fighters and more transports. The Rebel shuttle *Mercy* will have docked with the freighter by this time, and you must stop the transports before they can interfere with the rescue. Note that there are a total of three enemy transports and that each requires two torpedoes to kill. After you have eliminated these, switch back to lasers and finish off the TIE fighters. As soon as the *Mercy* makes it into hyperspace, you get the Mission Complete message.

Win Conditions

SHU *Mercy* must board FRT *Hampton* and then survive. TRNs *Omicron 1*, *2*, and *3* all must be destroyed.

MISSION 6: INTERCEPTION AND CAPTURE

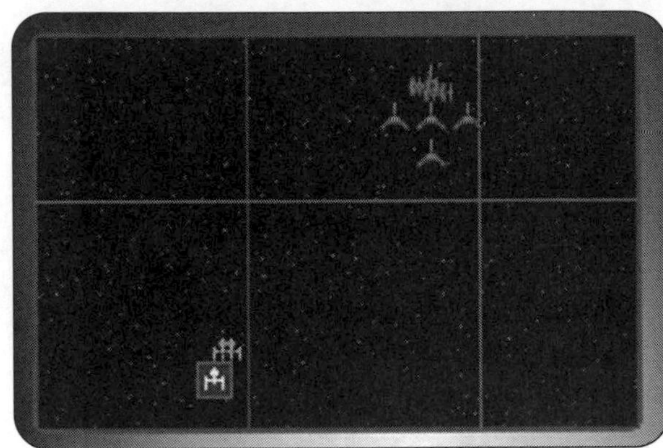

File Name: ackbar

Mission Briefing

This mission re-creates one of the most dramatic moments in Alliance history. You play a critical role in the rescue of the great Mon Calamari Admiral Ackbar.

Dafid's Training Objective

"This is your 'final exam' for the Y-wing. You have to use pretty much all your skills, particularly your ability to identify and disable a ship, and then protect the other mission participants until they complete their jobs. You have to move quickly and efficiently to find Ackbar's shuttle in time and then destroy anyone who tries to attack it or the *Hasti.*"

Tactical Summary

Five Imperial shuttles with TIE fighter escorts are en route to the Frigate *Vehemence.* One of them is carrying the Calamarian leader Ackbar.

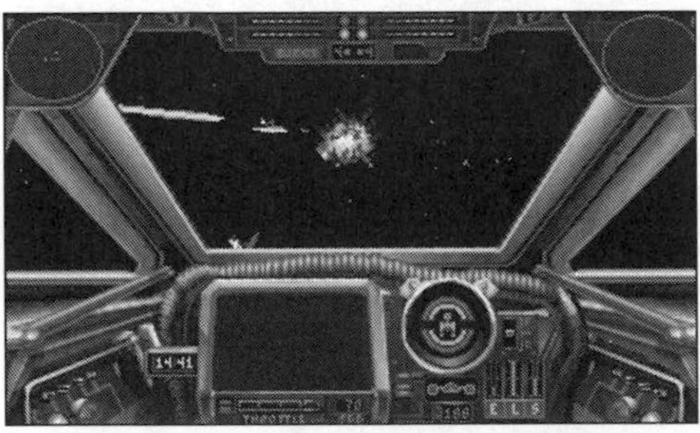

Try to get a TIE or two on the first pass.

Use the normal mission start sequence. Query the CMD for the nearest TIE fighter and engage with lasers. This fighter is part of a group of three, so if your marksmanship is good, you can take out two on the first pass. Try to get as many as you can as quickly as possible, but don't waste too much time chasing them around.

Target the first shuttle and switch to torpedoes. Fire a single torpedo as soon as you have a lock, and then target the next. Proceed to launch one

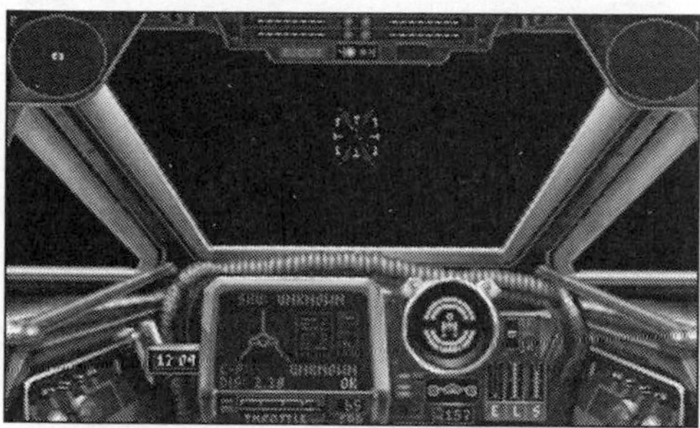

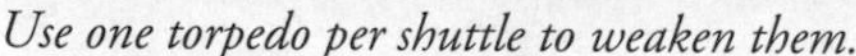

Use one torpedo per shuttle to weaken them.

Then fly close to ID the shuttles.

torpedo per shuttle, and then switch to ion cannons. Select dual-fire mode and make sure that they are fully charged. Now carefully close in on the shuttles to identify them. This maneuver requires getting very close, so try to adjust your speed accordingly and be careful.

When you find Ackbar, use ion cannons.

When you have identified the shuttle carrying Ackbar, use your ion cannons to disable it. This should require only two or three shots. The Rebel shuttle *Hasti* will have arrived and should be attempting to dock. Your job now is to protect it. Stay nearby and eliminate any TIE fighters that come close. Watch for T/F *Gamma*, in particular, because its primary target is the *Hasti*. When the *Hasti* escapes into hyperspace, the mission is complete and you can hyper out yourself.

Win Conditions

SHU *Hasti* must board SHU *Epsilon 5* and then survive.

Mission Note: SHU *Epsilon 5* is always the one carrying Ackbar, and it is always in the same position on the target list in the CMD. Also note FG #6 should be Planet 9.

A-WING HISTORICAL COMBAT MISSIONS

MISSION 1: REPAIR DEPOT RAID

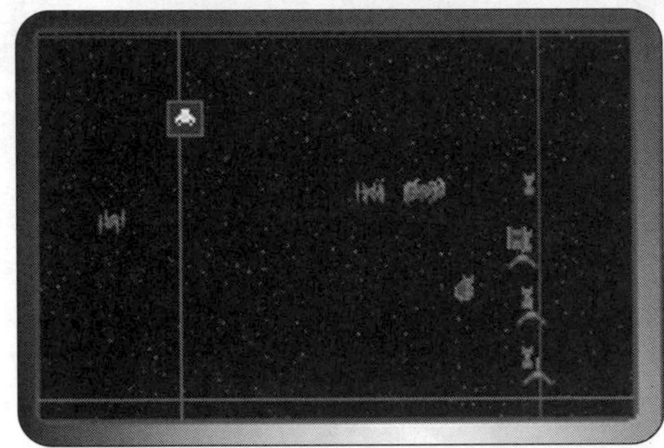

File Name: awaistem

Mission Briefing

This mission familiarizes you with the A-wing fighter. You learn to configure your power system, use your targeting system, and fire your lasers.

Dafid's Training Objective

"The A-wing is the fastest 'fighter in our fleet. Learn to fly it with respect for its advantages. Get used to the thrust and weapons controls. By the time you finish this mission, you should be ready for something a little more challenging."

Tactical Summary

There are no defenses to trouble you at the beginning of this mission. Take your time as you methodically destroy all Imperial craft in the area. The Empire's response will come too late to stop you.

Target the Bombers first.

When you drop out of hyperspace, you will find the Repair Dock directly ahead. (It is really two stationary freighters placed together.) Ignore it for now and query the CMD for the nearest enemy fighter. This is one of seven stationary TIE Bombers. Lower your speed to one-third ([) as you approach them. When you are about

Target the nearest shuttle.

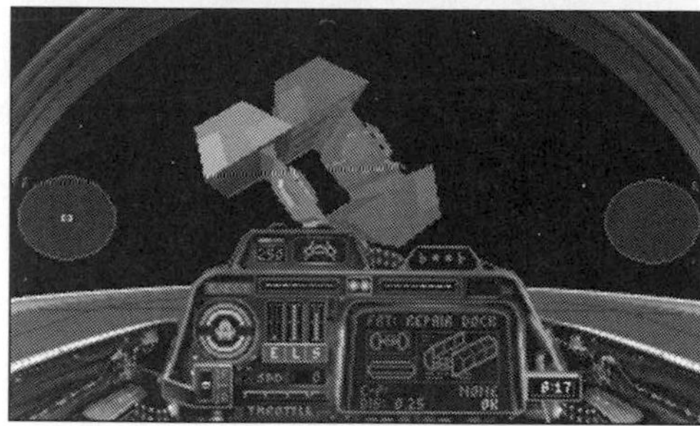

The Repair Dock.

one-half click away, lower your speed to zero (\) and finish them off.

Query the CMD again and throttle up to one-third ([) as you head toward the group of three stationary TIE fighters. After these fighters are destroyed, query the CMD again and throttle up to full power (Backspace) to chase after T/F Delta. This group of two TIE fighters attempts to evade your attack. They are unarmed and do not fire back.

These were the last of the fighters, so point back at the Repair Dock and lower your throttle back to one-third ([). Target the nearest shuttle (there are three in all); work your way through these and then the five transports. Cycle forward on the CMD to locate the first of two Space Tugs. These are very small and hard to hit.

Finally, cycle forward again to target the first half of the Repair Dock. Lower your speed to zero (\) and fire away until it blows up. Be sure to transfer shield energy to the lasers as necessary to keep them supercharged. For the last part of the Repair Dock, switch to concussion missiles and dual-fire them all into the Dock. Switch back to lasers to finish it off and hyperspace home.

- If you're feeling bold, stick around for the arrival of the Imperial Frigate *Virulence* and its TIE Interceptors.

- If you're really bold, attack the upper half of the repair dock as soon as you enter the area!

Win Conditions

All enemy craft must be destroyed *except* Space Tug T-34, the FRG *Virulence*, and T/I Zeta.

MISSION 2: AGGRESSOR SQUADRON TRAINING

File Name: waaggr1

Mission Briefing:

In this mission, you learn respect for the speed and maneuverability of the A-wing fighter by flying against Rebel starfighters!

Dafid's Training Objective

"This time you get to test your A-wing against our own fighters. Not only will you learn about the speed and maneuverability of the A-wing, but you'll also take on a series of simulated pilots ranging from Novice to Top Ace. Don't take any of them for granted. You can get shot just as dead when there's a moron at the helm as when there's a genius."

Tactical Summary

This is a pure dogfighting exercise. The "enemy" fighters enter one at a time: first an X-wing and then, a minute later, a Y-wing. And then, another minute later, an A-wing. As each is "destroyed," it is replaced by another.

Shoot Novices quickly before others arrive.

On the tail of this Y-wing; he's finished.

Get the A-W Top Aces; they'll fire missiles.

Each replacement is more skilled than the last. There are 15 in all, but you never have to deal with more than three at one time.

Query the CMD to locate the first X-wing and engage with lasers. Save your torpedoes to use against the Ace- and Top Ace-level X-wings and Y-wings.

Beware of the Novice level enemies because they make head-on passes at you. If you aren't quick to evade, they collide with you! Whenever you have more than one attacker at a time, target the A-wing first. These are the fastest and deadliest in a dogfight, and they have concussion missiles! The concussion missiles are the greatest danger. When the Ace and Top Ace X- and Y-wings arrive, switch to torpedoes and select dual-fire. This is the quickest way to eliminate them.

Win Conditions

All "enemy" craft must be destroyed, *except* those flown by Novice- and Officer-level pilots.

Mission 3: Intercept TIE Bomber Run

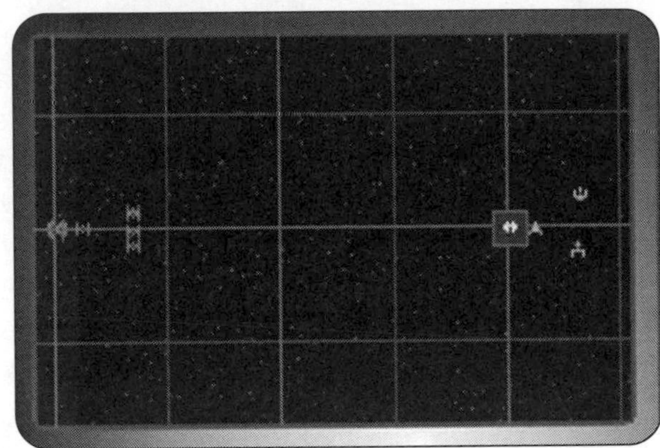

File Name: max2

Mission Briefing

This mission highlights the A-wing's superior interception capabilities. You learn to employ concussion missiles against incoming TIE Bombers.

Dafid's Training Objective

"Learn to use all that speed to some advantage. You've got to protect the *Maria* from the TIE Bombers. Get used to it. If you ever see any real action, TIE Bombers are going to be one of your main problems. Practice here to find the solution. If you don't, a lot of our people are going to suffer. Don't let me down."

Tactical Summary

The Star Destroyer *Malice* has chanced on the Alliance shuttle *Maria* undergoing emergency repairs. The *Malice* has launched an assault wave of seven TIE fighters and three TIE Bombers. The *Malice* leaves the scene, but

Move out to meet T/B Mu 1.

T/B Mu 2 *is about to go.*

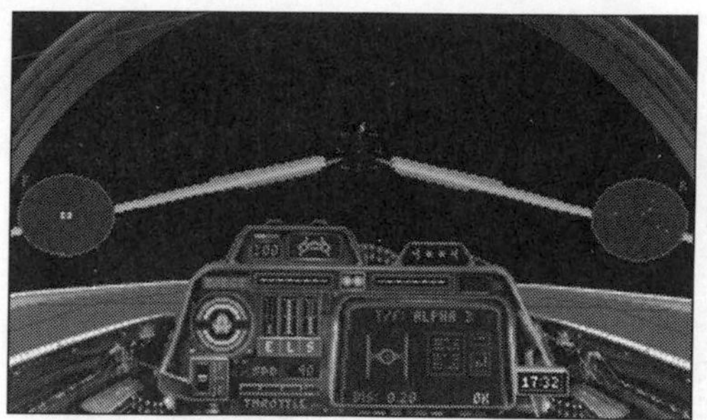

Head on at the TIE fighter.

returns later for the TIEs. An X-wing and a Y-wing remain near the shuttle while you move to intercept the attacking TIEs. The TIE Bombers are the greatest threat. You must stop them before they get close enough to use their missiles against the *Maria*.

Go to full throttle ([Backspace]) and switch to missiles as you head toward the nearest attacking TIE fighter (T/F *Alpha 1* at about 11 clicks). Cycle through your targets in the CMD and assign the TIE Bombers and T/F *Alpha 3* to memory locations ([Shift]-[F5]-[F8]). (*Alpha 3* is the close escort for the Bombers.) As soon as this is done, query the CMD for the nearest enemy ([R]) and fire your first missile as soon as you have a lock-on. Next, switch back to lasers, and fire a few blasts at his wingman as you pass. This causes the enemy fighters to break off their attack run to engage you.

Target T/F *Alpha 3* ([F8]) so that you can evade his attack. Now, return to missile mode and call up T/B *Mu 1* ([F5]). Launch as soon as lock-on is made, and proceed in a similar manner to eliminate T/Bs *Mu 2* and *Mu 3*. You should then mop up the remaining TIE fighters. If you're quick, you can get them all by yourself! When the *Maria* is repaired and makes it into hyperspace, you are done (about six-and-a-half minutes).

Win Conditions

TIE Bomber group Mu must be destroyed, and shuttle *Maria* must make it into hyperspace.

MISSION 4: ATTACK RUN ON FREIGHTERS

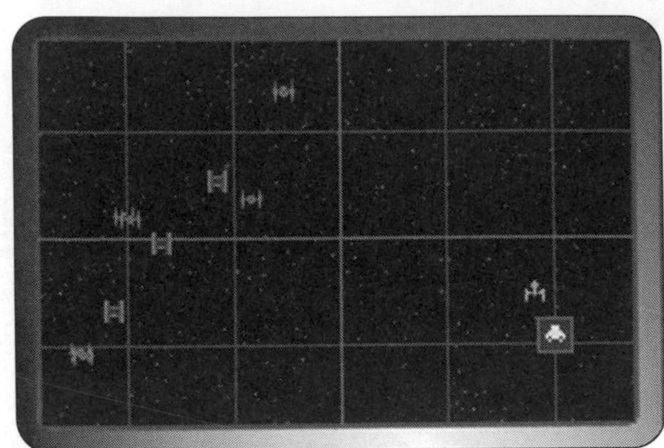

File Name: convoy2

Mission Briefing
In this mission, you learn to escort and support Y-wings while on a torpedo attack run against a convoy of Imperial supply freighters.

Dafid's Training Objective
"Everyone out there is a team player. If you're not, you should go home now. Protect the Y-wing, or the mission is a failure. Of course, the best way to protect him is to get rid of all his enemies as fast as possible. If you learn anything in this mission, it's how to destroy TIEs—fast!"

Tactical Summary
You are part of a composite strike team combining the speed and agility of the A-wing with the strength and firepower of the Y-wing. Eight TIE fighters are escorting three freighters.

Engage and destroy the TIE fighters as quickly as possible to keep the Y-wing safe. Use missiles when the target is more than one click away, but switch to lasers when you're in close. TIE fighters take only two supercharged laser blasts; this is much quicker than waiting for a solid lock-on. Remember that you have 12 missiles, so don't worry if a few miss. Keep in mind, however, that they can be useful later against the freighters.

If the Y-wing is killed, you have lost the mission. Therefore, if you have a hard time protecting him, send him home at the beginning of the mission and do the entire job yourself!

Win Conditions
All three freighters must be destroyed.

MISSION 5: PROTECT RETURNING STARFIGHTERS

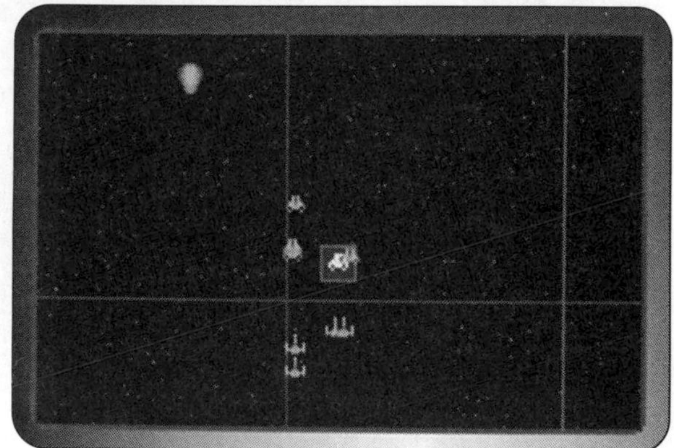

File Name: max15

Mission Briefing

This mission emphasizes the importance of protecting vulnerable Rebel fighters as they return from a combat mission.

Dafid's Training Objective

"The A-wing carries a full load of missiles. This is where you're going to learn to use them effectively. Learn to lock on early, fire, and move on to the next target. Otherwise, your friends are going to be dead meat! Also, don't try to do everything yourself. You've got a good wingman with you. Assess the situation and distribute your forces."

Tactical Summary

You have been sent to fly area security while the cruiser *Cathleen* recovers her starfighters and other craft. These ships have just conducted a raid against Imperial shipping and are battle-weary and low on energy. They make for the safety of the *Cathleen* as quickly as they can.

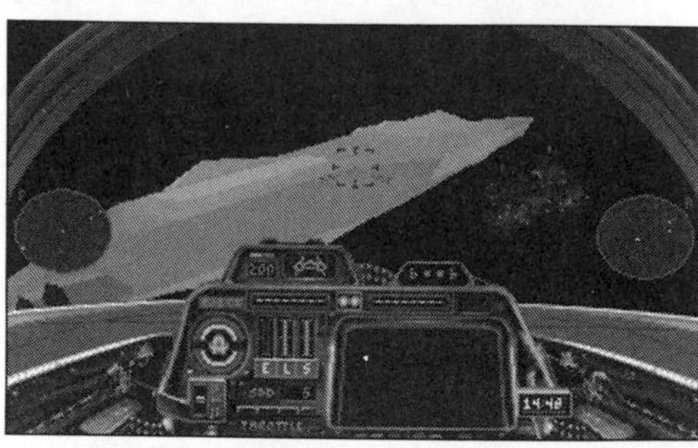

The Calamarian cruiser Cathleen.

As you drop out of hyperspace, hold course and give a look around. You have two minutes before the Imperial counterattack. Use the time to build up your shields and lasers. While you're waiting, you may fly around the cruiser and observe the recovery operations, but stay nearby.

The Imperial Frigate *Terminator* drops out of hyperspace about eight

Head toward the Imperial frigate.

Shoot the T/Bs with missiles.

clicks off the port (left) side of the *Cathleen*. A six-ship group of TIE Bombers is launched; the Frigate then hyperspaces away. The Frigate is no match for a Calamari cruiser, but the TIE Bombers cause a great deal of damage if they're left unchallenged.

Use the targeting system to select targets for your wingman and give him the attack order. Your concussion missiles are the best choice for intercepting the Bombers as quickly as possible.

Stay alert for the reappearance of the *Terminator* on the starboard (right) side of the *Cathleen*. Whenever an Imperial capital ship launches TIEs and then leaves, you can bet that it's coming back.

If you haven't wiped out the first attack wave by now, you are in trouble! You have to disengage to go after the next group of six TIE Bombers coming from the Frigate. Continue to order your wingman to attack targets in the first wave while you attack the second.

Keep in mind that there are only 12 TIE Bombers and that you have 12 concussion missiles. You should be able to stop them all yourself. This is what makes the A-wing such a deadly interceptor . . . even better than the X-wing!

As the friendly ships arrive to be recovered, keep an eye out for X-wing *Gold 4*. This is the last ship that returns and is usually the one the Imperials manage to kill. If you have been successful, you may want to finish exploring the cruiser in high detail, but be careful that you aren't in the way when she hyperspaces out!

Win Conditions

X-wing *Gold 1-4*, A-wings *Blue 5*, *8*, and *9*, and shuttles *Blue 1* and *2* all must return to the cruiser *Cathleen*.

MISSION 6: DEEP SPACE RECONNAISSANCE

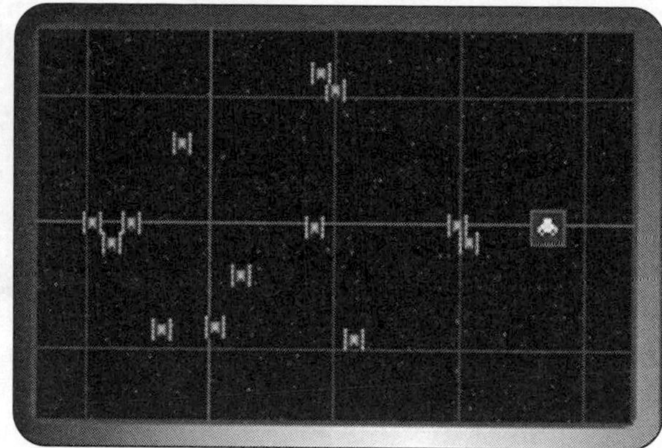

File Name: warecon1

Mission Briefing

In this mission, you learn the value of the A-wing's speed and special sensors for deep-space reconnaissance missions.

Dafid's Training Objective

"Reconnaissance is the A-wing's forte, my friends. Use your speed and maneuverability to identify enemy craft. Then use your firepower and dogfighting skills to eliminate any opposition that shows up. Put all your skills to work and you'll be ready for real A-wing action!"

Tactical Summary

Thirteen containers are strewn across space, and a nasty surprise is waiting for you! Cycle backward on the CMD (Y) to target the last container and assign it a memory location (Shift-F5). Cycle back again and assign this container a memory location (Shift-F6). Continue to cycle through the targets in reverse order, but make a close fly-by of each from now on to ID it before proceeding to the next.

Head for the containers.

Come close to ID the container.

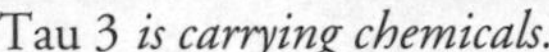

Tau 3 *is carrying chemicals.*

Get on the T/I's tail and he's as good as gone.

When all but the two assigned to memory have been ID'ed, recall the first of these (F5) and ID it. This step causes a trio of TIE fighters (group Beta) to come out and attack you. Engage and destroy them as quickly as possible. When these have been eliminated, ID the last container. Another trio of TIE fighters will come out; then the Imperial Frigate *Merciless* will arrive and begin launching waves of TIE fighters. Destroy T/F *Alpha* as quickly as you can and leave.

The destruction of T/Fs *Alpha* and *Beta* triggers the creation of two additional groups of Top Ace-level TIE Interceptors, so don't hang around unless you're up for a serious challenge!

Win Conditions

All containers must be identified, and T/F groups Alpha and Beta must be destroyed.

Mission Note: T/I *Sigma's* mother ship is wrong. It should be FG 14 (the FRG), not FG 9 (a CON). This doesn't affect the mission; it just looks strange.

PART FOUR

PART FOUR

ORIGINAL TOURS OF DUTY

That's not a moon. It's a space station.

— Obi-Wan Kenobi

Tour of Duty #1— A New Ally

I had just completed the last of the A-wing historical training missions, and was climbing out of the cockpit of the simulator when Commander Dafid called me on the comm.

"Farlander. Report to my office. Dafid out."

Jan-lo was nearby. She had been going through the training with me, although I had the idea that she would be going into intelligence training before long. She gave me one of those looks. You know, like, "Uh-oh. What did you do now?" I just shrugged. I had no idea what "TIE-Die" wanted. Jan-lo offered me an encouraging thumbs-up as she entered the simulator.

I walked along the row of simulator pods and turned left. Dafid's office was just down the hall from the simulator room; as I approached, I noticed someone standing in his doorway and facing into the office. I could see only the back of the man, but his bearing was very military, and from his shoulder insignia I could see that he was a lieutenant commander. I slowed my pace to see whether I could overhear what they were saying. Best to go in as prepared as possible.

". . . he seems to know his way around a blockade runner, commander," the man in the door was saying.

I couldn't hear the reply.

"I know he's green. But you said yourself that his simulator scores were nearly perfect. And General Dodonna himself . . ."

The man's voice trailed off as a slightly louder, but still incomprehensible, reply emerged from within the room.

"With all due respect," continued the first man, "we could use his help. There are so many operations in planning stages at this time. Well . . . We can't wait for every . . ."

The man was interrupted as a voice bellowed from inside the room. "Farlander! Where are you? Get in here. Now!"

By now only a few meters away, I spoke up. "I'm here, sir." As I walked up to the door, the man standing there turned. I didn't recognize him, but that was nothing to be surprised at—thousands of people were aboard the *Independence*.

"You're Keyan Farlander?" asked the man, sounding a little dubious.

"Sir!" I saluted crisply and stood at attention. Rebel officers were pretty lax about such things, generally, but I thought that this officer would appreciate the gesture.

"At ease, lieutenant. Relax." The man smiled, seemingly at some private joke. He didn't look like a man who smiled often. "Commander Dafid tells me that you aren't ready for active duty yet. What do you think, lieutenant?"

He was asking my opinion? "I think that whatever the commander says is probably true, sir."

"Listen, Farlander . . ." The man hesitated a moment and then turned back to Dafid. "I'm just the envoy, anyway, Dafid," he said. "General Dodonna seems to want this pilot in service as soon as possible. Don't ask me why." Turning back to me and giving me a sort of skeptical look, he added, "Have you completed the historical simulator training?"

"Yes, sir. But . . ."

The man held up his hand to stop me. "No buts, lieutenant. If the general wants you, he gets you. You're to report to the duty officer for Red Squadron tomorrow at 0600 hours." He saluted to me and sort of tipped his head to Commander Dafid, and then he spun around and left before I could answer. I stood there, stunned, watching him disappear down the hallway.

"Farlander . . ."

I faced Dafid, not really sure what to say. "Sir?" was all I managed.

The commander stood up from his desk and put his hand on my shoulder. It dug in a little too hard. He sometimes had trouble gauging the strength of his mechanical hand. "Farlander, that was one of the general's staff officers. They want you. You're to be the sacrificial lamb. Just remember everything you've learned here, and don't take this hero business too seriously. Heroes who fly starfighters most often meet with a quick end."

"Yes, sir," I said. I couldn't have agreed more. "But, sir?"

"What is it, Keyan?"

This was the first time—ever—that he had called me by my first name. It made me nervous.

"I was just going to ask . . . Am I really not ready yet?"

Dafid laughed so abruptly I almost jumped.

"Ready? Who's ever ready? You'll be all right. Keep asking yourself whether or not you're ready yet, and when the answer is yes, that's when you might consider a nice desk job. The end is near." He was still chuckling, the scar on his face stretched white, but then his smile faded and he spoke more seriously. I had never seen the commander in such a mood before. "In answer to your question, lieutenant, you're a damn good fighter pilot. If you can stay alive through your first few missions, you've got a chance. Just watch your back . . . and don't try to take on a Star Destroyer in an X-wing." I smiled then, but later I was to remember the commander's caution, and it would not seem humorous at all.

Reporting for Duty

I reported for duty early the next morning, and was sent to Briefing Room 7, a small room dominated by a large 3-D holo projection map. I recognized a few of the pilots who had arrived before me, and some nodded in my direction, but there was little conversation. I looked for a spot as far in the back as possible, and settled nervously into the auto-contour seat.

When Hamo arrived, he grinned and said, "Here we go," and then went off to talk to some other pilots I didn't know. Shortly thereafter, the briefing began.

"We've had some success lately against the Empire forces, but that only means that we have to be more careful. Our hit-and-fade tactics are working well enough to provoke a response from the Emperor."

Commander S'man began the briefing. I had seen him a few times before: He was hard to miss at nearly seven feet tall and close to 300 pounds. People said that he was a frustrated fighter pilot—too big to fly one—and that he had become a tactical genius and a mission planner just so that he could stay near the action. Whatever his story, people also said that he was tight with General Dodonna and Admiral Ackbar, and that S'man had planned many of the most successful Alliance missions.

For a moment he stood before the large holo sphere, with nothing displayed.

"A response from the Empire isn't exactly what we want, but our informants tell us that a response is what we're going to get. So, our first priority is to find out what what we can expect, and where it will take place. All we can know for sure is that the Empire will respond with a warhead to scratch an itch."

"Fortunately, we have several advantages. First, we have good intelligence about the Empire's movements through our network of informants. It's hard for the Empire to keep secrets when everything they do is on such a large scale. Second, we are few and hard to find. Third, our starfighters can hyperspace into combat and back out again while theirs are not hyperspace-capable. Fourth, we have a dangerous new starfighter which all of you have trained on—the A-wing."

Some shouts of agreement came from the assembled pilots and staff—the A-wing was popular with most pilots—but S'man put one of his great hands up and order was instantly restored.

"Don't get too confident, men. This is a life-or-death struggle, and the Empire still has the upper hand. Now, the general and his staff have worked hard to set forth the following goals, and you men will be risking your lives to accomplish these goals, so we want you to hear them.

"First, our informants are working hard to gain more information about the Imperial counterstrike, but we are also looking for ways to help ourselves. We hope to intercept some Imperial convoys, or perhaps capture some Imperial officers and find out what they know.

"Second, we have decided to evacuate our current base at Briggia. Our security is very tight, but nothing will remain a secret forever. We will have to mount a rear-guard action to protect the evacuation in case the Empire discovers the operation.

"Third, we must mount effective counterstrikes to delay the start of the Empire's response. In other words, we'll muck up the works."

There was general laughter at this uncharacteristic comment, but it faded quickly, and the commander went on as though he hadn't said anything out of the ordinary.

"Fourth, we expect to have several opportunities to capture military supplies as the Imperial operation begins to build up its ordnance.

"Fifth, we must seek new allies in our fight against the Empire. Several worlds are learning, through first-hand experience, that the Empire brings oppression when it promises peace, and we must work to prove ourselves a worthy alternative. One such world is Sullust, and, like the Calamarians, the Sullustan are a strong spacefaring race. Their superior navigation skills would be a great help to us.

"Sixth, well, sixth is to seize any target of opportunity. The High Command is studying several plans designed to hurt the Empire, and help our cause throughout the galaxy. We'll need your help to get it done.

"All that said, let's get to your first mission . . . ."

OP 1: DESTROY IMPERIAL CONVOY

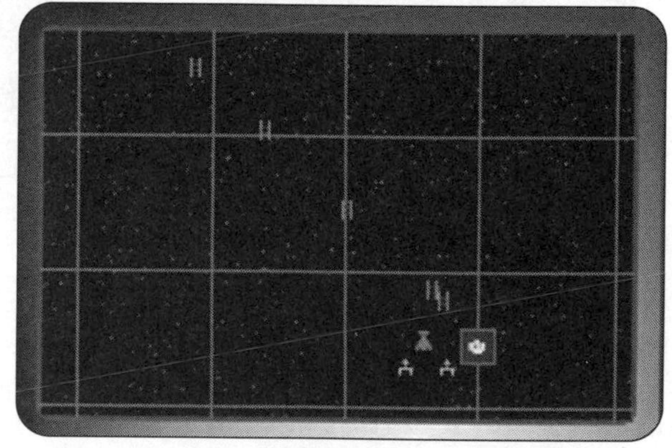

File Name: defect

Mission Briefing

You will fly an X-wing as wingman in a quick-strike mission against an Imperial convoy. The X-wings will fly cover, while Y-wings attempt to disable the lead ship. In addition, we plan to blow up the Emperor's supplies and get out before reinforcements can arrive.

Farlander's After-Action Report

I flew an X-wing in a hit-and-fade strike against an Imperial convoy. I was the wingman, and Hamo was my flight leader. During the mission, a corvette assigned to escort the convoy decided to defect to the Alliance, and a pair of Y-wings was ordered to disable the Imperial corvette so that one of our transports could capture it.

I used my normal mission-start sequence with the following exception: After hyperspacing into the engagement area, I transferred all laser power to my shields. (In retrospect, since no one shot at me, I could have redirected all shield power to the engines and just worried about maintaining full lasers.)

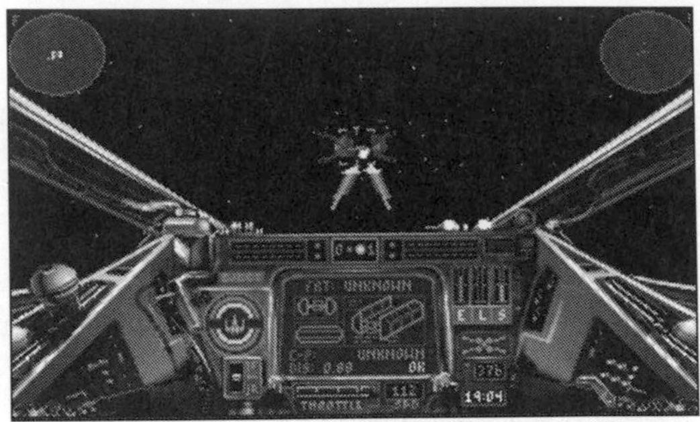
Targeting a freighter.

Anyway, I redirected all cannon power to the engines and got my speed up to 125. My map readout showed five enemy freighters in the area. The nearest two already had their shields down, and Hamo went after them. The next three formed a line stretching away toward their hyperspace jump point, and my job was to prevent the first two of them from escaping. I cycled through the targets until I located the third freighter. It was approximately eight clicks away. I headed toward it while Hamo began his run on the first two freighters. As soon as he destroyed them, he headed home.

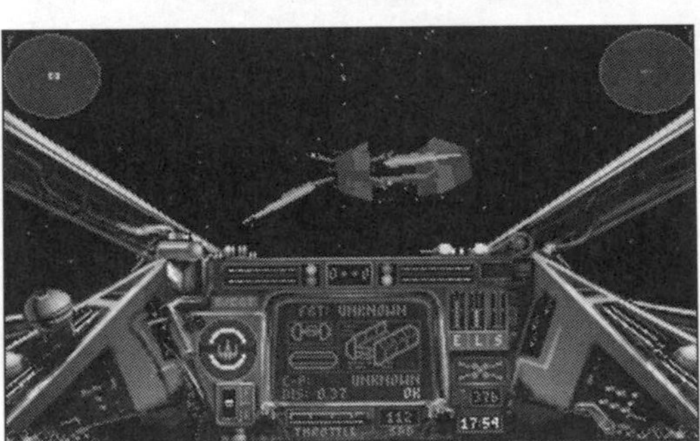
Using supercharged lasers.

Now, although I needed to get only the next two, I figured that if I moved quickly enough I could get all three, so I switched to torpedoes and selected dual-fire mode. As soon as I got a red lock, I fired two salvoes of two torpedoes and then switched to cannons. When I was two clicks from the target, I reset the cannon and shield recharge rates to maximum and transferred shield power to the lasers until they were fully supercharged. I began firing as soon as the target box turned green (1.50 km).

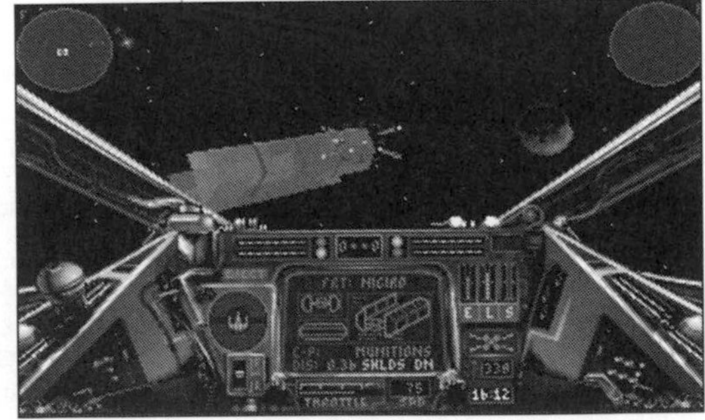
Coming in on the side.

I like to aim for a side of the freighter; it's bigger than the middle and easier to hit. This way, I took out freighter *Arreis* on the first pass. To prevent closing on the target too rapidly, I reduced throttle to one-third. As soon as the *Arreis* was finished, I transferred cannon power to my shields. Then I redirected cannon power to the engines and reset the shield recharge rate to normal.

I cycled forward to target the next freighter (the *Nigiro*) in the CMD at approximately four clicks away. As soon as I had a lock, I fired my remaining pair of torpedoes and then switched back to lasers, repeating the tactics I used on the *Arreis*. With my mission objectives completed, I headed back toward the corvette *Bixby*, which was being captured, and waited for my Mission Complete orders.

C.O.'s Analysis

"A fair job, lieutenant, and your report is clear and complete. However, there is always room for improvement," said the debriefing officer, the same man I had met outside Dafid's office. His name was Commander Lagrane.

"Here, read this report," he said. "Then go to the simulators, where you can try these new strategies." He handed me a holo, which I placed in my reader.

Debriefing (Win Conditions)

FRTs *Orcim*, *Esorp*, *Arreis*, and *Nigiro* must all be destroyed. The CRV *Bixby* must be recovered.

Mission Note: If you attack the third freighter, *Murtceps*, an Imperial Frigate will arrive two minutes afterwards. You still have time to wipe out the convoy, however, before its TIE fighters become a threat. Also, it's best to use two torpedoes apiece for each freighter. To get maximum points (and challenge) from this mission, you can send your flight leader home as soon as the mission begins. If you do so, you have to destroy all five freighters, but the first two go easily because their shields are already down; you can simply use your lasers on them. After destroying the convoy, you can stick around to fight the Frigate and its TIEs, or, any time after the Mission Complete message appears, you can go home.

Transcript of Interview with Captain Nogdra of the Imperial corvette *Bixby*

INTERROGATOR: *So, captain, why have you decided to come over to us?*

NOGDRA: It's . . . you don't know what I've seen. I can't . . . (pause)

INTERROGATOR: *Go on.*

NOGDRA: I can't condone their actions. Before I became captain of the *Bixby*, I was stationed on a Star Destroyer. I watched them destroy entire cities just to make a point. I watched them load intelligent beings into freighters with almost no life support and ship them off to who knows where . . . I held my tongue, but I'm not like that.

INTERROGATOR: *Like what?*

NOGDRA: I grew up on a Hub planet. I grew up with all kinds of beings. I can't accept the policies of hate and repression I've been ordered to uphold. I'm here to help you, if you'll have me.

INTERROGATOR: *How can you help us?*

NOGDRA: I'm a good captain. And I have some information. Not much, I'm afraid, but a little.

INTERROGATOR: *Tell me what you can.*

NOGDRA: Well, we were recently near Dellalt. The Imperials are using it as a staging point for supplies and equipment. I'd expect them to start operations in that sector. I'll give you the coordinates of the staging point . . . .

"Farlander!" It was Commander S'man himself.

"Yessir!" I answered. I had been walking down the hallway toward Ops when he caught up with me.

"Come with me," he said, walking alongside me.

"Where are we going?" I ventured. It was like talking to a giant; your neck bent at a strange angle when you tried to look him in the eye. It made me feel small.

"I've got an assignment for you," he said.

OP 2: RECONNAISSANCE MISSION

File Name: id-recon

Mission Briefing

Based on information gained from a defector, you will scout an area near Dellalt for Imperial ships. Identify all ships encountered, but leave at the first sign of a Star Destroyer.

Farlander's After-Action Report

I was in a lone A-wing with no missiles. As fast as the A-wing is, I felt pretty exposed; it was my first completely solo mission. I reminded myself that my job was to ID the enemy ships and that, to do so, I had to have each one targeted in the CMD as I approached it.

I began my normal mission checkout and start sequence. There was a Frigate about 4.5 clicks away when I hypered in, and I noticed two TIE fighters on patrol. With laser and shield recharge rates at maximum, I turned my A-wing toward the Frigate, but I targeted the nearest TIE fighter—it was just to the right of the Frigate and a little high. I shot both TIEs on the first pass and noticed that two more were launched immediately, but I kept

Shooting TIEs.

ID the Frigate.

Close encounter with a corvette.

heading toward the Frigate. I put it in the target box and executed a close (0.7 click) fly-by to identify it as the *Warspite*.

By this time, a pair of corvettes had jumped in. As I headed toward them, I checked to see that my shields and lasers were fully charged, and then reset recharge rates to normal. The TIE fighters flew in pursuit, and I let them come on. The farther they got from their mother ship, the better. I knew that destroying them at a greater distance would buy me time before the next wave could reach me.

As I closed on the two corvettes, a freighter appeared. It was closer than the corvettes, so I targeted it and flew close to identify it. I discovered that I had to get very close, within 0.30 click, to identify freighters and corvettes. After identifying the FRT *Ruggert*, I continued toward the corvettes. With the TIE fighters still in pursuit, I used the weave pattern we were taught to avoid their fire.

While I was identifying CRV group 327, three more corvettes appeared on my screen. I identified them as group 758, and with all five corvettes accounted for, I kept flying past them until I was out of their laser range.

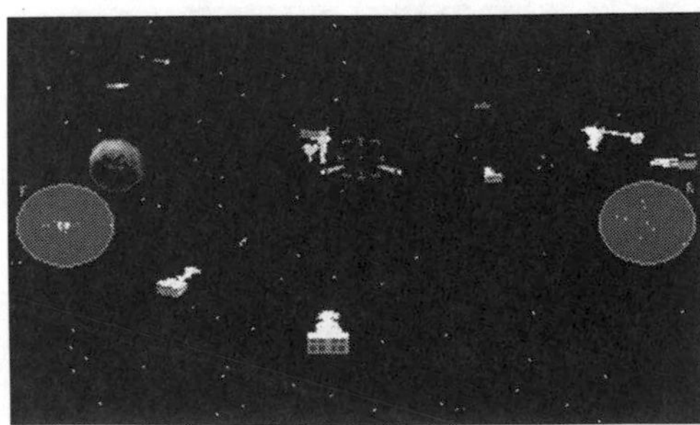

Scanning the area with cockpit off.

Finally, I decided to finish off the TIE fighters, which were still following me. I noticed that TIEs with hull damage would head for their mother ship, and that the mother ship generally would not send out reinforcements as long as the wounded TIE was still operational, so I let one TIE get away, buying even more time.

The Invincible *arrives.*

Soon, three more corvettes appeared. As before, while I headed toward them, a freighter (*Eichler*) entered nearby space, followed by two more corvettes. I ID'ed the first group as 427 and the second as group 524.

Finally, two Frigates came out of hyperspace. I checked to be sure that my shields were fully charged, and hurried toward them, aware that they were launching TIE fighters. After I identified them as Frigates *Harasser 1* and *Harasser 2*, a Star Destroyer (the *Invincible*) appeared. My Mission Complete message flashed on, and I hypered home.

C.O.'s Analysis

Commander Lagrane was his usual serious self, but he seemed happy enough. "Excellent report, lieutenant, and excellent job. There's not much to add, but you might hone your dogfighting skills in the simulators. Check out this additional report."

Again, he handed me a holo.

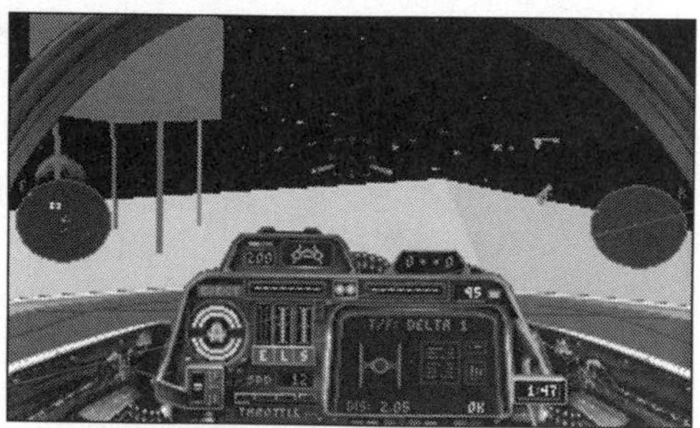
Getting to know the Invincible.

Debriefing (Win Conditions)

CRV groups 327, 427, 524, and 758, as well as FRTs *Ruggert* and *Eichler* and FRGs *Harasser 1* and *2* all must be identified.

Mission Note: If you're in the mood for some serious dogfighting, go ahead and engage the TIEs. Including those on the *Invincible*, there are 170 in all! The first 20 are Novices, and the rest are Top Aces. (This is about twice the normal complement for these ships, of course, but that's what makes it such a challenge.) Since you can also destroy the FRTs and CRVs without much effort, this can be a very high-scoring mission if you are up to it. Also, note that a transport and a shuttle arrive soon after the Star Destroyer does.

A few days after I got back from my solo mission, I began to suspect that something big was about to happen. We weren't told anything at first, but the senior officers seemed agitated, and I couldn't help but notice that many senior staff meetings were taking place. Nobody was talking about it, but there was a strong feeling of anticipation onboard. I asked Hamo whether he knew anything. He had made captain after his last mission, and his irrepressible confidence seemed to have gone up a notch, if that was possible.

"I figure we'll find out soon enough," he said. "After they plan what has to be done, you know who'll do it, don't ya?" He grinned. "Stop worrying, Farlander. Me, I can't wait to get back into the action."

The suspense ended the next day. We were called into Briefing Room 1 with several other squadrons. This time it was General Dodonna himself who led the meeting. He stood at the podium and watched the room as we settled into our seats. His face appeared calm, but I thought that I detected some worry in his expression. When we were all settled, the general began.

"Operation Strike Fear," he said quietly. "This is the Imperial response we have been anticipating.

"Some of you already know that we have planned to evacuate the Briggia base and move to a new location. However, recent events have forced us to take action sooner than expected: We have learned that the first target of Operation Strike Fear is Briggia itself."

The general paused again, stroking his gray beard, as a murmur went through the crowd of pilots. Finally, he consulted his personal holo-player, then activated the master holo display.

Immediately a small blue planet appeared in the center of the display, and several ships were launched from its surface. The general motioned to someone behind him, and the entire display was magnified several times until the planet filled about a quarter of the holo sphere and the ships were recognizable as various Rebel shuttles and transports.

"In a matter of hours, we will hyperspace to the Briggia area and mount a series of operations designed to protect the evacuation. Red Squadron, you'll be responsible for protecting the senior staff shuttles. Gold Squadron, I want you to lend one Y-wing in support of Red Squadron's X-wings."

As the general described the mission, more ships appeared in the display. I knew that the entire briefing was being recorded and would be handed out when we disbanded.

"Blue Squadron, you'll prepare for a separate mission to protect our base equipment transports," the general continued. "Now here is where the mission will begin."

OP 3: FLY POINT DURING EVACUATION

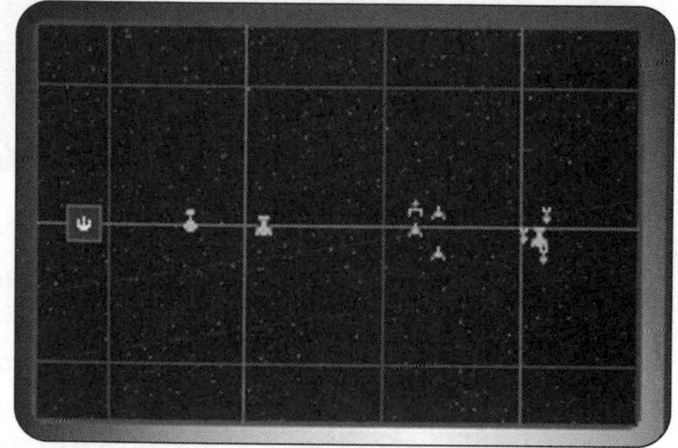

File Name: wxrgard1

Mission Briefing

The Imperial Fleet is ready to attack Briggia. You must protect key Rebel officers evacuating the planet in shuttles. Protect the shuttles until they reach their hyperspace jump points and are safely away.

Farlander's After-Action Report

I took the wingman position in my X-wing, teamed up with a flight leader I had never flown with before. I began with my standard mission-start sequence, but cut throttle to two-thirds, following X-wing *Red 1*. I cycled through the targets until shuttle *Arroyo 1* appeared in the CMD, and I assigned it and the next two shuttles to memory locations in the targeting computer. Since these were the ships I had to protect, I wanted to be able to find them quickly.

Targeting TIE fighters . . .

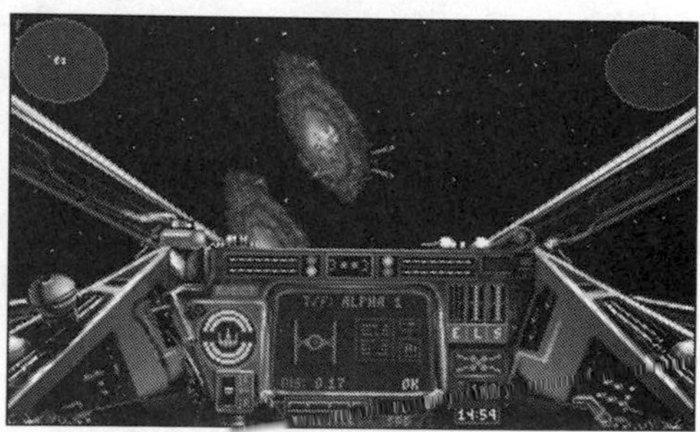

. . . and shooting them.

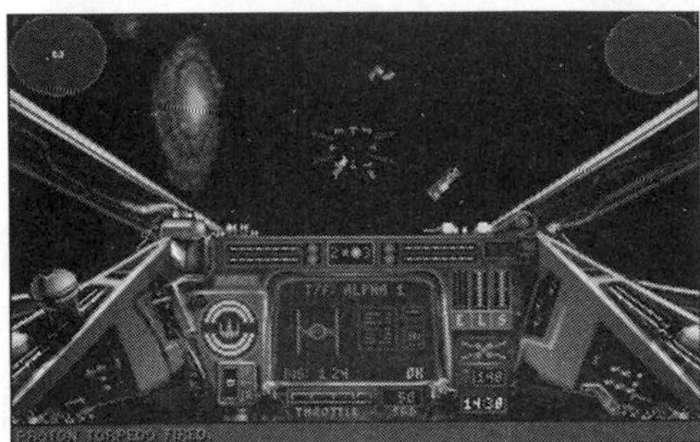

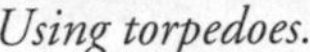

Using torpedoes.

Checkin' out R2.

About the time we reached the shuttles, the Star Destroyer *Invincible* dropped out of hyperspace. I queried the CMD to target the nearest TIE fighter, *Alpha 1*, communicated to *Red 1* that he should attack it, and then cycled forward to target T/F *Alpha 2*. If any of T/F Alpha or Beta were to get by me, I knew that I could use torpedoes on them, just as long as they didn't escape. After all three shuttles entered hyperspace, the mission was complete.

C.O.'s Analysis

Lagrane was in a hurry. "Look, lieutenant, there's no time for a thorough debriefing. We've got to get you spaceborne again. Here are some notes about the mission."

Debriefing (Win Conditions)

All three shuttles must escape.

Mission Note: TIE fighter groups Alpha and Beta turn out to be the keys to this mission, because they target the shuttles. Don't let them get by you, and if they do, chase them down. T/F Alpha are Veterans, and are succeeded by two waves. T/F Beta are Aces, and have nine succeeding waves, although the shuttles should escape before the third or fourth wave. The survival of Rebel FRG *Fugazi* was also necessary to the success of the mission, but because it jumps right at the start, you don't have to worry about it. TRN group Rhoon and CRV *Mahan* begin the mission with their shields down, so they are killed relatively easily.

I barely had time to grab something to eat before I was back in the cockpit again. The Empire had hit us hard, and we were all scrambling to salvage whatever we could. They sent me alone in an X-wing to help protect the wounded who were being transferred to a Medical Frigate.

OP 4: PROTECT MEDICAL FRIGATE

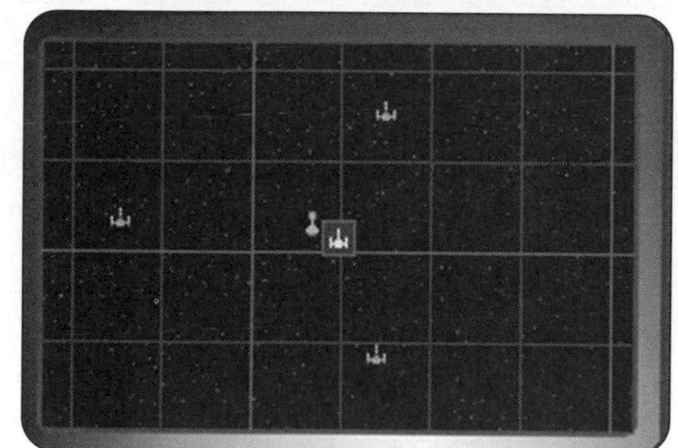

File Name: wxprot2

Mission Briefing

The wounded from the attack on Briggia are being brought to a Medical Frigate, and you must provide security while the transfer is made. Three Medevac shuttles and the corvette *Korolev* all must escape into hyperspace after delivering their cargo of wounded. First the shuttles and then the *Korolev* will dock and unload.

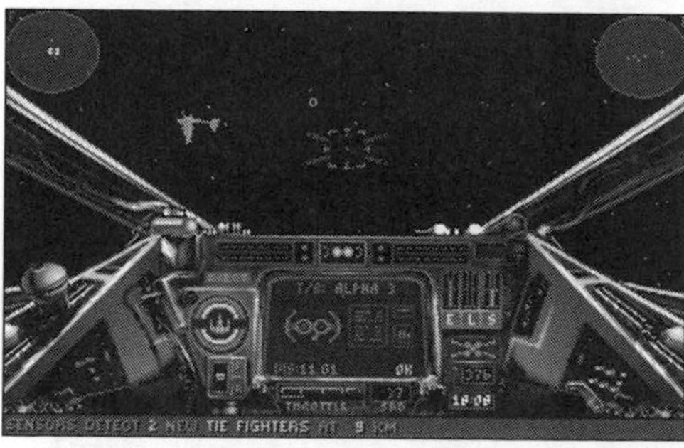

Targeting the Bombers.

Farlander's After-Action Report

I hypered in and began my mission-start sequence, charging up shields first. The mission began quietly, but then an Imperial Frigate, the *Warspite*, dropped out of hyperspace about 11 clicks from our position. The Frigate launched a group of three TIE Bombers and two TIE fighters, and then hyperspaced away.

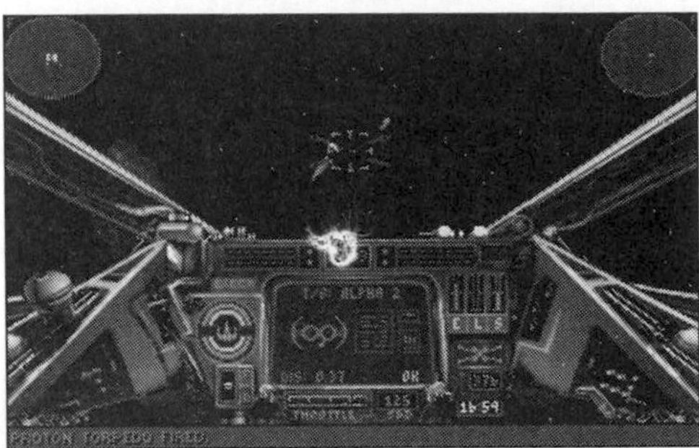

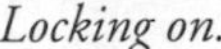

Locking on.

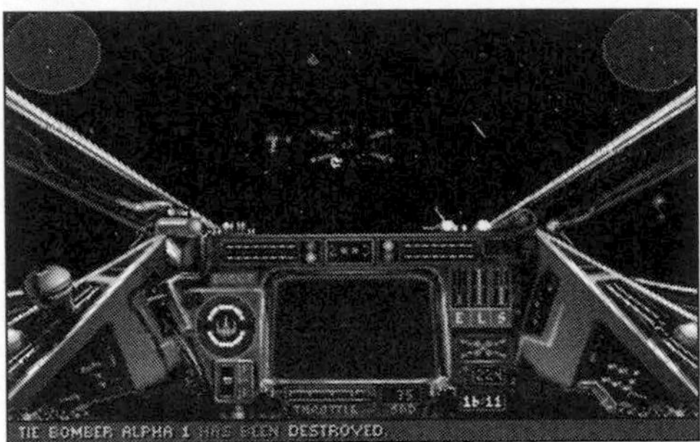

Scratch one Bomber.

Immediately I targeted a Bomber, and headed toward the Bomber squadron at full throttle. With fully charged shields, I set the shield recharge rate to normal and redirected all cannon power to the engines, pushing my speed up to 125.

I switched to torpedoes, and then, when I got within three clicks of my target, I reset shield and cannon recharge rates to maximum to bring my speed down to 50. Keeping my hand steady on the controls, I fired my first torpedo head-on, because the distance between us was still greater than 1 click. Any closer and I would have had to turn on the Bomber's tail and then fire.

As quickly as I could, I locked up and fired on the other two Bombers. I knew that I couldn't afford a miss because my computer told me that the *Warspite* had returned to normal space—on the side of the Medical Frigate opposite me—and it was launching more TIEs!

Again, I redirected cannon power to the engines and set the shield recharge rate to normal. When the TIE fighters got too close, I used the Wotan Weave to evade them. I knew that I couldn't stop to dogfight and still hope to intercept the second wave of TIE Bombers the *Warspite* had launched. I slowed down when I was within three clicks of those Bombers, and fired torpedoes as soon as I had a solid lock. I was also able to finish off the other two Bombers before they could launch their own missile salvos.

Finally, I turned my attention to the TIE fighters that had been dogging me the entire time. As I was engaged in the ensuing dogfight, the Mission Complete message came up on my display.

C.O.'s Analysis

"I barely made it through that one," I told Lagrane. "I was sure that the *Korolev* was a goner."

"We've analyzed your performance, lieutenant, and it was nearly flawless. Either you were very lucky or your skills are improving. Either way, we're thankful for your efforts. There's nothing more to add."

"I suppose that I could have attacked the *Warspite*," I joked, but Lagrane didn't look amused.

"Let's just stay alive, shall we?" he told me.

"Yessir!" I replied.

Debriefing (Win Conditions)

The corvette *Korolev* and the three Medevac Shuttles must all survive.

Mission Note: If you have a great deal of difficulty with this mission, try sending the shuttles home at the very beginning. This tactic takes unfair advantage of a small loophole, but it enables the *Korolev* to begin docking right away. Also, because there are six TIE Bombers and you have only six torpedoes, if you miss, you may find that the expedient way to destroy one or two is by ramming them. This strategy is not recommended, but it is quick and effective!

Also, note that since your 'wingmen' in this mission are not actually in your flight group, you can't give them attack orders.

We were all pretty worn out after the evacuation and the Imperial attack. I know that I was ready for a long rest, and I could see in the faces of my fellow pilots that they had also tested their limits. Many of the men were unshaven, and their faces looked drawn. The women seemed to have held up a little better, but they all showed the strain. It was harder to tell about the alien races, but it was easy to assume that they, too, were tired.

Then there were the faces that were missing from our circle of comrades. The memory of them seemed to occupy a space that made everyone less comfortable. I still expected to see Karka or Dontal whenever I saw Misch'an, but I knew I would never see them again. It was the missing people that got to me, and it was as though a cold wind blew through the ship when I thought of them.

There was no rest. There was no time for a break. We had been hurt, but the Empire had also suffered losses. There was already talk about mounting another raid on Imperial supply convoys. We were called in to a briefing the day after the *Korolev* affair, and I was surprised to see Sunnar Jan-lo in attendance.

"Hey, Farlander. Looks like I'm going out on this mission with you." I was surprised, and I guess it showed. Her expression soured a little, and she added, "You're not the only one who can pass the training, you know."

"I didn't mean . . ." I began. "I mean, I thought you wanted to go into intelligence."

"Yeah. Maybe eventually, but the Alliance needs more pilots. At least that's what the brass think. You heard about Poussan, didn't you?"

"No," I answered.

"Bought it. In the evacuation," she said tersely. "He collided with a TIE fighter, and his shields were too low."

"But how did he get into the action in the first place?" I asked, astounded. "When I left training, he was behind you."

"Don't know. I think he was just in the wrong place when they needed another body in a starfighter. Bad luck, I guess."

"What about Gart?" I asked, thinking about the quiet young man who had come up with us. I had never really gotten to know him, but now I was curious.

"Washed out. Disorientation problems," answered Jan-lo. "But he told me that he's going to try again. He doesn't talk a lot, but he seems to want to make it through the training. Wants it real bad. We might see him out there eventually."

It was sobering. One of my fellow Agamarians was already a casualty. Another a washout. It brought back feelings I had suppressed. Feelings of home, and with them feelings of frustration and anger. "Just make sure you don't buy it, Sunnar," I told her seriously.

"I'll be all right. Watch your own back, hotshot."

Then the briefing began.

OP 5: AMBUSH IMPERIAL SUPPLY CONVOY

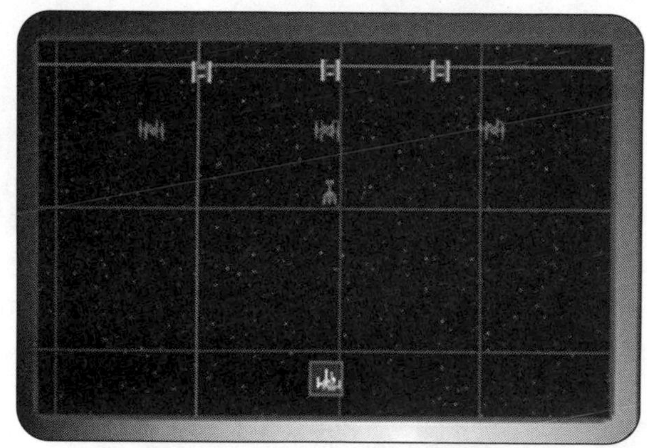

File Name: attackxy

Mission Briefing

The Imperial Fleet is low on resources after the attack on Briggia. Stop a supply convoy and the Imperial campaign can be set back several weeks. The convoy consists of three freighters with a corvette and several TIE fighters for escort. The convoy is less than four clicks away. The Star Destroyer *Invincible* is a nice, safe, 50 clicks away, but it will send reinforcements, so be quick!

Farlander's After-Action Report

I began my normal mission-start sequence, but then switched to torpedoes and selected dual-fire mode. Querying the CMD displayed a TIE fighter from group Beta. I sent my wingman to attack it and then targeted the corvette, which was directly in front of me.

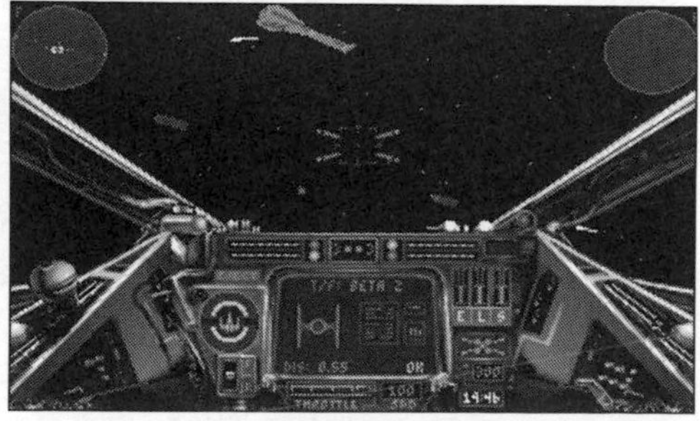

Targeting TIE Beta 2.

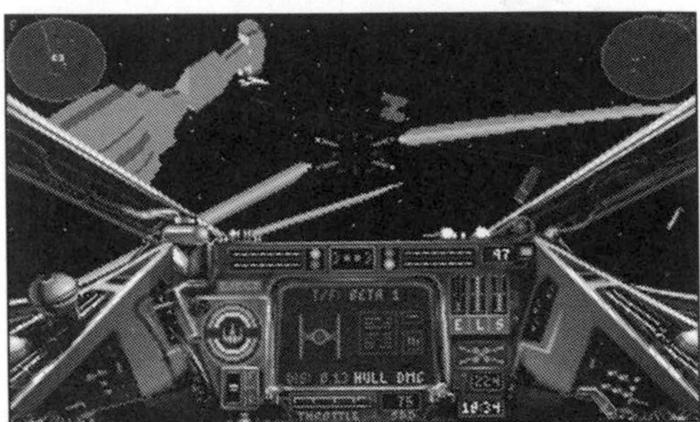

Dogfight around the corvette.

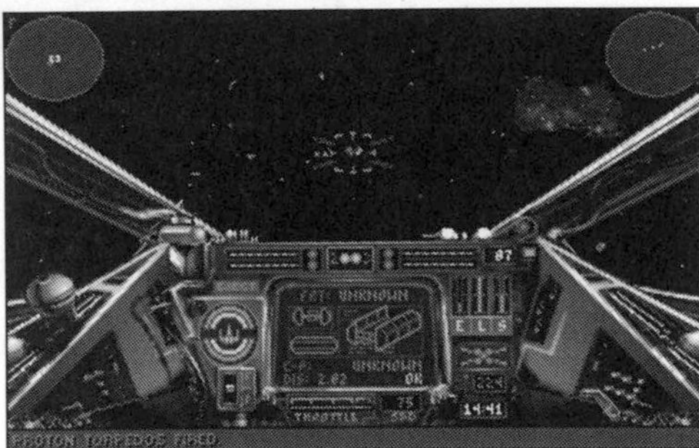

Targeting a freighter.

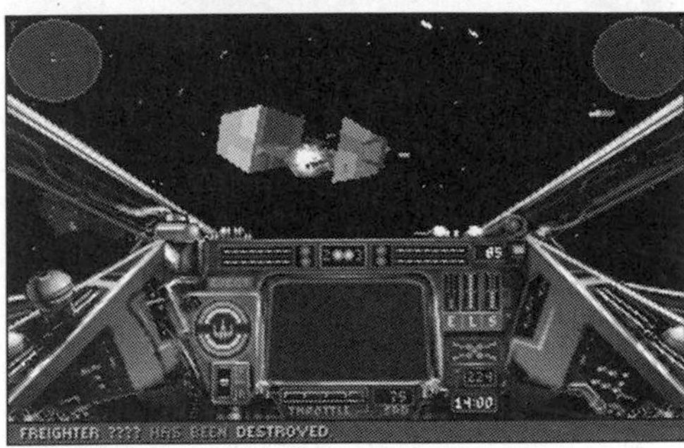

Bye-bye, freighter.

As soon as I had a lock, I fired all six torpedoes as quickly as I could. After firing the last pair, I queried the CMD again for the nearest fighter and switched back to lasers. Still angry over the news about Poussan, I engaged T/F groups Alpha, Beta, and Delta.

The Y-wings came in a minute after I arrived, and I kept the TIEs busy and away from them. When all the escorts were destroyed, I went to help the Y-wings destroy the now defenseless freighters. I targeted the closest freighter and called my wingman to help me. Of course, we had no trouble with the freighters, and then we got our Mission Complete message and hypered home.

C.O.'s Analysis

"Good mission, Farlander," Lagrane told me. "It was risky, firing all your torpedoes at the start, though. Still, it worked out, so you're to be commended. Here are some suggestions to try out in the simulator."

Debriefing (Win Conditions)

All three freighters must be destroyed.

Mission Note: If you're doing well enough, send your wingman and the Y-wings home, and destroy all the freighters yourself. Also, there are a ton of TIE Interceptors heading your way, and you can polish them off and gain valuable experience. For yet another challenge, attack the Star Destroyer and receive even more TIE target practice.

"Sorry, Lieutenant Farlander, no ops today," said the hangar requisition officer.

"But I have orders to go out on recon," I said. "Check the roster on the computer."

The man shrugged. "It's not that I don't want to send you out, but I have no more ships."

"What about all those?" I asked, pointing to a row of X-wings lined up and down the hangar.

"Look, lieutenant, I can't make 'em fly without more R2 units. You get me some 'droids, and I'll give you the starfighters. Deal?"

I stared in frustration. "I'll do my best," I answered after a moment, but the man had forgotten about me already, and was arguing on the comm with somebody else.

OP 6: RAID FOR R2 UNITS

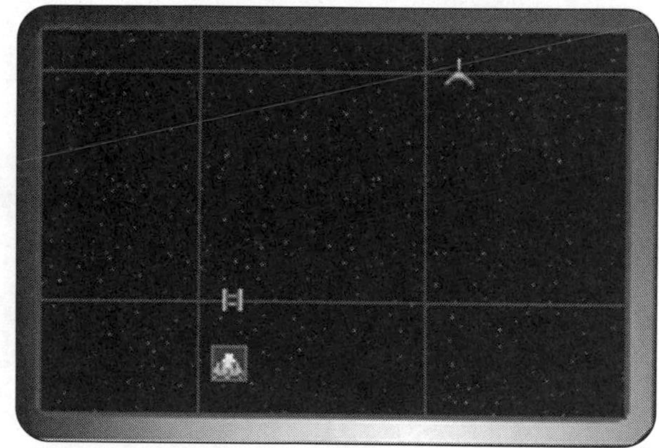

File Name: max13

Mission Briefing

The Rebellion does not have enough R2 units in supply. Capture a damaged freighter that contains desperately needed R2 units. Beware of pirates who are active in the area. You will come out of hyperspace with the disabled freighter directly in front of you, while the shuttle with the repair crew is almost three clicks away.

Farlander's After-Action Report

I checked out my A-wing's systems and performed normal mission-start procedures. I found the freighter *ARS Opus*, the one with the R2 units, and stayed close. Pirate Y-wings (showing neutral blue in the CMD) appeared about 30 seconds after I had hypered in. I queried the CMD for the nearest one, and ordered my wingmen to attack it.

Realizing that a Y-wing's cruising speed is only 80, I was careful to keep my own speed under control. Anticipating the arrival of enemy reinforcements, I conserved my missiles and used lasers against the pirate Y-wings.

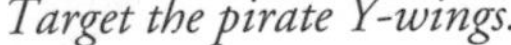

Target the pirate Y-wings.

Y-wings are easy prey.

I watched the computer readout with one eye, and within two minutes our shuttle, *Rescue Riker*, had docked with the freighter. I noticed that none of the Y-wing pirates went after it, a fact that would make my job easier. However, when four transports entered, I quickly realized the threat they presented, targeted them, and ordered my wingmen to attack.

I switched to missiles and selected dual-fire mode, figuring that the transports would try to disable the freighter as soon as the *Rescue Riker*

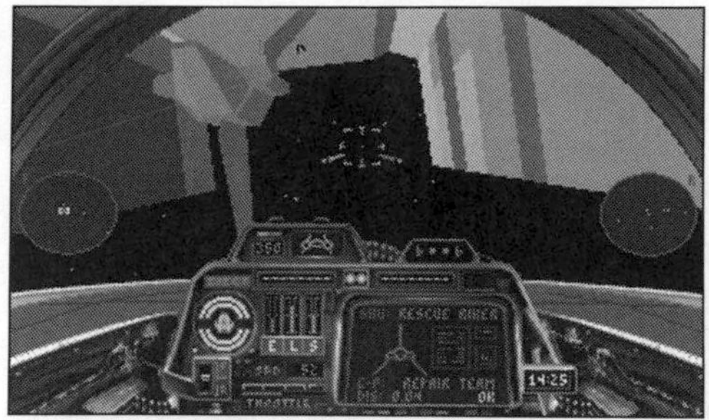

Closely guarding Rescue Riker.

Here comes a pirate transport.

captured it. I found that each transport required either three missiles or two missiles and a couple of laser blasts. After taking care of the first four transports, another wave of four appeared. My wingmen and I attacked them quickly, as well.

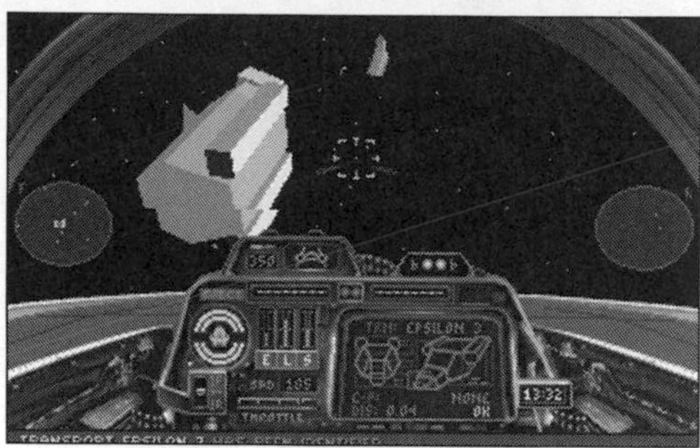

Epsilon 3 *has a problem.*

After the *ARS Opus* was captured, Blue Squadron's A-wings hypered in to form an escort. A pirate shuttle appeared, but it wasn't able to do anything with the freighter now operational and Blue Squadron's A-wings protecting it. I continued to attack enemy ships, however, until my R2 beeped and the Mission Complete message came over the computer.

C.O.'s Analysis

Commander Lagrane was in one of his better moods.

"Not bad, Farlander. Those R2 units are going to be a big help. Keeping the *ARS Opus* functional was your top priority, and you recognized correctly that the main threat came from the transports. You might have destroyed the Y-wings and the shuttles as well, but that wasn't necessary to complete the mission objectives."

Debriefing (Win Conditions)

FRT *ARS Opus* must be captured, and A-wing group Blue must arrive.

Mission Note: If you take on the pirate Y-wings for extra points, destroy groups Alpha and Beta first, because they have no successive waves. Then go after the others.

"Farlander! Jan-lo here." The comm link hissed a little, and I could hear many voices in the background. I sat in the darkness of the simulator pod, reviewing some of the most recent missions. "You copy, Keyan?"

"I'm here," I answered. "What's up?"

"Problems. I'm working in Operational Section today, and a message just came over that I thought you would want to know about."

Not liking the urgency in her voice, I said, "Go on. What's the problem?"

"I think that you should get up here. Your friend Captain Blastwell is in some trouble."

I was already headed out of the simulator. "I'm on my way," I replied.

I ran full speed down the hallways, dodging other crew members and receiving a few unpleasant stares, especially from the Quarren crew, who seemed disturbed by humans moving quickly in air. I suspected that I would feel the same way if I were in water with them, but I had no time to worry about such things.

I ran into Ops and found Jan-lo behind one of the holo readouts. She was already pointing to three ships on the display.

"See? That's Blastwell's X-wing," she told me. "Those other two are his wingmen. Something's gone wrong with the R2 units, and the ships are out of control."

"What could be going on?"

"We think sabotage. Remember the R2s we recently recovered?"

"Sure. I was on that mission."

"Well, they may have been tampered with. The engineers are checking out the others right now. In the meantime, you might want to get in a ship and help out your friend."

"I'm on my way," I called as I sprinted for the door.

OP 7: RECOVER STOLEN X-WINGS

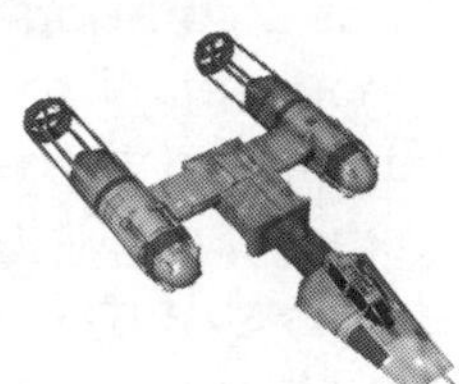

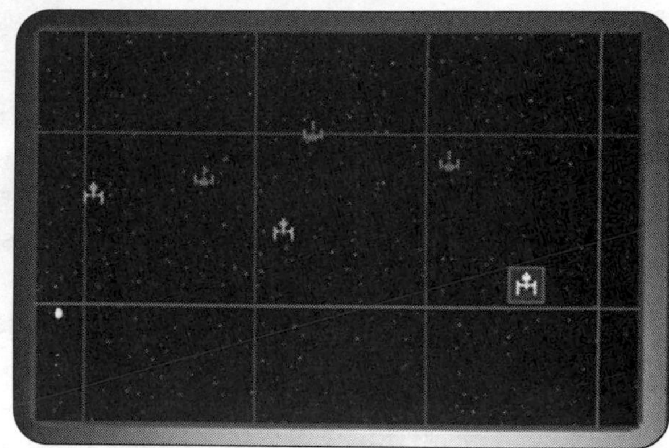

File Name: max10

Mission Briefing

Some R2 units stolen from the Empire had hidden programming that allowed them to take over X-wings. You must track down the X-wings and recapture them. You will drop out of hyperspace less than 1.5 clicks from the three stolen ships. An Imperial Star Destroyer is waiting about 45 clicks further on, and will immediately begin launching pairs of TIE Interceptors. You and two other Y-wing pilots are each responsible for one of the X-wings. Yours is *Blue 2*.

Farlander's After-Action Report

As soon as I hypered in, I quickly checked out my Y-wing's systems as usual, but I kept my recharge rates at normal. I saw immediately that the nearest threat was still far away, and more than anything else, I needed speed to catch up with the rogue X-wings. Fortunately, the X-wings were not traveling at full speed, so I kept my ship at full throttle; a speed of 80.

I tried to reach Hamo or one of the other pilots on the comm, but got no answer, so I cycled through the target list until I saw X-wing *Blue 2* in the CMD. As I came into range, I used my lasers to drop his shields. I fired slowly and carefully until I saw his shields begin to fail, and then I switched to ion cannons to disable him. After X-wing *Blue 2* was disabled, I reset recharge rates to maximum.

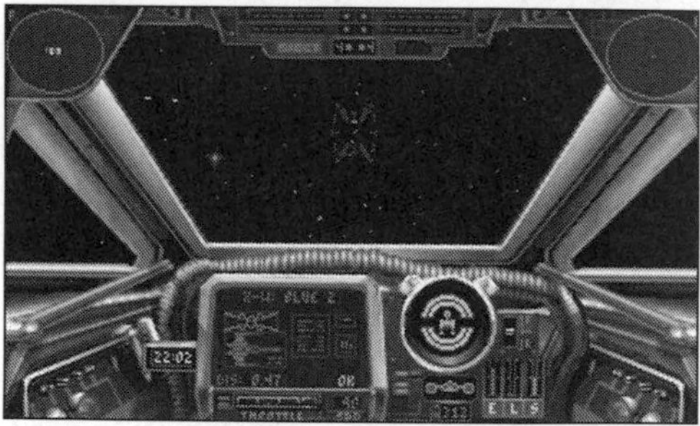

Catching up with Blue 2.

Quickly I cycled forward through the target list until the nearest TIE

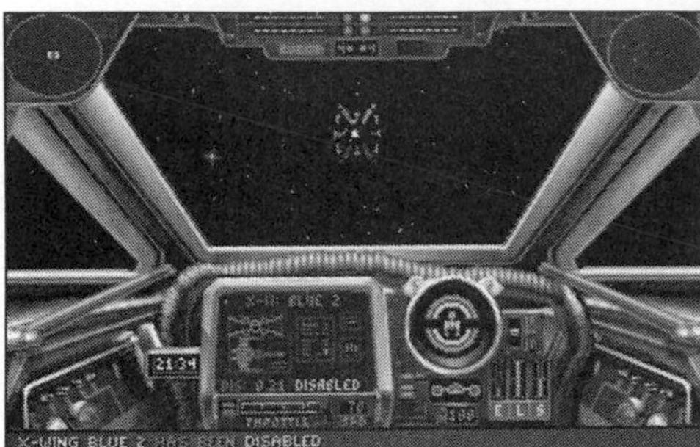

Blue 2 *is disabled.*

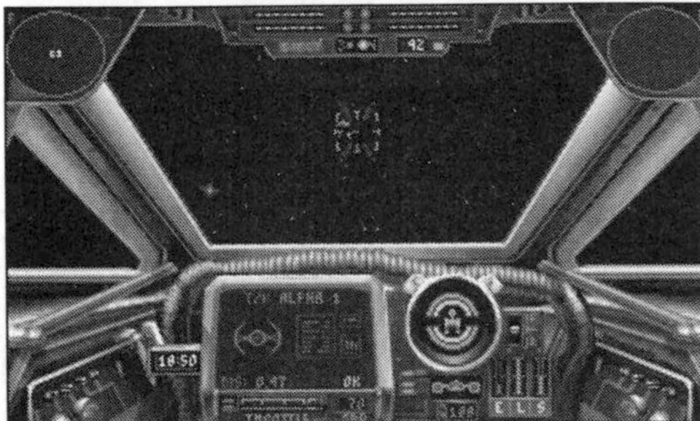
Shooting an Interceptor with a torpedo.

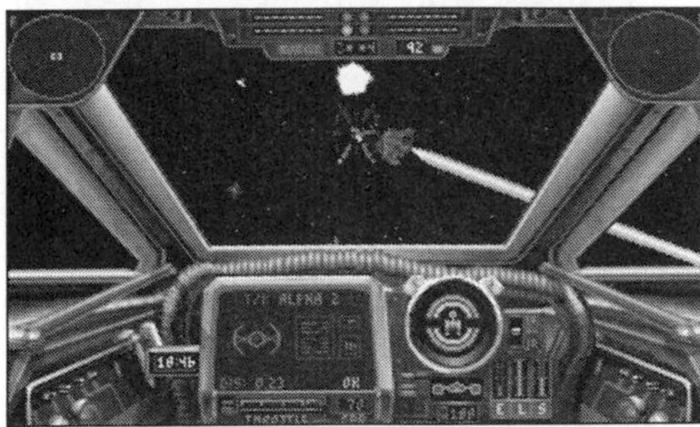
Going after TIE Interceptor Alpha 2.

You've got a TIE on your tail.

Interceptor, *Alpha 1*, was displayed in the CMD. I saw that it was about 33 clicks away. I assigned it to a memory location, then cycled forward to *Beta 1*, which was also about 33 clicks away. I assigned *Beta 1* to the next memory location, and then did the same with *Gamma 1* and *Delta 1*.

As soon as my shields and cannons were fully charged, I reset the recharge rates to normal and headed directly for *Alpha 1*. The other Y-wings were busy disabling their target X-wings, and when they finished, they hypered home. That left me alone to stop the TIE Interceptors!

With *Alpha 1* in the CMD, I switched to torpedoes. I fired a head-on torpedo shot at T/I *Alpha 1*, and then switched to lasers to blast *Alpha 2* before he got by me. Next, I increased the recharge rate one step for my cannons.

I realized that I had to shoot these TIE Interceptors before they got passed me. If even one got by, the helpless X-wings would be destroyed. I still had my torpedoes, however. I knew that if I could get a lock on one of the T/Is before it got more than 1.5 clicks away, I could still shoot it down, but I didn't want to have to do that. I kept checking my Inflight Map screen to be sure that no one slipped by.

I engaged the Beta group, dog-fighting and also using torpedoes if I had a clean lock, and after that the Gamma group. Delta came directly for me, and I had to dogfight their superior fighters; by this time, however, the X-wings had been refitted with new R2s and were headed for the cruiser *Maximus*, which had jumped in nearby.

This isn't what you want to see.

I kept the T/Is busy to be sure that the operation was successful. Then, when I received the Mission Complete message, I hypered home.

C.O.'s Analysis

"What was going on out there?" I asked angrily. "Why did the other Y-wings leave the scene with that Star Destroyer nearby?"

Commander Lagrane held out his hand to quiet me. "We're investigating the incident, lieutenant. I think that it was a communication failure. Fortunately, you were able to take up the slack. Good job."

"That's not supposed to happen, is it?" I asked, still not appeased.

"Look, Farlander, you know it's not supposed to happen. We hope that it won't ever happen again. But it did happen, and we're glad that you were there to do the job. Leave it to us. We'll get to the bottom of it."

Debriefing (Win Conditions)

The shuttles each must dock with their assigned X-wing. X-wing Blue must be recovered.

Mission Note: If you'd like a little extra dogfighting, try sticking around and shooting TIEs from the Star Destroyer. There are 52 in all. Also note that, as Farlander learned, Y-wings *Red 1* and *Red 3* are in separate flight groups, and cannot receive wingman commands.

For a few days things were quiet, as the technicians wiped the R2 units clean and checked all of them out. Hamo and I spent some time in the pilot's lounge talking about old times and playing Horansi, a particularly ruthless card game that was becoming popular among the Rebel pilots.

Hamo had a badly sprained wrist from the incident with the R2, but he was in good enough spirits, even if he couldn't fly for a while.

While we took our leisure, the High Command was busy, and Hamo and I were called into a private briefing with Commander S'man on our first shift, three days later.

"Several of our phase goals have been accomplished," Commander S'man was telling us. "Now we are ready to proceed with the fifth of our stated goals—namely, to help the Sullustans resist Imperial oppression. It's time we give them a reason to join the Alliance.

"We have discovered a secret operation that has been transporting important Sullustan prisoners from their home world to the Imperial capital; no doubt for interrogation, torture, and servitude. In four hours, we will launch a rescue operation as the prisoners are shuttled to a waiting Imperial Frigate. If successful, this mission should obtain widespread support for us on Sullust, and hopefully the Alliance will gain a powerful new ally in support of our cause."

The commander looked down at us then, as though assessing our worth, before continuing.

"We want to keep this mission quiet for now. There's a significant risk that, if we send in too many ships, the Imperials will kill the prisoners. We've decided that one pilot in a Y-wing should begin the rescue attempt, and we'll send in rescue transports after the shuttles carrying the prisoners have been disabled. It's a risky undertaking, and I tell you that I was opposed to it."

The commander checked a wrist display and then looked down at me.

"Failure could be disastrous. Remember that, Farlander. Be ready at 04:15," he said.

"Me?" I asked, somewhat incredulously.

S'man looked amused. "That's right: You. We've seen your ability to assess a situation, and then take the appropriate action under extreme pressure. This will be tougher than anything you've accomplished so far, but we think you're the right choice. And Blastwell?"

"Sir?" Hamo replied.

"You go over the mission plan with Farlander, and make sure that he knows everything you know. Check?"

"Check," Hamo told him. "Come on, Keyan. And don't worry. It'll be fine."

OP 8: RESCUE SULLUSTAN TECH STAFF

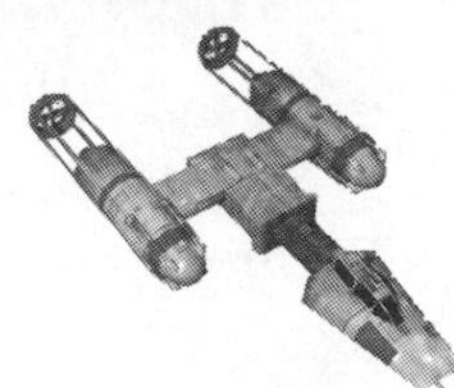

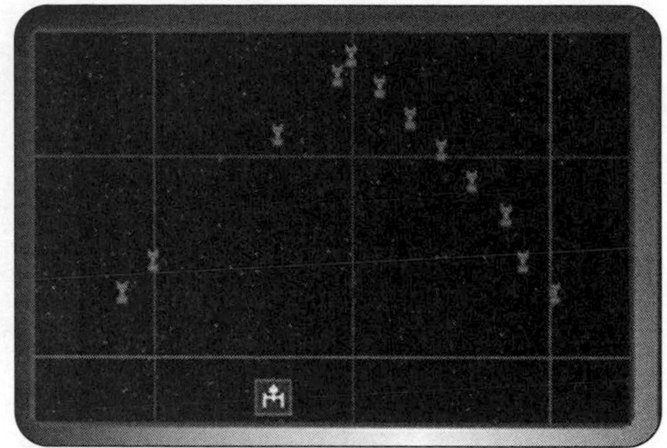

File Name: attack3

Mission Briefing

In an attempt to win the support of the Sullustans, you will lead an effort to rescue Sullustan prisoners held onboard Imperial transports.

Farlander's After-Action Report

I dropped out of hyperspace behind a large formation of a dozen transports, the nearest less than two clicks away and to my left. A pair of Nebulon-B Frigates, about 12.5 clicks away, launched two TIE fighters approximately 30 seconds after I arrived on the scene.

I performed my normal mission-start sequence, and then checked the Inflight Map to see how the transports were deployed. Most of them were on the right side of an extended vic formation. I targeted the rearmost ship on the right, which put me in a good position to move up the line quickly, identifying each transport in turn. I set my speed down to about 40 as I worked my way through the formation.

I switched to ion cannons, but held fire until I had finished my identification run. I figured that shooting at them now would just make

Approaching the transports.

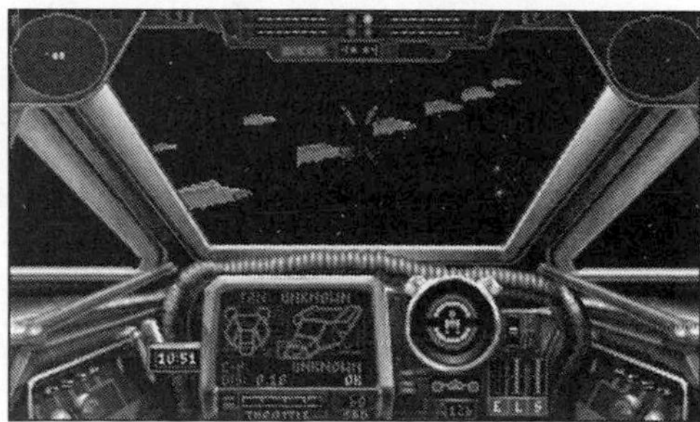

ID run on the transports.

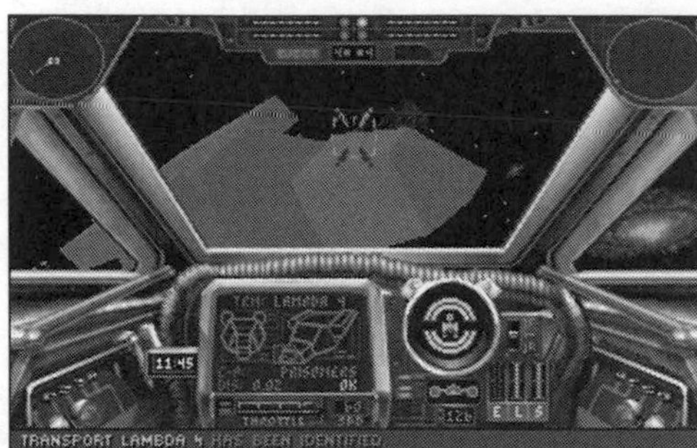

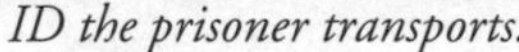

ID the prisoner transports.

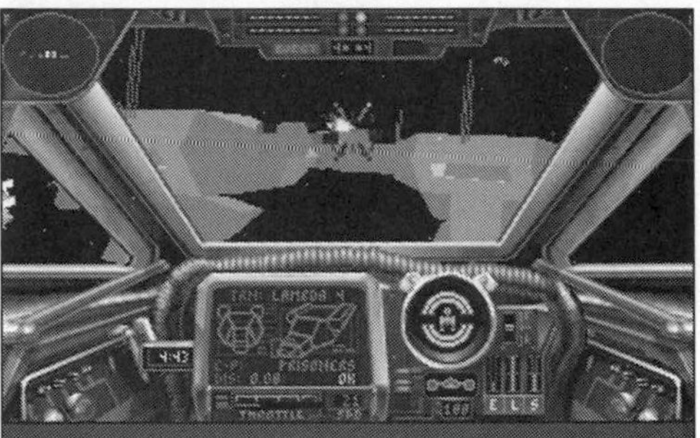

Disable the first prisoner transport.

them take evasive action, which would make my job more difficult. For now, they were just continuing on course without reacting to my presence, and I didn't want to do anything to change the situation.

I flew through the entire formation, keeping my speed under control so that I wouldn't collide with one of the slow-moving transports. I came very close to each transport so that my Y-wing's weak sensors could ID the craft. When I located a transport with prisoners, I assigned it a memory location. I proceeded until I had checked all the transports, discovering that only two of them were carrying prisoners.

When I was sure that I had found all the prisoners, I switched to torpedoes and fired one torpedo into the second prisoner transport to weaken its shields. After that, I switched to ions to disable it, which took only two supercharged dual-fire blasts.

Immediately I called up the other prisoner transport from memory and looped back to give it the same treatment. I did my best to disable them close to each other to make it easier to offer protection while the rescue operation began. I located *Rescue 1* and *Rescue 2* in the CMD and assigned them to my two unused memory locations. I wanted to check their status quickly in case I missed any messages about them.

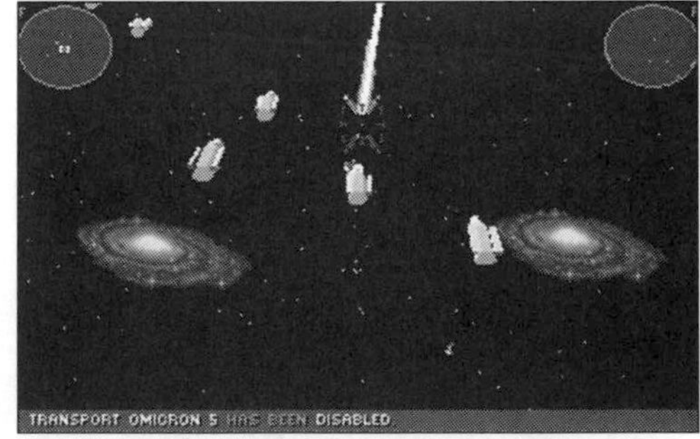

Disable the other prisoner transport.

Next, I called up the nearest TIE Interceptors, realizing that if they were still far enough away (at least six clicks), I could take out the Zeta group, which handled themselves like novice pilots. I kept watching the approach of T/I groups Alpha and Beta, though, knowing that TIE Interceptors were rarely flown by novices and that they represented a real threat.

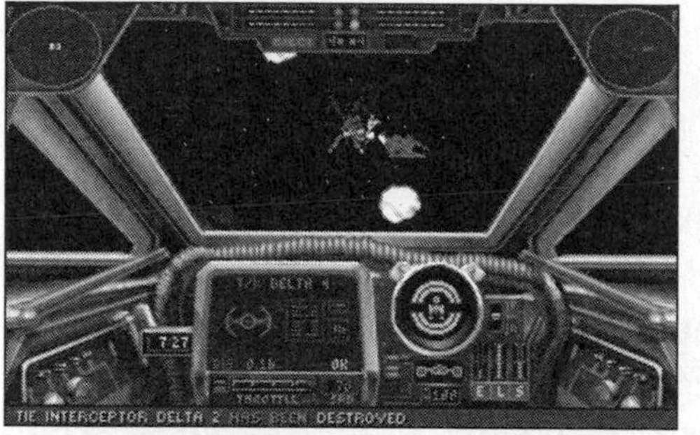

Shooting down TIE Interceptors

I finished off the Zeta TIEs quickly, but stayed near the transports as Alpha and Beta closed in. I used torpedoes to take out the leaders from a distance, and then engaged with my cannons to finish the wingmen. This tactic was pretty much the same one I had used previously with good results.

I noticed that a new wave of T/Is was launched as I destroyed the first. After Alpha and Beta were destroyed, I waited until the rescue mission was complete and *Rescue 1* and *Rescue 2* made it into hyperspace. When the Mission Complete message flashed on, I hypered out as well.

Debriefing (Win Conditions)

TRN *Lambda 4* and TRN *Omicron 5* must be boarded by *Rescue 1* and *Rescue 2*, which then must survive.

Mission Note: Toward the beginning of this mission, the CMD displays two TIE fighters from group Zeta when queried, but they are Novices, so ignore them unless they become a problem. Also, notice that the briefing is misleading, because you do not have to destroy any of the transports.

There are two groups of six transports, and the ones carrying the prisoners are always number 4 in the first group and number 5 in the second. At the start of the mission, you can cycle forward through the target list to the fourth transport, assign it to a memory location, then cycle forward seven more times and assign that one to a memory location. Go after this one first, and then carry on as just described.

You can get a maximum score by killing the disabled transports, (after the prisoners have been rescued, of course) and all the other transports, as well. Then fire at least one blast at each Frigate to get them to launch additional TIE Interceptors for more target practice. There are 80 TIEs in all, and they are Top Aces.

I arrived at the hangar on the *Independence* just as the rescued Sullustan prisoners were being escorted from the shuttles. With their wide eyes blinking in the bright light, they seemed momentarily disoriented, but quickly began chattering to themselves in high-pitched voices, looking around and pointing at various ships and other features in the hangar.

Another Sullustan came up to the group. He was dressed in Rebel uniform, and I recognized him as a navigator aboard the *Independence*. The Rebel Sullustan greeted the newcomers in their language, and they fell silent as he gave some sort of speech. Then they all began talking at one time.

I was turning toward the exit, on my way to report for debriefing, when I heard my name called in a sibilant, high voice.

"Lieutenant Farlander? Sir?"

I turned, and saw the *Independence* navigator facing me, his large, coal-black eyes unblinking and his oversized ears twitching slightly. Behind him stood the entire group of Sullustan prisoners, likewise favoring me with their disconcerting gazes. Once before, I had met the navigator, a very mild, kindly being whose name I never could figure out how to pronounce. But now I would have to do my best. I saluted.

"Lieutenant Commander Chiithii'n," I answered.

"Lieutenant, my friends from Sullust wish to thank you personally for your role in securing their rescue from the Empire. They want you to know that, if you should ever happen to visit our home planet, they will feast you on the choicest drutash grubs from the deepest caverns of Sullust, and bathe you in our most caustic green mud from the hot springs at Piringiisi."

Unsure how to respond, I gave a half bow. They came up to me, touching my face with their delicate fingers and speaking very broken Basic. Finally, an officer from protocol came with a droid who spoke to them in their language. They all laughed and followed the officer after waving good-bye to me. I hurried to meet Commander Lagrane and complete my belated debriefing.

For two weeks we flew routine missions while negotiations took place between the leaders of Sullust and the Rebel High Command. Finally, a summit meeting was arranged. Hamo was at last ready for action again, and we were assigned to fly Combat Space Patrol for the event.

OP 9: DIPLOMATIC SUMMIT AT SULLUST

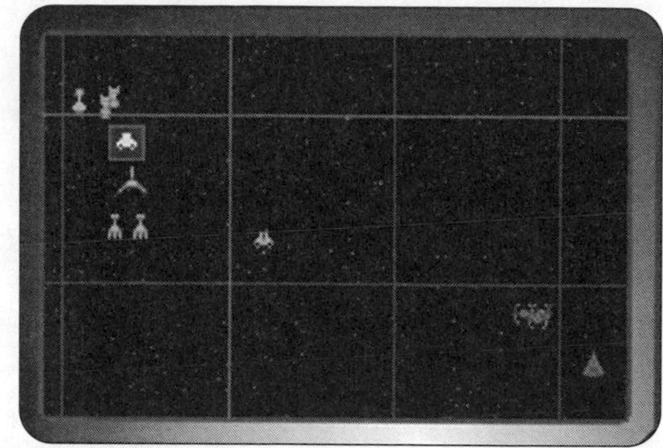

File Name: sullust

Mission Briefing
Protect the Sullustan leadership and their staff during a meeting with the Alliance. The Sullustans may be convinced to aid the Rebellion, so you must protect this summit.

Farlander's After-Action Report
We dropped out of hyperspace and surveyed the meeting location. It was all clear, and a few seconds later the rest of the summit participants began to arrive: two corvettes, four transports, the Frigate *Sor-SuLL II*, and two shuttles. I began my normal mission-start sequence and stayed close to Hamo, my flight leader, as the shuttles and transports began their slow dance around the larger ships. We saw no sign of Imperial intervention, but kept our eyes open.

A few minutes later, the Star Destroyer *Invincible* appeared behind the *Sor-SuLL II* and launched TIE Interceptor group Alpha, followed shortly by TIE Bomber group Zeta. Each group consisted of three ships. I figured that Hamo, out of real action for some time, would happily handle the threat without much help, but I wasn't about to let him go in alone.

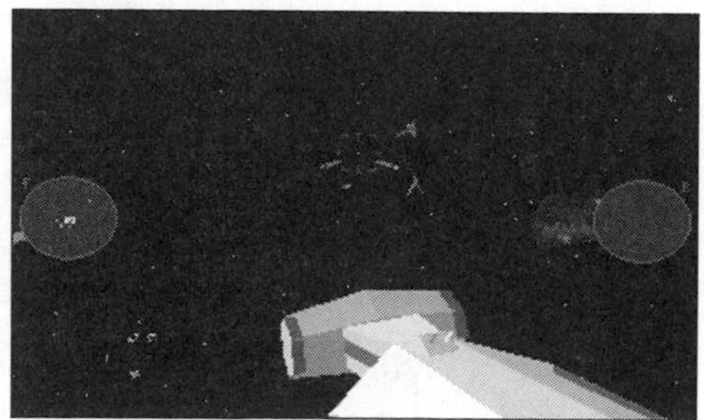

Escort the diplomats.

Watch over the Alliance ambassador.

Target the Bombers and destroy them quick!

The first two groups were rather poor pilots, and we took care of them quickly, firing torpedoes at the Bombers and then destroying the T/Is. A second wave was launched almost immediately, but they also flew poorly, and we had no real trouble with them.

No serious threats evolved, and we kept the meeting safe until, finally, the last ship jumped. As soon as the *Sor-SuLL II* hypered out, we got the Mission Complete message, and left for home.

Debriefing (Win Conditions)

All friendly ships except the two corvettes and your own flight group must survive.

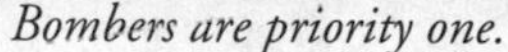

Bombers are priority one.

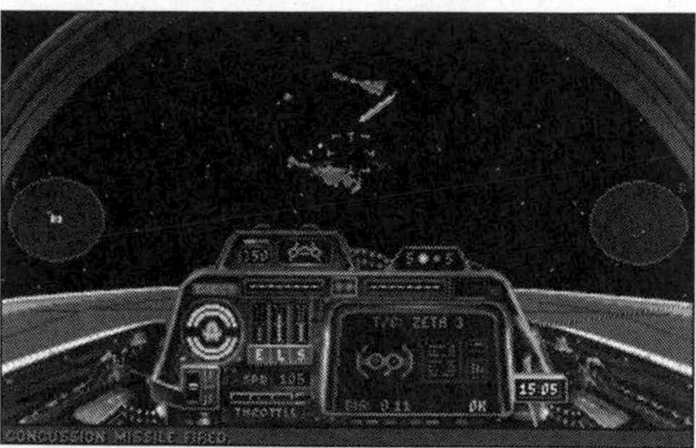

Destroy Bombers with missiles.

Mission Note: Switch to low detail because of all the large craft in this mission, unless you have a very high-speed machine. This mission is not a tough one, but if your dogfighting ability isn't up to it, leave one TIE Bomber from group Zeta alive. By itself, it won't destroy either of the corvettes.

"Well, now we know why the Imperial attack on the summit was so feeble," said Hamo, bursting into my cabin unannounced.

Looking up from the holo novel I was enjoying, I asked, "What do you mean?"

"Look, kid: Didn't you wonder why the Empire would send a Star Destroyer after the meeting and then launch some bunny pilots at us? It was just a diversion!"

"Diversion? For what? Cut to the dogfight, Hamo."

"*They got the Sullustan leader*. While we were out there meeting with the delegation, stormtroopers *kidnapped* the Sullustan leader."

I was dumbfounded, and I think it showed.

"So what are you waiting for, rookie?" said Hamo. "Let's go!"

"Hey," I called as I followed him out the door. "Where are we going? And who are you calling a rookie?"

OP 10: RESCUE SULLUSTAN LEADER

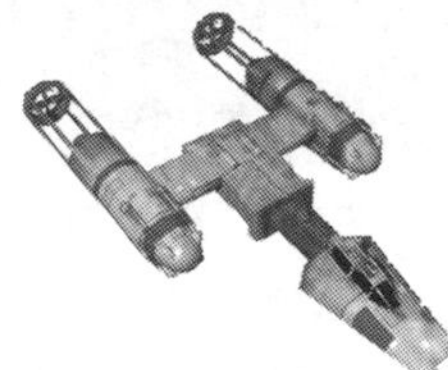

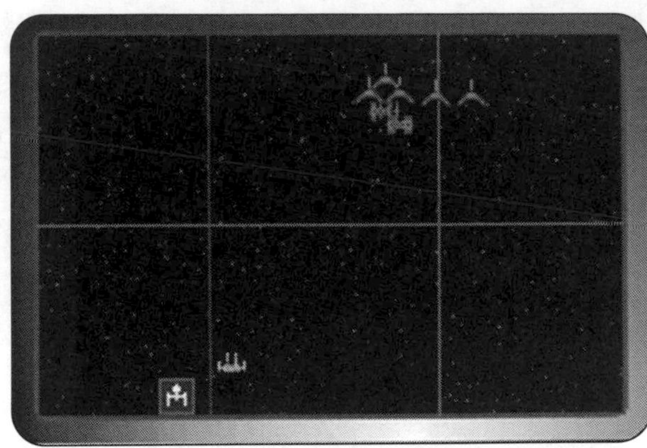

File Name: ack-hard

Mission Briefing

The Empire has kidnapped the Sullustan leader, and you must rescue him in order to secure Sullust as an ally of the Rebellion. You will drop out of hyperspace about three clicks behind a formation of five Imperial shuttles, escorted by a half-dozen TIE fighters. They are on their way to the Star Destroyer *Invincible*, 22 clicks distant. With your Y-wing, you must identify and disable the shuttle with the Sullustan leader. You are accompanied by a pair of X-wings.

Farlander's After-Action Report

Well, I'm not sure why I got to fly the Y-wing while Hamo got an X-wing. Maybe it had something to do with my success when I rescued the prisoners. Whatever the reason, I had the task of identifying and disabling the shuttle with the Sullustan leader in it.

I began my standard start sequence, but dropped throttle to two-thirds and switched to lasers. A quick survey of the CMD showed that TIE fighter group Alpha was about to turn and attack me, and I let them, taking out one in a head-on pass. Then I switched to torpedoes, as the remaining T/Fs continued past me, and fired one torpedo at each shuttle—not to destroy them, of course, only to weaken their shields.

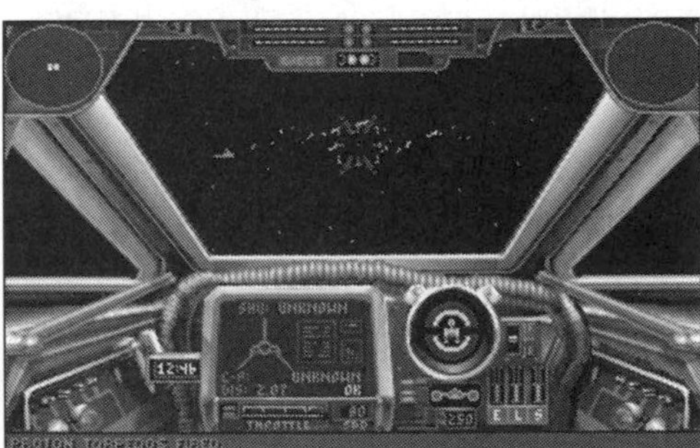

Firing on the shuttles.

Now I noticed that some shuttles turned to fight back; clearly not the

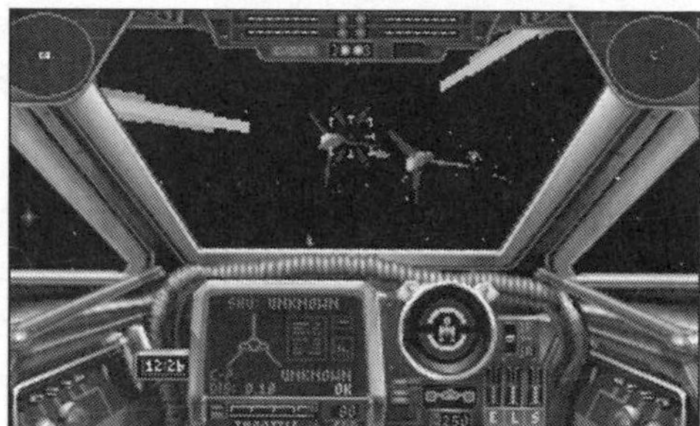

These shuttles fight back.

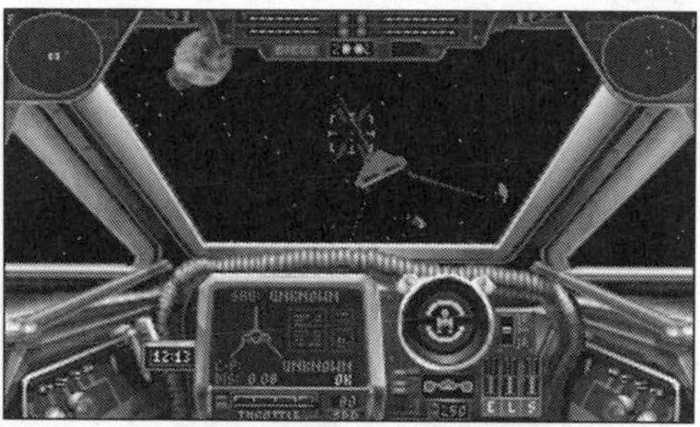

On the tail of a shuttle.

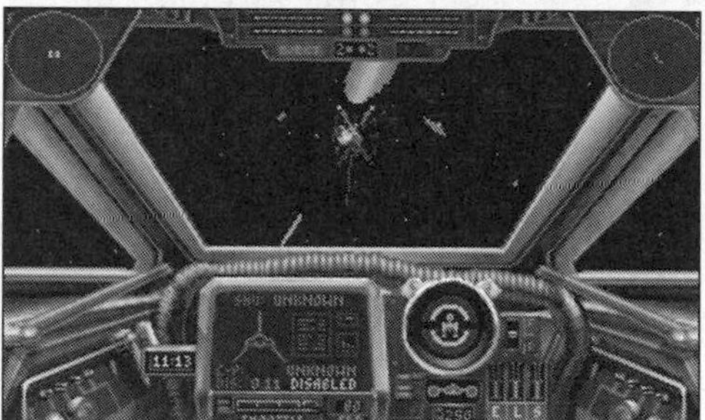

This shuttle is disabled.

Using cannons to take out TIEs.

ones with the prisoner. I reselected my lasers and took them out. The one remaining shuttle was the one I had to disable, and it was still on course for the *Invincible*.

So that I wouldn't lose it, I targeted it in the CMD and assigned it to a memory location, using the Wotan Weave as I closed in because the remaining TIEs from group Gamma were on my tail. Some TIE Interceptors from group Beta seemed to want to join in as well, but I couldn't take time to fight them yet. I had to disable the shuttle before it got too close to the *Invincible*.

After switching to ion cannons and checking that they were on dual-fire, I disabled the shuttle as soon as I was in range, then switched back to lasers.

The Alliance shuttle *Rescue 1* jumped in when the shuttle was disabled. Now I had to protect both shuttles until the mission was complete and the Sullustan leader had escaped into hyperspace.

I brought up *Rescue 1* in the CMD and assigned it to the next memory location. At the same time, I checked the computer and noticed a new TIE Interceptor group, Delta. I targeted *Delta 1* and assigned it to a memory location, and then I turned my attention to the TIEs nearest the shuttle. I concentrated on T/I Beta group as my highest priority, determined to eliminate them before T/I Delta came into range.

Next, I brought up *Delta 1* in the CMD, and switched to torpedoes—I had three left—and fired as soon as I could lock on, one for each Interceptor. They avoided engaging me, going instead toward *Rescue 1*, so I was able to get good shots.

If I had missed with any of the torpedoes, I would have had to redirect all my shield power to the engines, and set the cannon recharge rate to one step above normal, in order to catch up with them and still be able to keep firing.

As soon as these Interceptors were destroyed, the *Invincible* launched more of them. I turned toward the next wave, reset the shield recharge rate to normal, and began transferring cannon power to the shields until the shields were fully charged again. This time I had to engage the new wave of T/I Delta with lasers. Again, I redirected all shield energy to my engines in order to keep up with them.

The good news was that as I eliminated this group, *Rescue 1* had also gotten the job done. I received the Mission Complete message after the shuttle had jumped to hyperspace. With the shuttle gone, the Interceptors homed in on me, and I decided to stick around and shoot them up, even though the mission was over.

The Invincible *keeps launching T/Is.*

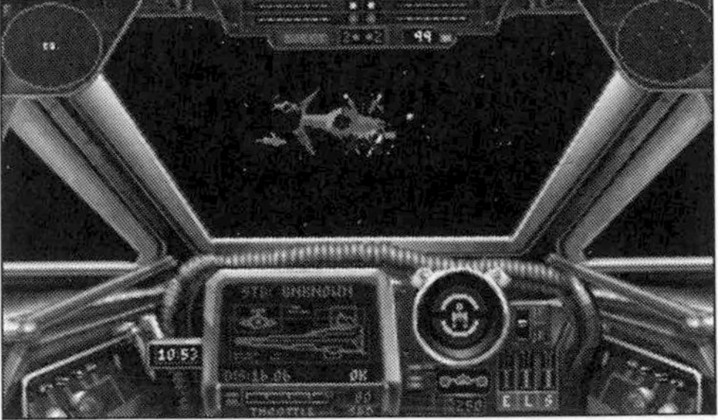

TIE Interceptor, point blank.

Debriefing (Win Conditions)
SHU *Kappa 5* must be boarded, and SHU *Rescue 1* must survive.

Mission Note: As you cycle through the target list, the last shuttle of the five is the one with the Sullustan leader. Stay back about 1.5 clicks from the group, and fire off two torpedoes at each of the other four shuttles. They won't turn to engage you unless you get within one click, so you can eliminate them without having to dogfight. You will still have a tough time with the TIE Interceptors, of course, but try to stay between the Rescue shuttle and the *Invincible*, and follow the procedure just given for dealing with the second wave of T/I Delta.

Lagrane was characteristically dour, even following missions that went exceptionally well. Oh, the occasional smirk would force itself onto his lips, like a brief distortion of time and space, but today his expression was especially linear, almost as though he were holding back emotions following some great tragedy. I wondered what could have gone wrong, and a hundred catastrophes burst forth, full-blown in my imagination. I sat and did not dare speak.

I think that he held the moment as long as he could, and then, finally, he broke into a great smile, a very un-Lagrane sort of thing that frightened me almost more than the tragic look, and said;

"Welcome back, Captain Farlander."

He held in his hand a set of captain's epaulets, and proffered them to me.

I took the patches from his hand and stared at them.

"Thanks," I said.

I couldn't really think of anything else. I wondered briefly what being a captain would do to me, and whether anything would change, but I was tired after the strain of the past few missions, and, making a few quick excuses, I made my way out of the debriefing room and into the corridor.

Of course, my retreat into solitude was not to be. Hamo was there with a few friends: Jan-lo, Gart, and a surprise.

"Hey, kid: Not bad," Hamo said, slapping me on the back and then standing back for a crisp salute, which prompted me to blush and pull his hand down. He pretended to struggle with me, throwing a few shadow punches that I blocked ineptly. I was amused, even touched, but my attention kept returning to the figure standing back just a little from the others. After a few more moments of joking and small talk, I excused myself and walked over to her.

"Lynia."

"Captain."

She half smiled and her eyes twinkled with azure and aquamarine. Like gemstones, her eyes seemed to change color from different angles. I was in danger of becoming lost in them. I mentally shook myself awake.

"I thought that I would never see you again."

"I promised to come visit you, didn't I?"

"But it's been . . ."

"I've been gone," she interrupted. "With Mon Mothma. We just got back to the *Independence* today. But I've been hearing about you. It seems you've achieved your dream."

"My dream?" I asked.

"To be a starfighter pilot, and destroy Imperial ships."

To be honest, the Keyan Farlander who had ridden up on the planetary shuttle from Agamar with this young woman seemed so long ago and so far away that it took me a moment to realize what she was talking about. I no longer dreamed of doing anything other than what I was doing. When I flew in a starfighter, I was more at home than anywhere else I had ever been—certainly more at home than I was standing before Lynia and realizing how happy I was to see her again.

"I guess you're right. I . . ."

"Keyan!" It was Hamo. "Are you coming? We're going to have a party!"

"I—I'll be right behind you. I'm coming."

"Well, come on, then," Hamo hollered. "And bring your friend."

"Yeah," echoed Jan-lo. "Come on, Keyan. This is your party."

"You go on," said Lynia. "I've got to get back anyway." She must have seen my disappointment, because she smiled and kissed me on the cheek.

"I'll be back soon," she said.

Then she turned and walked away, and I watched her until she rounded the corner at the end of the hall. I could hold my own against five-to-one odds in a starfighter; you would think that I'd have better defenses against one female with heavenly eyes.

I saw Lynia on only two other occasions before she had to ship out with Mon Mothma again. We were rapidly becoming friends, but there was still a reserve. I knew that she liked me, kept tabs on me. But she would always make our meetings short and wouldn't let things get too personal between us. Not knowing whether I would ever see her again made the frustration even worse.

But duty called, and we went out on sorties nearly every day. Some were uneventful scout missions or escort details where no enemies showed up. Then, every once in a while, a really significant mission would drop in our laps without warning.

OP 11: CAPTURE STAFF FROM CYGNUS

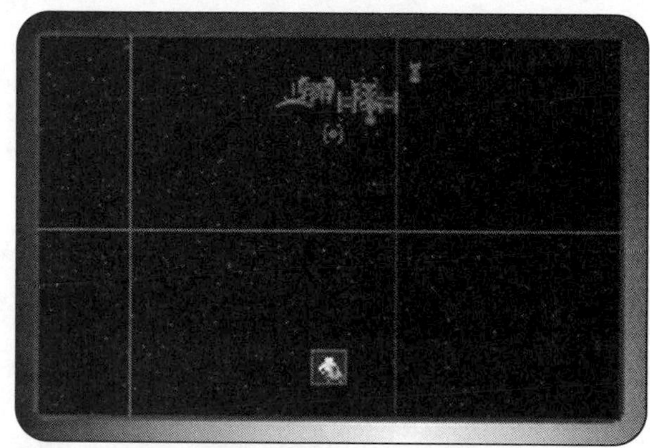

File Name: cygnus

Mission Briefing

Lead a raid on the Cygnus Corporation's starfighter performance trials, and capture their technical staff.

Farlander's After-Action Report

I was flight leader for this mission, and Jan-lo took the wing position.

We popped out of hyperspace practically in the middle of an uncomfortably large number of Imperial ships, but, fortunately, many of them seemed inert and posed no threat. We were looking for the transport that carried the Cygnus technical staff. Our job was to protect the strike team until they could escape.

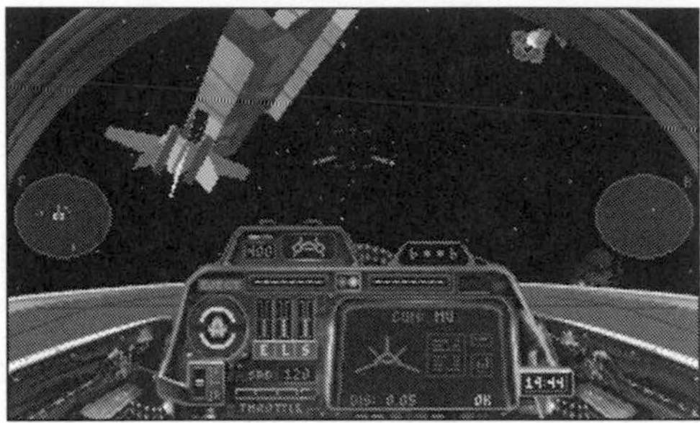

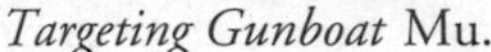
Targeting Gunboat Mu.

Find the technical staff.

I went through my start-of-mission check-out procedure, and, while Janlo attacked a few stationary craft, crippling or destroying them, I cycled through the target list until I found a transport. I headed toward it, and passed close by to ID it. I continued to ID transports until I found the one carrying the Cygnus staff. This one, *Kappa*, I assigned to a memory location.

When the Rebel transport *Lightning* arrived with the strike team, I brought it up in the CMD and assigned it to another memory location. As soon as I had identified TRN *Kappa*, TIE fighter group Zeta appeared in the target computer. Time to take on some enemy starfighters!

Another Imperial transport.

Breaking up a T/I formation.

T/F Zeta attempted to destroy the *Lightning*, but I saw to it that their plans went horribly awry. Two more waves followed the first from group Zeta. When I attacked *Dock 2* (the second freighter in the target list), two waves of TIE Interceptors were launched from *Dock 1*. I fought them and then, after the technical

Shooting Zeta 2.

staff was captured, I destroyed TRN *Kappa*. This seemed to trigger the launch of two more waves of TIE fighters from *Dock 1*. I proceeded to destroy everything, even after the *Lightning* was safely away, and then I got the Mission Complete message.

Rear view of freighter and transports.

C.O.'s Analysis

"Nothing new to report, sir. Just the usual TIEs and transports," I was telling the commander. Then I remembered. "There *was* something unusual . . ."

"Unusual?" asked Lagrane.

"Yes. There was a heavy craft, strange shape. Not a capital ship or a transport, but a little like a transport. It had heavy shields. Someone called it a 'Gunboat,' sir. Never saw anything like it before."

"A 'Gunboat,' you say?"

"That's what Jan-lo called it. Whatever it was, I'd bet it wasn't there to make our lives any easier."

"No, I'm sure you're right about that. We'll have to study the holo films from the mission to see what we've got here. OK, Captain. Good work. You're done."

"Yessir."

I put the 'Gunboat' out of my mind for the moment, and headed to the pilot's lounge for some R&R.

Debriefing (Win Conditions)

TRN *Kappa* must be boarded by TRN *Lightning*, which must then survive.

My promotion to captain had changed my life very little. Maybe I noticed a bit more deference on the part of junior officers, and perhaps a look of jealousy from some of the pilots, but all in all, I was just the same Keyan Farlander I had been before. The one big exception was the meetings.

Now, I'm not fond of meetings, preferring to spend my time resting, socializing with the other pilots, or practicing in the simulators. But now I was required to attend more planning meetings. That's how I learned of the plan to blow up the *Invincible*, one of the Emperor's premier Star Destroyers.

"We've discovered a massive explosive device the Empire has created. We don't know what they want to do with it, but we think that it would be effective against a Star Destroyer."

We stood around a large war map in one of the planning rooms. Commanders S'man and Lagrane were there, in addition to a few other commanders and captains. Hamo was there as well. I even spotted old Halley Kadorto, sitting in a corner of the room. He waved cheerily, and I waved back quickly.

"How do you think we should go about securing it?" asked Lagrane.

"We've intercepted some transmissions, and decoded parts of them. The device is scheduled to be loaded onto a freighter at the Celanon space port."

"But we'd never get away with a raid there," interjected Marskan, who usually flew with Blue Squadron.

"That's correct. Celanon is too busy and too well defended," agreed S'man. "However, the freighter appears to be bound for one of the deep-space transfer zones the Empire has been using for the past couple of weeks. The zone is heavily mined, but otherwise lightly defended most of the time. We think that we can get in and capture the freighter before the Imperials can respond.

"We'll assemble a small team. The first phase is to destroy the minefield. Then we'll send in a boarding party and capture the weapon."

He turned on the field map and began entering data from the computer. Soon, a large minefield took shape.

"Let's look at how we'll approach the minefield and where the hyperspace jump points should be," he continued. It was my first taste of mission planning. I began to find it interesting, after all.

> **HAN:** It's not wise to upset a Wookiee.
> **C-3PO:** But sir, nobody worries about upsetting a droid.
> **HAN:** That's 'cause droids don't pull people's arms out of their sockets when they lose. Wookiees are known to do that.
> **C-3PO:** I see your point, sir. I suggest a new strategy, R2: Let the Wookiee win.

OP 12: RECOVER EXPLOSIVE WARHEAD

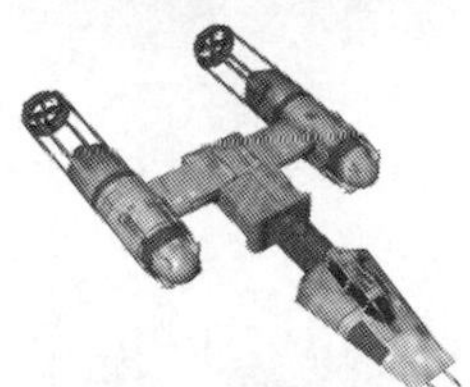

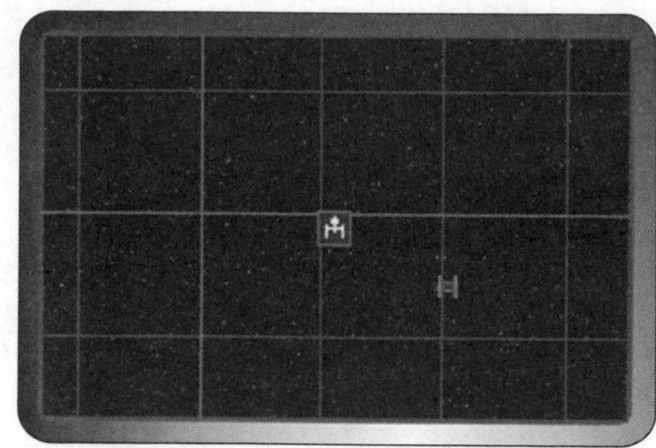

File Name: max20

Mission Briefing
Capture a massive explosive device from the Empire. It will be used in a modified shuttle to blow up a Star Destroyer. You will lead this effort. There are 18 mines in the minefield surrounding the target freighter, and they must be cleared so that the shuttle *Herald* may safely board the freighter and capture the device.

Farlander's After-Action Report
During my start-of-mission systems check, I turned away from the minefield and charged the secondary shields on my Y-wing to maximum. Then I headed for the mines, my throttle at one-third and my recharge rates on full. I decided to leave my lasers on single-fire, because a mine would explode with one hit, and I could shoot faster in single-fire mode.

Shooting a mine at point-blank range.

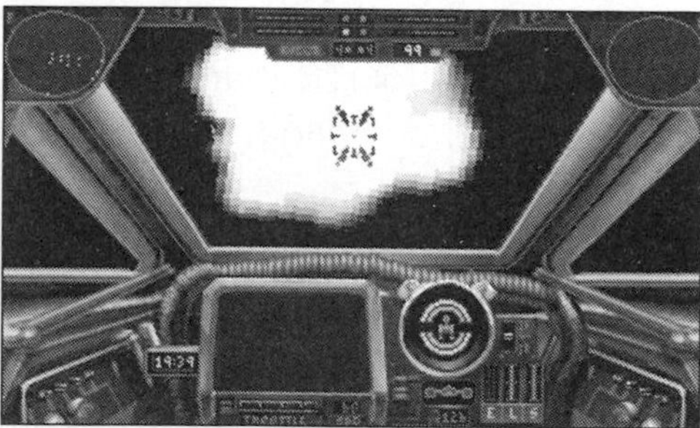
One less mine.

I came in carefully, bringing up a mine and shooting almost in one quick series of motions. I watched my shield levels carefully, transferring energy from lasers to shields to keep them charged, and redirecting the shield

power to keep the coverage even, fore and aft. I had to break off the attack once to reset and recharge.

As soon as I had cleared all the mines, I switched to ion cannons in dual-fire mode, and proceeded to disable the freighter *Gafra*. I throttled up to full power, and began to patrol the area while the *Herald* came in for the capture. We figured that it would take about one minute to complete the capture after docking had been accomplished.

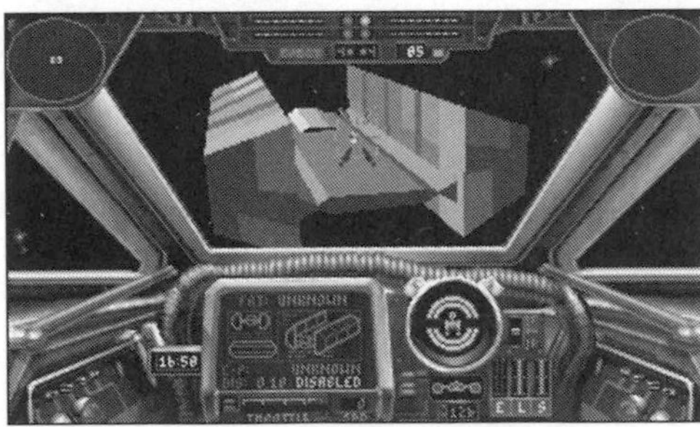

Disabling the freighter.

The Herald

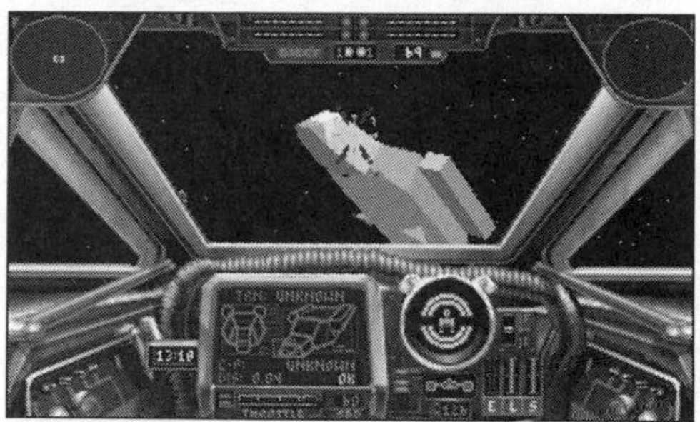

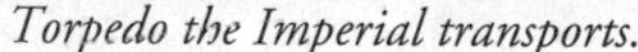

Torpedo the Imperial transports.

Use cannons when you run out of torpedoes.

As soon as the *Gafra* was captured, the *Herald* hypered out. At the same time, Imperial reinforcements arrived—two shuttles and two transports. Quickly I determined that the shuttles were going after me, but the transports were after the *Gafra.* I took evasive maneuvers to avoid fire from the shuttles, but I kept my computer locked on the transports. I switched to torpedoes and set them up in dual-fire mode.

The transports weren't going to make it easy, and I had to fire my torpedoes at practically point-blank range, keeping one eye on my shields because the shuttles were still after me. I knew that I could not afford to miss, but it was hard to get a solid lock. I concentrated on getting rid of the transports as quickly as possible, and then went after the shuttles. While I was hunting them down, the freighter escaped into hyperspace.

Debriefing (Win Conditions)
The FRT *Gafra* must be recovered.

When I finished debriefing, I headed back to my cabin, and found a message flashing on the comm. I accessed the message idly, one hand unbuttoning my shirt, when I stopped dead still. The message was from my aunt and uncle on Oorn Tchis!

Dear Keyan,

We hope that this message finds you well. We thought that you would want to know that your sister is being cared for around the clock. Although she is not responding yet to treatments, the doctors say that she has a strong will, and that we should not give up hope.

Rest assured, Keyan, that everything is being done for her. We are truly sorry for all that has happened.

May the Force be with you,

The message was signed "Aunt Mimya and Uncle Trinn." It was dated almost a month earlier.

Tour of Duty #2—The Great Search

It took me only an hour to discover just how difficult it was to send a message to anyone outside. It took me days to go from Communications to Logistics to Sector Command, back to Communications (to someone completely uncommunicative) to Intelligence and finally to Logistics again. In the end, I was assured that my message to Oorn Tchis might arrive in a few weeks. Or it might not. Generally, I was discouraged from trying to send any more messages.

When I wasn't trying to get by the numerous clerks and petty officers controlling outside communications, I kept to myself. Hamo was gone on some assignment off-ship, and Jan-lo had begun some additional duties as a junior trainee with Intelligence. And only the Force knew where Lynia was.

So I guess I missed some of the elation that had affected the other pilots and ops crew. We had beaten Operation Strike Fear, people were saying. We had blown up the *Invincible*. We *could* defeat the Empire. There was a sense of hope and anticipation among the crew on the *Independence*, a sense of growing confidence. It lasted right up until Admiral Ackbar gave his speech.

It started out all right.

"Beings of the Alliance, I have come to congratulate you," he told us, standing on the stage at the back of the large assembly hall.

"And to warn you," he added.

My mind was ahead of him, or so I thought. He would deliver the standard speech about overconfidence so that we would realize that the Empire was still a tremendous power and a genuine danger, that the *Invincible* was only one Star Destroyer and the Emperor had many more. That's what I expected him to say. I whispered something to that effect to Jan-lo, who sat next to me, but she gave me one of those looks that says, "Behave yourself," and returned her attention to the Calamarian admiral.

"We have beaten Operation Strike Fear," he began simply, his huge, dark eyes blinking slowly in the brightness directed at the podium. He turned his domed head back and forth, deliberately including everyone in the room.

"*You* have beaten Operation Strike Fear," he said.

We all cheered. Even me. We *had* done it. Hadn't we?

While the admiral waited, the uproar died down, and soon just a small undercurrent of whispering and murmuring remained as background noise. Ackbar continued.

"Now you must prepare for something far worse," Ackbar said, and paused. "*Far* worse."

It was as if someone just dropped a muffle on us. Or sucked all the air from the room.

"We have reliable information that the Empire is developing a terrible secret weapon," the admiral went on, without seeming to notice the deflated mood of the crowd.

"We don't yet know what it is, or where it is, but we must find out. If our information is correct, it is a weapon so powerful that it could destroy entire planets, obliterate civilizations, wipe out species, and give total dominance to the Empire. The fate of the Alliance, and of all free beings, rests with you, my friends. I ask you only to do your best."

Ackbar continued somewhat longer, but I hardly heard what he said. I was too busy trying to imagine what this super weapon could be, and in my mind I conceived endless horrifying variations on its power, and of its effects on the human body. I'd guess others in the room were thinking the same way.

General Dodonna took the stage when the admiral had concluded. He outlined the objectives worked out by the High Command.

"First, we must discover everything we can about this new secret weapon.

"Second, we will try to obtain its technology or the technical specifications for the device itself.

"Third, we are developing a plan to destroy another of the Emperor's Star Destroyers.

"Finally, as always, we will respond to opportunities as they present themselves.

"Any questions?"

✘ ✘ ✘

I met Lieutenant Cardacs just after he was assigned to the wingman position in my flight group. We had been briefed on an emergency rescue mission, and were on our way to the hangar.

"It's good to meet you, Captain Farlander; Cardacs here." We shook hands without breaking stride. Cardacs was a young man with sandy hair and pale, green eyes. He wasn't what you'd call handsome, I guess, but he didn't seem the type to notice. His face was darkened by exposure to some kind of radiation, and there were white circles around his eyes, where he must have worn protective goggles.

"Just transferred in?" I asked.

"Right. Been knocking about with some rogue squadrons in the Outer Rim. Sector Command, a little planet duty. You know."

"These protection missions are tough," I told him, looking for something to say.

"Yeah. I know. I'll stick close to you, captain. You know, I have a special interest in this mission."

"Oh?"

"Yeah. I had a friend we think was captured and sent to Mytus VII. I'm hoping he's one of the ones we're going after. Good pilot. Good friend."

"Let's make sure we get him," I answered as the hangar door irised open in front of us. "Time to go."

OP 1: RESCUE FROM STAR'S END

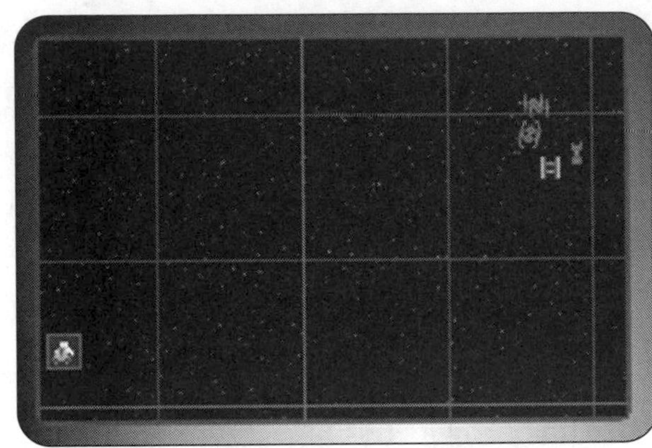

File Name: starsndb

Mission Briefing

Rescue our escaped pilots, who have stowed away aboard a freighter. Destroy the accompanying Imperial transport, and secure the area for a Rebel Rescue shuttle. The freighter is approximately six clicks from your entrance point from hyperspace. An Imperial transport is preparing to board the freighter, and a pair of TIE fighters and TIE Interceptors is each patrolling the area. The Star Destroyer *Intrepid* waits 11 clicks away.

Farlander's After-Action Report

I led my two-ship A-wing flight group into the area, and immediately sped toward the freighter *Genue*. With the Imperial transport already in the process of docking, I knew that I didn't have much time, so I left all my energy settings as they were to hold my speed at 120.

I ordered my wingman, a new transfer named Cardacs, to attack the second of the two TIE Interceptors that were coming toward us. I targeted the leader myself, and switched to missiles. As soon as I had a solid lock on my target, I fired, destroying him as we passed.

Taking care of the Interceptors

Next was a pair of TIE fighters. Having ordered my wingman to attack the number-two TIE, I switched back to cannons and took out the leader in a head-on pass. I knew that there wasn't time to get caught up in a dogfight. Now I was closing on the freighter.

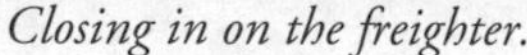

Closing in on the freighter.

Freighter and transport.

The transport had docked, but I knew that I should still have a minute or so. Since I didn't want the *Genue* to be in the line of fire, I reduced throttle to one-third and positioned my ship behind the transport, lining up a clear shot at point-blank range.

I Switched to missiles again and selected dual-fire mode, dropping my speed to zero and resetting cannon and shield recharge rates to maximum. As quickly as the launcher would let me, I fired four missiles to wipe out the transport's shields and damage its hull. Then I toggled back to cannons for the *coup de grace*.

Returning to full throttle, and resetting the shield recharge rate to the normal 50 percent position, I went to assist my wingman with T/F *Beta 2*. At this point, the *Intrepid* launched some reinforcements—a four-ship group of TIE fighters from Delta Squadron. After destroying *Beta 2*, we turned to engage the newcomers. As we battled Delta, the R2 let me know that more TIE fighters had been launched. These were replacements for Beta Squadron. Shortly after that, still more Deltas joined the fray.

By now, we were within gun range of the *Intrepid*, but I figured that as long as we were dogfighting the constant maneuvering would make us difficult targets. I was wrong, and my miscalculation carried a heavy price. My wingman was caught by enemy fire, and destroyed.

Then a three-ship formation of TIE Bombers (Eta) was launched. Recognizing the danger the Bombers posed, I decided to ignore the fighters for now.

I switched to missiles and reset them to single-fire mode, redirecting cannon energy to the engines so that I would close the distance quickly. As soon as I was in missile range, I reset the recharge rates for lasers and shields to maximum, reducing the rate of closure so that the computer would have time to get a solid lock.

I proceeded to take out all three Bombers with one missile apiece. A replacement wave of TIE Bombers was launched, and I eliminated them just as I had the first. During the action, I noticed that the shuttle *Drago* had arrived with the Rescue team.

I switched back to cannons and went after the nearest TIE fighter—There always seemed to be three or four chasing me. I quickly took out a couple of them, and then noticed a group of three TIE Interceptors from Gamma Squadron: They seemed to be headed directly for the rescue shuttle.

I targeted the leader of the Interceptors and chased him down, then did the same for Gamma 2. Gamma 3 got past me, so I switched back to missiles—I had only one left—and took him out from a distance. Figuring that there would be a replacement wave for T/I Gamma, I turned back toward the Intrepid. Sure enough, one was soon launched. I still had several TIE fighters from Beta and Delta chasing me, though, so I had to weave until I was in range to engage them.

During this battle, the Rescue Team completed its capture of the *Genue*. I kept after Gamma until they were eliminated, and I got the message that the *Drago* and *Genue* were safe. I finished off the last of the TIEs near me and hyperspaced home.

C.O.'s Analysis

Lagrane wasn't in one of his better moods. But then neither was I. I hadn't known Cardacs more than a few minutes, but that didn't make me feel less guilty over his death. And the computer analysis of my mission revealed some flaws in my strategy as well. The Commander was explaining it all to me.

"There was enough time at the beginning of the mission that you could have transferred some laser power to shields, and reset the cannon recharge rate to maximum as you closed the distance. This would have brought your speed down to 90, but that would have been fast enough. Also, you could have saved your missiles and blasted the transport with cannons instead. This would have allowed you to use missiles on the TIE Bombers and Interceptors that came later. More importantly, better attention to your Inflight Map might have alerted you to your wingman's situation, and you might have been able to come to his aid."

I must have looked like a whipped musti pup, because Lagrane suddenly lightened up a little. "Look, Farlander, he was an experienced pilot. He knew the risks. You act like you never saw anyone frag before."

"Never a wingman, sir," I answered, truly aggrieved.

"It happens, captain. Let it go. Learn from it and go on. Or next time, it could be you."

Lagrane was a master of pleasant thoughts.

Debriefing (Win Conditions)

SHU *Drago* must dock with and capture FRT *Genue*. Both must then survive. TRN *Lambda* must be destroyed.

The next day, the rescued pilots were taking a break from their extensive debriefing, and three of them were in the mess, grabbing a bite, when I entered the room. I noticed them talking with some of the other pilots, and looking my way. I paid it no mind, and proceeded to collect some porf (which I had begun to like, much to my surprise). I sat alone, still brooding a little over the last mission, and not really wanting company.

"You Farlander?"

One of the rescued pilots, a captain by his uniform, stood at the head of my table, leaning over with his hands placed flat on its surface. I looked up in surprise.

"That's me," I answered, a little defensive at the man's obvious breech of etiquette. I studied him, assessed him almost instantly. He was dark-skinned, hard-edged, and dangerous. "What do you want?"

"I'm Samuel Raider," he said, as though it should mean something to me.

"I'm afraid you've got me there," I told him. "Do I know you?"

"You knew my friend," he said. He wasn't going to make this easy on me, whatever his problem, but something in his tone clued me in.

"You're Cardacs' friend," I said with sudden insight. He said nothing. "Listen, I'm sorry about Cardacs. He was—I didn't really get to know him. He said that you were a great pilot," I added lamely.

"Just watch yourself," Raider said at last, and then turned and walked back to his friends. They all sat there then, watching me.

So much for gratitude.

I didn't see Raider again until I was called in to a squadron briefing the next day.

"This is Captain Raider," S'man was saying. "He recently escaped from Stars' End prison, and he has brought us important information. It seems that a slave ship carrying Wookiees is en route to a mysterious Imperial project. Wookiees are allies of the Alliance, and we must attempt to rescue them."

S'man nodded to Raider, who continued the briefing from that point.

"We think that some of the Wookiees may have information about their destination." The new captain was dead serious. "The rumors about a new weapon were everywhere at the prison, but we could never get close enough to anyone who had been there. Some of these Wookiees may know more. I'm going to lead a team of A-wings to get them back. I need two other pilots."

"You." He pointed at Jan-lo.

"And you," he said, pointing at me.

Why would he choose me? I quickly ruled out gratitude as a motivating factor.

Then one of the other pilots who had been rescued spoke up; "Hey, Raider. Come on. I haven't seen action in months. Let me go."

The captain turned to his friend and said, "OK, Toalagar: You're in. You and Farlander over there."

He pointed at me again, and I had a distinctly unpleasant sensation, as though his finger was a charged laser cannon, and I was its target.

OP 2: RESCUE WOOKIEE SLAVES

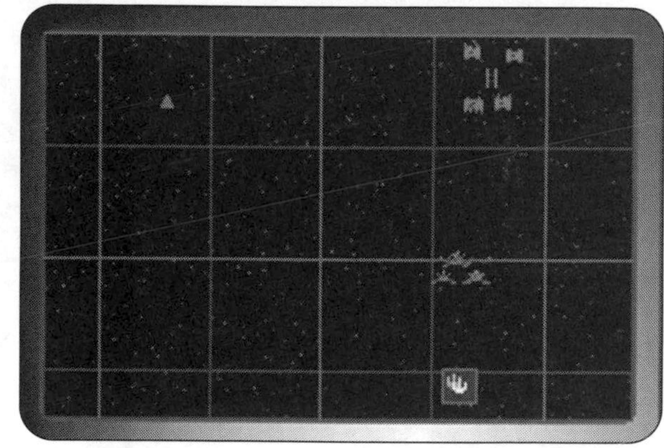

File Name: rescue1

Mission Briefing

You must capture a freighter containing Wookiee slaves. Look out for the new Imperial starfighter, the Assault Gunboat, which is now operational in this sector. You are in the number-three spot in a three-ship group of X-wings. Three groups of Assault Gunboats are three clicks immediately ahead. The Star Destroyer *Intrepid* is about 12 clicks away, and to the left. The freighter with the Wookiees is another six clicks beyond the Gunboats, and has a full TIE fighter squadron escorting it.

Farlander's After-Action Report

Went through the standard mission-start procedure. Between us and the freighter were six of the new Assault Gunboats we had been warned about. They all seemed intent on *Red 1* and *Red 2*. My threat indicator wasn't even flashing! Maybe they thought that the number-three spot

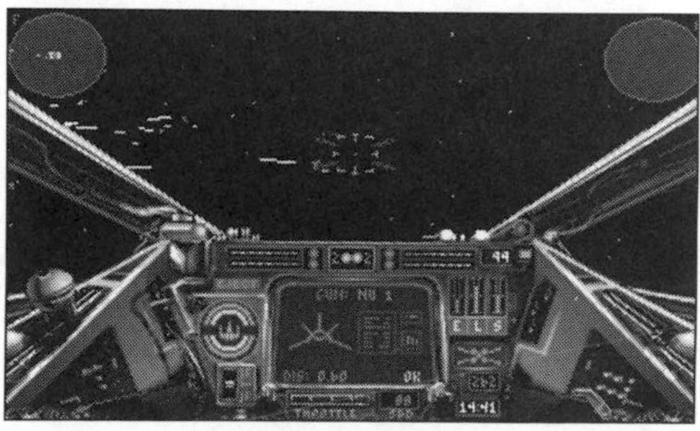

Targeting GUN Nu.

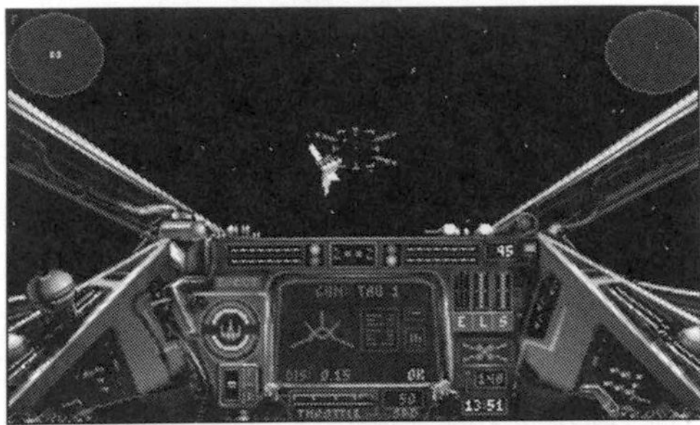

Lining up GUN Tau 1.

Another Gunboat novas.

was for rookies or something. *Red 1* and *2* proceeded with a head-on attack against the nearest enemy fighter, Gunboat *Mu 1*, while I made a flank attack with torpedoes.

Red 2 was lost to missiles on the first pass, but I managed to get off three torpedoes before anyone began to pay attention to me. By now, I was in the thick of it, along with *Red 1*, and I fired one more torpedo at short range. The target evaded at just the right moment, so I decided to switch to cannons and get back to basics. At one point, we both went after the same enemy, and Raider's cannon fire raked my shields. Accident? Or not?

"*Red 3*," he called over the comm. "Why don't you go find another ship?"

Finally, we destroyed all six Gunboats, then proceeded toward the freighter.

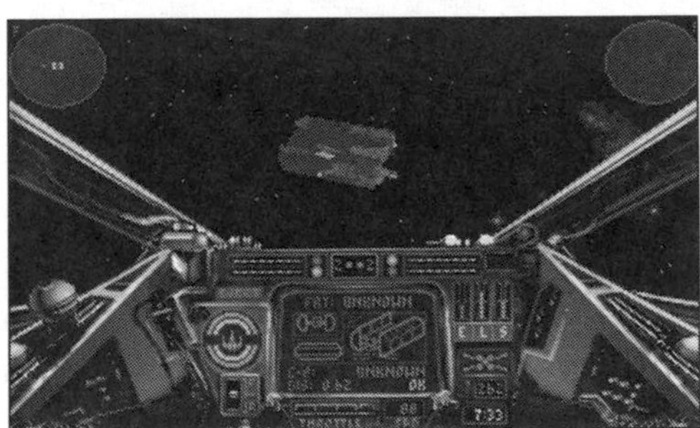

Approaching a freighter.

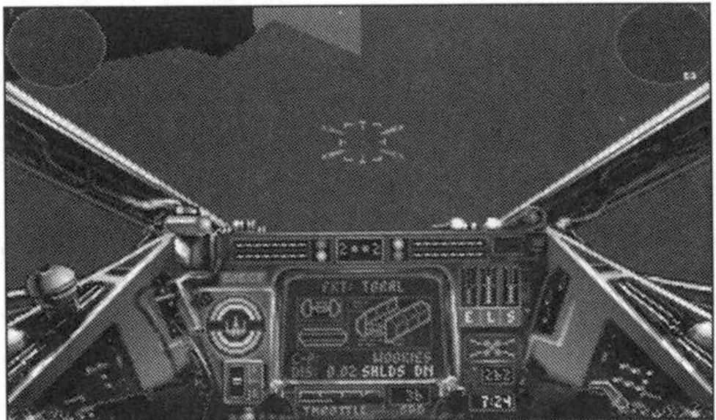

Getting a bit closer than necessary to ID.

The escorting TIE fighters were split into four groups of three apiece. They had the odds—six to one. It didn't look like a promising situation, but Raider was a good pilot, and we managed to hurt them pretty badly pretty quickly. After we had cut their numbers in half, I figured that it was time to confirm the identity of the freighter. *Red 1* continued after the TIEs while I peeled off for an ID run, and then I rejoined him.

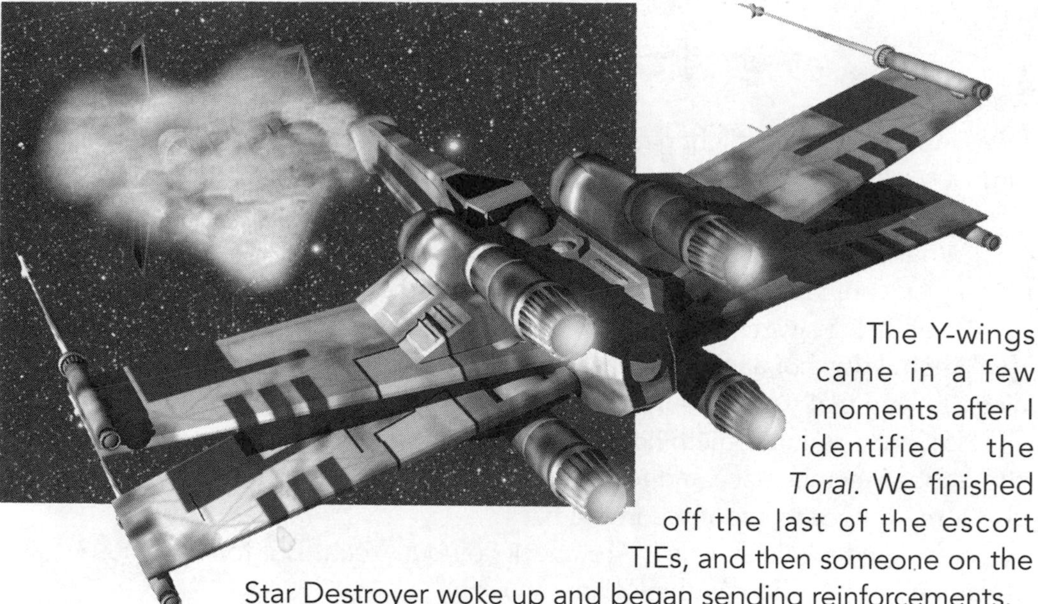

The Y-wings came in a few moments after I identified the *Toral*. We finished off the last of the escort TIEs, and then someone on the Star Destroyer woke up and began sending reinforcements.

The next three-ship group of TIE fighters was from Theta Squadron. These guys must have been ordered to stop the Y-wings, because they were pretty single-minded about it—which made it all that much easier for us to get behind them and blow them away. By now the Y-wings had disabled the *Toral*, and *Rescue 1* had arrived.

As soon as we finished off Theta, a replacement wave was launched, followed soon afterward by another flight of three from Zeta Squadron.

We were so caught up with Theta that I almost missed noticing that Zeta had gone right by us. Apparently, they were going after *Rescue 1* before it could escape into hyperspace. Worse, they were already more than two clicks away!

I quickly transferred my cannon power to the shields, and then redirected all cannon and shield energy to the engines. Switching to torpedoes—I still had two left—I targeted *Zeta 1* and launched as soon as I got a lock. I was just about to launch the last one at *Zeta 2* when I realized that I was close enough for cannons.

As I reconfigured the ELS levels and transferred some power back to the lasers, I began shooting. *Rescue 1* made its jump, and I finished off Zeta. *Red 1* had finished off another wave of Theta, so I formed up on his wing and followed him out.

Debriefing (Win Conditions)

TRN *Rescue 1* must dock with FRT *Toral*, and then escape into hyperspace.

I was stripping off my flight gear when Captain Raider came up behind me. I almost ducked. I was afraid that he might blame me for Toalagar's death, too.

"Farlander . . ." he said quietly.

"What is it?" I was a little defensive.

"I just wanted to apologize," he said. "For the stray shots."

"Yeah?" I answered.

"Yeah. I was hot about Cardacs, but . . ." He hesitated, then said, "Toalagar died . . . and that wasn't your fault . . . It was mine."

"Let me ask you something, Captain Raider," I said, deciding to get things straight between us once and for all. "Did you chose me for this mission to check me out, or to shoot me in the back?"

He looked a little shocked. "To check you out. Yeah. But to shoot you? What kind of pilot do you think I am, anyway?"

"A pretty good one, from what I saw," I told him sincerely. "But you were . . . You seemed to blame me . . ."

"I was wrong. Let's leave it at that. Come on. I've got some drinking to do, and I need some company."

He offered a handshake, and I complied. His grip was firm, and his eyes were steady.

"Oh, and Farlander . . ." he added as we strode up the path from the hangar bay, "You're not a bad pilot yourself."

As he started toward the hangar exit, I heard him say, more to himself than to me; "Yeah. You're OK."

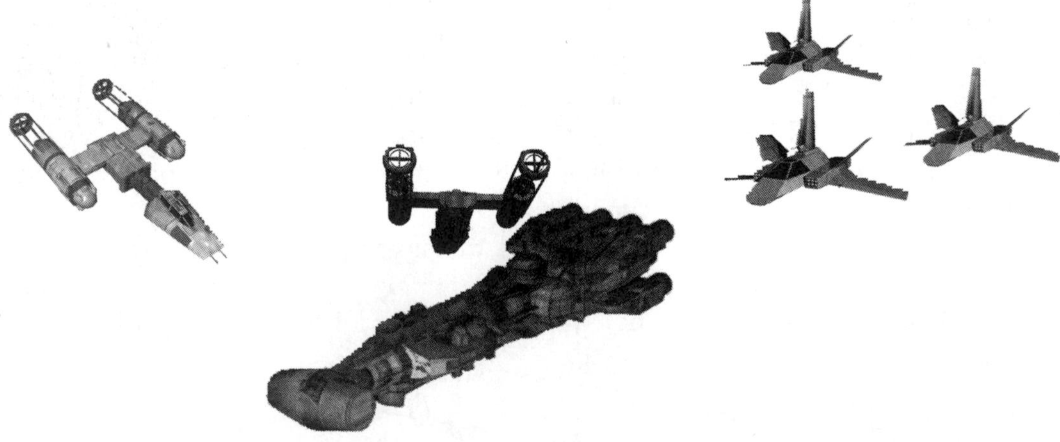

OP 3: ATTACK WEAPONS CONVOY

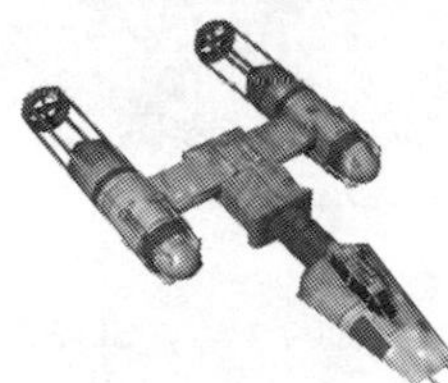

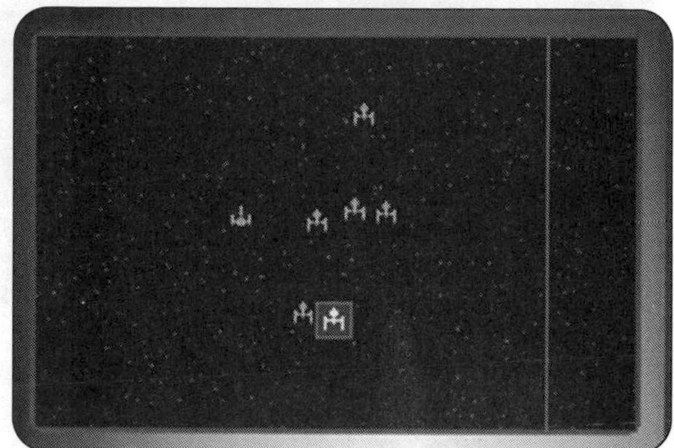

File Name: ystrike5

Mission Briefing

A vital Imperial convoy is expected to hyperspace into the area around our Comm Sat near Orron III. Assist your wing leader in destroying the convoy. You will be in the number-two spot of a three-ship group of Y-wings. The remainder of the strike force is made up of a lone X-wing and another three-ship formation of Y-wings. You will enter an empty area of space to prepare your ambush of the Imperial convoy. The first elements of the convoy will arrive in less than two minutes.

Farlander's After-Action Report

We all went through the standard mission-start procedure. I fully charged my shields and cannons, and reset the recharge rates to normal.

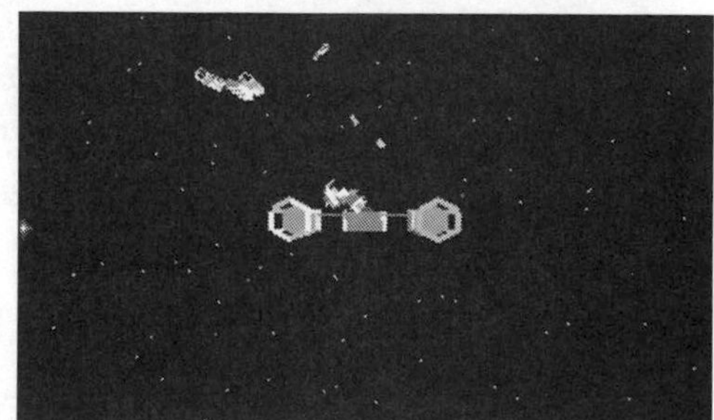

Approaching the corvettes.

The first two corvettes dropped out of hyperspace and flew right past us, so we all turned to make an attack from their left rear quadrant. X-W Blue got off the first torpedoes at the number-one corvette just as three Imperial transports dropped in.

I had targeted the same corvette, but I wanted to save my torpedoes. As I was closing in to cannon range, a pair of Imperial shuttles dropped in. Next was another pair of transports, and then a pair of Assault Gunboats from Tau squadron. I kept boring in on the corvette, and saw that its shields were failing, so I reduced my throttle to one-third. I got close enough to ID

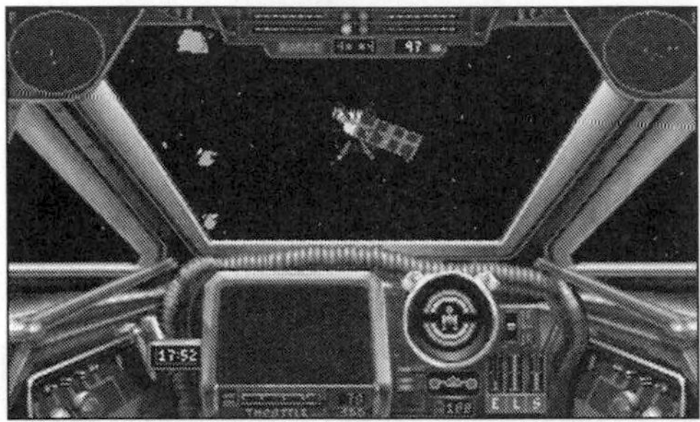

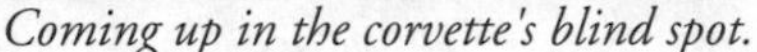

Coming up in the corvette's blind spot.

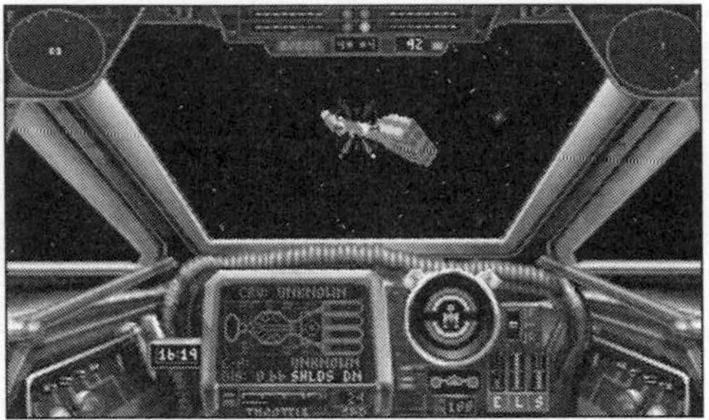

This corvette's ready to go.

it as the *Hyko 1* before I broke off to make another attack run. My speed was still too high to just take up position behind it and blast away.

A pair of freighters arrived as the *Hyko 1* finally began to disintegrate. As I turned to attack the other corvette, *Red 1* launched a pair of torpedoes at it. In a few moments, it joined its twin in oblivion.

I went back to full throttle and targeted one of the three transports. I switched to torpedoes and was just about to get a solid lock when GUN *Tau 1* opened up on me from behind. I held on a moment more, until I got the lock, fired, and then pulled back hard. It was then that I realized that *Gold 1* was already blasting away at the same transport. Another torpedo wasted.

I turned to go after *Tau 1*, and noted the unfortunate arrival of another pair of Gunboats. I switched back to cannons, and, while I was engaging my target, yet another pair of Gunboats dropped out of hyperspace!

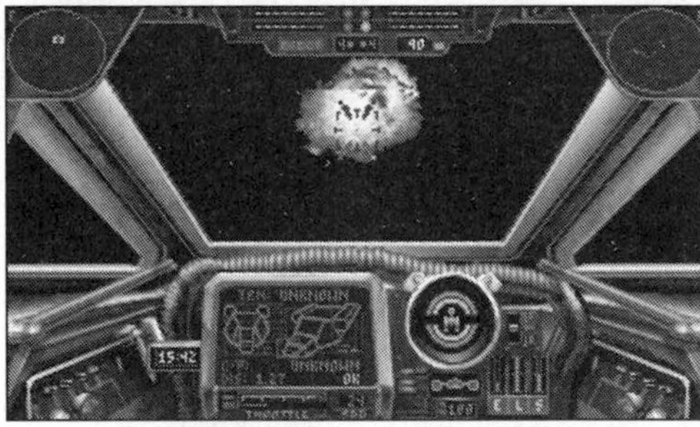

Destroy the transports.

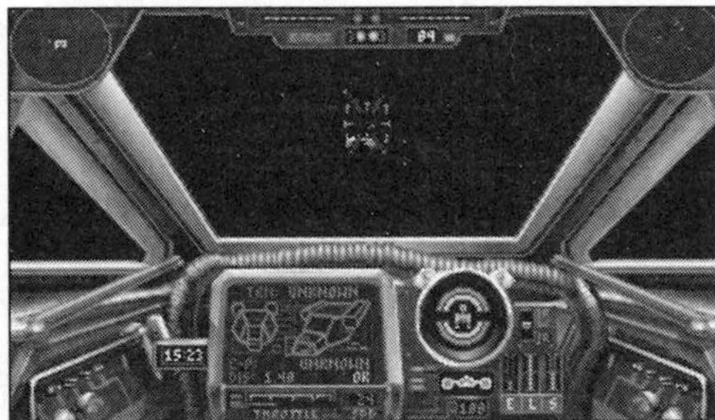

Locked onto another transport.

As soon as *Tau 1* exploded in a storm of electrical flashes and incandescent gas, I queried the CMD for the next-nearest enemy. It brought up *Mu 2*, which was still some distance away.

I began to cycle through the target list to find the newcomers designated as flight group Rho. I decided to go after *Rho 2*, and, as I turned to engage it, my R2 warned that I had a missile homing on me.

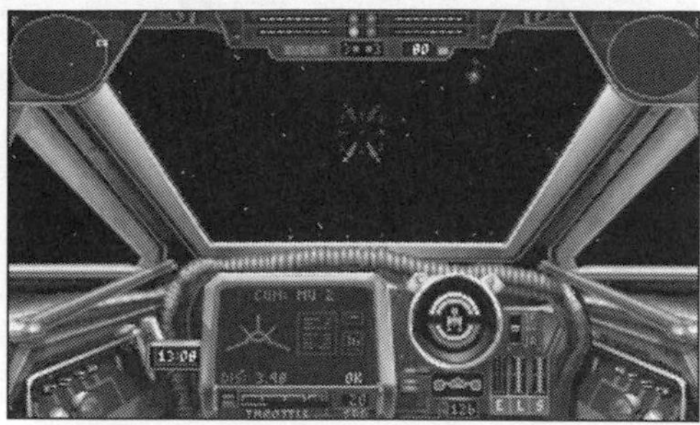

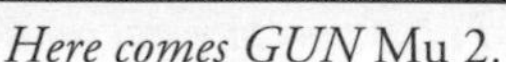

Here comes GUN Mu 2.

Scratch another Gunboat.

I targeted the missile and tried to evade, but it caught me anyway. Y-wings weren't made for evading missiles, but, fortunately for me, they did have strong shields.

I rebalanced and recharged my shields, then queried the CMD again for the nearest fighter threat. This time it brought up *Rho 1*, and I turned toward him for a head-on pass. By now I had a healthy respect for the Gunboat's firepower, so I went into a weave as soon as he began firing lasers. When we were less than half a click apart, I came out of my weave and maneuvered onto his tail. A minute later, he was history.

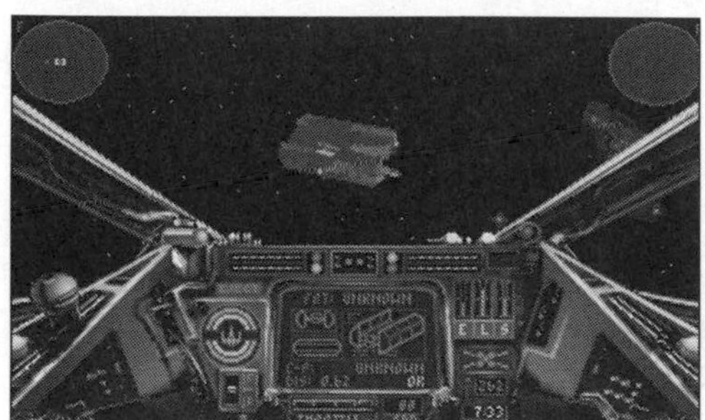

Coming up on a freighter.

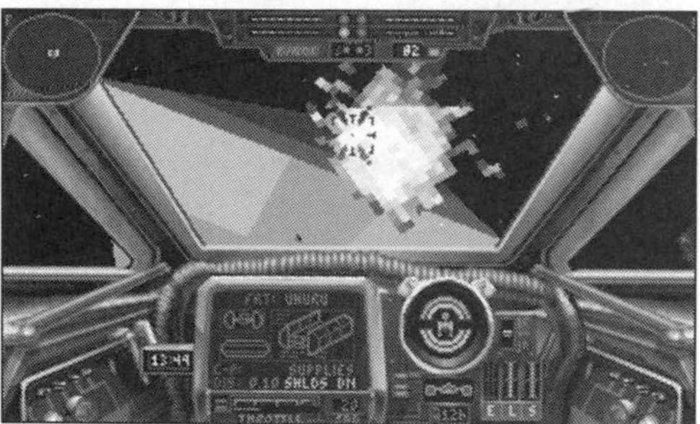

Shooting the Uhuru.

The chase had led me near the two freighters, so I targeted one and requested assistance from my wingmen. I switched to torpedoes, and, because I was so close, I didn't bother waiting for a lock. I launched two torpedoes in single-fire mode, and both hit. I came around for another run, and, just as I launched, I heard *Red 3* take a hit. Then *Red 1* bought the farm. Each had turned its tails on the enemy Gunboats in their haste to help me with the freighters. This was suddenly turning into a very bad day.

I had identified one of the freighters as the *Uhuru* and the other as *The Tone*. I kept looping back and forth between them, firing cannons mostly, but adding on a few torpedoes when I could close to point blank range.

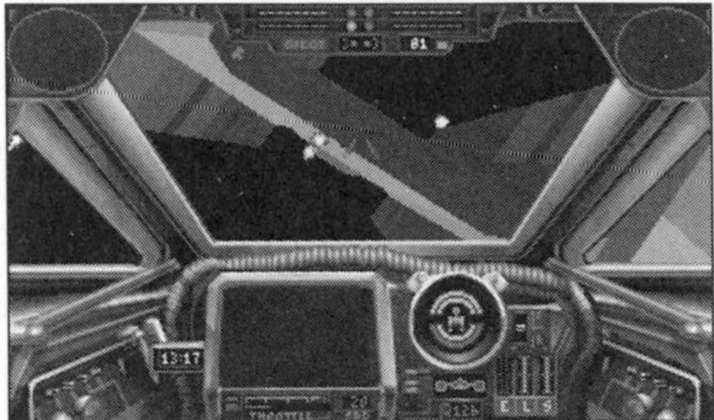

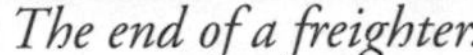

The end of a freighter.

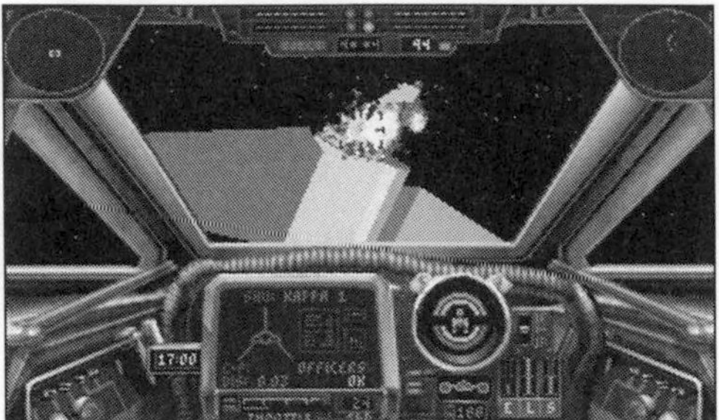

Take out the Imperial shuttles.

During firing runs, I reduced speed by cutting my throttle to one-third.

Finally, both freighters were destroyed, and I cycled through the target list a few times to get an idea of how things were going.

Y-W Gold was fine, as was X-W Blue. There was one Imperial shuttle left, and four Gunboats.

I headed off toward the Gunboats, having selected *Tau 2* as my target. After destroying *Tau 2*, I went after the shuttle. When I had eliminated it, I got the Mission Complete message, but I decided to finish off the last of the Gunboats before I hyperspaced home.

All three had ganged up on X-W Blue. I destroyed *Rho 2*, only to have two more show up to replace it. I reconsidered the merits of staying in the area, and decided that it was time to leave after all. The other pilots concurred. As I might have guessed, more Gunboats arrived to make life difficult. Y-W *Gold 1* didn't make it, but I kept the Imperials occupied while the others escaped. In the end, it was just me and one Gunboat, and then it was just me.

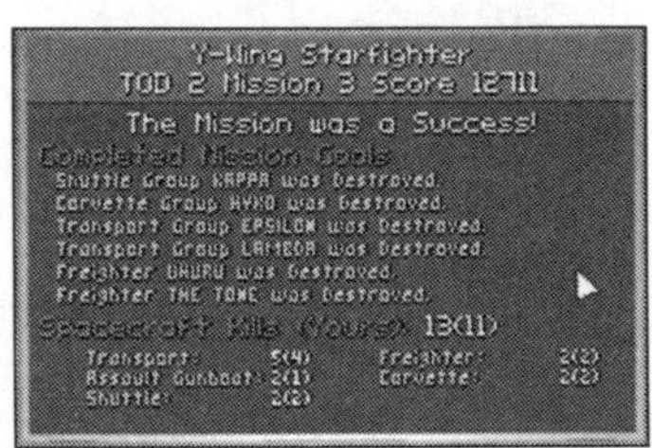

Mission summary

C.O.'s Analysis

Lagrane was really unhappy today. No, to be honest, he was furious.

"We're losing too many pilots, Farlander. It's time you learned to be more careful. To begin with, you should probably refer to your map more often, especially when requesting assistance from your wingman. If you see that your wingman is engaged and cannot safely disengage, don't order him to help you!

"Also, analysis suggests that you might have had fewer losses if you had taken care of all the threats before bothering with the freighters. By leaving shuttles and Gunboats active, you risked the safety of your group. Moreover, you took some risk that the shuttles and transports might get away. You probably should have made them your first priority. The freighters and the corvettes weren't going anywhere soon.

"Losing two wingmen this way is unacceptable. There will have to be an official inquest regarding the incident. I'm afraid that, in the meantime, you're to be suspended from flight operations, captain. That is all. You're dismissed!"

I never got in a word.

Debriefing (Win Conditions)

SHU *Kappa,* CRV *Hyko 1* and *2,* TRNs *Epsilon* and *Lambda,* and FRTs *Uhuru* and *The Tone* all must be destroyed.

I blamed myself for the deaths of Tan'tro and Ahsmar. Maybe I had been lucky up to this time. Maybe I wasn't a very good pilot after all, pulling such a stupid stunt. And here I was, grounded. Maybe it was for the best.

My cabin door irised open. Only Hamo ever entered like that, without announcing himself first. I looked up slowly.

"Hey, tough break," he said.

"You heard," I said miserably.

"Don't get down on yourself. We all have our moments."

"Yeah?" I asked cynically. "Did you ever . . ."

I stopped short. Hamo was wearing some new additions to his uniform. He had made commander! Somehow, it only accentuated my own misery.

"You're a commander," I said after a moment.

He looked a little embarrassed. "Yeah, well, it's a long story. You want to go grab some porf and something to drink? Come on. You need to get out of here."

I mounted a token resistance, but I let Hamo coax me into going with him. I was happy to see him again, but I dreaded meeting anyone else. I felt like a failure. Like a murderer.

When we reached the mess, I spotted Raider and a couple of other pilots sitting around, just passing the time between missions. Raider got up and joined us after a few minutes, sliding easily into one of the seats across from me.

"Porf, eh?" He made a face that adequately expressed his opinion of our meal. I made the introductions, figuring that Hamo and he hadn't met before.

Raider looked a little uncomfortable.

"Look, Farlander," he said. "Everybody's getting a little edgy. Losses are piling up, and replacements aren't coming in fast enough. But we think that you got a raw deal. I've watched you pilot a fighter, and I'd personally go up with you again any time."

I sat there pretty well floored. I still felt like a murderer, but at least I was a murderer with friends.

"Let me buy you a drink, captain," said Hamo.

After a rocky start, my friendship with Sam Raider grew. He and Hamo and I began spending a great deal of time together. The inquest came and went, and I was returned to active duty with a warning and a compulsory visit to TIE-Die and his simulators for some specific brushing up. The incident passed, and, like many situations that seem to offer nothing but tragedy, some good came of it. I cleared my head a little, gained back my self-respect, and made a new friend.

But I couldn't bring back Cardacs, Tan'tro, or Ahsmar. I'd learned that people die in battle, sometimes even people close to you, but I didn't think I would ever get used to it.

My next two missions were solo missions: No wingmen.

OP 4: CAPTURE STOLEN FREIGHTER

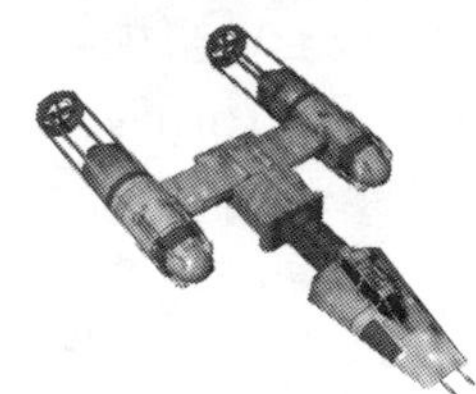

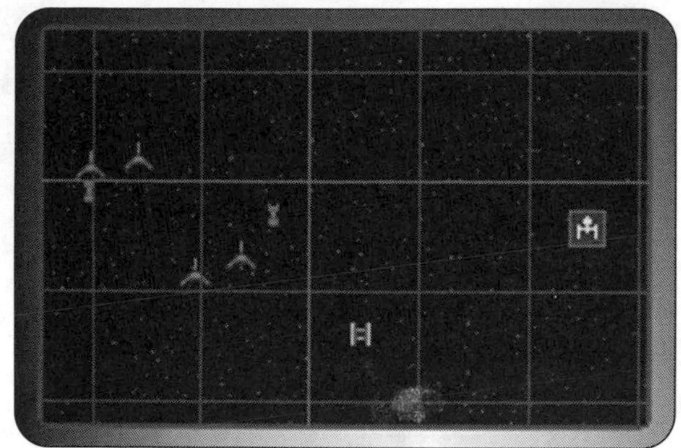

File Name: wycapt2

Mission Briefing

Fly cover for a Rebel shuttle while it attempts to capture an Imperial freighter. The Star Destroyer *Intrepid* is known to be in the vicinity. You enter the area alone in your Y-wing, and the freighter *Phoenix* is directly in front of you. Two Imperial transports and two pairs of armed Imperial shuttles must be neutralized first for the capture operation to proceed. The Alliance shuttle *Wilsey* arrives after the freighter has been disabled.

Farlander's After-Action Report

Straight by the book, standard mission start. Cycled through the target list and decided to go after the nearest transport. I selected torpedoes and, as I closed to firing range, the transport opened up with ion cannons on the freighter. I passed right by two of the shuttles as I got a lock and fired, and then switched back to laser cannons to finish off the TRN.

As soon as the transport blew up, another dropped out of hyperspace. I figured that if the new one was going to make the same attempt to disable the freighter, I'd let him proceed and save myself the trouble. I launched a couple of torpedoes at the freighter to help the process along.

The other transport probably had the boarding party, so I targeted that one next. I intended to use the same strategy—a torpedo followed by a few laser blasts—but while I strove for a solid lock, I was getting hammered by the shuttles, which were shooting me from behind.

Each had eight forward-facing laser cannons, firing four at a time, so even as I stretched the distance between us, they didn't have to be very accurate to hit me. I was just moments from achieving a lock on my target, however, so I held on just long enough to fire the torpedo, and then broke

off and went into evasive maneuvers, rebalancing my shields and redirecting power to them quickly.

I was able to shake my tormentors long enough to finish off the transport with a few blasts of laser fire. Again, a replacement dropped out of hyperspace almost immediately. I realized that I was going to have to get rid of the shuttles sooner or later anyway, and it might as well be sooner.

The situation was a little challenging at first: Although they're relatively slow compared to a Y-wing, shuttles are very maneuverable. I couldn't slow down to get a bead on one of them without risking exposing myself to fire from one of the others. But my superior speed kept me out of harm's way while I destroyed most of them. From then on, the battle was routine. There were still a couple of Imperial transports, so I went after them next.

The freighter had been disabled by this time, and the Alliance shuttle *Wilsey* had arrived to board and capture the *Phoenix*. This phase of the operation took a few minutes, during which I patrolled the area. All was quiet, and I was figuring on a peaceful end to this mission. On the other hand, I kept my speed up and my guns and shields charged, just in case I needed to get going in a hurry. After the freighter was under our control, the *Wilsey* departed and the *Phoenix* got under way.

Targeting the first transport.

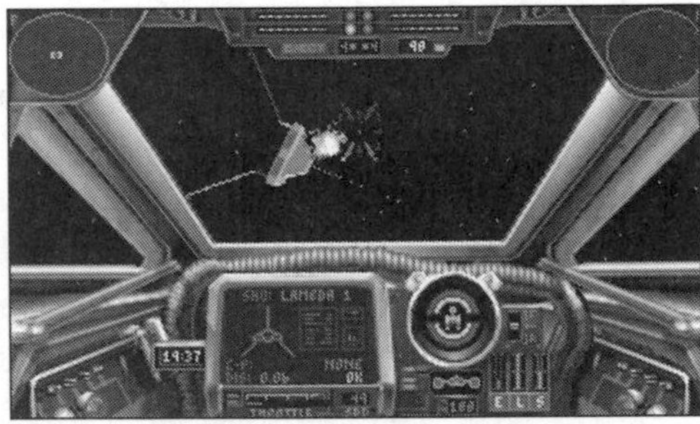

Going after shuttle Lambda 1.

No sooner had the *Wilsey* made it into hyperspace than a Star Destroyer popped up! Almost immediately, it launched a group of three TIE fighters (Alpha), which I sped off at maximum speed to intercept. As I did so, it launched a group of three TIE Bombers (Gamma). These would have to be stopped first.

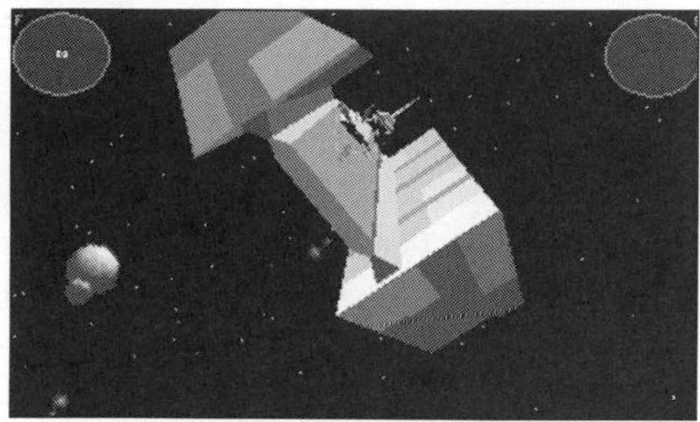

Keep guard over the Wilsey.

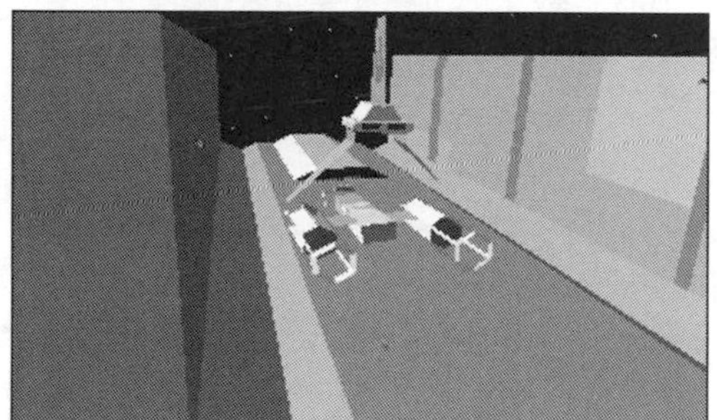

There's time to explore.

Getting close to the docking operation.

As it happened, I was able to eliminate two of T/F Alpha in a head-on pass while speeding toward T/B Gamma. There was another launch of three TIE fighters (Beta), but I ignored these as I concentrated on destroying the Bombers with my torpedoes and cannons.

After Gamma was eliminated, however, another wave was launched to replace them. I attacked the new Bomber group, and then kept after the TIEs until the *Phoenix* finally made it into hyperspace, and I received the Mission Complete message.

Before I could safely disengage, I had to take out any enemy fighters that might shoot me in the back as I tried to leave. This strategy took some time, but eventually I was able to break away and head for home. Before I left, however, I fired a torpedo at the STD *Intrepid*, just to spite them.

C.O.'s Analysis

"Very fine mission, captain, but you were a little lucky to get away with such a reckless attack on the first transport."

I hung my head. He was right, of course. I had let the shuttles get behind me and pelt me with laser fire. I knew what was coming next.

"Our analysis of the mission indicates that you might have attacked the shuttles first, perhaps slowing down by increasing shield energy, taking out a few with torpedoes and finishing them with your cannons.

"One torpedo and two supercharged laser shots will handle a shuttle. Let's face it—they're pretty slow targets. You should have been able to wipe them out and then go for the transports. After the shuttles were taken care of, there wasn't much to challenge you until the *Intrepid* arrived. If you saved a few torpedoes for the Bombers, you could have handled the latter half of the mission without much difficulty."

"You're right, of course, sir," I answered. "I was trying a little too hard."

Lagrane gave me one of those half smiles of his. "Yeah. That's right. But it was a damn fine bit of piloting. Just try to survive, Farlander. We need good pilots alive, not fragged and burned."

"Message received, sir," I told him.

Debriefing (Win Conditions)

SHU *Wilsey* must dock with and capture FRT *Phoenix*, and both must then survive.

Mission Note: The player's ship, the shuttle *Wilsey*, and the Star Destroyer all have three different start positions. These were designed to give three levels of difficulty for this mission.

When I heard that Mon Mothma was back on board, I hurried to contact Lynia. I caught up with her as she was coming out of a High Command meeting, along with General Madine, whom I had never met, Admiral Ackbar and Dodonna, among others.

"It's good to see you," I told her.

Her smile made me feel better than I had in weeks. She began to speak, and then stopped herself and looked at me as though seeing something new. Had I grown a wart on my nose or something?

"How are you, Keyan?" she asked. "You look different . . ."

I had no idea what she was talking about, but before I could respond, Mon Mothma came out of the meeting room, followed by a gold-colored protocol droid. It wasn't often one caught a glimpse of the Alliance head of state, and it was even less common for her to come over to chat, but that's what she did.

"Lieutenant . . . Oh, make that *Captain* Farlander, it's good to see you again."

She held out her hand. Rather timidly, I took it, not sure whether I should shake it, kiss it, or just sort of bow over it. OK. I had a hard time being comfortable with her. I was just an ordinary pilot, after all, and ordinary pilots didn't consort with galactic leaders. Besides, the last time I talked with her, she had told me a lot of stuff I didn't want to hear. Things about the Force . . . and destiny.

"Ma'am," I managed, taking her hand and releasing it quickly.

Now Mon Mothma studied me the way Lynia had done before. What was it? Maybe I was turning purple from eating too much porf.

"You've grown up, captain," was what Mon Mothma concluded. I was grateful that I wasn't turning purple.

"I guess so, ma'am. It's the war. You can't stay young for long. The young die young." I didn't really know what I was saying, but it sounded pretty good.

"Have you done as I suggested?" Mon Mothma asked me.

"I'm sorry. What was that?"

"Have you found someone to instruct you in the Force?"

"Ma'am, I've been instructed in all kinds of things, and I'm certainly becoming familiar with some force or other, but as to the Force . . ."

She smiled, probably seeing right through me.

"Keep your eyes open and your mind clear, captain. One day you'll meet someone strong in the Force, and you'll know it. Take it in. Absorb it as much as you can. Never waste your gifts. Take care, captain. And be good to Lynia. She's very special, too. And she likes you, you know."

With that, Mon Mothma winked at me and walked away. I think I was so shocked to see the head of the entire Rebel Alliance—one of the most powerful beings in the galaxy—*wink* at me, that I was a little slow to notice that Lynia was standing there, turning a rather hot shade of crimson. So she wasn't unflappable after all, I thought. But then, look at me.

Lynia and I managed to have some time together that night. We ate dinner in the executive dining room. They didn't call it a "mess" like the pilots did, and I could see why. The whole thing looked like something surface-side, not what we were used to on a starship. The tables were covered with fabric of some kind, soft yet apparently resistant to staining—as I found out when I spilled some Veronian wine. The plates were bright and clean and felt fragile and precious. Even the food was something that made me instantly forget about porf or mugruebe stew.

I don't want to give the impression that the executive dining room was extravagant, and in all honesty the menu wasn't so different from ours. It was the preparation. You could tell that the food here was made in individual portions; not in big vats of 40 servings at a time, ladled onto metallic trays in an assembly line. All right, so rank had its privileges.

"Mon Mothma seems quite interested in you, Keyan," said Lynia over a delicate bite of angel hair chintassa grass.

"Don't worry, Lynia. She's not my type."

She looked at me strangely at first, and then realized that I was joking and persisted.

"No, really, Keyan. She's not fanciful. If she sees something, you should pay attention. What exactly did she tell you?"

"Oh, nothing really. Something about the Force. It didn't make much sense to me."

"Oh," she said. "I see."

I got the feeling that she was sort of disappointed for some reason.

Just to change the subject, I asked; "Lynia, just exactly what is it you do?"

I had been wanting to know this for so long, but for some reason had always been reluctant to bring it up.

"Oh, I just observe things for Mon Mothma," she said coyly.

"What does that mean, 'observe things'?"

"I have certain . . . abilities . . . with ideas. It's hard to explain. My ancestors were a little . . . different."

"Different?" I persisted. "What do you mean?"

I waited for her to go on, but she seemed to have said all she was planning to say for the moment. Her one answer had only created a hundred new questions, but I found myself suddenly shy about probing further. Perhaps someday she would tell me more—when she was ready.

We ate in silence for a moment. Then, to break the tension, I asked; "What brings you and Mon Mothma to the *Independence* then?"

She smiled, obviously happier to be on safe, impersonal ground again.

"We're meeting with the High Command to set up an important operation. It has something to do with Imperial communications. I'm sure you'll learn more about it soon."

"No doubt, I will. As my friend Hamo says, 'You plan it; we man it.'"

She laughed and asked; "How is your friend Hamo?"

"He's very well. He made commander, but he seems kind of uncomfortable with it. He hasn't told me exactly how he got his promotion."

I got the distinct impression that she knew more about this than she was letting on. All she said was, "I'm sure he'll tell you when he's ready."

The rest of the evening passed pleasantly, and the next day Lynia was gone again with Mon Mothma.

OP 5: PROTECT CAPTURED SATELLITES

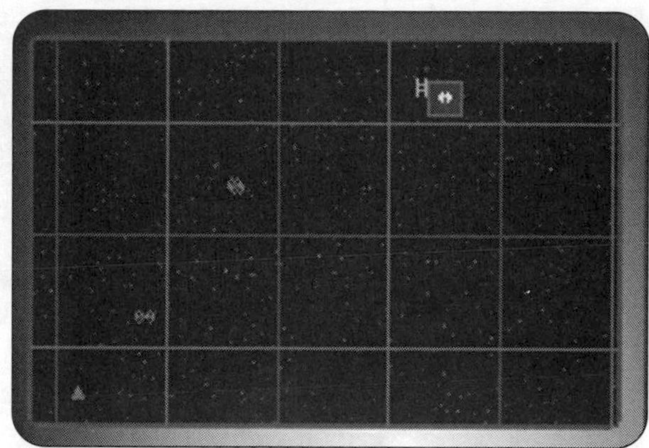

File Name: max9

Mission Briefing

A freighter carrying important satellites is waiting for the cruiser *Maximus*. You have been assigned to protect the freighter until the cruiser arrives. You will hyper in alone in your A-wing, and the freighter will be directly in front of you. The Star Destroyer *Intrepid* is a little over 13 clicks away, and has launched a pair of TIE Bombers and a pair of TIE Interceptors.

Farlander's After-Action Report

I was under immediate attack from two TIE Interceptors (Alpha) and two TIE Bombers (Beta), so I had to begin evasive maneuvers the moment I dropped out of hyperspace, carrying out abbreviated start procedures as I evaded. They had me at four-to-one odds, and the TIE Bombers were launching missiles, which I did my best to outmaneuver.

The *Intrepid* had already begun launching additional fighters, so the odds were going to get worse soon enough. I took out one of the Interceptors, came up behind one of the Bombers (controlling my speed), and sent a missile directly up its engine port.

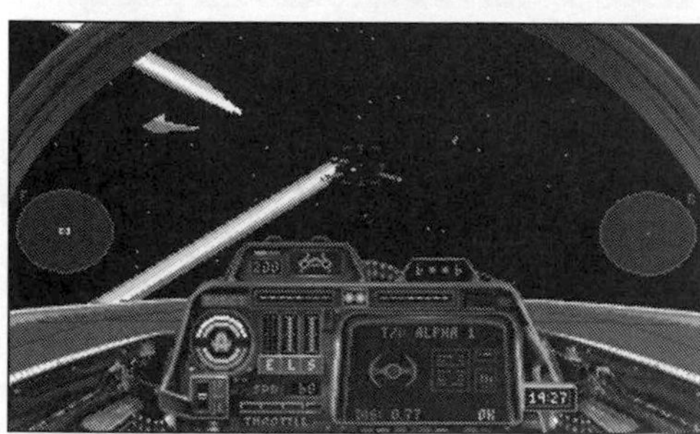

Shooting T/I Alpha.

I handled the second Interceptor then, and finally the other Bomber. As soon as I had destroyed the second Bomber, a replacement wave was launched from the Star Destroyer. Meanwhile, the new fighters were

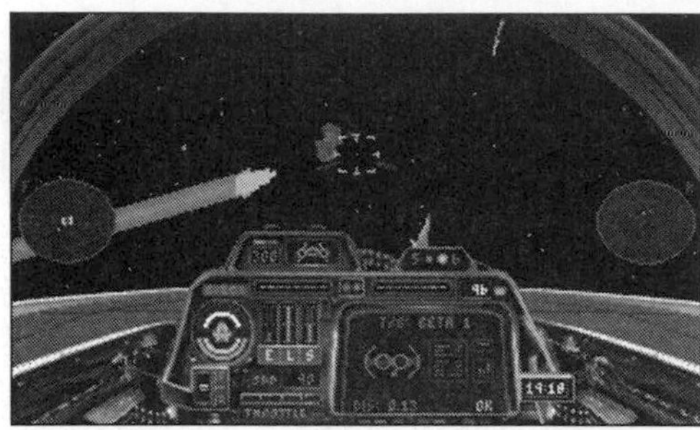

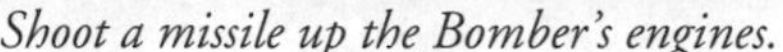

Shoot a missile up the Bomber's engines.

Someone's got you locked.

coming into range. First came a single Interceptor from Delta Squadron, and, coming up behind him, another from Zeta.

The Star Destroyer continued to launch TIEs in ones and twos. (Maybe they had some problem in the hangar bay?) Only once did one get by me. I quickly redirected all power to the engines and took off after him. I switched to missiles to take him out before he could do much harm. He did manage to make one attack run on the *Phoenix* before my missile caught him. Luckily, he wasn't a Bomber.

Finally, the *Intrepid* stopped launching TIEs. Then, when the *Maximus* arrived with the freighter *Ojai*, the Star Destroyer simply departed. Could it

Freighter Phoenix

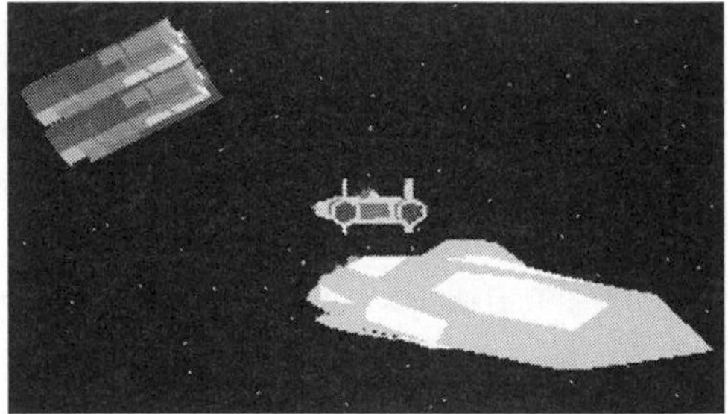

Cruiser, freighters, and A-wing

Close up on the docking operation.

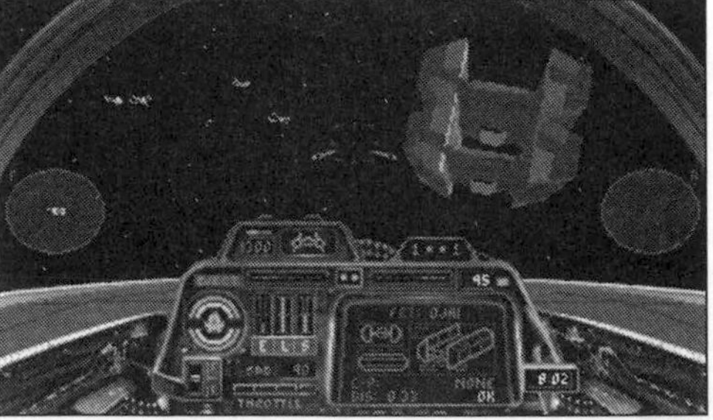

Watching over the Ojai.

be that the *Intrepid* is suffering an acute shortage of starfighters or pilots?

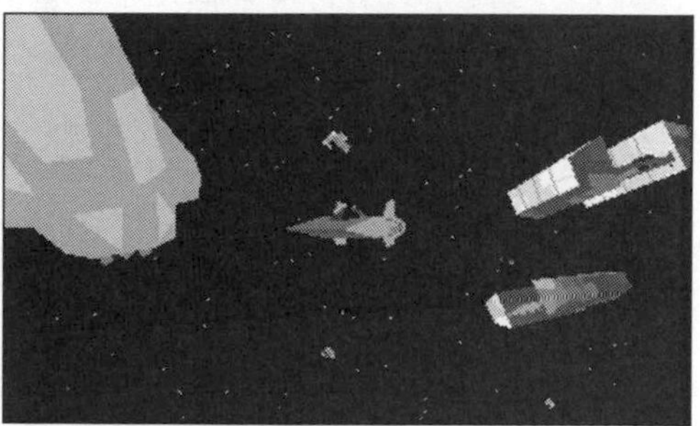

The Ojai *is on the way to her jump point.*

C.O.'s Analysis

"Good tactic, captain. Shooting each Bomber with a single missile at point-blank range gets rid of the threat immediately. With good dogfighting ability, you were able to overcome the odds."

"But tell me, why didn't I have some backup?"

"Yeah, Farlander. Good question. Get us some more pilots. Well, the truth is, we didn't anticipate a very heavy response on this mission, so we sent you alone. Go take a break, captain. You look a little tired."

"I wonder why."

Debriefing (Win Conditions)

The FRT *Ojai* must dock with the FRT *Phoenix,* and then survive. You must wait until the CRS *Maximus* arrives.

Mission Note: T/I Alpha and T/B Beta have two different start positions, designed to provide two levels of difficulty for this mission. In one, you have time to get your bearings; in the other, they are right on top of you.

We sat around the lounge, a bunch of pilots, doing what we loved to do—talk about starfighters and flying them.

"What's your favorite target?" Raider asked me.

"My favorite? That's a hard question to answer. I guess a TIE Bomber might qualify. I mean, it's not that I like them at all. In fact, I hate them. But I always have to target them before they get me or the ships I'm protecting."

"How do you fight the Bombers?" asked a new pilot, a Sullustan we called Speedy because we couldn't pronounce his name. He had just earned his wings and gone out on two tough missions. The fact that he was still here meant that he showed promise.

"You try to get them from a distance, with torpedoes or missiles. If you have to use cannons, put shields and cannons to max, and then come up from behind and blast away. If you're in a hurry . . ."

"If you've got shields," interrupted Raider, "just ram 'em."

The Sullustan's oversized eyes seemed to grow even wider, if that was possible.

"Me," interjected Hamo, "I like to go one-on-one with a TIE Interceptor."

Raider laughed, and said; "Really? They're too easy. I mean, they always seem to think they can outrun our lasers. Haven't you noticed how they turn after an attack run and vector directly away from you? As if our X-wings and A-wings couldn't keep up!"

"Yeah," conceded Hamo. "But they usually have better pilots than the TIE fighters."

"Those are my favorites," said Jan-lo, grinning. "I just like how easy it is to blast them."

"My last mission, I caught a TIE with a fantastic shot," said Naeco, one of the new veteran transfers. As he spoke, he used his hands to demonstrate the action he was describing. "I'd slowed down to blast a TIE Bomber, and this TIE fighter comes up behind me too fast. I caught him coming on the rear sensor, and just pushed my nose down a little. Then, as he came over me, I raised the nose and squirted a laser blast. He went nova on one hit. It was a beautiful deflection."

"I hate the Gunboats," said Speedy. "One jumped out of hyperspace right behind me on my last mission. Just about scared the scarns out of me."

"Scarns?" Both Hamo and I asked at once.

"Yeah," Speedy answered. "Scarns. You know . . ."

I didn't know, but I decided not to press the issue. Hamo just nodded as though he had just remembered what scarns were, but I was sure that he was bluffing.

"Gunboats are tough, but they're slow," said Raider, smiling inscrutably. Did he know what scarns were? "They're a nuisance, but you've got the advantage of speed and maneuverability. Me, I like to shoot a container. Just sits there, doesn't shoot back."

We laughed. Every one of us could agree with that.

"Oh, come on, Samuel," said Hamo. "You're kidding, right?"

"Yeah. Well, those chemical containers sometimes blow up nicely. Pretty colors, eh Speedy?"

"Actually, we see in a different range from you humans. I guess we probably have different esthetics."

"Different esthetics, is it? Hey, to me an explosion is an explosion."

"Yes," answered Speedy. "But to me, a human is a human."

None of us knew exactly what that meant, but the Sullustan was smiling, so we figured that it was a joke and laughed.

"The truth is, I like to shoot up corvettes," said Raider a moment later. "Maybe someday, I'd like to tackle a Star Destroyer."

"You're crazy," said Naeco. "You can't take on a Star Destroyer in a fighter. Stick to something five or ten times your own size."

"Yeah. Just give me 20-to-1 odds, and I'm a happy spacer," said Raider, winking across the table at me and Hamo.

"Me, I like a nice, dense minefield," said Hamo. "Or maybe a crossfire between two Nebulon Frigates."

Speedy was beginning to look a little nervous. Then the mission call indicator came on, and a klaxon blared. We all scrambled for the briefing room.

OP 6: AMBUSH IN THE CRON DRIFT

File Name: crndrft1

Mission Briefing

Fly escort for two Rebel ships, the freighter *Ojai* and the transport *Magnus.* They are to rendezvous with the corvette *Jeffrey.* Make sure that this convoy delivers its cargo. You will lead a two-ship flight of X-wings as you escort the freighter and transport to where the *Jeffrey* awaits. The *Jeffrey* is on the edge of the Cron Drift, so you must beware of the danger of collision with asteroids.

Farlander's After-Action Report

After a standard mission-start procedure, I assigned my wingman (Naeco) and the other three friendly ships to memory locations in the targeting computer. Less than a minute after we arrived, a pair of Assault Gunboats (Mu) appeared about three clicks behind us, and we turned to engage. I ordered Naeco to assist me with the lead 'Boat.

I decided to make some adjustments from my normal firing mode, and changed the cannons to quad-fire-linked and then switched to torpedoes. I fired as soon as I had a solid lock, and then targeted *Mu 2.* Immediately after launching my next torpedo, I switched back to cannons and quickly destroyed the target.

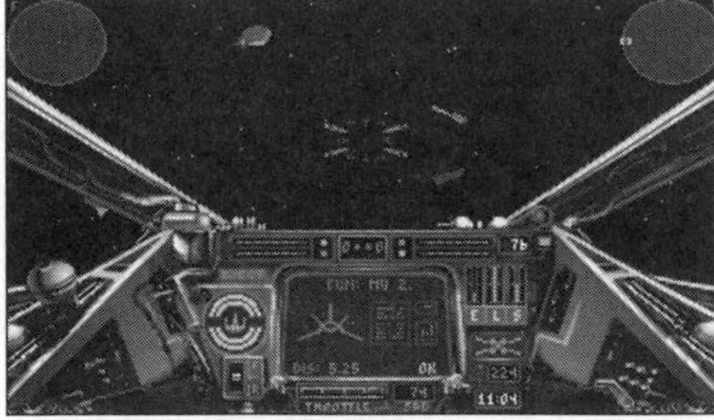

GUN Mu 2 *is 5.25 klicks away.*

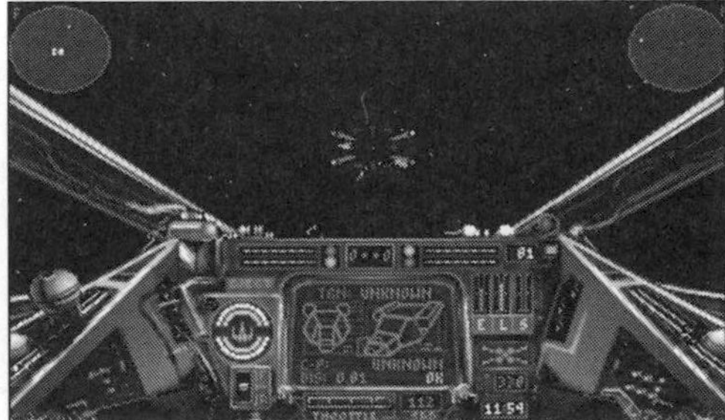

Imperial transports can be a threat.

Another pair of Gunboats arrived, followed shortly by a transport. Since a transport can be armed with torpedoes, I saw it as a serious threat to the *Ojai* and the *Jeffrey*. I left my wingman to finish off *Mu 1*, and took off after the interloper.

I brought up the transport in the CMD and switched back to torpedoes. Since it was about six clicks away, I redirected everything to the engines and got my speed up to 150. As soon as the targeting computer began locking on, I reset the recharge rates to maximum. I decided that I would use the same method which had worked on *Mu 2*.

Unfortunately, the transport was able to launch one of its torpedoes at the *Ojai* before I could completely close the gap, though I then made the ship pay the ultimate penalty for its transgression.

Next, I targeted the nearest enemy fighter, GUN *Mu 2*, part of a replacement wave for the original Mu group. As I engaged it with cannons, another transport arrived about nine clicks away. *Mu 2* was almost dead, so I stuck to it a moment longer before locating the new transport, and heading off after it.

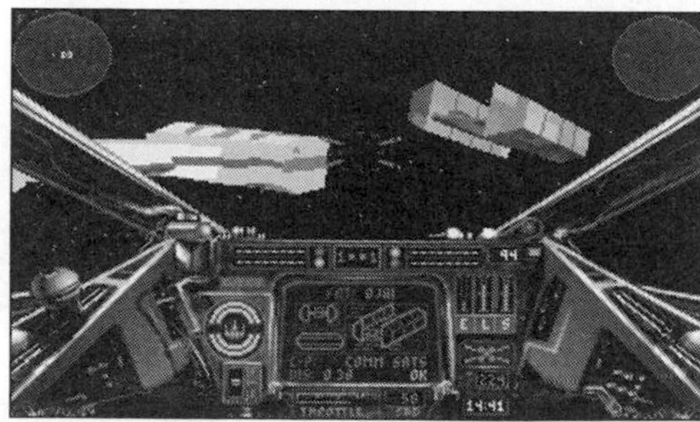

The Ojai *is approaching the Corvette.*

The Ojai *is docking.*

Between the Jeffery *and the* Ojai.

GUN Nu 2 is close.

I followed the same tactics and procedure as before, but this transport was farther away, and was able to get off two torpedoes before I could take it out. Also, during the chase, a Gunboat fired a missile at me that I couldn't take the time to evade! The missile hit me right after the transport blew up, but my shields were charged and my ship withstood the hit. I quickly rebalanced and recharged my shields. The *Magnus* made it into hyperspace after that, leaving me with one less ship to worry about.

Mu 1 was the nearest enemy now, so I turned to engage him with cannons. I was just starting to hit him when another transport came in about five clicks away. I broke off to engage the transport, intending to use the same tactics as before, and right away R2 indicated that I had another missile homing in on me.

I let it hit me, and, as I was balancing the shields, *Mu 1* began blasting me with lasers. Then the R2 gave me another missile warning. The new transport was still some distance away, and my shields were getting pretty thin, so I did some weaving this time. I straightened out and destroyed the transport as before, taking another missile hit in the process. R2 made a plaintive "bleep," and I decided that it was time for *Mu 1* to die. Yet another transport arrived as I was finishing him off.

I targeted the new transport about seven clicks away. As I headed toward it, another replacement wave for GUN Mu arrived, but they were a good nine clicks distant.

Using my now-standard procedure, I launched a torpedo at my target, and was surprised to see it sail astray! I would have to kill this transport with lasers, and as quickly as possible. I reduced speed by raising both shield and cannon recharge rates to maximum, and then began firing.

Something must have glitched with that torpedo I'd fired, because it missed in a second pass. Finally, my cannons did the job the torp had neglected, and I turned toward the nearest Gunboat, *Mu 2*. My wingman and I proceeded to destroy the Gunboats as fast as we could get on their tails.

Finally, *Ojai* had completed docking, and we just kept dogfighting while we waited for the *Jeffrey* to leave the area. A new Gunboat group arrived from Tau squadron. Soon afterward, I saw the Mission Complete message, but I wanted to bag a few more Gunboats. GUN Tau must have had some rookies, 'cause some of them went back into hyperspace as soon as they saw us coming! Eventually, no enemy ships were left, and we went home.

C.O.'s Analysis

"Good mission, Farlander. Good to see you're back to your old form," Lagrane told me. "Just one thing our analysis suggests: We think that you might have taken out all the Gunboats before turning to the transports. It's a small point, though. Well done."

Debriefing (Win Conditions)

The CRV *Jeffrey* must dock with the FRT *Ojai*, and then escape into hyperspace.

The practical jokes began soon after Naeco joined Red Squadron. Little things, like Naeco would come talk to you while you ate, and the next day your pee would glow in the dark! Or you would be strapped into the simulators and absorbed in a dogfight exercise, and a feminine voice would begin talking seductively over the comm. Things like that.

Naeco was an excellent pilot—a little reckless sometimes, but a superb deflection shooter. We all liked him immediately, but after falling victim to his little jokes, a bunch of us decided to get revenge.

One day, Jan-lo struck up a conversation with Naeco, sort of showing a little more than ordinary interest. We could all tell that Naeco liked Jan-lo, so she had no trouble getting him to agree to meet her later in a storage area of the Quarren section.

"It'll be more private," she told him. "Be sure to wear something comfortable."

Naeco was like a little kid; all excited. After Jan-lo departed, he approached me.

"Hey, Farlander. You know Jan-lo better than anyone else. Tell me about her. What's she really like?"

"Jan-lo? She likes a man to be really aggressive," I said, setting him up. "Don't waste time with her, or she'll lose interest."

I almost felt bad at that point, seeing him this way, but then I figured that he had it coming.

Later, Naeco went down into the Quarren section, where it's always kind of dark, opened the door to Storage Room V-2117 and walked in. Our little group huddled in a corner observantly.

"Jan-lo? You here?"

"Over here," she answered. "Come here and kiss me, Naeco."

She sounded really seductive. "This is a different Jan-lo," I thought.

So the poor guy walked up to what he thought was Jan-lo—it was really dark, remember, so he couldn't see very well—and planted this big kiss. Only, of course, that it wasn't on her.

Just then, Raider turned on the lights and we saw Naeco, lips puckered in the direction of a Quarren who works in the kitchen. Good sport, the Quarren, to go along with our twisted little revenge plot.

So there's Naeco, wiping his mouth and looking around, blinking in the sudden light. He saw us all, and joker that he is, realized immediately that he had gotten what he deserved. Laughing, and being a remarkably good sport about the whole thing, Naeco went so far as to grab the Quarren again, and plant another kiss, saying; "Sorry Jan-lo. I guess I've been taken."

We all ended up laughing, even the Quarren, although its laughter sounded like plumbing backing up.

After that, the practical jokes eased up a bit, though I think we all kept one eye out for Naeco. You never knew.

OP 7: PROTECT A DISABLED X-WING

File Name: max18

Mission Briefing

An X-wing carrying vital intelligence data has broken down near the Cron Drift. Assist in the rescue operation by flying cover. You will lead a three-ship flight of A-wings to where the disabled X-wing is stranded. Patrol the area, and keep any Imperial forces at bay until a rescue can be completed. The X-wing is directly in front of you as you drop out of hyperspace.

Farlander's After-Action Report

I used the standard mission-start procedure, and then assigned X-W Blue to a memory location in the targeting computer. Just over a minute went by before two groups of three Gunboats came in (Mu and Nu) about three clicks away. I turned to engage the nearest one and ordered my wingmen to attack.

I had destroyed one of the Gunboats (*Mu 1*) when an Imperial shuttle arrived less than one click away, headed straight for X-W Blue. I ordered my

Tailgating GUN Nu 3.

Nu 3 *is space dust.*

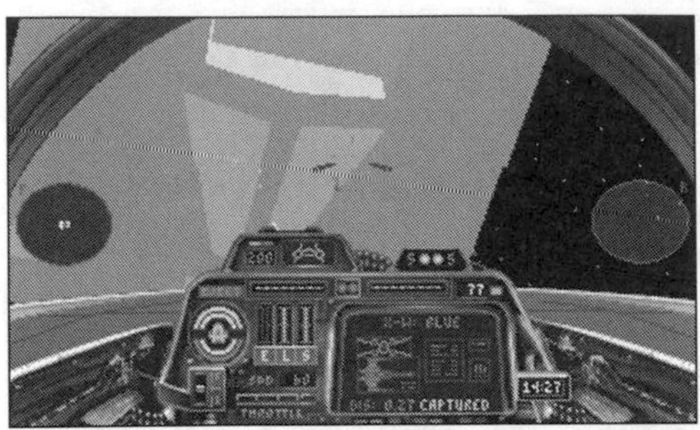

Dogging the enemy.

Don't let the Imperials get close.

wingmen to attack. When I checked the map, I saw that *Red 3* was getting battered by *Nu 1*, so I targeted *Nu 1* and came to the rescue while *Red 2* finished off the shuttle.

Another shuttle came in, and I ordered my wingmen to engage it. The dogfight was getting pretty furious, with the Gunboats launching missiles constantly. A few of them had hit me, and *Red 3* caught one, but *Red 2* was doing pretty well.

As soon as the shuttle was disposed of, another dropped in to take its place. *Red 3* finally succumbed to another missile, but *Red 2* and I were able to get this last shuttle. No sooner had we done so than the shuttle *Rescue* arrived, with its escort of three corvettes.

We turned our attention to the remaining Gunboats: There seemed to be an inexhaustible supply of them. Eventually, X-W Blue was repaired, and jumped to safety. After our shuttle and X-W Blue made it out, we followed them home.

C.O.'s Analysis

"It was an adequate mission, but you didn't take advantage of the safety area near the corvettes," Lagrane was saying. "Their extra cannons would have made an excellent killing zone to draw the Imperial fighters into. It would also have made you a much more difficult target to get a missile lock on."

"I lost another wingman, too," I offered, still a little baffled at how that happened.

"Yes, you did. Mission analysis suggests that *Red 3* failed to rebalance shields after that first missile hit him. It wasn't your fault, captain. However, destroying the shuttles quickly is important to your success. You might also have tried killing the shuttles more quickly by hitting them with two salvos of dual-fire missiles. That would leave them weak, and you could finish them off quickly with cannons."

"Sir?"

"What is it, captain? Something bothering you?"

"Well . . ." I began. Losing another wingman was bothering me, but what more could I say?

"I guess not, sir," I said at last. "Is that all?"

Lagrane studied me a moment, seemed about to say something, and then just told me; "Nothing more, Farlander. You're dismissed."

Debriefing (Win Conditions)

SHU *Rescue* must dock with and repair X-wing Blue. X-wing Blue must survive.

The pilot we had rescued in X-wing Blue turned out to be Biggs Darklighter, a veteran of many Alliance battles, and he joined us in the lounge after finishing his debriefing. It was quiet. Most of the other pilots were on scout or escort missions. Just me and Raider and Darklighter, who was doing most of the talking.

"So when I left Tatooine," he was saying, "I joined the Imperial Academy. I used to dream about flying a starfighter. My friend Luke and I were going to leave together—seek our fortunes in the Imperial Academy—but he had to stay behind and help his uncle on their moisture farm. He'd make a great pilot, Luke would, if he could just get off that dirty little planet."

Darklighter was a medium-built man with dark, straight hair that fell like a round bowl over his head. He had happy eyes, the kind that laughed a lot, and he sported a mustache.

"I couldn't wait for Luke. I went off alone and began my training. But I could see almost immediately that the Empire and I weren't going to get along. So, with a couple of friends, I hijacked an Imperial starship and brought it over to the Alliance."

He smiled and spread his hands. "It was touch and go. They almost blasted us away before we could convince them that we were just three Rebel sympathizers flying this whole ship by ourselves. Since then, I've been flying X-wings for the Alliance."

Darklighter paused to take a drink, leaning back in his chair and stretching his legs.

"So what's it like to fly a TIE fighter?" I asked. I had always wondered how the Imperial pilots felt about flying without shields and all.

"I tell you, captain . . ."

"Call me Keyan, please."

"OK. Anyway, Keyan, I wouldn't climb into one of those death traps again for love or money. You're just waiting for someone to catch you with a laser blast. Let me tell you, most TIE pilots are at least half-scared to death. The others are too stupid to be scared."

We laughed. It made us feel good to hear how bad the other guys had it. But Darklighter wasn't finished.

"Don't get me wrong. In the right hands, a TIE fighter has good maneuverability and fair speed. But the Empire doesn't invest all that much in training its pilots. The ones that get good are the ones who survive their first few encounters. Unfortunately for them, a lot of TIE fighter pilots don't."

"What about the newer Imperial ships, like the TIE Interceptor?" I asked him.

"Good question. I never flew one," he said thoughtfully, then added with a chuckle; "But I've shot a lot of them."

"They're faster, and more maneuverable than other TIEs," he continued. "They carry more weaponry, too. I've never had too much trouble with them, though, unless the odds were about ten to one."

"I always figured ten to one was pretty routine," said Raider.

Darklighter stared at Raider a moment, and then grinned. "I was just trying to be modest," he said. "Hope I get to fly with you some time, captain."

"Call me Sam," Raider told him.

"Hey, Keyan, Sam: Enough shop talk. I've got some new holos from Celanon City. Come on. We'll go check them out."

OP 8: STOP HYPERDRIVE REPLACEMENT

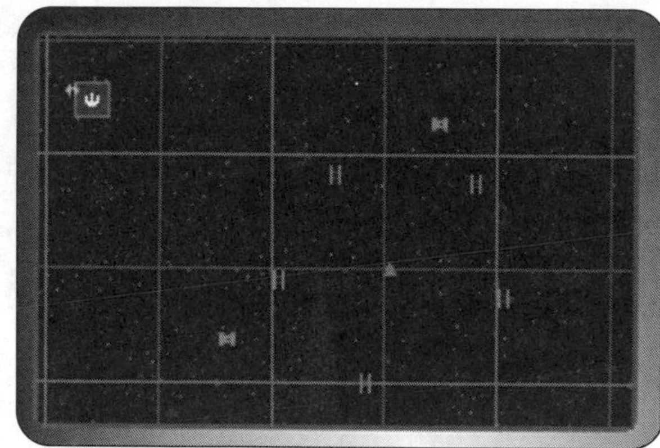

File Name: max1

Mission Briefing

Several freighters are unloading cargo onto the damaged Star Destroyer *Intrepid.* You must locate and destroy the freighters containing the hyperdrive replacement. Escorted by a pair of A-wings, you will fly an X-wing for this attack. The *Intrepid* is approximately ten clicks away, ringed by five freighters. Two pairs of TIE fighters are on patrol, and will move to intercept you.

Farlander's After-Action Report

I used the standard mission-start procedure, as the patrolling TIE fighters came right for us when we popped out of hyperspace. My escorts turned toward the nearest pair (Beta), and I joined them in a head-on attack. Soon, Alpha joined the melee, and I fought my way toward the nearest freighter.

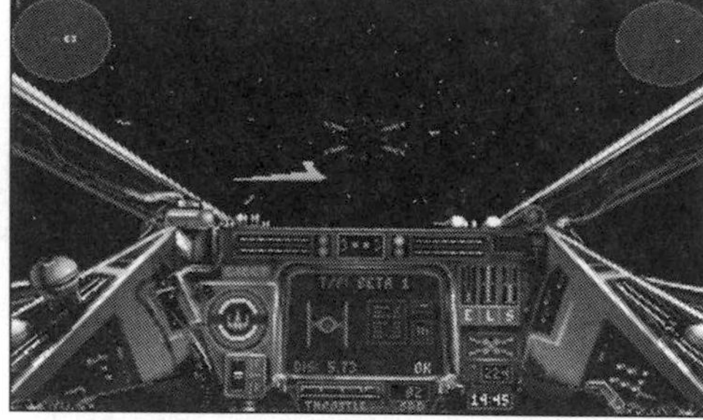

TIE fighter Beta 1 *is headed this way.*

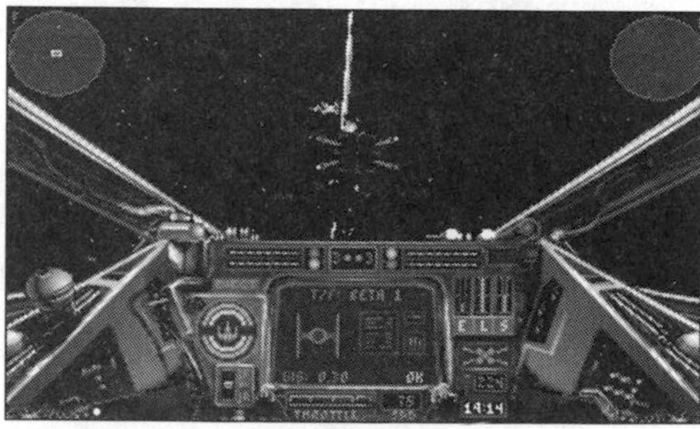

Blasting T/F Beta 1.

Before we could take care of all the fighters, a two-ship group of TIE Interceptors from Delta squadron was launched from the *Intrepid.* A minute later, a four-ship group from Theta squadron was also dispatched.

About four minutes into the mission, I made it to the first freighter, the *Kiam IV.* It was loaded

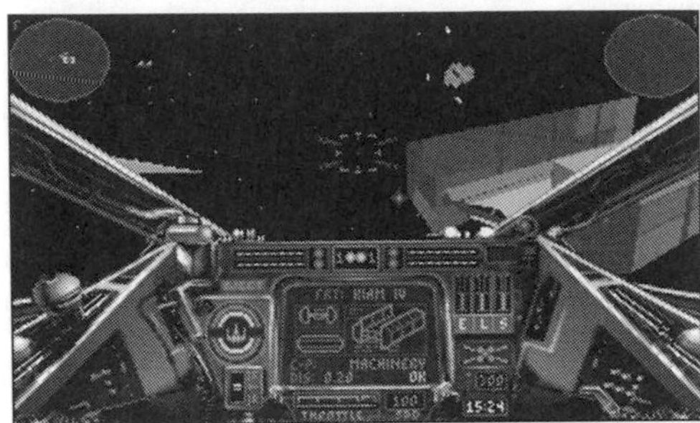

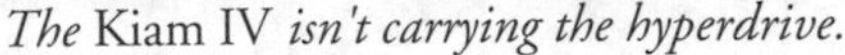

The Kiam IV *isn't carrying the hyperdrive.*

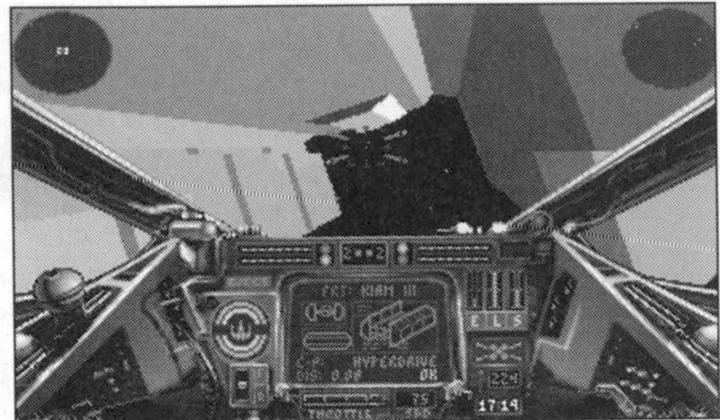

Freighter Kiam III *has hyperdrive parts.*

with machinery, so I continued toward the next in a counterclockwise rotation around the ring. Another pair of TIE Interceptors, these from Zeta squadron, joined the fray at that point.

The next freighter was *Kiam III*, which had hyperdrive spares, so I switched to torpedoes and selected dual-fire mode. Since I was so close, I didn't bother waiting for the targeting computer; I just fired them point-blank as fast as they would launch. That was the end of that freighter, and I set off toward the next.

The *Kiam II* was loaded with supplies, so I passed it up.

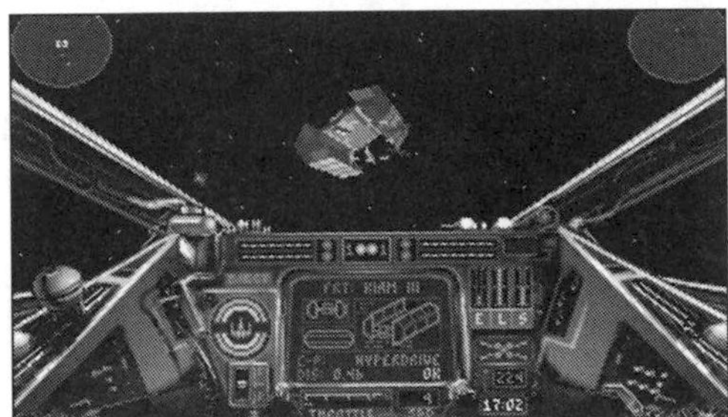

Torpedo Kiam III.

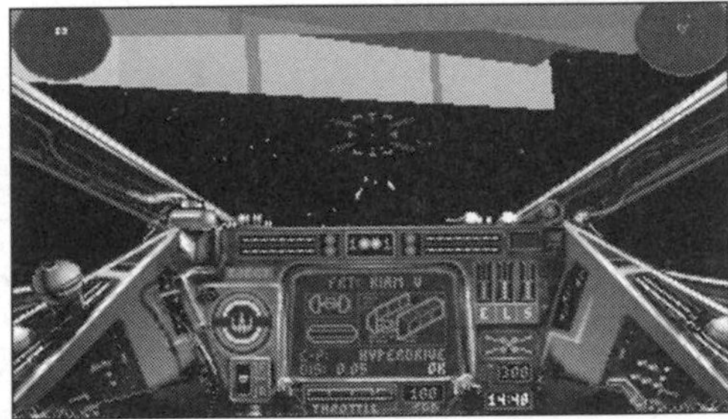

Here's another freighter to destroy.

Another pair of Interceptors launched, from Gamma squadron this time. I was constantly weaving to evade all these TIEs, and, even with the recharge rates at maximum, my shields were slipping.

Next was the *Kiam V*, carrying more hyperdrive parts. I tagged it in memory and decided that it was time to reduce the number of Interceptors hounding me.

I proceeded to engage and destroy several of my pursuers, while circling the *Kiam V* and firing on it as opportunities arose. After destroying the *Kiam V*, I headed off toward the last freighter. I received the Mission Complete message before I got close enough to ID it, though, so I withdrew as soon as I had fully recharged my shields and headed for home.

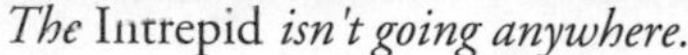

The Intrepid *isn't going anywhere.*

Get R2's view of your handiwork.

C.O.'s Analysis

I slumped in the chair in the debriefing room. Lagrane was looking me over critically. I could feel his eyes on me, but I couldn't meet them. I was feeling discouraged, despite my success. I had simply run out of energy, and there was no source to replenish it. Lagrane began his analysis of the mission.

"It was very risky to use all six torpedoes like that on the first freighter with the hyperdrive spares. You couldn't know how many of the five would have to be destroyed. As it turned out, there was only one other, but at that point you were in the middle of a hornet's nest of TIE Interceptors!

"You really had a hard time keeping your shields up, and constantly shunting cannon power to the shields was robbing you of the maximum effect of your lasers. Keeping your recharge rates at maximum forced your speed down to 50. You were asking for trouble, captain.

"Our analysis of the mission suggests that you should have redirected the shield energy to the engines and kept your speed up to at least 100. You would still have had to transfer cannon power to the shields constantly, but you would have been better able to evade your attackers, and as a result you would have lost less energy overall by better avoiding their cannon blasts.

"You know, Farlander, every pilot is only human. Don't take this too hard, but I see that your concentration seems below par. You're feeling the pressure, aren't you?"

I nodded.

"Now don't take this personally, captain, but I think you need to take a little time off."

"No, Commander. Wait. I'll be all right. It's just . . . I've been having these dreams."

"Dreams?" Lagrane asked.

"They've been going on for a few weeks. It's like a war is taking place in my head at night."

"Look, Farlander, I'm not equipped to deal with your dreams. You report to Sick Bay and see what you can do about it. If you don't get focused, I'm going to have to put you on inactive."

"Yes sir. I understand. Don't worry. I'll visit the med droids and see what they can do."

Debriefing (Win Conditions)

FRTs *Kiam III* and *Kiam V* must be destroyed.

"Good afternoon, Captain Farlander. Please describe your symptoms." The droid spoke in a pleasant voice, designed to make you feel at ease. Even so, I was nervous.

"I'm having strange dreams, and I'm not getting enough sleep."

"You're having dreams," repeated the droid. "Tell me about your dreams."

"Well," I began, somewhat reluctantly. "I'm always in a glowing sphere, and I have the feeling that it's very large."

"A sphere. Go on," said the droid.

"And there are voices," I continued.

"Tell me about the voices."

"I don't really understand them. I get bits and pieces, but I can't quite grasp the thoughts."

"Bits and pieces, nothing more," responded the droid.

"All I know is that there are two voices, and they're completely the opposite of each other. I think if I knew which one to listen to, I'd feel better."

"Tell me about feeling better," the droid requested.

"I'd feel a whole lot better if you'd stop asking questions, and give me something to help me sleep."

"One moment, please."

The droid wheeled out of the small cubicle, and I waited. And waited. Finally, an older woman entered the room, followed by the droid, or perhaps one that looked just like it.

"M4 here tells me you've got some attitude problems," the woman said. "Maybe I can help."

She was probably about 60 years old, gray hair, cerulean blue eyes. She seemed a little put out, as if I was intruding.

"Look, doctor . . . You are a doctor, aren't you?" I asked.

The woman nodded and offered a concerned smile, saying; "We're here to help you, captain."

She was treating me like some kind of a mental case, and my danger signals began flashing accordingly. I didn't want to end up on the inactive list. I took a deep breath and said; "Doctor, I've just had some bad dreams . . . the war, you know. But I'm fine. I just wanted to get something to help me get a few good sleeps. I think M4 there misinterpreted what I said."

The doctor looked dubious, so I repeated myself, adding a good-natured chuckle for emphasis:

"I'm *fine*, doctor. Everything is fine."

I can admit this now, but I never would have mentioned it to anyone back then. I felt something connect between me and the doctor. I felt my will reaching out to her; convincing her of what I was saying. It was the first time I had ever felt anything like that—like my will was actually emanating from me as a conscious force—and just as quickly I made a conscious effort to somehow shut it off.

By that time, however, the deed was done.

"Captain Farlander is fine, M4. He just needs a few good sleeps. Give him some sedatives and recommend him for active duty." And she smiled at me; a warm, sincere smile.

"It was good to meet you, captain. Good luck." Then she turned and left.

I made it back from Sick Bay just in time to grab an assignment.

OP 9: TAKE OUT INTREPID'S ESCORT

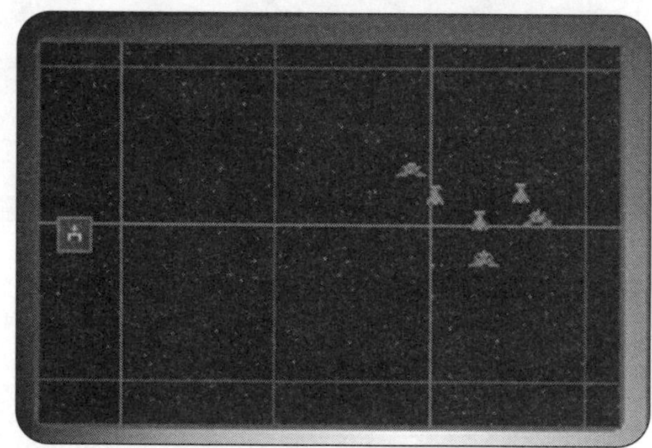

File Name: std1

Mission Briefing

A group of corvettes and several Assault Gunboats are on their way to protect the Star Destroyer *Intrepid*. Your mission is to intercept and destroy the would-be escort. You will lead a three-ship flight of Y-wings in this attack. The *Intrepid* is more than 50 clicks away. Three Imperial corvettes are located about 8 clicks away. Each is accompanied by a group of three Assault Gunboats. An X-wing has been assigned to escort you as you make your attack.

Farlander's After-Action Report

It promised to be a great mission. We hyperspaced into the area—Raider, Hamo, and I—ready for action, and certain to see plenty of it. Our escort, Captain Marskan, in X-wing *Blue*, arrived a moment later.

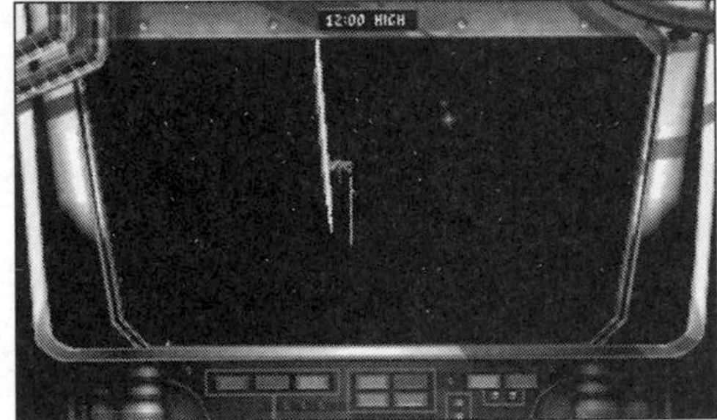

Your X-wing escort passing overhead

I ordered X-W *Blue* to wait while we built up our shields, meanwhile targeting the nearest Gunboat, *Mu 3*. As soon as we were fully charged, I ordered my wingmen to attack *Mu 3*, then ordered our escort to resume his mission.

I felt that if we could lure some of the Imperial fighters out to fight us, away from the corvettes, we could destroy them more easily. The Empire's pilots proved quite cooperative in that regard, and, with the assistance of my wingmen, I was able to wipe them out, one group after the other.

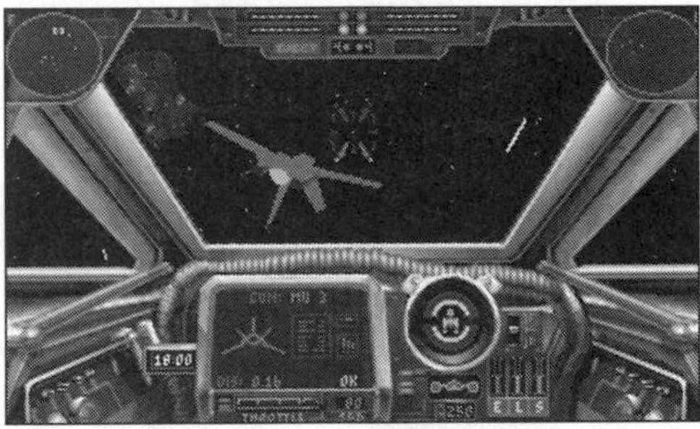
Taking out GUN Mu 3.

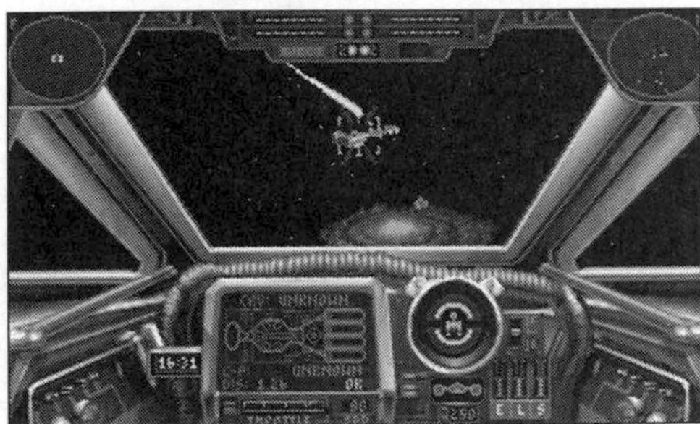
Locking onto one of the corvettes.

Finally, the three corvettes were alone, and I took up a position outside their cannon range. I cut my throttle to zero, and then switched to torpedoes, selecting the dual-fire mode.

I targeted the middle (lead) ship of the Vic formation, and ordered my wingmen to do the same. By removing the lead ship first, the other two were left with a blind spot that had previously been covered.

I launched as soon as I had a lock, and then targeted the next corvette and fired another pair of torpedoes at it. My wingmen had each fired two torpedoes at the first corvette, and it was soon destroyed. I then targeted the third corvette, and fired my remaining four torpedoes into it.

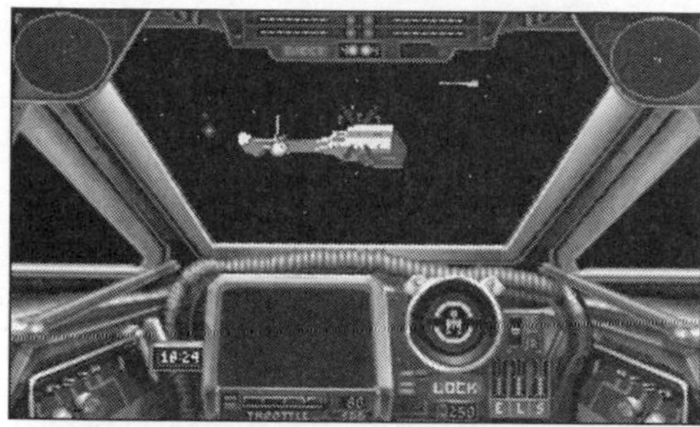
Approaching a corvette.

This is the best place to attack a corvette.

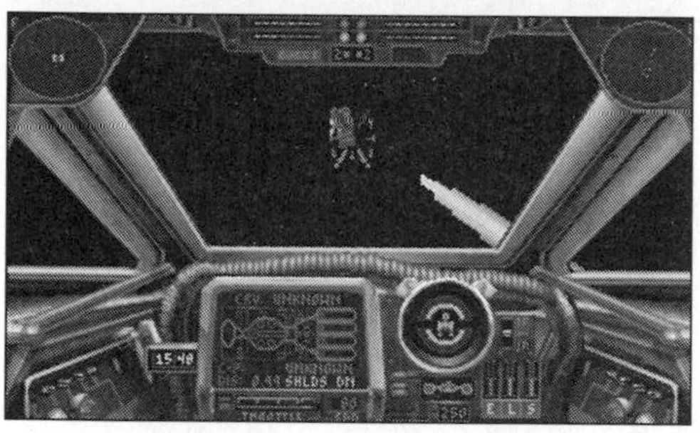
This corvette is ready to go.

I retargeted the second corvette at that point, so that I could order my wingmen to attack it. As soon as they acknowledged, I switched back to lasers and made a final attack run on the third corvette, coming in at full throttle. My wingmen finished off the last one on their own.

X-W *Blue* was of little help, frequently targeting the same ship I had. This led to my being hit by his lasers several times! Since he failed to account for a single kill, I see no justification for what appeared to be a reckless disregard for our safety.

C.O.'s Analysis

"Captain, didn't I tell you to see the medics?"

"Yessir. I did, sir."

"Good."

I noticed with relief that the commander seemed to consider the issue closed.

"I must say you handled yourself well in this mission. An excellent job. We've got some other suggestions for attacking corvettes, but they haven't been tested.

"We think you might be able to concentrate on the gun emplacement on one side of a corvette. Once it was taken out, you could attack from that angle without fear of reprisal. However, our analysis also suggests that the corvette might roll before it was completely disabled, bringing you into point-blank range of the guns on the opposite side. Needless to say, you should be very careful, and stay alert, if you try this technique. Back off from the corvette when its shields go down, and finish it from a distance."

"Again, your performance was very good. However, X-wing *Blue* did very poorly."

"I don't know what got into Marskan. He's never been so erratic," I agreed.

"This was a very difficult mission, and your success was marred by X-W *Blue's* performance. He arrived late, and was reckless in combat, endangering the very ships he was charged with protecting. Rest assured, he will receive an official reprimand."

"Listen, commander . . . Marskan's a good pilot . . . I just hope he's OK."

"I would think that you'd be pretty angry with him," said Lagrane.

"I am," I said. "But I also know that we all make mistakes."

Lagrane nodded, understanding me.

Debriefing (Win Conditions)
All three corvettes and all nine Gunboats must be destroyed.

The *Intrepid* sitting out there helpless in space was just too good an opportunity to pass up, and we scrambled within the hour. Raider was going to get his wish: Our mission was to attack the Star Destroyer!

OP 10: DESTROY THE INTREPID

File Name: std2

Mission Briefing
To begin your assault on the Star Destroyer *Intrepid,* take out the ship's shield-generator towers. You will lead a pair of X-wings in this most critical phase of the attack. After the shields are down, the Intrepid is vulnerable to proton torpedoes. Two A-wings will escort you, and Y-wings will come in four at a time to press the attack. The *Intrepid* is just under 16 clicks away. A

group of four TIE fighters will block your path at a distance of 6.5 clicks, and another two-ship group waits at 9.5 clicks. Finally, a pair of TIE Bombers is near the *Intrepid*.

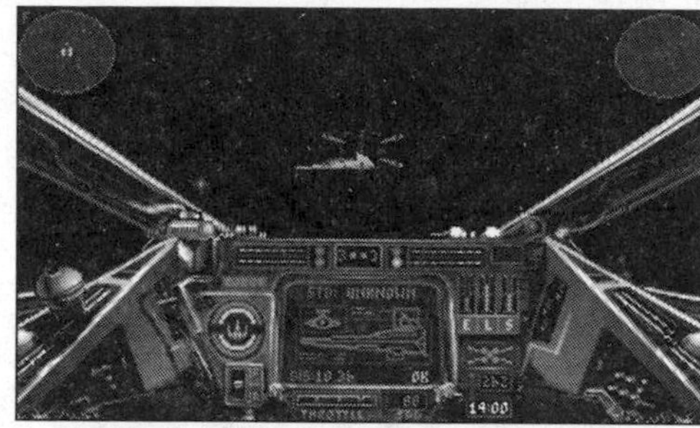
There she is. Go get her.

Farlander's After-Action Report

I used the standard mission-start sequence, with the following exception: Because it would be up to me to take down the shield generators, I had to get in there as quickly as possible. Consequently, I redirected all shield power to the engines and set the cannon recharge rate to maximum. This would allow me to maintain a constant speed of 100. As I neared the *Intrepid*, I was constantly transferring power from the lasers to the shields.

The first attack wave of Blue Squadron's Y-wings was already in front of us, and T/F Alpha was moving to intercept. Jan-lo was flying my wing, and I ordered her to attack the nearest of these, *Alpha 1*.

The A-wings from Gold squadron arrived and quickly went to the aid of the Y-wings as well. T/F *Alpha 2* was directly between me and the *Intrepid*, so I targeted him and killed him in a head-on pass. The CMD showed *Alpha 3* to be right next to me. When I turned to look, I saw that he was on Jan-lo's tail, so I changed course to take him out. *Alpha 1* and *Alpha 4* had been destroyed, so this left only T/F Beta and T/B Gamma to worry about.

By now I was about six clicks from the *Intrepid*, and T/B *Gamma 1* was waiting as I approached the Star Destroyer, preparing to launch a missile. I kept going, and we opened up on each other simultaneously. My shields took a beating and *Gamma 1* survived the first pass, but only momentarily, as Jan-lo finished him off when he turned away.

T/B Gamma will fire torpedoes at you.

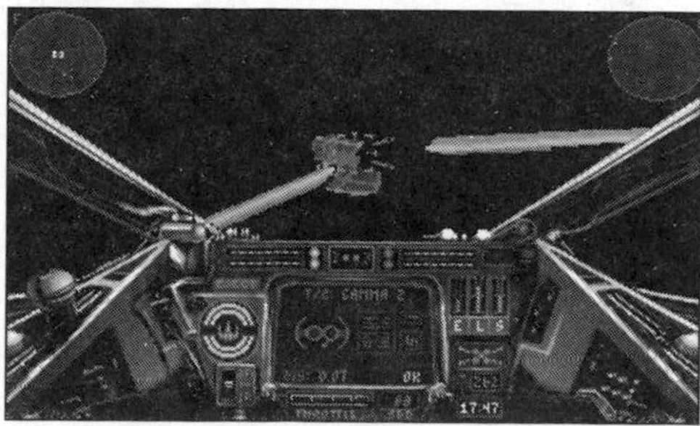
Shooting Gamma 2.

Continuing toward the *Intrepid*, I could see that Y-W *Blue 1* and *Blue 2* had been destroyed. A missile from *Gamma 2* caught Jan-lo with her shields too low, and I lost communication with her.

Then she was gone.

Raider, in one of the A-wings, blasted *Gamma 2*, but too late. I heard Raider on the comm but didn't catch what he said. The R2 was announcing the launch of a replacement wave for Gamma, and I was preparing to make my run on the shield generators.

Towers straight ahead.

I approached from the port side, maneuvering to bring both generators in line so that I could get them both in a single pass. With torpedoes selected in dual-fire mode, I closed in on the towers. Next, I reset the shield recharge rate to normal. The targeting computer wouldn't lock on a single part of the ship, so I had to be perfectly lined up when I fired. R2 signaled an incoming missile as I got ready to shoot, but my shields were still strong, so I pressed on, thinking momentarily of Jan-lo and then putting her out of my mind.

I launched the first pair of torpedoes at the nearest tower and then quickly lined up on the second. I was hit by two missiles just as I fired another pair of torpedoes. I lost my rear shields and took some damage to the hull, but quickly rebalanced the shields and transferred energy.

I was practically on top of the Star Destroyer now, as I selected single-fire mode and swung my aim back to the first tower. My next torpedo went low and passed underneath the shield generator. I had better luck with my last torpedo, firing it point-blank into the second generator and destroying it. I was furiously transferring energy to the shields as I switched back to lasers and swung around to take out the other generator.

An occasional lucky shot from the *Intrepid*'s gunners, and the constant attentions of T/B Gamma, were making this procedure difficult. I fired several laser blasts, but the tower still wouldn't blow, and I swung around again for another run. This time it went on the first shot, and the Star Destroyer's shields fell!

I was determined to put some distance between myself and the *Intrepid*, but first I would have to eliminate some TIEs. Another two-ship group of Interceptors (Zeta) had launched during my torpedo run, and I joined A-W

Gold in engaging them and T/B Gamma. The last Y-wing was eventually destroyed while firing the last of its torpedoes at the Star Destroyer, but another wave of Y-wings arrived to continue the attack.

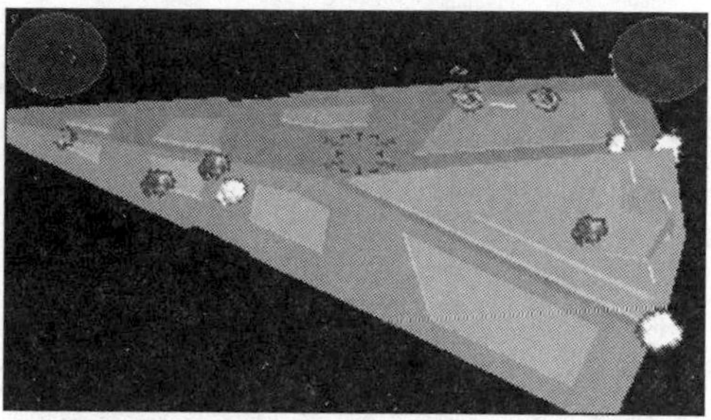
End of the Intrepid.

I kept dogfighting the TIEs, keeping them occupied while Y-W Blue closed in. Their attack finally overcame the *Intrepid*'s defenses, and the Star Destroyer began to break up as it was wracked by explosions. A four-ship patrol of Assault Gunboats (Rho) arrived, but they were too late to help the *Intrepid*. Y-W Blue headed home, and A-W Gold and I wiped out the last TIEs. We then overcame the Gunboats and decided to withdraw just as another wave appeared on the sensors.

C.O.'s Analysis

Lagrane had launched in without preamble.

"It's all very well to protect the Y-wings, Farlander. But your job was to attack the towers. And it should take only three torp . . ."

Then he noticed my expression, seemed puzzled by it, and said; "You look mighty miserable for someone who just helped blow up a Star Destroyer."

"It's Jan-lo, sir. She was from Agamar. We joined up together."

Lagrane looked at me strangely. "You haven't heard, have you?"

"Sir? Heard what, sir?"

"They snatched her. She's in a med tank now. They say she'll probably make it."

My heart missed a beat.

"Uh, Commander?"

"Yes, Farlander, you can go see her. Just one thing first."

"Sir?"

"I'm a little surprised you didn't take out that whole Star Destroyer yourself."

"Yessir," I said, smiling now. "I just wanted to let the other guys have some fun, too."

"Dismissed, captain."

Debriefing (Win Conditions)

The Star Destroyer *Intrepid* must be destroyed.

Mission Note: You must hit the Star Destroyer's towers with three torpedoes apiece to destroy them.

Jan-lo floated in a vat of bubbling blue slime. I coaxed and argued my way in to see her. Part of her face was burned, and I could see other seared patches and deep gouges in her arms and legs. Her body was mostly wrapped in some sort of bandage, but what I saw made my heart sink again. I found the nearest droid.

"Is she going to be all right?"

"Her prognosis is favorable, sir. Our med baths are remarkable at repairing burn damage."

"How long?" I asked.

"How long is what?" the droid replied. Damn literal creatures.

"I mean, how long will she need to be in that stuff?"

"Two or three days is the usual prescription."

"So if I come back in a couple of days, I can talk to her?"

"I can make no guarantees about that, sir."

"Take good care of her," I said at last, realizing that there was nothing else I could do. "She's my friend."

"Yes, sir. Don't worry. We always take good care of our patients."

✘ ✘ ✘

"Princess? What princess?" I asked.

"Princess Leia," Hamo told me. "She's one of the Senators from the Old Republic, originally from Alderaan. We're supposed to escort her while they hand-deliver something important to her. I get the impression our covert listening operation was a success."

It had been a few days since the *Intrepid* missions, and most of us had been off-duty to rest up. Naeco and I had looked in on Jan-lo, and she was beginning to seem like her old self remarkably fast.

Even after nearly buying it at the wrong end of a missile, she wanted only to get back in the cockpit. I had a feeling she might be grounded, though: It was tough taking all the damage she had suffered. Maybe she could enter Intelligence training now, the way we had always figured she would.

Later, as Hamo and I walked down one of the endless corridors inside the Calamarian cruiser, he was filling me in on the scuttlebutt about the upcoming mission. We often knew a great deal about what was going on before we were briefed. The veteran pilots had a good network of information—particularly Hamo, now that he was a commander and all.

"I guess I've never met a princess before," I said, kind of intrigued by the idea.

Hamo just shrugged and grinned. "Who has?"

"Think we'll get to see her?" I asked, feeling a little starstruck, a little stupid.

"Nah. We'll just pull escort duty and then hyper back here. She's not going to waste any time."

Something made me ask, "Hey, Hamo . . . You know her or something?"

Hamo blushed. Yes, he actually blushed.

"I met her," he admitted.

"So what's she like?" I asked, giving him a good-natured prod in the ribs.

"A looker," he confided, and immediately acted guilty for divulging that much. He clammed up then, and I could get no more out of him on the subject.

OP 11: DELIVER PLANS TO PRINCESS LEIA

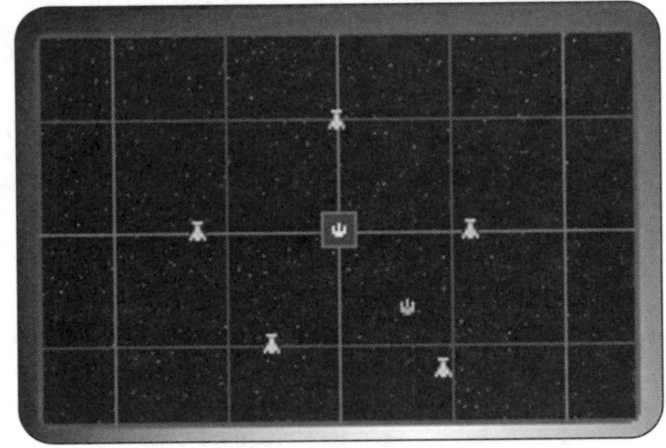

File Name: leia

Mission Briefing

Identify Princess Leia's corvette, the *Tantive IV*. Protect our shuttle as it delivers the secret plans to the princess. You will drop out of hyperspace in the midst of five neutral corvettes. They are all about four clicks away. In addition to your X-wing, another pair of X-wings is in the area to assist you, should Imperial forces intrude. The shuttle *Maria* will arrive after you identify the *Tantive IV*.

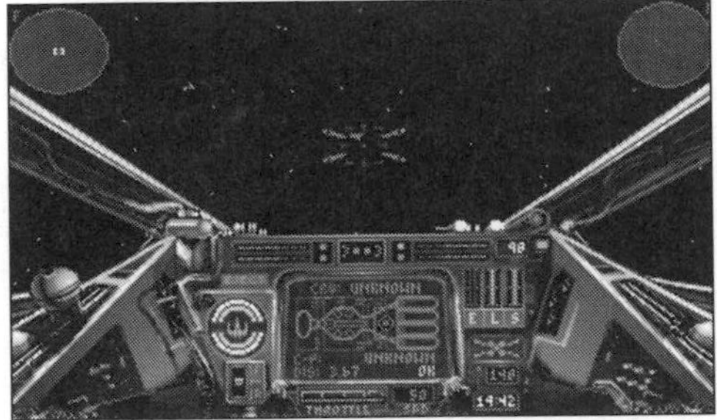

Searching for the Princess' CRV.

Farlander's After-Action Report

I quickly went through my standard mission-start procedure, and then initiated my search for the *Tantive IV*, targeting the nearest of the corvettes and heading toward it.

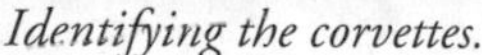

Identifying the corvettes.

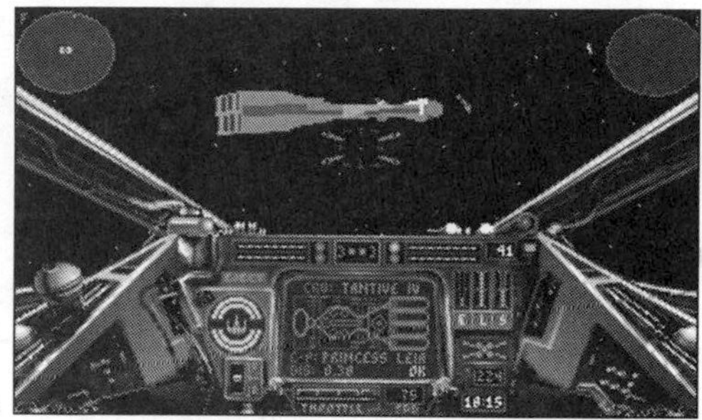

The Tantive IV

After identifying CRVs *T-Force 2* and *3*, I found Princess Leia's ship, and the shuttle *Maria* dropped out of hyperspace right on cue. I assigned both to memory locations, and took up a patrol of the immediate area.

About the time I got to thinking that everything was too quiet, an Imperial Star Destroyer arrived. It launched two four-ship groups of Assault Gunboats (Mu and Tau) and then departed.

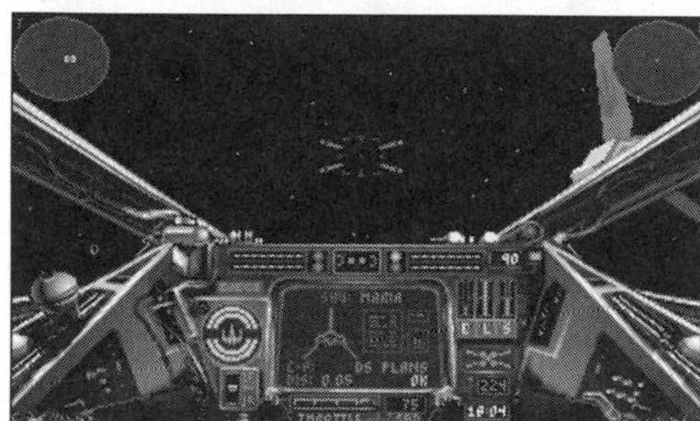

Here's the Shuttle Maria *with the plans.*

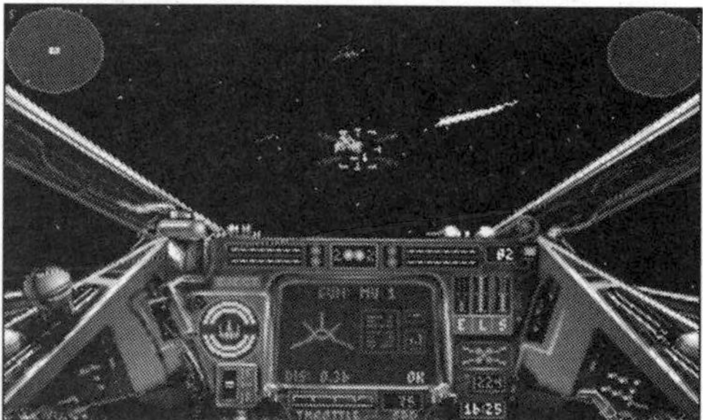

Target GUN Mu 1 *with torpedoes.*

I set my cannons to quad-fire, and then switched to torpedoes in dual-fire mode. I targeted the nearest of the Gunboats, *Mu 2*, and took off after it. I fired as soon as I had a solid lock, and then I turned to go after the rest of Mu squadron. *Mu 1* and *Mu 3* gave me no trouble: I hit them with two torpedoes each, and they fragged.

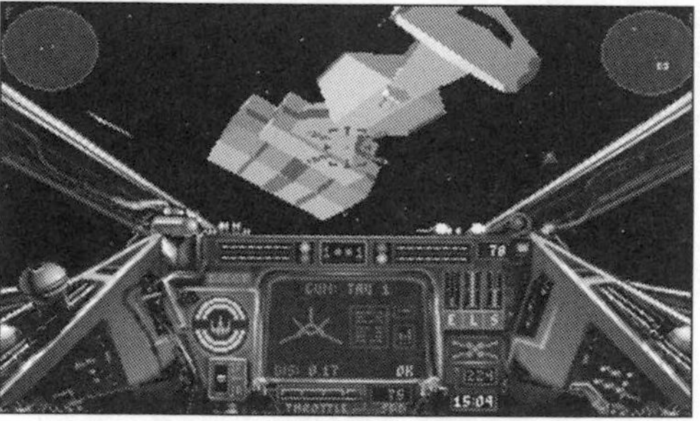

This Gunboat's behind the CRV.

Mu 4 had split off, and I saw that it was attempting to disable the *Tantive IV* while GUN Tau was firing missiles and engaging X-W Gold and myself.

The *Maria* made it to safety as I was destroying *Mu 4*. I was hit a couple of times by missiles, but was able to redirect power to the shields before taking any real damage. X-W *Gold 1* wasn't so lucky, and succumbed to missile fire.

The *Tantive IV* hyperspaced to safety as I was taking out GUN Tau. With Princess Leia and the Death Star plans on their way to High Command, I turned about and headed home.

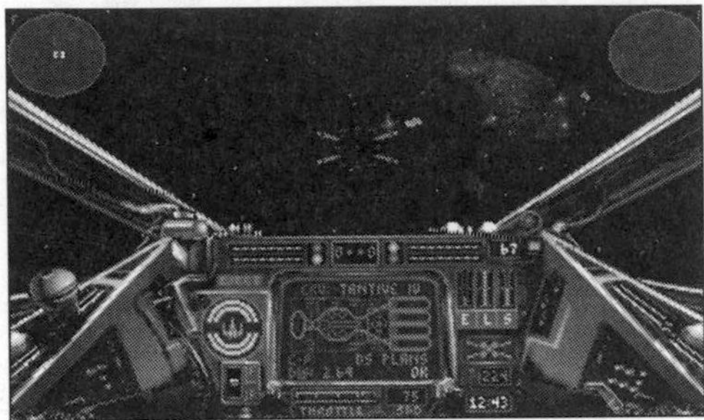

The Tantive IV *is taking off with the plans.*

Debriefing (Win Conditions)
SHU *Maria* must board CRV *Tantive IV*, which must then escape into hyperspace.

An hour later, we were back in the cockpits of our fighters. All we knew was that the princess was under attack. We weren't about to let anything happen to her.

OP 12: PROTECT PRINCESS LEIA

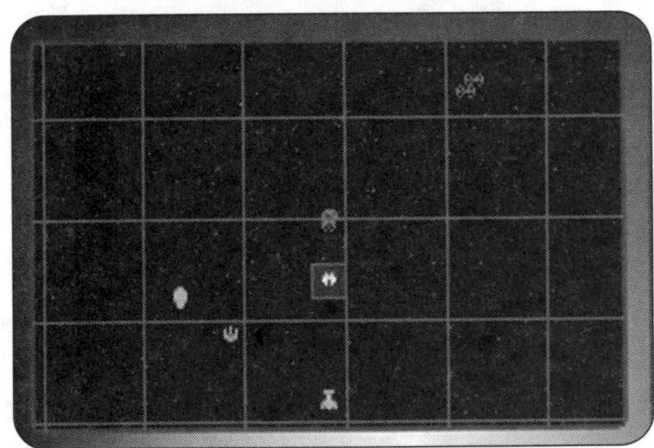

File Name: intcep1

Mission Briefing
The Star Destroyer *Immortal* has launched an all-out assault on the *Tantive IV*. Intercept the attacking TIE squadrons and secure the hyperspace jump

point. You are in the number-two spot in a pair of A-wings. Princess Leia's ship is about 8.5 clicks in front of you, and the cruiser *Liberty* is about 10 clicks to your right. Two groups of three TIE Interceptors are less than three clicks behind you, and closing fast. Another two groups of TIE Bombers are more than 13 clicks away, and the *Immortal* is more than 30 clicks away. A pair of X-wings is near the *Liberty* and will assist you.

Farlander's After-Action Report

We hypered in, Hamo and I in a pair of A-wings, went through the standard mission-start sequence, and then headed toward the nearest group of TIE Interceptors, Alpha.

Take a quick shot at the Interceptors . . .

. . . on your way to the Bombers.

I noticed several TIE Bombers also headed in our direction, so I decided to leave the Interceptors to X-W Gold. The Bombers were in two groups, one of three ships (Gamma) and one of four ships (Delta). I targeted the nearest Bomber and moved to intercept.

As I closed on my target, I found that three of the Interceptors were on my tail. I didn't even have to ask *Red 1* to help out, though: He was right behind them, giving them serious second thoughts about their reckless pursuit. *Beta 2*, the most persistent, got himself killed while he was closing in on me. Thanks to *Red 1*, I had enough time to lock and launch a missile at the nearest Bomber, *Gamma 1*.

Take care of the Gunboats.

It was about this time that a group of three Assault Gunboats entered the area, but I decided to finish off the Bombers before dealing with that threat.

I brought my ship around and came in behind the remaining Bombers, cutting my speed to avoid overtaking them. I carefully locked on each in turn, and fired one missile. When all but two were eliminated, the survivors began to evade, so I switched back to cannons and finished them off with lasers. I had kept one missile for an emergency.

Now I targeted the nearest Gunboat, and proceeded to engage it with cannons. After that, the nearest enemy starfighter was T/I *Alpha 1*, which, along with two Gunboats, was dogfighting X-W Gold in the vicinity of the *Tantive IV*. I immediately went to join them.

The Star Destroyer had launched replacement waves for Gamma and Delta, but they wouldn't get here for a while. On the way towards *Tantive IV*, I noticed that *Gold 2* had hull damage, so I pulled rank and ordered him to head home. Princess Leia's ship finally hypered out, and, after finishing off the remaining enemy ships in the area, *Gold 1* and I followed in its tracks.

Debriefing (Win Conditions)

The CRV *Tantive IV* must escape into hyperspace.

Princess Leia must escape into hyperspace.

We were celebrating our victory in the mess when we heard the news. The *Immortal* had ambushed the *Tantive IV* suddenly when she returned from hyperspace. The fate of the princess and the information she carried was unknown. Our celebration turned to a wake. We feared the worst.

Tour of Duty #3—The Gathering Storm

There were those on the *Independence* who were feeling confident, as though, in defeating now two Star Destroyers and successfully outwitting the Empire several times, we had truly gained some advantage.

But those of us who flew the missions, and watched the coming of raw recruits who left their belongings in freshly-scrubbed cabins without time to unpack, and went out on missions and died without our ever knowing their names . . . We felt the uneasy twinge of fear lurking silently in the recesses of our hearts, and deeper, in our guts.

The news that the princess had disappeared—that neither she nor the plans to the Emperor's secret weapon were still in Rebel hands—had served to lower our shaky morale even more. It made the sacrifices seem meaningless. We could take the pressure, the attrition, when we saw our successes before us, in the destruction of a Star Destroyer or the silent blossoming of an exploding weapons container. But this . . . Many of us began to doubt.

Those of us who had survived a few missions developed instincts that kept us alive. I could sense the direction my enemy would turn, anticipate his twists and loops, and stay on his tail until I had blasted him into space particles. I could lead him into my cannons without thinking, blasting empty space only to watch him fill the void and connect solidly with the red death in my lasers.

I had hardened, and I no longer questioned my right to kill. I questioned only my ability to remain alive in the chaos and uncertainty of battle.

But for many, the first mission was the last. For others, even after many successes, their luck ran out. It was a rare privilege to have friends like Hamo and Sam, Jan-lo and Biggs. But it was a tenuous friendship. You had to be ready to say good-bye at any time.

Still worse, I had begun to question our ability to win the war. I badly needed some good news.

We were gathered for one of those periodic events the High Command felt obligated to organize, where various awards and promotions were handed out. I even received a medal—for some mission I had already forgotten. And now General Dodonna was speaking about our goals. I kept thinking what a miracle we would need if the rumors I had heard were true. I kept hope alive, but just barely.

"We know now what the Empire's new weapon is," the general said flatly, as though he were reading the menu for dinner. That's how I knew that he was really worried. "It's called the Death Star; a very large, moon-sized spacecraft reportedly capable of generating immense energy bursts.

"We have several operations planned that should delay the completion of the Death Star, and our intelligence network is working to discover the location of the construction site for this massive project."

At this point, the general seemed to come alive a little, and some passion reentered his voice. I aligned myself with his conviction, using it to revive my spirits and my resolve.

"It is time for us all to realize that we are in a fight for more than our lives, for the principles on which the Rebel Alliance was formed. It's up to us to find a way to defeat this weapon. Rest assured, we in the High Command are not without resources. We are still strong, united, and ready to fight!

"Now here are our current goals. We will send out missions almost immediately, so from here, pilots and crew should report directly to briefings as posted on the holos outside.

"First, we will begin to stockpile military equipment and weapons for the assault against the Death Star.

"Second, we will use sabotage to delay the construction of the Death Star. We will also mount missions designed to capture key scientists and military staff.

"Third, we will redouble our efforts to locate the Death Star's construction site.

"Fourth, we will plan a massive assault on the Death Star to destroy it before it is completed.

"As always, we will respond to opportunities as they present themselves.

"Please report to your duty officers now, and thank you for coming. Dismissed."

I was on my way to the hangar when Jan-lo caught up with me.

"I wanted to see you before you went out," she said.

"What is it, Sunnar?" I asked.

"I'm being transferred. I'm going on a long assignment for Intelligence. I wanted to say good-bye. And to wish you luck."

"You're leaving?"

"Yes. I can't talk about it. But I'll most likely be gone a long time."

Then she came up and hugged me. "Take care of yourself, Keyan. Be careful."

"I'll do my best. You, too. Stay out of trouble, OK?"

She laughed. "I'll do my best," she answered, parodying me.

Then she turned and walked quickly away, and I continued to the hangar, where I climbed into an A-wing and prepared for another mission.

OP 1: GUARD WEAPONS TRANSFER

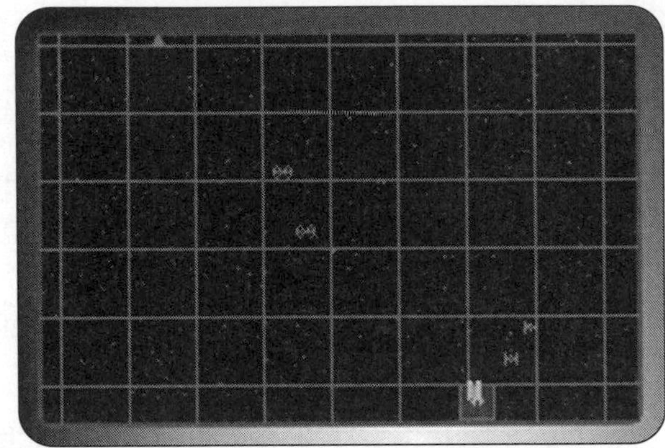

File Name: defend2

Mission Briefing

Guard the freighter *Sidral II* until the corvette *Frazier* has transferred its cargo. Your mission objective is to protect a transfer of contraband military materiel. This cargo comes to the Alliance from outlaw pirates and represents the latest in Imperial technology. The Star Destroyer *Immortal* is about 45 clicks away, but has already launched a TIE fighter and Bomber assault.

Farlander's After-Action Report

I went through the standard mission-start procedure, noticing that the *Frazier* and the *Sidral II* were less than a click from where we entered normal space. The *Immortal* had four three-ship groups of TIEs already closing in on us. The closest to us were two groups of TIE fighters—Alpha at four clicks and Beta at about eight clicks. Behind them were two groups of TIE Bombers—Gamma at 23 clicks and Delta at 29 clicks.

I ordered my wingman to attack the nearest enemy TIE fighter, *Alpha 1*, and then targeted the next for myself. I took out *Alpha 2* while keeping an eye on the message line. After we had eliminated Alpha and Beta, we

The CRV Frazier.

Assigning T/F Alpha 1 *to the wingman.*

turned to engage Gamma, which was now less than 12 clicks away. I knew that we couldn't let them get within torpedo range. The TIE fighters had succeeded in destroying one of the cargo containers, but the corvette and freighter were still untouched.

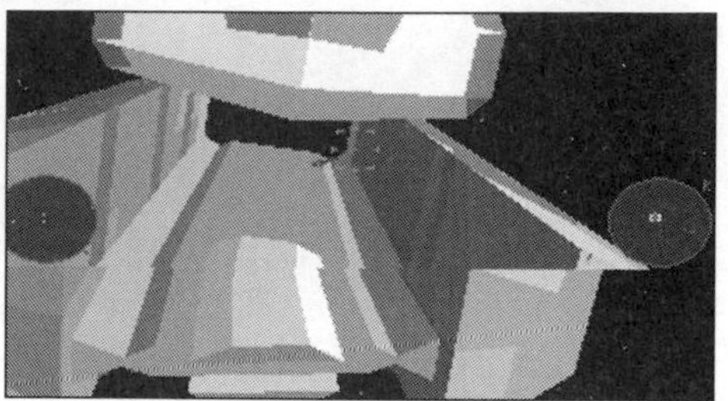

Flying over a freighter.

As we headed toward the Bombers, I switched to missiles. Also, I noticed that replacement waves for Alpha and Beta had been launched. While we were closing on our targets, I called up the *Frazier* and the *Sidral II* in the CMD, and assigned them to memory locations. I ordered my wingman to attack *Gamma 2*, and I took the leader. I fired as soon as I had a solid lock, then switched back to cannons and targeted *Gamma 3*. My wingman took care of *Gamma 2* with a missile, and we proceeded to attack Delta group using the same tactics.

After destroying Delta, we took up a position between our ships and the Star Destroyer, about eight to ten clicks from where they continued the cargo transfer. Here we could intercept the replacement waves from the *Immortal* without getting too far from our charges. As soon as the transfer was completed and our ships were safely into hyperspace, we headed home. This process occurred before the next assault wave could reach us.

C.O.'s Analysis

"You handled the mission well, captain," Lagrane told me. "However, there are a few comments I'd like to add. First, given the distance to the *Immortal*, you might have been able to eliminate some of the TIE fighters, even though you correctly targeted the Bombers as the primary threat. There was plenty of time between waves to shoot up the TIEs as well. You had missiles to spare, so you might have even used one or two on the TIEs that were attacking the cargo containers. If you noticed, T/F Beta was attacking the cargo containers, so only Alpha was specifically targeting you."

"I'll try and pick up on that next time, sir," I said.

"It's just some constructive criticism, Farlander. Don't take it wrong. You did a fine job. Fine job."

"Yes, sir. Thank you, sir."

Debriefing (Win Conditions)

The CRV *Frazier* must dock with the FRT *Sidral II*, and then both must escape into hyperspace.

"Who let them on this ship?" asked Raider.

"Who knows?" Naeco answered. "Come on. Let's go see what they want."

The leader was a tall, obese Calamarian whose tunic was military issue, covered with ornate commendations and battle patches, and whose face was scarred in three places. He wore a long cape and an iridescent headband that covered his bald head.

Surrounding the Calamarian were two Gamorreans who looked nervous and kept fingering the empty holsters where their blasters should have been. One Quarren stood silently by the leader's side, and also nearby was a human, who was dressed in the style of a Corellian, and started forward as we approached, seeming about to say something to us.

The portly Calamarian reached out a huge hand and grabbed the shoulder of the Corellian, who spun around angrily and then visibly calmed himself before retaking his place again.

"I am Tuz, the great trader," the Calamarian announced in a booming voice. "No doubt you have heard of me?"

He paused expectantly. We stared back, blankly.

"Well, no matter," he continued. "I've just delivered some prime Imperial timers and fusion shells. A few trinkets I came across in my travels."

"Probably defective," muttered Raider under his breath.

"What was that?" asked the Calamarian, gazing at Raider for a long moment as though searching for something he had lost. An uneasy silence ensued.

Finally, the Calamarian smiled, and said; "Stealing from the Imperials is thirsty work. . . ."

And Naeco responded, somewhat hesitantly; "O great Tuz. We would be honored if you and your friends would join us in the pilot's lounge."

Raider shot him a look, but Naeco just shrugged and whispered; "What's the harm? It might prove interesting."

After introducing ourselves, we led the Calamarian and his entourage to our familiar lounge, where we sat at one of the large tables in the back.

The pilot's lounge was really our ready room, but we spent so much time there that we had renamed it. It was a large area of the Calamarian ship, fitted with holo decks, tables, and some food dispensers that provided us with various snacks. We had made deals with the kitchen crew, and could get a wider variety of food sent over to us from time to time. Some of the pilots had fashioned a makeshift bar in one corner, which was tolerated though not condoned by the high brass.

Tuz sat at one end of the table, with the Quarren to his right and the Corellian to his left. The two Gamorreans stood behind the pirate, still looking uncomfortable. Naeco brought drinks for Tuz and his two lieutenants, and I figured that they would be excreting fluorescence by tomorrow. Nobody offered anything to the Gamorreans, whose eyes darted rapidly from one of us to the other.

"You're probably wondering why I donated all that nice Imperial technology to your Alliance," Tuz announced after tasting his drink and nodding to indicate his approval.

"Because you made a tidy profit?" suggested Naeco.

The Calamarian cocked his head to one side, staring at Naeco with one huge, unblinking eye—his left. I learned later that staring with the left eye was a way of showing surprise. On the other hand, if a Calamarian stared at you with his right eye, it was either a challenge to fight or an expression of love, depending on the circumstances.

"Actually, Captain, we made nothing on the deal at all."

"I find that hard to believe," stated Raider flatly. "The great Tuz giving away cargo? Not likely."

Tuz cocked his head three-quarters to the right, a defensive posture but not an outright challenge. "It seems that you have heard something of me, after all, Captain Raider?"

"Let's just say that we've met, and I found out you're a swindler and a cheat."

A Gamorrean suddenly lunged at Raider, his two ham-size hands swinging wildly. As I learned at that moment, Gamorreans would fight at the slightest provocation.

Raider ducked under the Gamorrean's attack with practiced ease and answered with a thunderous uppercut to the soft spot just under the creature's jaw. The Gamorrean fell backward, and Raider stood over him, shaking his hand and examining it for damage. Apparently there was no truly soft spot on a Gamorrean.

All this happened very suddenly, but the other Gamorrean was already on his way to attack. The Corellian was halfway out of his chair, and Naeco and I were about to rise to Raider's defense. The Quarren hadn't moved, and I suddenly noticed that the Gamorrean on the floor was smiling. There was nothing a Gamorrean liked more than a good fight.

Tuz raised his hand and everybody stopped.

"Friends. There's no need to be at odds. We're here to enjoy a simple drink with our new acquaintances from the Alliance." He turned to the Gamorreans and said; "Behave yourselves or I'll send you back to the ship."

"You handle yourself well, captain," he said, smiling in Raider's direction.

Raider slowly settled back into his seat, but his eyes were like coals, burning with anger. The Gamorreans looked disappointed.

Tuz continued.

"There was a time, Captain Raider, when I might have taken advantage of a gullible young trader and perhaps profited at his expense. But those times are long past. Now I am in the service of our common cause, although I don't wear the uniform you so admirably represent."

Raider was beginning to relax a little as the Calamarian spoke. Finally he grinned. "So it's 'let bygones be bygones' then, is it, Tuz?"

The trader grinned back hopefully, his hands spread, palms up. "As I said. We are on the same side."

"Are we to believe there's no ulterior motive for this change of heart?" Raider asked then.

The Quarren, who had to that moment done nothing to call attention to himself, leaned over and whispered something. Tuz then readjusted his headband and looked toward the Corellian on his left.

The Corellian, who was called Fortune, then spoke for the first time.

"Captain Tuz has been working for several months with the Alliance, under my supervision and that of Vice Admiral Wirriz, the quiet Quarren to my right. Captain Tuz has certain Imperial contacts that we have found . . . useful."

Now Raider looked even more dubious than ever. "You're not telling me that Tuz is doing all this for the sake of ideals?"

Fortune laughed and slapped Tuz on the back. The Calamarian winced but said nothing. "Let's just say that Captain Tuz has a very long and involved history with Admiral Ackbar, and that his participation in these undercover operations is not precisely voluntary."

It was interesting to observe how the tables had turned. Now, Fortune was in charge, and Tuz was the subordinate. The Quarren, however, remained silent and impassive, his only commentary consisting of an occasional rumbling that reminded me of the sound my stomach made after eating too much porf.

Tuz spread his hands wide in what I now saw was his characteristic pose of conciliation and said; "Commander Fortune is not entirely correct. I was, at first, a reluctant participant in this charade, but I have come to admire your commitment and dedication. I have no love for the Empire, after all."

He smiled at us all then, but it was hardly reassuring.

Raider looked doubtful, and even Fortune gave a short, staccato laugh. Finally, Fortune told us; "We will have to be departing soon. We've left some additional information with Commander S'man and Commander Blastwell, concerning an Imperial repair facility that is ripe for the taking."

He stood up, and we all followed his lead. We shook hands all around, except for the Gamorreans, of course, and ushered the pirates back to their ship, which was docked in Hangar Bay 4. As soon as we left the lounge, Tuz took over his role as leader and began a bombastic diatribe against "cheap Alliance negotiators" who wouldn't pay fair market value for such excellent cargo.

We watched their small freighter as it lifted on repulsor jets and floated out of the airlock. Raider stood rubbing his hand and shaking his head. "I wouldn't trust that Calamarian for an instant. He's as treacherous as they come."

Nobody responded, so I asked; "How's your hand?"

OP 2: Destroy Repair Dock

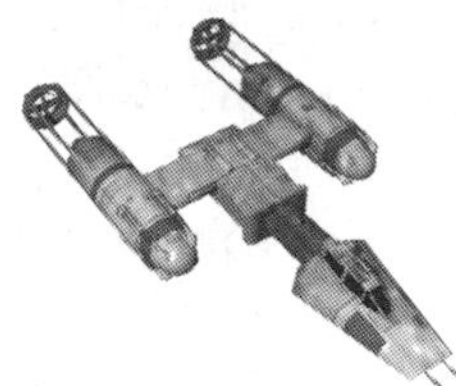

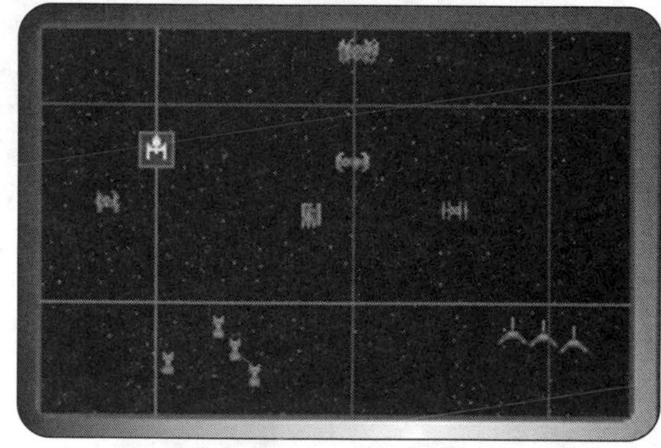

File Name: yraid

Mission Briefing

Assist your flight leader in destroying an Imperial Repair Dock and the surrounding ships. You are to attack an Imperial weapons supply and repair depot in order to cripple the Empire's ability to protect the Death Star. The Repair Dock is a converted freighter, and has a protective minefield surrounding it. An Imperial corvette is among the many vessels in the area.

Farlander's After-Action Report

I went through the standard mission-start procedure, noticing that the Imperial corvette was near the dock, and several other groups of ships were also nearby. Two groups, T/F Beta and T/B Gamma (two ships each), moved to attack us as we dropped out of hyperspace, so I

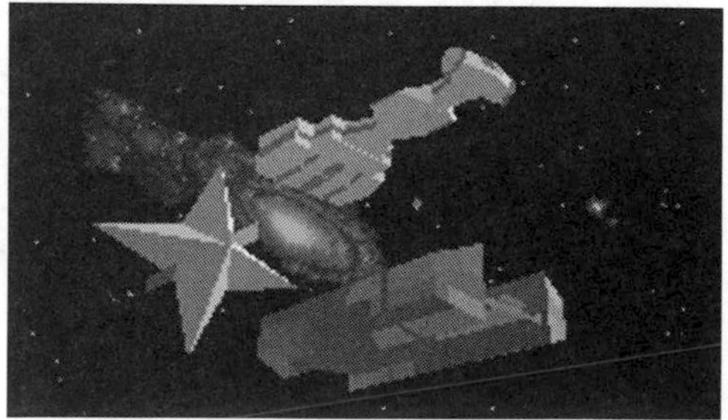

Freighter, corvette, and mine.

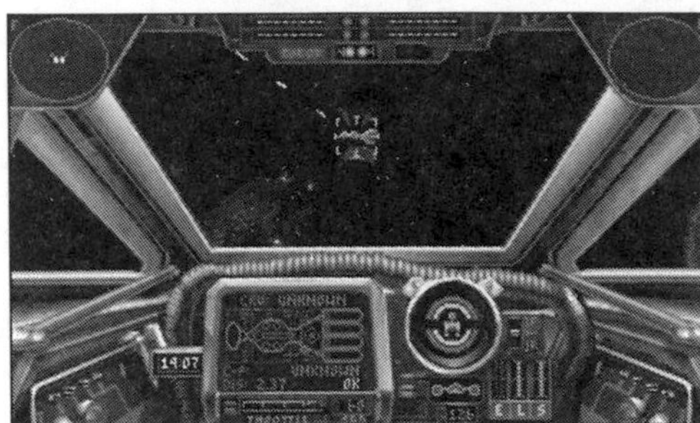

Targeting the corvette.

Going after the transports.

Coming up and under.

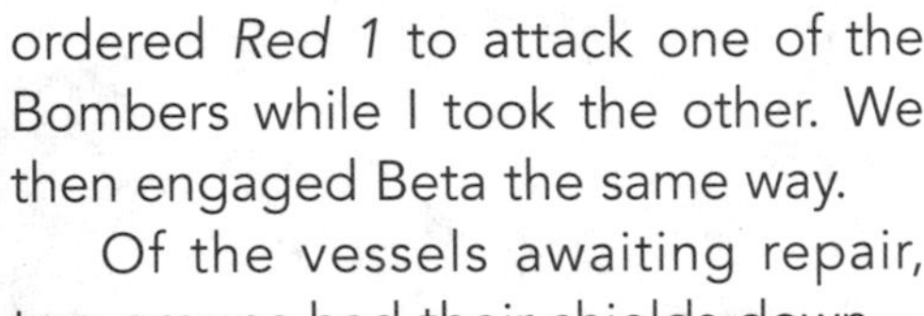

Heavy pursuit.

ordered *Red 1* to attack one of the Bombers while I took the other. We then engaged Beta the same way.

Of the vessels awaiting repair, two groups had their shields down—one group of four transports and one group of three shuttles. I ordered my wingman to attack the shuttles one after another while I took out the corvette and the minefield. I switched to torpedoes for the corvette and attacked it from just beyond the range of the mines. This maneuver also gave me some time to build my shields back up.

As *Red 1* moved to attack the Repair Dock, I headed toward a stationary group of three TIE fighters (Delta). While I was on the way toward Delta, an Imperial Frigate arrived and began launching TIE Interceptors and TIE Bombers. I broke off my attack on Delta to deal with the Bombers.

As soon as *Red 1* had destroyed the Repair Dock, he began heading for the jump point. I was concerned that I was being left to complete the mission alone, but I pressed on. Evading my pursuers as best I could, I destroyed the transports and continued on to a group of six stationary TIE Bombers (Zeta).

Occasionally, I would break off to dogfight with one of the Interceptors or Bombers when they made it easy for me. I noticed that every time I killed off a group, the Frigate would launch replacements, so I tried to rely on my shields and evasive maneuvers as much as possible. After I had eliminated T/B Zeta, I turned to engage the Interceptors and Bombers that were still on my tail. As soon as they were gone, I headed home. As I prepared to jump into hyperspace, R2 told me that another wave of Interceptors was launching.

C.O.'s Analysis

"Good mission, Farlander."

"Yes, sir. I could have used more help from *Red 1*, though, sir."

"He left a little too soon, didn't he?"

"He did, sir. I didn't feel that the mission was complete until the last of the Imperial ships was taken care of."

"We'll get *Red 1* on some teamwork simulations, captain. Don't worry."

"Thank you, sir. I sometimes get a little nervous out there all alone."

"Nervous?" he smiled. "You?"

I think I blushed. "Yessir. I don't mind having a little company out there."

"Don't blame you for that. We'll see what we can do."

Debriefing (Win Conditions)

TRN group Lambda, SHU group Omega, T/B groups Zeta and Gamma, T/F groups Beta and Delta, and the Repair Dock (FRT) all must be destroyed.

Mission Note: Pick targets for your wingman, but save the Repair Dock for last. The attack on it triggers the arrival of the Frigate. Also, although it is not a win condition, the corvette should be taken out as early as possible to reduce the chances of losing your wingman.

The Frigate and the player's flight group each have three possible start positions that vary the difficulty of the mission.

We flew many missions that seemed to lead nowhere. Lots of picket duty, watching planetary systems from a distance, or keeping tabs on the movements of certain ships the High Command suspected of involvement with the Death Star project. It was all routine.

We got new recruits every few days, and they had to be oriented and assigned. Some of them even managed to survive to become LTS on future missions. (LTS was our slang for Likely To Survive. You didn't learn what it meant until you were one.)

Namrhe and Omin-Oreh were two promising LTSs who had made it through a couple of tough dogfights. Namrhe was a nomad, having come originally from Bestine IV, where the Emperor had set up a high-security base and sent all of the small planet's population packing with promises of a "new and exciting home." The promises weren't kept, of course, and most of the people of Bestine IV had scattered to other systems.

Omin-Oreh came originally from one of the systems at the bottom tip of the Rim. He spoke softly and said little when he did speak. His deflection shooting showed great promise.

I chose both Namrhe and Omin-Oreh for what sounded like a routine escort mission. We launched our Y-wings at 0455 hours. By 0547, Namrhe was dead and Omin-Oreh was floating in a tank on Med Deck.

OP 3: CAPTURE MILITARY TRANSPORT

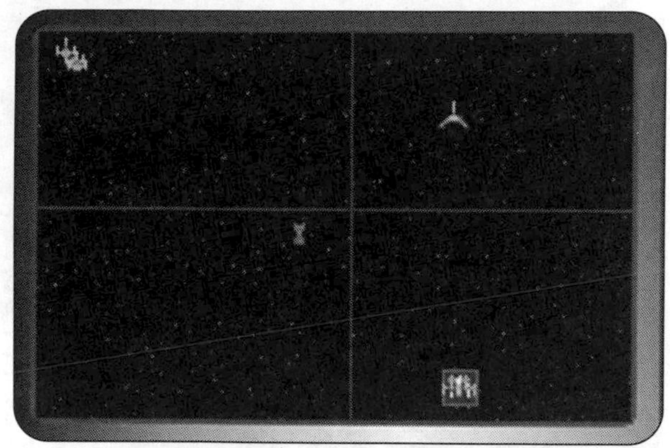

File Name: max14

Mission Briefing

Special operations forces have managed to sabotage a key Imperial military transport in order to cause its hyperdrive to fail. Now stranded, the transport is carrying military advisors who are connected to the Death Star project. Lead your Y-wing squadron to oversee its capture. An Alliance shuttle will deliver a commando team to board the transport, and you will be assisted by three X-wings from Blue Squadron.

Farlander's After-Action Report

After a standard mission-start procedure, I brought up the shuttle *Hunter* in the CMD and assigned it to memory. Then I targeted the enemy transport and flew in close enough to ID it, assigning it to memory as well. My shields and cannons had reached a full charge, so I reset the recharge rates to normal and went to full throttle.

ID the transport.

I decided to stay close to the shuttle in case of trouble, and, sure enough, about a minute into the mission, two three-ship groups of Imperial Assault Gunboats arrived (Mu and Rho). I queried the CMD for the nearest one and ordered my wingman to attack it. By the time the boarding party had captured the transport *Omicron*, I had destroyed three of the GUNs.

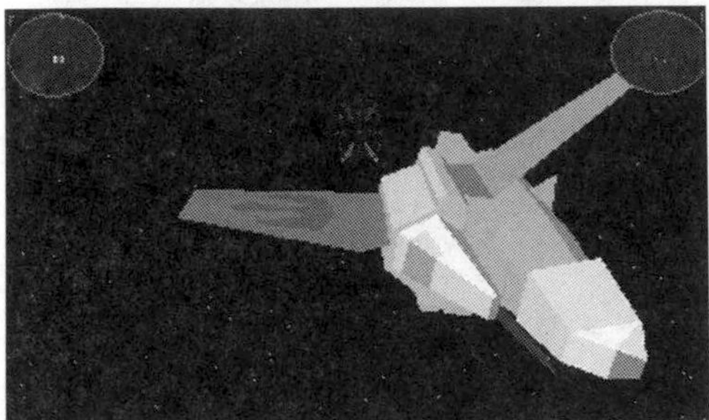

The Rebel shuttle.

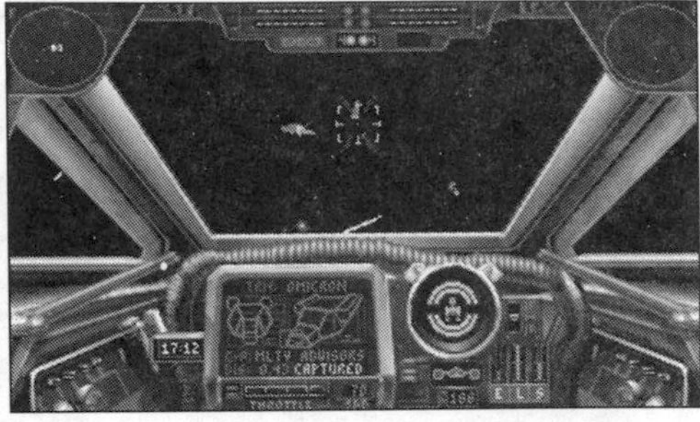

Guard the Omicron.

Shooting GUN Rho 3.

While I was fighting the GUNs, I had noticed X-W *Blue 1* getting hit pretty badly. I ordered him to head for home, and tried to keep the GUNs away while he prepared for the jump, but they ganged up on him, and I couldn't distract them all. *Blue 1* was destroyed just seconds before he could make it to safety.

The Alliance Frigate *Inad* arrived a moment later, so I turned back to the *Omicron,* staying close to keep the Imperials at bay. I destroyed another Gunboat, and saw that X-W *Blue 2* had been shot up also. *Blue 3* was gone as well, but I didn't see what happened. My wingmen, at least, remained in good shape.

Then my heart sank, as an Imperial Star Destroyer arrived a mere four clicks away. The *Inad* was still over 13 clicks distant, and the *Omicron* had more than ten clicks to go to reach it.

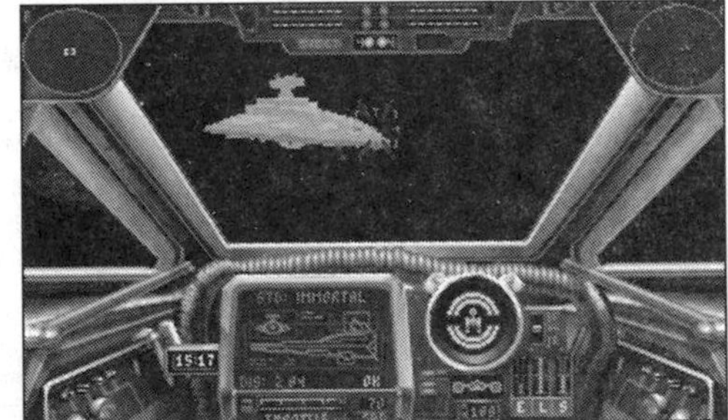

The Immortal *is very close!*

I decided to stick to the *Omicron* to make sure that it made it to the *Inad.* An Imperial transport dropped out of hyperspace near the *Omicron* and immediately moved to attack it, so I targeted it and switched to torpedoes. I selected dual-fire mode so that I could kill it as quickly as possible.

The Star Destroyer had launched a three-ship formation of TIE fighters from Beta Squadron. The GUNs and the TIEs kept after me, so I requested assistance as I kept on after the enemy transport. My torpedoes finally caught it after two near misses, but another transport arrived to take its place. I destroyed it and the one that followed, as both my wingmen were hit while trying to keep the enemy fighters off my tail.

When I was sure there were no more Imperial transports to worry about, I began dogfighting with the remaining starfighters. The Gunboats seemed to have endless replacements, so as soon as the *Omicron* was safely aboard the *Inad*, I hypered home.

C.O.'s Analysis

"You were quick to recognize the threat posed by the transports. In fact, all the enemy starfighters were preoccupied with attacking our starfighters and ignoring our shuttle and the captured transport. Not so the transports.

"It was a good thing you held on to your torpedoes, but you could have used some against the Gunboats to adjust the odds a little in your favor. You would have had to rely more on your wingman to assist against the enemy transports, though."

Debriefing (Win Conditions)

The TRN *Omicron* must be recovered.

Mission Note: If the GUNs arrive far enough away, you may want to try a head-on attack against them using torpedoes. Switch to dual-fire mode because the Gunboats are fairly tough. The Imperial transports are the greatest threat, and must be stopped quickly, so stay close to the *Omicron*.

Gart was a soft-spoken boy with jet-black, rather unruly hair, lazy eyes, a smile that was just a little too wide for his face, and a burning desire to be a starfighter pilot. He had good reflexes and took instructions well, and he loved our ships, which seemed deadly and sophisticated.

And he loved the Alliance, which had become his real home.

He devoted himself to his training, and I saw him emerge more than once from the darkness of the simulators with a look like he had been on some exotic and beautiful journey.

There were at least a dozen other duties to perform aboard the *Independence,* and opportunities in many departments, but for Gart, the youngest of the trainees, the only people who really existed were the pilots.

Gart had tried, twice, to qualify as a starfighter pilot, and though he was only 16 years of age, there was every indication that he would make a good one. Unfortunately, due to circumstances entirely beyond his control, it appeared he would be prevented from attaining his fondest dream.

When Gart was very young and still living with his family on Agamar, he had contracted a rare and, for most people, a harmless though incurable illness. The disease attacked the brain stem in a subtle way that left its victims with an outward appearance of perfect health. But the peculiar conditions involved in piloting a starfighter revealed the damage that had been done.

In simulators, Gart performed as well as any student, and better than most. In actual flight, however, his damaged brain stem caused him to suffer terrible pain behind the eyes and at the base of the neck, and his sense of direction became affected.

The loss of directional sense, called "disorientation syndrome," could come from a variety of things, but Gart's disease was one of the more obscure causes. For some time, the medics aboard the *Independence* couldn't diagnose the problem properly. When an extensive battery of tests finally revealed the illness, the medics told Gart and his commanding officers that under no circumstances would he ever be able to be a pilot.

For perhaps anyone else, that would have been that.

Except that Gart, whose single interest in life was to be a pilot, would simply not accept it. He dedicated every moment of his life, even, I think, in the subconscious world of his dreams, to proving them wrong.

Overcoming his natural shyness, he came to us, asked us questions, begged time from the instructors, and got himself into real-space simulators and finally, somehow, into fighters.

I doubt any of us could imagine the pain he endured, as his damaged brain stem retaliated against his efforts along his healthy nerve endings. But, remarkably, with unflinching determination, he gradually accustomed himself to the sensations.

Perhaps it was a medical miracle, but I think of it more as a testament to the sheer power of the mind: Gart became a pilot on his third try.

Even the most dubious of his instructors had to admit that he handled a starfighter not just well, but with an exceptional grace and certainty and precision no one had seen in a rookie in years. He was, perhaps, the best of us all; anxious to see the enemy, to fire his cannons in battle, and to return to the approbation of his fellow pilots.

Everyone respected him for his accomplishments, and Gart found, it seemed to his surprise, that he had friends, and even admirers.

Gart was sent to me, as I was now helping to orient new pilots to Red Squadron since Hamo was more and more involved in strategic planning and special missions that took him off-ship. Gart and I had a natural bond, being fellow Agamarians. We talked a great deal during those first few days, and I have never known anyone so single-minded and purposeful. Somehow, his concentration both attracted and repelled me.

I had taken Gart with me on a temporary assignment to the Cruiser *Defiance*, where I was sent to observe and train some new pilots. We were there only an hour when the attack came.

I had intended to take Gart slowly into action, to give him a milk run and sort of observe him while he eased into his new role. But suddenly we found ourselves in the thick of battle without any warning, and most of the experienced pilots stationed on the *Defiance* were on other missions. I needed him, and besides, if ever a pilot was ready for action, it was Gart.

OP 4: SCRAMBLE!

File Name: max17

Mission Briefing

Defend the Calamari Cruiser *Defiance* from a surprise attack by the Imperial Star Destroyer *Immortal*. This is a scramble mission. Your flight leader will lead your three-ship group out of the hangar bay. A pair of Blue Squadron's A-wings are already intercepting the attacking TIEs. The *Immortal* is nearly 16 clicks away, off the port side of the *Defiance*. The first wave of attackers is about 4 clicks off the starboard side, so you will exit the hangar directly toward them. A six-ship group of TIE Bombers (Gamma) is being led by a three-ship group of TIE Interceptors (Beta). Another six-ship flight of Bombers (Delta) has just left the *Immortal*.

Premission Note: Use the lowest detail level for this battle, because of the many ships (2 capital ships and 26 fighters) involved.

Farlander's After-Action Report

I went through the standard mission-start procedure with the following exception: I redirected shield power to the engines and reset the cannon recharge rate to maximum. I then transferred cannon power to the shields and targeted the nearest Bomber, *Gamma 1*. I Ordered my wingman to attack, then switched to torpedoes before selecting another Bomber for myself.

X-wings over the Defiance.

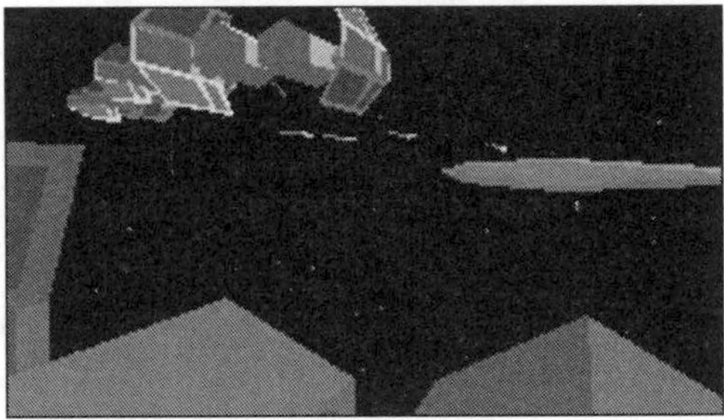

Bombers on the attack.

The Bombers had already launched their first salvo as my targeting computer began to acquire a lock. I fired as soon as possible, then saw that yet another six-ship group of Bombers (Alpha) had been launched from the *Immortal*.

As I closed in on T/B Gamma, I switched back to lasers and put the shield recharge rate back to normal. Hoping to force them to break off their attack, I began firing along the length of their formation. A few did turn about, but most kept going as I swung in behind them. I had to be careful when I fired—we were still so close to the *Defiance* that she was a wall against the sky, and I didn't want any of my shots to hit her.

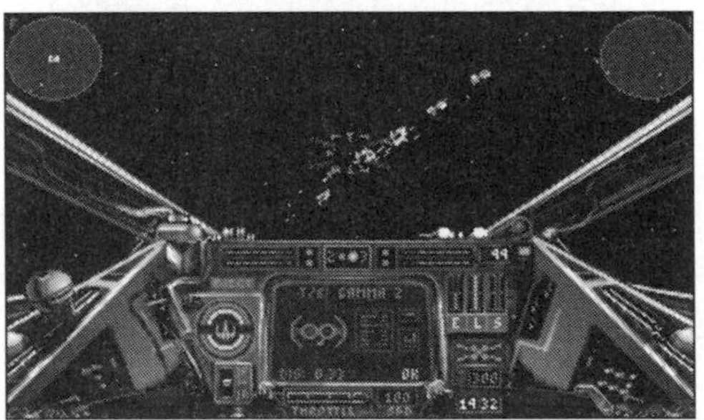

Targeting the Bomber formation.

The cruiser's gunners were doing an excellent job, but we knew that we couldn't let up for a second. I proceeded to search out the Bombers and ordered my wingman to go after them, and then I targeted others for myself. I chose to ignore the Interceptors for now. First, there were only a few of them, and anyway, their lasers weren't going to do much damage to the *Defiance*.

We continued to attack the TIE Bombers and were happy to see the *Immortal* jump into hyperspace. Our joy was to be short-lived, though, as she re-appeared off the starboard side of the *Defiance*. We were chasing down the last hull-damaged enemy starfighters when R2 reported the return of the Star Destroyer.

Protect the Defiance.

I decided to leave the remnants to the others and head off toward the *Immortal* on my own. The Star Destroyer soon began to launch TIE Interceptors (two groups: T/I Theta, three ships; and T/I Zeta, four ships) and then four more TIE Bombers (Beta). I targeted one of the Bombers and saw that A-W Blue and my wingman had come out to join me. T/B Beta began firing missiles at us, but we kept our shields up and avoided the missiles or absorbed them in our shields. Before long, the *Defiance* made it to safety, and we took that as our cue to disengage and hyper out.

C.O.'s Analysis

"It's a good thing Calamari cruisers are as tough as they are!" Lagrane said. "Even with all your efforts, this was a close one."

"I wasn't sure myself if we could hold them off long enough," I told him.

"You beat four-to-one odds, Farlander. You and the other pilots. Keep up the good work."

"I'll do my best."

"Oh, and Farlander?"

"Yes?"

"It's unusual to take a rookie out on this kind of mission. . . ."

"I know, sir."

"But I've studied his performance, and he did all right. Keep working with him, but, for the time being, try to keep him out of anything that serious."

"He is good, isn't he?"

Lagrane gave me one of his rare smirks.

"He's good enough for a rookie," he said. "Let's try and make sure he lives long enough to fulfill his potential."

Debriefing [Win Conditions]
The CRS *Defiance* must survive.

Mission Note: When the *Immortal* returns, it has two possible entrance points: one about ten clicks away and the other about five clicks away.

Gart was a happy spacer. He couldn't get enough of it, and, even after the mission was over, he had to talk about it, reliving every moment and savoring every cannon blast and every twisting, wrenching loop. You would never think, to hear him talk, that he had been ravaged by pain the entire time, and that he had forced it away by sheer willpower.

Still, it *was* a good mission he had flown; at times brilliant, in fact. Just maybe, I thought, Gart had made the leap from rookie to LTS.

For the next day, back on the *Independence* and with no missions scheduled, Gart followed me around most of the time. I didn't mind. It was uplifting to see how happy he was.

". . . and then I pulled out and pushed the stick hard. I came around and there he was, 30 degrees off my port laser. I fired and he just seemed to float into the beam and explode. It all happened so fast . . . but to me it was slow-motion. And then, this other TIE came . . ."

It was uncanny listening to Gart describe his experiences. He remembered every detail and seemed to know instinctively what to do in every situation. I could see that he would be one of the best pilots we had ever had. It was good to think of him in Red Squadron. Good pilots helped you stay alive.

Gart was in the holo film room, reviewing his mission. I was taking a breather, looking to see whether Raider or Naeco or one of the other pilots was up for a game of Horansi, but no one was around. I was just sitting and thinking about getting something to eat when Hamo appeared in the lounge.

"Keyan, we're on to something big."

"Hamo! Good to see you, too."

Hamo had been gone for several days. He tended to come and go frequently now, and rarely came on missions with us anymore, although technically he was still with Red Squadron.

"No, listen," he said earnestly. "You're going out on a really important mission. I've been working on this for a week. We think that we can grab some of the Death Star design team. I want you to fly a Y-wing. You ready to go?"

"Sure," I said. Not that the Y-wing was my favorite starfighter, but I had completed some good missions in one, and the commanding officers tended to remember those missions. "What do I have to do?"

OP 5: Intercept and Capture

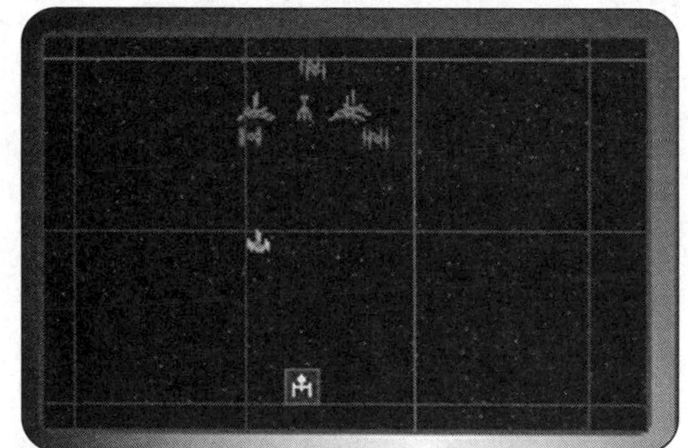

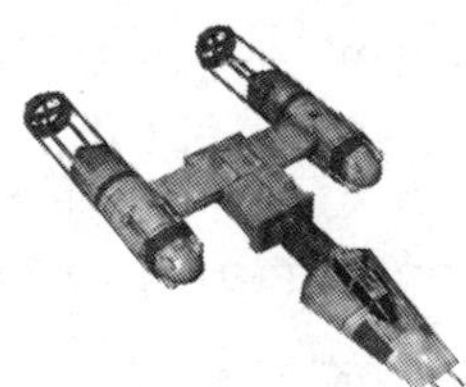

File Name: wyresc3

Mission Briefing

You will be part of an assault on an Imperial corvette carrying members of the Death Star design team. You are responsible for disabling the corvette while two X-wings from Blue Squadron draw off its starfighter escorts. The primary objective of the mission is to capture the design team members. You will pop up about four clicks from the target. It is being guarded by two groups of Assault Gunboats (Rho and Tau, two ships apiece) and three groups of TIE fighters (Alpha, Beta, and Gamma, two ships apiece). The corvette is headed toward the Star Destroyer *Immortal*, which is about 16 clicks away.

Farlander's After-Action Report

I went through the standard mission-start procedure, then targeted the corvette right away. I switched to torpedoes, and set my cannon and shield recharge rates to maximum. While the targeting computer was acquiring a lock, I switched to dual-fire mode and launched two salvos as soon as I had confirmation. I then targeted the nearest Gunboat, *Tau 2*, and fired a pair of torpedoes at it, following with a similar attack on *Tau 1*.

Next, I switched to cannons and targeted the nearest TIE fighter (*Beta 2*). I had to reset the shield recharge rate to normal and the cannon rate to one above normal to be effective in the dogfight. I destroyed the TIE and brought the corvette up in the CMD. Its shields were down. I began weaving toward it while slowly charging my cannons, switching to ions and selecting the dual-fire-linked mode.

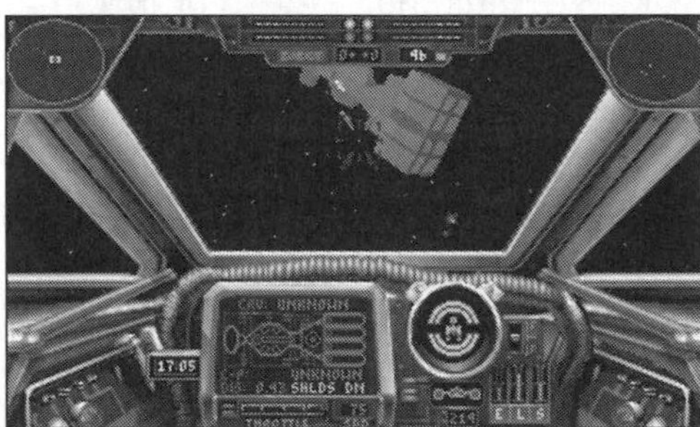

Coming in on the Imperial corvette.

The *Immortal* had launched two three-ship groups of TIE Interceptors by this time (Delta and Zeta), so I knew that I had to get the corvette disabled quickly.

When I had closed to less than one click from the target, CRV *Godar*, I opened up with the ion cannons. I reset the cannon and shield recharge rates to maximum and tried to make my attack from within the corvette's blind spot. It didn't take many blasts before it was disabled.

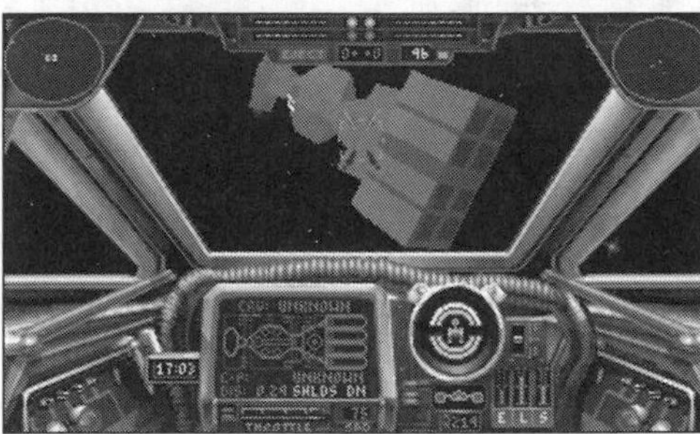

Firing away.

I was now three minutes into the mission. I knew that SHU *Rescue 1* would arrive about a minute later, so I targeted one of the remaining Gunboats, *Rho 2*. Because of their concussion missiles, they were more of a threat than the TIE fighters were. Besides, X-W Blue was doing pretty well against the TIEs. I destroyed *Rho 2* with lasers and proceeded to attack and destroy *Rho 1* in the same way.

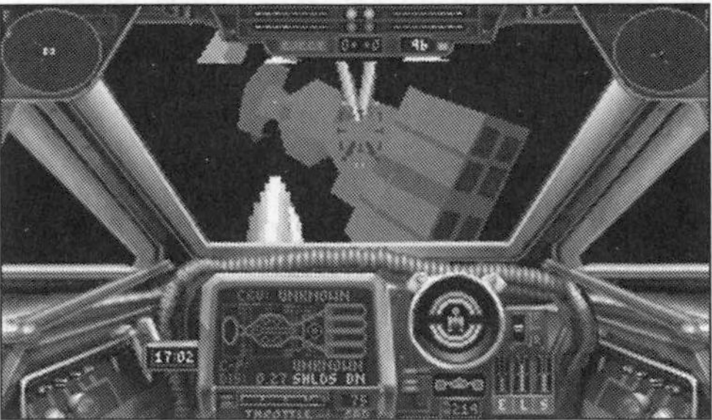

Using ion cannons to disable the ship.

I queried the CMD for the next-nearest enemy fighter, and targeted T/F *Gamma 1*. After that, it was T/I *Delta 2*, still some three clicks away.

Dogfighting TIE Interceptors is a real challenge in a Y-wing, but I was confident that X-W Blue and I could prevent any of the Interceptors from getting past us to interfere with the Attack Team, which had by now boarded the *Godar*.

I redirected my shield power to the engines and set the cannon recharge rate to maximum so that I could keep up a little better. I had to remember to transfer energy from the cannons to the shields every few seconds, but that wasn't much of a problem.

Finally, the Attack Team had secured the Imperial design team on-board *Rescue 1*. A little while after they had escaped into hyperspace, I disengaged from the dogfight and headed back toward the *Godar*. I wanted to destroy it before leaving the area. One Interceptor (T/I *Zeta 1*) was quite persistent in chasing after me, so I turned about for one last dogfight. When it was over, I proceeded to destroy the *Godar*, and then I hypered home.

C.O.'s Analysis

"You did it again, Captain Farlander," Lagrane told me.

"Sir?" I said, not quite sure what he was getting at.

"Once again, you showed an instinct for the mission that let you take the best approach. The Gunboats were, in fact, the primary danger to the shuttle. Eliminating them first made the rest of the battle that much easier.

"Just as a matter of policy, it's a good idea to identify the greatest threat and attack it first. This strategy ensures that your battles will get easier as you go, and it is also effective psychologically. Your opponents see their toughest fighters defeated first, and they become demoralized. Remember, most of the battle is psychological in the first place. If your opponents believe that they are going to be beaten, often they will *allow* themselves to be beaten!"

Not that I minded, but Lagrane seemed unusually philosophical today.

Debriefing (Win Conditions)

The SHU *Rescue 1* must dock with the CRV *Godar*, and then escape into hyperspace.

We pilots tended to spend most of our free time in our own lounge, but sometimes we would venture out into the common areas of the *Independence.* Several large concourses of the Calamarian cruiser were devoted to supporting the crew, which, when the ship was fully staffed, numbered more than 5,000.

The *Independence* was almost like a small city, with various zones and support services roughly located in four quadrants of the ship. Much of the planning and navigation was performed in the bow quadrant, but pilots liked to be close to their craft, and our lounge was somewhat aft of amidships. When we ventured out of our specific area, we often found ourselves in the aft quadrant.

Time was artificially synchronized aboard the ship to coincide with the light and dark cycles of our most recent planetary outpost. Naeco and Raider and I took Gart to Lucky Lower 13 during one of the night shifts.

All the Calamarian ships had once been pleasure craft, converted to war machines in support of the Alliance, and Lucky Lower 13 had once been some kind of ballroom (although I have never actually seen a Calamarian or a Quarren dance). It was a meeting place for many of the crew who worked in the engineering and administrative departments. At any rate, the cavernous room was darkened to accommodate the large segment of Quarren clientele it catered to, and tables and chairs fashioned from some faintly luminous material glowed diffusely pink in the dusk.

We sat at one of the glowing tables and surveyed the room. A Quarren came to the table carrying a flat, empty tray stuck tight to one suckered hand. We ordered some non-intoxicants because we were all on active duty, and then took up surveying the room.

A fighter pilot rarely sat alone for long, and we were counting on that. Soon we had attracted a small crowd of curious crew members, and had consented, with minimal prompting, to regale them with combat stories. Pilots were celebrities on the ship, and with good reason.

We risked our lives every time we flew a mission, and most of the crew had never saw a laser blast, or smelled the peculiar oily scent of an X-wing cockpit, or felt the jolt of a concussion missile striking shields. Most of them only went about their duties with the sameness and predictability of peacetime work. We were objects of admiration, curiosity, and wonder—which was why we often kept to ourselves.

But tonight we wanted Gart to enjoy the attention he deserved for having become a pilot. We wanted to see him grow up a little, have some fun, loosen up. Anyway, it was Naeco's idea.

Before long we had managed to maneuver Gart between two attractive young women who worked in computer operations. He was obviously nervous and said little, squirming somewhat uncomfortably as they plied him with questions about being a pilot and all the danger and excitement of combat. We all encouraged him, telling the women what a special pilot he was, and generally making the situation worse.

When I finally made my excuses and prepared to retire, Gart rose and made to accompany me. One of the young women looked disappointed, and I said; "You stay, Gart. Have some fun."

Then I leaned over and whispered to him; "The one on the right likes you. There's more to life than starfighters, you know."

But Gart was one of a kind. He gave me a blank look, grinned, and rubbed his hand through a wavy shock of hair. "I'll just go back with you, sir. If you don't mind."

"Sorry, girls," I said with a sigh. "I guess you'll just have to wait for another night."

They laughed, and tried to cajole us both into staying, but I was thinking of Lynia, and I suspect that Gart was thinking of X-wings. At any rate, we left the young women in the more than capable company of Raider and Naeco.

OP 6: DESTROY IMPERIAL BASE

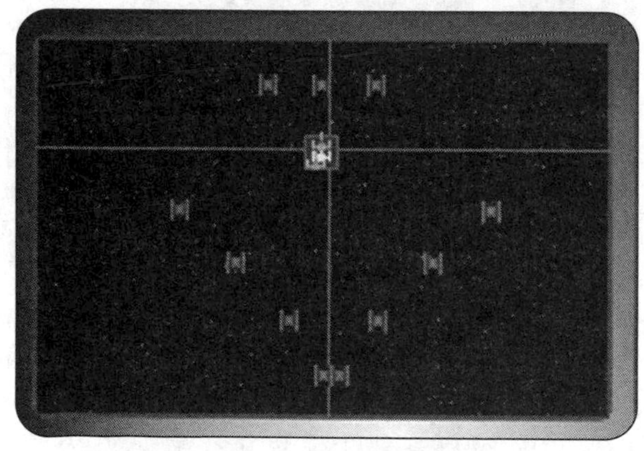

File Name: larry1

Mission Briefing

Lead an assault on the Imperial base near Kalla VII, and destroy all equipment and supply ships you find there. Your three-ship group of X-wings will come out of hyperspace less than four clicks from a large Imperial base. The base consists of 11 cargo containers protected by a large minefield. There are 32 mines. We have reason to believe that at least two Imperial freighters may arrive during the raid. Speed is essential, since the Imperial Frigate *Priam* is in this sector with orders to respond to any Rebel attacks.

Farlander's After-Action Report

I went through the standard mission-start procedure, except that I ordered a full stop and reduced my throttle to zero. This way, we could charge up our shields fully while planning our initial attack run. The cargo containers that made up the base were arranged in the outline of an arrowhead—three along the base and four along the two sides.

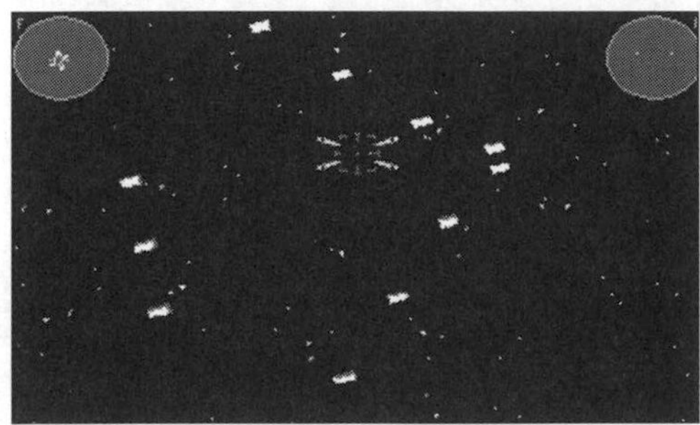

Containers in an arrowhead formation.

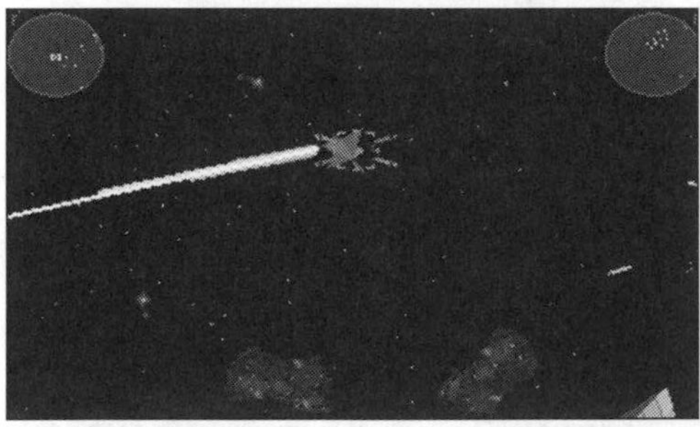

Shooting a mine.

I ordered my wingmen to attack one of the three containers along the "bottom" of the arrowhead. Meanwhile, I would take out the minefield. I went to full throttle with my cannons at full recharge and shields at normal. I set my firing configuration to dual-fire mode even though mines need only one hit to be destroyed—the wider spread would increase the odds of a hit.

If it could be said that an X-wing has a weakness, I'd have to say that it is in the kind of "target" shooting you must perform in clearing a minefield. I hate to waste cannon energy, but I also hate to waste time. I felt that this was the type of mission for which a Y-wing would be much better suited, but Red Squadron's Y-wing group had taken some bad losses recently, so we were in X-wings.

As I proceeded through the minefield, I kept up a constant transfer of power from the cannons to the shields. Every so often, I rebalanced the shields as well. Also, whenever R2 signaled that my wingmen had destroyed a container, I assigned them a new target.

As soon as I had destroyed all the mines, I reduced my throttle to one-third and started in on the containers myself. We had destroyed more than half the base when two freighters popped up out of hyperspace. I targeted one and ordered my wingmen to attack it, and then I targeted the other and switched to torpedoes. I selected dual-fire mode and launched all six as soon as I had a lock.

I then switched back to cannons and targeted the first freighter again. The three of us proceeded to destroy it in short order. We continued our assault on the base, and had just finished destroying it when the FRG *Priam* arrived. One of my wingman was killed, rammed by the FRG as it decelerated from its hyperspace jump. It was horrific to witness, and there was nothing I could do. My remaining wingman and I escaped into hyperspace.

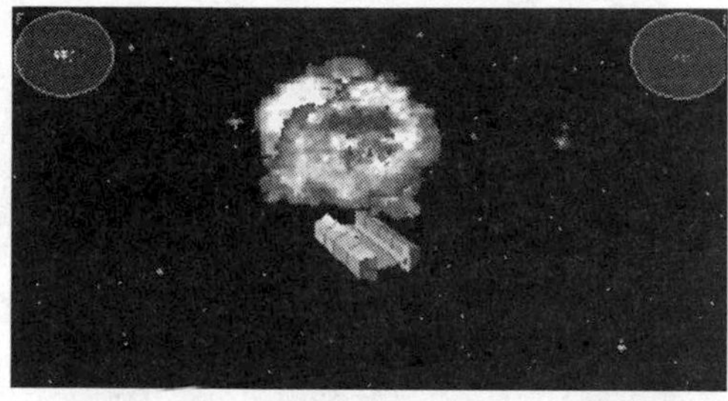

Nice explosion.

C.O.'s Analysis

Captain Farlander was a no-show at the debriefing. However, the mission went very well. Holding on to the torpedoes to use on the freighter was good anticipation. Tough luck with the wingman who died in a rather bizarre accident. Recommend Farlander for evaluation and psyche work-up.

— Lagrane

Debriefing [Win Conditions]

FRT group Diputs and CON groups Yar, Enna, and Evad all must be destroyed.

Mission Note: FRT Diputs and FRG *Priam* have three different starting positions to vary the difficulty of this mission. The farther away they are when they arrive, the easier the mission should be.

Later, alone in the holo film room with all the lights turned down, completely isolated from everyone, I replayed the mission holo a dozen times. Part of me still denied that it was real.

Finally, I had to accept that Gart was dead.

After returning to the *Independence*, I had walked numbly from the hangar, my legs moving with wooden, repetitive motions that seemed completely separated from my consciousness. I had no thoughts that I was willing to acknowledge, even to myself. Only a dumbstruck refrain: "He's dead. Gart is dead."

I couldn't quite believe it—couldn't *comprehend* it—however many times it went through my head.

I had seen so many pilots shot. Some had survived; most had died. But none had died as senselessly as Gart.

In such a short time, Gart had become almost like a brother to me—a younger brother for whom I had become responsible. He couldn't be gone. His death was not only a personal tragedy for me, but, I felt, a personal *failure.*

In the darkness, I wept for Gart, for myself, and, I think, for all those who had come before us. I was tired; worn out. My reserves failed me. In my grief, I fell into a deep, exhausted sleep.

I dreamed that I stood on a vast plain. Thin, irregular bands of smoke or gas floated a few feet above the ground. There was nothing else. The horizon was lit by an opalescent crimson glow, cut across by long, horizontal strands of blackness, as though I stood within a giant gemstone. The colors around me pulsated slowly and rhythmically.

At first, I thought I heard Gart speaking to me, but soon I realized that it was not his voice. It was a soothing voice. It helped ease my pain. It instructed me to seize control of my life, to use my power to help others. The voice told me how easy it was to achieve power. Power to do as I pleased, to win the war, to defeat my enemies, to avenge Gart's senseless death. It was a good voice.

It told me, finally, who I was.

I awakened, hours later, groggy and disoriented. I got up stiffly from the chair and walked slowly to my cabin, careful not to meet anyone along the way. I felt the passages ahead of me, mentally scanning for any intruding beings, and walked on only when no one was about. I felt strange, my dream only half remembered.

The next day I awoke refreshed, with no trace of grief or disorientation, and my dreams completely forgotten. My comm was flashing, and I saw an order to head back to medical. What for, I wondered.

I made my way back to the Med Deck and reported as ordered. An orderly made me sit and wait until one of the droids could see me.

Soon I was ushered into a cubicle with a psyche droid. I could see a holo recorder in the corner.

"Captain Farlander. I trust you are well."

"Well enough," I answered. "How are you today?"

"We are here to evaluate your fitness for duty, Captain Farlander. Please tell me about your last mission."

I thought about the question a moment. What did the machine want to know?

"It was successful," I answered.

The droid nodded its head. "And nothing unusual happened?"

"Unusual? No . . . Nothing unusual."

After a momentary silence, the droid asked, "And how do you feel about the death of Flight Cadet Gart?"

Ah. So that was it. Didn't they understand anything?

"He died in the line of duty. It was really too bad, but it seems a lot of us die every day. Learning to live with that is part of the war."

The machine nodded again, and seemed to consult something inside itself, because the silence lasted several long seconds. Finally it said; "Thank you, captain. You may go now."

"That's all?" I asked.

"You may go now," the droid repeated.

I left the Med Deck and headed for the ready room. Raider was already there, sitting with a couple of the newer pilots. Omin-Oreh was there, freshly out of the tank and looking none the worse. So was Captain Marskan of Blue Squadron. As I walked into the room, their conversation halted abruptly.

Raider looked up and said; "Damn shame about Gart."

The others nodded sympathetically in agreement.

"Yeah. Well, he probably shouldn't have been out there anyway," I said, helping myself to a strong cup of red Calamarian C-tea. (We thought of it as C-tea, but it really was sea tea, which came from the vast oceans of Calamari.)

"But you know very well he was . . ."

"Only the strong will survive, Raider. You know that. Maybe Gart never belonged out there. That's all there is to it."

Raider sort of froze, his mouth half-open. He stared a moment, then turned to Marskan and asked; "So . . . How's morale over at Blue Squadron?"

I drank my tea in silence. Even Raider didn't understand. I got up and left them with a perfunctory "See you later."

I walked over to Ops and found S'man. He was busy looking over some reports on the holo, but quickly closed the files as I barged in on him.

"Commander."

"Ah, Captain Farlander." S'man was all smiles. "What can I do for you?"

"I want to go out today. I'm looking for an assignment."

The commander gave me an expression practically identical to Raider's.

"It's not exactly common for you pilots to come asking for assignments, Farlander. Don't we work you hard enough?"

"Actually, no," I told him.

"Well . . . We have several operations going out today. One of them is quite important, but of course you aren't scheduled for it. . . ."

The commander seemed to be implying that that was all, but I had other ideas. It was my duty, the voice in my head was saying, to take these missions; so that other pilots would be safer; so that the Alliance itself would be safer.

I knew that S'man was about to ground me. I really didn't know why, but I knew that it had something to do with the psyche droid and the reports he had been reading.

"I think I would be ideal for this mission," I told him, filling the words with the force of my will. Somewhat to my surprise, he responded; "Yes, come to think of it, you would be ideal. Report to Briefing Room Three at 0200 hours."

"I'll be there, sir." I saluted and left. Looking back as the door irised closed behind me, I saw the commander rubbing his forehead, a slight look of confusion on his face.

OP 7: DESTROY PRIAM'S ESCORT

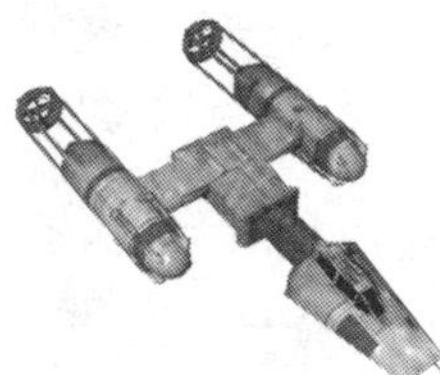

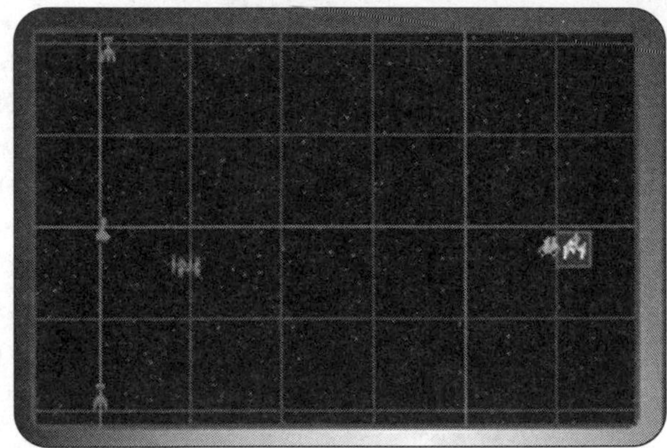

File Name: larry2

Mission Briefing

You'll lead a flight of two Y-wings, assigned to eliminate the Frigate *Priam's* escorts, leaving the ship vulnerable to capture. The *Priam* is less than nine clicks directly in front of you. Two corvettes have been assigned to protect it from raiding starfighters and are circling about three clicks from the Frigate. A three-ship TIE fighter group (Alpha) is also on patrol in the area. The *Priam* is surrounded by 18 mines.

Farlander's After-Action Report

I went through the standard mission-start procedure, while noting that there was a corvette stationed on either side of the *Priam.* I chose to target the one on the right, then ordered my wingman to attack it, as well. As we closed, I switched to torpedoes and selected dual-fire mode. Meanwhile, A-W Blue intercepted T/F Alpha, killing *Alpha 1* and *Alpha 2* on the first pass. When *Alpha 3* was destroyed, a replacement wave was launched from the *Priam.*

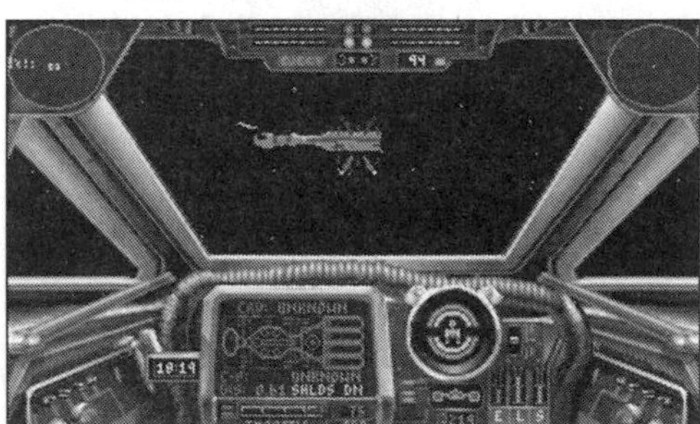

Approaching a corvette.

As soon as I had a solid lock on my target, I fired a pair of torpedoes, and so did my wingman. I then switched back to cannons to finish it off. I made my final approach through

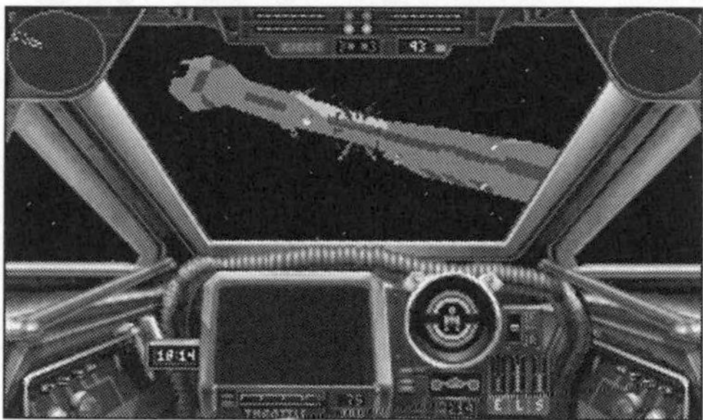

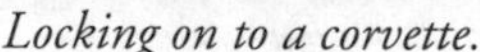

Locking on to a corvette.

Passing by the Priam.

the corvette's blind spot, but came in a little high, and took several hits myself before finishing the ship. I noticed that two more three-ship groups of TIEs had been launched (Beta and Gamma), and saw A-W *Blue 1* break up in a head-on pass with two of them. The pilot was later rescued.

Next, I brought up the other corvette in the CMD and ordered *Red 2* to attack. As I worked my way toward it, I engaged some of the TIEs, killing one. *Red 2* had been occupied with several TIEs, and as of yet had been unable to attack the assigned target.

Another corvette dropped out of hyperspace, accompanied by an Imperial transport. I continued to press forward toward the second corvette and switched back to torpedoes. I was already in range, so as soon as I had a lock I fired all six of my remaining torps as fast as the launcher would let me. Meanwhile, the third corvette and the transport were heading directly for the *Priam.*

Because the transport was moving faster, I targeted it next, switching to cannons to make an attack run, and passing close enough to ID it.

I had begun to make this technique a habit; identifying a particular ship and its contents helps me make better decisions about which craft to attack and when. It was loaded with supplies, so I circled around and finished it off.

Next, I turned my attention to the third corvette. After I had it targeted, I ordered my wingman to join me in attacking it. By luck, I found myself already in this one's blind spot. It didn't take long to finish it off, and we got the Mission Complete message soon afterward. Except for a handful of TIEs and a small minefield, the *Priam* was looking pretty vulnerable. We disengaged and prepared to hyper home.

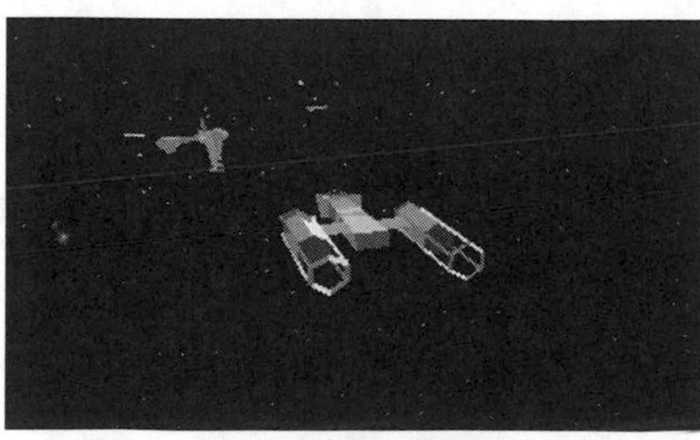

The Priam *is looking pretty vulnerable.*

C.O.'s Analysis

"What were you doing out there, Farlander?" Lagrane was angry. "I gave *specific* orders that you were to report to the medics for evaluation."

"Yes sir," I said. "I did. And as you can see, sir, I'm fine."

The commander looked me in the eyes, staring me down, and I returned his stare with a calm, open expression. Finally, he sighed and said; "Other than losing *Blue 1*, and that was his fault, it was a very good mission. I'll grant you that. But I want you to take some time off now, captain."

"I don't need to take any time off, commander," I said, slowly.

Lagrane seemed to shift before my eyes. It was as though I could see his mind phasing to a new state.

"You don't need to take any time off," he repeated, his eyes somewhat distant.

"I need to go out and help capture the *Priam*," I said.

"Yes. Good idea. Go out and help the Y-wings of Gold Squadron. Get going now, Farlander. What are you waiting for?"

Debriefing (Win Conditions)

CRVs *Dar Es I*, *Dar Es II*, and *Dar Es III*, and also TRN *Omega* all must be destroyed.

I rushed from Commander Lagrane's office to the hangar. Gold Squadron's Y-wings were already out of the airlock, so I reported to the duty officer quickly, signed out an A-wing, strapped in, and did a quick system checkout as I fired up the repulsors and floated the starfighter toward the hatch.

I was feeling pretty good. I felt no fatigue. My mind was clear and strong. I found myself wondering why I had taken so long to realize my power, to understand the Force. Why had I been so afraid of it? With the Force, I could do anything. I looked forward to killing more TIEs. For Gart, I thought. For the Alliance.

OP 8: Capture the Frigate Priam

File Name: larry3

Mission Briefing

Provide cover for both waves of Y-wing groups as they disable the Imperial Frigate *Priam.* Rebel commandos will then board and capture it. You are to advance ahead of Y-W Gold and clear the minefield for them. You will drop out of hyperspace less than four clicks from the target. There are eight mines left around the *Priam.*

Farlander's After-Action Report

As I went through the standard mission-start procedure, the targeting computer detected a three-ship group of TIE fighters (Alpha) launching from the *Priam.* I decided to worry about the mines later, and deal with the fighters first.

I queried the CMD for the nearest one and targeted *Alpha 2.* T/F Alpha was making a head-on attack on Y-W Gold, so I edged out to the right and made a flank attack against them. I had planned to disrupt the TIEs attack run, but was less successful than I had hoped. As they turned to follow the Y-wings, however, I was able to get on *Alpha 2's* tail and destroy him, and I proceeded to take out *Alpha 3* and then *Alpha 1* in short order.

Getting on Alpha 2's *tail.*

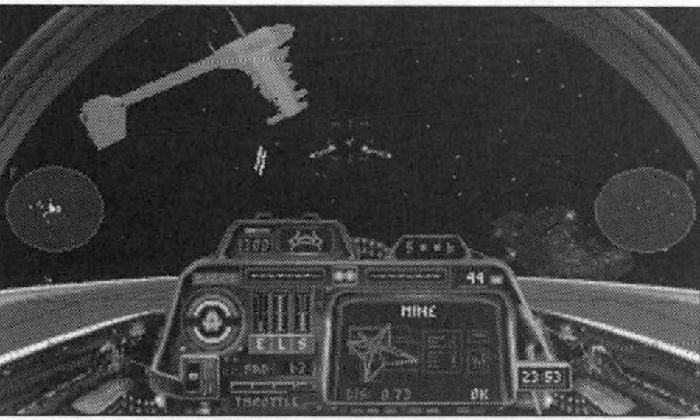

Clear out the mines.

Making my way toward the *Priam,* I took aim at the nearest mine. I had my cannons at maximum recharge, and kept up a constant transfer of power from the lasers to the shields. Y-W Gold was firing ion cannons at the Frigate, and ignoring both the ship's return fire and the minefield. I knew that I would have to be quick.

As the last mine of the field came into my sights, a TIE Bomber launched from the Frigate. My task with the mines completed, I rapidly brought T/B Beta up in the CMD, switching to missiles since it was almost 1.5 clicks away. I then boosted the shield recharge rate to maximum to bring my speed down. My first missile sailed wide of the target, but I had kept tracking the Bomber, and I quickly loosed another which scored a hit.

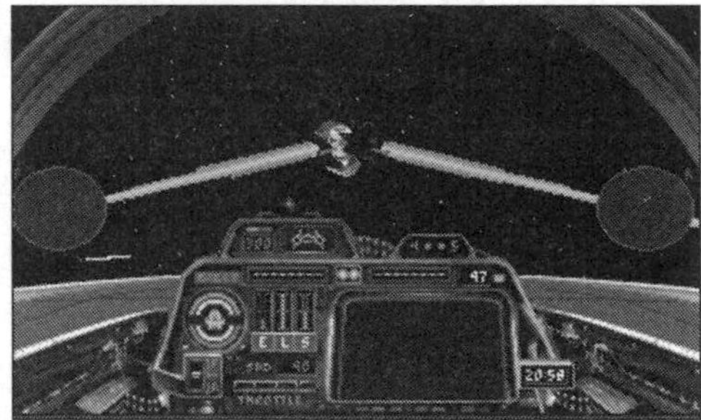
Blasting a Bomber.

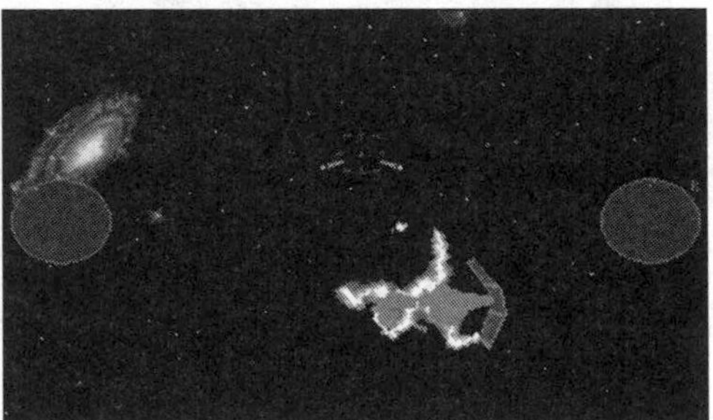
Death of a TIE Bomber.

After that T/B's destruction, another was launched, and I destroyed the newest arrival with a missile, as well. I had taken a few hits from the *Priam* while dogfighting close to it, so I decided to put some distance between me and those Imperial gun crews. While I spiraled out, I realized that no more TIEs had been launched, so I figured that that was probably it for the *Priam's* starfighters.

I turned about and targeted the *Priam* while selecting missiles in dual-fire mode. I fired the rest of them at the Frigate to help bring down its shields and aid the Y-wings. So far, two Y-wings had been lost.

After unloading my missiles, I noticed that my shields were getting thin, and once again I decided to disengage for a moment to recharge. As I turned around for another attack run, this time with lasers, I saw that the Frigate's shields were failing. I began to pour fire into it while Y-W Gold's remaining ships barraged the target with their ion cannons. With the shields down, the ions soon had the desired effect.

It was all over now, but we couldn't be sure that the Empire wouldn't send reinforcements. The second wave of Y-wings from Gold Squadron came in as the first wave returned to base. Seeing that the Frigate was already disabled, the second unit turned around and left. As the commando teams and Rebel crew came in and boarded the *Priam*, I began to circle the area. I continued to patrol until I saw that they had successfully captured the enemy ship. They took it into hyperspace as soon as they had control, and I followed them out.

C.O.'s Analysis

Lagrane was pleased.

"You did a good job on the Bombers, captain. Good job. Your performance was excellent. Very efficient. Thanks to your efforts, our losses were far smaller than anticipated. Take a break, Farlander. You've earned it."

Debriefing (Win Conditions)

The FRG *Priam* must be boarded.

Mission Note: The win condition for this mission should have been "must be recovered," a small loophole that doesn't usually become a factor.

As I left Lagrane's office, I reviewed the mission in my mind, and realized that I was beginning to reach out toward my opponents. The voice of the Force inside me was teaching me. I could almost take control of a TIE pilot and force him into my sights. I couldn't quite do it yet, but I thought that eventually it would come to me. Then, I could protect our pilots and craft almost through shear force of will: No one would get by me.

I decided to visit the lounge and see who was around. I saw Raider and a bunch of the newer pilots. Speedy was there. I hadn't seen the Sullustan pilot in a while. But as I walked up to Raider's table, he suddenly got up and began to walk away.

"Raider, where you going?" I asked.

"I've got some things to do," he said coolly, adding; "See you later."

"Wait," I said. "You don't want to go now." I didn't want Raider to leave, so I decided to make him stay.

He hesitated, just a moment, and then said; "See ya later, Farlander," and turned away.

I felt an intense frustration surge up in me, and unleashed a mind blast at him. I didn't even know that I was doing it.

Raider staggered a moment and then straightened himself and looked me in the eye. It was the old Raider. The one I had first met. Dangerous.

"Leave me alone, Farlander. I don't know what you're up to, but I don't want anything to do with it." Then he left.

Confused, I walked over to the bar and grabbed a drink at random. I don't really think that I was fully conscious of my actions. Then I sat at the table with Speedy and the new pilots.

"What's gotten into him?" I asked, laughing. "Must've eaten some bad porf or something."

The other pilots laughed, but Speedy said; "He was just fine until you got here, captain."

I shrugged my shoulders in an exaggerated gesture of bemusement and then asked; "Where you been, Speedy? Haven't seen you around."

"Oh, they took me for special training, because I'm Sullustan," he said proudly. "They want me to work in reconnaissance. Because of my navigational skills, I guess."

"Great," I said. "Maybe you won't get shot at so much."

The Sullustan blinked a couple of times, his dark, oversized eyes reflecting an inverted, fisheye view of the lounge behind me. I found myself thinking, quite incongruously, how a Sullustan could be used as a mirror to watch your back while you talked to him. I turned my attention to the other pilots. I already knew a few of them. There were a couple of new ones as well. They all watched me with something akin to awe. I had a pretty good reputation, and newer pilots often seemed to treat me with some deference. In the past, I had always been embarrassed by their admiration, but now I saw it as only appropriate. I smiled.

"You know, our mission is blessed by the Force itself," I told them. "We oppose a great evil. Anyone can join in the power."

They all looked at me with wonder. I could see that they were captivated by what I was saying, and the effect was intoxicating. Only one of them seemed to have a questioning look; it was Casal Marskan, younger brother of Captain Marskan from Blue Squadron.

"What are you talking about, sir?"

"The Force is the ultimate power. With it, you can destroy your enemies. Just open yourself to it, let it guide you, and you'll be unbeatable."

"Is that your secret, sir?" asked Marskan. "I mean, it's well known that you've never lost a ship or failed a mission."

"Yes. The Force is the secret. Let it guide you. Listen for the voice inside that tells you about the power. It's all there. You don't really have to do anything but pay attention."

I stayed with the pilots, talking, and at the same time formulating a new idea. What if the Alliance had an entire squadron of pilots guided by the Force? How could the Empire oppose them? We would be unstoppable. I could see the pilots listening to me, believing in me, and in their own potential. It felt good.

A few days later, we received word that two of our corvettes had been captured. I was asked to head a team of X-wings to support a recapture and rescue mission. I chose the younger Marskan and another of my 'followers;' Horodi.

OP 9: CAPTURE ETHAR I AND II

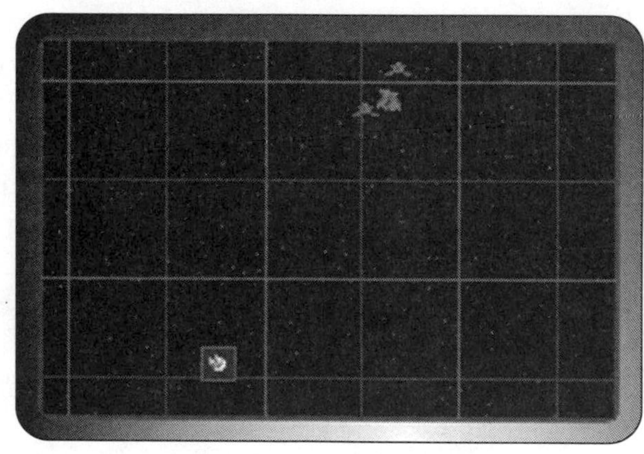

File Name: assault2

Mission Briefing

Provide escort for the Y-wings attempting to recover the corvettes *Ethar I* and *Ethar II*. Your three-ship group of X-wings will lead the attack. You are in the number-two position. The target corvettes are about ten clicks from the point where you come out of hyperspace. Two Imperial shuttles with repair crews are near the Alliance ships. Two groups of three Assault Gunboats are protecting the Empire's operations. Two groups of three Y-wings will follow the initial Rebel wave in three minutes. Shuttles *Rogue 1* and *Rogue 2* will bring in the Rescue Teams six minutes after those Y-wings arrive.

Farlander's After-Action Report

I went through the standard mission-start procedure, and, because we had some distance to cover, I redirected shield power to the engines and set the cannon recharge rate to maximum. I transferred energy from the cannons to the shields as we closed.

Switching to torpedoes, I targeted the nearest enemy fighter, GUN *Tau 3*, and ordered my wingmen to attack. R2 reported that the Imperial shuttles had docked less than 30 seconds after we came out of hyperspace.

As soon as I had a lock on *Tau 3*, I fired a torpedo. Someone had launched a missile at me, which hit right after I fired. I quickly reset the shield recharge rate to normal and balanced my shields, then I targeted *Tau 2* and fired a torpedo at it, as well. I boosted the shield recharge rate to maximum and switched to cannons, finishing off the Gunboat with a handful of laser blasts, and then targeting GUN *Rho 1*. I proceeded to destroy the remaining 'Boats as quickly as I could.

Both my wingmen had fallen victim to enemy fire, but the Y-wings were doing their job, having disabled both corvettes right after they were repaired. The corvettes and the Y-wings were nearly eight clicks away, and replacement waves for Rho and Tau had arrived.

Rho came after me, but Tau went after the Y-wings, so I took out two of GUN Rho and then disengaged to lend some assistance. Y-W *Blue 1* was destroyed, and I knew that I had to get there fast. I redirected everything to the engines, and began weaving in that direction.

The Y-wings began jumping into hyperspace by the time I got to the disabled corvettes, and I figured that our shuttles would be arriving soon, so I tried to destroy the remaining Gunboats as quickly as I could. There was only one left when the shuttles arrived.

The Rescue Teams were just getting ready to dock when I killed GUN *Tau 3*, and a new pair of 'Boats, Mu, hypered in. I targeted the nearest and turned to meet it as a new replacement wave for GUN Tau popped up.

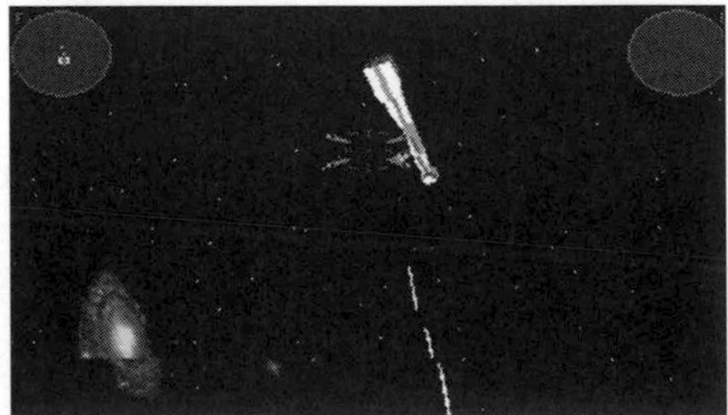

Disabling the corvettes.

GUN Mu ignored me, and went straight after our shuttles. I maneuvered to attack them from the side as they opened fire.

Just as I was taking out the second Gunboat from group Mu, Tau got close enough to launch a couple of missiles in my direction. The first took out my hull/shield integrity display, but I was able to evade the second. As I resumed the dogfight, I saw that the Rescue Teams had been successful and that the shuttles and recaptured corvettes were heading for their jump points. I continued to destroy Gunboats until SHU *Rogue* and the corvettes were safe, and then I got ready to follow them.

Another new pair of Gunboats arrived, Nu this time, in addition to yet another replacement for Tau. I hadn't received the Mission Complete message, so I turned to engage GUN Nu. After destroying Nu, I turned toward Tau, which had launched another missile attack. I wasn't so lucky evading this time, and was auto-ejected as my ship was destroyed.

I had plenty of time to think about the carnage of the mission while I awaited rescue.

C.O.'s Analysis

"That was a little more resistance than we expected over a couple of corvettes," said Lagrane when I finally reported for debriefing, after a couple of hours of recuperation on the Med Deck. "And apparently, there was some kind of communications problem getting you the mission complete signal."

"Just happy to among the living, sir," I replied. "Not everyone who went out was so lucky."

"Your superior dogfighting skills saved you," said Lagrane. "If the battle had still been raging when your ship blew, I don't know if we'd been able to pull off the rescue."

Debriefing (Win Conditions)

SHUs *Rogue 1* and *Rogue 2* must dock with and capture CRVs *Ethar 1* and *Ethar 2*. All four then must escape into hyperspace.

Marskan was in my face the minute I came out of debriefing. He shoved me up against the wall, one hand at my throat, the other cocked to strike.

"You killed my brother," he said, his voice tight and strained.

"Get your hand off me, Marskan," I told him.

I grabbed the hand at my throat and bent it slowly backward, my eyes boring into his. Still poised to strike, his right hand remained frozen. It was a test of wills, and I could hear the voice and feel the strength of the Force inside me. In silence our minds locked, until finally he let go and stepped unsteadily backward. I reached out with my mind and closed down his windpipe, watching as he clutched desperately at his throat.

I released Marskan, realizing in that instant that I could kill him with a thought. It frightened me, appalled me. I shut down the voice, the Force, the power, and backed away. But Marskan was looking at me as though I had just grown horns and was breathing fire. He backed away and ran down the corridor, his footsteps echoing against the walls, receding into the distance. I watched him go and felt numb and afraid.

I made my way slowly toward the lounge. As I walked, I felt the voice return, and my fear and confusion were wiped away. I had lost two of my young pilots, but there were still more. Marskan's brother and Horodi had obviously been unworthy of the Force, and Captain Marskan himself would eventually come to realize it. I would have to work harder with the other pilots.

But even as I walked and planned, I felt something tugging at me, nagging from somewhere deep and still, calling as though from a great distance. It caused my head to ache, and I tried to shut it out.

As I approached the ready room, I spotted Marskan with Raider and Speedy. They eyed me suspiciously as I walked by. I could feel a tingling sensation on my skin, at the back of my head, and, strangely, in the palms of my hands. But I continued without hesitation, walking slowly and deliberately into the lounge, where I found several young pilots eager to hear what I had to say.

Later the same day, the word came down that we were to be on active alert indefinitely. The Imperial Death Star was believed to be operational, and we were at Condition Yellow.

I was assigned guard duty to protect one of our main weapons-storage compounds.

OP 10: GUARD VITAL SUPPLY DEPOT

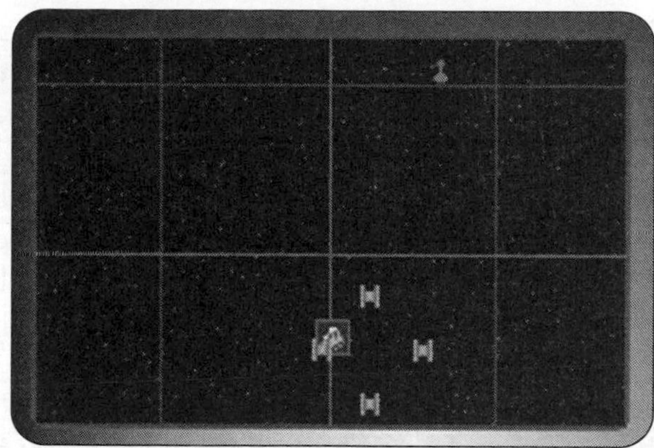

File Name: max19

Mission Briefing

Protect our hidden cache of weapons from Imperial attack. You are to lead your three-ship flight of A-wings on a defensive patrol around the cache until you're relieved by Blue Squadron. The cache is made up of 12 cargo containers.

Farlander's After-Action Report

I went through the standard mission-start procedure, switching to full throttle as soon as I had charged my shields and lasers to the maximum. We were on patrol for less than two minutes when the Imperial Frigate *Retsub* came out of hyperspace right through the middle of the depot. We were within gun range, and they opened up on us immediately.

We turned away to get out of range, and saw that a four-ship group of TIE Bombers (Alpha) had been launched. Switching to missiles, I targeted the nearest of these, *Alpha 3*, and ordered my wingmen to attack. I then targeted *Alpha 4* and launched a missile during a head-on attack, but *Alpha 3* turned in front of the projectile's path and was destroyed instead. This was unfortunate, because *Alpha 3* already had hull damage, and was about to be destroyed by my wingmen anyway.

Guarding the weapons cache.

I kept after *Alpha 4* and destroyed it with another missile, then targeted *Alpha 2*, saw that it had hull damage, and kept cycling backward to target

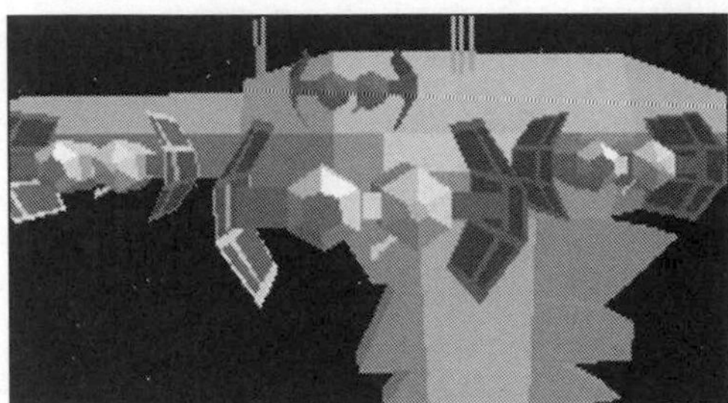

TIE Bombers coming at you!

Locking on to T/B Alpha 2.

Close encounter with Retsub.

Frigate in a bad start position.

Alpha 1. *Alpha 2* was killed by my wingman, and I used another missile to destroy *Alpha 1*. This action brought out a replacement wave from the *Retsub*, so we repeated our attack on the newcomers.

I had even less luck with my missiles this time; the Bombers at first managed to evade my first three! The missiles finally caught up with all but *Alpha 2*, but I saw that another four-ship group of Bombers, Gamma, launched about then.

So far, we hadn't lost any containers, and both my wingmen were in good shape. The *Retsub* then launched another four-ship formation of TIE Bombers (Beta). These must have been their best pilots, because they handled their Bombers much better than the previous groups had.

We engaged in an exchange of missiles and laser fire with the Bombers until they were all destroyed, fighting through three replacement waves for Beta and one for Gamma, and the *Retsub* departed before the battle ended. *Red 3* was destroyed by two quick, successive missile hits, but when A-W Blue arrived, all but one of the cargo containers had survived.

C.O.'s Analysis

Lagrane wrote 'Good Mission' on the bottom of my report and dismissed me. He looked exhausted, and I reasoned correctly that he had been preparing for a series of larger, even more important operations.

Debriefing (Win Conditions)

At least 50 percent of each group of CONs ZL, LT, and XZ must survive. A-W Blue must arrive to relieve you.

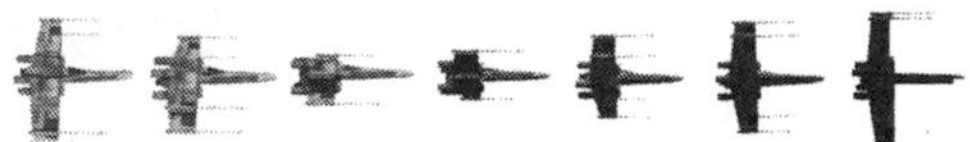

Hamo was waiting for me in the hangar as I climbed down the ladder from my A-wing. He looked impatient, so I took my time, stowing my helmet and checking the controls. Let him wait.

"Keyan," he called at last, seeing that I wasn't coming over to see him.

"Oh, hello, Hamo," I called back. "What's going on?"

He crossed the distance between us and stood near the nose of the A-wing I had just flown.

"That's what I was going to ask you," he said. "Are you all right?"

"Sure. I'm fine. Had a little trouble out there—Lots of Bombers—but we got 'em."

Hamo was studying at me with one of those looks I had been getting a lot lately: Heavy scrutiny. Trying to see inside me.

I smiled. I was just about to say something clever to get him off my back when a terrible emptying, sucking, draining flash of energy coursed through me. It made me stagger and clutch the battle-scarred hull of the A-wing. Slowly, I lowered myself to the ground and sat there holding my head.

To describe the feelings I was experiencing may be something that words cannot accomplish. It was as though your best friend had just disappeared from your life, suddenly and without warning. It was like that, multiplied several million times. I felt nauseated, and for a moment I forgot where I was.

To compound the disorientation I felt, an unholy glee superimposed itself on my mind. Whatever I was feeling, it frightened and repelled me. I felt myself shutting down.

I heard Hamo say, from a distance; "Keyan?" just before everything went black.

"Beware the dark side." I heard the new voice clearly. It was not like the other voice, which seemed to have abandoned me for the moment. "Feel the

Force around you. Use the Force for knowledge and defense. Never for attack. Free yourself before it is too late."

I could not have been unconscious for more than a few seconds, but, looking back, I think those few seconds might have saved me. When I came to, Hamo was kneeling by my side, calling my name and checking the pulse in my neck. When he saw my eyes open, he said; "Are you all right? What happened?"

"Something terrible." As I spoke, the words caught in my throat. "Something big . . . and *terrible*."

"Tell me. What is it?"

"I don't know, Hamo. I don't know."

Hamo helped me up after a few minutes, and we began to walk out of the hangar. He had to hold me up at first, but soon I got my legs under me again and walked without his help. I felt no voice, no power. It was an empty feeling, but not a bad one. I felt free.

Hamo wanted to take me to the medics, but I refused.

"No. The medics can't do a thing for me, Hamo. I'm afraid that I'm beyond their skills now."

"You're talking nonsense, Keyan."

"Am I? Have you talked with Raider and Marskan?"

Hamo looked uncomfortable.

"Yes," he said slowly. "But we can talk about that later. . . ."

"No. You don't understand. Whatever they've told you is true. I've been . . . I don't really know what I've been, but I don't like it. And I don't know how to prevent it."

I stopped, and he stopped with me.

"Hamo, take me to my cabin. Don't tell anyone about this. Please."

"But I have to . . ."

"Promise me," I said desperately. I didn't feel like I could (should?) use the Force to bend his will, but luckily my own sense of need and urgency was enough to sway him.

"All right," he said. "But only for now. If anything else happens, I've got to report it."

"Thank you, Hamo. I've got to figure this out for myself."

Hamo was as good as his word. He didn't tell anyone what had happened. And I sat in my cabin for hours, waiting for the voice to return. Dreading it. I was still there when the Imperial attack came.

OP 11: DEFEND THE INDEPENDENCE

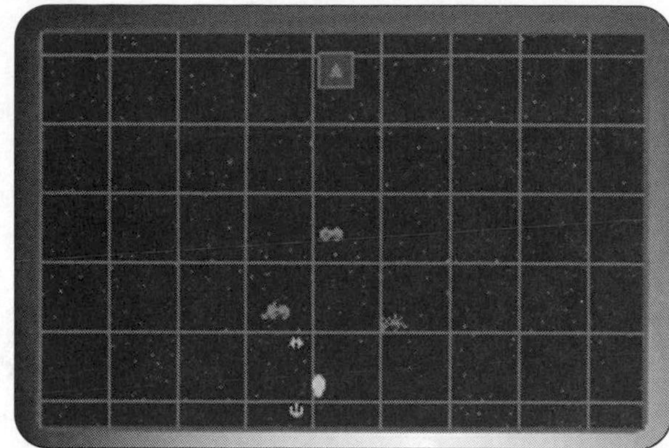

File Name: defend1

Mission Briefing

Intercept and destroy the attacking Imperial ships, providing cover until the CRS *Independence* can escape. You will lead a two-ship flight of X-wings in defense of the Alliance flagship. Two A-wings from Blue Squadron will assist you. You will come out of hyperspace about 3 clicks from the *Independence*. The Star Destroyer *Immortal* is more than 32 clicks away, and has already launched three groups of TIE Bombers; Alpha with six ships, and Beta and Gamma with four ships apiece. Two Assault Gunboat groups (Mu and Nu, two ships apiece) are escorting Beta and Gamma. The nearest attackers are more than 9 clicks away, and A-W Blue is already moving to intercept them.

Farlander's After-Action Report

I went through the standard mission-start procedure. The Imperial attack had split into three parts—T/B Beta and GUN Nu on one flank, T/B Gamma and GUN Mu on the other, and T/B Alpha coming right up the middle, but still almost 17 clicks away.

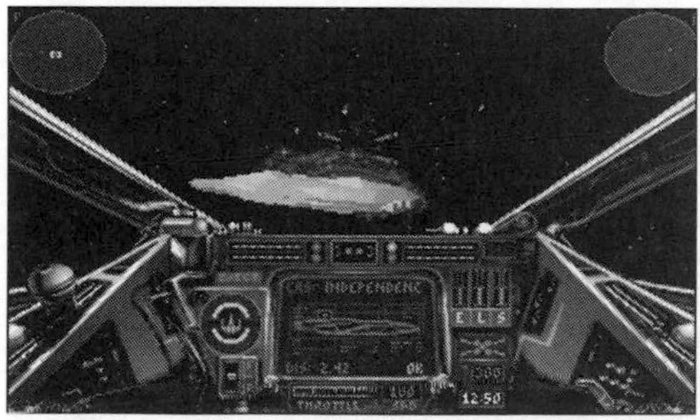

Defend the Independence.

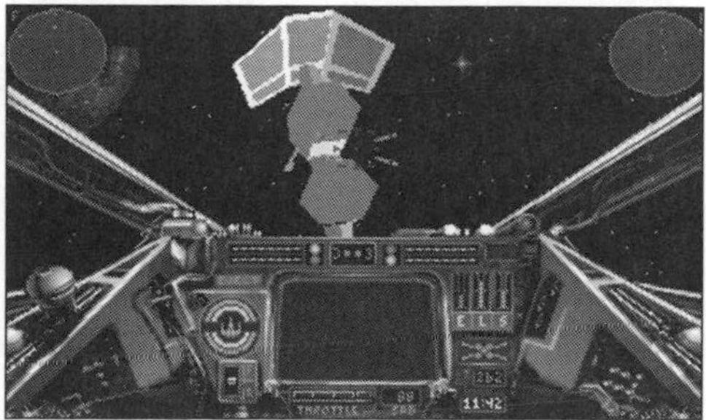

Ram the Bomber to take it out quickly.

Gamma 2 *is as good as finished.*

A-W Blue was already going to meet T/B Beta, so I led my flight toward T/B Gamma. To close the distance as quickly as possible, I redirected all shield power to the engines and boosted the cannon recharge rate by one. This gave me a speed of 112. On the way, I kept up a constant transfer of energy from the lasers to the shields, so that I would have them fully charged by the time we got within range.

I switched to torpedoes and ordered *Red 2* to attack *Beta 3*. I targeted *Beta 1* for myself. As soon as I began to get a lock, I reset the shield recharge rate to one above normal, and the cannon rate to maximum. This setting would allow me to better match speed with the Bombers and Gunboats. I launched as soon as I had a solid lock, and then switched to cannons. I began firing immediately, hoping to disrupt their attack, but I was too late: The surviving Bombers had begun firing their torpedoes at the *Independence*.

I wanted to ignore the Gunboats for now, but they were staying right with us. I kept getting hit by missiles, even though I evaded several. After taking a third hit, I decided that I would have to deal with the Gunboats quickly. I switched to torpedoes and fired one at the first Gunboat I saw, and then switched to cannons to finish it off.

I took care of another Gunboat with a similar tactic, and then turned my attention back to the Bombers, who were now all around the *Independence*. I redirected shield power to the engines to boost my speed again, and closed the distance rapidly. Now that we were within range of the cruiser's guns, we were able to make short work of the Bombers. What we didn't hit, the cruiser did.

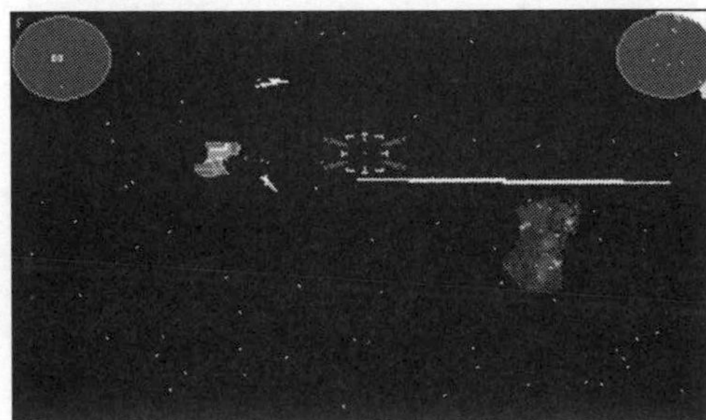

Leading the Bomber.

Taking out GUN Mu 1.

More attack waves were launched for all the enemy starfighter groups, but the *Independence* was able to reach its jump point and escape to safety before they could arrive. The cruiser had lost its shields but hadn't taken any serious hull damage. Two A-wings were lost, although they were replaced by a second wave before the *Independence* hypered out. We continued to battle with the nearest Imperial ships, then disengaged and made our jumps as soon as we could.

Debriefing (Win Conditions)
The CRS *Independence* must survive.

The voice returned during the attack on the *Independence,* but this time I did not welcome it. I struggled against its commands and refused to believe in its message of ultimate power and glory.

It even made me lower my shields, and for a moment I was helpless in the thick of the battle, but something else reached out to me, cast the voice away, and left me free to regain control. Quickly, I redirected energy to my shields and continued to defend the cruiser. After that, neither voice returned. I did not, of course, mention any of this in my report.

We arrived at Yavin in the middle of a night shift. Operations were already under way to repair the damage to the *Independence.* Fortunately, the cruiser had suffered very little; mostly damage to the shield coils and some electronics.

They sent Red, Gold and Blue Squadrons to Yavin Base on the planet's fourth moon almost as soon as we arrived. We were given the orders an hour before we rendezvoused with the *Independence,* so we were ready to depart even upon our arrival.

We flew our starfighters in tight formation until we reached the upper atmosphere, separating there and flying under ground control to avoid collisions. Most starfighters can operate in atmosphere, but they are difficult to fly, and don't perform that well.

Even though it was night time when we arrived, with the stars twinkling in the atmospheric haze and a cold breeze blowing into the open hangar, there was plenty of activity everywhere. We stood around for a few minutes, and I noticed that Raider, Marskan, and a few others kept together, away from me, while the newer pilots I had influenced stayed close. I had not spoken to any of them other than to give necessary commands, but they still seemed enthralled.

How was I going to tell them the truth? Maybe it would be easier if I even knew the truth myself.

Biggs was already on Yavin with a few more pilots. Red Squadron got several transfers, including Biggs, Wedge Antilles, Jek Porkins, and a few other veterans. Gold and Blue also gained personnel as the High Command gathered its resources in preparation to meet the Death Star. There was a sense of doom over the entire base, although everyone was working hard and no one said anything.

We were given quarters deep inside the base itself, and told to get some rest. High Command expected the Imperial Attack within the next day or so. None of us rested, though. We were all too nervous, and each of us found a different way to relieve the stress.

I was feeling isolated and alone. Now that the voices had left me, I realized the damage I had done, and I couldn't face anyone. I kept to myself, wandering the hangars aimlessly, staying away from the other pilots.

So I was there when the light freighter flew recklessly into the main hangar. The pilot was either crazy or very good. Or both.

I waited around to see who came out. The base commander showed up just as a strange crew of humans and droids, with one huge creature I recognized as a Wookiee, emerged. A small shuttle vehicle arrived, and the three humans piled onto it. The Wookiee fussed around the ship, and then the droids—a beat-up R2 and a nervous protocol droid (I swear it was a nervous droid if ever there was one)—were led off by some operations personnel.

One of the passengers, a young woman, jumped off the shuttle and ran to greet the base commander. I overheard him say something about Alderaan and "fearing the worst." They hurried off, leaving the other two humans to fend for themselves.

One of them was a Corellian, by his outfit. The other was a young man of indeterminate origin. By his clothing, I guessed that he was from an outlying world where dress standards were not too rigorous. He was blond, medium built, and very young. About my age, I guessed, but not battle-hardened. I could see that. The Corellian, on the other hand, seemed to know his way around, and watched everything with wary eyes. I guessed that he was the reckless pilot of the light freighter.

The young man headed over to examine an X-wing nearby. He seemed fascinated, and again, I saw parallels with myself from what seemed like lifetimes ago. Still feeling isolated from my friends, I decided to approach this boy and see whether I could be of any help.

"Hi," I said, holding out my hand. "I'm Keyan,"

He was down on one knee, studying one of the laser-cannon heat deflectors. He straightened and turned in one motion. Smiling, he took my hand.

"I'm Luke," he said.

As I touched his hand, I had the distinct impression of another energy, a very strong energy, inside him or around him. I think that he, too, felt something, because he gave me a strange, puzzled look. I probably looked equally puzzled.

"Are you really a pilot?" he asked after a moment, the puzzled look replaced by a guileless expression of wonder.

"Sure," I answered. "I've flown a few missions."

"Wow. I'd like to fly an X-wing. I'm sure I could do it. I used to hunt womp rats in Beggar's Canyon back home. In a T-16 Skyhopper. They tell me the controls are almost the same."

"I used to fly a T-16," I said. "I modified the fusion activators to push the acceleration, and also the thruster jets to get more speed."

"I hadn't thought of that," he replied with understanding. "I set my ion afterburners just to the point of overload. I guess I pushed the old buggy pretty hard."

"Hey," I asked him. "You want to climb in the cockpit of this X-wing?"

His eyes turned saucer-sized, and his grin cut through the gloom I still felt in my heart.

Luke and I spent about an hour at the X-wing. I stood outside the cockpit and showed him how all the controls worked. He was quick to grasp everything. As he said, the T-16 and the X-wing were designed along the same lines. As he was climbing out of the cockpit, I happened to catch a glimpse of an unfamiliar cylinder hanging from his belt. It had been hidden beneath the cape he wore.

"What's that?" I asked.

"Oh. My lightsaber. It belonged to my father."

"I thought only the Jedi used lightsabers," I said.

He looked a little embarrassed. "My father was a Jedi," he said. "I want to be one, too."

"The Jedi know a lot about the Force, don't they?" I asked.

"Yes. The Force is where they get their powers," he told me. "I'm just now learning to trust the Force, and to let it guide me."

My heart was racing, but I had to ask him what I really needed to know. "But how can you know you're not trusting the wrong side? The dark side?"

He looked at me in surprise. "You know about the dark side?"

"I'm really afraid I know *too much* about it," I answered.

I desperately needed to talk to someone, to find a way to fight the voice, to find my way to the light. And there was something about Luke. An innocence, yes. And a sense of power waiting to be released. No one else I had ever met, other than possibly Mon Mothma, would understand what I had been through. But somehow I thought that maybe, just maybe, Luke would be able to.

I opened up to Luke; told him what I had done. I could see that my story affected him. He asked some questions, and thought seriously about what I told him.

Finally, he said; "I wish that old Ben were here. Ben Kenobi. Obi-Wan. He was my teacher; a great Jedi master. But he's dead. Darth Vader killed him."

And suddenly I could feel his sense of loss as though it were my own.

"I saw it happen," he added.

"I wish I had a teacher," I said.

"You know, sometimes I think Obi-Wan is still around. I hear his voice . . . inside my head . . . you know?"

"I've heard voices, too. They scare me."

"Ben taught me a little before he died. He said that a Jedi never uses the power of the Force for revenge or personal gain. It's supposed to be used to defend, to help others, to learn your own heart. The dark side is all about power over others. Ben was always saying; 'Trust the Force, Luke.'"

They way Luke said those words, it was comforting just to hear them. Although I wasn't sure that I could trust the Force, I trusted Luke. I saw no deceit or hypocrisy in him.

"Come on," I said on an impulse. "You want to fly an X-wing?"

"You bet!" he answered without hesitation.

"We're about to fight a battle we probably can't win. The Emperor's gigantic space station, the Death Star, is coming to destroy the Alliance," I told him. "But I'd like you and your Ben Kenobi on our side."

"The Death Star?" Luke looked surprised.

"Yes. Supposedly it's going to come after us."

"I just *came* from the Death Star. Han and I—and Chewbacca; that's the Wookiee—we just rescued Princess Leia from there. She had important information for the Alliance about a flaw in the station's design."

"You just *came* from the *Death Star*?" I asked incredulously.

"It's true."

"And that woman was the princess?"

"Yes. Princess Leia," he said earnestly. "She has information that might help us destroy the Death Star."

Luke was completely sincere, and perhaps even more incredibly, I found that I had no trouble believing him.

In what I'm sure was record-breaking time, Luke became a part of Red Squadron. We needed anyone willing to man a starfighter and he showed a remarkable aptitude on the hastily arranged tests.

Another Gart, I caught myself thinking. It wasn't a pleasant thought.

Then the Death Star was detected, and Yavin Base went into high gear. The station had come out of hyperspace on the opposite side of Yavin from our moon, and for the moment we were shielded by the planet itself. But that situation wouldn't last long.

We were called into the briefing room. They hadn't yet found a way to destroy the Death Star, but they were still analyzing the data, and we weren't going to sit here helplessly waiting for the imminent attack. Our mission would be to destroy their communications satellite and disrupt operations. Any delay, we were told—even an hour—might spell the difference between the total destruction of the Alliance and the biggest defeat the Empire had ever known.

OP 12: BEGIN DEATH STAR ASSAULT

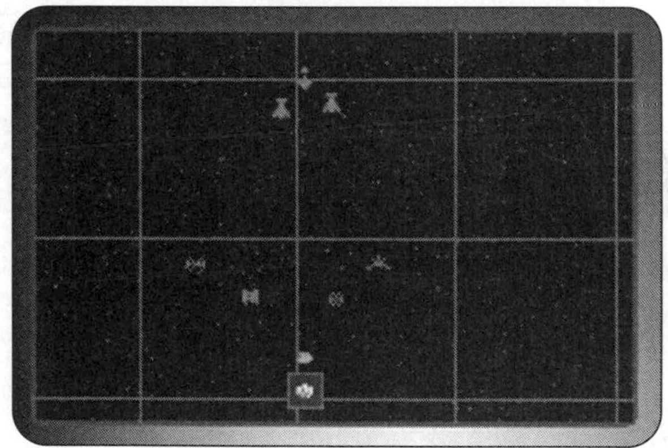

File Name: dstar1

Mission Briefing

Use your X-wing to destroy the Comm Sat that is coordinating the defenses of the Death Star. Also destroy as many ships as possible. You will be in the number-two spot of a three-ship group of X-wings. Two A-wings will escort you into the target area. The Comm Sat is approximately 12 clicks away. To reach it, you have to run a gauntlet of TIE fighters, Bombers and Interceptors, as well as Assault Gunboats. In addition, two corvettes and a Frigate are in the immediate vicinity of the satellite. The Death Star itself is some distance away.

Farlander's After-Action Report

After going through the standard mission-start procedure, I wanted to get to the Comm Sat as quickly as possible, so I redirected all my shield power to the engines and set the cannon recharge rate to one above normal. I had to maintain shields by constantly transferring energy from the lasers. I then cycled through the target list until I located the satellite and headed toward it. My wingmen followed me.

Approaching the Death Star.

The Death Star is guarded by a Frigate.

We came under immediate attack, as the nearest enemy fighters were less than four clicks away from our entry point. I decided not to engage at all, and went into the standard evasive weave while maintaining my heading toward the Comm Sat. I knew that the enemy fighters would have an almost impossible time hitting me with anything but missiles, and as long as they didn't overwhelm me, I could recharge my shields fast enough to overcome the occasional hit.

Heading for the Comm Sat.

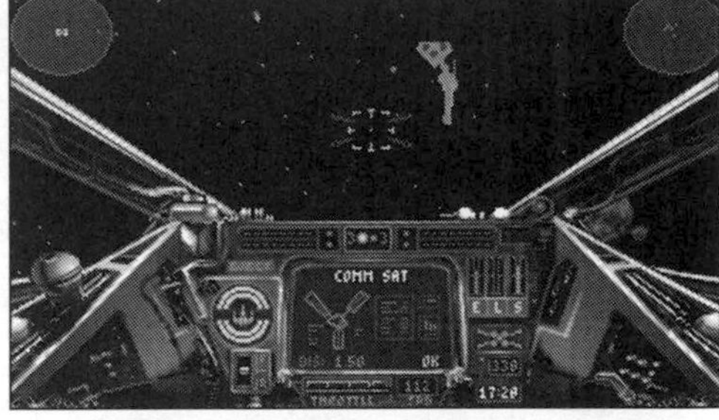

Targeting the Comm Sat.

X-wings over the Death Star.

About a minute into the mission, R2 alerted me to the launch of a group of four TIE fighters of some new type we hadn't seen. As I closed on the target, I switched to torpedoes so that I wouldn't have to get too close. By the time I got within range to fire, both my wingmen were shot up, though they were later rescued. I fired on the Comm Sat, and when it was destroyed, I received the Mission Complete message and promptly hypered home.

C.O.'s Analysis

"Good job, Farlander. Very good. I've been worried about you lately, but you handled yourself well. Better get going, though. They're going to need you again right away."

"Yes, sir. By the way, sir. Did you get any data on the new TIE fighters?"

"We're analyzing them now from the recorders. They're definitely an advanced design. We're calling them TIE Advanced for now."

"Yes, sir." I said. "And sir?"

"What is it?"

"I'm sorry, sir."

"Sorry for what, captain?"

"I'm just sorry, sir, for a lot of things. But I am definitely ready for this battle."

"You'd better be, Farlander."

Debriefing (Win Conditions)

The Comm Sat must be destroyed.

When I came out of debriefing, I looked around for Luke, but couldn't find him. I had to hurry anyway. Another mission was already getting started. I had missed the formal briefing, but I picked up the basics from Hamo, who was flying again in another group.

"The engineers have decided that a single fighter can destroy this thing," he said. "Which sounds like a crock to me, but we're out of good options."

"A single fighter? How can that be possible?" I asked.

"Beats me. Something to do with an unshielded exhaust port."

"What do we need to do?"

"Just kill TIEs," he answered.

"That I can do," I replied.

I was teamed up with a new pilot I didn't know, and it didn't look as though there would be time to get to know him now. We were spaceborne within minutes.

OP 13: ATTACK DEATH STAR SURFACE

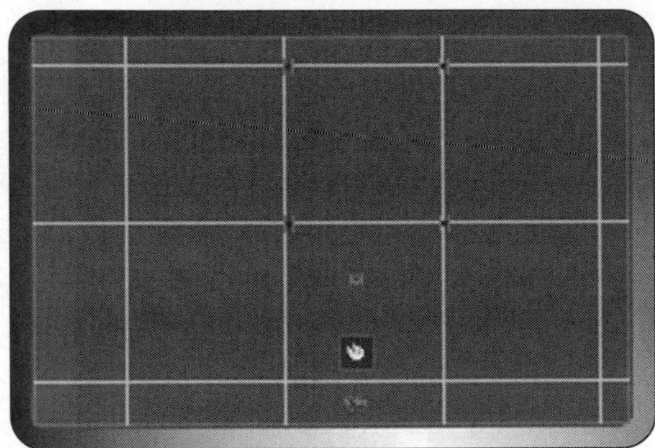

File Name: dstar2

Mission Briefing

In preparation for a Trench Run, you must clear the Death Star surface defenses surrounding a Nav Buoy. You and your flight leader will bring your X-wings out of hyperspace directly above the surface of the Death Star. A group of three TIE fighters (Alpha) and a group of two TIE Bombers (Iota) will try to intercept you. There are four hangar ports to be destroyed. They are arranged as the corners of a square about six clicks on a side.

Farlander's After-Action Report

I went through the standard mission-start procedure, and we were immediately engaged by enemy fighters. As I evaded them, I cycled through the target list, finding the hangar ports and assigning each one to a memory location. I then ordered *Red 1* to attack the nearest hangar while I turned to engage the TIE Bombers.

I matched speed with the Bombers by turning up the recharge rates of my shields and lasers. I tried to stay at least two kilometers above the surface to stay out of range of the Death Star's gun towers. *Red 1* took a great deal of damage from T/F Alpha as they all ganged up on him, then

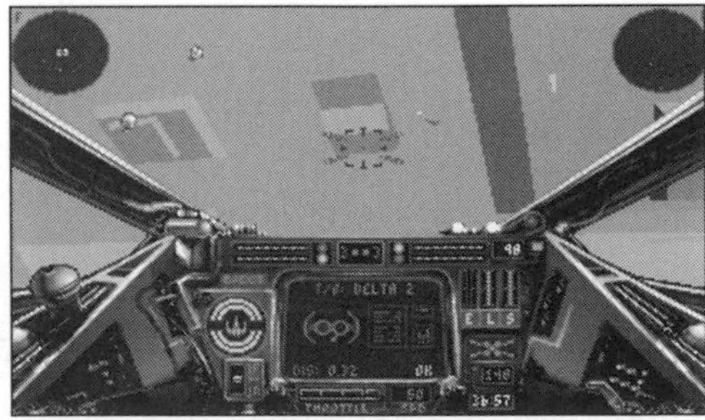

TIE Bombers are hard to see here.

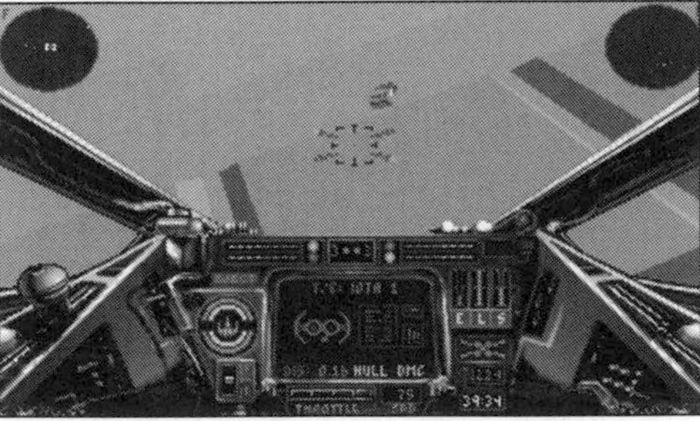

T/B Iota 1 *is hurt.*

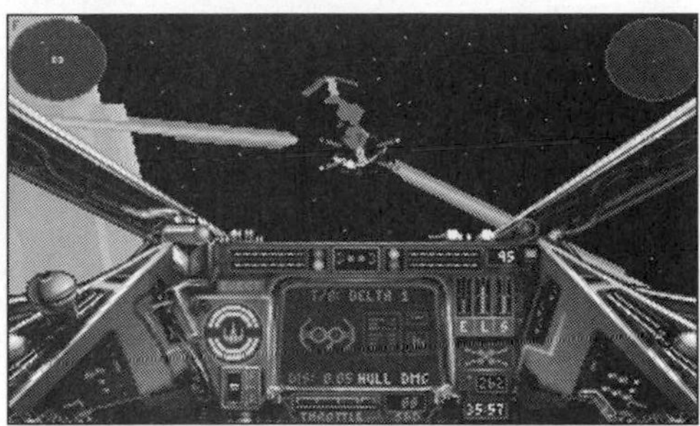

This is better.

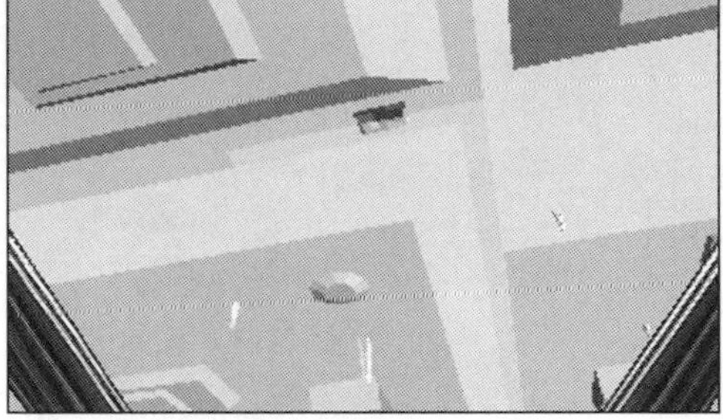

Passing over a hangar.

one of the Bombers finished him off with a missile. When I had destroyed T/B Iota, a new group, T/B Delta, rose to take its place.

I redirected shield energy to the engines and pressed on toward the nearest hangar. When I was close enough, I switched to torpedoes, launched two into it, and then finished it off with cannons. I continued in similar fashion to destroy the next two. Occasionally, I broke off an attack run to kill a TIE or two, but mostly I tried to evade them. I knew that if I could destroy all the hangar ports, they wouldn't be able to launch any more TIEs at me, and then there would be plenty of time to finish off those that remained.

The last hangar was the hardest, because I had used up all my torpedoes by that time, and had to rely on my cannons alone. I had five TIE fighters chasing me, so I decided I needed to finish them off before going after the final hangar. I turned about and engaged them one after another until they were all destroyed. As soon as the last of them blew, two more were launched from the remaining nest.

I was directly above the last hangar, so I dove down toward it with cannons blasting at these new TIE fighters. I took out one but suffered several hits myself, then reset the shield recharge rate to maximum and balanced my shields. Ignoring the last TIE for a moment, I decided to make

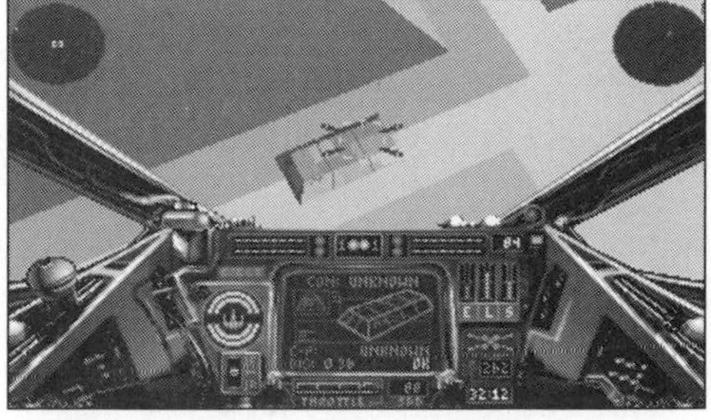

Coming at the hangar with cannons armed.

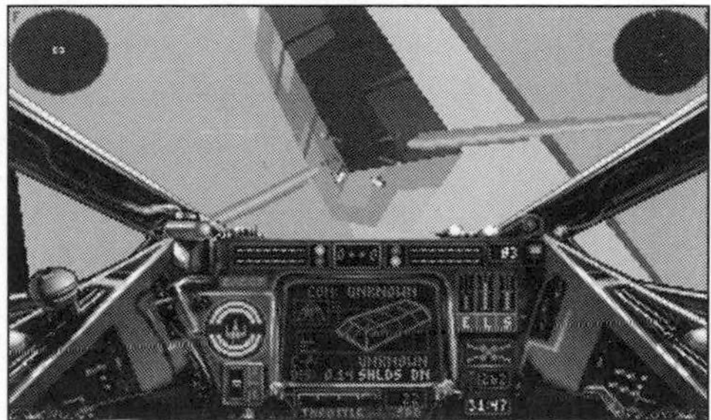

Shooting the hangar.

Taking aim on a gun tower.

Another gun tower goes boom.

my attack on the last hangar. As I got closer and began to fire, I shifted my shields to the rear for protection from the last fighter. Finally, the hangar blew and I quickly turned to engage the last TIE.

After destroying this last TIE, I targeted the Nav Buoy and turned in that direction. It was more than three clicks away, and, when I got to within two clicks, I dove down toward the surface and began taking out gun towers. There were an awful lot of them, and I had to transfer cannon energy to the shields several times to keep going. Eventually, I got the Mission Complete message and left for home.

Debriefing (Win Conditions)

All four Hangar Ports must be destroyed, as well as all laser towers within two clicks of the Nav Buoy.

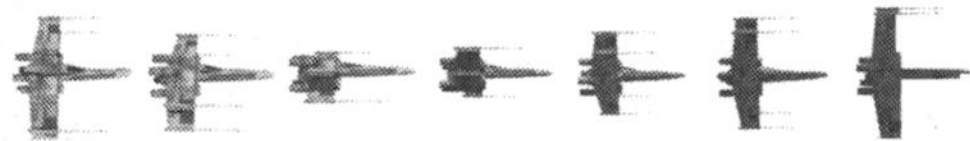

The final assault was about to begin, but I had some business to take care of first.

"Friends, I have to tell you something," I said. "I made a mistake."

They all stood there in a semicircle around me—the pilots who thought of me as their leader. "The Force isn't as I described. You've got to understand this. It's not about power. It's about knowledge. It's not about controlling. It's about trusting."

"But we saw you . . ." one of them began.

"What you saw was foolishness," I told them. "You saw me endangering you all. You heard the voice of the dark side speaking through me."

They looked uncomfortable. As if they didn't believe me. I knew I had to persuade them.

"Please . . . you mustn't trust anything I've told you about the Force. Trust your own instincts. Everything I said was horribly wrong!"

By the time I finished, I was practically screaming at them. Couldn't they get it through their heads?

I left them standing there. I could think of nothing else to say. As I whirled around to get away, I spotted Raider. He was watching from a distance, but he said nothing to me—just turned and went about his business.

I hurried to my assignment. I was to fly a Y-wing, temporarily assigned to Gold Squadron. I wasn't happy about the reassignment, but it wasn't up to me.

We were to launch the final attack on the Death Star in five minutes. I spotted Luke talking to the Corellian he had called Han. Then the princess came up and talked to Luke, and kissed him on the cheek. I thought of Lynia. Where was she right now? I had heard that Mon Mothma was somewhere at the base. . . .

There was no time left. I closed the hatch and fired up the repulsorlifts to guide the craft out of the hangar. This was a do-or-die mission, and we all knew that, for most of us, it was time to die.

OP 14: DEATH STAR TRENCH RUN

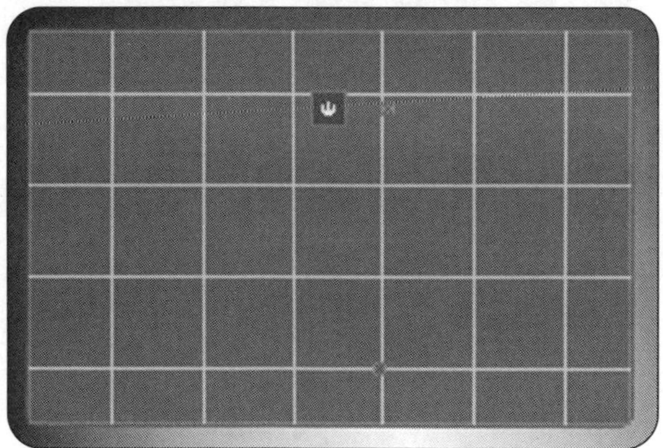

File Name: dstar3

Mission Briefing

Complete the final assault on the Death Star by attacking the exhaust port at the end of the trench. This is it! Our best hope is for a single starfighter to slip through the Death Star's remaining defenses to attack its weak spot. You will come out of hyperspace near the surface with the trench directly ahead. Stay high and out of range of the surface until you are ready to enter the trench.

Skywalker's After-Action Report

As I went through a standard configuration procedure, three TIE fighters from Alpha group were rising from the surface about 4.5 clicks away. Three

TIE Advanced from Omega were nearly 20 clicks away. I targeted the nearest TIE and charged it head-on. I switched to torpedoes and reset the shield recharge rate to maximum to slow the closure rate, firing just as I got a lock and T/F Alpha's laser blasts reached me.

I took out *Alpha 1*, but almost lost my forward shields in the process. I quickly balanced the shields, and also transferred some laser energy to them. Now I reset the shields to normal recharge rate and targeted the next TIEs. I switched to cannons to dogfight them. These pilots were really skillful, and it took me so long to kill them that T/A Omega was able to get to me before I could make it to the trench.

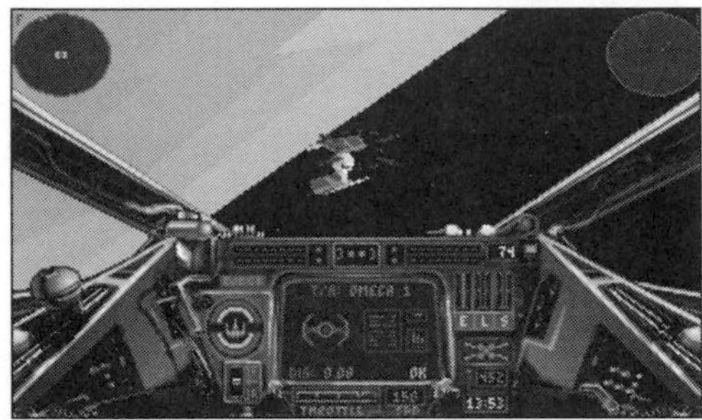

Chasing down a TIE Advanced.

TIE Advanced.

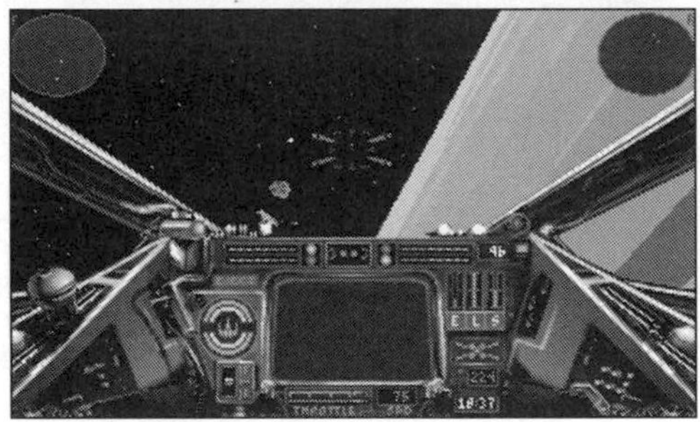

Dogfight over the Death Star.

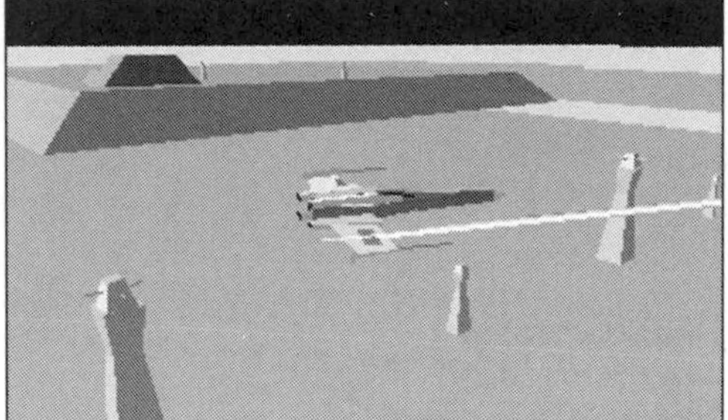

Brushing the gun towers.

These new TIEs were incredibly fast and hard to hit. I redirected all shield power to the engines and set the cannon recharge rate to one above normal. At least I would be almost able to keep up. I also selected quad-fire-linked mode because I noticed that the TIE Advanced had some sort of fast-charging shields! I would have to make every shot count, and I wanted to do maximum damage with each opportunity. It took quite awhile, and they put up a determined fight, but eventually I prevailed.

I set my sights for the trench and reset my recharge rates to maximum. I wanted to have full charges all around before entering the trench. I had

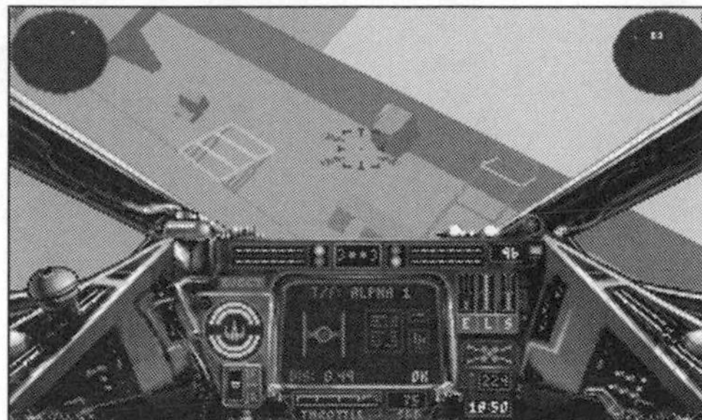

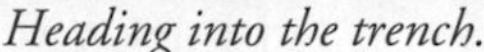

Heading into the trench.

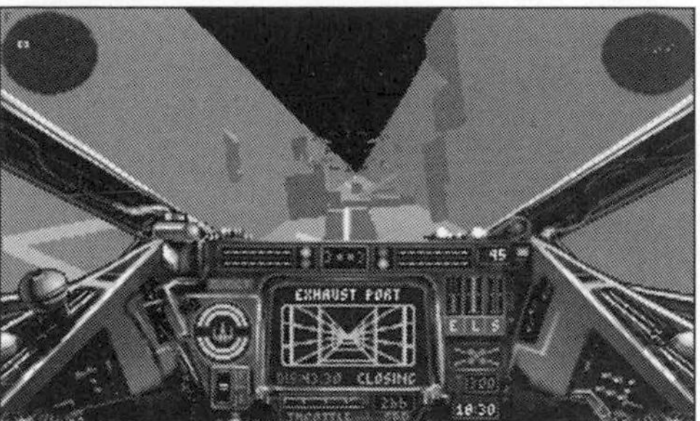

Starting the trench run.

worked my way to a position directly above the trench, and, as soon as I had full charges, I redirected everything to the engines and dove inside.

The rim of the Trench was lined with gun towers, so I had to do some jinking to gain entry without sustaining heavy damage. Then I was in! I reset the cannon recharge rate to maximum and moved the shields forward.

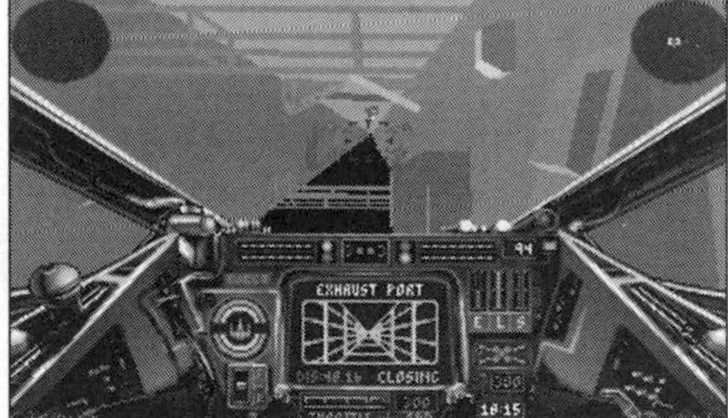

Note the X-wing's speed in these pictures. R2 boosts your speed to about three times normal!

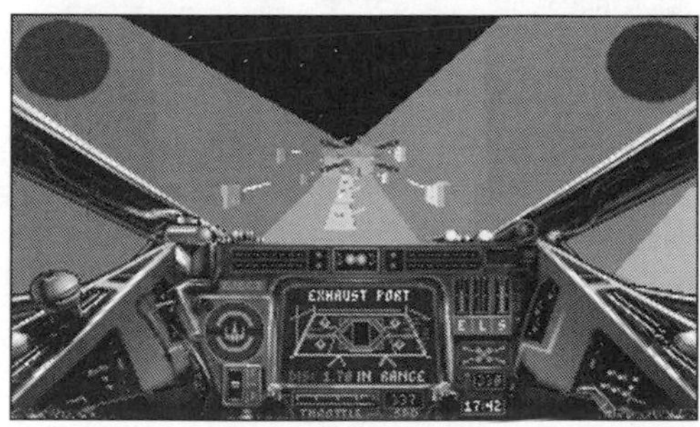

Ready to fire.

The trench was full of obstacles and gun emplacements, and I tried to evade them as best I could. I kept up a constant transfer of laser power to my shields as I closed on the exhaust port. I switched to torpedoes, and when the port came into view, I steered directly for it. I launched my torpedoes at point-blank range, and scored a direct hit!

I immediately pulled up and away, retreating to a safe distance before pausing to relish the explosive finale of the Rebellion's greatest victory.

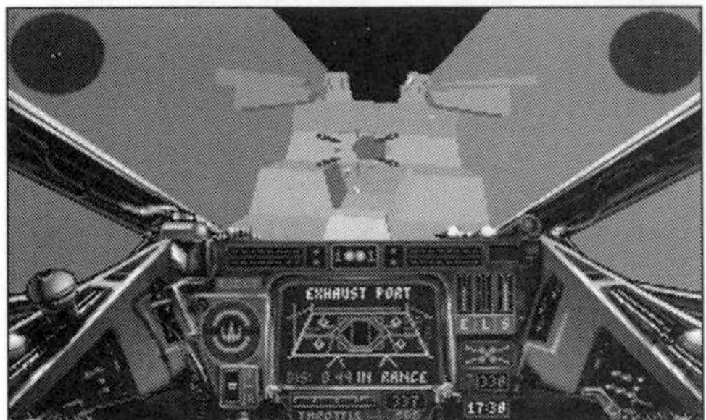

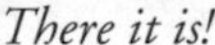

There it is!

Leaving the trench.

Debriefing (Win Conditions)
You must destroy the Death Star.

The battle was furious and deadly. Every ship in my Y-wing group was destroyed except for mine. I could do little, though, except clear away some TIEs, and give Gold Squadron a chance at the exhaust port. I was too far away to help when the new TIEs came up behind and destroyed the three Y-wings in the trench. I wanted to swing around for a shot, but by that time I was being attacked from all sides and my own shields were failing.

I heard the chatter from Red Squadron and recognized Luke's voice as well as that of Biggs and Wedge. I heard it when Porkins bought it, and then Red Squadron launched an attack on the trench, but missed. I was trying to stay out of the way of the TIEs and get into position to do some good, but the Y-wing was just too slow. If only I had an A-wing.

Then I heard Luke, Biggs, and Wedge head in for their attack run. I missed some of the chatter because I found myself too close to the Death Star's surface guns, and had to dodge a crossfire. Then I heard Wedge bail, too damaged to continue. Shortly afterward, Biggs nova-ed. There was a lot of static, but I thought that I heard ground base asking Luke why he had turned off his targeting computer.

I had finally shaken the TIE fighters and was turning my Y-wing back toward the trench. I couldn't see Luke, but I did see the Corellian freighter, the *Millennium Falcon*, fly into view above the Death Star, firing down into the trench. There were two explosions, and an odd-looking TIE fighter went careening out of control and off into space.

Over the comm line, I clearly heard Han say; "You're all clear, kid. Now let's blow this thing and go home."

Only moments later, I was able to join formation with Luke, Wedge, and the Falcon as we headed away from the Death Star. Luke's shot had gone straight down the port, and I swiveled my head for a better look at the doomed station as we pulled clear. Ahead of us, no longer eclipsed from our view by Yavin, was the moon that served as the Rebel base.

I put rear shields full-on and transferred maximum energy to my engines to keep up with the other ships. When the Death Star blew, she didn't just explode—she was obliterated. We were barely past the main force of the blast. My poor Y-wing bucked and twisted, but the shields held, and I was able to keep control.

Over the comm, Han was whooping.

"Great shot, kid! That was one in a million!" he yelled.

Later, I stood among the troops as the heroes took the stage and received their award. I had previously been promoted to commander, and, after hearing their story, I felt proud to have helped Luke, Han, Chewbacca, Leia, and even the two droids, R2-D2 and C-3PO, in any small way.

I felt little of the joy all around me, though. I don't know where or how, but Hamo had been killed. I couldn't accept that he was lost, but there was no sign of him. No one had seen him shot, but he was gone. So were Biggs and Porkins and so many others.

The Death Star was destroyed, and the Empire routed. For now. But the fight would go on. I knew that I had much to make up for. Marskan still hated me, and for good reason. Raider still wouldn't talk to me, and many young pilots had died because I had made them feel invincible. I doubted that I would ever be able to atone for my mistakes.

At least Lynia didn't hate me. Now that the immediate threat was over, she had promised to spend more time with me. So I had hope. And I had a mission. Like Luke, I hoped to one day learn to master the Jedi way, and once and for all banish the taint of the dark side within me.

PART FIVE

PART FIVE

X-WING CD MISSIONS

X-WING CD MISSIONS

Special Note: In this section you'll find basic strategies for completing the following missions: Imperial Pursuit (Tour of Duty 4), B-Wing (Tour of Duty 5), plus all B-wing Historical Missions and the Bonus Missions included with the X-Wing CD-ROM. Good luck.

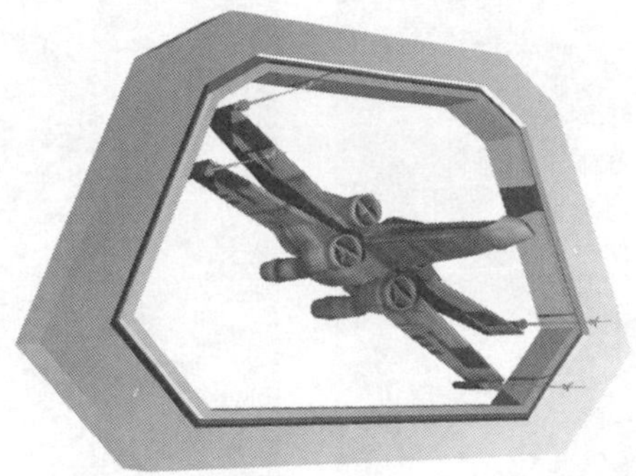

Tour of Duty #4—Imperial Pursuit

OP 1: Evacuate Yavin

File Name: t4mo1am

Mission Briefing

Following the destruction of the Death Star, a retaliatory strike on the base at Yavin is imminent, and so all personnel must be evacuated. You will fly an A-wing and escort corvette group Crescent, carrying the last of the evacuees. The corvettes will take 17 minutes to reach their jump point.

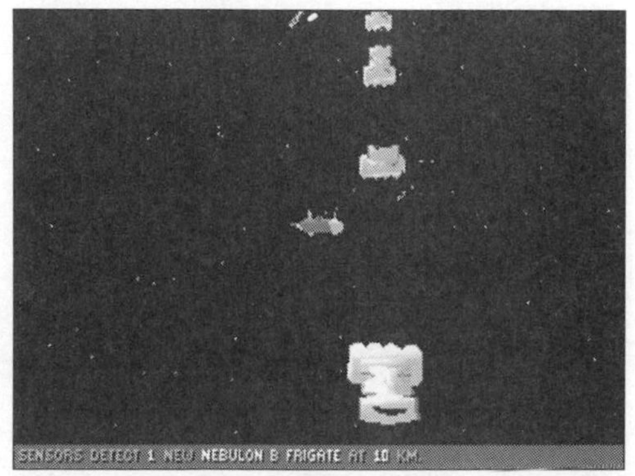

The Frigate arrives.

Farlander's After-Action Report

As I began the mission, piloting A-wing *Red 1*, I looked at the Inflight Map and examined the formation of the five corvettes. About 16 kilometers away, some Gunboats were attacking a group of four

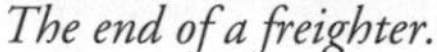
The end of a freighter.

Going after the Bombers.

supply freighters. The freighters' shields were already failing, and they were too far away to be saved. Anyway, my orders were to guard the corvettes.

I went through my mission start-up procedures and cycled through the corvettes to see what each one was carrying, then I assigned the lead ship to memory at F5. Just as I got my shields to maximum, I noticed a Nebulon B Frigate, the *Red Wind*, entering the area about ten kilometers away. Soon after, the freighters were destroyed and the Frigate launched two TIE fighters and four TIE Bombers.

I targeted the nearest Bomber and went in after the enemy. I intercepted the TIE fighters on my way to attack the Bombers, taking some shots as the T/Fs flew by. T/F *Eta 1* sustained hull damage from my onslaught, and turned back to the Frigate.

I continued my approach toward the T/Bs, shooting them quickly with my laser cannons. Even though the remaining TIE fighters were still a threat, I wasn't too worried about them; I kept after the Bombers.

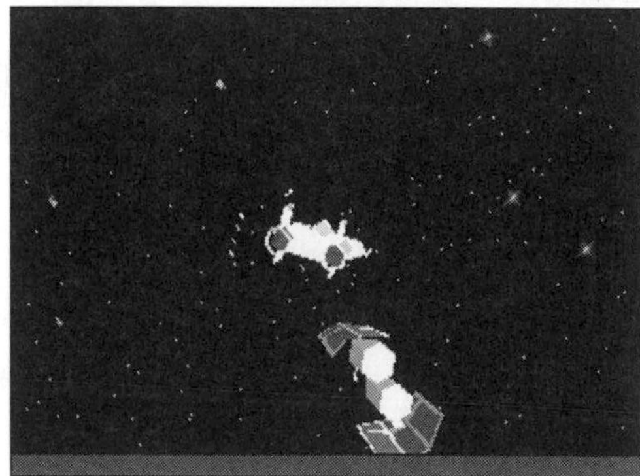
Bomber on my tail.

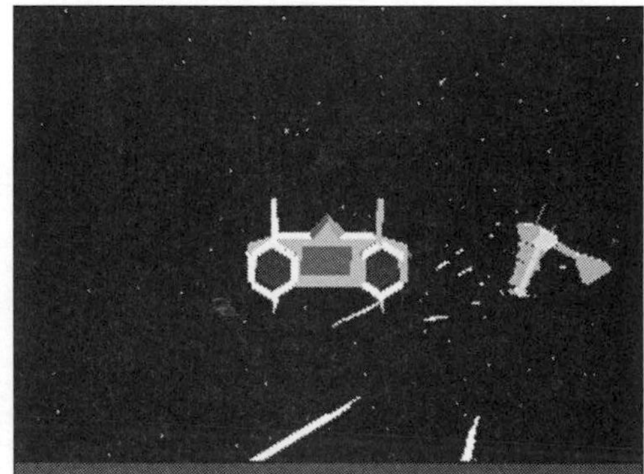
Taking fire from the Frigate.

TIE Bomber Delta 3 *is dead.*

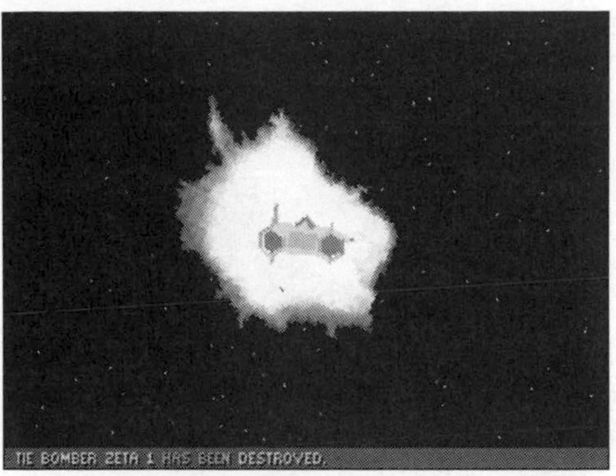

Destroying T/B Zeta 1.

The Frigate launched more T/Bs from group Beta, and I went after them with my lasers. I was close to the Frigate, though, and I had to keep away from its gunners. I put my shields on maximum recharge and kept them balanced, sustaining quite a few hits from the big ship.

The Assault Gunboats were now attacking the corvettes, but because the GUNs didn't have any missiles or torpedoes to launch, I figured that the five corvettes could handle the four Gunboats. I stayed near the Frigate after finishing off the Bombers, and took on TIE fighters until four T/Bs from Gamma group appeared. I took a quick look at the Inflight Map to make sure that I hadn't missed anyone, and then I closed in on the Bombers with quick missile shots, making short work of them.

Next came T/B group Delta. I took out a couple more Bombers with missiles, then switched back to lasers and went after the rest. I was able to make them break off their attack run, and then I mopped them up as they scattered.

For a moment, the area was clear; then, at around 9:40 on the clock, T/B Zeta launched from the Frigate. I did a weave to avoid the Frigate's fire and looped around to attack, putting both lasers and shields at maximum and boring in amongst the Bombers.

As soon as I finished off the last of T/B Zeta, a replacement wave launched, and I also noticed a new Gunboat group appear about 22 kilometers away.

I had three missiles left, but I decided to save them for the moment. While the GUNs were traversing the distance between us, I targeted the Bombers, again closing within range of the Frigate.

I shot the first Bomber with cannons, and then went after *Zeta 2* and *Zeta 3*, also with cannons. *Zeta 2* received hull damage, and began evasion

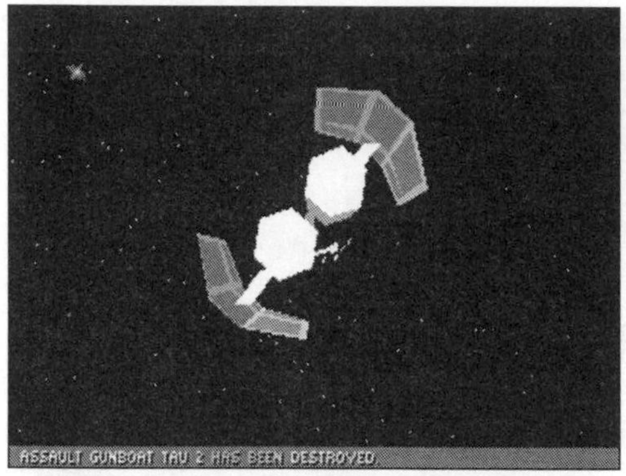

Point blank range.

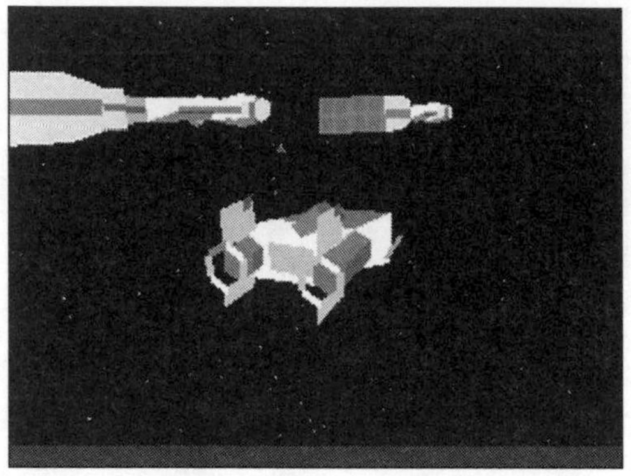
Close escort on the corvettes.

CRV Crescent 1 *escapes.*

maneuvers. I set my recharge rates to speed up again, noticing that *Zeta 3* was getting too far away. I caught up with him and took him out. The clock read 5:40.

Gunboat group Tau was now at about 13 kilometers, and I began circling about 3 kilometers from the Frigate, ready for any new TIE Bombers that might appear. Meanwhile, I kept an eye on the GUNs. After awhile, I decided that no more T/Bs were coming, so I took some ritual potshots at the Frigate and headed out to intercept the Gunboats just as they were about to attack the escaping corvettes.

The second group of Gunboats fared no better than the first, getting cooked by the corvettes before I could reach them; shortly after that, the corvettes began changing formation in preparation for their jump into hyperspace. I set my recharge rates to maximum and watched for any new danger. At just less than one minute on the clock, the corvettes began their jumps, and I got the Mission Complete message.

Debriefing (Win Conditions)
Corvette group Crescent must survive.

Mission Note: The key to this mission, as with many others, is stopping the Bombers before they can launch torpedoes.

OP 2: PROVIDE AREA PROTECTION

File Name: t4mo2xm

Mission Briefing

You will fly an X-wing, protecting Alliance forces as they head towards jump points during the retreat from Yavin.

Farlander's After-Action Report

I was assigned to X-wing *Red 2* in a two-ship group. After the last mission, when we lost some important food-supply freighters, we knew that it was important to protect what remained of the Alliance's supplies. We were to guard two three-ship groups of transports, one three-ship group of shuttles, and a pair of freighters.

I ran through my mission-start procedures: There were no enemies around. I placed X-W *Red 1* in memory at F5, and TRN *Lebo 1* at F6.

At just under 14:00 on the mission clock, a pair of Assault Gunboats appeared about six kilometers away. I redirected shield energy to my engines, set laser recharge rates to normal, and sped toward the GUNs.

As I came within laser range, I set my shield and laser recharge rates to maximum. Just as I began shooting at him, *Mu 2* fired a missile at *Red 1*. I closed in and blasted him into fragments, then turned my attention quickly to *Mu 1*, setting my shield recharge rates to normal to close the distance between us, and then giving him the same treatment.

Another pair of Gunboats followed the first, only three kilometers from me. I closed quickly on them and went after *Mu 2*, and *Red 1* followed, absorbing a missile hit in the process. As I destroyed *Mu 2* and took off after *Mu 1*, *Libra 1* entered hyperspace.

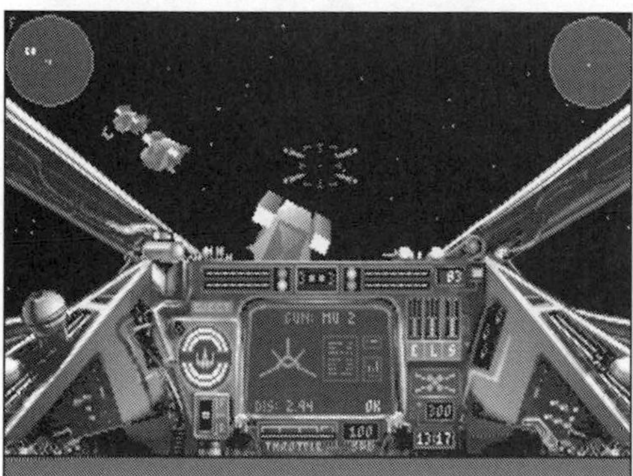

Going after Gunboats and transports.

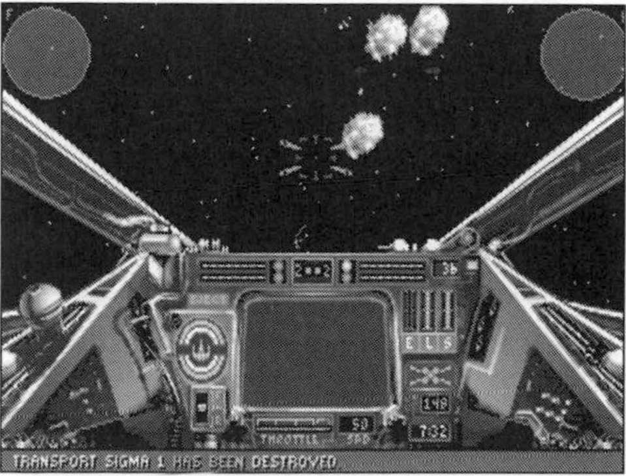

Clearing the area.

Shortly after that, I finished off *Mu 1*, about the same time shuttle group Chipr arrived. The mission clock read just under 11 minutes as I placed *Chipr 1* in memory location F6. All was quiet for the moment, but I was sure that it wouldn't last long.

Assault Gunboat group Nu fulfilled my prophecy, jumping into the area about three kilometers away. As I headed for the new threat, I routed more energy to my engines. The shuttle group entered hyperspace quickly, which was a relief. Without anyone else to attack, the Gunboats came after me, of course, but I was ready to fight them off.

Meanwhile, two bulk freighters from group Bo arrived about six kilometers away, and also two Imperial transports, those about four kilometers from me. *Nu 2* was still harassing me, so I asked my leader to attack him and took off toward the transports, arming my torpedoes and getting ready to fire.

The transports were quick, and launched two torpedoes apiece before I could get a lock on them. I blasted the first transport with one torpedo, then closed quickly on the second with lasers, energy recharge settings back to maximum. The first transport was still trying to attack the freighters, even after the torpedo hit, so I finished him off as well.

As Alliance TRN group Goat arrived, I noticed that *Red 1* was still dogfighting GUN *Nu 2*, so I set my recharge settings for more speed so that I might be of some help. Then the situation went from bad to worse: A Star Destroyer suddenly popped into the area, and that could only mean big trouble. The STD was about 24 kilometers away, so at least it wasn't an immediate threat. I flew in to finish off *Nu 2* as five TIE fighters from group Alpha were launched from the Star Destroyer.

After I finished off GUN *Nu 2*, a replacement wave arrived about a kilometer away, and I turned to engage *Nu 2* while *Red 1* attacked *Nu 1*. I made quick work of *Nu 2* and helped *Red 1* destroy the other Gunboat. TIE fighter Alpha was still quite a distance away, so I looked for closer prey. Gunboat group Rho jumped in about two kilometers away to oblige me as transport group Goat was entering hyperspace. Freighter group Bo was still in danger, however; those freighters move pretty slowly.

I closed at maximum speed to intercept GUN Rho as they began attacking the freighters with their lasers. I took out *Rho 1* as quickly as I could, and then went after *Rho 2*, wondering why *Red 1* wasn't more effective. T/F Alpha had closed within 17 kilometers.

More Gunboats arrived a couple of kilometers away, but two more transports also arrived, and because they were more dangerous, I switched to torpedoes and fired as soon as I got a lock on each ship. *Red 1* and I closed in to finish the job after firing the torpedoes.

Red 1 went after *Rho 2* and destroyed him, but *Bo 1* was under heavy attack by *Rho 1*. I headed toward *Rho 1* as the freighter entered hyperspace and safety. Soon after, I finished off *Rho 1* and got the Mission Complete message, just as T/F Alpha arrived on the scene. I stayed around to take out the TIE fighters even though X-wing Blue had arrived to relieve us. I set my cannons to quad-link and continued dogfighting until all the T/Fs were gone. After that, I decided to jump home and call it a job well done.

Debriefing (Win Conditions)
Transport groups Leeo and Gort, shuttle group Chipr and freighter group Eo must all survive.

Mission Note: The key to this mission is stopping the Gunboats quickly, while keeping an eye out for Imperial transports. The TRNs must be intercepted as soon as possible.

OP 3: EVACUATE CRUISER MAXIMUS

File Name: t4m03xw

Mission Briefing
The Alliance Cruiser *Maximus* has been caught in an Imperial ambush, and the crew, escaping aboard shuttles and transports, must be protected. You will fly in a two-ship group of X-wings, assisted by the remaining A-wings of Blue Squadron.

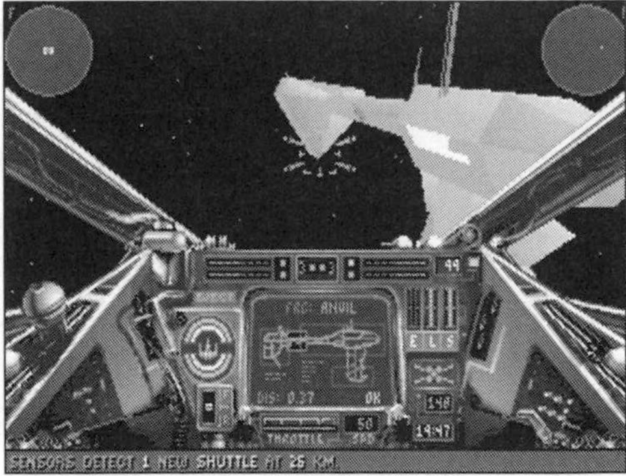

Flying by the Anvil.

Farlander's After-Action Report
I flew X-wing *Red 1* for this mission, checking my Inflight Map as the operation got underway to note the locations of the other ships. Frigate *Anvil* was nearby. A-wing Blue was about 9 kilometers behind my position, and the escaping transports and shuttles were stretched out between the Frigate and the doomed cruiser. The nearest enemy fighters were T/F Gamma, nearly 12 kilometers away.

We used all available laser energy to charge shields, and redirected shield energy to engines to achieve the greatest speed, leaving laser recharge rates at maximum.

I placed X-W *Red 2* at memory location F5, shuttle *T'ur 1* at F6, transport *Uzbe'k 1* at F7, and transport *Tadjyyyk 1* at F8. In this way, I could quickly relocate the endangered transports and shuttles.

I kept shunting laser energy to shields until they were fully charged, and then reset the laser recharge rate, redirecting the energy to my engines. My speed reached 150 as I closed within five kilometers of T/F *Gamma 1*, where I reset laser recharge rates back to maximum before ordering my wingman to attack *Gamma 1*. At about 18:30 on the mission clock, I got the message that the Calamarian cruiser *Maximus* and also A-W *Blue 2* were destroyed.

I took out *Gamma 1* in a head-on pass, relying on my shields to protect me, then ordered my wingman to attack *Gamma 2*. He took out *Gamma 2* quickly, and I searched for the next-nearest target, which turned out to be TIE Bomber *Alpha 2*, less than six kilometers away. I kept my laser recharge rates at maximum, and shield energy redirected to the engines, setting my cannons on quad-fire mode as I closed on *Alpha 2*. As I came around on the T/B's tail, I reset my shield recharge rate to maximum to match the Bomber's speed, and took him out.

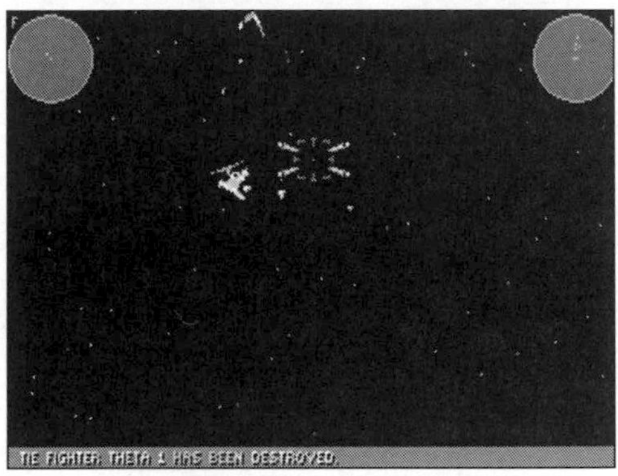

Taking out the TIE fighters.

I noticed then that TIE fighter group Theta had gotten past me, so I channeled all power to the engines, armed my torpedoes, and took off after them. I assigned my wingman to *Theta 3*, and I headed after *Theta 1*. The enemy was already firing on the escape craft by the time I launched my first torpedo. As I came in close, I reset laser recharge to maximum and took out *Theta 2* with cannons.

T/I group Beta was in the area by now, so I blasted *Beta 1* with a torpedo, then switched my attention to *Beta 3*. About that time, finally, transport group Uzbe'k entered hyperspace. Checking for other enemy craft, I located T/B *Zeta 2*, and turned to attack, blasting him until my CMD indicated hull-damage. Not feeling particularly merciful, I finished him off with a couple more shots.

My next target was T/I *Beta 3*, and as I went after him, someone pegged me twice. Checking the Inflight Map, I noticed that some T/Bs had gotten past me, but were only about one kilometer away. I switched to torpedoes and sent them a message.

My little area of space was full of TIE Interceptors, but my attack on the TIE Bombers made them break formation and begin evasive maneuvers. More of the Alliance escape craft were entering hyperspace as I continued to dogfight.

Finally, I got the Mission Complete message, though I decided to keep fighting the Imperials a while longer. Then my wingman caught one too many laser blasts, leaving me alone. It was getting far too hectic in the area, but I had little choice other than to continue to fight until I could get some clear space around me to jump out.

Debriefing (Win Conditions)
SHU groups Khaaza'k and Tur, and TRN groups Uzbe'k and Tadjyyyk must survive.

Mission Note: The key to this mission is to make sure that you stay between the fleeing Alliance ships and the Imperial fighters. Use the Inflight Map frequently. SHU Khaaza'k is the last to leave, so pay special attention to it.

OP 4: PROTECT FRIGATE ANVIL

File Name: t4m04aw

Mission Briefing
A-wing Red and X-wing Gold are assigned to protect the Frigate *Anvil* as it receives supplies from the corvette *Lauhu*.

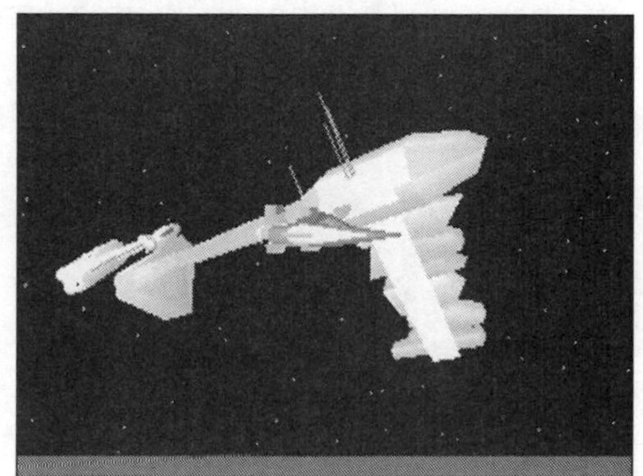
Guarding the Anvil.

Farlander's After Action Report
For this mission, I flew the number-two position in a two-ship group of A-wings. As the operation got underway, I checked the Inflight Map, noting that X-wing Gold was about nine kilometers away, and that the Frigate *Anvil* was just around six kilometers away.

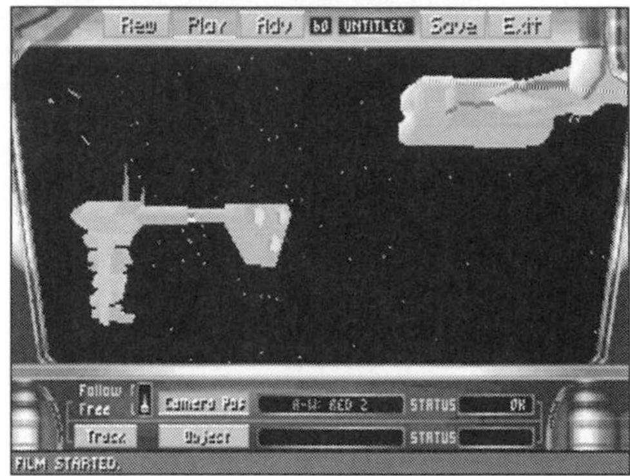

The corvette and the Frigate.

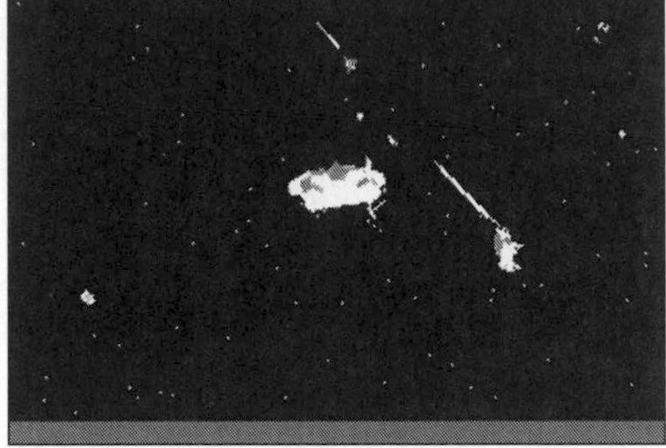

A-wings attacking.

As a precaution, I accounted for all the key Alliance ships in memory locations, putting A-wing *Red 1* in memory location F5, X-wing *Gold 1* in F6, the *Anvil* at F7, and the CRV *Lauhu* at F8.

About that time, four Assault Gunboats, designated Rho, arrived about 13 kilometers from my location. I quickly set my laser recharge rates to maximum, and redirected all shield energy to my engines to achieve a high speed, closing on the Gunboats. A-W *Red 1* and X-W Gold were also heading to intercept the enemy. At about 18:30 on the clock, I had closed within missile range, but I stayed with lasers. The Gunboats began firing missiles at the X-wings.

I reached laser-firing distance, and reset my shield recharge rates to maximum to slow down my A-wing, which otherwise would close too quickly on the slower Gunboats. I began firing steadily from behind *Rho 1*, making quick work of him. I next targeted *Rho 2*, and noticed that all three remaining craft—*Rho 2*, *Rho 3*, and *Rho 4*—were flying in a tight formation. As I assessed the possibilities, a Nebulon B Frigate arrived on the scene about six kilometers away.

Targeting T/B Beta 1.

T/B Alpha in formation.

I stayed on the Gunboats, firing quickly but watching for any sign of activity from the Frigate. I didn't have long to wait. Within moments, a group of TIE Bombers was launched, and I immediately switched to dual-fire missiles and fired to soften up *Rho 4*. I used a few laser shots to complete the job, and then I turned on *Rho 3* and gave him the same treatment.

By this time, T/B *Alpha 3* was within range, so I switched to single-fire missiles, waited until I got close, and fired one up his tail. Then I targeted *Alpha 2*, and gave him one as well. With the first two down, I switched my attention to *Alpha 1*, and chased him down with laser cannons.

The party was joined by TIE Interceptor group Gamma at that point, so I went after T/I *Gamma 2* as soon as the Bombers had been reduced to floating particles. The TIE Interceptors were faster than the Gunboats and Bombers, and I had to readjust my speed a little, reducing my shield recharge rates to normal.

My next target was *Gamma 3*, and as I turned toward him, I got the message that the docking operation was complete. So far, so good. The mission clock read 15:15, and all of Gamma group was destroyed.

Another group of T/Is from Delta group were on the way, currently at about seven kilometers. I redirected shield energy to the engines and headed for the nearest enemy, noting that more TIE Bombers had also arrived.

I intercepted T/I *Delta 3*, quickly shot him down, and then sent my wingman after *Delta 1*. Without shields, the T/Is and T/Bs went fast. I turned my attention to T/B *Eta 1* and switched to missiles. I was a little slow, and someone had already launched some torpedoes. *Eta 1* ate one of my missiles, however, and that was that. I gave *Eta 2* a missile as well. Then I noticed that another T/B group, Theta, had begun launching torpedoes.

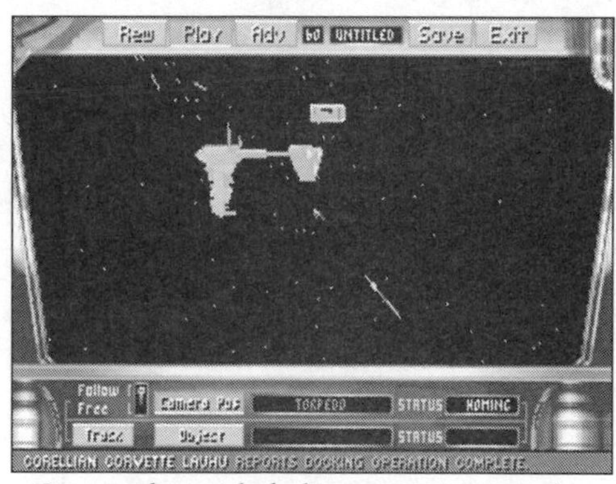

Camera shot with docking operation complete.

I kept after the T/Bs with missiles and cannons, finishing them off as quickly as I could. In an A-wing, I was able to move rapidly among the T/Bs, and destroy them with little danger to myself. Soon after, the *Anvil* made its jump into hyperspace, followed by the *Lauhu*. I was still in the thick of the action, so I kept after the Bombers until I had cleared my little area of space of all enemy fighters.

I decided to swing by the enemy Frigate, and identified it as the *Fire Lance*. There wasn't much left to do. The X-wings had jumped out of the area, and I wasn't quite crazy enough to go after an Imperial Frigate by myself. After the Mission Complete message flashed on my CMD, I turned on the hyperspace unit and headed home.

Debriefing (Win Conditions)
The Frigate *Anvil* and the corvette *Lauhu* must survive.

Mission Note: The key to this mission is, again, to prevent the T/Bs from launching their torpedoes. Protect the *Anvil* and the *Lauhu* from the Bombers' attacks.

OP 5: ABANDON SHIP

File Name: t4m05xw

Mission Briefing
The Frigate *Anvil* has been irreparably damaged, and must be abandoned. X-wing Red will guard the evacuation process, assisted by two Y-wings from Gold. After the corvette *Hart* and a group of three transports rescues the *Anvil*'s crew, X-wing *Red 1* must destroy the *Anvil* to keep it out of Imperial hands.

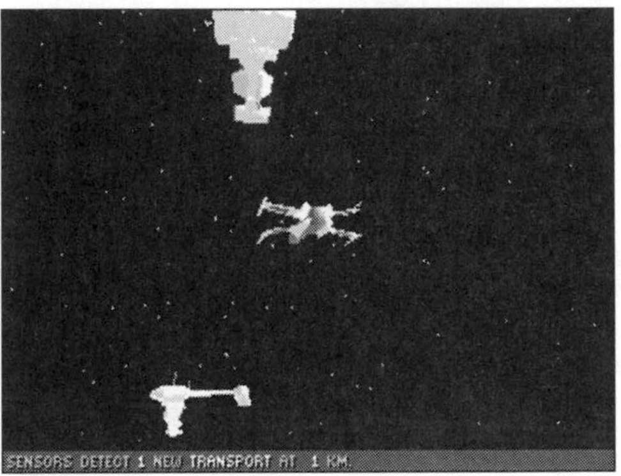

Hart & Anvil.

Farlander's After-Action Report
I flew X-wing *Red 1*, the leader of a three-ship group. I jumped in about 6.5 kilometers away from the *Anvil*, and immediately checked my Inflight Map to determine the status of the area. Then I went through my mission start-up procedures, and saved the *Anvil* at F5. The corvette *Hart* arrived, and I placed it at F6. I placed the Nav Buoy at F8—it was about 18 kilometers away—then I put X-wing *Red 2* at F7.

Transport *TT4449* arrived then, but so did three Imperial Gunboats, at a distance of about 18 kilometers. I turned toward them, resetting both laser and shield recharge rates to normal. As I set out after the GUNs, another

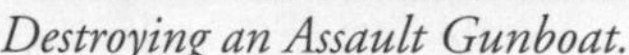
Destroying an Assault Gunboat.

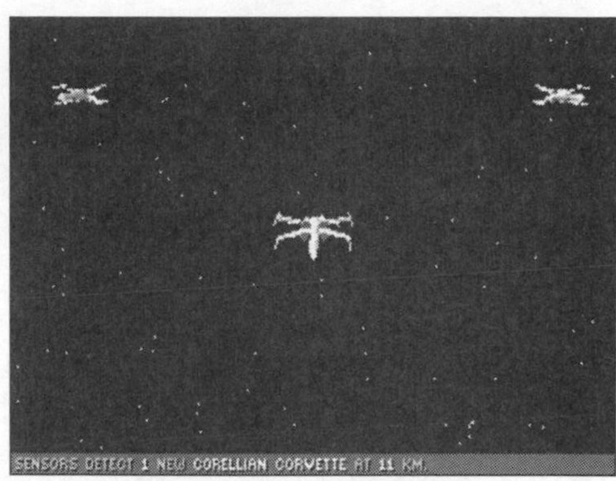

X-wing formation.

TRN arrived; *TT4472*. I looked again at the Inflight Map, and saw that the transports and the *Hart* were closing on the *Anvil*. The Gunboats were about 15 kilometers away, and also closing. The mission clock read 19:30. The third transport, *TT4475*, arrived about then.

I set my lasers on quad-fire as I reached a position nine kilometers from the *Anvil* and about five kilometers from the Gunboats. I didn't want to get much farther away from the evacuation operation, just in case an attack might happen from some other direction. The Gunboats fired missiles at me, which I evaded by going into a tight loop.

I assigned my wingmen to attack the Gunboats, while I waited for the missiles to self-destruct, which I knew they eventually would. Then I turned in toward the nearest enemy; GUN *Mu 3*. I set my recharge rates to maximum to match speed with the craft, and began firing lasers. I got the message from my R2 unit that the transports had entered the *Anvil's* hangar, as my wingmen and I quickly finished off the Gunboats.

The transports had emerged from the *Anvil*, carrying the evacuees. The mission clock reading 16:20.

I headed at full speed toward the *Anvil*, which was now about 10 kilometers away. The corvette *Hart* had docked with the *Anvil*, but now the situation took a bad turn, as an Imperial corvette appeared on the other side of the Frigate, just one kilometer from it. I quickly set my X-wing to maximum speed, with all energy redirected to the shields, and headed for this newest threat.

Meanwhile, Rebel Y-wings from Gold group launched and appeared to be going after the new corvette, as well. Two Imperial transports appeared then, also near the Frigate, and I quickly ordered my wingmen to go after one of the TRNs while I switched to single-fire torpedoes and drew a bead on the other.

As I closed within range of the blossoming dogfight, I reset shield and laser recharge rates to maximum. The enemy corvette began firing at me, and I had to redirect cannon energy to keep my shields up. When I had a good shot, I fired a torpedo at the first transport. As I switched my attention to the other TRN, I got the message that the *Hart* had completed docking operations with the *Anvil*.

One of the Imperial TRNs was using ion cannons against *Red 2*, presumably planning to use the same weapon to disable the Frigate so that they could capture it. We made sure they never got that chance.

When we had finished off the transports, more arrived, but a combination of torpedoes and lasers spelled their doom, as well. Soon the area was completely clear of enemy craft.

Now it was time to destroy the *Anvil*. The *Hart* was on the way to its jump point, so I made a pass on the Frigate, firing my lasers. My wingmen would not join me in attacking the *Anvil*, so I just shot until the craft was destroyed. I wanted to save my four remaining torpedoes, just in case.

I had almost finished scuttling the *Anvil* when two more Imperial corvettes arrived. I immediately ordered my wingmen to attack one of them, and, after the *Anvil* blew, I dropped all recharge rates to zero and sped to intercept the new CRVs. I switched to dual-fire torpedoes, intending to draw the corvettes fire away from the transports.

The evacuation transports were about 6 kilometers away, the enemy corvettes were 16 kilometers away, and the *Hart* cruised at a distance of about 2.5 kilometers.

As I closed within six kilometers of the corvettes, I reset my laser recharge rates to maximum and my shield recharge rates to normal. When I

Scuttling the Anvil *as CRVs arrive.*

Death of the Anvil.

got a red lock, I fired all four remaining torpedoes at the first corvette, *Viper 1*, dropping its shields.

With my shields at maximum charge, I strafed *Viper 1* with lasers, managing to damage his hull on the first run. I turned away, and wove out to let my lasers recharge before circling around to finish him off.

Going after the CRVs of Viper group.

My wingmen were still awaiting direction, so I ordered them to join me in attacking the other corvette. A three-ship group of Gunboats from Tau arrived, but we stayed with the CRV. We had inflicted serious hull damage on *Viper 2* by the time the evacuation transports began entering hyperspace. The clock read 6:20.

With *Viper 2* destroyed, I went after the Gunboats with my cannons on quad-fire and all recharge rates at maximum. I ordered my wingmen to attack one of the Gunboats while I went after another. When I finished off the first of the GUNs, I redirected shield energy to my engines, speeding toward the next enemy craft before returning the shield setting to maximum recharge.

All the transports had entered hyperspace by the time I finished off the last of GUN Tau. The clock read about 5:00.

The corvette *Hart* was still about nine kilometers from the Nav Buoy and its jump point. Three more Gunboats arrived then, and we went back to work.

By the time I had finished off Gunboat group Tau, corvette *Hart* was about five kilometers from a safe jump. Another wave of GUN Tau arrived, and I went after them. The process was beginning to seem routine: quad-fire; match speed; cut them down. I think *Red 2* would have disagreed, however, as I got the message he had been destroyed.

Still another wave of GUN Tau arrived, and we kept fighting, wishing just for the moment that corvettes were a little faster in normal space.

X-W *Red 3* was lost then, but the Y-wings were still out there firing. The next wave of Gunboats took a new tack: Two of them went after me, while the third went after the *Hart*. I got the incoming missile warning and began evading, and finally, the *Hart* made it to its jump point. The mission clock read 0:00.

I got the Mission Complete message, but I was still under attack from the Gunboats, and decided to finish off the remaining enemy craft before heading back home, right behind the Y-wings.

Debriefing (Win Conditions)
The CRV *Hart* and all three of the Alliance transports must survive. The Frigate *Anvil* must be destroyed.

Mission Note: The Alliance TRNs are never in serious jeopardy, so concentrate on protecting the corvette *Hart*.

OP 6A: GUARD REPAIR OPERATIONS

File Name: t4m06xma

Mission Briefing
The Alliance freighter *Op Mus*, carrying a vital supply of grain, has broken down, and must be protected while repair operations are made. The transport *Jaamn* is on route with a repair crew, and you will fly one of a pair of X-wings to secure the area until the *Op Mus* can leave under its own power.

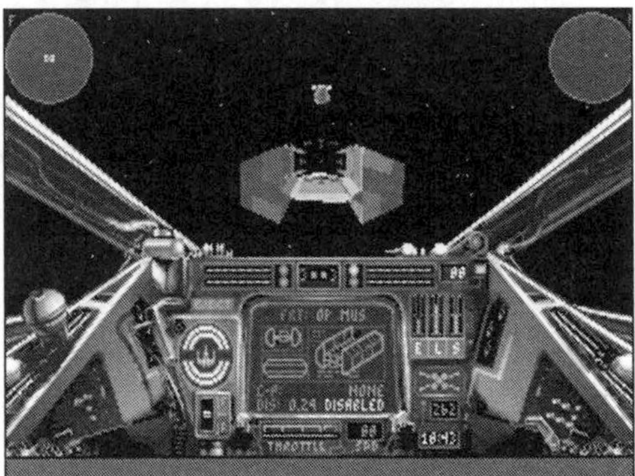

The Op Mus *is disabled.*

Farlander's After-Action Report
I was the flight leader, and I went through my standard mission-start procedure after arriving on the scene. No enemy craft were nearby, and I put the freighter *Op Mus* in memory location F6. When transport *Jaamn* arrived, I put it in F7, all the while fully charging my shields and lasers.

Just as I achieved maximum charge, a two-ship Gunboat group entered the area, and I immediately sent my wingman after *Mu 1*, while I moved to engage *Mu 2* with lasers.

My wingman was still struggling after I had polished of *Mu 2*, so I helped him destroy *Mu 1*, provoking the arrival of two new Gunboats: *Nu 1*

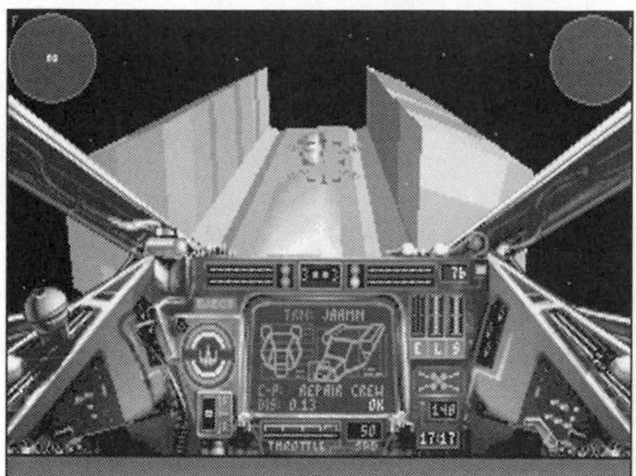

Repairs under way.

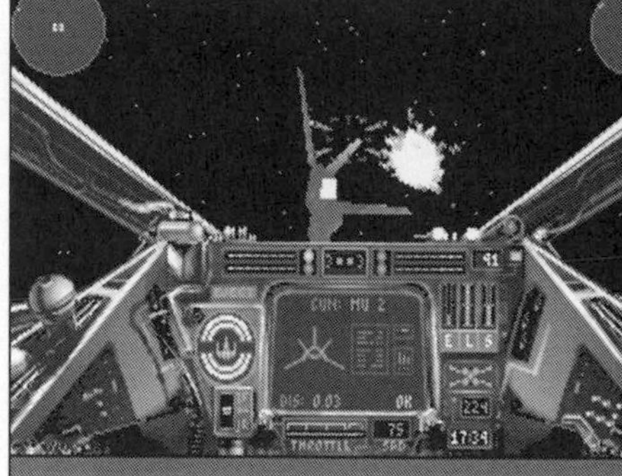

Blasting GUN Mu 2.

and *Nu 2*. I assigned my wingman to *Nu 1* and went after *Nu 2* with lasers, though once again I had to come to my wingman's aid when I had finished off my own target.

By this time, the transport *Jaamn* had docked with the freighter, and repair operations were under way. Meanwhile, two more Gunboats arrived, this time from Tau group. After sending my wingman after *Tau 1*, I plastered *Tau 2* with a torpedo from right on his tail. About five more laser shots finished him off. I had to move quick to take out *Tau 1* at that point, as he had eluded my wingman (who was this guy, anyway?) and was headed for our transport. A torpedo and a few laser bursts did the trick.

Another wave of GUN Mu arrived, but they seemed intent on the transport, so I decided to wait until they had passed, then turn in behind them for a few torpedo shots. In retrospect, this was far from the best idea I'd ever had, as one of the GUNs loosed a missile that I was forced to absorb with my forward shields.

Targeting GUN Mu 1.

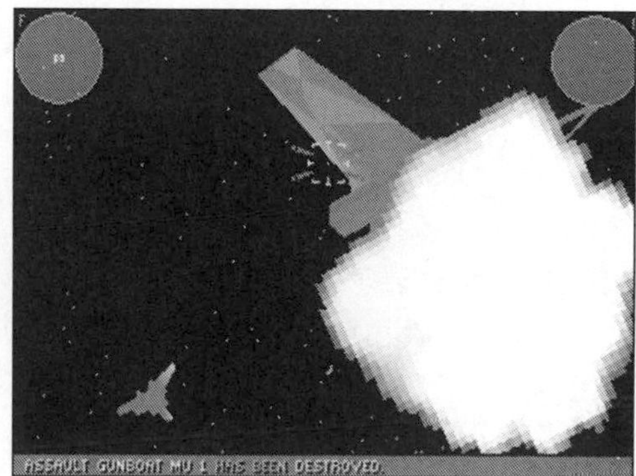

Torpedoing GUN Mu 1.

After rebalancing my shields, I turned in behind the Gunboat and fired a torpedo, finishing him off with lasers. I quickly recharged my shields by transferring energy from the lasers, then joined my wingman in destroying *Mu 1*.

Two more waves of Gunboats, from groups Nu and Rho, arrived on the scene, but we made quick work of them. My wingman seemed to finally be finding his bearings. Some Y-wings also entered the area, but did nothing aggressive, so we left them alone.

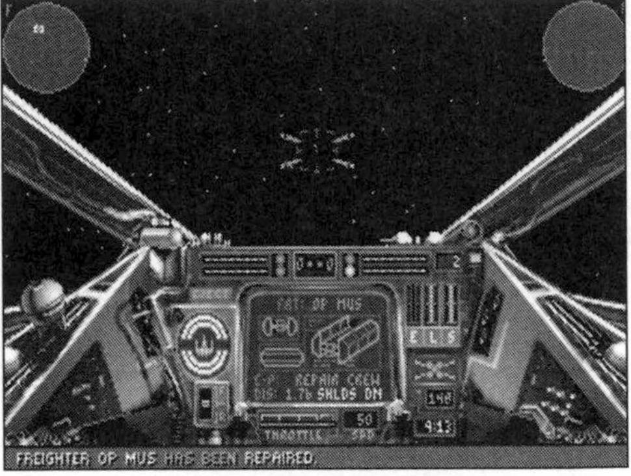

Repairs are completed.

Throughout our dogfighting, I was careful that we didn't get lured too far away from the freighter. Whenever any enemy moved to attack either the transport or the freighter, I broke off my current engagement and hurried to provide defense.

I had learned by now that a torpedo, even fired from a distance of a kilometer or more, would divert a Gunboat long enough for me to close that gap, though I had also learned to be careful that the Alliance ships I was protecting weren't in any danger should a missile go astray of its intended target.

The docking procedure was completed 10:55 into the mission, and with 8:30 remaining on the clock, transport *Jaamn* entered hyperspace. Soon after that, the freighter followed, and I got the Mission Complete message. I was still engaged in battle with some Gunboats, so I took care of the immediate threat and then left the scene.

Debriefing (Win Conditions)

The freighter *Op Mus* and the transport *Jaamn* must survive.

Mission Note: There is a chance, depending on when you destroy the first waves of Mu and Nu, that the second waves will arrive together. Take on the nearest threat to the freighter and transport first, and work your way through them. If you have torpedoes, you may want to use some.

OP 6B: PROTECT SUPPLY CONTAINER

File Name: t4m06xmb

Mission Briefing

An Alliance ship evading Imperial attack was forced to drop and abandon a container full of grain in the Lesser Plooriod Cluster. Fly escort in a two-ship group of X-wings while the freighter *Trips* attempts to recover the cargo. Also, beware a specially modified Imperial corvette rumored to be on patrol in the area.

Farlander's After-Action Report

I was assigned to Red Squadron—flight leader in a two-ship group of X-wings. I jumped into the area and immediately checked for the closest enemy craft, spotting only T/F Alpha at a distance of around 18 kilometers.

I checked the Inflight Map, and discovered that behind the TIE fighters were some TIE Bombers. I knew that I'd have to keep them away from the supply container, and since TIE Bombers can begin launching torpedoes at a distance of 5 kilometers, I figured that that was my radius of operations.

I decided to head in the direction of the enemy craft and wait about 5 kilometers from the container. I ran through the standard start-of-mission sequence, and put the throttle to full. I put the container *D3RM3* into memory at position F5. After I arrived at my desired location, I circled, awaiting the enemy craft, resetting shield recharge rates to normal to gain a little more speed. The T/Fs were still about 3 kilometers away.

When the fighters were within about two kilometers, my wingman took out after them. As I turned to engage the T/Fs, three of them turned toward me in response. In general, I try to avoid head-on attacks—much better to have the enemy in your sights when he doesn't have you targeted—and facing three-to-one odds, I decided to evade.

I looped around behind the closest fighter and shot him down with a dual-fire spread, then continued after the remaining T/Fs, although I kept my eye on the T/Bs. I knew that I could always send my wingman after a fighter; the Bombers were certainly a greater threat.

When an enemy corvette jumped into the area, I wasted no time: We had been warned in our briefing that this was a particularly dangerous CRV, a prototype of some kind, and I decided I didn't want to know what tricks it had up its metallic sleeve.

Switching to dual-fire mode, I acquired a red lock quickly, and launched all six of my torpedoes at the new arrival. Back to the drawing board, Imperial scum.

Next, I took off after the TIE Bombers. This was risky, and, in hindsight, I might have waited until they came a little closer before engaging them, but I was greedy for my share of kills. My wingman had already broken up their formation, and I was able to go in with lasers and help finish them off.

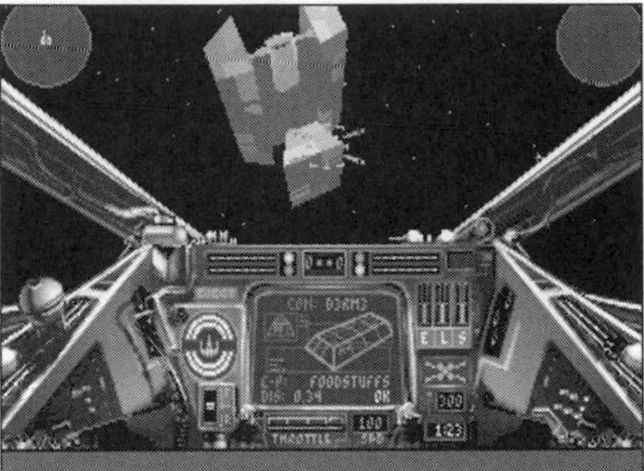

Freighter and container docking.

After the T/Bs were destroyed (at about six minutes remaining), I headed at high speed back toward the container.

At five minutes remaining, a pair of Gunboats from Mu group jumped into the area. Both myself and the GUN group were about four kilometers from the container, on opposite sides. I ordered my wingman to attack *Mu 1*, and went after *Mu 2* myself.

FRT Trips *is loaded and leaving for hyperspace.*

At 3:12 remaining, the freighter *Trips* finally docked with the container. I finished up with *Mu 2* and went to help my wingman.

At 1:08 remaining, the freighter reported that its docking operation was complete. The latest Gunboat arrivals seemed more interested in attacking our X-wings than the container, so it was relatively easy for the *Trips* to escape to hyperspace after that. The Mission Complete message came up, and my wingman and I hypered home.

Debriefing (Win Conditions)

The container *D3RM3* must be boarded, and the freighter *Trips* must survive.

Mission Note: If you can destroy the modified corvette within 30 seconds of its appearance (at 9:40 of the mission clock), it prevents the CRV from launching a TIE Bomber, which is followed by two additional waves of single T/Bs. Also note that, during this operation, a neutral freighter jumps into the area and leaves a neutral container. If you want, you can go destroy the container. This action triggers an impressive battle between a Calamarian cruiser and two Imperial Frigates, which you can join or observe.

OP 7: HIDE AND SEEK

File Name: t4m07ym

Mission Briefing

An Imperial convoy is scheduled to pass through a region of space near an asteroid field. According to intelligence reports, at least one of the craft will be carrying much-needed grain, and the asteroid field would make a good area from which to launch a sneak attack. Identify any vessels carrying foodstuffs, disable them, and X-wing Gold and transport *Raider* will arrive to help retrieve the cargo.

Farlander's After-Action Report

I flew a solo mission in Y-wing *Red 1*, and went through my standard procedure, setting my throttle to zero at first and charging my lasers and shields fully while sitting in the asteroid field. At 18:45, I headed at full throttle toward the freighters, with both shields and lasers at normal recharge rates. At 17:45 on the clock, five transports entered the area, and, shortly after that, one more appeared. I had a hunch that the last transport to enter was important.

I flew by the freighters, making a loop through them to ID them all. None of them was carrying the grain I was after. The five transports that had entered earlier were now turning on me and attacking. I was ready to return fire, but I had to ID them before destroying them, so I had to be sure to damage, but not destroy, until I had seen what they were carrying.

I kept my shields even, and raised the recharge rates on my lasers and shields, taking evasive maneuvers to avoid being raked by their combined fire.

Even with recharge rates at maximum, I was faster than the transports, and found myself using the throttle-down keys to slow my craft after I had a TRN in my sights. I kept after the transports until I found *Kappa 6*, loaded with grain. He was aggressive, but I disabled him with ion cannons before mopping up the other TRNs.

A group of three shuttles entered the area after I had disabled *Kappa 6*, and I turned to engage. I maneuvered in behind the shuttles and hit them with one or two torpedoes, then finished them off with a flurry of laser blasts.

After the first two shuttles were destroyed, I went after the third exclusively with lasers, saving my torpedoes just in case. At about 12 minutes remaining, an Imperial corvette entered the area, approximately six kilometers from the disabled transport. I headed toward it. Meanwhile, X-wing Gold entered, along with a special transport, *Raider*, and moved towards *Kappa 6*.

With six torpedoes remaining, I got ready to open fire on the corvette, launching the whole load as soon as I had a red lock.

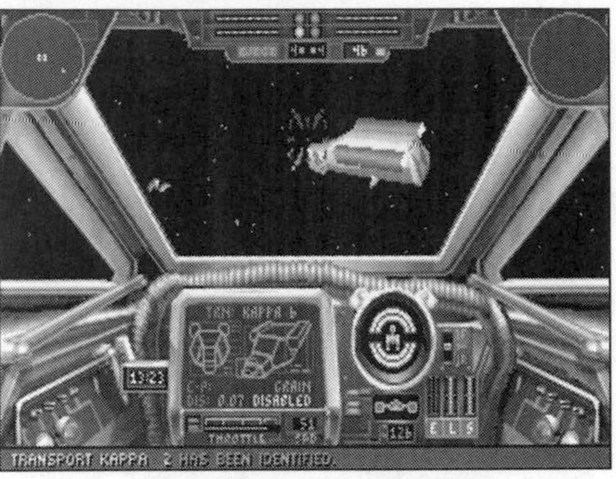

TRN Kappa 6 *is disabled.*

With ten minutes remaining, I got the Docking Complete message. At about the same time, the corvette received my six torpedoes, and was obliterated. At just more than nine minutes remaining, I received the Mission Complete message. Almost simultaneously, I noticed that three Gunboats from group Mu had appeared, and I dispatched them before heading home.

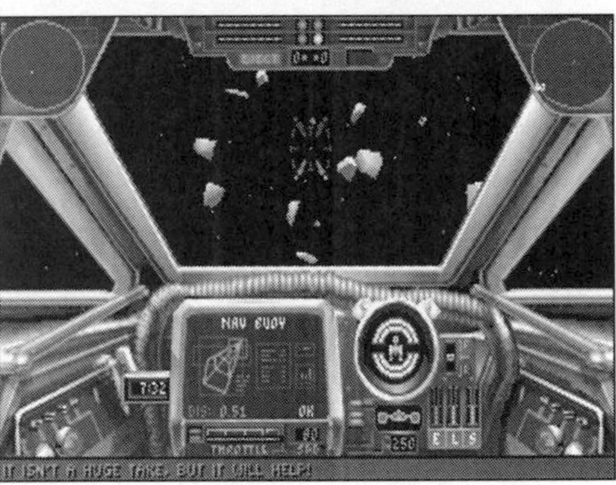

End of the mission.

Debriefing (Win Conditions)
Transport *Kappa 6* must be boarded, transport *Raider* must survive.

MISSION 8A: CLEAR MINEFIELD

File Name: t4m08xma

Mission Briefing
Overlord Ghorin, ruler of the Greater Plooriod Cluster, has agreed to sell grain to the Alliance. The transfer of the much-needed food supply will be made near a hyperspace jump point that has recently been mined by the Empire. You will fly a Y-wing into the area and clear it prior to the arrival of an Alliance freighter. You will have about seven minutes to take care of 57 mines.

Farlander's After-Action Report

I performed the standard mission-start procedure, making sure to charge up shields to their maximum. I surveyed the area, locating the mines and noticing that many of them were oriented on flat, imaginary planes. I decided to attack along those planes.

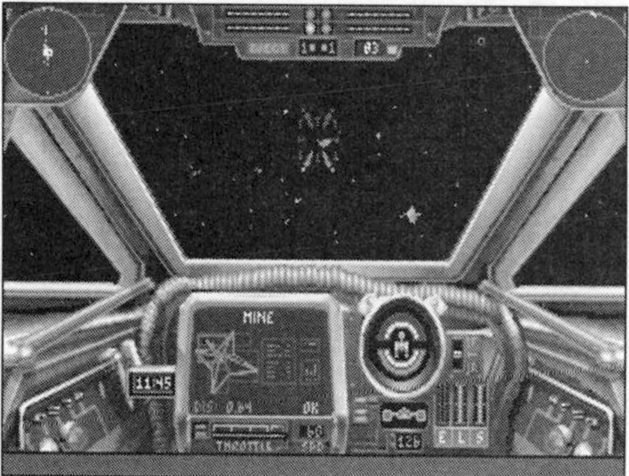

Targeting a mine.

After I was among the mines, I began firing in single-shot mode, using the joystick button to target the next mine, and then shooting again as quickly as possible. Usually, one shot was all it took, and it was important to keep moving to avoid being hit. I didn't shoot randomly, however, because every missed shot was wasted energy that could have gone into my shields. I used the single-shot mode because, with the guns so close together on the Y-wing, there was no advantage to dual-shot.

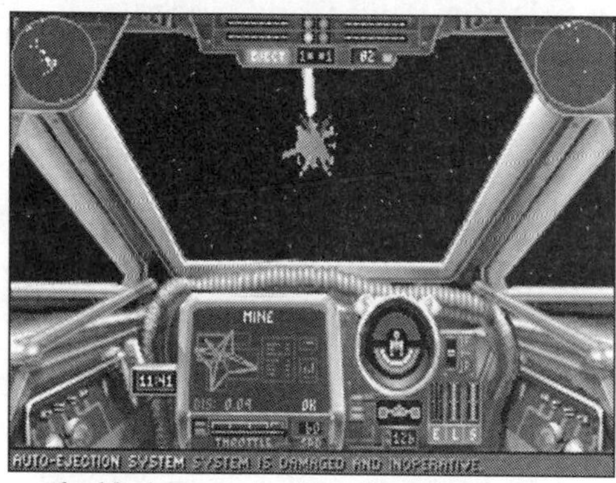

Shields down and taking damage to systems.

I kept transferring laser energy to my shields and balancing them. There was no need to keep the lasers supercharged, because even the weakest shot would take out a mine.

When my shields began to ebb, I headed away from the mines, shifting protective power to the rear. The mines' range was about two kilometers, so I went beyond that to recharge. I shot some torpedoes at the mines while I waited for the shields to build back up again.

At about eight minutes remaining, as I was destroying the final mine, freighter *Plee'h 1* entered the area.

I had been very efficient, but even if a few of the mines had remained active, I could have continued to destroy them after the Alliance ship arrived. The freighter could have taken a few hits, and I also could have flown among the mines, distracting them from the freighter while I finished the job.

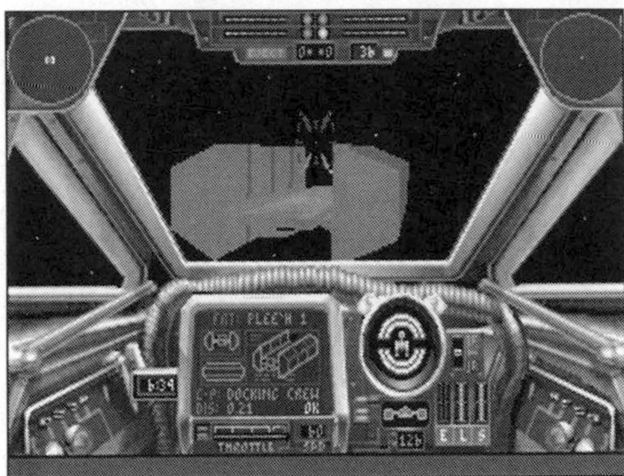

Flyby of the Plee'h 1.

End of mission.

I kept close to the freighter, and at five minutes on the clock, a second freighter, *Plee'h 2*, hypered in.

At 2:45 on the clock, the first freighter jumped to hyperspace, and the Mission Complete message appeared on my console. I headed for home.

Debriefing (Win Conditions)
All mines must be destroyed. The freighter *Plee'h 1* must survive.

OP 8B: DESTROY COMM AREA

File Name: t4m08ymb

Mission Briefing
Imperial corvettes are deploying mines around a communications satellite near Saheelindeel, far from any Alliance outposts. An attack would divert attention from Rebel operations near the Greater Plooriod Cluster. You will fly an X-wing, charged with destroying the mines and intercepting any Imperial response. Y-wing Blue will handle the Imperial corvettes.

Farlander's After-Action Report
When I first entered the area, piloting X-wing *Red 1*, I noticed the corvettes nearby. Since they were not my primary objective, I ignored them, and focused instead on the minefield.

I was about eight kilometers from the nearest mine, giving me time to execute my standard mission-start procedure. As I was surveying the minefield, I noticed that some enemy Gunboats were also in the area, and were, in fact, close enough to be launching missiles at me!

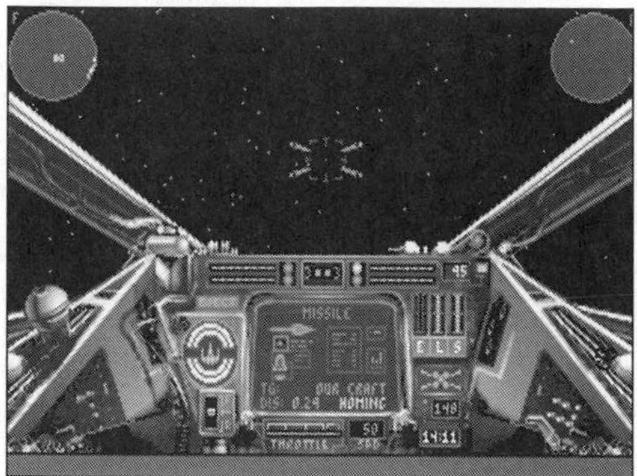

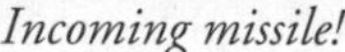
Incoming missile!

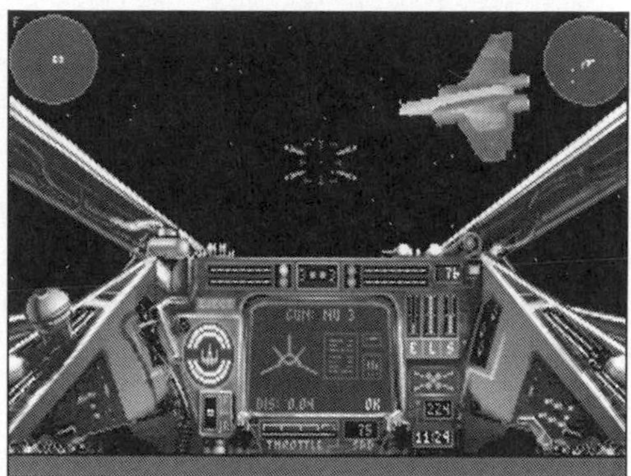
Gunboats from Mu Squadron.

I broke off my approach to the minefield and turned to engage the GUNs. My first task was to evade the missiles as best I could, looping until they exhausted themselves. Then I turned to the attack, setting laser and shield recharge rates to full, thus dropping my speed to match the Gunboats.

I used my lasers to take out GUN *Mu 1*, then found *Mu 3* nearby and took him out as well. I thought about leaving *Mu 2* alone and going after the minefield, but he wasn't going to let me go, so I had to destroy him as well.

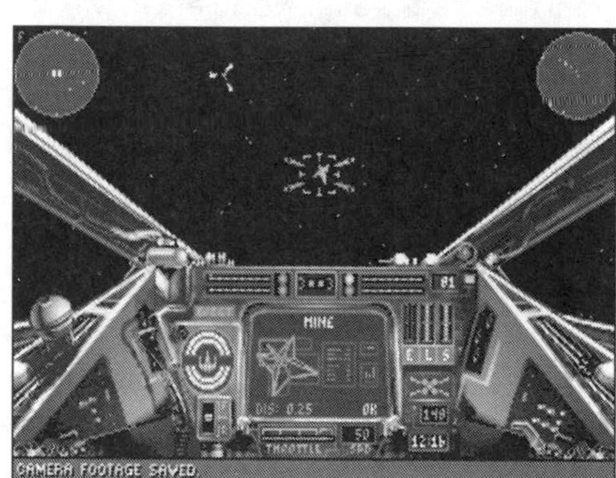

Mines & satellite.

At about this time, I got a message that one of the corvettes had been destroyed. I also noticed that another corvette had hull damage, so I fired a torpedo at it to collect the kill.

Now, as I approached the minefield, I made sure that my shields were fully charged. There were only 14 mines, so I figured that it would be a simple job. I proceeded to wade in, shooting quickly and dodging the incoming fire. After the mines were destroyed, I shot the communications satellite. With my mission accomplished, I looked around for any remaining enemy craft, then jumped back home.

Debriefing (Win Conditions)

All mines and comm sats must be destroyed.

Mission Note: In an X-wing, using dual-fire mode works best against mines, because of the spread pattern caused by the cannons' placement.

OP 9: GUARD CARGO TRANSFER

File Name: t4m09am

Mission Briefing

Freighters from Overlord Ghorin's fleet will rendezvous with Alliance ships to deliver the much-needed grain supply. Fly escort, and keep your eyes open; though Ghorin claims he has become sympathetic to the Rebel cause, he is not to be trusted.

Farlander's After-Action Report

I was flight leader in a three-ship group of A-wings, and we found the area all clear at the beginning of the mission, so I ran through my standard mission-start procedure. Soon, a neutral freighter entered the area, and I flew toward it to find out what was inside.

Transmor 3 contained a cargo of grain. *Khan 3* followed; a Rebel freighter carrying the docking crew.

Things seemed to be going according to plan, then, to the surprise of almost no one, Gunboats *Mu 1* and *Mu 2* appeared on the scene.

I targeted *Mu 1*, and told my wingmen to attack, as I went after *Mu 2*. These GUNs were not carrying any torpedoes, so they weren't much of a threat to the freighters. The transports that followed at 17:52, however, were loaded with torps and much more dangerous.

I immediately went after the transports, and assigned my wingmen to join me. Our objective was to stop the TRNs before they could get within five kilometers of the freighters or else they would be able to lock and fire.

On my way to intercept, one of the Gunboats got in my way and paid the ultimate price. Then my wingmen and I were on the transports and, within minutes, they were destroyed. We turned our attention back to the

Point blank shooting on GUN Mu 2.

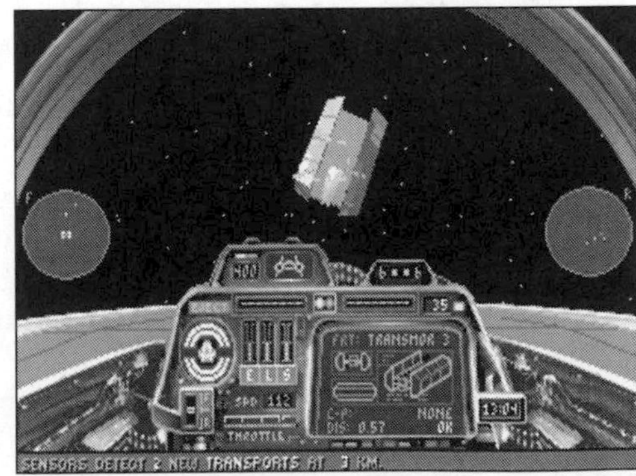

Transmor 3 *getting ready to jump to hyperspace.*

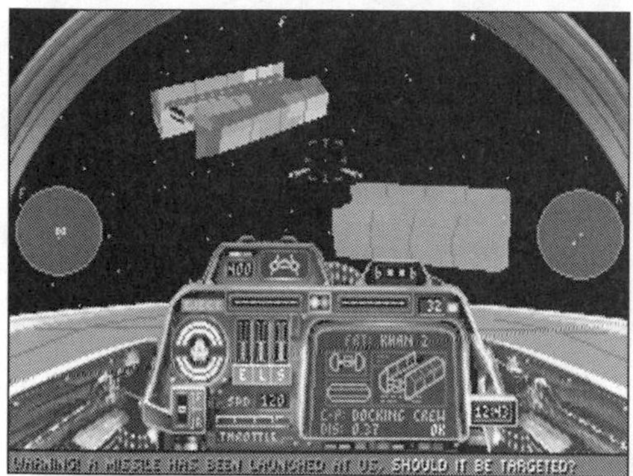

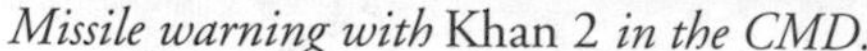

Missile warning with Khan 2 *in the CMD.*

Freighters docking.

remaining Gunboats then, and finished them off. I attacking with lasers only, saving my missiles in case I really needed them.

After the first group of Gunboats had been destroyed, another group appeared. I kept one eye on the message line to watch for any ships that might carry torpedoes, or for missiles that could endanger the freighters.

At 15:35 on the clock, the two freighters docked and began transferring cargo. I kept checking the Inflight Map to assess the locations of ships in the area. At 14:20 on the clock, another neutral freighter appeared.

At around 12:30 on the clock, two more transports from Kappa group appeared, and I took my wingmen after them immediately. These transports got in closer than I liked, so I switched to missiles and fired two before finishing off the second TRN with lasers.

After this most recent threat was eliminated, I returned close to the docking point to stay near the freighters. You never knew where a threat would appear, or when.

At about 8:40 on the clock, two ships of GUN Tau entered the area, accompanied by two transports designated *Lambda 1* and *Lambda 2*. The TRNs would have to be my top priority. Again, I used two missiles on each transport, followed with a few spurts of the laser, and the transports were rubble. I wasn't able to prevent them from shooting off some torpedoes, but I managed to destroy them before they had emptied their payload.

With the last satisfying explosion of TRN Lambda, I turned my attention back to the Gunboats from Tau group and took care of them, finishing up just as two more transports arrived. I used my missile strategy on them, as well.

At 5:00 on the clock, *Khan 1* and *Transmor 4* had completed their missions, and the final Docking Complete message came through. At 4:10 on the clock, the final freighter had jumped to hyperspace, and I got the Mission Complete signal.

When I had finished mopping up some stray Gunboats, I initiated the jump sequence. More Gunboats appeared as I was getting prepared for hyperspace, but I figured that the job was done, and allowed the countdown to continue.

Debriefing (Win Conditions)

All freighters must dock and transfer; Alliance freighters must survive.

OP 10: GRAIN SNATCH

File Name: t4m10aw

Mission Briefing

The grain provided by Ghorin was tainted, and would have caused widespread illness had the treachery not been detected. Fortunately, our intelligence operations have uncovered a cache of grain at a nearby Imperial storage facility. Fly an A-wing and make a reconnaissance of the facility. The freighter *Sarsuma* will arrive to load any grain detected.

Farlander's After-Action Report

I came out of hyperspace and immediately checked the Inflight Map, discovering two groups of TIE fighters in the immediate area. Each group consisted of five craft, and the nearest, T/F Alpha, was about 3.5 kilometers from my location. They seemed to be escorting a pair of neutral shuttles. About 9 kilometers away, the second group of T/Fs seemed to be guarding a formation of six cargo containers, located about 6 kilometers from my position.

I quickly ran through my mission-start procedures, but didn't have time to fully charge my shields. I placed laser recharge rates at maximum and shield recharge at normal, then, with the throttle at full, I turned away from the oncoming T/Fs, charging my shields from laser energy as quickly as I could. The TIE fighters were slowly gaining, but my shields were quickly charging.

After my lasers had recharged fully as well, I turned to engage. The enemy was about two kilometers away.

Because A-wings aren't known for great shield strength, I chose to do a Wotan Weave as I approached the TIE fighters, avoiding their combined fire. I switched to dual-fire mode and turned in on the first T/F, blasting him and moving on to the next. My laser recharge rate was at maximum, and my shields were recharging at the normal rate. They were going down like flies, but then T/F group Beta joined the fray, and I had eight (and then seven) T/Fs after me.

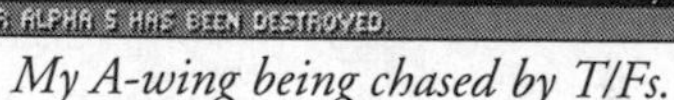

My A-wing being chased by T/Fs.

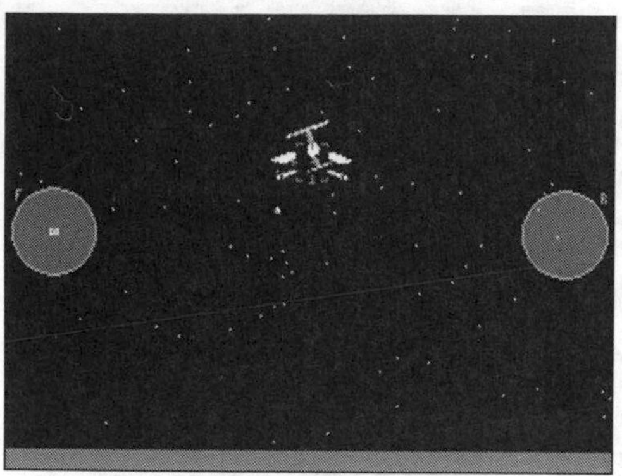

Getting a shot on a T/F.

My shields took a few hits, but I dodged a few shots as well, and kept up my own attack. The number of TIEs dwindled rapidly.

By the time I finished off the TIE fighters from Alpha and Beta groups, I was about eight kilometers from the containers. The two neutral shuttles were about six kilometers away. I inspected the shuttles, and found that they were both bearing government officials.

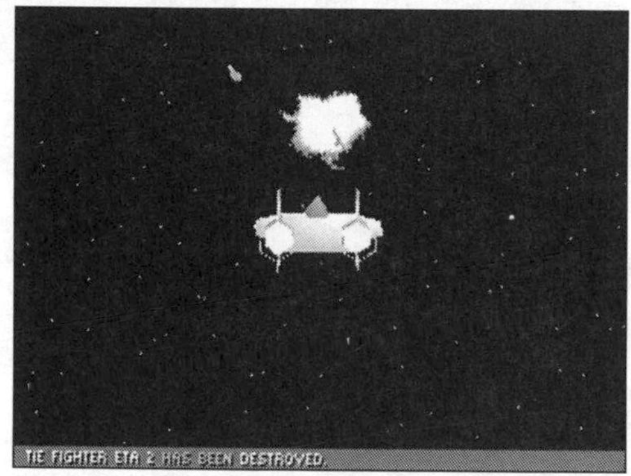

Death of a TIE fighter.

Since they were neutrals, I chose not to attack them. Even though they were dealing with the Imperials, they might have had no choice. Maybe at a later date, they would turn out to be our allies. I left them and headed for the containers.

As I approached the CONs, I slowed down to one-third speed to inspect them for grain. There were six, arranged as three stacked pairs. I had just inspected the second of CON group Pi when an Imperial freighter came out of hyperspace nearby. The freighter dropped a container, then quickly jumped back into hyperspace. Having found nothing in the original six, I went over to inspect this new container (*Psi 1*) and found the grain I'd been looking for.

I knew that our freighter would come in now, so I was dismayed to see a Star Destroyer appear instead. Sure enough, and not without a certain irony, FRT *Sarsuma* jumped in practically on top of the STD *Badi Dea*. The Star Destroyer's turbolasers immediately began spitting death.

The Sarsuma *in the CMD, with Star Destroyer.*

I popped my throttle to full speed, as TIE Bomber group Beta launched and immediately helped the Star Destroyer's gunners finish off the doomed freighter. There was no longer any reason to stay in the area, so I jumped for home. I had done my part, but we had come up empty. I knew that we were going to have to find a source of grain soon.

Debriefing (Win Conditions)

Container groups Chi, Xi and Pi must be identified. Container *Psi 1* must be identified. TIE fighter groups Alpha and Eta must be destroyed. The freighter *Sarsuma* must arrive.

OP 11: CAPTURE GHORIN'S Y-WINGS

File Name: t4m11yw

Mission Briefing

As part of a plan to retaliate against the traitor Ghorin, the Alliance will ambush a convoy of the Overlord's ships, and abscond with six of Ghorin's Y-wings. The Y-wings and the corvette *Halifax,* carrying payment to Ghorin for a shipment of grain, must be disabled. The payment will be confiscated, and the *Halifax* destroyed.

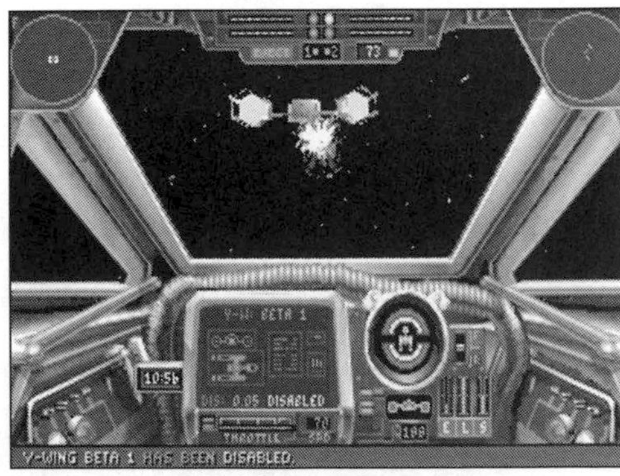

Disabling Y-W Beta 1.

Disabling a corvette.

Farlander's After-Action Report

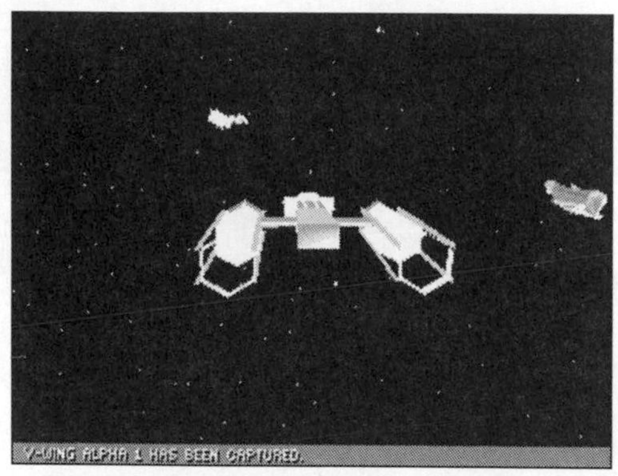

Transport and corvette ahead.

I flew the lead in a two-ship group of Y-wings, and checked the Inflight Map as I came out of hyperspace. There was no activity in the area, so I went through my standard mission start-up procedures, making sure that my shields and my weapons were fully charged.

There were two Nav Buoys nearby—one at about a kilometer away and the second at about six kilometers. I began a figure-eight pattern between the buoys, waiting for Ghorin's forces.

Two Y-wings, Gamma, appeared, and I softened each up with a torpedo, switching to lasers to bring down their shields, and finally to ion cannons to complete the disabling process.

Two more two-ship groups of Y-wings, from Alpha and Beta, appeared in rapid succession, and my wingman and I applied the same tactics to render them immobile.

Now it was time to go after Ghorin's corvette, the *Halifax*. I shot both my remaining torpedoes at it in dual-fire mode, then I went in with ion cannons while other forces went about capturing the crippled Y-wings.

I noticed that my wingman was a little confused, and decided to send him home and handle the situation on my own. The Calamarian cruiser *Maria* entered the area on schedule, with 7:00 elapsed on the mission clock, and the TRN *Storm* was launched from the cruiser to board the *Halifax*. I stuck close to be sure that things went as planned.

TRN Storm *docks with the* Halifax.

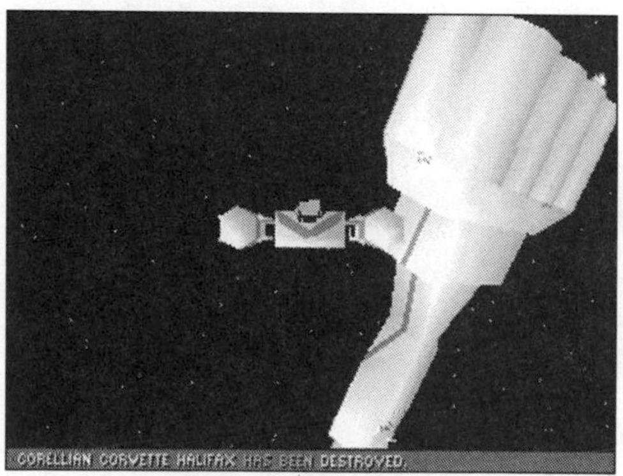

Taking out the Halifax.

At around 2:15 on the clock, the docking operation was completed, and I went in and finished off the disabled corvette.

Now it was just a matter of time before the *Maria* jumped into hyperspace, which it did at about 0:40 on the clock. I followed shortly afterward.

Debriefing (Win Conditions)
The TRN *Storm* must complete its mission. The CRS *Maria* must survive. Half of the Y-wings from Alpha, Beta and Gamma groups must be recovered. The CRV *Halifax* must be boarded.

Mission Note: Try to disable the Y-wings in pairs, as each has a corresponding pair of shuttles that appear to complete the capture operation. The pairs of shuttles appear as soon as one Y-wing in a group is disabled. Y-wings can survive one torpedo hit, so using a torp to soften them up speeds along the disabling process.

OP 12A: RAID STORAGE AREA

File Name: t4m12xma

Mission Briefing
As part of the plan to discredit Overlord Ghorin, the Alliance will use his captured Y-wings to eliminate an Imperial grain storage area in the Hollan D1 sector. The Imperial Frigate *Sentinel* is currently stationed at the depot, but will probably flee upon our arrival. The cruiser *Cathleen* will arrive after the initial strike force to pursue the Frigate. X-wing Red will support the mission, charged with eliminating any mines, satellites or other Imperial ships in the region.

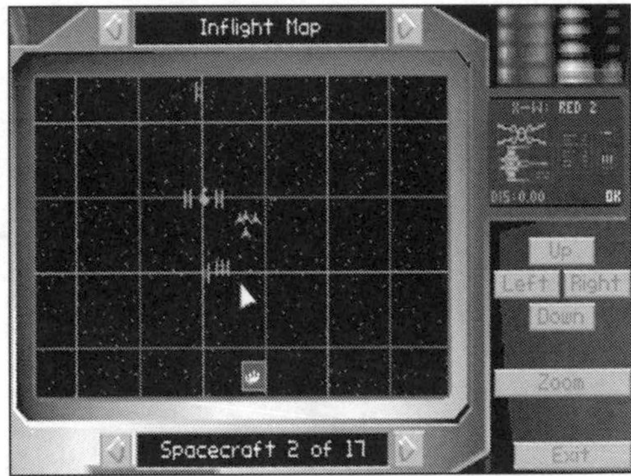

Mission start map showing FRT to destroy.

Farlander's After-Action Report
I flew the wingman position in a group of X-wings, and, as we entered the area, I noticed two freighters in the distance. I targeted the lead ship and switched quickly to torpedoes, firing off four in dual-fire mode as soon as I had a red lock.

Going after an enemy shuttle.

Next I targeted the freighter behind the first one, switching to lasers, and increasing my recharge rate. I began strafing, and the other pilots in my group seemed to know what to do to assist me; I didn't have to ask them to help.

Once both freighters were destroyed, I began to go through the rest of my standard start-up procedure, until an attacking shuttle group interrupted. I went into a tight turn and toggled through the CMD to locate the enemies, then pulled out when I had one targeted. Suffice it to say they were sorry they'd ever messed with X-wing Red.

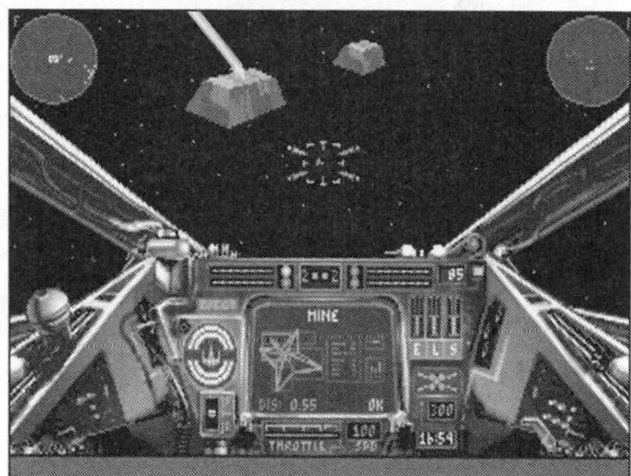

Targeting a mine with containers nearby.

No enemy fighters were in the area, but there was an enemy Frigate, which began launching ships. I ran through the list until I found a shuttle group, instructing Red to attack while I chose a target for myself.

At 18:00 on the clock, the Imperial Frigate left the area, pursued by the Rebel cruiser *Cathleen*. I held on to my torpedoes, shooting the shuttles with lasers only. By the time they were taken care of, TIE Advanced *Iota 1* and *Iota 2* had joined the party, but since dogfighting them would take a great deal of time, I began evasive maneuvers.

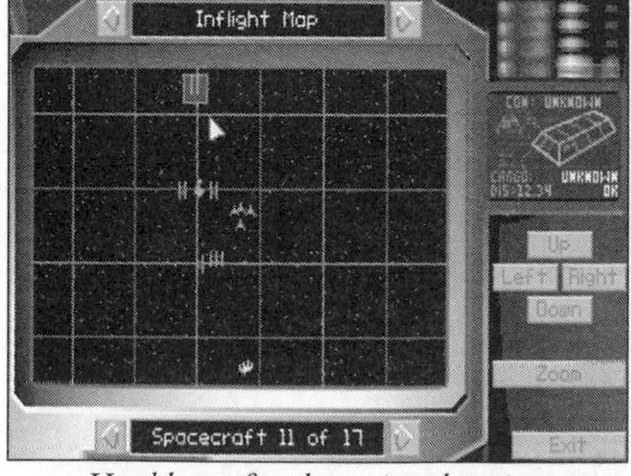

Head here after destroying the mines.

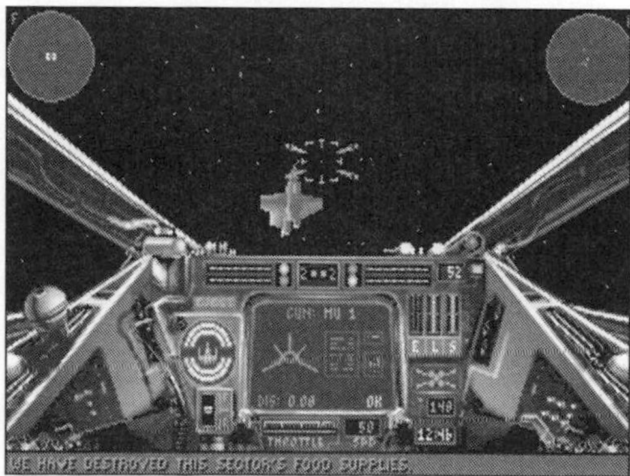

GUN Mu 1 *in CMD, win message displayed.*

There were some containers in the area also, but the contingent of Ghorin's Y-wings was going after them, and I decided to head for a nearby minefield to remove that threat.

I used the Inflight Map to get my bearings and check out the locations of potential targets, noticing as I did so that the Y-wings were laying waste to the grain. As I traveled, I readjusted my recharge levels to gain speed. At about 14 minutes on the clock, three Gunboats from group Mu entered, heading in our direction, and we engaged. Then a freighter arrived, and I quickly targeted it and fired my remaining four torpedoes.

Debriefing (Win Conditions)
Freighter groups Figii and Motti must be destroyed. Container groups Psi, Phi, Pi and Chi must be destroyed.

Mission Note: This mission requires quick responses from the beginning, if you expect to get both freighters before they leave. The second FRT enters near the group of containers, and doesn't stay long, so make sure you're in the vicinity or the mission is lost.

OP 12B: CORVETTE ALLEY

File Name: t4m12xmb

Mission Briefing
To further discredit Overlord Ghorin, we will use his captured Y-wings to destroy a corvette convoy carrying an important Imperial grain shipment. Five of the Y-wings will be utilized, and two X-wings from Red Squadron will support the mission.

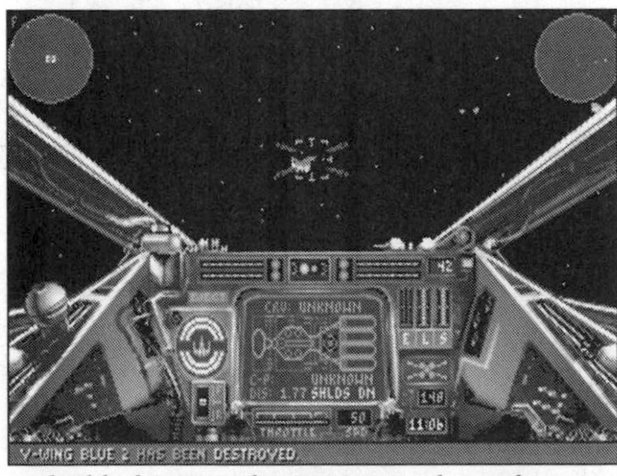

Shields down on the CRV. Missile on the way.

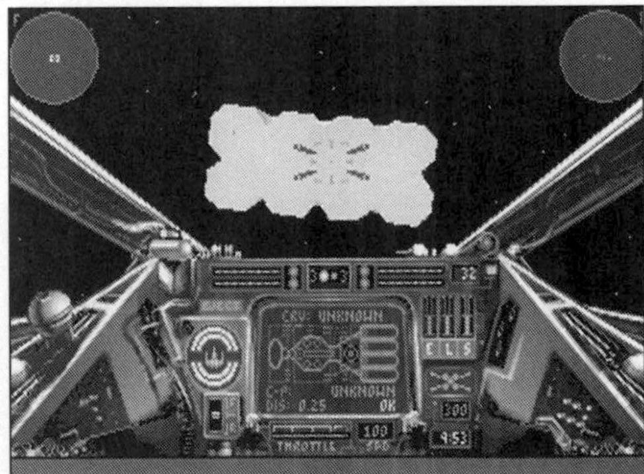

In the blind spot of the corvette.

Farlander's After-Action Report

I was the flight leader in a two-ship group of X-wings, and as I went through the standard mission-start sequence I noted seven corvettes about 9 kilometers away. Four Gunboats from group Rho were about 20 kilometers away, but I stuck with the Y-wings, who were going after the corvettes.

I ordered my wingman to attack the top corvette of the back-middle two, giving him a chance to use his torpedoes. After my systems were fully charged, I dropped laser and shields recharge rates down to gain some speed, staying just ahead of the Y-wings.

When I was close enough, I fired a few laser blasts at the two corvettes in the back-middle of the formation, drawing their attention away from the Y-wings. I knew that I could evade better. Meanwhile, the Y-wings fired torpedoes at the bottom corvette, destroying it quickly.

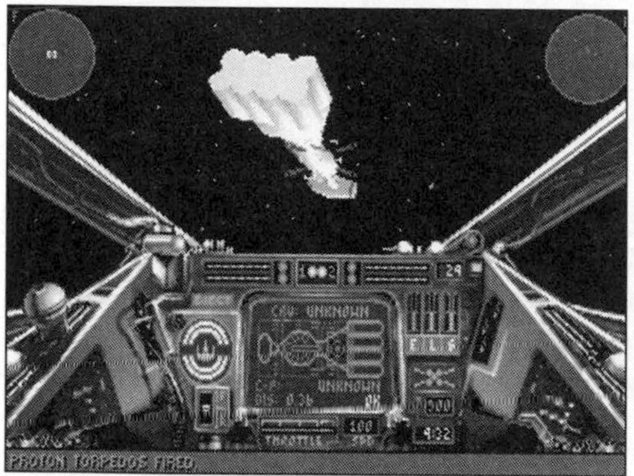

Firing torpedoes at a corvette.

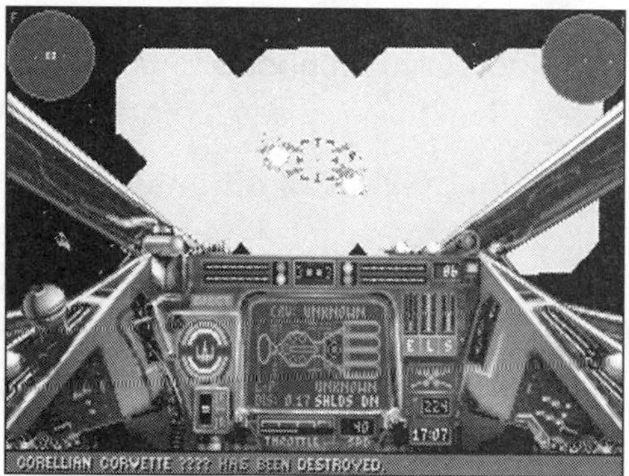

Another corvette bites it.

I set my shield and laser recharge rates to maximum, and checked the location of the incoming Gunboats. Then I slipped into the blind spot behind the top-middle corvette and used lasers to blast it away.

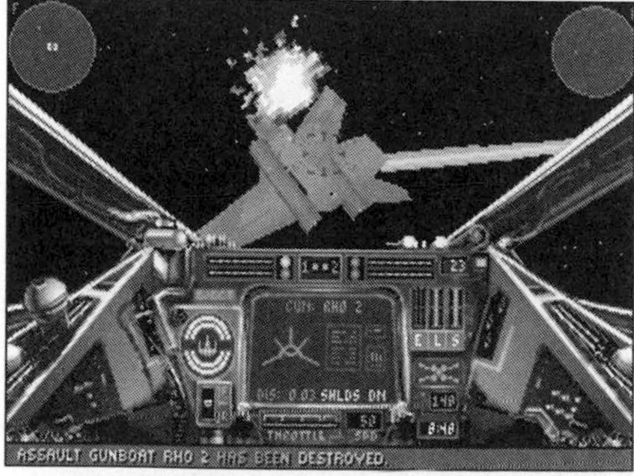

Close attack on GUN Rho 2.

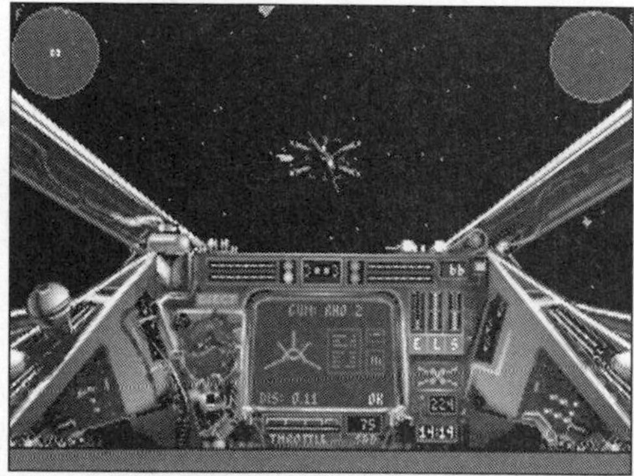

My ship is damaged, but I'm going after Rho 2.

Next, I targeted the lead corvette, switched to torpedoes, and fired all six of them in dual-fire mode, achieving the desired result.

My wingman and I then helped the Y-wings overwhelm their chosen target, and I noticed during the CRVs destruction that the Gunboats were now about four kilometers away.

After the GUNs had closed to within about 3 kilometers, I broke off my attack on the remaining corvettes and headed toward them. The Gunboats shot missiles at me, and I broke off my run temporarily to evade. I waited until the first missile was close, within .4 kilometers, and then began my tightest turn at a speed of 80 or better. I kept the missile in front of me as it attempted to loop around and go after me again.

As I destroyed Gunboats, more arrived. I tried to keep an eye on the Y-wings, though, just in case one of the GUNs attacked them: Making sure the Y-wings completed their mission was the highest priority.

I dogfought Gunboats until the Mission Complete message came up on my screen, then fragged a few more just for good measure before heading home.

Debriefing (Win Conditions)
Corvettes *Geedon 1-7* must be destroyed.

Mission Note: The two corvettes in the back-corner of the formation call in more Gunboats when attacked, so you should deal with them last.

OP 13: GRAIN EXCHANGE

File Name: t4m13yw

Mission Briefing
To culminate our efforts against Ghorin, we will ambush a shipment of grain he is sending to the Empire, and replace it with the tainted grain he supplied to the Alliance earlier. All craft must be disabled so that the crews and cargo can be replaced. Y-wing Gold will be responsible for the freighters, and Y-wing Red will handle all other ships.

Farlander's After-Action Report
I flew *Red 1* in a two-ship group of Y-wings. My job, specifically, was to disable the freighters' Y-wing escorts. We knew we would have to work quickly to keep from being discovered by the Imperials in the area.

When we came out of hyperspace, I went through my standard mission-start procedure. I put *Red 2* at memory location F5 and *Gold 1* at F6. Then I entered the Nav Buoy at F7; it was just a little less than three kilometers away.

Three Y-wings arrived then; the advance for the grain convoy. I ordered my wingman to attack Y-W *Alpha 1*, as Ghorin's freighters arrived on the scene. I switched to torpedoes, and fired a couple into the third freighter, following with a couple for the second.

About that time, a pair of transports arrived. Y-W Gold was going after the freighters, and I continued to go after the Y-wings for the moment. As I was fighting the enemy Y-wings, *Gold 2* was destroyed.

Launching torpedoes at the second freighter.

I finished off Y-W *Alpha 1* and went after *Alpha 2*. We came at each other in a head-on pass, trading hits, and I lost half my front shields, though I quickly rebalanced and turned in behind him. A few laser shots finished him off.

I noticed that a few shuttles were in the area now, but decided that it was time to help disable the freighters. I went after the nearest of them with my ion cannons, firing quickly until the job was done.

I disabled another freighter, then decided to check out the shuttles and transports. I flew in toward SHU *Lambda 2*, discovering it filled with trade officials. They tried their best to evade my attack, but a few well-placed shots left the craft disabled, and I also gave SHU *Lambda 1* the same treatment.

I checked on the transports then, and discovered that they were about a kilometer away. I was afraid that they might be running for it, so I redirected shield and laser energy to the engines and quickly caught up with them. SHU *Kappa 1* and *Kappa 2* were carrying workers, and I quickly disabled their craft as well.

Inspecting the FRTs.

I went back to full throttle then, checking the Inflight Map. The two Rebel freighters, *Rand* and *Talli*, were on their way to dock with Ghorin's freighters. Four Rebel transports were also coming in.

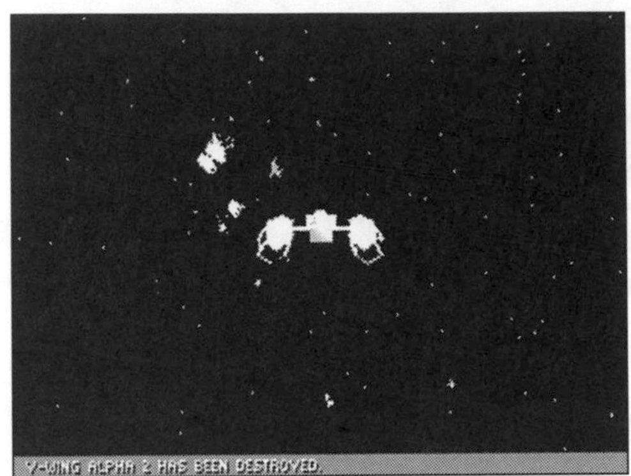

Taking out some Y-wings.

Everything seemed to be under control. I decided to fly close to Ghorin's freighters to ID them. Four minutes remained on the mission clock as I approached the freighters.

Before all the docking operations had been completed, some more of Ghorin's Y-wings arrived. I disposed of both Y-W *Beta 1* and *Beta 2* with two torps apiece, then finished off *Beta 3* with cannons.

A crowd of freighters and shuttles.

As *Beta 3* fragged, some of our ships began entering hyperspace, but the freighters were still engaged in their transfer operations. The clock read 2:15: We were running out of time, and I hoped that no more ships would arrive before we finished.

Finally, at 0:20 on the clock, the last Rebel ship completed docking, and the *Tally* and *Rand* headed for their jump points. Just before they took off, an Imperial Star Destroyer jumped into the area and began launching TIE Bombers. I was forced to engage some, and feared that the mission was a failure. Finally, when the two freighters had jumped out, I sent my wingman back home and followed him.

Apparently, the Imperials didn't understand what had happened. They must have figured that they chased us off before we could attack the convoy, because we received information later that confirmed the mission's success.

Debriefing (Win Conditions)

Y-wing groups Alpha and Beta must be destroyed. Freighters *Talli* and *Rand*, and transport groups *Kaffir* and *Khirvan*, must dock and escape. Transport *Kappa*, shuttle *Lambda* and freighters *Hugo* and *Grotius* must be boarded.

Mission Note: The key to this mission is to disable Ghorin's freighters as quickly as possible, to speed along the docking process. Order your wingman to help; he'll be useless dogfighting Ghorin's Y-wings. You have only 13 minutes before the Imperials arrive.

OP 14: CONFIRM GRAIN DELIVERY

File Name: t4m14am

Mission Briefing

As the final phase of the plan against Ghorin, confirm that the tainted grain is delivered to the Imperial forces. The Imperial Frigate *Elite* is awaiting the grain shipment, which will be arriving via transports. Identify any transports carrying grain, but do not engage. Be on guard for the TIE Advanced models that are reportedly part of the *Elite's* forces.

Farlander's After-Action Report

I flew the lead position in a three-ship group of A-wings. We jumped into the area, and I went directly to my Inflight Map to check the situation. I saw only two other ships—a Frigate and a TIE Advanced. I began charging my shields and going through my normal mission-start procedures, ordering my wingmen to go after T/A *Alpha*. The Advanced had other ideas, however, and charged me in a head-on pass.

Before I could react, the T/A had collided with my A-wing, relieving me of my forward shields. The Advanced fared even worse in the incident; obliterated instantly. The T/A moved faster than I'd anticipated, and, as I rebalanced what was left of my shield energy, I wished I had the confrontation to do over again.

I decided to stay about three to four kilometers from the Frigate so that I wouldn't get shot at while awaiting the incoming transports.

The Frigate launched a two-ship group of TIE Bombers, designated as Zeta, and my wingmen rushed to engage, but I hung back until the T/Bs were outside the Frigate's turbolaser range. My wingmen handled one of the Bombers, and, fully recharged, I moved to engage the other.

TIE Interceptors *Delta 1* and *2* launched at about that time, so I switched targets on the fly, selecting T/I *Delta 2*. The Frigate was launching still more craft, and I kept my laser and shield recharge rates at maximum.

One of the Bombers launched a missile, and I quickly redirected all energy to my engines to evade. I went into a tight turn, keeping the missile directly in front of me. I set my recharge rates back up while in the turn, sustaining the maneuver until the projectile had exhausted its fuel supply. Finally, I rolled into the battle again, deciding to concentrate on the Bombers for obvious reasons.

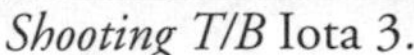

Shooting T/B Iota 3.

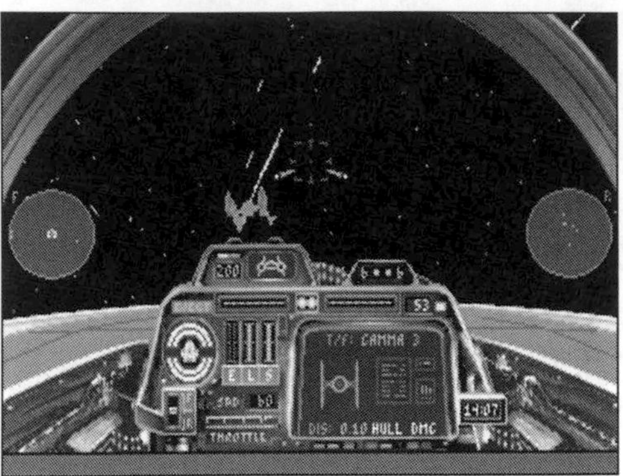

Going after T/F Gamma 3.

Another TIE Advanced showed up, but I didn't go after him right away. I kept checking the Inflight Map, watching for the transports, but still they hadn't arrived. I decided to dogfight on the Frigate's hangar side, keeping just out of its gun range while maintaining a good intercept position for the much-anticipated TRNs.

When the clock read 13:35, three transports finally arrived in the area. I broke off the dogfight and headed for them. A second group of two TRNs also appeared as I was getting my bearings.

The enemy didn't want to let me go after the transports, of course, though they couldn't guess at my true motivations. T/A *Theta 1* got on my tail then, and unloaded on me. He was a pretty good pilot, and certainly much better than that of the first Advanced.

I called my wingmen for help while I quickly switched to missiles and destroyed a pair of TIE Bombers. My next target was a TIE Interceptor, and I had to get very close to him—about .15 kilometers—to be sure of a missile hit. I've found that with the faster craft, if your missile misses once, it will often exhaust its fuel before catching up with the intended target.

There were still 11 enemy starfighters in the area—five TIE Advanced from Theta and Beta groups, and six TIE Bombers from Alpha and Delta groups—and my primary concern was identifying the transports.

I had to work hard to get near the TRNs, going into a weave to avoid being hit by my pursuers. Finally, I got close enough to ID TRN *Sigma 1*, which was carrying troops, and *Sigma 2*, carrying a load of grain. I was the center of attention, and I had to call my wingmen in to help me out again.

To make matters worse, as the clock read 12:00, three Gunboats from Eta group arrived. Having found the transports with the grain, I spent several anxious minutes wondering which message I'd get first; Mission Complete or Incoming Missile.

Finally I received the message I'd hoped for, and, after transferring all my laser energy to my shields just to be safe, my wingmen and I made the jump for home.

Debriefing (Win Conditions)
Transport group Sigma must be identified.

Mission Note: This mission is meant to be a challenge even for Top Ace dogfighters. If you're having trouble completing it, try flying away from the Frigate for about three minutes, and then turning back. You should arrive in the area about the same time the transports do. This strategy reduces the amount of dogfighting you have to do, but it leaves your wingmen out in the cold. If you stay and fight, have your wingmen gang up on one T/A at a time, and save missiles for Bombers.

OP 15: STEAL TIE ADVANCED

File Name: t4m15aw

Mission Briefing
It is imperative that the Rebellion secure one of the new TIE Advanced ships for study. To that end, we will attack an Imperial Research and Development site during a routine staff rotation. A-wing Red will be responsible for intercepting the shuttle filled with replacement pilots, clearing a nearby minefield and destroying the upper containers of the facility. The freighter *Ashanti* will arrive to dock with one of the fighter sheds and complete the mission.

Farlander's After-Action Report
We jumped into the area, and I immediately checked the Inflight Map. At 16 kilometers was a container with a pair of TIE fighter drones nearby. Another four containers were located about 8.5 kilometers away. Several TIE Advanced that were parked near the containers had their shields down, and others were engaged in exercises, attacking the T/F drones. There was also a shuttle about 6 kilometers away, which appeared to be on its way out of the area. Finally, there was a transport near the containers.

I set my shields and lasers to maximum recharge and went through my standard mission start-up procedure. A new shuttle arrived, and I ordered my wingmen to go after it while I targeted the original one. I switched to dual-fire missiles, launched at the shuttle, and tried to follow with cannons. I must have hesitated too long, though, because it got away into hyperspace.

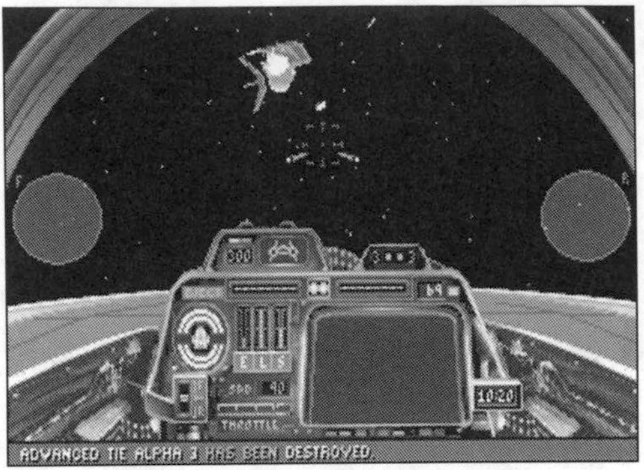

Destroying a TIE Advanced.

Meanwhile, as I redirected all shield energy to my engines, my wingmen finished destroying the incoming SHU. I ordered them to attack the transport, and I moved to destroy a nearby minefield. One of my wingmen went down while I was clearing the last of the mines.

After all the mines were gone, I reset my shield recharge rates to normal, targeted TIE Advanced *Alpha 5*, and shot it with dual-fire missiles as soon as I got a lock. I gave T/A *Alpha 6* the same treatment. A pair of Gunboats arrived in the area, but I kept after the TIE Advanced, shooting them with lasers. Thankfully, my wingmen came to help out. By that time, I had shields down on *Alpha 5*, and then finished him.

GUN Tau 2 *eats laser.*

My wingmen made quick work of *Alpha 6*, and I sent them after the incoming Gunboats. Switching to missiles, I launched two apiece at two of the Gunboats, closing with cannons to finish them off.

The freighter *Ashanti* arrived, and, during a break in the action, I discovered that *Red 2* had suffered hull damage. I sent him home.

More Gunboats arrived, but I held on to my last pair of missiles, preparing to attack with cannons. I assigned my remaining wingman to help me with this new wave of GUN Tau, and he went after *Tau 1*, while I attacked *Tau 2*.

While we took care of Tau, the *Ashanti* was docking with the containers. I thought that it might be a good idea to go in and ID the CONs, so I redirected energy to my engines and hurried in that direction. The nearer containers held TIE Advanced fighters. I then went to take a look at the one distant container, but two Corellian corvettes arrived just as I started out. The mission clock read 5:50.

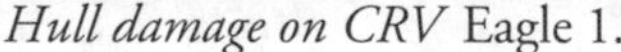

Hull damage on CRV Eagle 1.

Destruction of Eagle 1.

I decided to shoot off my last two missiles on the lead corvette, *Eagle 1*, as my wingman joined me in battle. I went in with lasers to try to finish off the CRV, as an Imperial transport suddenly entered the area and began launching torpedoes at the *Ashanti*.

The TRN managed just the one salvo before I had redirected my hostility and disposed of him, returning then to finish the confrontation with the corvettes.

My wingman must have sustained serious damage, because he entered hyperspace without my orders. I was on my own now. *Eagle 2* was closing on the *Ashanti*, so I kept after him to draw away his fire. I got the message that the docking operation was complete at 2:50 on the clock, as I maneuvered into the CRV's blind spot and began pummeling it with laser fire.

Staying safely away from the CRVs guns, I was able to do significant damage. However, the pilot was also getting shots on the freighter. It was a close call, but I breached the CRV's hull and destroyed it just as the freighter began its jump into hyperspace.

My mission was accomplished, but I was still curious what was in that distant container. I flew there quickly, destroying all the remaining containers along the way. The final container was the drone shed, and I could see no reason not to blow it up, which I did before calling it a day and jumping home.

Last gasp of Eagle 2.

Debriefing (Win Conditions)
Container group Chi and Shuttle *Epsilon* must be destroyed. The freighter *Ashanti* must dock and survive. Half of container group Psi must be boarded.

Mission Note: Order your wingmen to attack any active Imperial craft in the area while you take care of the minefield, and keep one eye on the *Ashanti* during its docking operation.

OP 16A: ESCORT BASE CONVOY

File Name: t4m16awa

Mission Briefing
Patrol a hyperspace jump point while three groups of freighters and corvettes pass through. The convoy carries supplies from the abandoned base at Yavin, and each group will arrive five minutes apart, taking 13 minutes to reach its jump point.

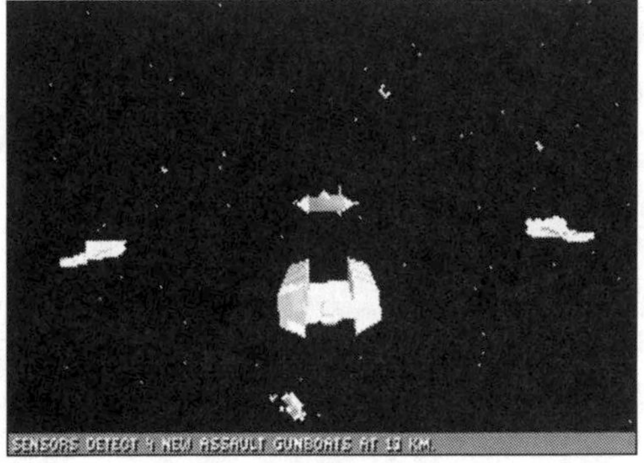

The Cielo *and the two CRVs.*

Farlander's After Action Report
I flew in A-wing Red Squadron, and my flight leader and I jumped into the area between the two Nav Buoys with no one else around. I assigned my flight leader to memory position F5, and went through my standard mission-start procedure. Freighter *Cielo* and the corvettes *Wasp 1* and *Wasp 2* arrived then, and headed for their jump position. *Wasp 1* carried troops, and *Wasp 2* carried droids. The freighter carried the base equipment.

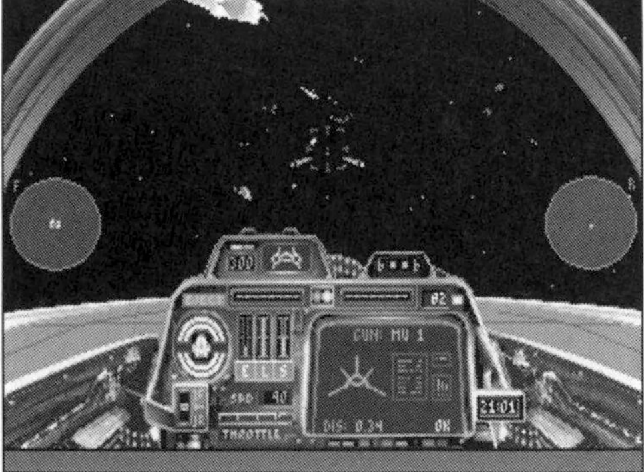

Attacking GUN Mu 1.

Within moments, four Imperial Gunboats arrived at a distance of 10 kilometers, and I immediately sent a message to my companion A-wing to attack. I put shield recharge rates at normal, and left laser recharge at maximum as I headed towards the GUNs. After my lasers reached maximum charge, I reset their rates to normal.

As soon as I was within range, I opened fire.

I reset my recharge rates to match speed with the Gunboats, and headed into what was by now a familiar exercise of destruction. *Mu 1* went down within moments, and I switched my sights to target *Mu 3*. *Mu 4* was on A-W *Red 1's* tail, so I fired a few shots to get him to break off his attack before returning my attention to *Mu 3*. Within a few minutes, Mu had been reduced to smoldering fragments.

Another group of four Gunboats arrived about seven kilometers away. We sped toward them, with *Red 1* in the lead. I went after the leader of the formation, knowing that the wingmen would probably attack me.

(That may sound like a pretty idiotic strategy, but if you think about it, the wingmen can't attack me and the convoy at the same time, and if I, in turn, make sure the leader is occupied, then I know the convoy is safe.)

Shooting T/B Gamma 1.

As I was fighting these Gunboats, a second group of Rebel convoy ships arrived—another freighter, *Namu*, and a pair of corvettes, *Orca 1* and *Orca 2*.

Momentarily distracted by the arrival, I clipped the enemy Gunboat, taking out part of my forward shields, but my ship held up. I transferred some energy from lasers to shields, and balanced the shields again, finishing off the Gunboat immediately afterward.

A third group of Gunboats replaced the second, but, though the names changed, the end result was always the same, and soon the space around the convoy was clearing of enemies once again.

The situation was under control—at least until an Imperial Frigate arrived and began launching TIE Bombers. I took out the last Gunboat of the third group and told *Red 1* to attack the T/Bs, while I redirected all energy to engines and switched to missiles.

There were two Bombers and two TIE Interceptors in the dogfight, and, since the Bombers were the greater threat, I positioned myself to deal with them quickly. Another pair of Bombers and Interceptors launched then, adding to the melee. I had closed within five kilometers of my target Bombers, and I then put my recharge rates to maximum; I didn't want to fight the Interceptors with my shields down.

I got a lock on T/B *Alpha 2* and fired one missile. Surprisingly, the missile hit *Alpha 1*, which just got in the way, I guess. I switched to lasers and went after *Alpha 2*, taking it out quickly. I next targeted T/Bs *Gamma 1* and *Gamma 2* with equally lethal results.

Red 1 was going after the TIE Interceptors, and I decided to help, but only for a moment. T/B Alpha had been replaced, so I switched to missiles and turned my attention to them. Then came a replacement wave of T/B Gamma.

I kept after the Bombers, shooting them as fast as I could. I ordered *Red 1* to attack the Bombers as well.

At one point, I found myself too close to the Frigate, which was called the *Red Wind*. The Frigate's gunners, I'm sure, had been itching to plaster me with cannon fire, and now they got their chance. Still I kept moving, rebalancing my shields and taking care of Bombers.

The T/Bs kept coming, and we kept after them. It was important that they not be allowed to continue their attack runs unmolested. When I had a chance, I tried to take out the TIE Interceptors, because they were making life difficult and dangerous. *Red 1* bought it, and I was alone with all these Imperial killers.

I continued to check the CMD for Bombers, and kept attacking them until all had been destroyed. Some of the Bombers had successfully evaded my missiles, and I had to hunt them down and shoot them with lasers.

Now that all the Bombers were taken care of, I went after the Interceptors, resetting my recharge rates so that I could gain some speed. The clock read 4:40, and the second convoy group entered hyperspace. The third and final group (FRT *Ox* and CRVs Wolf) had appeared just a little while ago, and still had a fair distance to cover.

I kept after the Interceptors, one at a time. Once I had cleared space of enemy fighters, the Frigate launched another pair of T/Is. Angry, I destroyed the Interceptors and fired a few shots at the Frigate; pointless, but it felt good.

The final convoy group was on its way to the jump point and the clock read slightly more than two minutes. I had one missile left, and no more enemy fighters were in the area. I watched the convoy with one eye and the Frigate with the other.

With nothing else to attack, I decided to strafe the Frigate. This strategy was foolish, but challenging. I had to weave and shoot in single-fire mode to get off as many shots as possible. The mission clock was running down, and still the last of the Rebel ships hadn't jumped.

Finally, seconds after the clock reached zero, the last of the convoy jumped successfully into hyperspace, and I followed them soon afterward.

Debriefing (Win Conditions)
Freighters *Cielo, Namu* and *Ox,* and corvette groups Wasp, Wolf and Orca must all survive.

OP 16B: SUPPORT ALLIES

File Name: t4m16xwb

Mission Briefing
Protect a neutral supply convoy from any harassment by the Imperials. Though they are neutrals now, they may someday be our allies. A task force led by the cruiser *Maria* is nearby, as is A-wing Gold. Either will provide assistance in the event it is needed.

Farlander's After-Action Report
I was the leader of a five-ship group of X-wings from Red Squadron. Coming out of hyperspace, I went immediately to the Inflight Map and surveyed the situation.

There were two pairs of TIE Advanced and two groups consisting of four TIE Bombers each, apparently launched from a Star Destroyer about 28 kilometers away. The nearest enemies were T/A Alpha at 6.7 kilometers, followed by T/B Beta at 12.8 kilometers.

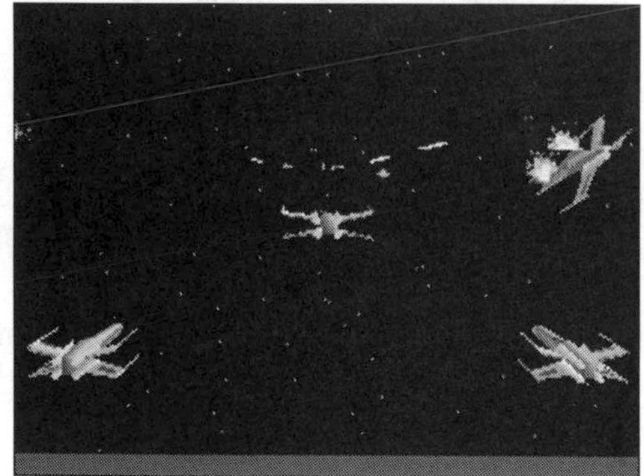

Starting a head-on pass against two T/As.

We turned to engage the TIE Advanced, and I set my lasers and shield recharge to maximum as I led us toward a head-on pass. I knew that the high recharge rates would slow me down, but, relative to the TIE Advanced, our closing speed would still be high enough to keep me from taking too many hits. I would also gain slightly more time to punish the enemy.

After completing the pass against the TIE Advanced, I redirected my shield energy to the engines, gaining enough speed to dogfight with the Imperials. I took a few shots, and ordered my wingmen to attack the T/As while I took off after TIE Bomber group Beta, realizing that they constituted a greater threat to the safety of the Leafar ships transiting the area. The second group of T/As joined the fight as I attacked the Bombers.

It was getting a little hot here, and I called my wingmen in to attack the TIE Advanced nearest me while I finished off the first group of Bombers and went after the second. As I approached T/B group Gamma, I reset my energy configuration to match speeds with the Bombers, toggling my lasers to quad-fire mode. My wingmen had by this time destroyed one of the T/As, so I ordered them to go after another.

Some of T/B Gamma slipped past me, so I returned to a speed setting and chased after them. By the time I had destroyed the last of T/B Gamma, a replacement wave of T/B Beta was about 12 kilometers away, and a replacement for T/B Gamma launched soon afterward. I ignored the T/As for now, and went full speed toward the Bomber groups.

Under attack by TIE Advanced fighters.

I checked to make sure that my wingmen were keeping the T/As busy, and noticed that I had lost *Red 2* in the battle. Three others remained to keep harassing the Advanced fighters.

As I approached T/B Beta, one of them launched a missile at me. I redirected energy to engines and began single-firing at the incoming projectile. My shields were fully charged, so I took the chance that I could hit the missile with my lasers before it reached me, and I was successful.

I closed quickly on the Bombers, switching energy configurations and putting lasers back to quad-fire. I destroyed the first T/B, but the rest of the Bombers continued past me, and I had to chase them down to take them out.

For the first time, I noticed that the A-wings of Gold Squadron were engaged with the Bombers, too. That was fine by me. As I noticed the arrival of Gold, I also noted one of the Advanced fighters on my tail. I called my wingmen to attack it, while I managed to evade a missile it launched from close range. Only myself and *Red 4* remained in our fighter group.

T/Bs *Gamma 1* and *Gamma 3* had gotten past me, so I went after them at maximum speed and applied the torpedoes, finishing off this most recent threat. Another wave of T/B Beta was on the way, however, about 13 kilometers distant.

T/A *Alpha 2* was heading back to its mother ship with hull damage, but a couple of other T/As were still in the area. I went after T/A *Delta 2* before attacking the next wave of T/B Beta. As I headed toward the Bombers, I switched to single-fire and began spraying the area to break up their formation, and to protect myself from any missiles they might try to launch. Then I closed in and began systematic destruction. The next wave of T/B Gamma was on its way by this time, so I worked quickly.

I fought T/B Gamma, evading missiles and blasting the Bombers as quickly as I could. These latest waves of Bombers were aggressive, and tried to gang up on me, but I kept moving and shooting; quickly and accurately.

No new waves appeared, so I figured that I had taken care of the main threat. The nearest enemy was T/A *Delta 2*, about 4 kilometers from my ship and heading for the Star Destroyer, which was 10.5 kilometers away. The A-wings were still going after the remaining TIE Advanced, so I joined in. Fighting TIE Advanced, I redirected shield energy to engines and kept transferring laser energy to shields to keep them from discharging.

As I was fighting the T/As, some reinforcements arrived on our side. Checking the Inflight Map, I noticed that the Rebel Frigate *White Hawk* was about 20 kilometers away, and that some new A-wings from both Blue and Gold Squadrons had entered the area. The cruiser *Maria* was about 22 kilometers away as well.

The situation looked good for the Rebel side. I decided to head for the Star Destroyer and see whether I could do some damage. I had four torpedoes left, so I decided to try to take out its shield towers. If I could do that, I might be able to finish off the Imperial ship with lasers. OK. It sounds far-fetched, but you can't blame me for trying.

I had gotten my Mission Complete message a few moments before, but decided to keep attacking the STD up until the time it launched some TIE Bombers in retaliation for my bold attack.

Rethinking my plan, I decided to head for hyperspace.

Debriefing (Win Conditions)

Three corvettes, two freighters and four shuttles must make it into hyperspace. The Nebulon B Frigate *Whitehawk* must arrive.

OP 17: ATTACK FRIGATE RED WIND

File Name: t4m17am

Mission Briefing

The Frigate *Red Wind* appears to be undergoing repairs near Plooriod IV; it is stationary and the Imperials have laid a small minefield around it. Two A-wings from Red Squadron will clear away the mines so that a group of Alliance corvettes can attack the Frigate.

These Bombers are firing torpedoes at our CRVs.

Farlander's After-Action Report

I was the flight leader, and when we jumped into the area I quickly noted that the nearest enemy was a TIE Advanced about 9.5 kilometers away. I wasn't worried about the TIE Advanced: They weren't carrying torpedoes. What worried me was the possibility that the Frigate might launch some TIE Bombers.

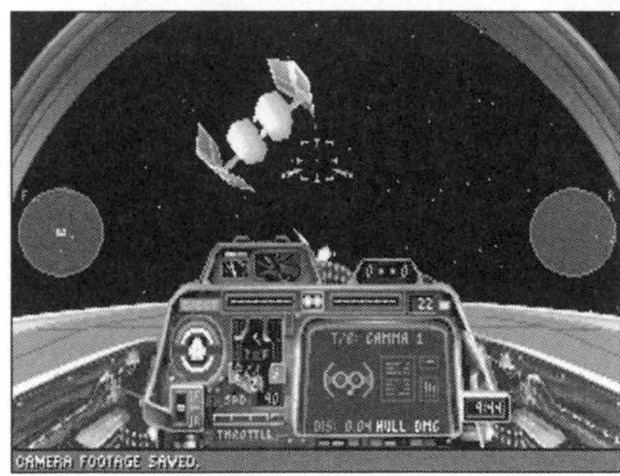

T/B Gamma 1 *is almost gone.*

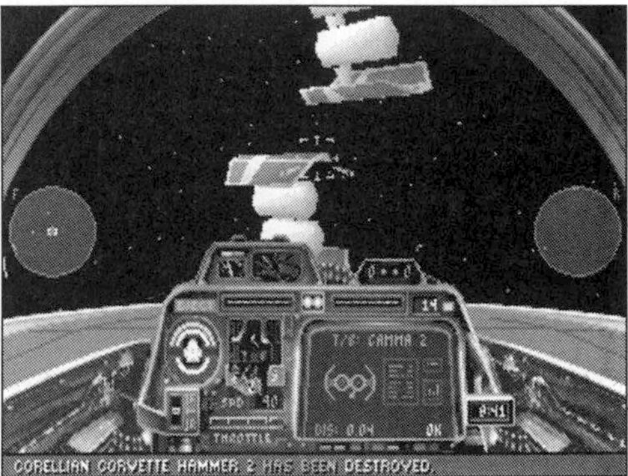

Harassing the Bombers.

I knew that I would have to intercept any Bombers at least five kilometers from our corvettes, or else the CRVs would come under missile fire.

After I had evaluated the situation, I went through my standard start-up procedure and watched the corvettes enter above us. I went directly after the TIE Bombers as soon as I saw them: T/Bs *Delta 1* through *4*.

I headed toward them as fast I could, ignoring the TIE Advanced and firing my own projectiles. I took the first two Bombers out with missiles, noting that at 16:45 on the clock a freighter entered the area. I paid no attention to it, and mopped up the rest of T/B Delta with my lasers.

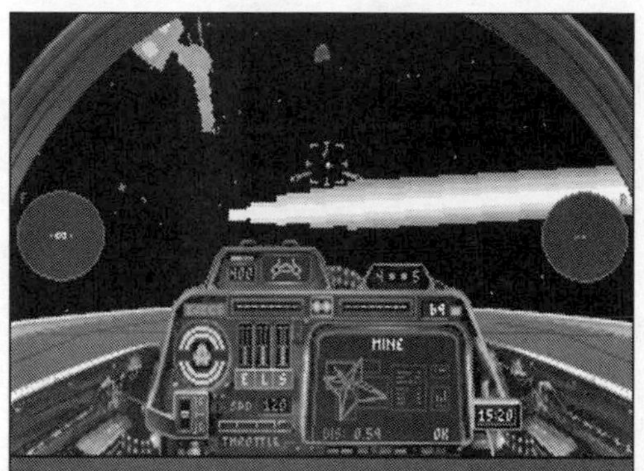

Targeting a mine.

While I waited for another wave of Bombers to appear, I toasted T/A *Alpha 2* with lasers to give my wingman a breather. Then I headed for the minefield to clear the way for the corvettes. I was pretty familiar with mine shooting at this point, but I had drawn the ire of the TIE Advanced, and had to call my wingmen to cover me.

Having my wingmen in the area also drew some of the Frigate's fire away from my ship. In dual-fire mode, I took out the mines, one after the other. I took some hits myself, but I was careful to watch my shield levels. Finally, I had cleared the mines, and I pulled out of the area to recharge. By this time, the corvettes were closing within firing range of the *Red Wind*.

Three CRVs from Striker group.

T/B group Gamma launched then, and I immediately went after them with missiles, firing at point-blank range as quickly as I could. I didn't bother waiting for a red lock, but shot when I had a good angle from right on their tails.

When the corvettes finally made their attack run on the Frigate, I joined in. I figured that any shots I scored on the enemy weakened it more, and also, that my presence helped divert some of the Frigate's guns from the CRVs, increasing their lifespan and thus their effectiveness.

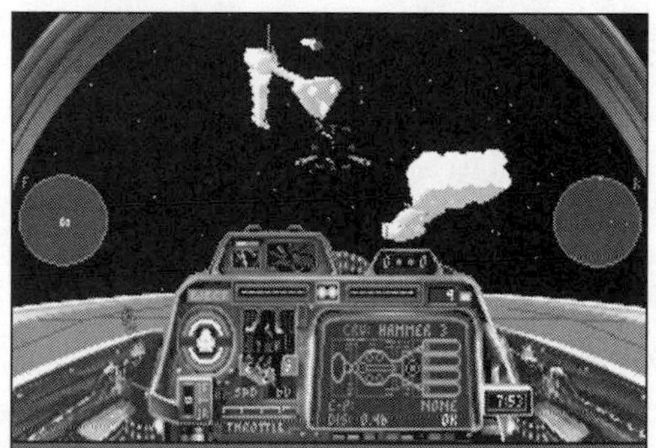

CRV Hammer 3 *getting hammered by the FRG.*

The first wave of corvettes didn't last long under the Frigate's guns. The second wave—*Hammer 1, 2,* and *3*—arrived, and I flew out to join them, recharging my shields and lasers on the way.

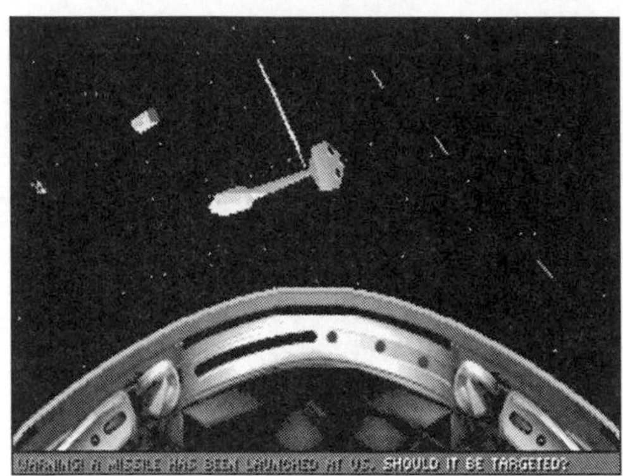

Flying away from the Red Wind.

The Bombers were scoring some hits on the corvettes, and I redoubled my efforts to stay on top of the Bomber threat. The CRVs were also taking major punishment on every attack run, but their brave crews kept at it, whittling down the Frigate.

The corvettes weren't the only targets of the TIE Bombers. T/B Gamma group, which showed up at about seven minutes on the clock, seemed to have a special disregard for the safety of myself and my wingmen, which I took exception to.

I was tempted to dogfight the TIE Advanced, which were causing me all kinds of trouble, but the Bombers remained my primary focus. Then, with about 5:00 on the clock, some shuttles appeared, followed quickly by our last three corvettes from Arrow group.

The *Red Wind* still had shields, and I knew that this was it. I decided to help blast away at the Frigate after the corvettes were in attack position. Until that time, however, I kept after the TIE Bombers.

Finally, I had destroyed all the Bombers that the Frigate had to throw at me, and meanwhile Arrow group had gotten within attack range. I wasn't having much luck against the TIE Advanced, which buzzed me almost constantly, so I decided to fly among the corvettes to hopefully utilize some of their firepower against the elusive Advanced fighters.

The *Red Wind's* shields had began to drop as Arrow group went to work: The mission clock had run down to zero, so I had no sense of the time that had elapsed. I flew in with the corvettes to help bring down the Frigate, thinking perhaps I would get that lucky hit that finished her, and credit for the kill. Not bad, if you can get a Frigate kill in an A-wing.

FRG Red Wind's *shields are down.*

As I headed in to the attack, I called my wingmen for cover as the TIE Advanced pursued. The Frigate went down quickly. It had a freighter docked with it, apparently trying to repair the stricken ship before we destroyed it, but it was too late.

Just as we completed the operation, and the Frigate began to tumble and break up, five Gunboats entered the area. Our mission was complete. All three CRVs of Arrow group survived, but the other groups were not so lucky. Before the last corvettes left the area, they went after the freighter and the container, and then they jumped out. One of them had been hit by a torpedo from the Gunboats, but they all made it to safety, and I decided to join them.

Debriefing (Win Conditions)
The Nebulon B Frigate *Red Wind* must be destroyed.

Mission Note: This is a mission where your Bomber-battling techniques must be at their peak. Note that, since they follow a predetermined flight path during launching, T/Bs are particularly vulnerable for the first few seconds. Also, in an A-wing, if someone shoots a missile at you, you want to evade. Hit the spacebar, divert full power to the engines, and make that missile miss. After the missile runs out of steam, go after the guy who shot it, or else he'll probably try it again.

One more thing: Don't attack the container, unless you want more enemies. Destroying the container causes two additional Gunboats to jump into the area.

OP 18: CAPTURE IMPERIAL GUNBOATS

File Name: t4m18ym

Mission Briefing
In preparation for a sneak attack on a secret Imperial research site, The Alliance will raid an Imperial arms depot to steal Assault Gunboats. The Gunboats will be used as part of a 'Trojan Horse' maneuver in the later campaign. Y-wing Red will lead the raid, first eliminating any defenses and then disabling any Gunboats. After the GUNs are recovered, with the assistance of shuttle group Leary and the Calamarian cruiser *Cathleen*, the depot must be entirely destroyed.

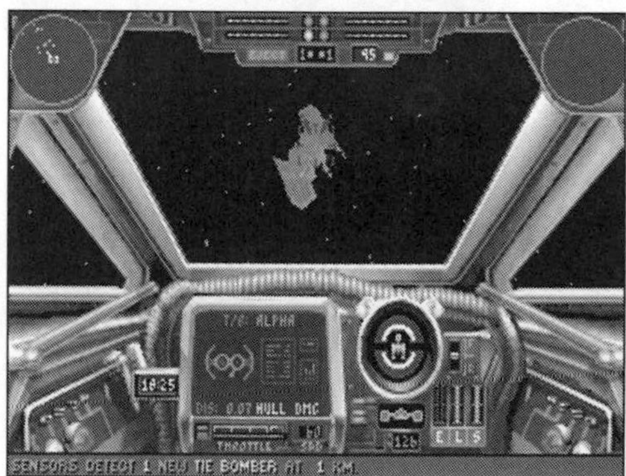

Bomber patrol.

Farlander's After-Action Report

Taking heat from the enemy CRV.

I flew the lead in a two-ship group of Y-wings. We jumped into the area and immediately checked the Inflight Map to confirm the situation. Three corvettes were present, near a group of Gunboats, and in the distance were TIE Bomber groups Alpha, Beta, and Gamma.

My first objective was to neutralize the corvettes. After going through my standard mission start-up, I targeted a corvette, placed it in memory location F5, and told my wingman to attack it. Then I targeted the next corvette and switched to dual torpedoes, firing six as soon as I had a red lock. Immediately, I recalled the first corvette and fired my two remaining torpedoes at it. All the while, I was heading toward the CRVs and closing within range of a small minefield.

There were eight mines, and I blasted them with lasers as I headed toward the corvettes. The Bombers, alerted to our presence, were vectoring to attack.

When T/B Beta arrived, I tried to fend off the Bombers while helping my wingman destroy the second corvette. When the second corvette was history, I targeted the next one and told my wingman to go after it, helping him out as best I could. More T/Bs were being launched, however, and I decided to deal with them before they overwhelmed us.

My wingman fragged, so it would be up to me to handle the third corvette. I had eliminated some of the Bombers, but many remained. I picked one of the closest, and pressed the attack. Once the T/B threat was dissipated, I headed toward the remaining corvette. One more T/B was launched as I flew up behind the CRV, trying to get into its blind spot. The parked Gunboats floated eerily nearby; they were no threat.

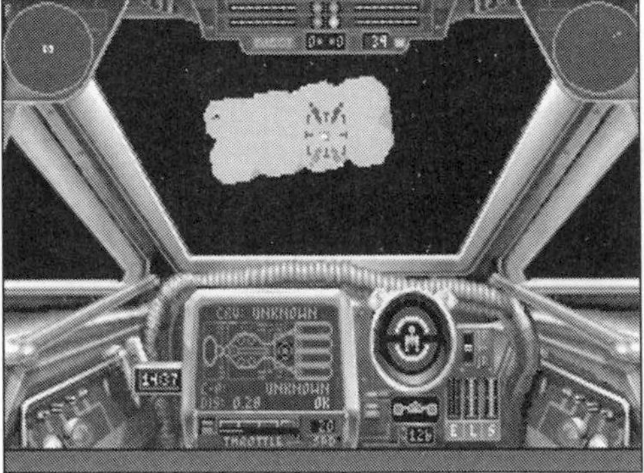

Parked in the CRV's blind spot.

T/B *Gamma 1* launched a missile at me, and I knew I couldn't outrun it, so I continued to fire missiles and checked my shields, waiting to absorb the hit. Afterward, I chased the Bomber down.

The corvettes would each have three Bombers on board, so I had the option of destroying each wave until there were none left, and then taking out the corvette, or attacking the CRV vigorously to try and prevent the Bombers' launch. Since I could wait outside the CRV hangar bay and peg the Bombers with relative ease, that's the route I chose.

Once the Bombers had been taken care of, I recharged my ship, then increased my speed and dropped in behind the corvette, firing as I approached. I dropped my throttle to one-third and rebalanced my shields full forward, protecting against the shots that would, almost inevitably, get through.

Once in the ship's blind spot I parked there, blasting away with my lasers until the CRV began to tumble. I had to be careful once it rolled, because its guns continued to fire until it had blown up. I put on full throttle, rebalanced my shields, and got out of there as fast as I could.

Taking out Gunboat Tau 2.

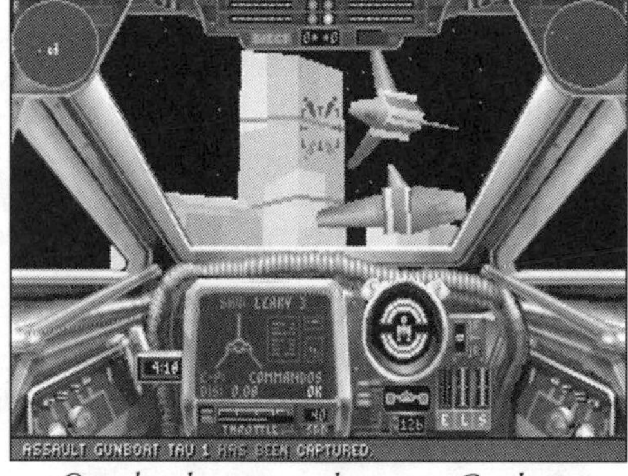

Our shuttles capture the enemy Gunboats.

Shuttles landing on Gunboats.

Finally, with all the other threats gone, I switched to ion cannons and disabled each Gunboat. I placed myself in a good position to see all the Gunboats, then parked my ship and fired at will.

As soon as I had completed the operation, I went to full throttle, just in case, and checked the Inflight Map. Three Rebel shuttles, *Leary 1, 2* and *3*, had arrived, carrying pilots for the disabled Gunboats. I flew out to escort the shuttles, switching back to lasers as I did so.

A group of enemy shuttles arrived then, and I attacked immediately. I was careful not to attack the SHUs head-on, and risk a missile launch, but turned in behind them at two-thirds throttle, blasting with dual-fire lasers and wishing that I still had torpedoes. By the time I had taken care of the Imperial shuttles, the three Rebel shuttles had begun docking and capture operations.

Moments after the last Gunboat was captured, the Calamari cruiser *Cathleen* jumped in about three kilometers away, and all the Rebel ships headed for her. I kept guard on the group, holding the rear position. After everyone was safely within the cruiser, about three minutes, the *Cathleen* took about two minutes to reach its jump point.

I went after the remaining Imperial containers then, destroying them before I, too, jumped for home. Imperial Gunboats had arrived, but weren't able to affect the mission. After the *Cathleen* had jumped out of the area, three Imperial corvettes had arrived, but they couldn't close before I made my exit.

Debriefing (Win Conditions)
The shuttle group Leary must dock and survive. The cruiser *Cathleen* must survive.

Mission Note: As an alternative strategy, you can stay outside the mines and corvettes when the mission begins, and dogfight the Bombers until none remain. This lets you go after the corvettes and Gunboats without being harassed by the Bombers. Also note that disabling any one of GUN Lambda triggers the launch of three Imperial shuttles. To delay the shuttles arrival as long as possible, attack each Gunboat and weaken its shields, and then go back to each for the final disabling.

OP 19: CAPTURE IMPERIAL CORVETTE

File Name: t4m19ym

Mission Briefing
Using the captured Gunboats, Alliance forces will attack a secret Imperial research site, with the ultimate goal of stealing a new corvette prototype. This new CRV has been outfitted with shield technology similar to that in the TIE Advanced models, and would prove a very formidable foe in combat. Y-wing *Red 1* will lead the assault, escorted to the site by the captured GUNs, who will claim to be themselves escorting a defector. *Red 1* must disable the target CRV, and then protect the capture operation.

Farlander's After-Action Report

Piloting Y-wing *Red 1*, I jumped into the Imperial testing area escorted by the captured Gunboats, and immediately checked my Inflight Map. Three pairs of Corellian corvettes were arrayed around a group of containers. The nearest corvette was about 8.5 kilometers away, and the containers were about 12 kilometers away.

I went through my standard start-up procedures and put GUN *Eta 1* at memory location F5. We headed for the nearest corvette, and when we got to within about four kilometers, I ordered the three Gunboats to wait while I disposed of the mines. I headed for the corvettes, redirecting energy to the engines to gain speed, and firing on the mines as I approached.

After I had taken out the mines, some Imperial Gunboats entered the area. I ordered my escorting Gunboats to proceed with their mission, and reset laser recharge rates to maximum and shields to normal as I headed toward the enemy GUNs to help my escorts take care of them.

Still more Gunboats appeared about ten kilometers away, but I was still busy with the first group. I then returned to the main mission and headed in among the corvettes to ID them. As I approached the CRVs, the new group of Gunboats got on my tail, and I had to take care of them. They began firing missiles at me, and I had little choice but to keep after them until I had eliminated the threat.

As soon as I had finished them off, I flew in a weave pattern to approach the CRVs. Neither of the first two were the ones I was looking for, however, so I headed for the next pair.

More Gunboats closed in on me, of course, and I had no choice but to fight them off. In the battle, I lost one of my escorts, but I had little time to worry about it. I kept fighting, rebalancing my shields and redirecting some laser energy to them as necessary.

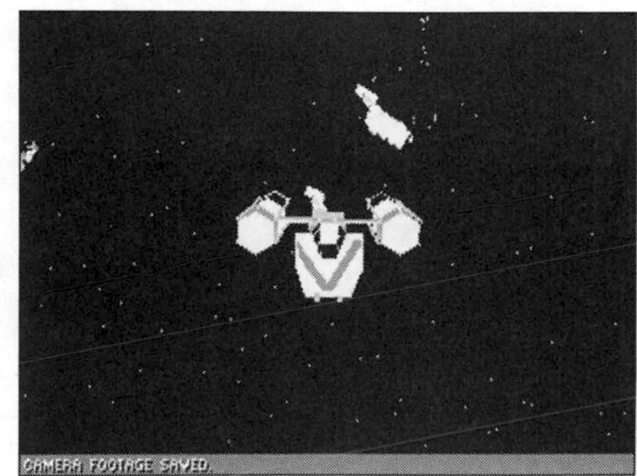

IDing a corvette.

Finally, the latest wave of Gunboats was finished off and we headed back toward the second pair of corvettes. I told my escort to wait once again, and took care of the mines as before.

The respite from attack lasted only until I had finished off the last of the mines, then more enemy Gunboats appeared, and I ordered my escort to join me as we headed toward the next pair of corvettes. The new enemy fighters were still some distance away.

The second pair of corvettes did not include the one we were after, so we headed toward the third pair. I realized that our path would take us near the containers, and decided to take advantage of the situation, redirected shield energy to lasers and angling in the direction of the CONs. As I approached the containers, the enemy Gunboats had pulled within range, and began firing missiles at me. I had little choice but to engage the new threat.

With all the maneuverability of a brick, my Y-wing still proved sufficient to take out the enemy 'Boats. I finished them off and headed in to ID the containers, finding nothing of interest.

By this time, another wave of Gunboats had come within missile range, and I was forced to absorb some hits, rebalancing and recharging my shields before beginning the dogfight anew. It took several minutes of intense concentration and maneuvering, but I was able to defeat the latest threat, and turn my Y-wing's nose toward the final pair of corvettes.

Again, I told the escorts to wait while I went in to destroy the mines. I decided to fire a couple of torps into each of the remaining corvettes, figuring that one of them had to be the craft I sought. Then I went back to cannons and destroyed the mines. Next, I identified CRV *Blade 5*, and found that it was the one I was after, which meant that I had no need to spare the other one.

I flew out of gun range and switched to torpedoes, firing off two more, then I switched to cannons and corkscrewed in with laser recharge rates at normal, blasting the unwanted CRV into oblivion. More enemy Gunboats appeared, and I decided to take care of them. It wouldn't do to have to avoid fire from the corvettes and dogfight the Gunboats at the same time.

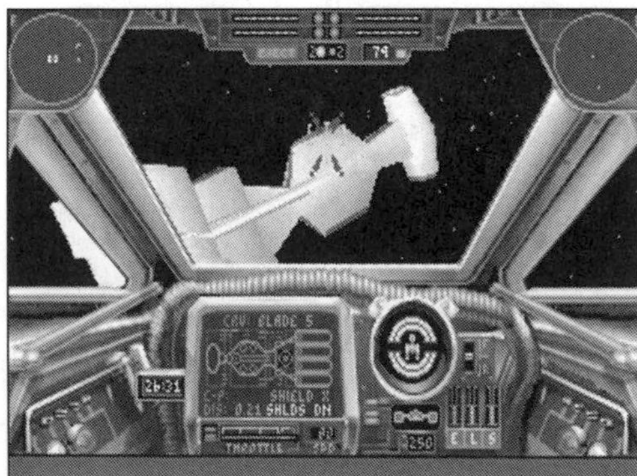

Shields down on CRV Blade 5.

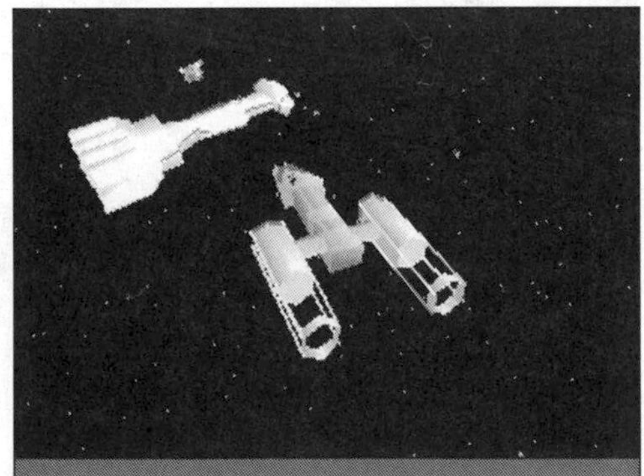

Transport Storm *and CRV* Blade 5.

After the GUNs were destroyed, I switched to single-fire torpedoes and fired one at *Blade 6*, and also one more at *Blade 5*. *Blade 6* withstood the single torpedo, so I went in with cannons to finish her off. It took two strafing runs to complete the job.

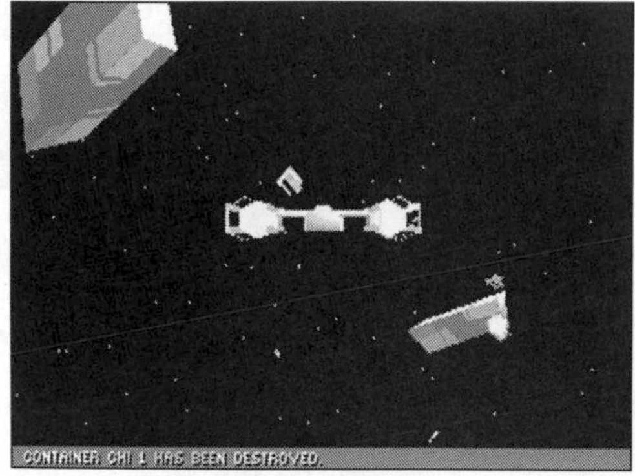

Destroying the containers.

Now it was time to disable *Blade 5*. I worked my way to the corvette's blind spot and began firing with ion cannons. I was in no danger, so I simply throttled down and fired until the corvette was disabled. At that point, transport *Storm* entered, and I placed her at memory location F6.

While I waited for the docking to be completed, I decided to do some additional damage, and I went after the containers.

After the containers were reduced to rubble, I headed for *Blade 1* and *Blade 2*. About that time, I got the message that *Blade 5* had been captured, and another Gunboat arrived about six kilometers away.

I redirected all energy to engines and headed back toward the new threat before they could prevent the *Storm* from completing its job. I also ordered what remained of my escort to join me. After I got within two kilometers, I reset my laser recharge rates to maximum and began firing on the enemy, which by this time was strafing *Blade 5*, and making me wish I'd stayed closer to the capture point.

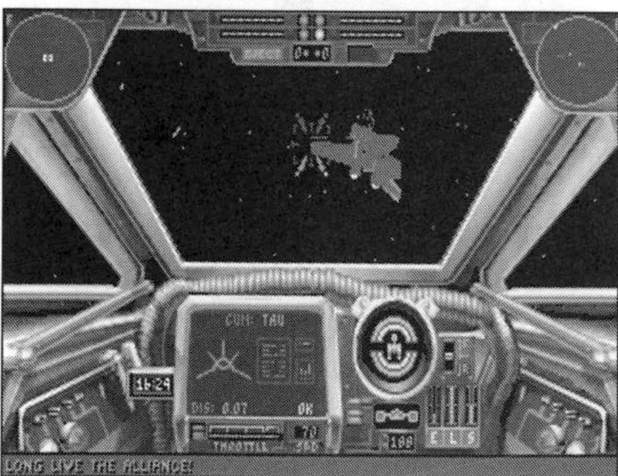

Mission complete!

As I was chasing GUN Tau, TRN *Storm* entered hyperspace. I kept patrolling until *Blade 5* also made the jump, and then got my Mission Complete message. I sent the remains of my escort home, and cleaned up a few of the remaining corvettes before jumping out myself.

Debriefing (Win Conditions)

Corvette *Blade 5* must be recovered. Transport *Storm* must dock and survive.

OP 20: DEFEND RAM'S HEAD

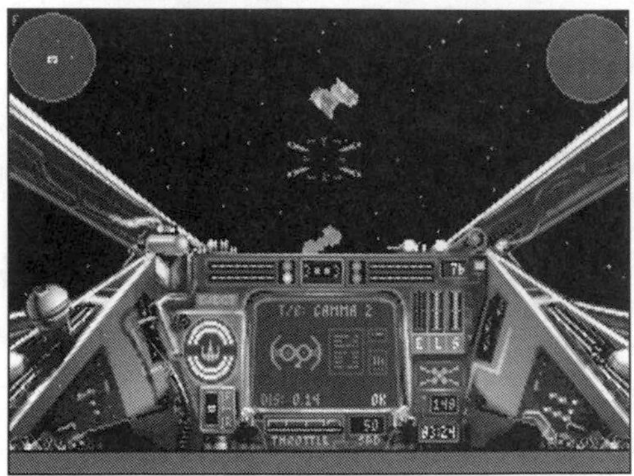
Targeting T/B Gamma 2.

File Name: t4m20ym

Mission Briefing

The newly-captured Imperial corvette, dubbed the *Ram's Head*, must be prepared for its final mission. The CRV will be used to plow through the bridge area of several Star Destroyers in an act of multiple starship decapitation. Technicians aboard a second corvette, the *Libra,* are waiting to board the *Ram's Head* and make final preparations for the mission, which will take place in an Imperial Deep Dock that has been left relatively unguarded thanks to an Alliance ruse. X-wing Red will secure the area.

Farlander's After-Action Report

I was flying the lead X-wing in Red Squadron, accompanied by two wingmen. We jumped into the area and checked it out, noting only the corvette *Libra* nearby. I began my standard mission start-up procedures, circling the CRV and putting her in memory at F5.

At 0:40 into the mission, the CRV *Ram's Head* appeared, followed by an Imperial Frigate, *Darkness*, which launched TIE Advanced Alpha. I headed directly toward the Frigate. After launching the T/A, the Frigate followed with three TIE Bombers, and I immediately made these my primary targets. Their torpedoes were the greatest immediate threat to the safety of the *Ram's Head*, which was moving to dock with the *Libra.*

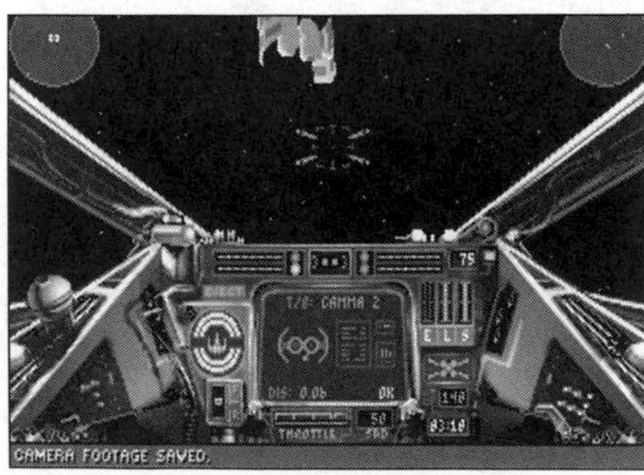

On the tail of T/B Gamma 2.

I put the three T/B of Gamma group into memory at F6, F7, and F8, just in case they might get by me. Then I ordered my wingmen to attack *Gamma 1*, while I went after *Gamma 2* with lasers only. I wanted to save my torpedoes for later.

I reset my recharge rates after I had closed with the Bombers, matching speed with them, and took out *Gamma 2* with four dual-fire blasts. *Gamma 1* flew into my view screen, and I shot him on reflex. He blew up, already weakened by my wingmen. I looked for *Gamma 3*, but it was also gone. My wingmen must have caught up with him, as well.

Two more T/Bs launched then—*Eta 1* and *Eta 2*. I ordered my wingmen to attack T/B *Eta 1*, while I hurried to intercept its twin. We took out the Bombers easily, as they were concentrating on the *Ram's Head*, which had docked rapidly with the *Libra*.

Destroying *Eta 1* and *2* only cleared the area temporarily. Another wave of T/B Eta launched almost instantly, and this time I went after both Bombers alone, since my wingmen were mixing it up with the TIE Advanced, and ordering them to break off might seriously endanger them.

Still another wave of T/B Eta followed the second group, and once again I engaged. The Bombers were easy prey. I simply stayed about two kilometers from the Frigate to avoid its fire, and picked off the T/Bs as they came within my range.

The fourth wave of T/B Eta raced into battle, accompanied by another T/B group, Beta, which came directly after me, firing a missile almost immediately.

I took the hit, and my shields were depleted, but I quickly rebalanced and went after *Beta 1*. I thought about using a torpedo, but I wasn't in such bad shape, so I stuck with lasers and blasted him and his buddy.

Unfortunately, by the time I had finished off both of Beta's Bombers, group Eta had gotten past me by about five kilometers. I ordered my wingmen to attack *Eta 1*, and set my recharge settings for maximum speed as I chased them. They would be launching torpedoes at any moment!

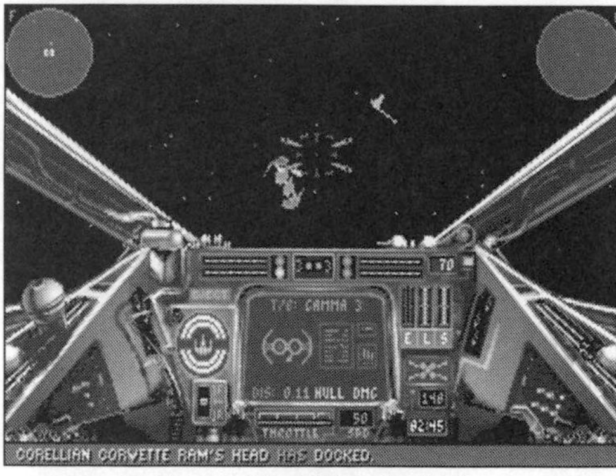

Ram's Head *has docked.*

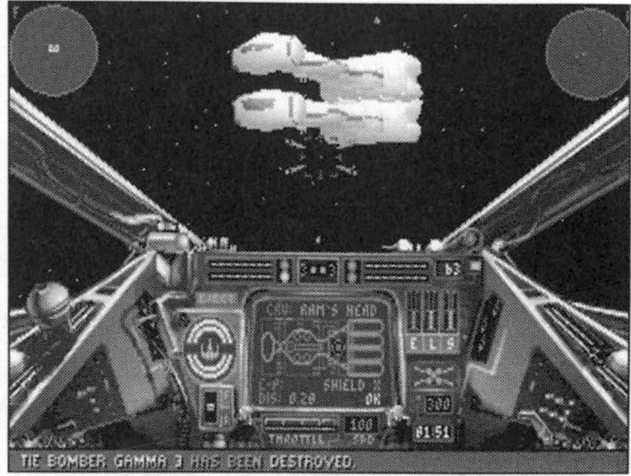

Ram's Head *has Shield X.*

I was trying to get a lock on *Eta 1* with a torp, but T/A Alpha was hammering me. I worked to recharge my shields and keep Alpha ahead of me, so that he couldn't continue firing. Finally, I was able to shoot down both of T/B Eta.

I continued engaging waves of Bombers until the Frigate ran dry of them; a lengthy process. Then an Imperial corvette arrived and seemed to be going after the *Ram's Head* and *Libra*. Four Rebel Y-wings of Gold group also appeared, but too far away to be an immediate help.

I headed toward the Imperial corvette, arming my torpedoes to open fire on it as soon as I could. I ordered my wingmen to attack, hoping that they would fire torpedoes, which they did. Each of my two wingmen launched two torps apiece, and I added my own pair after that to collect the kill.

At 75:10 on the clock, an enemy transport entered the area, and I ordered my wingmen to intercept it. I was afraid that the transport might be carrying torpedoes, and so it constituted a serious threat to our corvettes.

I then checked the Inflight Map to make sure no one had snuck into the area. By now, I was some distance from the docking operation, and wary of an ambush from the far side of the coupled CRVs.

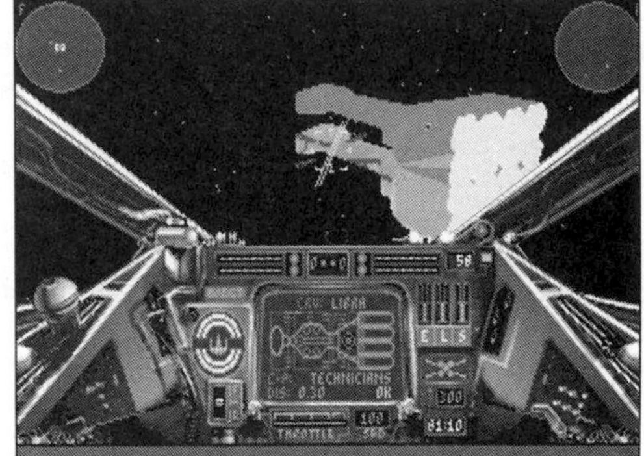
The Libra *during docking operations.*

I kept a position about five kilometers from the Alliance corvettes while my wingmen went after the transport. The Y-wings had closed on the Frigate, and were targeting the enemy craft with their torpedoes.

Another TIE Advanced was launched, and I went to intercept it, fearing for the safety of the Y-wings. I didn't necessarily need to destroy the T/A, just distract it. Meanwhile, I got the message that my wingmen had taken out the transport, so I ordered them to go after T/A Delta as well.

At 71:00 on the clock, the two corvettes *Ram's Head* and *Libra* jumped to the safety of hyperspace. The Mission Complete message came across my CMD, but I decided to stick around and help the Y-wings finish off the Frigate, which appeared to be in bad shape. I figured that I might get the kill credit for this ship if my timing was good. I also ordered my wingmen to attack.

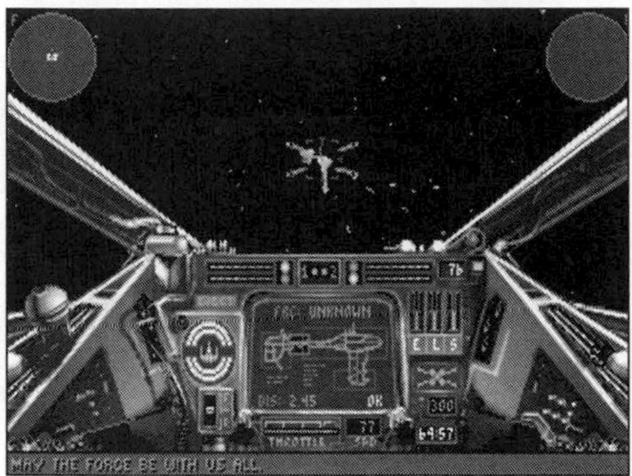

Mission complete.

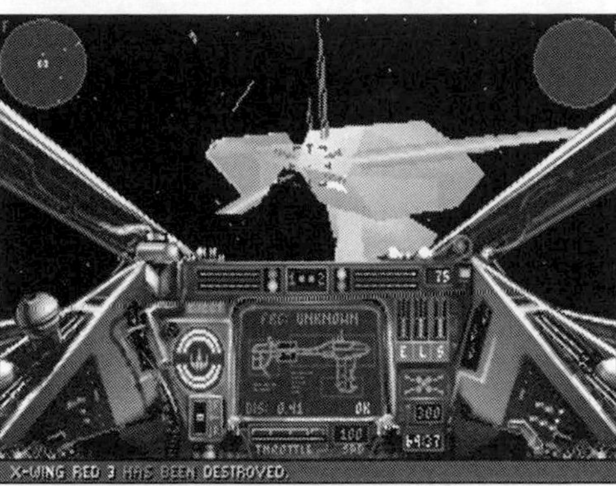

Attacking the Imperial Frigate.

Attacking the Frigate with lasers was dangerous, but it was already reeling, so it took only a few more moments to finish the job. With the Frigate gone, I jumped for hyperspace and headed home.

Later, I had the satisfaction of viewing a holo of the *Ram's Head* in action, tearing apart several Star Destroyers in the most impressive display of destructive power I had witnessed since the eradication of the Death Star.

Debriefing (Win Conditions)

The corvette *Libra* must be boarded, and the corvette *Ram's Head* must escape.

Mission Note: The key to this mission is to concentrate on the TIE Bombers early, and take out the corvette *Assassin 8* and the transports when they appear. You don't have to destroy the T/As, and doing so can waste a great deal of time. Unless you're a Top Ace dogfighter, you may not want to set that as a goal; simply keep the T/As from messing up the mission.

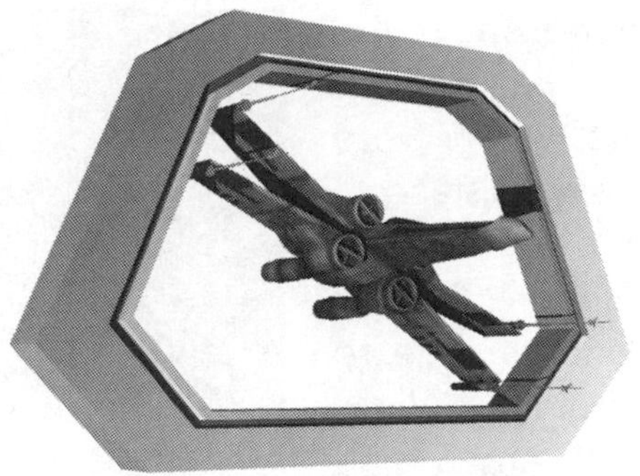

TOUR OF DUTY #5— B-WING

OP 1: PROTECT B-WING ASSEMBLY AREA

File Name: t5m01wx

Mission Briefing

While the Alliance continues searching for a place to house its new main base after the evacuation of Yavin, the Rebel forces have also been engaged in developing new offensive strategies, and are now close to deploying a devastating new starfighter; the B-wing. The makeshift assembly area for the B-wing requires constant protection, and Red and Gold Squadrons have been taking turns escorting freighters into and out of the area.

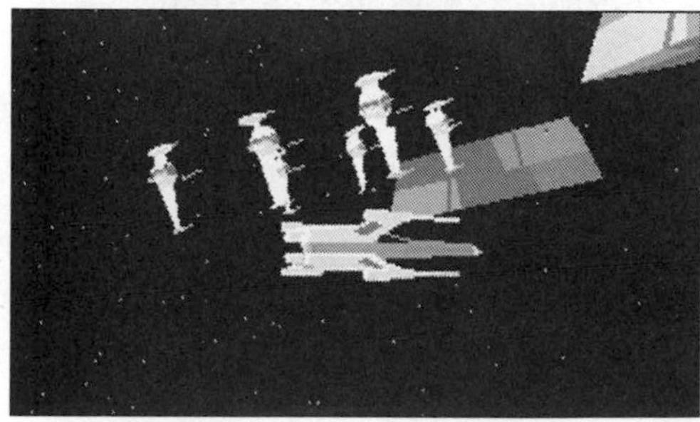

Looking out over B-wing Blue.

Farlander's After-Action Report

I was the flight leader in a four-ship group of X-wings, charged with protecting the assembly area. Coming out of hyperspace, I checked the Inflight Map, and located X-wing Gold. They were less than three kilometers away, headed out of the area. B-wing Blue was near a group of storage containers, which were about 5.5 kilometers in the distance.

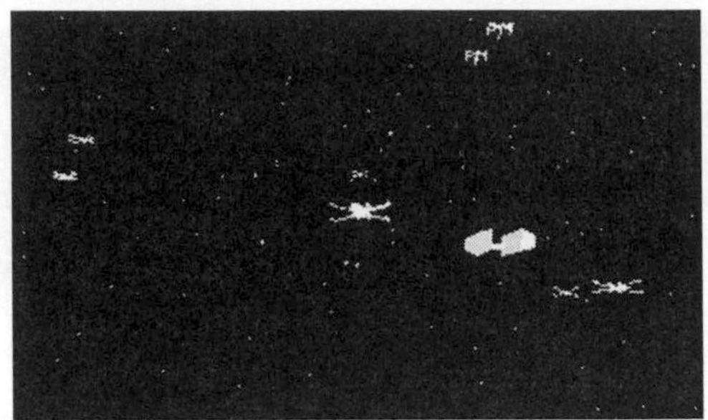

FRT Niven *and X-W Gold head for home.*

I went through my standard mission start-up procedure, setting my recharge rates and throttle to maximum. I put the freighter *Niven* into memory position F5, and B-wing *Blue 1* at F6. I then set the container with the Control Deck at F7. Meanwhile, X-W Gold entered hyperspace, leaving the guard duty to my group, X-W Red.

About the time X-W Gold made the jump, as if on cue, a pair of Imperial Gunboats arrived about eight kilometers away. I shifted all energy to my engines, and accelerated toward them.

I put my cannons on quad-fire, and ordered my wingmen to attack the nearest Gunboat. The enemy was able to launch missiles, but we quickly destroyed the GUNs without losing any X-wings. After the first two Gunboats were destroyed, two more appeared.

I repeated the procedure of ordering my wingmen to attack the first Gunboat, while I redirected energy to my engines for more acceleration. At about half a kilometer, I channeled energy to shields and lasers to match speed with the 'Boats, and we proceeded to blast them into oblivion.

While I was finishing off the second wave, Gunboat group Rho arrived on the scene, accompanied by two enemy corvettes. The first Gunboat group, Mu, was also replaced. Suddenly the situation had become much more challenging.

I sent my wingmen to handle *Mu 2*, while I turned my attention to one of the corvettes. Meanwhile, another pair of corvettes arrived, and suddenly I was getting worried. I ordered my wingmen to help me attack the first corvette, designated *Purple Claw 1*.

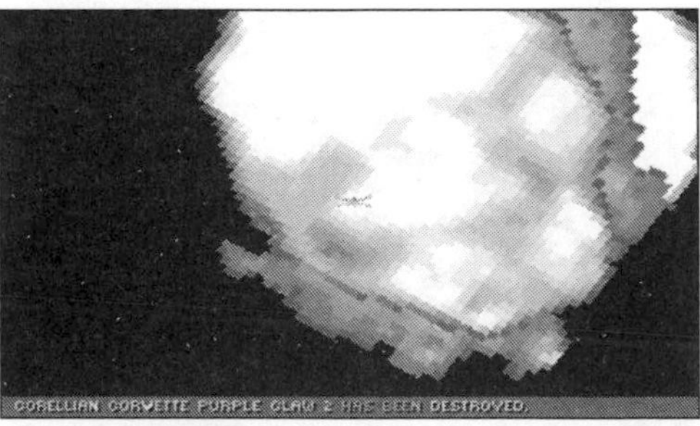

Death of the Purple Claw 2.

I noticed that Gunboat *Rho 2* had gotten by our line of defense, so, as my wingmen finished off *Purple Claw 1*, I ordered them to engage *Purple Claw 2*, and headed for the assembly area at full speed.

By the time I arrived, *Rho 2* was in the assembly area, and doing some damage. I got on his tail and quickly destroyed him, noting that the B-wings still seemed to be all right.

A shuttle arrived on the scene, so I flew close by to inspect it. It was the neutral SHU *Lambda*, out of Habassa, and I left it alone.

GUN Rho was replaced by another group, but they were about 11 kilometers away. My wingmen had shields down on *Purple Claw 2*, so I flew over to help them finish off the corvette, keeping one eye on GUN Rho.

By the time *Purple Claw 2* was disposed of, the new Gunboats had closed to within about seven kilometers, and I ordered my wingmen to intercept. The second pair of corvettes was also about seven kilometers away, and I switched to torpedoes, firing six of them at the lead ship in that group as soon as I had a red lock.

By this time, the new Gunboat group had closed to within 1.5 kilometers of my position, so I switched to lasers and went after *Rho 2.* A couple of shots took care of him, so I switched to *Rho 1* and finished him off as well. I quickly checked the condition of my wingmen, and found that one was no longer among the living; that left just three of us.

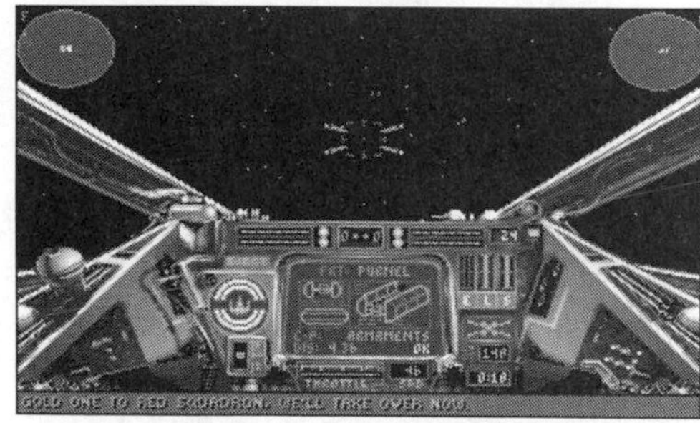

My wingmen head for home.

Two more Gunboats replaced Rho, but they jumped in about nine kilometers away, giving me time to slip into the remaining corvette's blind spot, slow to one-third throttle, and blast it until it exploded. Suddenly the situation was looking much better.

We went after the replacement wave for GUN Rho after that, and quickly took care of business. *Rho 2* was after the B-wings, and slipped past us while we were killing *Rho 1*, but I quickly caught up and destroyed the interloper.

By this time, the mission clock read 1:15. I headed back toward the assembly area with all recharge rates at normal, and lasers and shields fully charged. Another freighter arrived then, and at 0:35 on the clock, X-W Gold showed up as I got the Mission Complete message.

Debriefing (Win Conditions)

B-wing group Blue, and containers *R-Gamma*, *L-Gamma*, *R-Beta*, *L-Beta* and *C-Alpha* must all survive. The freighter *Purnel* and X-wing Gold must arrive.

OP 2: COVER B-WING EVACUATION

File Name: t5m02wx

Mission Briefing

Now that the Imperials have discovered the B-wing assembly area, it must be evacuated. Four X-wings from Red will protect the operation while tug pilots fly the B-wings. The B-wings will be helpless if attacked. The Habassa have generously offered to send a corvette to help evacuate the assembly area crew.

Farlander's After-Action Report

Again, I was the flight leader in a four-ship group of X-wings. Our job was to intercept any Imperial attacks during the evacuation process.

When I arrived in the area, no enemy craft were nearby, so I was able to proceed with standard mission start-up. I headed toward the B-wings, as X-wing Gold headed out, and the freighter *Purnel* followed them into hyperspace.

I placed my wingmen into memory positions F5, F6 and F7, so that I could call them up at any time. After my shields and lasers were fully charged, I reduced my recharge settings to normal, maintaining a high speed as I circled the B-wings in anticipation of an Imperial attack.

Guarding the base.

The Star Destroyer Relentless *arrives.*

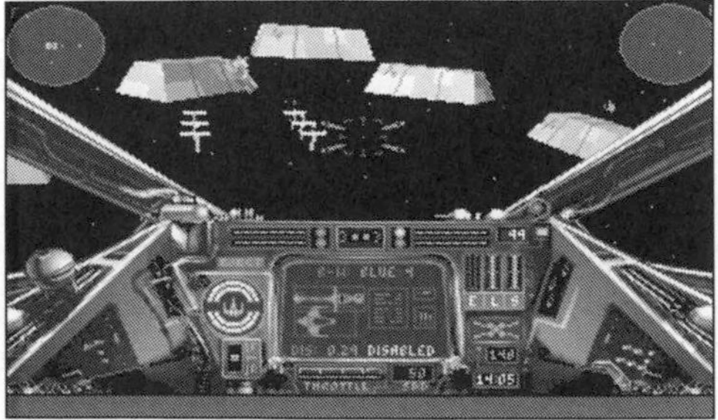

B-wing Blue 4 *needs repair.*

The tug docks as I attack T/F Alpha 2.

The clock read 14:15 when the Star Destroyer *Relentless* appeared, emerging from hyperspace about 13.5 kilometers away. I headed toward it as soon as I had it up on the Combat Multiview Display, telling X-W *Red 4* to wait near the B-wings. My other two wingmen followed me. About one kilometer out, I told X-W *Red 3* to wait, then proceeded towards the Star Destroyer, accompanied by *Red 2*.

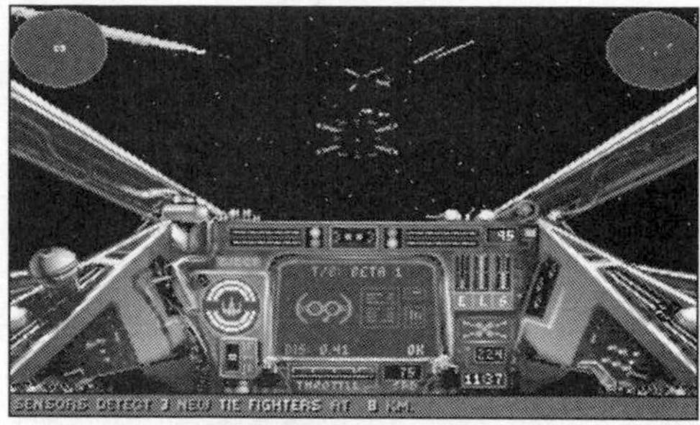

Attacking T/B Beta 1.

Within 30 seconds of its appearance, the *Relentless* launched three TIE fighters. *Red 2* attacked the TIE fighters without special instructions from me, and I joined him, singling out *Alpha 3* for a quick death.

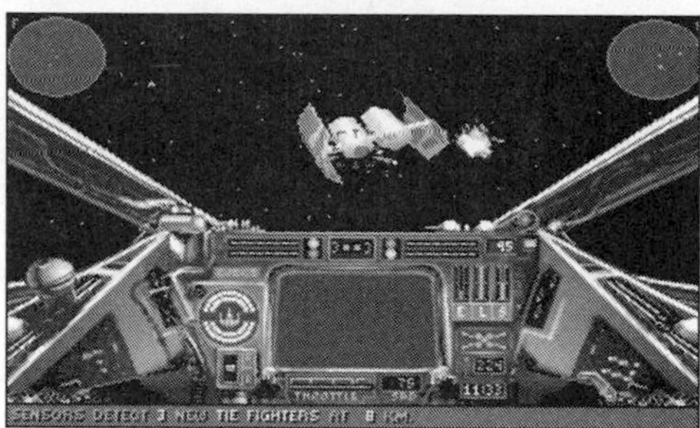

On the tail of a T/B.

Soon after the TIE fighters were launched, a wave of TIE Bombers also joined the fray, but we were able to engage the fighters first because the Bombers were a couple of kilometers behind them. I kept one eye on the Bombers, however, to be sure that they didn't get past us.

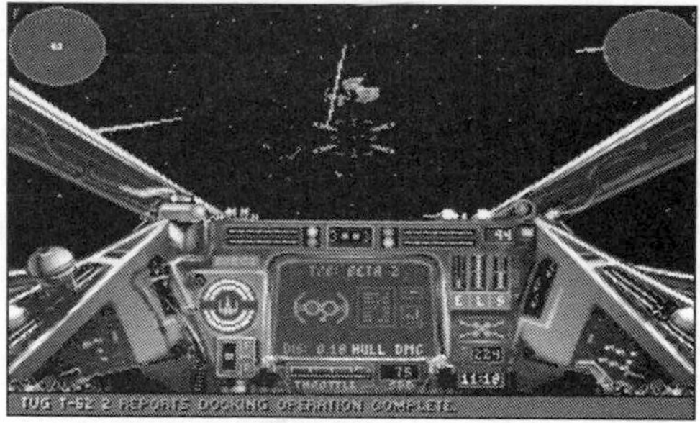

Finishing off T/B Beta 2 *as the tug docks.*

With dual lasers, I caught T/F *Alpha 3* on the first pass and destroyed him. Then I targeted the Bombers, increasing recharge rates to match their speed, and closing in behind *Beta 2*. I made short work of him, and went on to attack the next target, T/B *Beta 3*, which was already a few kilometers past our position.

I redirected energy to my engines to catch up quickly, then got on his tail and finished him. T/B *Beta 1* was nearby, and I turned on him and gave him a dose of my laser cannons. In my CMD, I could see that he had hull damage, and he turned to head back to his base aboard the Star Destroyer.

Some pilots believe in letting hull-damaged ships return to their base if they try to do so, but we have observed that the Imperial ships often begin

Beta 3 *is next. B-W* Blue 2 *is repaired.*

heading home until you stop firing on them, and then turn around and resume their mission. Having occasionally been victimized by this irritating tactic, and not being in a particularly merciful mood, I decided to finish him off.

A second group of T/F Alpha had been launched, and was about a kilometer away, so I engaged the new ships and ended up in a tight-turning dogfight. TIE fighters go quickly if you can get a shot on them, and within moments we were going after *Alpha 3*. By the time we had destroyed all of Alpha, however, three more TIE fighters from Gamma group had joined in.

We continued dogfighting, and watching for the emergence of any more Bombers, which would be my first priority. Meanwhile, Alliance tugs were ferrying pilots to the B-wings so that they could take them out of danger.

I stayed between the Star Destroyer and the evacuation so that I would be in a position to intercept any serious threat to the B-wings' safety. I also made sure that I stayed out of range of the Star Destroyer's turbolaser batteries, and, between each kill, I checked the Inflight Map to be doubly sure that no Bombers had gotten by us.

I also watched the fighters, because they would go after B-wings, even though they didn't pose as great a threat. I noticed, in fact, that T/F *Alpha 3* had slipped away from the dogfight, and was attacking the B-wings. In response, I ordered my wingmen to go after him, while I turned to attack T/B group Theta, which had just launched from the Star Destroyer.

The Habassan corvette, *Habatok 2*, arrived in the area to help evacuate the personnel from the base. Meanwhile, I got jumped by a pair of TIE fighters and lost my targeting computer for a moment. I continued the fight without it, seeking out the enemy visually, which is much more difficult. I switched to my Damage screen and found that I had also lost my hyperdrive. The targeting computer, of course, was what I needed most just then, and I instructed the on-board R2 unit to prioritize the repairs.

Eventually, my systems were functional, and I kept dogfighting, using lasers and torpedoes as necessary, until all the B-wings and base personnel had safely evacuated. Exhausted, I jumped into hyperspace right behind them.

Mission Note: The key to this mission is to let no one get by you. Form a wall to protect the B-wings. If anyone gets through, use torpedoes to stop them, or send your wingmen after them. Any breach may very likely cost you this mission.

Also, early in the mission, if you employ the strategy of leaving wingmen behind in a defensive position, remember that a Shift-A command will cause all your wingmen to attack, and you'll have to toggle back to *Red 3* and *Red 4* and tell them to wait again. The Wingmen Attack order covers all wingmen simultaneously, which does prove useful if any enemy craft gets too far by your forward position to pursue personally.

Be careful not to get too close to the Star Destroyer! If it is attacked, or hit by a stray shot, the *Relentless* launches T/B Delta, a six-ship group of Top Aces with three waves.

Debriefing (Win Conditions)

B-wing group Blue must survive, the CRV *Habatok 2* must dock and survive, and the freighter *Purnel* must arrive.

OP 3: PROTECT B-WING DELIVERY

File Name: t5m03wa

Mission Briefing

Protect the B-wings as they arrive at their new mother ship, the Calamarian cruiser *Maria*. Once again, the B-wing pilots are inexperienced. Two A-wings from Red Squadron will guard the operation.

Farlander's After-Action Report

I was the flight leader in a two-ship group of A-wings. When we entered the area, no enemies were in sight, so I went through my standard mission start-up procedure, placing my wingman at memory location F5, the cruiser *Maria* at F6, and B-W *Blue 1* at F7. I headed toward the *Maria*, six kilometers away.

Soon enough, an Imperial Nebulon B Frigate arrived, launching three TIE fighters within moments. I ordered my wingmen to engage. Switching to dual-fire mode, I attacked, taking out the first fighter quickly, then reset my shield recharge rate to normal to pick up a little speed and went after the next.

Checking the Inflight Map, I discovered that the Frigate had launched more fighters, although none had gotten past us. There were also some enemy TIE Bombers, however, which might pose a threat.

Looking over the scene as the Frigate arrives.

I sent my wingmen to go after T/B *Beta 1*, while I went after *Beta 2* with missiles, taking the Bomber out quickly. I switched to cannons to take out *Beta 3*, and also eliminated him in short order. Two new X-wings arrived, but I was too busy taking on the TIE fighters to see who they were.

Someone fired a missile at me, and I didn't have time to dodge. I took some damage, and while reworking my shields, I noticed that T/B Beta had been replaced by a second wave. I sent my wingmen after *Beta 1*, and switched to missiles to fire on *Beta 2*. Once my missile was away, I switched back to lasers and destroyed *Beta 3* before returning to engage the TIE fighters. T/F *Alpha 6* went down, and I received a message at 18:00 on the clock that some of the B-wings were entering the hangar.

I went after T/F *Alpha 1* next, and then I noticed that TIE Interceptor group Gamma had been launched. I sent my wingmen after T/I *Gamma 1*, and then, to my consternation, I noticed that a second Imperial Frigate had arrived.

I kept shooting up the TIE fighters nearby, hoping to clear things up, before noticing that the second group of B-wings was under attack. I had to head out quickly to take care of them before too much damage was done. I wove back and forth to keep from being hit from behind as I flew.

The new B-wings were dangerously close to one of the Frigates, so the situation was difficult at best. I checked on the TIE Interceptors and made sure that my wingman was after them, discovering in the process that X-wing Gold was also in the melee. Meanwhile, I was still being harassed by the TIE fighters.

The destruction of a T/B.

I stayed close to the B-wings, and continued to shoot up the T/Fs. I had missed T/B Delta, and they were able to launch torpedoes against the *Maria*, but I quickly flew in and shot down the Bombers before they could make a second pass.

When T/B Delta was destroyed, the immediate area was clear of enemy fighters. T/I group Gamma was about seven kilometers away, and I decided to fly by the nearest Frigate, which was only 1.5 kilometers distant. After I had ID'ed the Frigate, I headed toward T/I group Gamma, adjusting my recharge rates to gain speed.

More TIE Bombers were launched—a replacement wave of group Delta. I switched to missiles to take care of *Delta 2* in a hurry, and then went after *Delta 1* with cannons. *Delta 1* had already taken some damage, so he fell quickly. With the Bombers finished, I turned back to the Interceptors.

By this time, one of the Frigates had moved within firing range of the cruiser, and they were exchanging volleys. I fired on another Bomber from a replacement group of T/B Delta, and then had to move fast to shake loose some TIE Interceptors. X-wing Gold came in and took them off me at the last moment.

The Frigate and the cruiser exchange fire.

The first Frigate had left the area, but the second one was still around. I flew in to identify it, and then shot another missile at T/B *Delta 2*, which missed. *Delta 2* was being harassed by X-wings, though, and I was able to get on his tail and finish him.

We were getting the area under control. All the TIE fighters, Bombers, and Interceptors had been eliminated. That left only one Frigate, about 5.5 kilometers from the *Maria*.

I was about four kilometers from the *Maria*, which was heading for its jump point, when a group of Gunboats appeared in the cruiser's path. More X-wings appeared as well, and quickly engaged the 'Boats. I flew in to help out, as one of the X-wings bought it.

I went after GUN *Tau 2*, resetting recharge rates to match its slower speed. Unfortunately, I got tagged by one of the X-wings, and decided to break off and select another target.

We mopped up the Gunboats without much trouble, but they were quickly replaced by another wave. I switched to dual-fire missiles and let fly on GUN *Tau 1*, then fired on *Tau 4*, following up with two more missiles for *Tau 3* that didn't quite do the trick. Those were my last two missiles, so I went after *Tau 3* with laser cannons to finished him off, then completed the job by disposing of *Tau 4*. *Tau 2* was the only remaining Gunboat, and he had drawn a crowd of X-wings, so I stayed out of the way and let them finish him.

The Frigate was almost within gun range of the cruiser by this time, and another wave of Gunboats had arrived. I went back to work on the Gunboats, disposing of them quickly with the help of the X-wings.

Still another wave of GUNs appeared, but I decided to attack the Frigate to draw fire away from the cruiser. I was going to order my wingman to attack the Gunboats, but he was gone. I hadn't even realized it.

I flew in on the Frigate, which ignored me, so I tried a few strafing passes, figuring at least to damage her as much as possible for not paying closer attention. I even reduced speed to one-third to get a better look, and still she didn't fire on me, so I kept up a constant barrage from my cannons until her shields went down.

After a few more shots, the Frigate seemed to notice me at last. That's probably because the cruiser *Maria* had escaped to hyperspace, and my mission was complete. I kept up the attack, figuring that she couldn't last much longer with her shields down, but she deprived me of any final satisfaction by jumping out of the area.

It was time to leave, but some Gunboats were still in the area, and I decided to help clear them before heading home.

Debriefing (Win Conditions)

At least 50 percent of B-Wing Blue must survive and dock with the cruiser *Maria*. The *Maria* must survive.

OP 4: DESTROY TIE STAGING AREA

File Name: t5m04mb

Mission Briefing

For your first mission in a B-wing, attack a TIE staging area near Yunkor IX. The area is housing fighters that will be used to replenish the battle-depleted Imperial forces of nearby capital ships. Containers have been converted to hangars and work areas, and all CONs and parked fighters must be destroyed.

Farlander's After-Action Report

This was a solo B-wing mission, my first, and my craft came equipped with 12 torpedoes. The B-wing operated pretty much like other Alliance fighters, and I went through a standard mission start-up procedure when I arrived in the target area.

I checked the Inflight Map, locating Gunboats *Nu 1, 2,* and *3* between my position and the containers I was after. I immediately targeted the closest Gunboat while they began firing missiles at me.

The B-wing is too large and too slow to evade a missile, so I made sure that my shields were charged up before taking two missile hits in quick succession. Then I evened out the shields, transferring just enough energy from my laser banks so that I could still shoot at full strength.

I slipped in behind GUN *Nu 3* as its squadron past me, discovering that the B-wing's speed matched well with the Gunboat. I destroyed the first one quickly—my first kill in a B-wing!—and turned immediately to get on the tail of *Nu 2. Nu 1* was after me with his lasers, but, fortunately, he wasn't shooting any more missiles. I kept transferring energy from lasers to shields, an excellent tactic since the lasers charged faster.

I realized that I was losing time, so I broke off and headed toward the containers, and a small minefield protecting them. One of the Gunboats was still after me, but I couldn't afford to dogfight at the expense of my mission.

I targeted the closest container (the one on top of the stack), and I was still being harassed by one of the Gunboats when a pair of TIE fighters showed up. I couldn't afford to ignore fighters, but I did make

Going after GUN Nu 2.

Shooting the mines.

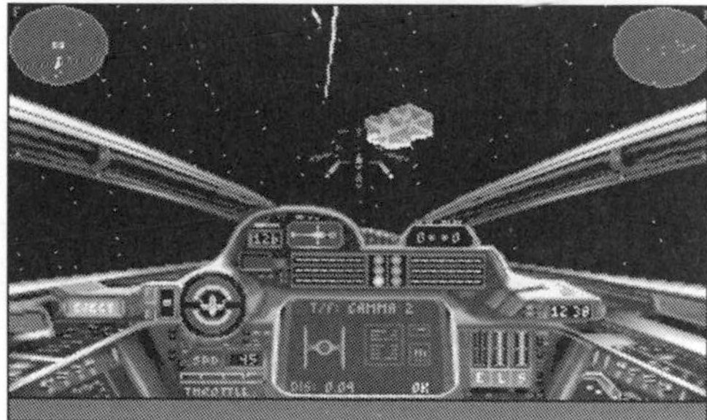

Attacking T/F Gamma 2.

Targeting a corvette.

quick work of them. Without shields, they lasted about half a minute.

I was still taking hits from the Gunboat, but I was able to switch back to torpedoes and get a lock on the container. At 4.5 kilometers out, I fired a pair of torps and then followed with one more, figuring three torpedoes per container should do the trick.

I quickly targeted the next container and repeated the process. I had to keep jinking to avoid the Gunboat's lasers, but I was able to achieve a red lock and fire at the large, stationary containers with relative ease. Because I was firing torpedoes, I kept transferring all laser power to my shields, rebalancing them as necessary.

I gave the third and fourth containers the same treatment, dispensing my last torpedo with one container remaining as I approached the minefield's range of fire.

I flew in circles before approaching the minefield, recharging shields and lasers for about half a minute before heading for the last container. I opened up a barrage of lasers at a distance of about 1.6 kilometers, for the most part ignoring the mines and concentrating on the container. I figured that I couldn't afford to waste any time completing this mission, so I shot any mines that came into my sights, but didn't make a special effort to seek them out.

Suddenly, someone hit me with a missile, and I worked frantically to recharge my shields as a couple more TIE fighters appeared. I turned to attack them, meanwhile transferring energy constantly to my shields.

As I kept after the TIEs, I was able to get my shields back to full charge. Then I went in after the last container, finally reducing it to floating debris. Whenever I could, I shot a mine, further reducing the threat to my craft. Once all the containers had been disposed of, I went after some unmanned TIE fighters that had been left in the staging area.

I shot a couple of those TIEs with my lasers, and then decided, with my shields fully charged, to simply ram a row of three, plowing through them in the well-armored B-wing. I took some damage, but most of the TIE fighters were destroyed.

One remained, and I was about to take it out with a quick burst of cannon fire, when a pair of Imperial corvettes, designated *TA-305 1* and *TA-305 2*, entered the area.

The corvettes had TIE bays, which meant that they could begin launching fighters or Bombers at any time. I destroyed the last of the parked TIE fighters and, thankfully, received my Mission Complete message. With no remaining torpedoes, I ditched the corvettes and jumped into hyperspace.

Debriefing (Win Conditions)
TIE fighter group Zeta, and containers *Chi 1-5* must be destroyed.

Mission Note: The key strategy for this mission is to destroy all the containers using three torpedoes apiece, except the one near the parked TIE fighters. Also, if you destroy only two of GUN Nu as the mission starts, you won't have to deal with the replacement waves, and the B-wing can take the punishment.

OP 5: DESTROY SECRET WEAPONS BASE

File Name: t5m05mb

Mission Briefing
The Empire is attempting to duplicate the super shield technology at a secret weapons research base. The base is constructed of cargo containers and protected by just two CRVs so as to appear unimportant. An A-wing/B-wing team from Red Squadron and an X-wing/Y-wing team from Gold Squadron will attack the compound.

Farlander's After-Action Report
After jumping into the area, I checked my Inflight Map and confirmed the situation to be sure that our intelligence was accurate. Six containers were in a row, with a corvette on either side. One TIE Bomber was also present.

I went through my mission-start procedures, then targeted the corvette on the right, switching to torpedoes and firing off five as soon as I had a red lock. Then I toggled up ion cannons and flew in to disable the craft.

As the X-wing was engaging the TIE Bomber, I quickly locked on to the other corvette, fired five more torpedoes, then switching to ion cannons to disable it, as well. I noticed an incoming missile, but had no other choice than to absorb the hit with my shields. After both corvettes were disabled, I moved

Disabling a corvette.

away from the action and recharged my shields and lasers before returning. I was shadowed by T/B *Alpha 1*, so I destroyed him, too.

Destroying the containers.

A massive dogfight had suddenly erupted all around me. Despite that, I turned my attention to the containers, firing my two remaining torpedoes into the first one and then finishing it off with lasers. I went after the rest of the containers with my lasers as well.

The A-wing and the X-wing were assisting both myself and the Y-wing by holding off the enemy fighters, so I was not in any great danger from random attacks. My shields were holding, and I kept moving, firing on the containers until all were destroyed. Finally, when the last of the containers exploded, I turned back to the disabled corvettes and finished them off one after the other.

After the second corvette was destroyed, I received the Mission Complete message. Two more corvettes and three Gunboats entered the area, but I had no orders regarding them, so I jumped for home.

Debriefing (Win Conditions)

Container groups Xi and Chi, and CONs *Phi 1* and *Phi 2*, as well as corvettes *Trigger 3* and *Trigger 7*, must be destroyed.

Mission Note: Destroying the first corvette triggers the arrival of the reinforcements, so disable the CRVs and save them for last.

OP 6: Prisoner Rescue

File Name: t5m06my

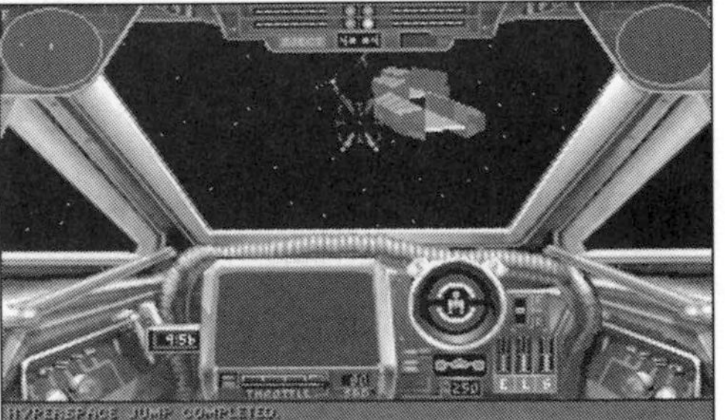

Beginning the mission.

Mission Briefing

A Y-wing starfighter is being sent to rescue Habassan prisoners from an Imperial slave convoy. Freighters carrying the slaves are due to rendezvous with the Imperial Frigate

Mayhem near Cificap VIII. The transport *Ranger* will rescue the slaves once the freighter carrying them is disabled. An A-wing from Blue Squadron will fly escort.

Farlander's After-Action Report

As I entered the mission area in my Y-wing, I lowered the nose of my craft and saw the three Imperial freighters, one of which was sure to be carrying the Habassan prisoners. Almost immediately, I saw the telltale glow of Imperial laser fire, and then three shuttles coming after me.

I took evasive action to avoid a head-on confrontation, quickly charging my shields and turning in behind the first of the shuttles. I would have to deal with them before I could inspect the freighters.

Even with my recharge rates at full, I was a hair faster than the shuttles, so I throttled down to two-thirds power and came in behind one of them, firing lasers.

After destroying one, I sought out the next, finally dispatching the third before flying in close to the freighters to ID them. I began with the one at the back of the formation, called *Strider,* which carried base equipment. The middle freighter, called *Treader,* also contained base equipment. The first one in the line was called *Walker,* and it was the one I was looking for. I had found the prisoners.

I checked my shield and laser charge, then switched to torpedoes and destroyed the other two freighters with six torpedoes apiece. I did this because the freighters were close together, and I needed to disable the first freighter but could not afford to let the others come crashing into it from behind.

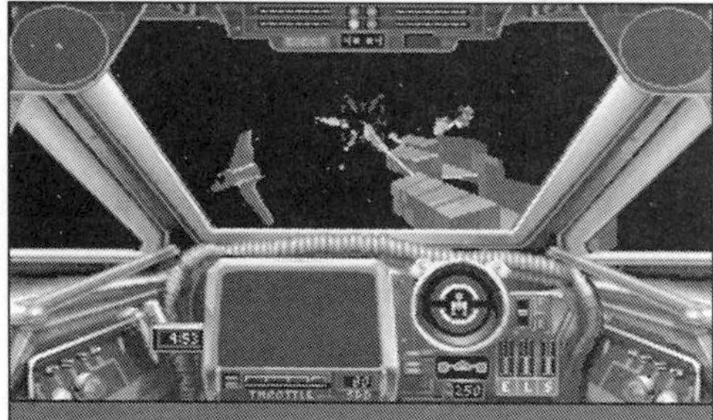

Shuttle attack!

After the two rear freighters were destroyed, I attacked the leader; first with lasers, to drop the shields, then with ion cannons, to disable it. I cut my speed to zero, since there was no apparent threat and I had an escort.

Almost immediately, Rebel transport *Ranger* arrived and headed for the freighter. Meanwhile, I set my throttle to full speed again. I wasn't taking it easy—I knew that an Imperial probe was 99 kilometers away, and that the Empire would know about our activities soon enough.

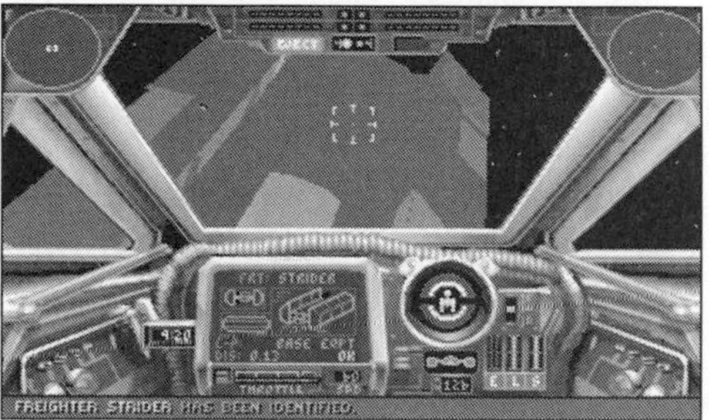

Getting ready to torpedo FRT Strider.

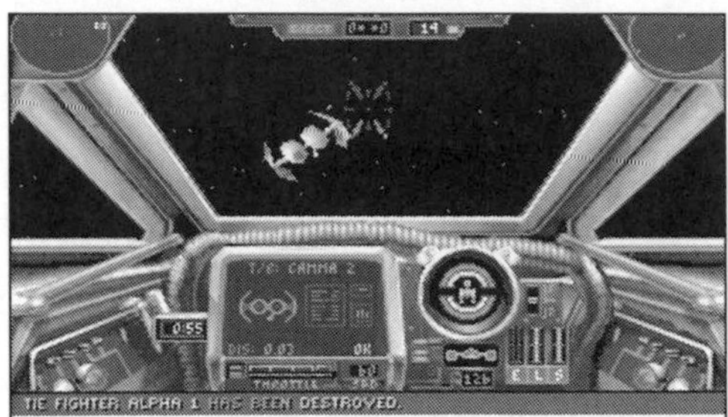

Taking out the T/Bs.

As the *Ranger* closed in, an Imperial Frigate arrived about eight kilometers out and began launching TIE fighters from Alpha group. I targeted T/F *Alpha 2*, and headed on an intercept course.

Soon after the fighters launched, a TIE Bomber group was also dispatched. The Bombers were the greater threat, of course, so I knew that I couldn't forget about them. But the fighters were closer, and I hoped to take them out before the Bombers came within range.

My escort, A-wing *Blue 1*, was much quicker, and he destroyed *Alpha 2* before I arrived on the scene. I turned my attention to *Alpha 1*, and, with recharge rates at normal, I came in at full throttle to destroy him on the first pass.

I switched vectors to go after the Bombers, which went down quickly but were replaced in a matter of moments by TIE Interceptors *Beta 1* and *Beta 2*. The A-wing engaged, and I went in to offer assistance, pegging T/I *Beta 2* even in my relatively sluggish Y-wing.

I kept checking the area and the Inflight Map to be sure that no one slipped by me. So far, so good.

The clock read 0:30 when I received the message that the docking operation was complete. The prisoners were on-board the transport. If we could hold out a little longer, the transport could escape to hyperspace, and the mission would be a success.

I kept dogfighting until the transport made the jump. The mission clock read zero as I prepared to enter hyperspace and leave the scene. We had done what we needed to do, and even though there were plenty of enemy starfighters buzzing about, I decided that discretion was the better part of valor.

Debriefing (Win Conditions)

Transport *Ranger* must dock with the freighter *Walker*, and survive.

Mission Note: The freighter with the prisoners can be the first or second one in line. Because this is a random occurrence, if you're having trouble with the mission, re-fly it. It's easier to complete this mission if the prisoner freighter is the second one, because then you have to destroy only the last freighter, rather than the last two.

OP 7: HELP NEUTRALS OUT OF AMBUSH

File Name: t5m07mx

Mission Briefing

The Habassa are leaning toward joining the Alliance, and if this mission is successful, and we can save a Habassan convoy from Imperial attack, they may finally be convinced. Imperial CRVs will stage the attack near Retep V, and all nearby Alliance forces will scramble to protect the Habassa. Red will send four X-wings, Gold will send two A-wings, and three B-wings from Blue will arrive within six minutes.

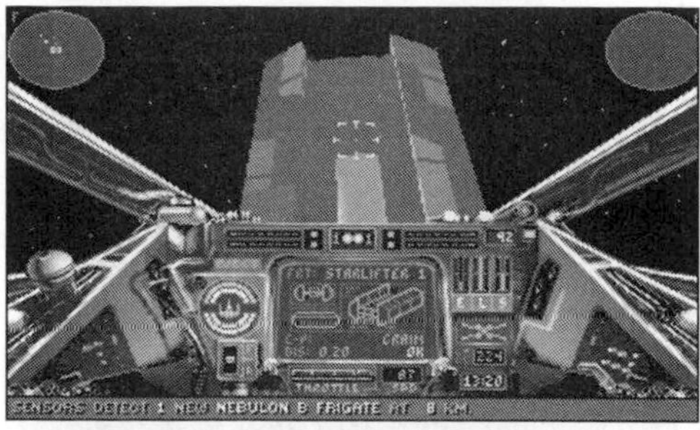

A grain freighter from Starlifter *group.*

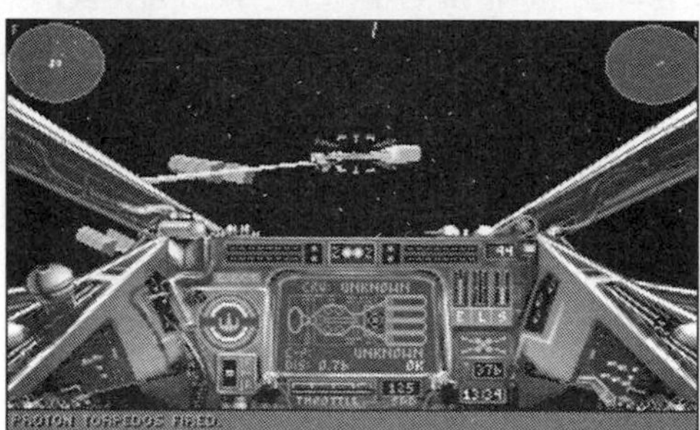

Firing on the first corvette.

Farlander's After-Action Report

When we jumped into the area, Imperial corvettes were plastering the Habassan freighters, and I knew right away that we would lose some of them. Habassan transports were returning fire on the corvettes, but they definitely needed some help.

I began to charge my shields at the normal rate, while redirected laser power to my engines, then shifting some laser energy over to the shields as well. At full throttle, I got to a speed of 125.

I targeted the second-closest corvette and ordered my wingmen to attack, then targeted the closest corvette myself. Switching to torpedoes, I fired two, then set my lasers at full recharge, transferring energy back to them as I was closing in for the kill.

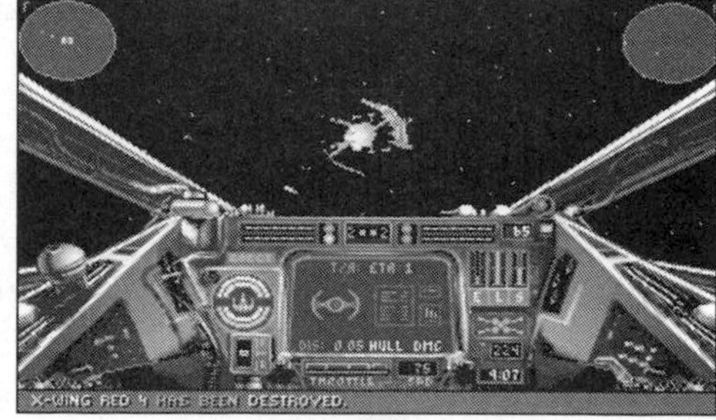

Finishing off T/A Eta 1.

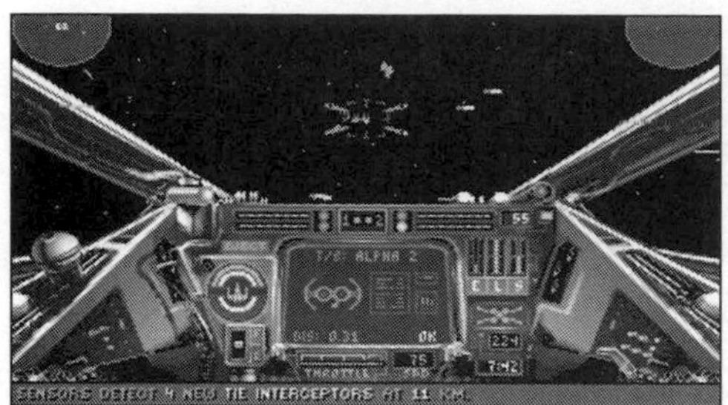

Firing on T/B Alpha 2 *in the distance.*

As both corvettes were destroyed, they tumbled in their death throes, firing off blasts even while disintegrating. I kept coming in closer to try and draw off their fire from the freighters, as every shot from their turbolasers did great damage.

An Imperial Frigate arrived then, about nine kilometers away, and immediately launched TIE Advanced *Eta 1*. I ordered my wingmen to attack the Frigate, hoping that they would launch torpedoes from a distance, and then I headed to intercept the enemy starfighter.

I set my recharge rates at normal, and set the Frigate in memory location F5. Because my wingmen would break off their torpedo run on the Frigate if they were attacked, I wanted to be sure to reassign them quickly to the Frigate, keeping them focused.

After disposing of *Eta 1*, I kept moving toward the Frigate, dogfighting my way in the direction of the Imperial ship. During their launch sequence, TIE Bombers must follow a predetermined flight path, and they're completely vulnerable at that time. Realizing this, I hung around near the Frigate's TIE bays, blasting Bombers into oblivion whenever they appeared.

One of the TIE Bombers slipped by me, but I'd been checking the Inflight Map to be sure that no one got too far. I followed at full speed, and nailed him with a torpedo before he could launch his missiles.

The Frigate was closing in on the freighters, and I knew that I would have to intercept the Bombers even more quickly now; there wasn't much room for error.

I continued rebalancing shields, keeping them charged up. At 7:15 on the clock, a second Frigate entered about ten kilometers away, and proceeded to launch four TIE Interceptors from Delta group. I still had my hands full with TIE Bombers, however, and they were my first priority.

The Bombers were able to fire torpedoes almost instantly when they emerged from the Frigate, so I had to kill them without delay. A-wing *Gold 1* and *Gold 2* had gone after the Interceptors, so at least I didn't have to concern myself with them for the moment. I was getting desperate, though, and even began to ram some of the Bombers to take them out quickly.

At 5:00 on the clock, some Habassan Y-wings entered the area and began launching torpedoes at the first Frigate. Relieved, I kept going after the Bombers. I noticed that a T/B was among the freighters by then, so I switched to torpedoes and launched one to take him out.

No more Bombers would be launched from the first Frigate, as it had sustained heavy hull damage, and I decided to close in and finish her off once I had cleared the area of the last T/B.

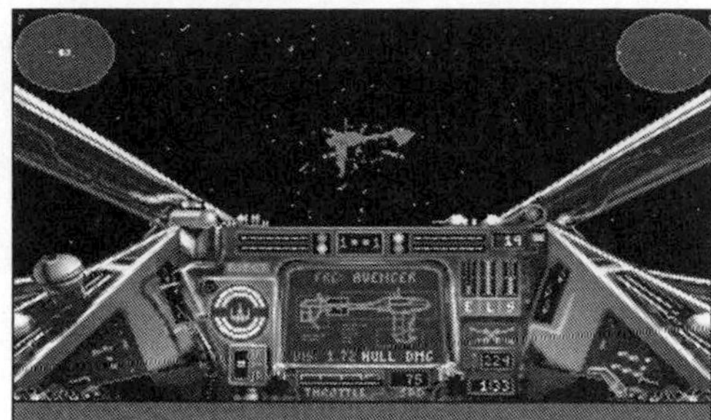

The Frigate Avenger *with hull damage.*

With the first Frigate disposed of, the only remaining threat was the Interceptors coming from the second Frigate. Habassan Y-wings and transports were firing torpedoes on the Frigate, and I headed in to lend assistance. I was about to order my wingmen to join me, up until the point that I noticed they had all been destroyed.

I was still ten kilometers from the FRG, and she was already failing, so I knew I wouldn't serve much purpose making the trip. I headed toward the Interceptors to help the A-wings. The clock read zero as the surviving three freighters jumped to hyperspace, and I received the Mission Complete message. I finished off the last of the Interceptors, and jumped out myself.

Mission Note: When the mission begins, quickly get to the first two corvettes, fire a couple of torpedoes at one, and have your wingmen fire at the other. Then concentrate on taking heat off the freighters until they can make the jump. You definitely will lose two of the freighters. It's necessary to stop the TIE Bombers at all costs. Use torpedoes as necessary against the Bombers to make sure that they don't get within missile-launching range, and have your wingmen use their torpedoes against the Frigate.

This mission also has a secret: Destroy the transport *Epsilon* to trigger the arrival of Habassan Y-wing reinforcements.

OP 8: ESCORT VIP TO ALLIANCE CRUISER

File Name: t5m08wa

Mission Briefing

A-wing Red is assigned to fly escort for the Habassan envoy, traveling aboard the transport *Bardictol*, on route to the cruiser *Independence* to sign a formal declaration of allegiance to the Rebellion.

Cruiser Independence *under attack.*

Farlander's After-Action Report

I was flight leader in a three-ship group of A-wings, assigned to escort the Habassan transport. We expected the Empire to attack, and it was at the request of the Habassan envoy that Red Squadron was assigned to the job.

At the beginning of the mission, I checked the Inflight Map and found only the cruiser, about 17 kilometers away. I put *Red 2* in memory at F5, and the *Independence* at F6. The Habassan transport arrived, and I put it in memory location F7. I then ran through my normal mission start-up procedure, and took a position near the transport to confirm its ID.

Soon after I had made the confirmation, an Imperial Frigate arrived to crash the party, jumping in right next to the *Independence*. Almost immediately, a second Frigate appeared, this one flanking the cruiser on its opposite side.

Some TIE fighters launched in quick order, and I assigned my wingmen to go after T/F *Alpha 1*, while I went after *Alpha 2*. There was also a second pair of TIE fighters from Beta group.

I reset my laser recharge rates to normal, traveling at 120 kps, and quickly took out *Alpha 2* with a head-on pass. We were now under attack by TIE Interceptors as well, and after disposing of the fighter, I quickly targeted T/I *Eta 2* with my cannons linked in dual-fire mode.

I kept checking the Inflight Map as a precaution, and that's how I learned that *Beta 1* had gotten by us. I quickly turned to pursue. *Beta 1* had closed to within 2.5 kilometers of the Habassan transport, which was now approaching the cruiser, so I switched to missiles and fired as soon as I had a red lock. I had *Beta 2* on my tail by then, and as soon as I had launched my missile I turned and engaged, ending the battle quickly. I then decided to give the transport a closer inspection.

The transport is heading for the hangar.

Entering the hangar.

Another Gunboat explodes. Mission is a success.

While checking the status of the transport, a pair of T/Is appeared and attacked, and I called in my wingmen to help out with the confrontation. The transport was being harassed by TIE fighters, and I needed to give that matter most of my attention.

I switched to lasers and took out one of the fighters, deciding then to keep close to the area, and engage any opposition forces until the docking was complete.

The dogfighting continued for some time, and I destroyed several more TIE fighters and Interceptors. They came in waves, and I had all I could handle, but I was able to keep the transport safe. Finally, the ship made it to the hangar.

I noticed that other Imperial craft had joined the fray, as had some friendly corvettes. The cruiser was still under attack, and now I began to battle with Gunboats and Bombers.

The dogfighting continued until the clock ran down to about 20 seconds, and it was then that the *Independence* jumped into hyperspace. More Gunboats arrived, and I was anxiously awaiting the Mission Complete message as I engaged this latest wave of Imperials. After I had the message, I finished off the rest of the Gunboats before heading for hyperspace.

Debriefing (Win Conditions)

The transport *Bardictol* and the cruiser *Independence* must dock. The cruiser must then escape into hyperspace.

OP 9: GUARD CARGO PICKUP

The Kielty 1 *begins boarding.*

File Name: t5m09ma

Mission Briefing

Two Alliance freighters are collecting food supplies left by the Habassa near Retep III, and will be escorted by a pair of A-wings from Red. The cargo transfer should take about six minutes.

Farlander's After-Action Report

As the mission began, I went through my standard start-up procedures, while two Habassan freighters dropped off a pair of containers. Two Alliance freighters, *Kielty 1* and *Kielty 2*, arrived for the rendezvous.

Another container was some distance away, but it was not critical to the mission. No hostile craft were in the area.

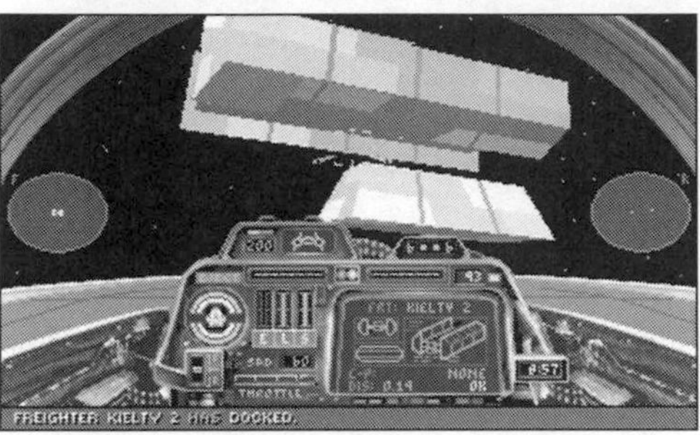

Kielty 2 *has docked with the Habassan.*

I circled the storage units while my shields and lasers charged to full. At 8:30 on the clock, an Imperial Nebulon B Frigate appeared, immediately launching four TIE Advanced from Delta group, as well as four TIE Bombers from Alpha.

Targeting T/A Delta 2.

Since the Bombers were the more dangerous craft, from the mission perspective, I led my group in to attack. If the Imperial fighters were following standard orders, the TIE Advanced would have an anti-starfighter directive, and would concentrate on our A-wings. I ordered my wingmen to attack T/B *Alpha 1*.

With the A-wing's speed and missile load, it was indeed a formidable craft, and I was happy to pilot one in this mission. I decided to place the four Bombers in memory locations F5 through F8, then fired one missile at T/A *Delta 2*, following up with some laser blasts to finish him off. After that, I punched up location F6, and went after T/B *Alpha 2*, this time exclusively with lasers.

I was too slow, and two of the Bombers, *Alpha 3* and *Alpha 4*, were able to launch missiles.

Firing a torpedo up the tailpipe of a T/B.

All four missile hit the freighter *Kielty 1*, but I exacted some revenge, destroying both the transgressors with a missile apiece. As soon as all of T/B Alpha was history, a second wave was launched from the Frigate, and I headed toward them to intercept as quickly as possible.

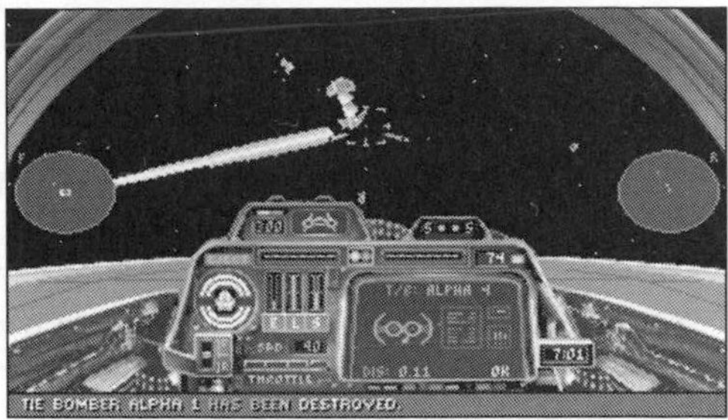

Finishing a T/B with laser fire.

This time I was quicker, dispatching all four Bombers within 20 seconds. I fired a missile at the first one, and switched to lasers to destroyed two more as I approached. I then swung in behind the fourth and took him out as well.

After that, I headed for the Frigate, closing to within about two kilometers on the hangar side. This time, when a new wave of T/B Alpha was launched, another four Bombers from Beta group were dispatched as well. I switched to missiles and obliterated three of T/B Alpha, then picked off one from Beta group.

I dealt with *Alpha 1* after that, as he had the misfortune of being the closest enemy craft, then toggled the CMD until I had T/B *Beta 3* targeted. I dispatched *Beta 3* with another missile, leaving me with only two.

By this time, my wingmen had destroyed all of T/A Delta, and there were no enemy craft in the area other than the Frigate. As I took stock of the situation, I received the message that the docking operation was complete.

A second wave of Beta was launched, but I was right next to them, working to avoid the turbolaser fire from the Frigate. I wanted to hold on to my two remaining missiles, so I went after the Bombers with lasers, getting one of them on my first pass, then falling in behind and destroying the remaining three.

The clock read 2:20 when the *Kielty 2* jumped to safety, with *Kielty 1* having entered hyperspace just before that. No more starfighters appeared in the area, and it looked as though the Frigate had run dry of them as well. At 51 seconds on the clock, I received the Mission Complete message. I destroyed the now empty containers before returning to base.

Debriefing (Win Conditions)

Container group Psi must be boarded. Freighter group Kielty must dock and survive.

Mission Note: The key to this mission is to engage the TIE Bombers as close to the Frigate as possible. Use missiles on a couple, and then finish them off with lasers. Be sure to save some missiles for when the two groups, Alpha and Beta, appear simultaneously. Leave your wingmen alone unless someone gets past you, and then send them after that craft.

Mission Note (continued): Also, if you destroy the container that's off in the distance, away from the others, Rebel reinforcements arrive—three X-wings from Blue group, two B-wings from Gold, and two Rebel transports from Badger group, as well. If you have trouble with this mission, therefore, you can call in the cavalry. For a little fun at the end, wait until after the freighters have made the jump, then summon the reinforcements and watch them attack the Frigate. Join in, and try to get the last shot on the Frigate to collect the victory points.

A note on general tactics that will serve you well in large dogfights, such as the one in OP 9: When a group is in formation, you can target the leader and fire a missile, and sometimes the missile will hit another craft while you still have a lock on the leader. This technique works well when the craft are bunched together. Also, when you're using lasers, you might try targeting the leader of a group, but going after a wingman. If you can stay on the wingman until he's destroyed, you can quickly find the rest of the group, because you still have the leader targeted in the CMD.

OP 10: PROBE CAPTURE

File Name: t5m10wb

Mission Briefing

As part of its surveillance operations, the Empire is distributing probes in the outer systems. The surveillance probes are being deployed from a transfer area near Bota II, and the Alliance will lead a raid to capture an Imperial freighter loaded with the devices. Gunboats and a small minefield protect the probes. B-wing Red will lead the mission, accompanied by A-wing Gold. The transport *Storm Unit* will arrive once Red disables the freighter.

Farlander's After-Action Report

I was flying a lone B-wing, and, checking the Inflight Map at the beginning of the mission, I found a cluster of Imperial craft about six kilometers away. There were two freighters and three containers. Three kilometers distant was Assault Gunboat group Rho, composed of three craft.

The Gunboats were already beginning to target me with missiles, but a B-wing can take some good shots, so I headed toward them while transferring cannon energy to my shields, and bumping up my shield recharge rate. My speed was 56 kps as I came in to attack GUN *Rho 3*. Dual-firing my cannons, I kept on the Gunboat's tail (while A-wing Gold occupied the other Imperials), then made quick work of both *Rho 1* and *Rho 2*.

Shortly after we had destroyed the first wave of GUN Rho, another contingent of three Gunboats arrived. I was busily recharging my shields as I turned to intercept. As before, they launched missiles at me, but I took one ship out in a head-on pass, and continued after the others when A-wing Gold disrupted the formation.

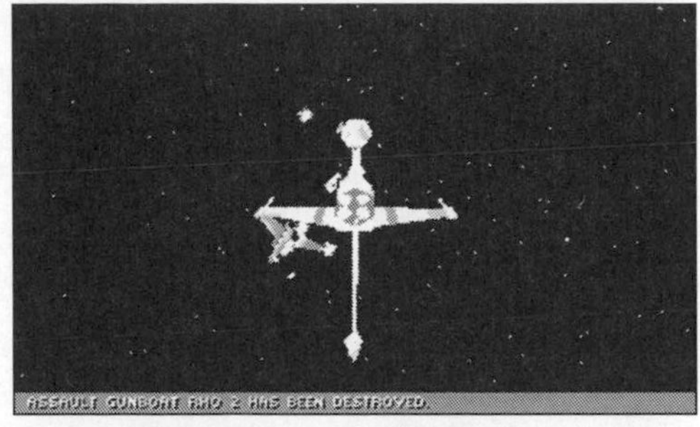

Destruction of GUN Rho 2.

When the Gunboats had been dealt with, I ordered A-wing Gold to wait while I headed in to clear the mines. As I entered the minefield, I bumped up my laser recharge rate one notch above normal and began a dual-fire assault. I took out the mines quickly and headed in to inspect the containers, finding nothing of consequence.

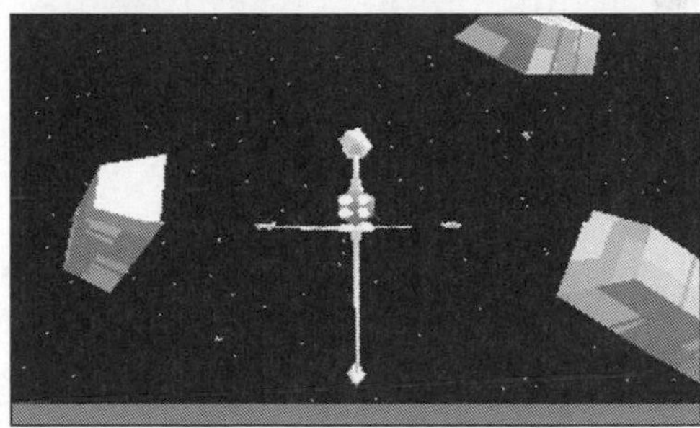

Flying through the containers.

I headed toward the freighters next, attacking the one in the lead as soon as I was within range. I lowered my throttle to one-third and began strafing in single-fire mode while I conducted a quick scan. Both were carrying toxic waste, and their shields fell quickly. I then switched to ion cannons and disabled the lead freighter, allowing the other to ram it from behind with destructive results.

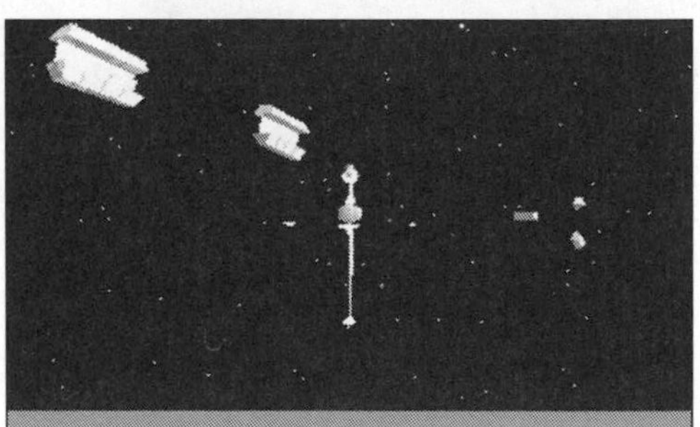

Looking back at the containers.

A pair of corvettes had arrived to divert my attention, and I complied, launching two torpedoes into the first while redirected shield energy to my engines, gaining speed with lasers at maximum.

I switched to ion cannons and disabled CRV *Spider 1*, then went after *Spider 2*, finding her blind spot while lowering my throttle to one-third. I dropped a couple of torpedoes to soften her up, then fired lasers until her shields went down. Finally, I switched to ion cannons and completed the disabling process.

A new freighter had entered the area, and I responded by returning to full throttle and opening fire. Suddenly, another corvette appeared as well. I switched my attention to the corvette, firing two torpedoes, then following with two more. I dispatched the CRV quickly, because it seemed to be heading toward the new freighter, and that made me a little nervous.

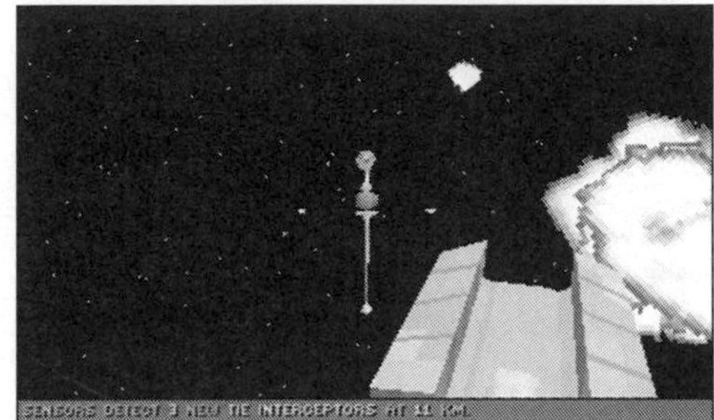
Scratch one corvette.

Three TIE Interceptors had just shown up, and I decided the time was right for the waiting A-wings to resume their mission.

Checking the Inflight Map, I found that a Frigate, obviously the launching vehicle for the Interceptors, had arrived about ten kilometers away. The situation was critical. The Frigate dispatched a TIE Bomber group while I flew in to ID the new freighter, discovering it was the *Libom*; carrying the probes. I took out the *Libom's* shields with my cannons, then switched to ions to disable her as another A-wing arrived.

Now I redirected all shield energy to my engines, and went to full throttle. The TIE Interceptors were attacking me frantically, so much so that I collided with one. I rebalanced my shields, and also redirected more laser energy to my defense, just in time to sustain a missile attack from some unseen foe.

I returned my shield recharge rate to normal as I came within gun range of TIE Bomber group Beta, taking out a couple of Bombers quickly and then blasting T/I *Alpha 3*, while transferring shield energy to my engines.

The Rebel transport *Storm Unit* was now in the area, so I placed him at memory location F8. I then disposed of *Alpha 1*, followed shortly thereafter by T/B *Beta 3*.

The *Storm Unit* had captured the Imperial freighter, and I kept all other threats at bay until both ships had entered hyperspace. Mission complete.

Debriefing (Win Conditions)
The freighter *Libom* must be recovered.

Mission Note: This mission has several entry points for Gunboat Rho, determined at random. In other missions, they can be as far as 11 kilometers away at the beginning. The strategy outlined here works best when the Gunboat group is relatively close. Also, the trick of disabling a lead freighter and letting following freighters collide with it may or may not work. If it doesn't, you can still go in with lasers and finish the job.

OP 11A: DESTROY CORVETTE BASE

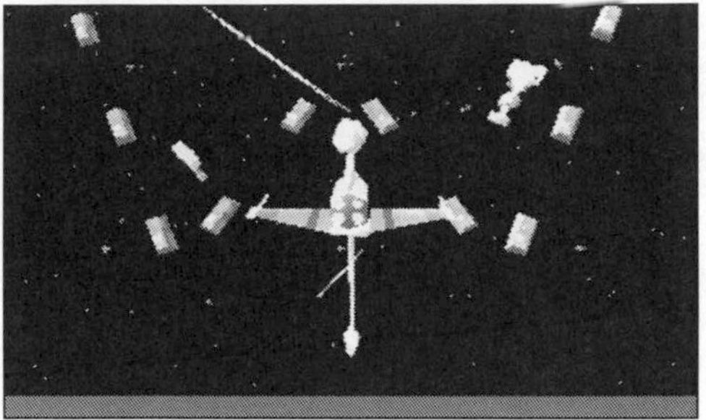

Heading into the base.

One corvette down, another to go.

File Name: t5m11wba

Mission Briefing

An Imperial System Patrol Squadron Base will be destroyed by three B-wings from Red. This should further frustrate the Empire's surveillance efforts. The base is protected by mines and a small number of TIE fighters.

Farlander's After-Action Report

At the mission start, we jumped in to the area above a W-shaped installation. Checking the Inflight Map, I located a three-ship group of TIE fighters already deployed to attack us, waiting less than three kilometers away. Some containers and a pair of corvettes were about five kilometers away, at the base. There were also mines and a tug in the area.

I ordered my wingmen to attack the nearest TIE fighter while I targeted a corvette. I noticed that one of the corvettes was disabled, and I ignored that one. I redirected shield recharge energy to my engines to pick up a little speed, switched to torpedoes in dual-fire mode, and waited for a missile lock. Meanwhile, my wingmen had finished off the first TIE fighter, so I ordered them to engage the next-closest T/F.

I fired six torpedoes into the first corvette, then headed toward the second. Because it was disabled already, there was no reason to waste torps in destroying it. I kept assigning my wingmen to the nearest enemy fighter as I trained my cannons on the disabled craft. Ignoring nearby mines, I made quick work of the defenseless ship.

Another corvette appeared on the scene, and I ordered my wingmen after it. Switching back to torpedoes, I recharged and rebalanced my shields, then turned and achieved a lock on the newest arrival. I shot four torpedoes into it, finally switching to cannons to finish her off.

I ordered my wingmen to go after the remaining TIE fighters, while I went in to clear the minefield. I kept my shields balanced and charged by transferring energy from my cannons, using the tri-fire mode to achieve an effective mine-destroying spread.

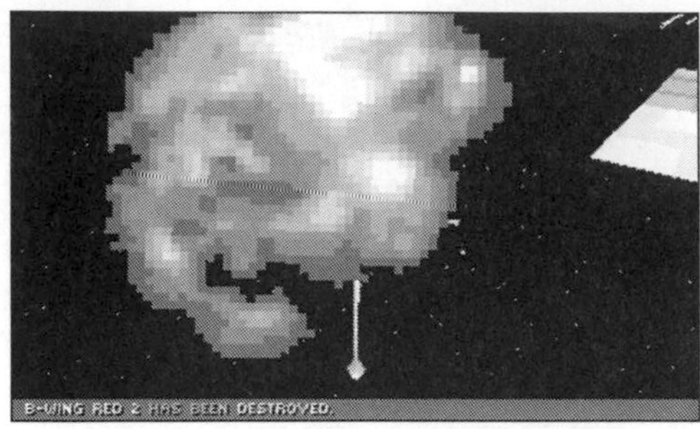

Death of a B-wing.

When the last of the mines had been polished off, I noticed that an Imperial Frigate had jumped in about five kilometers away. I ordered my wingmen to attack one of the containers while I flew out to engage the TIE fighters being launched from the Frigate.

Soon, some Gunboats also joined the party, and stuff began flying everywhere. I was taking hits and working hard to keep my shields up. One of the Gunboats targeted me with a missile, and I had no choice but to absorb the hit in the slow B-wing. While I took some abuse, my wingmen had destroyed one container, and I sent them after another.

The Gunboats were the biggest threat, because they kept firing missiles at me, and even a B-wing can't take an unlimited number of missile hits. I targeted *Tau 1* and shot him with linked cannons. By dogfighting with the Gunboats, I achieved two purposes: I got rid of them as I shot them to pieces, and I kept them from launching more missiles, as Gunboats generally will not fire missiles in close combat.

After destroying two of the Gunboats, I checked the Inflight Map and learned several pertinent facts: 1) One TIE fighter and one Assault Gunboat were still close by; 2) Most of the containers were about a kilometer away, and; 3) I had just lost both my wingmen.

I ignored the two fighters and went after the containers, keeping my shields up. I redirected shield energy to the engines to keep my speed relatively high, switching to single-fire mode before initiating a strafing loop on the remaining containers. When the tug came into my sights, I shot it, too.

While I was destroying the last of the containers, a new wave of T/F Beta had been launched. With the mission nearing its end, and having had enough dogfighting, I decided to make a pass on the Frigate to ID it. It was the *Dark Eye*, and I paid the price for my curiosity as the FRG nailed my craft with several hits.

I worked to recharge my shields as I headed away. The mission clock read six minutes, and I decided that it was time to leave. The Mission Complete message flashed on and I jumped out, right after I taught the persistent T/F *Beta 1* a lesson.

OP 11B: DESTROY IMPERIAL BASE

File Name: t5m11mbb

Mission Briefing

In this mission, an Imperial System Patrol Squadron Base in the Feenicks system will be targeted. All Assassin class corvettes in the area must be destroyed. The base is guarded by TIE Bombers, Gunboats, and a small minefield. Two B-wings from Red will lead the attack, with an X-wing from Blue flying escort.

Farlander's After-Action Report

As flight leader of B-wing Red, my main concern would have to be the corvettes. With 12 torpedoes at my disposal, I knew that I could take out two of them myself, leaving the third CRV to my wingman.

At the mission start, Gunboat *Mu 1* was five kilometers away, so I had time to perform standard start-up procedures. I then checked the Inflight Map to get a good idea of where everything was. You couldn't always count on the briefing to be accurate, and I liked to see the situation for myself.

To my surprise, no corvettes were present—just some containers, Gunboats, and mines.

I ordered my wingman to attack *Mu 1* and noticed that the X-wing was also engaging the Gunboats. *Mu 3* began targeting me and firing, so I corkscrewed out of his path and fell in behind him, blasting away in single-fire mode. I put my lasers at full recharge and my shields at normal to achieve a good dogfighting speed with the Gunboat.

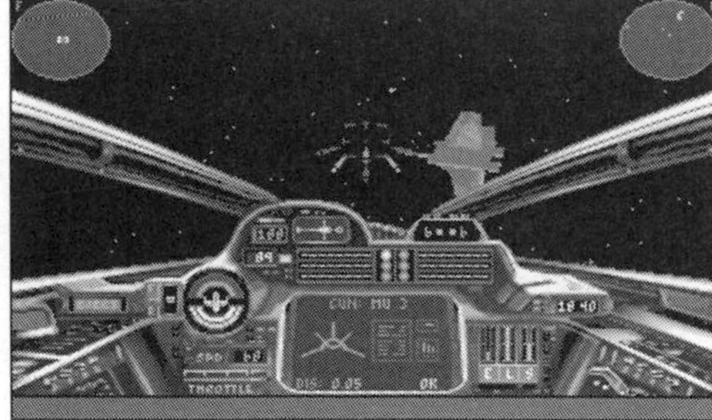

Deflection shot on GUN Mu 3.

I destroyed *Mu 3* and went after *Mu 2*, transferring laser power to my shields and rebalancing as necessary. At 18 minutes on the mission clock, my sensors detected the entry of a corvette four kilometers away. Checking the map, I noticed that, in fact, two corvettes had arrived, and they were heading for the container

GUN Mu 2 *is about to beome a fireball.*

Firing torpedoes at a corvette.

Another corvette flames out.

area. I finished off *Mu 2* and assisted in the destruction of *Mu 1* before turning my attention to the CRVs.

I ordered my wingman to attack one of the corvettes while I targeted the other, launching six torpedoes and reducing the CRV to debris as soon as I had a red lock. A third corvette also entered the area, so I locked on and fired my remaining six torpedoes with the same result.

Shooting the mines.

My wingman was going after the third corvette, so I decided to take out the mines.

Switching to tri-fire mode, I was busy clearing mines when I noticed that TIE Bombers were being launched from the third corvette. I went after them in a hurry, but as soon as I destroyed one, another joined the fray.

The obvious tactic at this point was to destroy the corvette—no sense in allowing it to keep launching Bombers—and I made that my top priority.

As soon as the shields went down on the third CRV, I disabled it with ion cannons and let my wingman finish the job. By disabling the corvette, I prevented it from firing in the last stages of its destruction.

I then destroyed the last TIE Bomber in the area, and ordered my wingman to attack the containers while I finished off the mines. With 12 minutes remaining on the clock, I received the Mission Complete message.

Debriefing (Win Conditions)

Corvettes *Assassin 55-57* and containers *Phi 1-3* must be destroyed.

Mission Note: There are a couple of ways to play this mission. You can stay outside the range of the mines and corvettes and dogfight all the enemy starfighters first, then, after all the starfighters are gone, you can go in and attack the corvettes. The easiest way to complete this mission, however, is by using the tactics described.

Note that after you have the shields down on a corvette, it's quicker and safer to disable it than it is to destroy it. After the ship is disabled, it can no longer fire, so it's easy to complete the job.

For extra points, you can order your wingman to attack the containers, but switch his target as soon as he has their shields down, then go in and finish the job yourself.

OP 12: INTERCEPT IMPERIAL ATTACK

File Name: t5m12mb

Mission Briefing

In this mission, scramble to the aid of an Habassan convoy near Pii II, under attack by Imperial Gunboats. Four B-wings from Red are the only ships available to respond.

Farlander's After-Action Report

I flew as a wingman in a four-ship group of B-wings. Entering the mission area, I checked the Inflight Map and found four Gunboats located on the opposite side of the freighters. There were two ships from GUN Mu and two from GUN Nu. Seconds later, eight more Gunboats arrived—four each from Rho and Tau groups. Now we had 12 Gunboats against four B-wings—the usual odds.

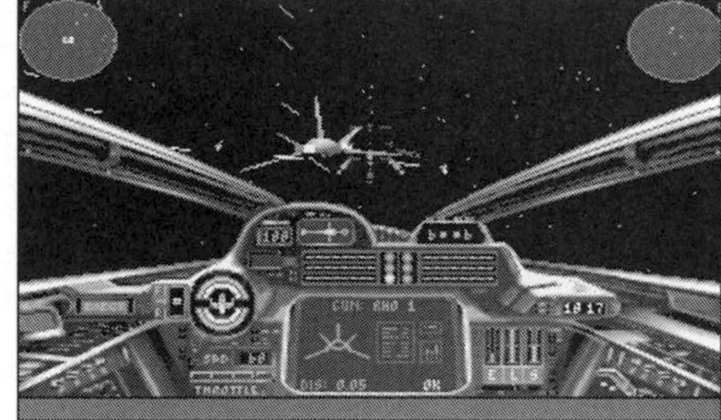

Dogfighting GUN Rho 1.

I targeted the closest Gunboat, which turned out to be *Rho 4*, and assigned my wingmen to attack him. Then I selected *Rho 3* for myself, reducing my laser recharge rate to zero to gain speed, and transferred laser energy to my shields. When I was close enough, I increased my laser recharge rate to maximum and began blasting.

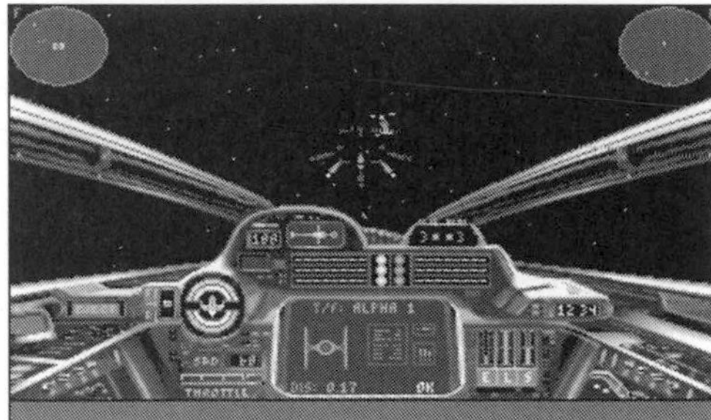

Fighting T/F Alpha.

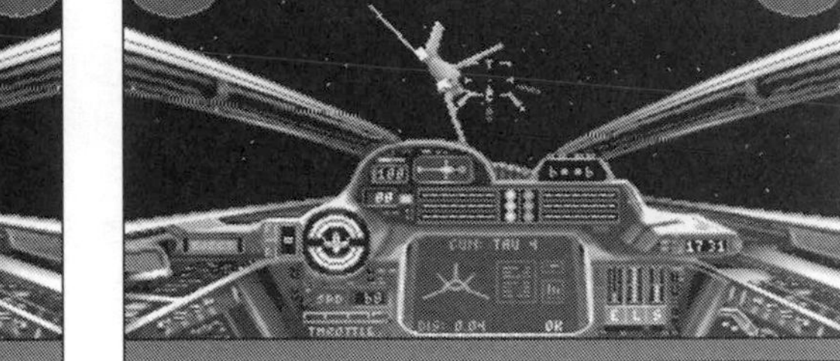

Shooting a Gunboat.

After destroying *Rho 3*, I shot up four more Gunboats very quickly before checking the condition of the freighters. I found that the first one in the group had been disabled, and I headed toward it to stand guard. Checking the Inflight Map one more time, I assessed the situation again.

I noticed that an Imperial freighter was closing in on the disabled Habassan craft, and I figured that the Imperials were going to trying for a capture. Quickly, I switched to torpedoes and fired six of them into the Imperial freighter, destroying it before returning to the dogfight.

At about 9:20 on the clock, the Star Destroyer *Maximus* entered the area, which was now filled with starfighters. I found myself thinking that this was one of the largest dogfighting battles I had ever been in.

The clock read 15:20 when three transports—*Kappa 1*, *Kappa 2*, and *Kappa 3* —arrived. I was afraid that they might be on their way to capture or destroy the Habassan freighter, so I set my course to intercept them and switched to dual-fire torpedoes. I had to keep weaving to avoid fire from the Gunboats.

I diverted all laser recharge rates to the engines and transferred all laser energy to shields. As soon as I had a red lock I fired two torpedoes, then locked on to the next transport. I wanted to take them out as quickly as possible, so I fired two torpedoes into each one and then turned my attention back to the starfighters.

Checking the Inflight Map, I looked for any other craft that might be able to board or capture the Habassan freighters, but there were none. By that time, I had had enough of the enemy starfighters blasting me from behind. Time to turn the tables!

A disabled freighter.

The Star Destroyer was launching TIE fighters, but only one at a time. I kept firing on the Gunboats and fighters at a comfortable pace.

Meanwhile, another Habassan freighter, *Jess 9*, had docked with *Jess 6*, and was presumably repairing it or taking on its cargo. I tried to dogfight near the two freighters to guard against any Imperial attacks. Some Habassan Y-wings were also nearby. At 7:00 on the clock, I received a message that the docking operation was complete. After the freighters escaped into hyperspace, the mission would be over.

At 6:00 remaining, I received the Mission Complete message. The Habassan freighters had made it safely to hyperspace, and my job was done. I destroyed one more TIE fighter and then headed home.

Debriefing (Win Conditions)
Freighter group Jess must survive.

Mission Note: As surmised, the Imperial freighter was moving to capture FRT *Jess 6*. .Once the Imperial FRT is destroyed, the arriving transports will try and destroy *Jess 6*, and you should save six missiles to quickly thwart that plan.

OP 13: PROTECT B-WING DELIVERY

File Name: t5m13ma

Mission Briefing
The Alliance freighter *Radley* is delivery a new group of B-wings to the cruiser *Cathleen*, and the operation must be protected. A-wing *Blue 5* was flying escort, but has experienced a shield failure. A-wing Red will relieve *Blue 5*, and guard the area until the *Cathleen* arrives in about 10 minutes. The B-wings involved will be flown by inexperienced pilots, and virtually defenseless.

FRT Radley *at mission start.*

Farlander's After-Action Report
At the start of the mission, no enemy craft were in the area, so I went through my standard mission start-up procedures. I was flying as wingman. Just as I finished setting my shields and lasers, an Imperial Frigate appeared about 15 kilometers away, and launched TIE Bombers *Alpha 1* and *Alpha 2*.

I headed to intercept, but before I did I placed the *Radley* at memory location F5, so that I could locate it easily. I didn't want to get too far away from the freighter.

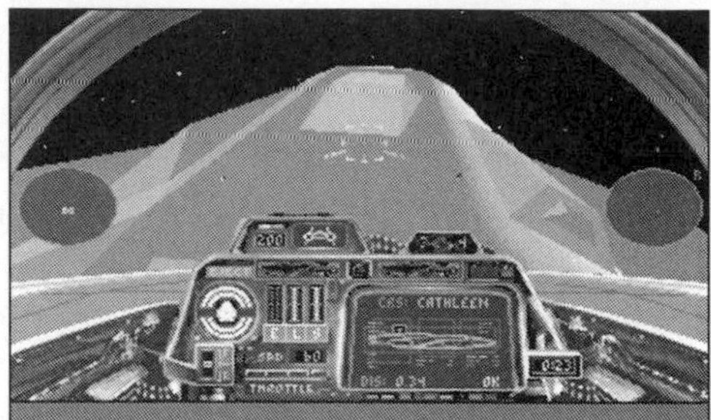

The Cathleen.

About a minute after launching the Bombers, the Frigate launched two TIE Interceptors from Beta group. I kept my attention on the Bombers, however.

I was fully recharged and at normal settings, and T/I *Beta 2* got to me first, so I blasted him into dust while I waited for the Bombers to get within range.

When the closest T/B was in my sights, I reset my laser recharge rate to maximum and took him out with a few blasts. I gave the second one the same harsh treatment. T/Is *Gamma 1* and *Gamma 2* had been launched, and T/I *Beta 1* was still buzzing about.

Another wave of T/B Alpha spewed forth just then, followed by a four-ship group of T/F Delta. I had three Interceptors, two Bombers, and four TIE fighters to contend with. Just another day in the Rebel Alliance.

As usual, I kept my attention on the Bombers and placed them in memory locations F6 and F7. I kept dogfighting the nearest starfighter until the Bombers came within range, and then I broke off and destroyed them quickly. The Bombers made for pathetically easy targets against an A-wing.

T/F Delta jumped me as I was going after the second wave of T/B Alpha, but I flew through them and destroyed the first Bomber. The T/Fs continued to harass me, and, in all the confusion, I had to recall the second Bomber from memory. As soon as I had destroyed that one, I went after the fighters, shooting three of them quickly. Meanwhile, the Frigate launched a three-ship Bomber group, Eta.

Checking the Inflight Map, I saw that T/F *Delta 1*, the one fighter I hadn't destroyed, was going after the *Radley*. I instructed my wingmen to pick him up while I continued after T/B Gamma.

The Frigate, unfortunately, was busy launching more ships; this time it was T/Bs *Zeta 1* through *Zeta 3*. Now there were six TIE Bombers to worry about.

I had 12 missiles, and this was the time to use them. I redirected all laser energy to engines, locked on to the first Bomber and fired a single missile. I repeated the procedure until I had fired on each of the six T/Bs.

Two Interceptors from Iota Squadron tried to jump me, but I noticed them while they were still about 1.5 kilometers away. I took one out with a missile on the first pass, then got a lock on *Iota 2* and destroyed him, too.

Eliminating one Iota.

I checked the Inflight Map to see whether any Bombers had escaped, but none remained, so I headed in to help my wingman, who was still going after T/F *Delta 1*.

I was, by this time, 15 kilometers from the *Radley*. I left my shield recharge rate at normal but redirected my laser energy to the engines, pushing my speed up to 150.

I told A-W *Red 1* to attack the TIE fighter again, just to make sure that he knew what he should be doing. He wasn't having a very good day. I noticed, in fact, that he was down to hull damage, so as soon as I got close enough to engage *Delta 1*, I sent *Red 1* home.

I fired a missile at *Delta 1* from a few kilometers out, but he avoided it. Still, it distracted him for a moment, giving me more time to get within laser range. Redirecting power to my cannons, I went after *Delta 1*—and got hit by my own missile!

Muttering an assortment of unsavory oaths, I recovered, and went in with lasers firing, blasting the TIE fighter to space dust. He had caused enough trouble already.

At 4:00 on the clock, the Calamari cruiser *Cathleen* finally arrived, and launched six Y-wings from Gold group to go after the Frigate.

At 1:22 on the clock, the freighter *Radley* jumped successfully into hyperspace, followed by the *Cathleen*, and I received the Mission Complete message.

Debriefing (Win Conditions)

The freighter *Radley* must dock with the cruiser *Cathleen*, and both ships must survive.

Mission Note: Stop all ships that might get by and destroy the freighter. With larger groups of Bombers, you can use missiles on one or two of them from a distance, and then follow up with lasers on the remaining ones when you get close enough. Also, missiles are good to save for those Bombers that do get past you.

OP 14A: CAPTURE IMPERIAL FRIGATE

File Name: t5m14wxa

Mission Briefing

A rendezvous between two X-wings and a pair of corvettes has been leaked to the Empire, in hopes of luring the Imperial Frigate *Mayhem* into a trap. The bait will be a secret list—compiled by the Habassa—of planets that would be suitable for the new Rebel base. When the *Mayhem* responds, B-wing Blue will launch the attack, protected from the Frigate's TIE Interceptors by the X-wings. Transports with commandos will arrive to complete the capture process.

Farlander's After-Action Report

As flight leader in the two-ship group of X-wings, I went through my standard start-up procedures when we jumped into the mission area. I then put my wingman at F5, a Rebel corvette at F6, and a Habassan corvette at F7. I flew in close to ID the Habassan corvette. After my lasers and shields were fully charged, I switched both recharge settings to normal and began to orbit the two CRVs.

At 20:40 on the clock, an Imperial Frigate arrived and began launching TIE Interceptors and Bombers. I switched to single-fire mode, ordered my wingman to attack T/B *Beta 1*, and then began firing rapidly as the TIE Interceptors approached.

By putting a barrage of fire up while approaching head-on, I hoped to damage or destroy one of the enemy ships. I inflicted hull damage on T/I *Alpha 3*, and quickly finished him off. Switching to quad-fire mode, I took out T/B *Beta 1* next, then ordered my wingman to join me in attacking *Beta 2*, resetting my recharge rates to bring my speed down.

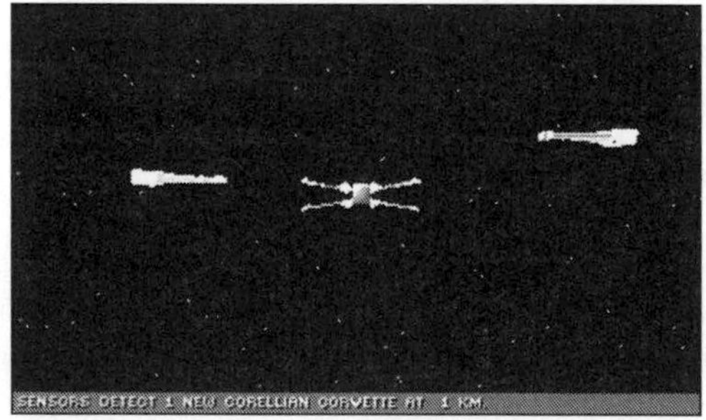

Rebel and Habassan corvettes.

I kept my shields charged and went after T/I *Alpha 1*, redirecting some shield energy to my engines to gain speed, and making quick work of the Interceptor.

Another wave of T/B Beta launched, so I ordered my wingman to attack *Beta 1* while I concentrated on *Beta 2* and *Beta 3*. More Bombers followed,

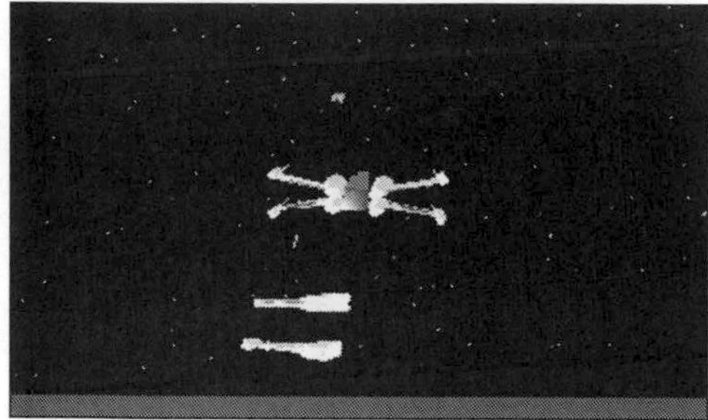

Two corvettes docking.

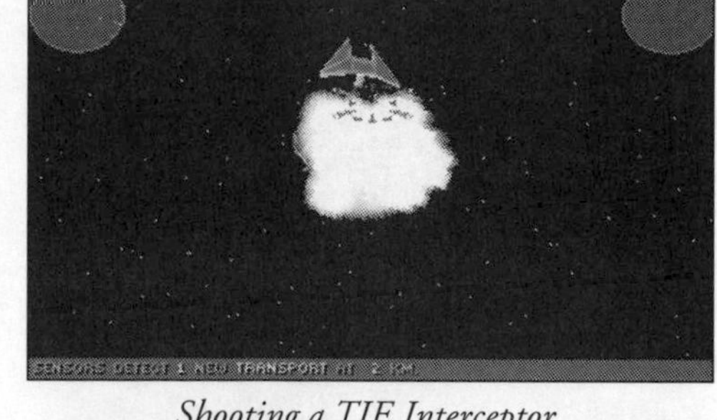

Shooting a TIE Interceptor.

as the corvette *Tilde* entered hyperspace. We went after this next wave of TIE Bombers, coming close enough to the Imperial Frigate to come under its fire.

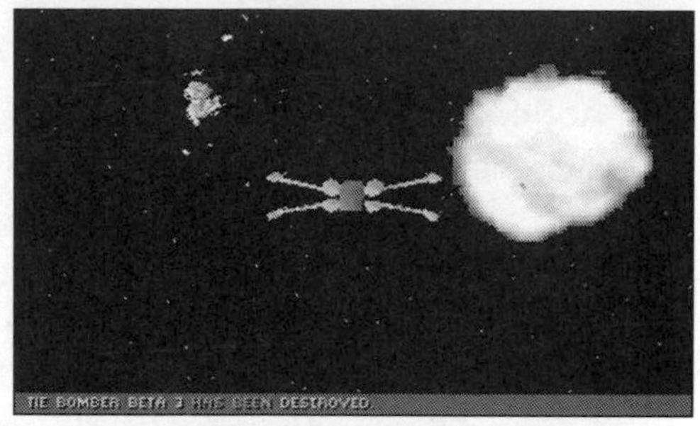

Destruction of T/B Beta 3.

We kept alternately attacking the TIE Bombers and the TIE Interceptors, making the Bombers our highest priority. It was dangerous, attacking the Bombers when the Interceptors were about, because they often got off good shots while we were otherwise engaged.

Approaching the enemy Frigate.

I checked the condition of the B-wings attacking the Frigate. B-W *Blue 3* was holding up all right, though *Blue 1* had hull damage. I didn't have time to check on *Blue 2*, but I did notice that T/B *Beta 1* was getting past us, so I ordered my wingman after him and took off in pursuit myself, redirecting all energy to the engines to get my speed up to the maximum 150.

T/I *Alpha 2* attached himself to my tail, so I ordered my wingman to attack and get him off of me. B-W *Blue 1* was being dogged by *Beta 1*, so I ordered him to take evasive action until I could get off a killing shot.

I turned back toward T/I *Alpha 1* next, resetting my recharge rates and blasting him head-on. A new wave of B-wings had arrived, and I noticed that the Frigate's shields were down. More Interceptors launched then, and

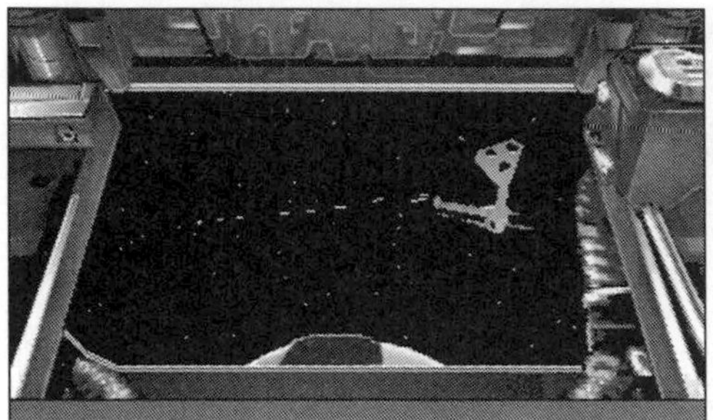

The B-wings are attacking the Frigate.

we went after them. The B-wings succeeded in disabling the Frigate with about 12:20 on the clock. As I flew in to attack the latest wave of Interceptors, I ID'ed the Frigate to confirm that it was indeed the *Mayhem.*

Then the B-wings, having accomplished their task, withdrew from the area, and the Alliance transports began to arrive. I was continuing to dogfight Interceptors, but then noticed that some Assault Gunboats from Mu group had appeared.

I switched to torpedoes and fired one into each of the three Gunboats, following that up with lasers to finish them off. Replacement Gunboats arrived almost instantly, and I headed toward their jump point as fast as I could.

On route, I ordered my wingman to attack, and switched back to torpedoes. I fired one torpedo in a head-on attack, and then switched to cannons and finished off the Gunboats—again.

When the second wave of GUN Mu was gone, the clock read 7:00. I headed back toward the Frigate, watching for any new Imperial craft. For a change, things were quiet, which made me even more uneasy. I charged up my shields and lasers and waited for the message that the Frigate had been captured, which came at 6:30 on the clock.

More Gunboats arrived then, accompanied by two corvettes. I went after the Gunboats, shot a missile, and switched to cannons. We were in the middle of the corvettes—not a good place to dogfight—when my wingman was destroyed in a crossfire, leaving me to handle the situation alone.

The mission's success was suddenly in doubt. The *Mayhem,* now in Rebel control, was about five kilometers away. I didn't think that she could escape before the corvettes came within firing range, so I decided to take on the leader to buy some time. I armed my torpedoes and fired the last two. Gunboats kept launching missiles at me, and the corvettes were firing on me as well, so I was in a bit of trouble.

Transport *Storm* entered hyperspace, which didn't help me much.

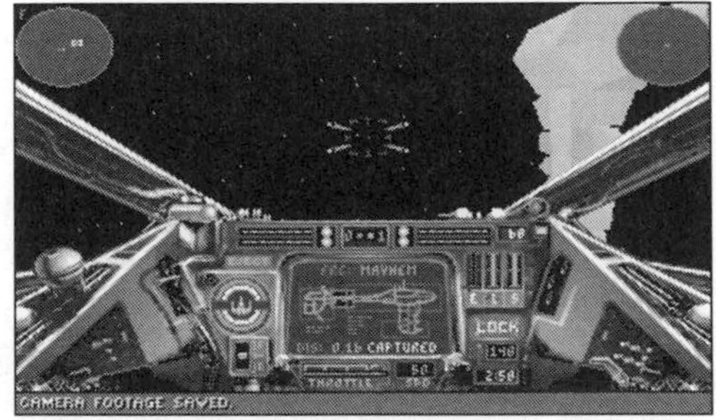

The captured Frigate.

I switched to cannons and flew towards the corvette, weaving my way in to make it more difficult for the gunners to target me. I made one strafing pass on the CRV, but took a great deal of damage, and lost some of my instruments. I decided at that point to go after another Gunboat, because they were making the situation much more difficult.

I switched to quad-fire and destroyed *Tau 2*, but my X-wing was in pretty poor shape. I wished that I had ion cannons to disable the CRV, but I didn't. As I tried to decide who to attack, the Frigate made it into hyperspace, and I high-tailed it out of there at the first possible moment.

Debriefing (Win Conditions)

The corvettes *Filve* and *Bilbringi* must dock and survive. The Frigate *Mayhem* must be recovered.

Mission Note: If one of the first waves of B-wings is able to bring down the Frigate's shields, they will continue their attacks. They must be ordered to go home so that the following waves can use their ion cannons to disable the Frigate. This is, of course, a critical point, so you must watch the Frigate's condition and be sure about which wave of B-wings is attacking.

OP 14B: CAPTURE IMPERIAL OFFICERS

File Name: t5m14mbb

Mission Briefing

A pair of B-wings from Red will intercept an Imperial troop convoy that was scheduled to rendezvous with the Frigate *Mayhem*. Identify and disable any transports carrying Imperial officers so that the Rebel TRN *Shock* can arrive for the capture. The officers will be interrogated to learn more about the Star Destroyer *Relentless* and its task force.

Farlander's After-Action Report

Entering the mission area, I went to the Inflight Map immediately, and saw that there were 18 transports located about 5.5 kilometers away. I set my laser recharge rate to minimum, while leaving the shield recharge at normal. I also transferred some laser energy to shields before heading for the transports, passing a couple of asteroids on the way.

The transports break up formation.

A wall of laser fire was coming toward me as I headed for the transport armada. There was no easy way to get behind the ships, so I simply waded in and fired a few shots at any transport that came into my sights.

I ID'ed *Sigma 2*, but it was carrying regular troops. I decided to destroy it so that it wouldn't be able to shoot at me. I kept redirecting energy to and from the shields to adjust my speed as I kept up the identification process, destroying irrelevant transports along the way.

I was taking some hits, but I kept destroying enemy craft and transferring energy back to my shields. Finally, I found the officers in TRN *Sigma 6*.

I placed the transport in memory at location F5, to be sure that I didn't accidentally lose or destroy it. Then I began to destroy the rest of the transports without bothering to ID them. Once the body of the force was obliterated, I would come back to disable *Sigma 6*.

Three Gunboats from Mu appeared about five kilometers away, and, since I still had 12 torpedoes left, I decided to use them in dual-fire mode to take out more transports before the Gunboats closed in.

I quickly took out six more transports with torpedoes, leaving half a dozen. The Gunboats were still four kilometers away, so I switched back to lasers and destroyed another transport quickly. Then I received a missile warning. The Gunboats had arrived.

I turned to attack them while I prepared to absorb the missile hit, ordering my wingman to attack the Gunboats as well. For some reason, only *Mu 2* engaged us. *Mu 1* and *Mu 3*, inexplicably, were sitting off in the distance.

I destroyed *Mu 2* easily, and went back to destroy the remaining transports. After that, I switched to ion cannons and fired on TRN *Sigma 6* until it became disabled.

I switched to the Inflight Map, and noticed that a Frigate had entered the area. Three TIE Interceptors were headed my way, but they were still 19 kilometers out, so they weren't an immediate threat. Some TIE Bombers were also launched, but they were even slower than the Interceptors. The remaining Gunboats were closer, so I went to destroy them. My wingman was gone, so I was on my own.

The clock read 1:40 when the Alliance transport *Shock* entered the area, sent to capture the officers.

As the *Shock* closed on *Sigma 6*, I fired on *Mu 1* and took him out. Mu 3 finally joined the battle, and managed to get a missile off, but my shields held, and I was able to destroy him from behind.

End of mission.

More Gunboats, *Tau 1* through *Tau 3*, were firing missiles at me; one scoring a hit. I didn't know where they had come from, but I knew that I had to keep them busy. With no time left on the clock, the docking operation was now complete. If I could just hold on until the *Shock* made it to hyperspace, the mission would be a success.

I kept dogfighting the Gunboats until all were destroyed, then turned towards the Interceptors. Before I engaged, however, I received the Mission Complete message. The Rebel transport had entered hyperspace, bearing the Imperial officers to our base for interrogation.

Debriefing (Win Conditions)
The transport *Shock* must dock with TRN *Sigma 6*; the *Shock must survive.*

OP 15: ESCORT B-WINGS ON ATTACK

File Name: t5m15wa

Mission Briefing
The last Frigate in the task force of the Star Destroyer *Relentless* is undergoing repairs, and vulnerable to attack. The FRG *Juvaini* is being serviced near Sunaj IV, and will be assaulted by two waves of three ships from B-wing Blue. A-wing Red will fly escort, charged with taking out any TIE patrols.

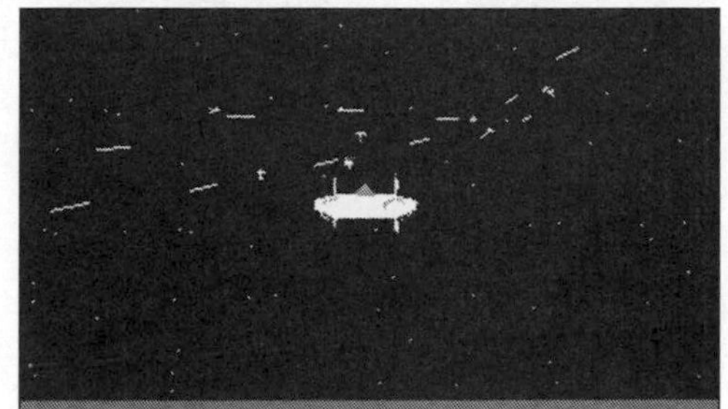

Heading toward the battle.

Farlander's After-Action Report
I flew the lead role in the two-ship group of A-wings from Red. We were to neutralize the Frigate's protective fighter patrol while the B-wings did their job.

At mission start, I checked the Inflight Map and discovered two groups of TIE fighters. T/F Alpha was about 13 kilometers away, and T/F Beta was about 7 kilometers distant. Almost 10 kilometers away were a freighter and a Frigate.

I went through my mission-start procedure, then placed A-W *Red 2* at memory location F5, and the Frigate at F8. When the B-wings arrived, I put B-wing *Blue 1* at F6. After that, I redirected shield energy to my engines to gain speed and caught up with the B-wings. I ordered my wingman to attack T/F *Beta 1*, and headed on in myself.

As I approached the T/Fs, I set my cannons to dual-fire, and reset my shield recharge rate to normal. I quickly shot *Beta 2*; TIE fighters were no match for an A-wing, as he learned the hard way.

By this time, T/F Alpha was in range, and so I went after *Alpha 1* with a destructive head-on pass. Next came *Beta 1* and *Alpha 2*. A new wave of T/F Beta launched and closed fast, and soon became my next prey.

I was just outside the Frigate's gun range (about two kilometers) and was continuing to attack the TIE fighters as they appeared. With no shields, they took almost no time to destroy. I wasn't quite fast enough to save all the B-wings, however; one of them went down.

A group of TIE Interceptors from Delta launched next, followed by T/I Gamma. I went after them as quickly as I could. Although the Interceptors were faster than the T/Fs, they were still pretty easy to kill. The biggest danger lay in colliding with one of the ships, because the area was getting pretty crowded. A second group of B-wings arrived, but so did some Imperial Assault Gunboats.

I was still mixing it up with TIE fighters and Interceptors, and ordered my wingman to go after *Gamma 1* while I went after *Delta 2*, which had just been launched in a replacement wave.

Between targets, I reset my recharge rates to minimum to gain speed, hurried to the next target, and then reset back to dogfighting configuration.

Targeting an incoming missile.

After I had taken care of the replacement wave of T/I Delta, I turned to engage GUN Tau, switching to missiles in dual-fire mode. More Interceptors were launched, and I received a missile warning as I let fly with two of my own on *Tau 1*.

After taking the hit, I rebalanced my shields and switched to cannons. I closed to cannon range on *Tau 1* and finished him off, then ordered my wingman to assist me with *Tau 2*, and went in with my cannons firing. A pair of corvettes were trying to cover the Frigate's retreat, and I tried to dogfight in that general direction.

With the Gunboats out of the way, I returned to T/I Gamma and engaged. The Frigate's shields were still holding, but the B-wings were launching more torpedoes even as I checked the CMD. This newest wave of torpedoes brought down the Frigate's defenses, and I knew that now it was only a matter of time.

I kept after T/I Gamma until the last of the group was destroyed. GUN Tau had been replaced, so again I shot two missiles at *Tau 1*, and then ordered my wingman to join me. Another missile launched in my direction, but I evaded it. With my cannons, I finished off the Gunboats, but not without taking a missile hit to the forward shields.

The Frigate was registering hull damage, and I switched to single-fire mode and cruised a little closer. I was interested in getting the kill, although I didn't want to commit suicide to do it. Still, I was preparing to go in firing when another torpedo salvo hit the Frigate broadside, and she went up in a colorful fireball. Though I was not directly responsible, it was still quite satisfying.

Our primary mission was accomplished, but I wanted to take out a few more of those pesky Interceptors. I turned to engage them even as I received the message that another missile was headed my way.

I began evasion tactics and then changed my mind, going after *Tau 1* with dual-fire missiles. I received the Mission Complete message, but still wanted to keep fighting a while longer. The B-wings destroyed one of the corvettes as I finished off *Tau 1* with my cannons. I then went after *Tau 2* with my wingman's help.

With their mother ship dead, I put T/I Gamma out of its misery, then decided to take out some mines and a Nav Buoy in the area for good measure.

While the B-wings entered hyperspace, I decided to check out an unidentified container I'd spotted nearby. A minute later, I ID'ed it as an Imperial supply container, so I blasted it with my cannons in single-fire mode. My wingman joined me, and we quickly destroyed it before making the jump home.

Debriefing (Win Conditions)

The Nebulon B Frigate *Juvaini* must be destroyed.

OP 16: ATTACK PROBE CALIBRATION SITE

File Name: t5m16wb

Mission Briefing

The Star Destroyer *Relentless* is conducting calibration tests on new surveillance probes prior to their deployment. B-wing Red will attack and destroy all the probes, which are arrayed between containers of test equipment. The containers must also be destroyed. This begins a series of missions that will culminate with the destruction of the *Relentless*.

The Star Destroyer arrives.

Firing torpedoes at the containers.

Farlander's After-Action Report

Attacking the first containers.

I was leading a three-ship group of B-wings, and as we came out of hyperspace I checked the Inflight Map, locating the first group of four containers about eight kilometers away. Another group of containers was nearly 35 kilometers away, guarded by a trio of Gunboats. Closer at hand was another trio of Gunboats. The Star Destroyer *Relentless* did not seem to be in the area, but there were plenty of probes around.

I went through my usual mission start-up procedure as a pair of A-wings jumped in to provide support for the mission. I was glad to have them along.

I ordered my wingmen to attack the nearest container as the Star Destroyer *Relentless* arrived, right in my path, dampening my mood considerably.

I targeted the next-closest container, and switched to torpedoes. As soon as I had a red lock, I fired one off, then switched to dual-fire mode and let fly with two more. After that I gave another container the same treatment.

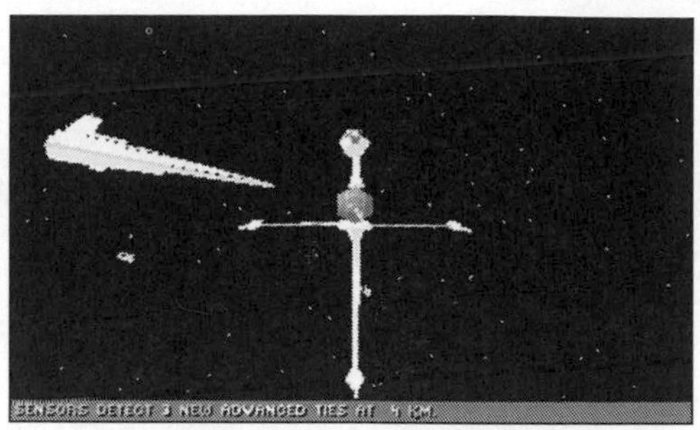
Looking back at the Relentless *as T/As launch.*

My wingmen had still not launched their torpedoes, but, soon after I blasted the third container, they seemed to get the idea. When they had finally gotten their shots off, I assigned them to attack the remaining CON.

Next, I switched to lasers in fire-linked mode. So far, no ships had emerged from the *Relentless*. I had to finish off the first container, and I repeated my orders to my wingmen.

After the fourth container was destroyed, I ordered my wingmen to go after the far grouping. GUN Mu was on our trail, but not gaining very quickly, so we all headed toward the distant containers. Finally, the suspense was over: Three TIE Advanced were launched from the *Relentless*. Trouble was on the way.

T/A Alpha was catching up with us quickly, and I was about to turn around to defend myself when the Advanced fighters engaged my A-wing escort. I set my shield recharge rate to zero to boost my speed up, anyway.

Someone fired a missile at me, and I discovered that TIE Bomber Beta was also in the chase. I kept going toward the far containers and, checking the situation, found that one of the Bombers was destroyed by an A-wing. So far, although I had absorbed one missile hit, the escort had kept us from attracting too big a crowd.

I kept transferring laser energy to my shields and rebalancing. One of the TIE Advanced came after me in a head-on pass, but I escaped damage. Likewise, there was a missile shot at me, but it apparently missed.

I then collided with T/A *Alpha 2*, the net result being minor shield damage for me, and complete destruction for him. I'll make that trade anytime.

I was coming up on the first of the probes, and I began mowing them down like so many practice targets.

I decided at that point to engage T/B *Beta 1*, which had been firing missiles at me for some time, but just then one of the A-wings beat me to it.

Another threat, GUN Mu, entered the scene at that point, and I reset my shield recharge rate to maximum and went after *Mu 1*. When he was dust, I looked for *Mu 2*, but all the other Gunboats had been destroyed. Another wave of T/B Beta launched, however, so I knew I wouldn't have time to get lonely.

The probes were separated at intervals of five kilometers, and, as I

Destruction everywhere.

headed out to destroy more of them, I received the message that B-W *Red 3* had been destroyed. I guessed that they'd run into trouble up ahead.

(In retrospect, I might have kept them closer to me for safety.)

I continued to destroy the probes, with my speed set at 91. I noticed GUN *Nu 3* nearby, apparently more interested in the A-wings than in me, but I decided to pay him a visit with my cannons.

After I was finished with *Nu 3*, I went after another group of probes. On route, I was tagged by two missiles, and had to quickly rebalanced my shields. All of a sudden, I had a great deal of company, and more missiles were incoming.

Torpedo hits on a container.

I had little choice but to keep after the probes, and destroy any enemy fighter that got too close. I blasted *Nu 2* and decided to take on *Nu 1*. The A-wings were some distance away, mixing it up with the TIE Advanced.

The B-wing is a tough bird, and she showed it on this mission, as I sustained many missile hits. I finished off the Gunboats and went after T/B *Beta 1*. After that, the next-nearest enemy was about 8 kilometers away, so I redirected shield energy to my engines and headed for another set of probes.

I had an easy time of it for a while, destroying many probes without further incident. With a little less than five minutes showing on the mission clock, I headed for the last group. The nearest enemy was T/B *Beta 3*, but it was now more than 10 kilometers away. The *Relentless* was 23 kilometers away. Could it be that the rest of the mission would be a cakewalk?

After I had destroyed the final group of probes, I headed for the last container group, about 4.5 kilometers away. I switched to torpedoes in single-fire mode and shot one at the nearest container. I used a torpedo or two to soften up each of the remaining CONs, then finished them off with lasers in single-fire mode and my throttle at one-third.

There were no enemies near me as I received my Mission Complete message, and I headed into hyperspace with 1:45 left on the clock.

Debriefing (Win Conditions)
Containers groups Chi and Xi, and all of the probes, must be destroyed.

OP 17A: AMBUSH IMPERIAL ARMS SHIPMENT

File Name: t5m17maa

Mission Briefing
A convoy of Imperial corvettes and neutral freighters is set to rendezvous with the Star Destroyer *Relentless*, and replenish its dwindling supply of TIE fighters. A-wing Red will initiate the attack on the arms shipment, joined by three Alliance corvettes.

Farlander's After-Action Report
I was the flight leader in a three-ship group of A-wings. To protect the corvettes that would accompany us, I had decided that the best strategy would be to take out any TIE Bombers first on this mission. When I arrived on the scene, however, I changed my thinking.

As we entered the area, the battle was already raging around us. I took a couple of hits before I had time to react, and then went into a steep turn. I powered my shields from my laser batteries, and set laser recharge rates up. I then targeted T/B *Delta 1* and rolled into position to destroy him.

I ordered my wingmen to attack the nearest enemy starfighter, while I put the top Imperial corvette in my CMD at F5. Our corvette was exchanging volleys with the enemy CRV, and I added my firepower to the attack, further damaging the enemy craft and simultaneously drawing off some of its fire.

I dodged between the freighters, using them as shields, and shooting at them whenever an opportunity arose. I noticed that the Imperial corvette, in its attempts to attack me, was actually scoring hits on the freighters I hid behind.

Using a freighter as a shield.

Eventually, the corvette was destroyed. At that point, I switched to missiles and fired a single missile into two consecutive TIE Bombers.

As soon as Rebel CRVs *Yogi 1* and *Yogi 2* arrived, I was about to rejoin the battle against the Imperial

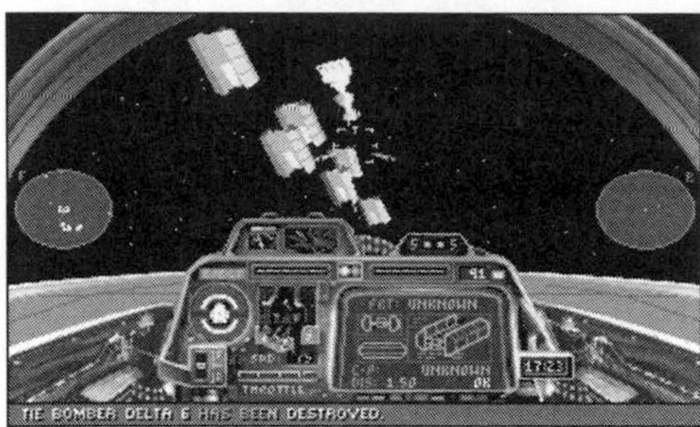

The freighter convoy.

FRT Sornsen 1.

corvettes, but then received an incoming-missile warning and had to evade.

I told my wingmen to cover me, and went after one of the nearby Gunboats. Then I repeated the procedure, this time targeting an Imperial corvette. Soon the second Imperial corvette was spinning in its death dance, and we went after the bottom—and last—Imperial CRV.

Rebel CRV *Yogi 1* had been destroyed, but *Yogi 2* was closing in. As soon as the enemy corvette's shields were down, I fired two missiles at him and finished him off.

Corvette *Yogi 2* turned and made a pass on the freighters. I appreciated his help. There were six freighters (*Dotermin 1-3* and *Sornsen 1-3*) carrying all kinds of TIE parts and supplies.

While shooting the freighters, I had to engage Gunboats periodically. After all the enemy starfighters were cleared, I ordered my wingmen to help me attack the freighters, making things move even more quickly.

The clock read 11:30 when two more Imperial corvettes showed up about seven kilometers away. They began dropping off TIE Bombers, and I hurried to destroy the rest of the freighters before the Bombers could get within range.

With my wingmen helping me, we made quick work of the freighters, and by 10:30 on the clock the last of them were destroyed. T/B Gamma was still four kilometers away. I received the Mission Complete message, and my wingmen headed for home. I decided to follow them.

Debriefing (Win Conditions)

Freighter groups Dotermin and Sornsen, and corvette group Shurik must be destroyed.

Mission Note: In this mission, it is useful to use the freighters as shields while attacking the corvettes. The Alliance corvette will be destroyed no matter what you do, but the enemy CRVs also must be destroyed.

OP 17B: DISRUPT DELIVERY OF NEW TIES

File Name: t5m17wbb

Mission Briefing

The Star Destroyer *Relentless*, which still has an undetermined number of TIE fighters and Bombers, is receiving a shipment of replacement TIE Interceptors near Sunaj. B-wing Red will fly a quick hit-and-fade, destroying all the containers holding the new Interceptors. The raid should take less than five minutes, and, if it is successful, a follow-up assault to destroy the *Relentless* is planned.

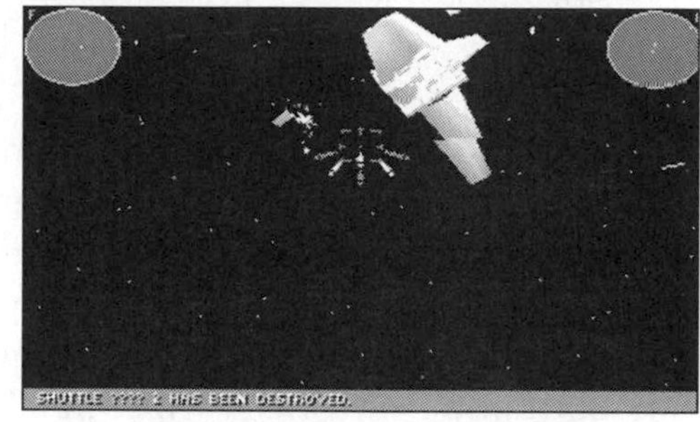

Destruction of the second shuttle.

Farlander's After-Action Report

I was the flight leader in a two-ship formation of B-wings. We came out of hyperspace and I checked the Inflight Map, finding the Star Destroyer *Relentless* dead ahead, 8.7 kilometers away. A neutral corvette was parked nearby, with a freighter 7.2 kilometers distant.

Also, Gunboat group Tau, consisting of three craft, was less than three kilometers away, and a pair of shuttles was close by. I ordered my wingman to attack a container that was dropped off by the freighter.

I quickly went through mission start-up procedures and then turned to take care of the nearest shuttle. GUN Tau had already begun launching missiles. I took out the first shuttle, and then the second.

I went after GUN *Tau 1* next, noticing that some new shuttles were in the area, and figured that they would be coming after us. Then I took out the other two Gunboats, calling my wingman to help me out.

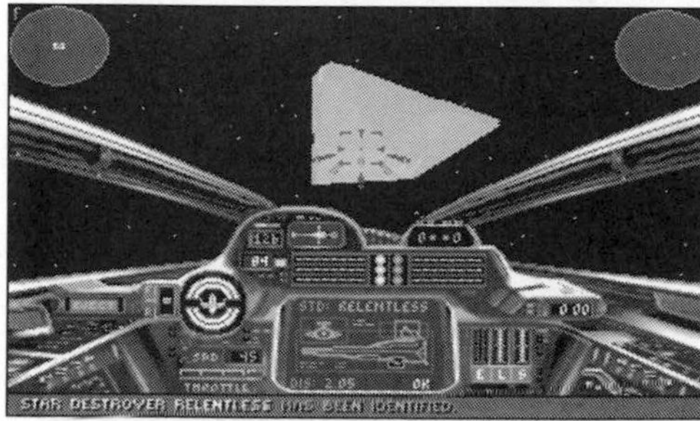

IDing the Relentless.

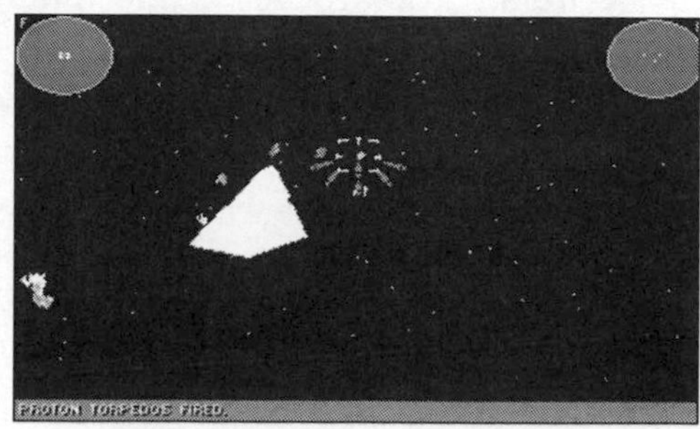

Torpedo attack on containers.

More freighters were arriving and dropping off containers. Some TIE fighters came in, attacking me, but it was the shuttle that was causing the heaviest damage, so I went to take him out. My wingman had already been destroyed, and I found myself asking why we hadn't been given some escort for this mission. I was going to be everyone's target.

Torpedoing more containers.

I put my shield recharge rates at normal and turned to engage the TIE fighters. This was no easy task, but I was able to destroy T/F *Alpha 3* within about 15 seconds, and then I went after the other three T/Fs. It took a minute or so, but I got all four of them.

I took a missile hit from T/B *Beta 1*, and noticed that more T/Fs had been launched. My mission orders were to avoid engaging enemy fighters, but I couldn't much help it under the circumstances.

I put my shields and laser recharge rates at maximum, and targeted the first container with my torpedoes. I fired one, and spun to avoid the oncoming TIE fighters, then shot two more torpedoes in dual-fire mode into the same container.

I switched to the next container and fired two torpedoes into it, then followed with a third. The next container got the same treatment as soon as I could get a red lock. That made three containers gone.

I then broke off my attack to charge and rebalance my shields, with four TIE fighters on my tail and another group of TIE Bombers on the way. I turned to engage the fighters and took a couple of missile hits, deciding then to give my attention to the Bombers, because they were giving me the hardest time.

I had three torpedoes left, and there was one container to receive them. I fired them off as quickly as I could, and then went back to battling the starfighters. I took more missile hits, and continued to maintain my shields manually.

Another shuttle appeared, but I was too busy to worry about it at the moment. I kept going after the Bombers and fighters as the Mission Complete message flashed on the screen. I decided to take out the rest of the starfighters and the shuttle before I returned to base. The *Relentless* kept launching more starfighters, of course, so I finished off a few more and then jumped for home.

Debriefing (Win Conditions)

Container group Chi must be destroyed.

OP 18: DESTROY THE RELENTLESS

File Name: t5m18wb

Mission Briefing

B-wing Red will lead an assault on the Star Destroyer *Relentless*, charged with taking out the massive shield generators prior to a full-scale attack. The *Relentless* has minimal starfighter support, but has been reinforced with Imperial Gunboats. A-wing Gold will escort the initial B-wing strike team, and B-wing Blue will provide two waves of support once the mission is underway.

Farlander's After-Action Report

I led Red's two-ship B-wing group, with two A-wings for an escort. Dropping out of hyperspace, I was directly above the *Relentless*. The massive Star Destroyer was only 6.5 kilometers away. T/F group Alpha was about five kilometers distant, and GUN Rho was about nine kilometers from our position.

I went through my mission start-up procedures, placing B-W *Red 2* at memory location F5, and the *Relentless* at F6. Some corvettes entered the area at that time, so I quickly targeted the first of them, firing off six torpedoes in dual-fire mode.

I redirected shield energy to the engines and headed in toward the Star Destroyer, turning to fire at the shield towers. I shot four torpedoes into one tower in dual-fire mode, then switched to single-fire. I received an incoming-missile warning as I came around on the shield towers again, but ignored it, and got off two more torpedoes at close range, bringing the shields down.

Taking out the first CRV as the other shoots me.

Ducking away from the laser fire in the vicinity of the Star Destroyer, I recharged my shields before switching to fire-linked cannons and targeting the nearest Gunboat, *Rho 1*. I put my shield recharge rate back to maximum as I came in behind *Rho 1* and blasted him.

Shields down on STD Relentless.

The dogfighting was intense, and in quick order I confronted and disposed of a corvette, a transport, a Bomber, a TIE fighter and two Gunboats. B-wing

Blue 1 met with a fiery death during an attack run on the Star Destroyer.

One of the Imperial corvettes had its shields down, so I switched to single-fire cannons and went in to finish him off. It took two passes, but I destroyed him.

T/B *Beta 2* was my next target, and another Gunboat after that. I was taking a pounding, but I managed to keep my shields up throughout the battle.

Another corvette was destroyed, and a new wave took its place, but it was too late for the *Relentless*. The Star Destroyer had heavy hull damage, and I flew in with cannons blasting just to add to the punishment it was sustaining. I absorbed another missile blast while making my strafing runs, but I continued to fire on the Star Destroyer, raking her hull with cannon fire on multiple passes.

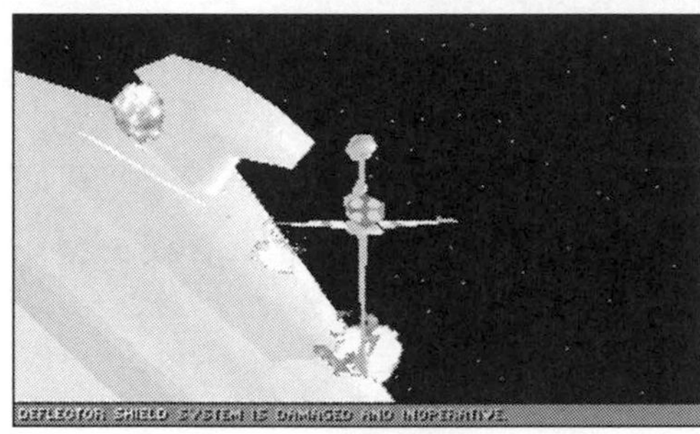

My B-wing is taking damage, too.

I received the Mission Complete message when the *Relentless* exploded, but I myself had taken one too many hits, as both my shields and my auto-eject system were gone. I figured that it was time to go home; the clock read 1:12.

Debriefing (Win Conditions)

The Star Destroyer *Relentless* must be destroyed.

OP 19: OPERATION "BLUNT STICK"

File Name: t5m19mb

Mission Briefing

With the Star Destroyer *Relentless* obliterated, all that remains is to destroy the remaining Imperial surveillance probes, and the path will be clear for the Rebel forces to escape to a new base site on the ice planet Hoth. The remaining probes, protected by small minefields, will be attacked simultaneously, utilizing almost every starfighter in the Alliance fleet.

Farlander's After-Action Report

I flew a solo B-wing in this mission, and, when I entered my assigned area, no other ships were in the vicinity. I targeted the probe I was after, and saved it in memory at F5. I placed the Nav Buoy at F6, and noted that several mines were located about ten kilometers away. With my shield recharge directed to the engines, and my laser recharge at full, I headed toward the probe.

As I flew, I transferred cannon energy to my shields to bring them to full charge. Three freighters then entered the area, one carrying a container, and almost simultaneously a six-ship group of Gunboats appeared and set a course to intercept me. So much for a peaceful mission.

The freighters clustered around the probe, effectively blocking me from getting a long-range torpedo shot at it. I noticed while considering a distance shot that I had only six torpedoes on this mission; half the usual load. Best to try and get closer.

I turned to engage the Gunboats, realizing that my best chance was to take them out as quickly as possible. I decided to use a torpedo on each one (setting my shield recharge rate to maximum after I was within torpedo range) and then switch to ion cannons to disable and neutralize them as quickly as possible. As I was engaging the Gunboats, two Corellian corvettes entered the area, and as I got on the tail of *Mu 1*, I sustained a couple of missile hits.

I had to chase the Gunboats to get off my torpedoes, firing from point-blank range. *Mu 1* evaded my first torpedo, and managed to stay away from it for a while. I went after *Mu 2* and then *Mu 3*. Checking *Mu 1*, I found that his shields were down, so eventually my torpedo must have found its mark. I dealt him a disabling dose of cannon fire, and continued on to take out all six Gunboats.

GUN Mu 2 *is disabled.*

Chasing Mu 3, *with Bomber in pursuit.*

Meanwhile, the corvettes had launched TIE Bombers, and they were closing on me in a swarm. Suddenly, this mission was turning out to be a death trap, and I wondered why I didn't have any escort. Things were bad enough already, and then another set of four Gunboats arrived.

Some of the Gunboats were managing to evade my torpedoes, so I had to go in with laser cannons to take them out. I continued to fight Bombers and Gunboats, and anything else I could set my sights on.

The mission clock read 12:30, and I realized that I needed to get to that probe. I couldn't stay there and dogfight forever. Fortunately, I had taken care of the nearby threat. Unfortunately, more starfighters were clustered around the probe—and its shield of freighters and corvettes. I recharged my shields and lasers fully, then headed toward the minefield.

As I passed them, I destroyed *Mu 1* and *Mu 2*. Waiting up ahead were four more Gunboats and two Bombers, who noticed me about the time I noticed them. They fired a pair of missiles at me, which I managed to evade before taking out both ships with my lasers.

I disposed of mines when the opportunity arose, but the turbolaser fire coming from the corvettes was intense, and I still didn't have a clear lane to get a lock on the probe. The Gunboats were beginning to attack, so I headed away from the mines and the corvettes to get some room to maneuver where I wasn't being plastered.

I kept dogfighting until I had cleared the area of active enemy starfighters, destroying the TIE Bombers and disabling the Gunboats.

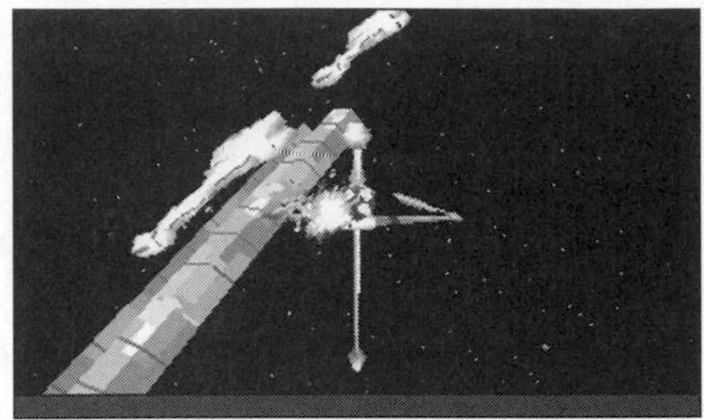

Heading toward the FRTs and CRVs.

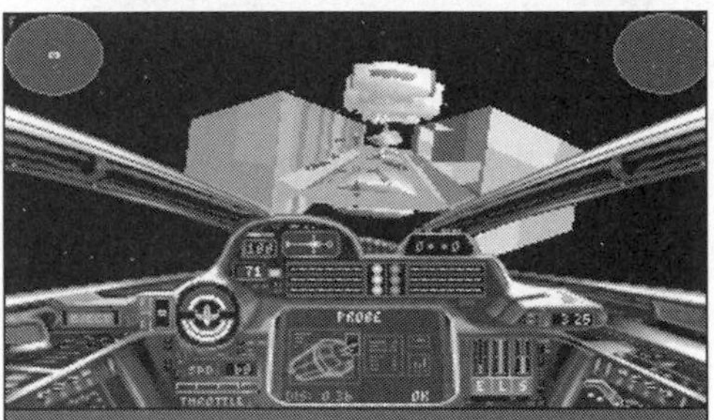

Getting a line on the probe.

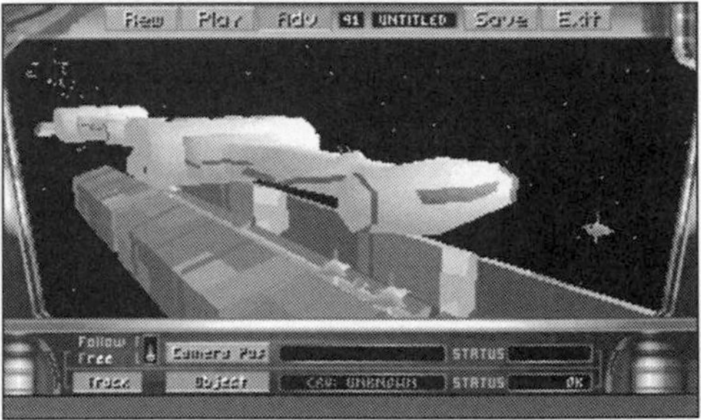

Another view of the probe and mines.

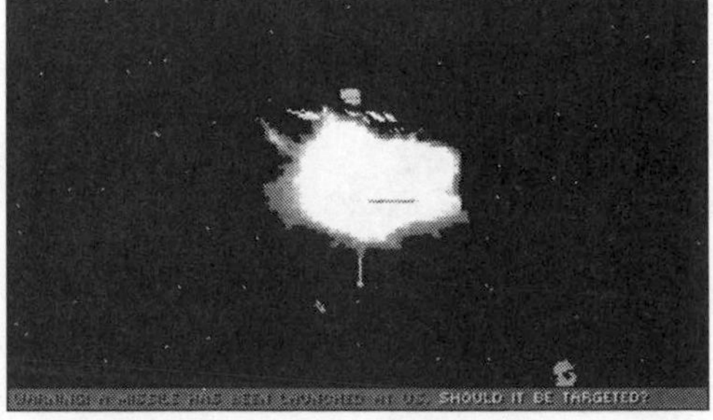

Taking a missile hit.

I took out some more mines, and then I flew around the "front" of the formation that was guarding the probe.

I got a bead on the probe, even though it was protected in a tunnel formed by the freighters and the corvettes. There was a great deal of fire coming from all the ships nearby, but I was able to get a lock on the probe, and the Mission Complete message shortly after I fired let me know I'd hit the target.

Of course, with about four minutes left on the clock, I decided to take out the rest of the Imperial craft that remained before heading for home. Some shuttles arrived as I was destroying the last of the freighters, so I took them out, too.

Debriefing (Win Conditions)
The probe must be destroyed.

Mission Note: If you destroy the container and the freighters, the corvettes will leave the area.

OP 20A: SAVE THE CRUISER CATHLEEN

File Name: t5m20mba

Mission Briefing
One of the last of the Alliance's capital ships on route to Hoth, the Calamarian cruiser *Cathleen,* has been ambushed near its jump point by an Imperial Frigate. The *Cathleen* has launched starfighters in its own defense, but needs help to make the jump undetected: Any Imperial ships in the area must be destroyed so that the course to Hoth remains a secret.

Farlander's After-Action Report
I was assigned to lead a three-ship group of B-wings in the *Cathleen's* defense.

As we came out of hyperspace, the cruiser was directly ahead, so I pulled up to avoid a collision and checked the Inflight Map. Some A-wings were about 2.5 kilometers

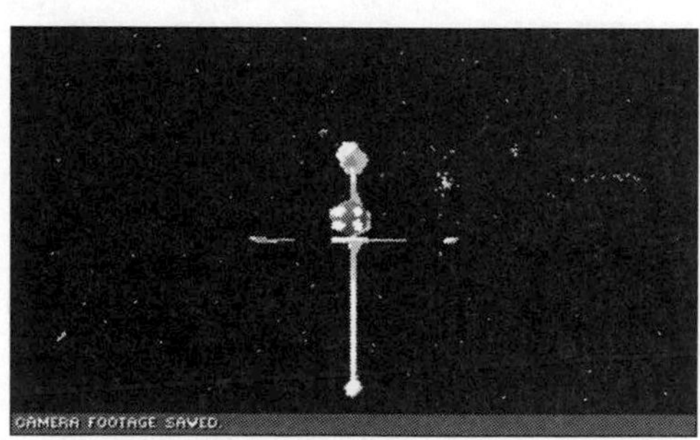

Heading in toward the Y-wings & Frigate.

away, and a shuttle, the *Minnow,* flanked the *Cathleen*. The Imperial Frigate's shields were already down, and a six-ship group of T/B Beta was on its way, probably about to begin launching torpedoes.

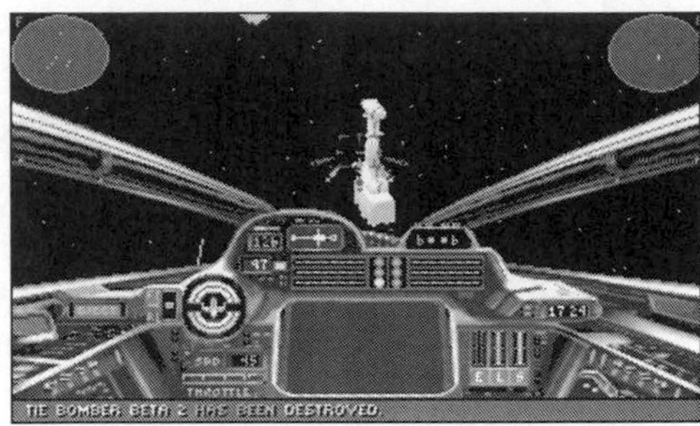

Last moments of a corvette.

Immediately, I targeted the first TIE Bomber and ordered my wingmen to attack. Some Y-wings had entered the area, and were going after the Frigate.

With more than 19 minutes left on the clock, the Frigate abandoned the fight, but the Bombers were still coming. With the help of my wingmen, we took out the remaining T/Bs quickly. More Imperial craft were entering the area, though—four corvettes and a group of Gunboats. The Gunboats were attacking us with missiles, but the greatest danger was from the corvettes.

The first corvette was destroyed before I could get near it, so I turned my attention to the next one. A torpedo here and there helped take down the shields, and cannons finished the job. We were able to destroy the corvettes within a minute or so, and then turned after some transports which had arrived and already launched torpedoes. The Gunboats were still after us, but we had to deal with the immediate threats to the cruiser.

Checking the Inflight Map again, I found that there were a large number of transports. One of the A-wings was still in the area, and three Y-wings and only two Gunboats remained. There were six transports, which I identified as the greatest threat, so I engaged, using some of my remaining torpedoes to deal with them as quickly as possible.

The Gunboats kept firing missiles at me, and I kept assigning my wingmen to attack one transport while going after another. As I destroyed the last of the TRNs, I got hit with a particularly wicked volley of missile and cannon fire, and lost my instrument panel.

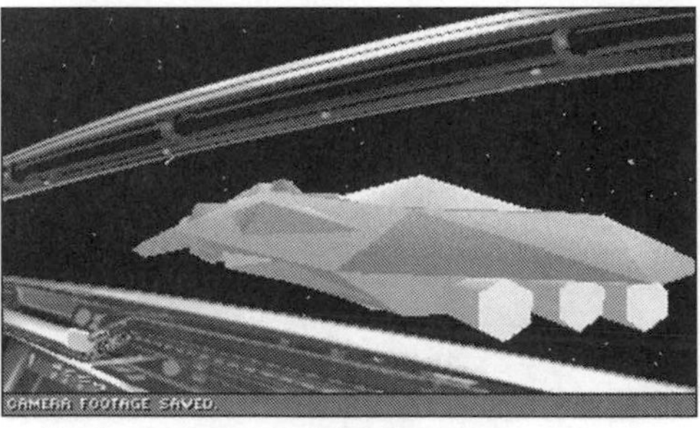

Close pass by the cruiser.

I was, however, able to finish off the Gunboats just then, giving myself a short reprieve. Another Gunboat group had arrived, and was currently mixing it up with my wingmen and the other remaining Alliance fighters. With 10:30 on the clock, we destroyed the last of GUN Mu. I had my instruments back by then, too.

The *Cathleen's* shields were down by this time, so the situation was critical. I got my lasers and shields fully charged, and waited for more Imperial incursions.

End of mission.

Taking up a position near the *Cathleen*, I throttled back to one-third. Checking my ship, all was well. I still had three torpedoes left. With about nine minutes left on the clock, the *Cathleen* jumped for hyperspace, and I received my Mission Complete message. Time to head for home.

Debriefing (Win Conditions)

The cruiser *Cathleen* must escape.

OP 20B: ESCAPE TO HOTH!

File Name: t5m20wbb

Mission Briefing

The Calamarian cruisers *Yali* and *Maria* are set to rendezvous before proceeding to Hoth. B-wing Red and A-wing Gold will patrol the area. When the *Maria* arrives, both ships will leave for the new Rebel base planet. Any interfering Imperial ships must be destroyed to keep the new base location a secret.

Farlander's After-Action Report

I flew as wing leader in a two-ship group of B-wings. As I entered the area, I checked the Inflight Map, discovering that the cruiser *Yali* was about 12 kilometers away. Two A-wings from Gold squadron were also nearby.

I went through my mission-start procedures, being sure to charge my shields to maximum as quickly as I could. I put my wingman at memory location F5, and the *Yali* at F6. I put A-W *Gold 1* at F7, and, when an Imperial Frigate arrived, I put it at F8.

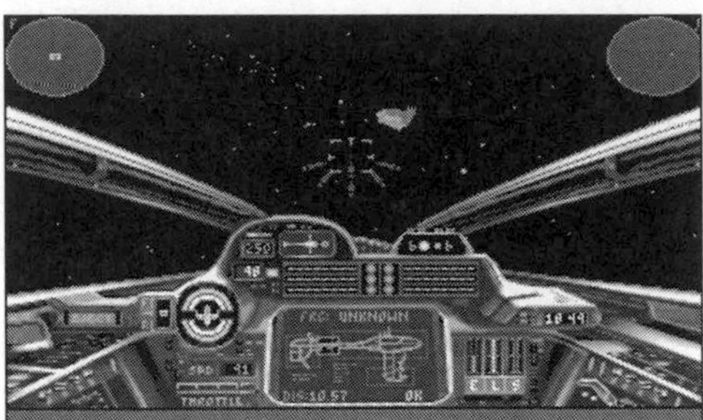

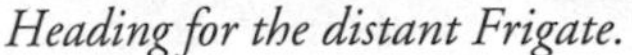

Heading for the distant Frigate.

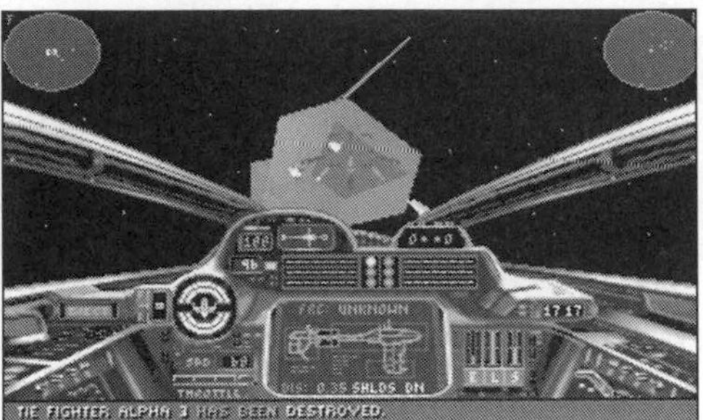

Coming in from the front of the Frigate.

I ordered my wingman to attack the Frigate immediately, and then switched to torpedoes. I redirected shield energy to the engines (with lasers still recharging at maximum) and headed toward the FRG, which had just launched a group of TIE fighters.

The Frigate came in close enough to begin firing on the cruiser, which began launching some Y-wings to counterattack. Another Imperial Frigate arrived then, about seven kilometers away, but I continued to head toward the first craft, resetting my laser recharge rates to normal to gain a little more speed.

Closing to within six kilometers, I acquired a red lock on the Frigate and shot all 12 torpedoes in dual-fire mode. I switched to cannons then, and continued toward the Frigate with my laser recharge rate set to maximum and my shields at normal. When I was within laser range of the Frigate, I began firing rapidly in single-fire mode.

About this time, a third Nebulon B Frigate arrived about 12 kilometers away. Meanwhile, the first Frigate's shields were down, and I ordered my wingman to attack the second Frigate while I went in for another strafing run (this time with ion cannons to disable the enemy craft, so that it couldn't return our fire while we finished it off). A couple of TIE Interceptors were on my tail, but I continued to fly over the Frigate *Fear* until she was destroyed.

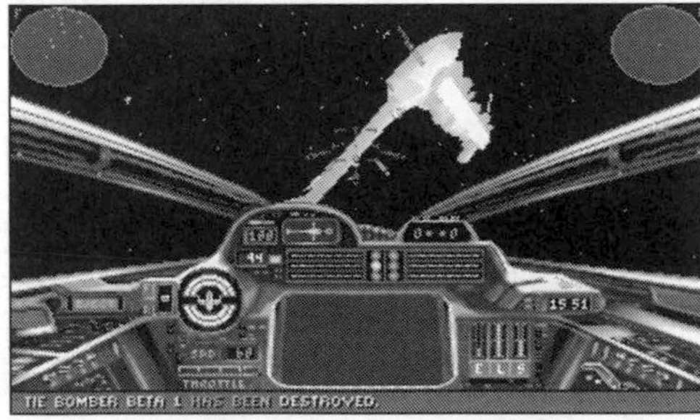

Final moments of FRG Fear.

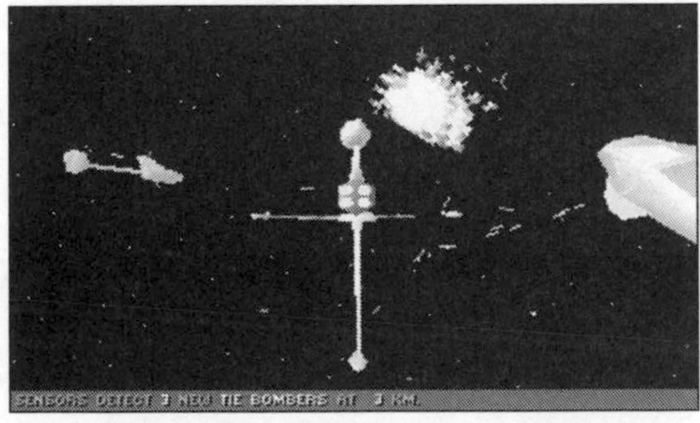

Starfighters coming in from the rear.

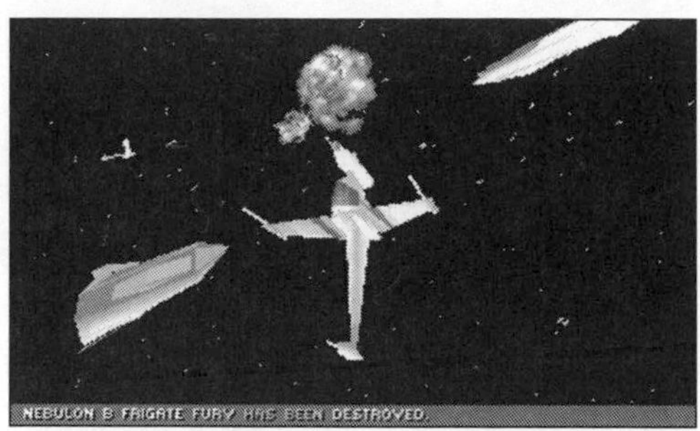
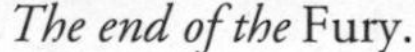

The end of the Fury.

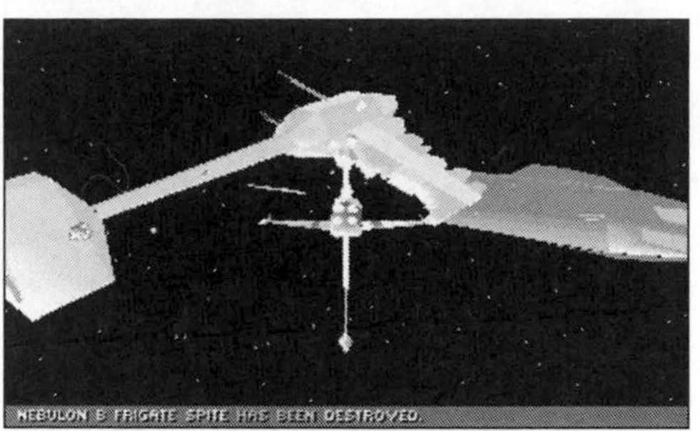

Last gasp of the Spite.

I ignored the pursuing T/Is, and headed toward the second Frigate, which was firing heavily on the *Yali* by this time.

I took evasive maneuvers whenever my shields got hammered too hard, but managed to keep going in and strafing the Frigate *Fury.* About this time, the second cruiser, *Maria*, arrived and joined in the battle. I decided to place her in memory location F7. Soon, the Frigate's shields fell under the combined fire of two cruisers and various fighters. Switching to ion cannons, I attempted to disable the *Fury,* which was soon destroyed. Now only one Frigate remained.

Checking the two cruisers, I found that they were in remarkably good shape. As I was about to go after the third Frigate, another one appeared less than two kilometers behind me. I ordered my wingman to attack this new entry, the *Spite,* and turned to go after it myself. Same procedure; same result.

Now just the one Frigate remained. I ordered my wingman to attack, but before heading in I decided to take out the TIE Interceptor that was making my life a living hell. Of course, one of his mates took his place in short order, but I reduced that one to space junk almost as fast.

The remaining Frigate, *Hate,* was already damaged from its battle with the cruisers. Its shields were down, and the rest of the job was pathetically easy.

A few Imperial starfighters were still in the area, so I prepared myself to go after the remaining enemies. I redirected shield energy to my engines, with lasers at maximum, and fought until the area was clear.

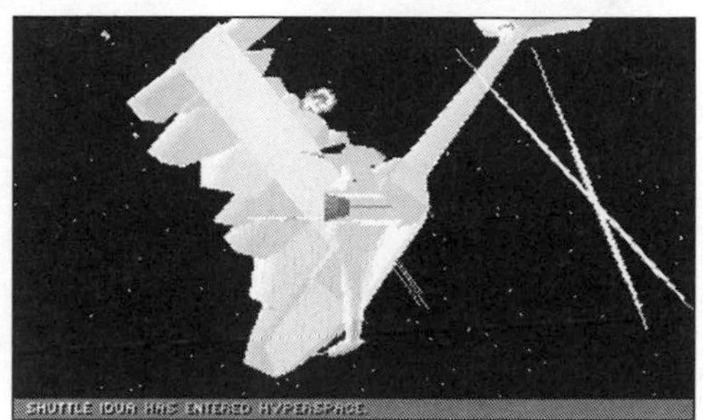

Another view of a Frigate destructing.

Soon afterward, the Alliance ships began entering hyperspace. I

The cruiser Maria *is headed for safety.*

took out the Nav Buoy just for grins, and then, with only a few seconds left on the clock, the cruiser *Maria* entered hyperspace. I received the Mission Complete message. Moments later, I followed the rest of the fleet, and jumped to our new base on Hoth.

Debriefing (Win Conditions)

The cruisers *Yali* and *Maria* must survive. The Frigates *Fear, Fury, Hate* and *Spite* must be destroyed.

X-Wing CD Bonus & Historical Missions

B-wing Historical 1: Project Shantipole

File Name: t5h1wb

Mission Briefing

Following the success of the Empire's Nebulon B Frigate during the Battle of Yavin, the Rebellion developed the B-wing heavy fighter as a tactical response. An insectoid race called the Verpine constructed the craft at the Shantipole Test

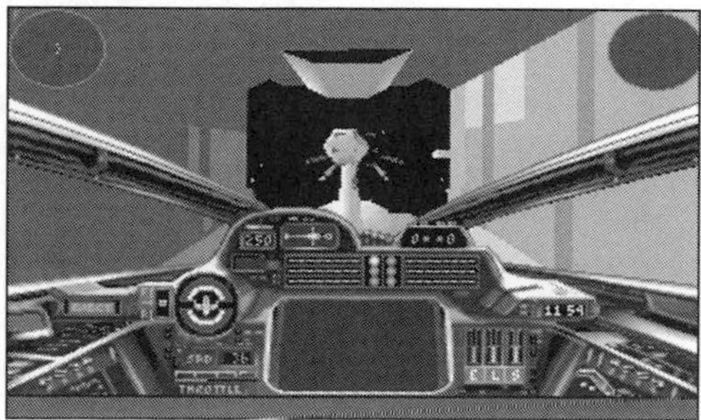

Beginning of mission, trailing #1 prototype.

Facility, but the secrecy of the compound was compromised by an Imperial spy. You will fly the only armed B-wing prototype during the subsequent evacuation. Protect your own craft, as well as another unarmed prototype and two evacuation vehicles. The corvette *Shantipole* carries the Verpine staff, while the shuttle *Falcon* is escaping with Admiral Ackbar and his aides.

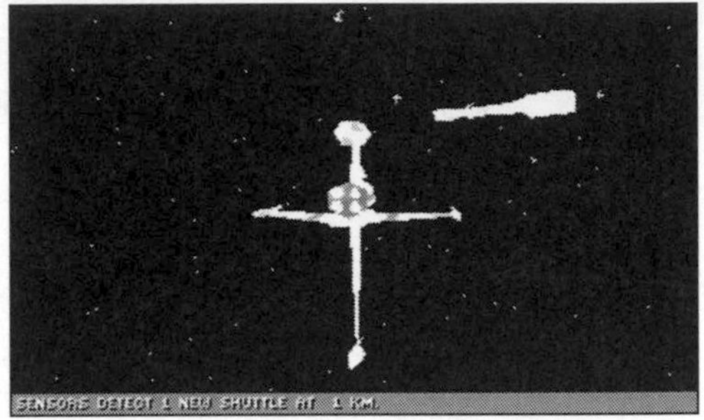

CRV Verpine *in the distance.*

Farlander's After-Action Report

At the beginning of the mission, I went through my standard start-up procedure and then did a fly-by of the corvette *Shantipole*. I placed the CRV in memory location F8, the number-one B-wing in F5, and the shuttle *Falcon* at F6. Enemy transports were attacking by this time, and I turned to engage them, quickly destroying the nearest one with lasers.

I noticed that some Imperial corvettes were in the area as well. I wanted to stay near the shuttle, but I also had to protect the *Shantipole*. I went after another TRN, and while I was taking care of business, the number-one B-wing made it safely into hyperspace.

SHU Falcon *has finished docking.*

Shortly thereafter, the shuttle began its docking operation. A new X-wing arrived to help escort the evacuees, as part of the testing facility went up in a fireball behind me. Four enemy corvettes were in the area now, and I was feeling a little outnumbered.

I began firing on the closest enemy CRV, drawing its attention away from the *Shantipole*. I was then able to turn and engage the nearest transport, which was in the process of attacking me. The X-wings were firing torpedoes at the Imperial corvettes, so I was able to concentrate on the TRNs.

The shuttle *Falcon* entered the safety of hyperspace, and I worked my way over toward the *Shantipole* to see if I could help out. My shields had taken a beating during the dogfight with the transports, and I had to keep fighting them as I surveyed the battle scene. The Imperial corvettes were going fast under the torpedo attacks of the X-wings, and I joined in to help destroy the last of them with my cannons.

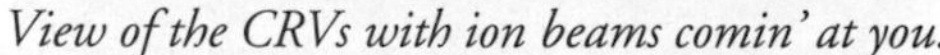

View of the CRVs with ion beams comin' at you.

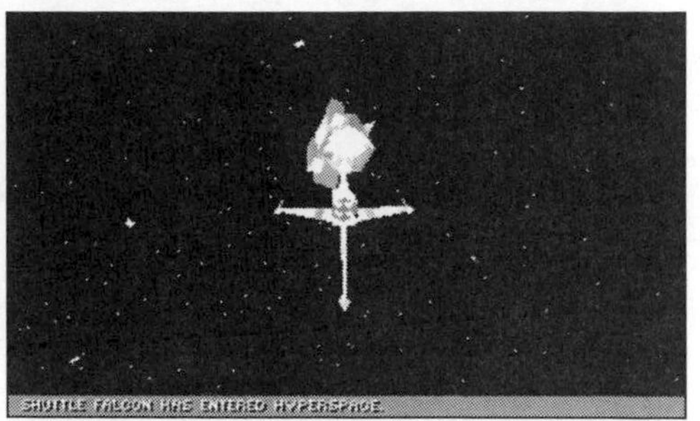

Taking out a transport as the Falcon *leaves.*

About five minutes remained on the clock; all that was left in the area were a couple of transports, and the X-wings were already going after them. I joined in and collected both kills with superior shooting. The area was clear for the moment, but then another pair of Imperial transports arrived.

I went after them, taking advantage of their slower speed, and reducing them to debris as the mission clock approached two minutes. With the area clear, some of the X-wings began entering hyperspace. A little later, the *Shantipole* jumped out, as well. Mission complete. Time to go home.

Debriefing (Win Conditions)

Both B-wing prototypes must escape, as well as the corvette *Shantipole* and the shuttle *Falcon*.

Mission Note: Remember that pressing [R] won't locate transports to target. Stay near the SHU *Falcon*, and keep one eye on the CRV *Shantipole*.

B-WING HISTORICAL 2: ASSAULT ON IMPERIAL CONVOY

Retreating TIE fighters.

File Name: t5h2mb

Mission Briefing

In this mission, use the B-wings overwhelming firepower to wipe out an Imperial convoy on route to Petrakis. The convoy is composed of shuttles, corvettes, and freighters loaded with TIE fighters. Two B-wings and one X-wing from Red Squadron will attack; beware of Gunboats, and do not harm any neutral craft.

Farlander's After-Action Report

I was the flight leader in a two-ship group of B-wings, and we had an X-wing escort. As the mission began, six TIE fighters were in view, and I blasted a couple though it was not part of our overall objective. To my surprise, the TIEs scattered and ran at that point, and so I turned my attention to the freighters.

I targeted the nearest freighter, *Ocean 2*, and sent my wingman after it. I then targeted the nearest corvette, *Manx 1*, switching to dual torpedoes on the fly. As I waited to get within range, I did some basic maintenance on my shields, rebalancing and transferring energy from lasers. I noticed that a transport was attacking my wingman, so I broke off my torpedo run and engaged the TRN with lasers.

Shooting the TRN Sigma 2.

Having taken care of TRN *Sigma 2*, I turned back toward the corvette and switched again to torpedoes. At about 5 kilometers away I got my red lock, and fired six into the corvette. About this time, two Gunboats jumped into the area, but they were still 10 kilometers distant, and not an immediate threat.

Having shot half my torpedoes at the first corvette, I decided to help my wingman destroy the freighter. I wanted to be sure that the lead freighters in the convoy couldn't jump to hyperspace before we got to them, and as I finished off the lead freighter with lasers, my wingman automatically targeted the next; *Ocean 1*. I joined him.

We still had one corvette to take care of, in addition to another pair of freighters. I ordered my wingman to go after the CRV, and I also attacked with lasers. About this time, the Gunboats I had noticed earlier had closed within range, and were firing missiles at me. I couldn't evade, but I turned on the Gunboats and destroyed the nearest one, staying aware that we had to finish the corvette and the other freighters before they could jump out of the area.

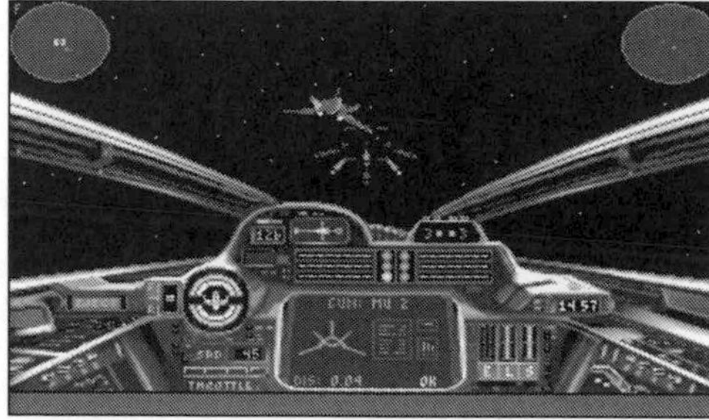

Shooting Mu 2.

Taking on the corvette.

After I had fragged the first Gunboat, I came in behind the corvette *Manx 2*, slipped into the blind spot while dropping my speed, and opened up with lasers. After the corvette's shields were gone, I switched to ion cannons to disable it before finishing the job.

About the time I destroyed the corvette, GUN *Mu 1* had found me again, and was trying to get a missile lock. I turned and engaged him, sparing myself another hit. Two more corvettes had jumped into the area, and my wingman went after them.

As soon as *Mu 1* had fireballed, I went to send my wingman after the nearest freighter, but he was gone. He had gotten the shields down on one of the new corvettes, but was wasted in the process. I was on my own.

I targeted the freighter myself, and went in with cannons blasting. I took a moment to send two torpedoes into the corvette that was now lacking shields, destroying it quickly.

I was getting hit by some heavy fire, which I first assumed was coming from the corvette, but it turned out to be a shuttle that was peppering me with laser blasts. I found the sneaky shuttle, *Lambda 2*, and destroyed him and his leader, *Lambda 1*. I then went back after the lead freighter, and, saving my last four torpedoes for the corvette, I used cannons to destroy both it, *Teve 1*, and its mate, *Teve 2*.

Firing on corvette Hornet 2.

Finally, it was time to take out the corvette, *Hornet 1*. I switched to torpedoes and let fly with all four, and then I moved in behind the CRV *Hornet 2*, disabling it with ion cannons before finishing the job. Two freighters were still in the area, but they were neutrals, so I let them alone. After the destruction of the CRV *Hornet 2*, I got my Mission Complete message.

Debriefing (Win Conditions)

Freighter groups Ocean and Teve, and corvette groups Manx and Hornet must be destroyed.

Mission Note: Always disable large ships when their shields are down, and then finish the job as necessary. Also, if you do attack the neutral freighters, four Y-wings will enter the area and go after you. This may make the mission more difficult, but you can use these Y-wings to gain extra points.

B-WING HISTORICAL 3: CAPTURE THE FRIGATE PRIAM

File Name: t5h3mb

Mission Briefing

Compare the B-wings performance with that of the Y-wing in this historic recreation of the Frigate *Priam's* capture. The Frigate is damaged and vulnerable. B-wing Red will eliminate the defensive minefield, and disable the FRG prior to the arrival of capture teams aboard transport *Jordi* and Shuttle *Panda.*

Farlander's After-Action Report

At mission start, I immediately targeted the Frigate *Priam*, placing it in memory location F5, and ordered my wingmen to attack. I knew that they would fire torpedoes as soon as they came within range.

I powered up my shield and laser recharge rates, and switched to dual-fire torps as well, firing all 12 as soon as I had a lock. Meanwhile, TIE fighters from Alpha squadron tried to engage me, but I ignored them, leaving them to our two A-wings to take care of. My mission was to get the *Priam*.

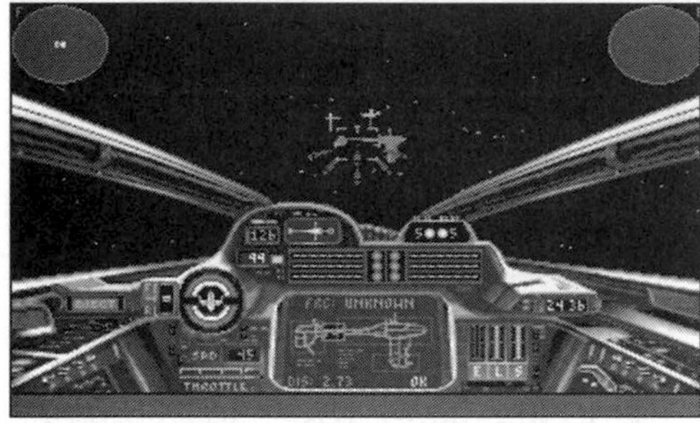

Heading toward the Frigate.

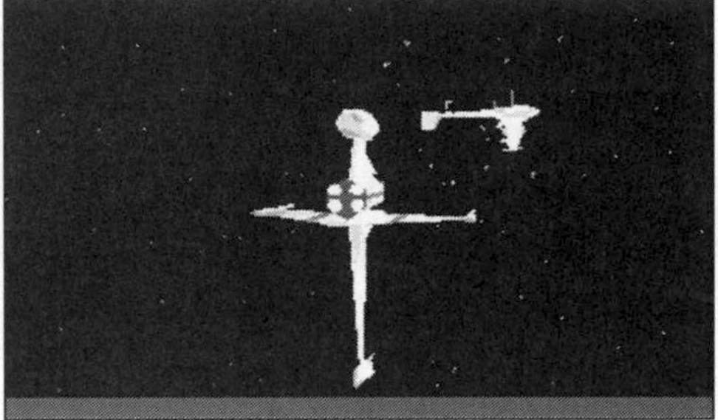

The B-wing approaching the Frigate.

As soon as I had launched the torpedoes, I switched to lasers in link-fire mode and went to the minefield, clearing the way for my wingmen to make their attack runs. Once the minefield was taken care of, I went in with lasers after the Frigate. I ignored the starfighters that the Frigate launched, and concentrated on my target. One of the Bombers came close to getting a missile lock on me, so I turned and took him out, a distraction of only a few moments.

I tried not to get in too close to the Frigate—to stay between 1.5 and .5 kilometers away, dodging fire while getting my hits in. The B-wing was too slow to go in tight on a fully functioning Frigate, but the more I could draw the Frigate's attention, the better chance my wingmen had of surviving.

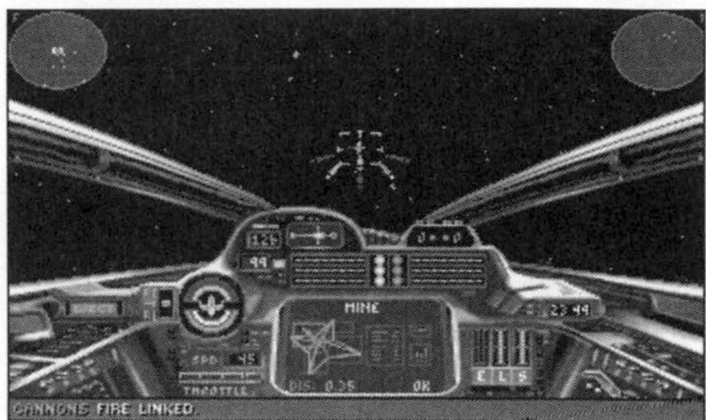

Enemy mine.

It took several passes with my lasers before the Frigate's shields went down. The only thing I stopped for was to destroy any TIE Bombers that came too close, as I couldn't afford to absorb missile hits on top of the damage the Frigate was doing.

At 21:00 on the clock, the *Priam's* shields dropped, and I switched to ion cannons. Moments later, the *Priam* was disabled. Now our job was to provide cover for the boarding party. Some Gunboats entered the area about 14 kilometers away, so I placed them in memory locations F6 and F7.

Transports *Assault 1* and *Assault 2* had entered the area, carrying commandos to board the *Priam*. Four other transports were carrying supplies and crew. It was up to us to protect these ships.

When the Gunboats got within range, they fired a missile at me to emphasize their arrival. I turned and corkscrewed in at them, swinging in behind to greet them with my lasers. I got GUN *Mu 2*, but I was too late to prevent *Mu 1* from destroying one of my wingmen. There was no way he was going to get away alive. I did a head-on pass, and then swung around behind and obliterated him.

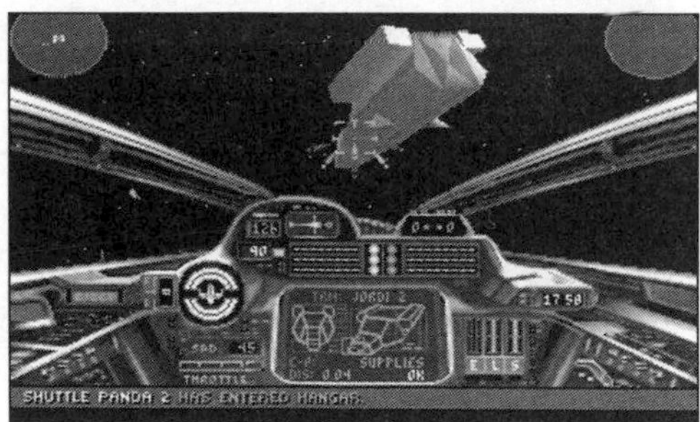

TRN Jordi *with supplies.*

A second wave of Gunboats jumped into the area, but they were about 10 kilometers away. The Rebels were in control of the Frigate by this time. The clock read 15:30.

The Rebels aboard the *Priam* headed toward the jump point, but then two Imperial transports and two Gunboats jumped in right along side the Frigate, and began firing lasers and torpedoes. I engaged them as quickly as possible, but the *Priam* took a couple of torpedo hits just as she escaped into hyperspace. The Gunboats were firing missiles at me even as the Mission Complete message appeared on my display.

The *Priam* was ours, and I knew that I could head home at any time. I stuck around to take care of the two closest Gunboats, and then fired up the hyperdrive.

Debriefing (Win Conditions)
The Frigate *Priam* must be recovered.

Mission Note: The key to this mission is to assign your wingmen to attack the Frigate as soon as the mission begins, protect them as long as possible by destroying the minefield, and then draw as much of the Frigate's fire as you can. Also, if your wingmen continue to attack the *Priam* after she's disabled, tell them to ignore the target, to wait, or to go home.

B-WING HISTORICAL 4: B-WING ATTACK ON THE *SHRIKE*

File Name: t5h4wb

Mission Briefing
Fly the B-wing for its intended purpose; evening the odds against a Frigate in battle. The Nebulon B Frigate *Shrike* will make for a nearby jump point, marked by a Nav Buoy, to try and escape. The Buoy is protected by a small minefield.

Farlander's After-Action Report
I was the flight leader of a three-ship group of B-wings. Two A-wings from Gold Squadron were to be our escort. As the mission got underway, the Imperial Frigate *Shrike*, was about 7 kilometers away. About 3 kilometers away was a two-ship group of TIE fighters from Alpha, and two more ships from T/F Beta were about 11 kilometers distant.

The A-wings hadn't arrived yet, so I went through my standard mission start-up procedures, and assigned B-wing *Red 2* to memory location F5. The Frigate I put at F8. I ordered my wingmen to attack the Frigate and switched

Firing two torps at the Frigate.

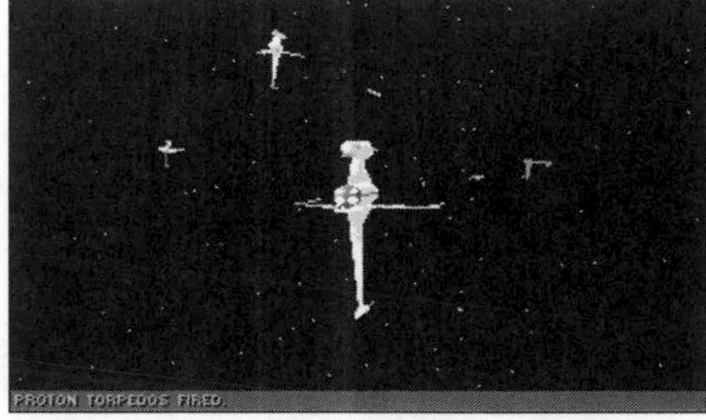

Engaging the enemy with B-wing support.

to torpedoes in dual-fire mode. By this time, the A-wings had arrived and were engaging the enemy fighters. I led my group directly toward the *Shrike*.

I fired all 12 of my torpedoes as soon as I could get a red lock, then switched to laser cannons in single-fire mode.

I reset my shield recharge rate to normal to gain some speed, and make it just a little more difficult for the Frigate's gunners to target me. When the *Shrike's* shields went down, I switched to ion cannons and went in to for the disabling.

With a little more than 12 minutes on the mission clock, the *Shrike* was busily launching a variety of craft, including some TIE Bombers. I was being hammered by the enemy starfighters, but I kept strafing until the Frigate was destroyed. It took several passes; I had to keep redirecting laser energy to my shields and rebalancing them.

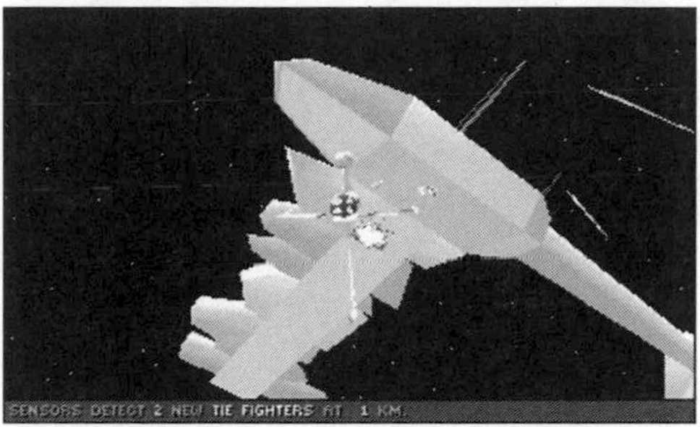

Strafing run on the Shrike.

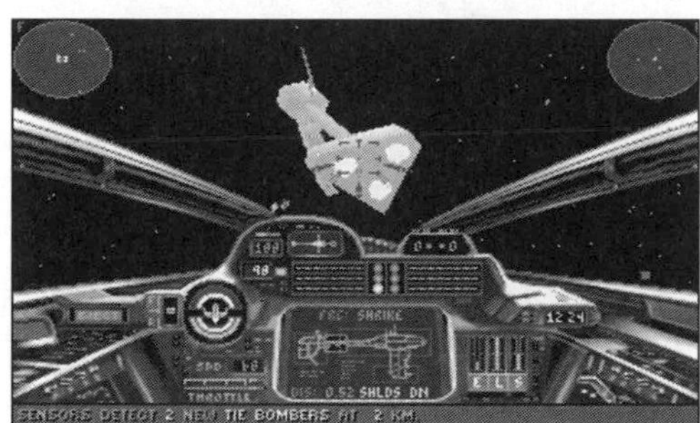

Shields down on the Shrike.

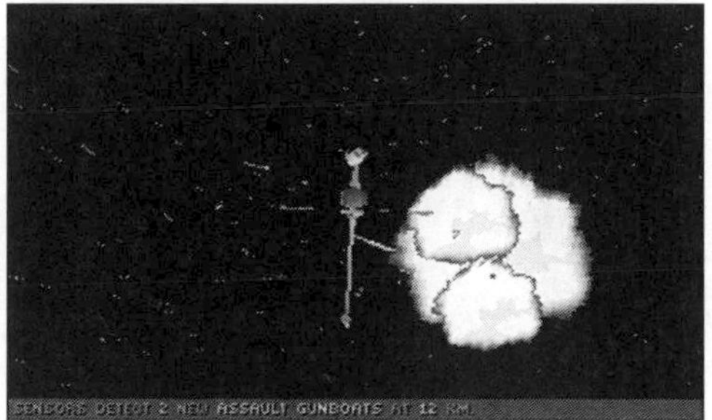

The Shrike *is history.*

A pair of Assault Gunboats appeared, followed by a pair of corvettes. I ordered my wingmen to go after the first CRV, while I attacked the nearest enemy starfighter, which turned out to be T/F *Beta 2*.

Taking out the remaining TIE craft from the Frigate, I reasoned, should make it easier for all of us to stay alive. I destroyed a Bomber, and next targeted a Gunboat. The Mission Complete message came on, but I wanted to duplicate the historical mission, so I kept after the enemy craft.

When there were no more Gunboats, I turned my attention to the corvettes, but then a new wave of GUN Eta was launched. I headed in toward CRV *Banshee 1*, discovering that my wingmen had already had an effect, and its shields were down. Before I could begin a new attack run, however, my wingmen finished the job.

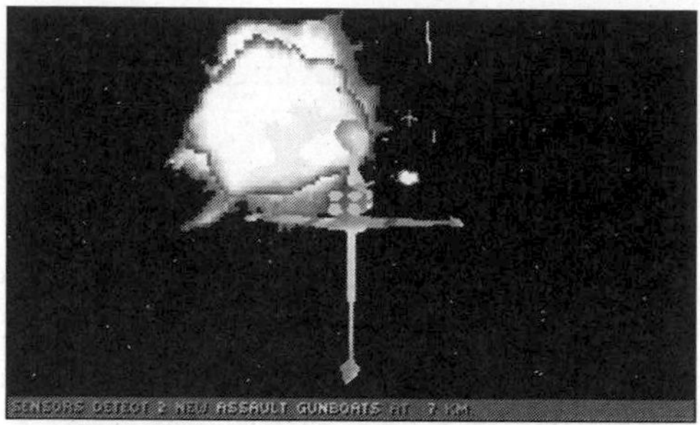

Another corvette bites the dust.

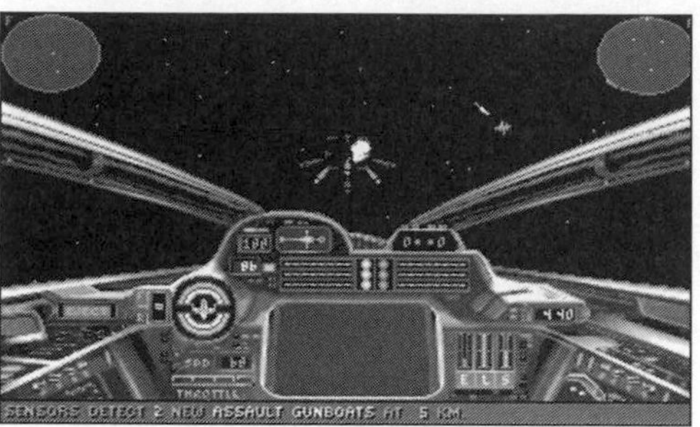

Blasting mines.

A targeted another CRV then, slipping into the sweet spot behind the Corellian craft and blasting away until it exploded.

The A-wings had taken care of the second wave of GUN Eta, but a new wave appeared, and I decided to go in after them, redirecting some energy to my engines to gain speed. At one kilometer from the nearest Gunboat, I reset my recharge rates to maximum and took out GUN *Eta 1* in a head-on pass. He was already damaged by the A-wings, so I finished him with just a couple of shots. *Eta 2* was my next target.

After finishing off the Gunboats, I headed toward the minefield, figuring that I wouldn't leave anything in this area. After destroying the mines, I blasted the Nav Buoy and decided that my work here was done.

Debriefing (Win Conditions)
The Frigate *Shrike* must be destroyed.

B-W HISTORICAL 5: ATTACK DEATH STAR SURFACE

File Name: t5h5wb

Mission Briefing
Compare the performance of the B-wing with that of the X-wing in the historic attack on the Death Star surface. B-wing Red will clear all Death Star defenses near the Nav Buoy, including any TIEs and all turbolaser towers within two kilometers. All four hangar ports in the vicinity must also be destroyed.

Farlander's After-Action Report
I was the wingman in a two-ship B-wing group: We came out of hyperspace above the surface of the Death Star, and went through standard mission-start procedures. I then assigned B-W *Red 1* to memory location F5, telling

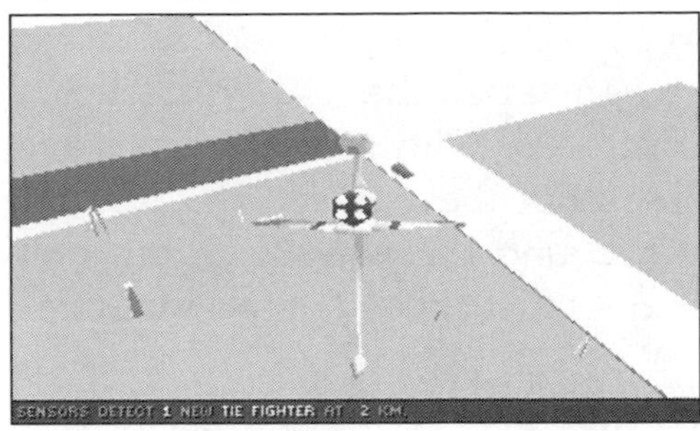
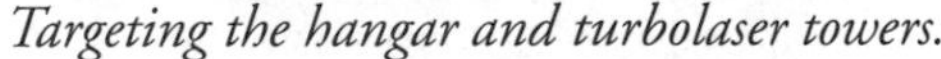

Targeting the hangar and turbolaser towers.

Taking some flak from the T/Fs.

him to go after the nearest TIE fighter. I put the nearest container, which was 5 kilometers away, at F6; the next one, also 5 kilometers away, at F7; and another, which was 10 kilometers distant, at F8.

I switched to torpedoes in dual-fire mode, and set my shield recharge rate to normal. The hangars were located at the bottom of some artificial canyons formed by the surface structure of the Death Star. To get a clear shot with my torpedoes, I positioned myself directly above the hangar, and then loosed three torpedoes into the nest.

That took out the first hangar, so I hit F7 and targeted the next. Someone had fired a missile at me, but B-wings were made to take some punishment, so I ignored it. I found the fourth container, and put it in memory at F6 before returning my attention to the one at F7. I kept transferring laser energy to my shields to make up for the damage being caused by the Death Star's defenders.

I fired another three torpedoes at the second hangar and then went after the next, which was 7.2 kilometers away.

As I went after the third container, I was pelted by several missiles, but my shields held thanks to some quick rebalancing. When the action got too hot, I called my flight leader to come to my assistance. As I was disposing of another hangar, B-W *Red 1* was destroyed, and I was on my own. I flew upside down over the Death Star, using "high" view to watch the surface pass by.

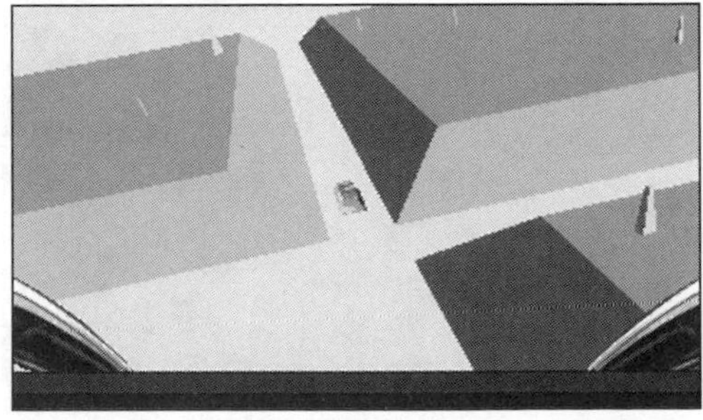

The Death Star surface.

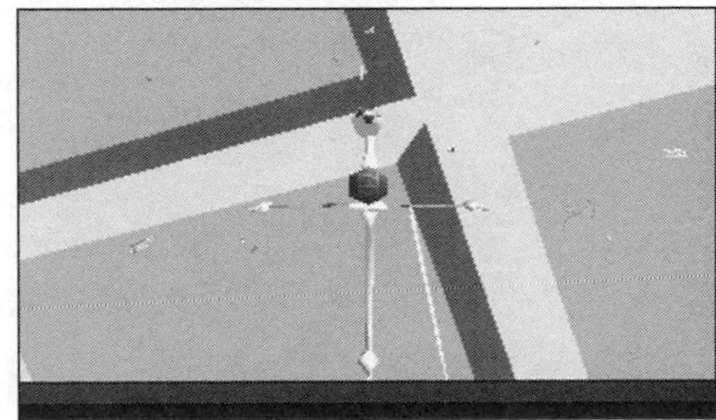

Wreaking havoc on hangar 4.

When I was over the last hangar, I turned and fired my torpedoes.

With all four hangars destroyed, I went after the TIE fighters and Bombers that were making my mission so hard. With my cannons linked and all recharge rates at maximum, I took out the nearest TIE Bomber. Many enemy starfighters were clustered around the Nav Buoy, but only three Imperial craft had gone after me. I guess that they figured that three against one would be enough. Wrong.

After destroying the nearest Bomber, I took on a TIE fighter, and then finished off another Bomber. More enemies joined the action then, and, as I destroyed T/B *Beta 1*, three more T/Fs got on my tail. I set my shield recharge rate to zero, reconfigured my shields to the rear, and kept redirecting laser energy to them. I was chasing T/B *Beta 1*, and wanted to finish him off before I turned my attention to the TIE fighters.

After I had shot *Beta 1*, I rebalanced my shields and reset shield recharge rates to normal, turning to go after T/F *Gamma 2*, my nearest tormentor. T/I *Delta 1* was the next enemy to go. Then came *Gamma 1* and *Gamma 3*, who was about four kilometers away in the direction of the Nav Buoy. I began recharging my shields as fast as I could. *Gamma 3* came after me, and I rammed him—not a good idea for a TIE fighter to try to play chicken with a B-wing.

I continued to destroy the defending TIE starfighters until the job was completed, and then headed toward the Nav Buoy. I still had to destroy all the turbolaser batteries within two kilometers of it.

Closing on the Nav Buoy, I dropped to the Death Star's surface and began firing on the towers. Switching to single-fire mode, I shot my lasers as fast as I could, destroying each tower quickly as I passed.

After I had destroyed innumerable gun towers, the Mission Complete message came across my display. Some gun towers were still nearby, but I figured that I must have gotten the ones our Mission Control wanted, so I jumped into hyperspace and headed home.

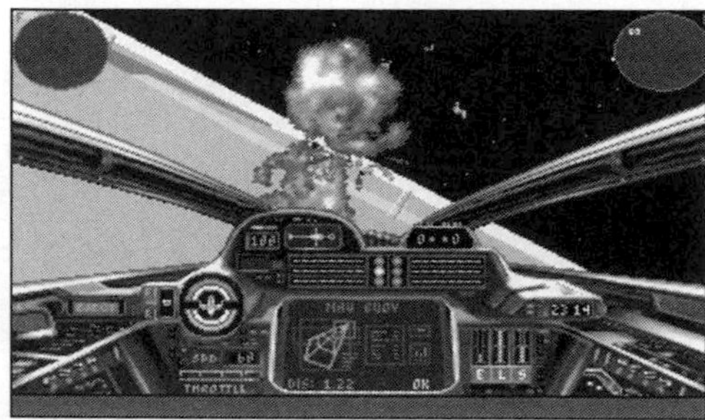

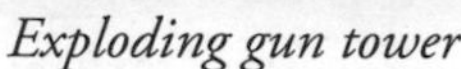
Exploding gun tower

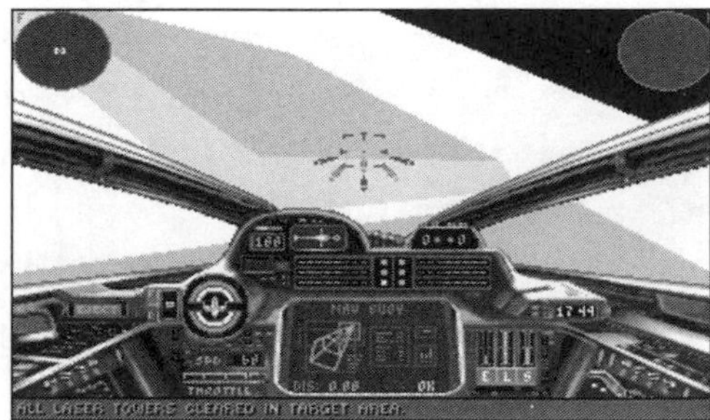

Win message

Debriefing (Win Conditions)
The four hangar ports and all turbolaser towers within two kilometers of the Nav Buoy must be destroyed.

Mission Note: Concentrate on the hangars disguised as containers, and dogfight only when necessary. You don't have to have a red lock to blast a hangar if you approach it from directly above.

B-W HISTORICAL 6: DEATH STAR TRENCH RUN

File Name: t5h6mb

Mission Briefing
Pilot a B-wing in this re-creation of the final trench run attack on the Death Star. Follow the Nav Buoys to the trench, then turn left and drop down for the run. Redirect all energy to your front shields once inside the trench, and switch to torpedoes when closing on the exhaust port. Also, once in the trench, redirect all energy to your engines; your B-wing has been modified to have triple the ordinary thrust.

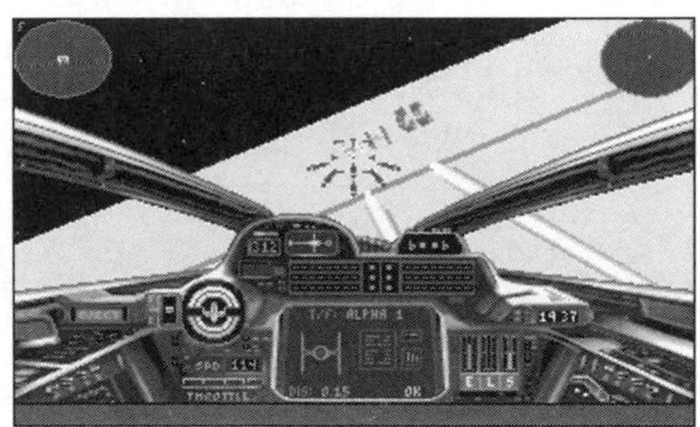

T/F Alpha in attack mode.

Farlander's After-Action Report
At the beginning of the mission, I set my recharge rates up and targeted T/F *Alpha 1*, which was directly in front of me. I set my lasers on link-fire mode and corkscrewed my way in, transferring laser energy to my shields as I flew by the group. I didn't engage them, but kept running toward the trench. I was about two kilometers above the Death Star's surface.

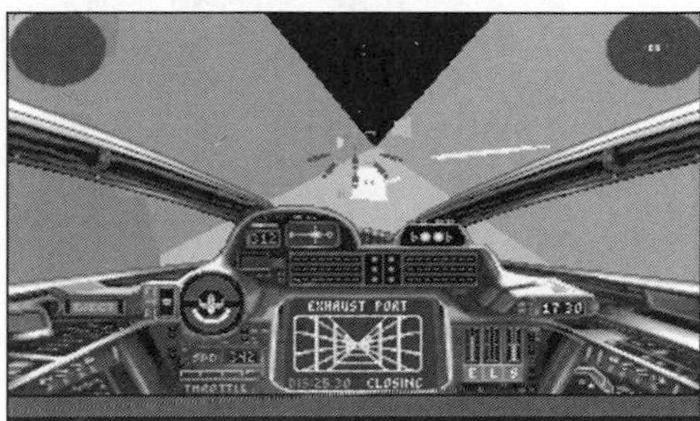

Heading down the trench.

After I was over the trench, I put my laser recharge rate at zero and my shield recharge rate at normal to gain speed before dropping down for the run.

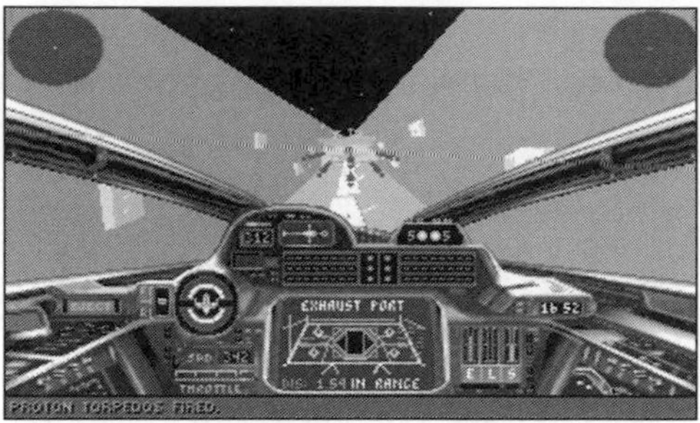

Shooting torpedoes down the tube.

I kept evading incoming laser blasts, not worrying about firing back. My mission was simple: Fire my torpedoes into the exhaust port. I tried to move in a sort of circular motion, getting the lasers to fire at me, and then moving around to avoid the incoming blasts. I switched to dual-fire torpedoes so I would be ready when the time came.

I was about seven kilometers away, but my shields were gone. The B-wing has a thick hull, which can take a great deal of damage, but this was cutting it awfully close. I kept dodging the incoming laser blasts as I sped toward my target. When the exhaust port came into view on my CMD, I fired my torpedoes two at a time. This was my chance, and I took it, scoring a direct hit. I had done it! I had destroyed the Death Star in a B-wing.

Debriefing (Win Conditions)
The Death Star must be destroyed.

Mission Note: The key to this mission is to avoid getting into any battles or firing lasers at anything. If you engage the TIE fighters at the beginning of the mission, the TIE Advanced catches up to you and finishes you off, so it's imperative that you don't waste any time or energy. Try different weaving motions to throw off the trench guns. You'll take some hits, but don't fire back. Transfer all the energy you have into your shields. As soon as you see the exhaust port in the CMD, fire all your torpedoes, and then pull back on the stick and get away from the Death Star.

Bonus Missions

BONUS MISSION 1: PROTECT CARGO TRANSFER

File Name: wotan1aw

Mission Briefing

In this A-wing mission, protect a cargo transfer during an attack by Imperial Frigates. A-wing *Red 1* will inspect a pair of containers hidden in an asteroid field. When the contents are verified, two transports will deploy to ferry the supplies to the cruiser *Stimsenj'kat*. TRN group Renhoek will require two or three trips. X-wing Gold and B-wing Blue will assist in fending off any Imperial patrols.

Passing a transport.

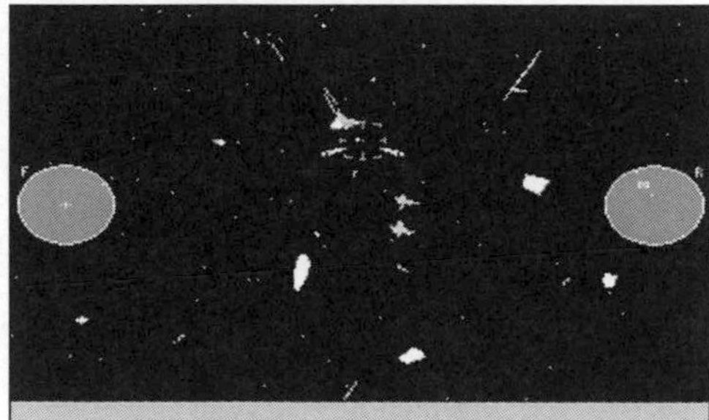

No-cockpit view of three Gunboats.

Farlander's After-Action Report

I was the leader of a four-ship group of A-wings. We launched from the cruiser *Stimsenj'kat*, and I saved *Red 2* at memory location F5 and the cruiser at F6 before heading towards the nearest container.

After my shields were at maximum, I reset the recharge rates to normal and inspected container *Xi 2*. It contained Lonsigar, as did the next one, *Xi 1*. Two transports designated Renhoek launched then, to begin the transfer of the cargo. I put *Renhoek 1* at memory location F7. Four Assault Gunboats had also entered the area, and I ordered my wingmen to go after the lead ship. I reset my cannon recharge rates to normal, and turned to join the battle.

As I got close to the GUNs, I set my recharge rates to maximum to slow my A-wing. *Rho 1* broke off his attack, but the other three Gunboats had gone after one of my wingmen. As sometimes happens when you attack the lead ship in a group, the other ships had abandoned their mission, and were out for revenge. This, of course, played right into our hands.

I finished off *Rho 1*, and then ordered my wingmen to attack *Rho 3*, which was the closest threat to the transports. I helped them finish off *Rho 3* and then *Rho 2*, then it was time for *Rho 4* to taste our lasers. We got the message that the transports had completed their docking operation—the first of several.

The situation darkened when an Imperial Frigate arrived. I hadn't finished off *Rho 4* yet, and while I did, three TIE Bombers launched from the Frigate. Almost simultaneously, X-wings from Gold Squadron came to our aid.

With *Rho 4* dead, we went after the Bombers. There were also some TIE Advanced, but the Bombers from Beta Squadron were the first priority. By the time I reached them, some had already taken damage from the X-wings, and those were easily disposed of.

A Gunboat remained, and T/B Delta launched along with a replacement wave of T/B Beta. I switched to single-fire missiles and fired on the lone Gunboat, which was attacking our TRNs, and then switched to lasers to finish him off.

Returning to the Bombers, I began firing on *Delta 1*, but not before the T/Bs had launched some of their torpedoes at the cruiser. Meanwhile, TRN *Renhoek* had entered the hangar aboard the *Stimsenj'kat*. Another wave would launch momentarily, but I had other problems, such as T/B *Beta 1*, whom I destroyed with a single missile before he could do any damage. I then fired a missile at *Beta 3*, which he evaded, but I decided to let it chase him and see what happened.

I went after T/B *Delta 1*, firing a missile at him as well, and firing a missile at point-blank range on *Delta 2*. I switched to lasers to finish off *Delta 3*, which had already been shot up by the cruiser's gunners. I noticed that another Frigate had entered the area while I was busy with the Bombers.

Meanwhile, another wave of transports completed their docking operation with the containers.

I decided to save the more distant Frigate at F8. It was launching more T/B Delta, and also T/A Gamma. The nearer Frigate was launching T/B Beta and T/A *Alpha. I* went after more T/Bs, firing missiles on *Beta 1*, and then going after *Beta 2* with cannons. I was losing count of the enemy craft, but just kept firing on the Bombers as fast as I could. B-wing Blue was attacking the Frigate.

Distraught, I shook off an attack by a TIE Advanced, and continued to go after Bombers, which kept coming in wave after wave. What was so important about this cargo transfer?

Both T/Bs Beta and Delta had launched new waves, and they were about the same distance away. I sent my wingmen after Delta while I stayed with Beta.

In a head-on pass, I fired a missile at *Beta 1* that went wide of its target. I then turned my attention to *Beta 2*, using cannons, hoping that my missile would catch up eventually. *Beta 3* was next: He was headed for the cruiser, and began to take fire. I finished him off and then turned to greet T/B *Beta 1*, which was still among the living. I finished him with cannons, and then went to intercept what was left of T/B group Delta.

Finally, all the Bombers were destroyed, at least for the moment, and I turned some attention to the TIE Advanced. *Alpha 3* was the nearest one, and I ordered my wingmen to attack. I was going to go help out the B-wings, which were attacking the Frigate *Rapier*, but then I noticed that the other Frigate, the *Firestorm*, was within range of the cruiser and exchanging fire.

I redirected shield energy to my engines and headed toward the *Firestorm*. By attacking the *Firestorm*, I hoped to draw some attention away from the cruiser, so I went in gunning in single-fire mode. Checking the situation, I noticed that the shields were down on the *Rapier*, and I decided to go help finish her off, again redirecting shield energy to the engines to gain speed. I continued to ignore the TIE Advanced, who were pursuing me relentlessly.

The B-wings were launching more torpedoes at the *Rapier*, so it was only a matter of time before she went. I came in firing with shield recharge rates reset to normal. In my first strafing run, the *Rapier* registered hull damage. Moments later, she blew.

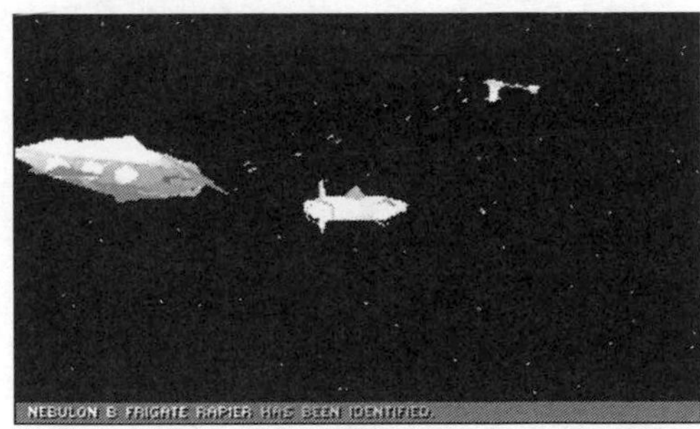

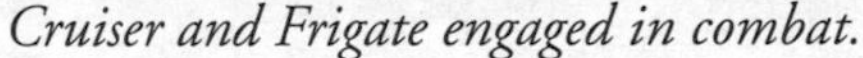

Cruiser and Frigate engaged in combat.

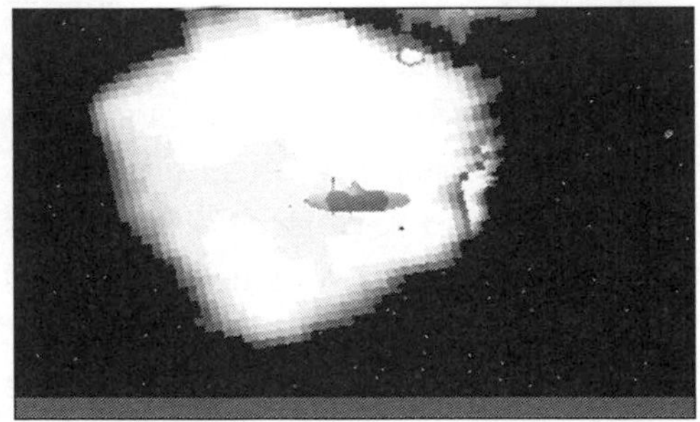

A grim ending for the Rapier.

Yet another Nebulon B Frigate arrived, and shortly afterward began spewing forth starfighters. The *Firestorm*'s shields were down, however, and I took the time to help finish her off while sending my wingmen after the newest group of TIE Bombers. After one firing pass, I switched to missiles and targeted T/B *Theta 1*. I was too late to prevent them from firing one salvo of torpedoes at the cruiser, but I didn't figure to let them fire any more.

As the *Firestorm* blew, I fired at *Theta 1*, and then went after the next Bomber.

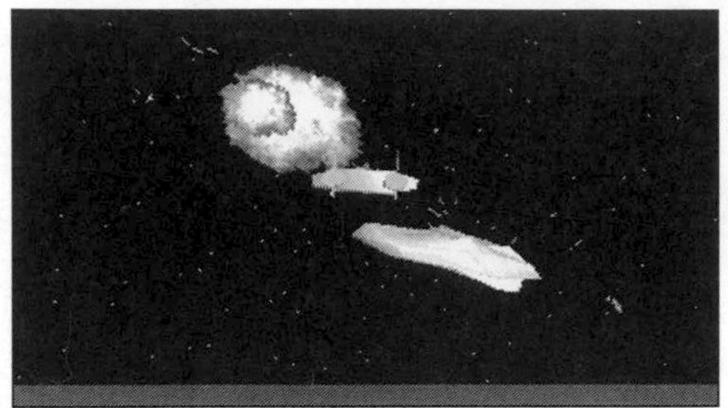

The Firestorm *blows, with a cruiser nearby.*

By this time, the transports had completed their third cargo run. *Theta 1* had evaded my missile, so I finished him off with cannons, triggering a second wave of T/B Theta. I sent my wingmen after *Theta 1* while I targeted *Theta 2* with a missile, switching to cannons immediately after the missile was away, and going after *Theta 3*. *Theta 2* proved evasive, so I went in and finished him off with cannons. Another wave of T/B Theta launched, and we went after them, as well.

As we were fighting the third wave of T/B Theta, the CRS *Stimsenj'kat* entered hyperspace, and the Mission Complete message appeared on my display. The mission clock read 74 minutes. I continued to fight successive waves of Bombers.

Without the cruiser to attack, the Bombers tried unsuccessfully to target me with their missiles, and were soon all destroyed. We then went after the Advanced fighters. I noticed a big battle going on where the cruiser had been, with X-wings and TIE Advanced mixing it up. B-wing Blue was still attacking the remaining Frigate, *Reaper,* and I decided to join in to help them out.

I could have jumped to hyperspace at this point, but there were still many enemy craft around, and I wanted to do my part. I kept ordering my wingmen to attack the nearest TIE Advanced while I strafed the Frigate. It looked as though the *Reaper* was getting ready to escape into hyperspace, so I tried to make my attack runs as quickly as I could. At the same time, however, I wanted to be sure that my guns were turbocharged and that my shields were high.

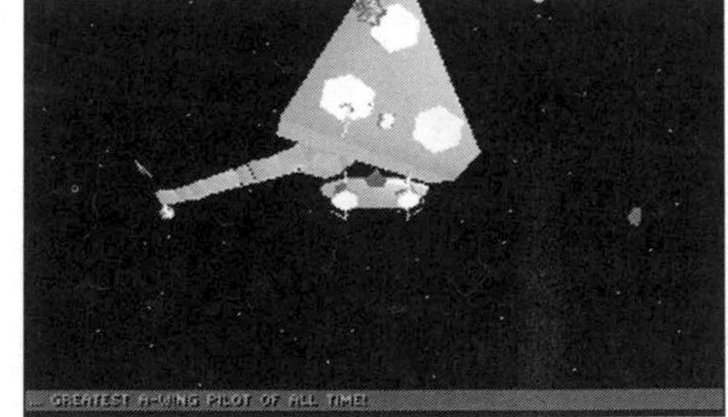

A Frigate ablaze.

All the B-wings had been destroyed, so it was up to me at this point. I kept strafing the *Reaper* until she finally blew up, and I took that as my cue to make an exit.

Debriefing (Win Conditions)

Container group Xi must be inspected. Transport group Renhoek and the cruiser *Stimsenj'kat* must survive.

Mission Note: Identifying the containers triggers the arrival of Gunboats Rho, which target the transports.

BONUS MISSION 2: DESTROY TROOP CONVOY

File Name: wotan2xw

Mission Briefing

Following the Battle of Hoth, the Empire became overconfident, but this mission proved that the Rebel Alliance was still a force to contend with. Fly an X-wing as part of a multi-ship task force assigned to take out a lightly-guarded troop convoy, which is composed of 40 freighters and 60 transports.

Farlander's After-Action Report

I was the flight leader in a four-ship group of X-wings. Our specific mission was to destroy as many transports as we could, and we would also assist B-wings, whose job was to take out freighters, and A-wings, who were to engage any starfighter escort. The convoy was huge, and we were charged with taking out at least half of it.

I looked at the Inflight Map when we entered the mission area, and noticed the B-wings directly ahead and the A-wings behind us. The closest ships in the convoy were about five kilometers away; freighters and Assault Gunboats. No transports were in the area at the moment, so I targeted *Tau 1* and ordered my wingmen to attack. The B-wings had already begun firing torpedoes.

The B-wings launching.

As soon as a six-ship group of transports entered the area, I ordered my wingmen to break off from the Gunboats and go after the closest TRN. I followed, and set my guns on quad-fire. We kept after the transports, which fell quickly under our combined attack.

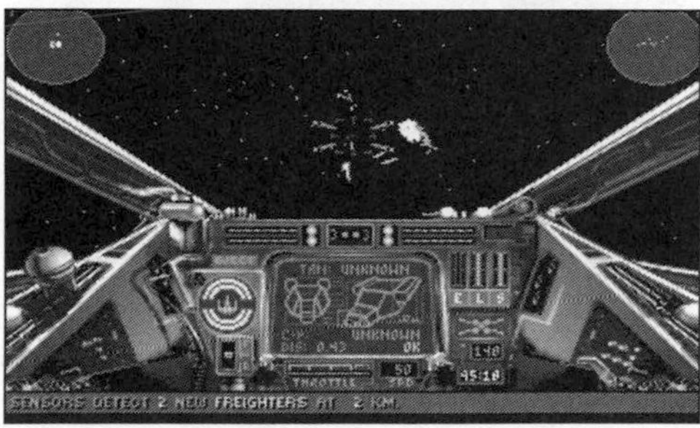

The wingmen converge on a transport.

When only one transport was left, I ordered my wingmen to attack it, and went back after the Gunboats the A-wings had missed.

A new group of TRNs followed the first, so we repeated our performance and took them out, again as quickly as possible.

The Gunboats were firing missiles at us, but we stuck with the transports as long as they kept coming. When there was one left, I again turned to the battle with the Gunboats.

Every time we destroyed the last of a flight group, more would appear. A second wave of GUN Tau arrived, and also a new transport group in addition to a new group of freighters. I was able to take out a couple of Gunboats before the next wave of TRNs showed up, then I was forced to break off and rejoin my wingmen.

I paid particular attention to any Imperial craft that were in a position to attack the B-wings, since they seemed to be drawing most of the heat.

The battle continued for nearly 20 minutes. Apparently we had destroyed the necessary percentage of the convoy, and our Mission Complete message appeared on the display. Time to go home.

Debriefing (Win Conditions)

Transport group Epsilon must be destroyed (there are 30 ships, arriving in five six-ship flight groups) as well as freighter group M-S (20 ships arriving in pairs).

Mission Note: The key to this mission is to take out the transports quickly, using your wingmen. After each wave of transports is down to one ship, assign that ship to your wingmen, and then go after the Gunboats until a new wave of TRNs arrive.

For die-hard dogfight fans, you can continue until you destroy the other half of the convoy. Save your six torpedoes for the Star Destroyer *Resolute*, which comes in a little later, so that you can take out its shield generators (with three torpedoes apiece). If you have any wingmen or B-wings left by that time, they'll help you take out the Star Destroyer. You have to dogfight its complement of starfighters, however. There are 201 enemy craft to destroy in this mission.

BONUS MISSION 3: ATTACK STAR DESTROYER

File Name: wotan3bw

Flight group and X-wings.

Mission Briefing

Fly in B-wing Red as part of a multi-ship task force assaulting the Star Destroyer *Kotiote*. During the attack, an Alliance freighter will arrive to raid several Imperial containers in the area. B-wing Red will attack the Star Destroyer's shield towers, while X-wing Gold will assist in the attack on the *Kotiote*, while A-wing Blue engages any starfighters escorts. Let no one escape aboard shuttle craft.

Farlander's After-Action Report

This mission group consisted of four X-wings, four A-wings, and four B-wings. I was the flight leader in the B-wing group, and our specific assignment was to take out the shield generator towers, rendering the huge ship defenseless.

Coming out of hyperspace, I checked the Inflight Map and found the Star Destroyer directly ahead, but almost 13 kilometers away. There were two groups of TIE fighters, one about 9 kilometers away and the other almost 15 kilometers away. On my way in, I went through a standard mission start-up, preparing for a head-on attack against the TIE fighters of Alpha Squadron.

I ordered my wingmen to attack a transport that was in the area as we flew in toward the Star Destroyer. I took out T/F *Alpha 1*, but didn't turn back to go after any other enemy starfighters. When T/F Delta came within range, I also took a shot at them. T/I Gamma joined the party, and I was able to take out *Gamma 3* before heading in to attack the Star Destroyer itself.

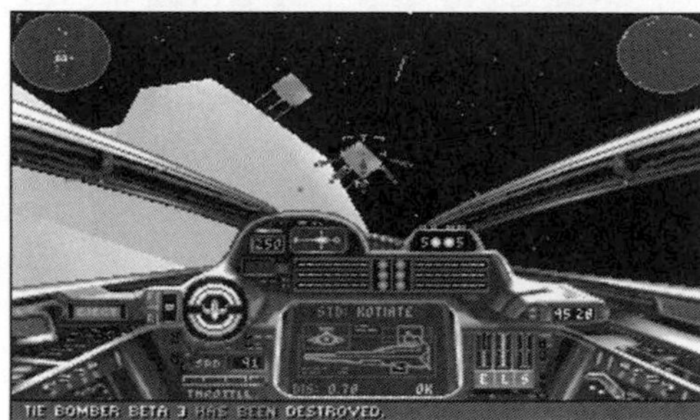

Targeting a tower.

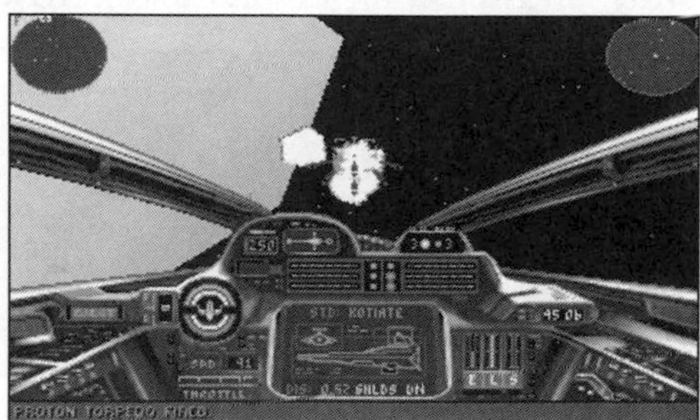

Firing torps again.

I switched to torpedoes in dual-fire mode, continually transferring laser energy to my shields. The other B-wings were already attacking the Star Destroyer. Meanwhile, TIE Interceptors were on my tail, and TIE Bombers were trying to get a missile lock on me. I shot the first two torpedoes at the nearest shield generator tower, and followed with two more for the second tower.

I switched to single-fire torps for my second pass, firing one torpedo into each tower and finishing the Star Destroyer's shields.

I switched to ion cannons immediately, and headed in to disable the Imperial ship. With the shields down, the ion cannons did their work quickly, and the Destroyer was helpless.

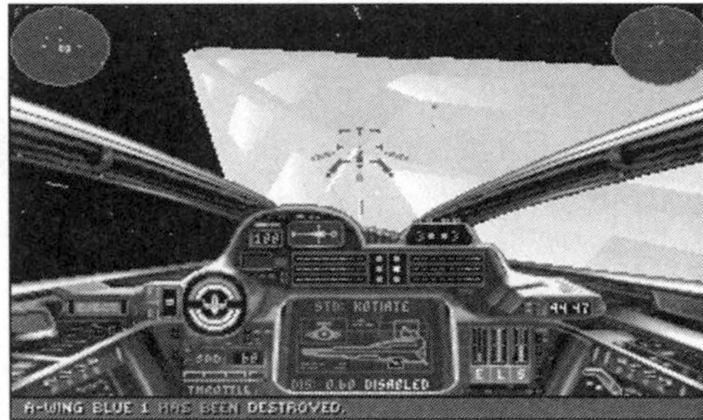

The Star Destroyer is disabled.

I checked the Inflight Map to see what else was out there. Twenty-three craft were in the area, including TIE fighters, Interceptors, and Bombers. Most of our forces were still alive. In fact, we had lost only one X-wing so far.

I began dogfighting, and one of the Bombers targeted me with a missile, which convinced me to pay particular attention to any T/Bs.

When an Imperial shuttle launched from the stricken Star Destroyer, I ordered my wingmen to go after it and went along with them. It was SHU *Lambda 1*, carrying officers. They were already abandoning ship, but it would do them no good. I had little time to gloat, however, as I was under heavy laser and missile fire from all sides.

My wingmen destroyed the shuttle, but then another launched, and we turned to pursue. While my wingmen hurried to intercept this new SHU, I decided to take care of T/B *Beta 1*, which was making my life miserable.

By the time I finished with *Beta 1*, the shuttle was almost five kilometers away, and I had to redirect all energy to my engines to catch up, rebalancing

Taking enemy fire while closing on the shuttle.

One less Star Destroyer in the Imperial fleet.

my shields to the rear because I was still getting plastered by missiles. My wingmen again reached the shuttle first, making short work of it, so I was able to reset my laser and shield systems, turn around, and go after my tormentors.

T/F *Alpha 3* turned out to be the closest target, so I went at him head-on—damaging him on the first pass and finished him on the next.

While looking for T/Bs, I noticed that an Imperial Frigate had arrived. Meanwhile, just as I was wondering about the fate of the Star Destroyer, the message came through that she had been destroyed.

The Frigate was launching TIE Advanced, and I ordered my wingmen to attack the FRG while I flew in for a head-on attack against T/A *Iota 1*. Meanwhile, his wingmen were trying to whittle down my rear shields, so I had to pay close attention to my ship's condition; a difficult task while dogfighting a much faster craft like the Advanced. It took awhile, but I finally got *Iota 1*.

Checking the Inflight Map, I saw that one of our freighters was docking with the containers, and all four A-wings were still in the action. X-W Gold and B-W Red were still active as well.

The X-wings and the B-wings were over by the Frigate, so I decided to join them and help take her out. I switched to torpedoes in dual-fire mode, and waited for a missile lock. The A-wings were engaging the T/As, so I was unmolested for a change, and my shields had a rare chance to fully recharge.

I fired all five of my remaining torpedoes at the Frigate. As they sped on their way, I got the Mission Complete message on my display.

I wasn't about to stop now, however, and set my cannons to single-fire in preparation for a standard loop attack on the Frigate *Bird of Prey*, strafing her hull with my lasers.

A torpedo's-eye view of a Frigate.

A few minutes later, the Frigate's shields were down, and I switched to ion cannons to quickly disable her. Now we could finish her off without much to worry about. With 80 minutes left on the clock, the Alliance FRT *Schwa* entered hyperspace.

Now I was free to dogfight the T/As, eliminating the last of the Imperial presence in the area. I knew that eliminating the TIE Advanced would cause a new wave to launch, since the Frigate could launch new waves of starfighters even though it was disabled. When I had had enough, I jumped for home.

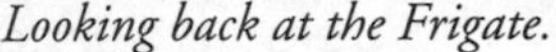

Looking back at the Frigate.

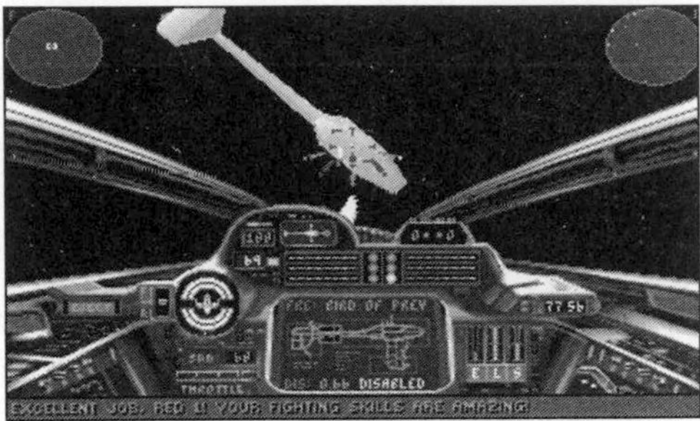

Cockpit view of disabled Frigate.

Debriefing (Win Conditions)

The Star Destroyer *Kotiote* and shuttle group Lambda must be destroyed.

Mission Note: For the die-hard dogfighter, leave the Frigate disabled and fight the TIE Advanced until there are no more waves. If you want to make it easier on yourself, destroy the Frigate as soon as she's disabled, and *then* clean up the rest of the Advanced fighters. You've got your Mission Complete, so you can go home at any time.

BONUS MISSION 4: PROTECT CONVOY

File Name: max101x

Mission Briefing

A Rebel convoy traversing the Mennaalii system dropped out of hyperspace to avoid an asteroid field, and was ambushed by a group of pirates. Fly in X-wing Red to intercept.

Farlander's After-Action Report

I was the flight leader of a three-ship group of X-wings. Since the attacking pirates flew some of the same craft the Alliance did, I knew that I would have to choose my targets carefully, using the CMD to identify which craft were friendly, and which were not. Pirate ships shown blue in the CMD readout.

As I entered the area, some Y-wings were already attacking a group of freighters. There was no way to stop the attack, but I headed at high speed toward the enemy.

When I arrived on the scene, FRT *Xroi 1* had been destroyed, and the other freighter's shields were down. I targeted the first of the Y-wings and

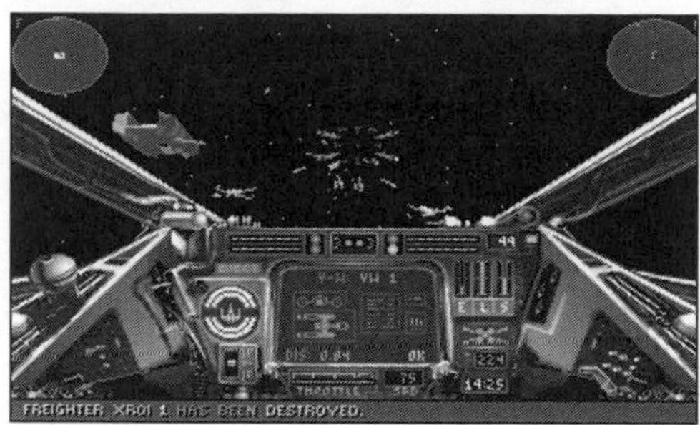

Engaging Y-wings as the mission begins.

ordered my wingmen to attack, while I took the next-closest one.

Y-wings could take some punishment, so we had to hammer on them for a while before getting any satisfaction. I took out mine, and then helped with the leader, as my wingmen were still trying to bring him down. That left only one pirate ship in this group, and I quickly finished him, as well. The superior speed of the X-wing, and the available quad-fire mode, makes Y-wings easy targets.

After I had destroyed these first three Y-wings, I went to the Inflight Map and surveyed the situation. Our Y-wings were going after an enemy Frigate, while enemy A-wings engaged them. I went after the nearest A-wing, also instructing my wingmen to attack.

The clock read about 18 minutes when four new X-wings appeared. They were enemy craft, so I aborted my wingmen's orders and sent them after the nearest of the new arrivals. I went after the second X-wing, switching to dual-fire torpedoes and setting my laser recharge rate to normal to pick up some speed.

I acquired a red lock, but didn't fire right away: I let him fly past me, and then came up behind him so that I could fire on a straight flight path. The two torpedoes hit, and that was one X-wing down. I picked up the next X-W and fired a pair right up his thrusters. I gave the same treatment to the fourth X-wing, leaving only the leader. As I headed toward him, my wingmen finished him off.

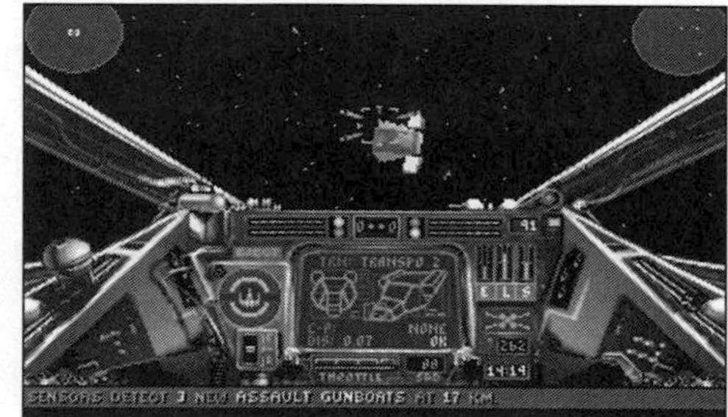

Shooting a transport.

As I cycled through the craft in the area, I noticed that only one enemy starfighter remained, an A-wing, but he was blown up as I looked on. Moments later, two more A-wings were launched. At about that time, a pair of transports appeared, dangerous chiefly because they carried torpedoes. Having shot my torpedoes already, I headed in to engage the transports with lasers, calling my wingmen in to attack one while I took on the other.

As I came in, I set my recharge rates to maximum so that I wouldn't overrun the TRNs, and then began firing on *Transpo 2*. After that, I went after the other transport, and helped my wingmen finish him off.

Now, from the opposite direction, three Gunboats from Mu Squadron arrived. I headed back toward the freighters. The Frigate had stopped launching new starfighters, so I decided that the Gunboats were the only significant threat for the moment.

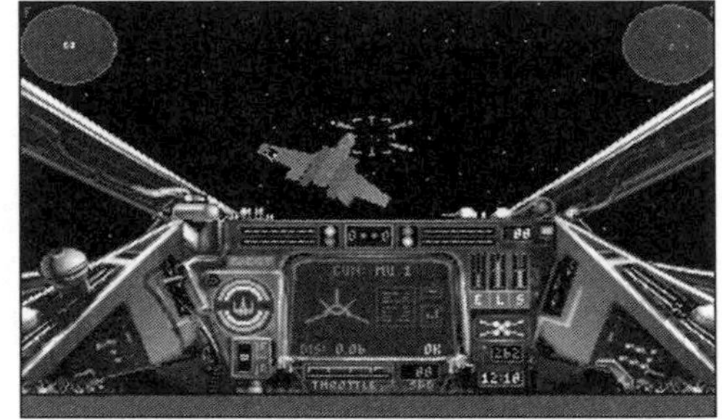

Dogfighting with GUN Mu 1.

The GUNs were already attacking the freighters and the corvette by the time I got within range, but fortunately, they weren't using missiles. When I closed on the battle, however, they reevaluated their tactics, and I was greeted with a missile that must have come from one of the Gunboats.

I told my wingmen to cover me, and made sure that my shields were fully charged. I tried to evade the projectile, but was unsuccessful. A moment later, I was frantically rebalancing and recharging my shields.

Just before I destroyed the third Gunboat, I got the message that the pirates' Frigate had been polished off. That would have been pretty good news, except that the next thing that happened, or so it seemed, was the arrival of an Imperial Star Destroyer.

There was still one A-wing left, but the Star Destroyer was the greater threat. Fortunately, the remaining freighter and the corvette jumped into hyperspace moments later, and the Mission Complete message flashed on my display. I didn't have to be told twice.

I knew that I could stay there and engage the Star Destroyer, and its complement of starfighters, but then I wasn't feeling foolhardy that day. I jumped into hyperspace and went back home.

Debriefing (Win Conditions)

All Rebel corvettes must survive.

Mission Note: Concentrate your attacks on X-wings, transports and Gunboats, in that order. The A-wings will attack you, while other ships target the corvettes. Also, the pirate's Frigate gets whittled down by the Rebel Y-wings. If you're going for maximum points, you might want to find a way to get the final blow on her with lasers, or with a torpedo, if you've managed to save any.

BONUS MISSION 5: ATTACK IMPERIAL STOCKYARD

File Name: max102b

Mission Briefing

Lead a hit-and-run B-wing attack on an Imperial Stockyard, consisting of several containers full of weapons.

Farlander's After-Action Report

I was the flight leader in a four-ship group of B-wings. Our mission was to destroy all the containers in the area—12 of them total.

At the beginning of the operation, I noticed some shuttles behind me, and took instant evasive maneuvers, redirecting all energy to my engines and hitting full throttle as I juked out of the way of any unfriendly fire. I found the nearest shuttle, and told my wingmen to attack. I found another shuttle nearby, and I went after him.

Three Imperial corvettes entered the area, presumably to protect the containers. As soon as the two shuttles were destroyed, I ordered my wingmen to attack one of the corvettes. I switched to torpedoes, and targeted another corvette, launching six torpedoes as soon as I had a red lock.

I was getting hit from behind, and after my torpedoes were launched, I turned and sought my attacker. It turned out that two more shuttles had taken the place of the first pair. Meanwhile, the corvettes had been able to launch some TIE Bombers.

I went after the nearest of the Bombers, T/B *Beta 2,* immediately, ignoring the shuttles for the moment and keeping my shields up. I linked my cannons to blast the T/Bs. After the first corvette was destroyed, I sent my wingmen after the third. The one I had shot was finished.

I helped my wingmen destroy the third CRV before resuming my Bomber hunting. I figured to get rid of the corvettes first, because they might launch more T/Bs after I had destroyed the first wave.

After I had destroyed T/B *Beta 2,* I went after *Beta 1.* My wingmen were already launching torpedoes on the containers, so I turned to engage the shuttles.

T/B Beta 1

After all the shuttles and Bombers were destroyed, I decided to clear the minefield that protected the containers. This would make it easier for my wingmen as they attacked the CONs.

With 13:30 on the clock, four new Gunboats jumped directly into the area with the containers. They were on us before we knew what happened; firing missiles before I could react. There was no time to waste, so I immediately targeted the closest GUN and ordered my wingmen to attack. I went after the next one I found.

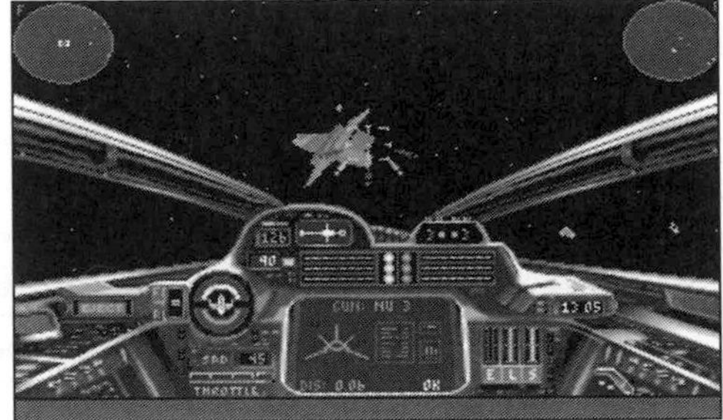
Dogfighting Gunboats.

I took two missile hits in short order, but I kept my shields up, and went in after the nearest Gunboat, *Nu 3*. After I finished off the first GUN, I went after *Nu 2*, shooting a couple of mines when the opportunity presented itself.

I knew that I could have taken out the Gunboats with my remaining torpedoes, but my cannons were doing the job nicely. Meanwhile, a couple of TIE Advanced had shown up, and were making things difficult.

Only three containers remained. I looked for my wingmen, but none were left. I still had six torps, and I decided to fire two at each container, hoping to finish them off and complete my mission. The T/As were blasting me with lasers, but my B-wing could take it.

At 5:15 on the clock, the last container went up in a ball of flame, and I got the Mission Complete message. The two T/As were still chasing after me, but I knew that I would have a great deal of trouble dogfighting them in a B-wing. It could be done, but not today: I jumped for home.

Debriefing (Win Conditions)

Container groups C558 and C442 must be destroyed.

Mission Note: The key in this mission is to do things in steps. First take out all the shuttles, then the corvettes, and then the Bombers. After this is done, have your wingmen attack the containers while you go after the mines. Engage the Gunboats when they appear, and then continue with the mission. You have to evade the A-wings, but you will probably be better off not trying to destroy them until your mission goals have been completed. Also, If you destroy the tug *Empleh*, an extra group of X-wings arrive to help you.

BONUS MISSION 6: PROTECT YOUR MOTHERSHIP

File Name: max103a

Mission Briefing

The Imperial Frigate *Blue Fox* is launching a Bomber attack on your mothership, the Alliance cruiser *Excelsior*. Two A-wings from Red will scramble to the cruiser's defense, followed by both X-wings and Y-wings once the craft are armed. More Imperial re-enforcements are on the way, so protect the cruiser until it can jump to safety; about 20 minutes.

Farlander's After-Action Report

I was the flight leader in a two-ship group of A-wings. At the beginning of the mission, I turned right and found the nearest Bomber, T/B *Alpha 6*, and ordered my wingman to attack. I got between the Bomber and the cruiser, and managed to intercept one of its torpedoes as it was launched, then I attacked using lasers.

At this point, I set my recharge rates to maximum. A pair of Gunboats were following the Bombers, and one of them fired a missile at me. I set laser and shield recharge rates to normal to gain speed, and waited for the missile to reach .3 kilometers. Then I went into a tight evasive turn, and even managed to dispose of a Bomber flying directly in my path with three quick laser blasts.

After the missile self-destructed, I found the nearest Gunboat and got rid of him, too.

Once I had destroyed both Gunboats, I went looking for more TIE Bombers, but there weren't any left near the cruiser. A new wave of T/B Beta was on its way, however, so I took my wingman after them. I switched to missiles and launched one at *Beta 1*, and then another at *Beta 2*.

Attacking Mu 1.

Beta 2 managed to evade, so I went after him with lasers, but a missile warning came through and I myself was soon dodging once again. After four loops, the missile was almost out of energy, so I went after the nearest Bomber.

I heard another missile warning, but I was able to destroy a couple more Bombers. Another Bomber group, Gamma, was after the cruiser, and I dispatched *Gamma 1* with a missile of my own. *Gamma 3* was hull-damaged, and I finished him off with a single laser shot.

More Bombers were coming in: First, a four-ship group called Delta, then another six-ship group designated Theta. The area was swarming with T/Bs. I fired missiles as quickly as I could get Bombers in my sights. Some of them were attacking me; others were going after the *Excelsior*.

Targeting T/B Theta with a missile.

I was wondered whether the situation could get any worse, so of course it did.

Three corvettes arrived, and angled towards the cruiser. I would have gone after the CRVs, but I was busy with Bombers. I noticed that flight groups Eta and Theta were the ones that were interested in me, although Theta seemed interested in both my ship and the cruiser. The others were after the cruiser exclusively.

One of the corvettes was destroyed by the *Excelsior*, while the others jumped into hyperspace after completing their attack run. I had destroyed most of the Bombers by this time, and went after the latest wave from the Frigate.

I had managed to use mostly lasers, so I still had six torpedoes left. I used my lasers to destroy two Bombers of Eta group, and, when no more were launched, I decided that that was probably the last of the starfighters the Frigate was carrying. Still, the Frigate itself was getting closer to the cruiser, and would soon be a direct threat.

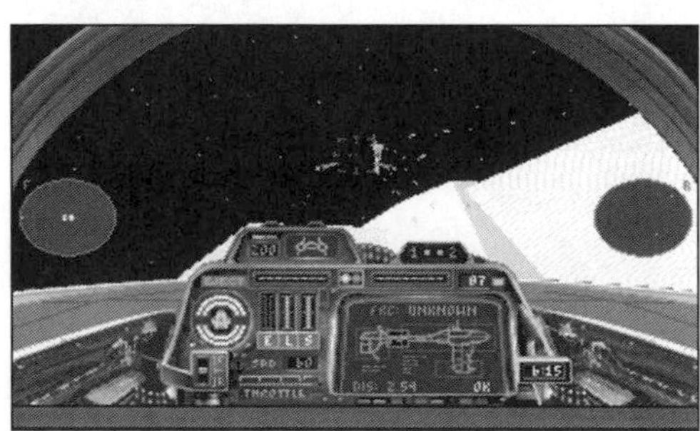

Cruiser and Frigate firing on each other.

Two TIE Interceptors were launched, and I called my wingmen to help out. I wasted a couple of missiles, but I still had four left.

At about 9:15 on the mission clock, the *Excelsior* launched a strike team against the Frigate—three Y-wings and two A-wings. Another wave of T/I Zeta launched, but was quickly destroyed.

The *Excelsior* had taken several hits, and I was afraid that the Frigate might have enough firepower to finish her off. I flew in close to the cruiser and prepared to attack the FRG; a move I also hoped would serve as a distraction.

I joined in the attack on the *Blue Fox*, and watched for hull damage, hoping to get the killing shot. At 5:10 on the clock, two TIE Advanced jumped into the area, but they were 15 kilometers away. I quickly put T/A *Iota 1* in memory at F5, so that I could find him easily later. I wanted to keep tabs on the T/As.

I introduce myself to the Frigate Blue Fox.

At 4:20 on the mission clock, the Frigate was finally destroyed, but the *Excelsior* had taken numerous hits as well, and her shields were down. The good news was that she was very near the jump point.

I transferred energy settings to normal to increase speed, and shot T/A *Iota 1* with a missile. Then I joined the remaining Rebel craft in going after *Iota 2*. When the clock read 0:30, CRS *Excelsior* jumped to safety. I stuck around to take out *Iota 2*, moments before the end of the simulation.

Debriefing (Win Conditions)

The cruiser *Excelsior* must survive.

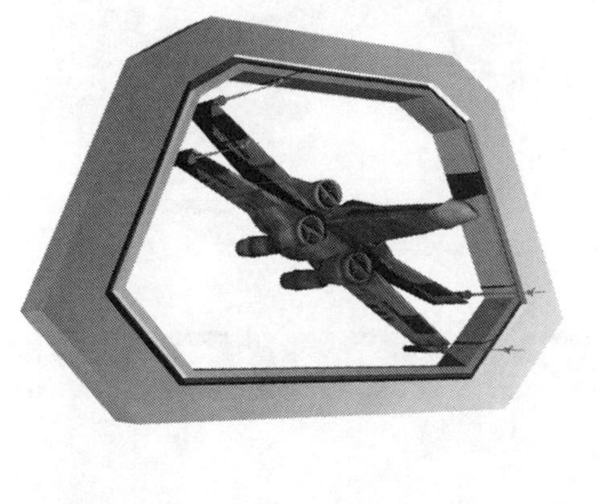

APPENDICES

APPENDIX A

Scoring and AI

Scoring in X-Wing

Points Awarded

Each laser/ion cannon hit 3
Each rocket/missile hit 100
Death Star buildings 20
Completing mission 1500
Destroying Death Star 7500

Craft destroyed (non-friendly)

Satellites/mines/probes 50
X-wing 600
Y-wing.....................................400
A-wing 800
TIE fighter 400
TIE Interceptor 600
TIE Bomber..............................600
TIE Advanced 1800
Assault Gunboat........................800

Transport 600
Shuttle 800
Tug 200
Container..................................800
Freighter.................................1200
Cruiser 6000
Frigate 4000
Corvette 1600
Star Destroyer 8000

Craft Captured

X-wing	3000	Shuttle	4000
Y-wing	2000	Tug	1000
A-wing	3200	Container	4000
TIE fighter	2000	Freighter	4800
TIE Interceptor	3000	Cruiser	30000
TIE Bomber	3000	Frigate	16000
TIE Advanced	9000	Corvette	6400
Assault Gunboat	4000	Star Destroyer	40000
Transport	3000		

Points Subtracted

Each laser/ion cannon fired 1*

* Refers to each individual cannon. If you fire in quad-fire-linked mode, you lose four points every time you squeeze the trigger.

Each rocket/missile fired............. 50

Losing your spacecraft 5000

Achieving Rank

As you play through the tours of duty, you gradually increase your score (assuming that you don't get killed or captured and have to revive your pilot).

Here's the list of accumulated scores required to rise up the ranks in the Rebel Alliance.

Officer	20,000
Lieutenant	50,000
Captain	100,000
Commander	250,000
General	500,000

The Kalidor Crescent

The Kalidor Crescent is given to pilots in recognition of exceptional performance in a single mission. Here are the single-mission scores required to win the medal and its upgrades.

Main Medal 10,000
Bronze Cluster 12,000
Silver Talons.........................14,000
Silver Scimitar......................16,000
Golden Wings.......................18,000
Diamond Eyes......................20,000

Enemy AI Characteristics

Here are the main criteria used to differentiate enemy pilots from each other. No hard statistics are available to list the differences between each type of pilot—for example, a Novice to a Top Ace. Better enemies have the following characteristics, however:

- Faster reaction times in all situations; decisions made more frequently
- Quicker, more intelligent target selection
- Better firing accuracy with laser and ion cannons
- Better missile and torpedo lock-on; consequently better missile accuracy
- More efficient management of weapons; more shots fired when the odds of a hit are better
- Better ability to stay on the tail of a target
- Faster response to attacks
- More radical defensive maneuvers to evade attacks
- Better formation flying, smoother maneuvers, and better exits from and entrance into ships (refers to both the launching speed of fighter craft and docking and separation abilities)
- Better avoidance of larger obstacles; in particular, large spacecraft

APPENDIX B

Using the Camera and the Viewing Room

During our training, we were taught to use the holo films of our missions to improve our performance and to learn better tactics. I always liked to watch my missions again from different angles. Our holo projection system lets us record in 3-D; when we play back, we can view the action from just about any angle or position.

This appendix presents a few tips for using the Viewing Room.

Getting to the Viewing Room

You can enter the Viewing Room in two ways. Aboard the *Independence,* select the lower right doorway to enter the Viewing Room. During a mission, you can begin recording by pressing [C] and then jump to the replay by pressing [V].

Main Controls

Your main holo film controls are Play, Advance, Rewind, Load, Enter Sim, and Exit.

- Press Play [P] to start and stop the recording. To see a few frames at a time, press Play repeatedly.
- Press Advance [A] to advance rapidly through a holo film clip without any sound. Press again to stop advancing.
- Press Rewind [R] to return to the beginning of the clip at any time.
- Press Load [L] to obtain a list of available clips.
- Press Enter Sim [S] to switch from viewing to full simulation, in which you then pilot your starfighter. When the simulated mission ends, you are back in the Viewing Room. You don't receive any mission scores or credit for missions completed in this way, however. Also, you can't record new clips when you enter a simulation in this way.
- Press Exit [E] to leave the Viewing Room.

View Modes

X-Wing has three view modes — Follow, Free, and Track.

- In Follow mode, the camera follows whatever object you select. Cycle through the objects to follow by pressing [C] until the one you want is listed in the Camera Pos. box. Press [Shift]-[C] to cycle backward.
- In Free mode, the camera remains in a fixed position. You can use the controller to zoom and pan to watch the action from a single position. Note that you can toggle between Follow and Free modes by pressing [F].
- In Track [T] mode, the camera angle moves to keep a selected object in view. Select an object by pressing [O] to cycle through all the objects in the holo film. Or press [Shift]-[O] to cycle backward.

If both Follow and Track modes are activated, the camera views the tracked object from the position of the object being followed.

Using the View Modes

After you understand the way the view modes work, you can use them to your advantage. Combinations of modes reveal different angles on the action. Try everything.

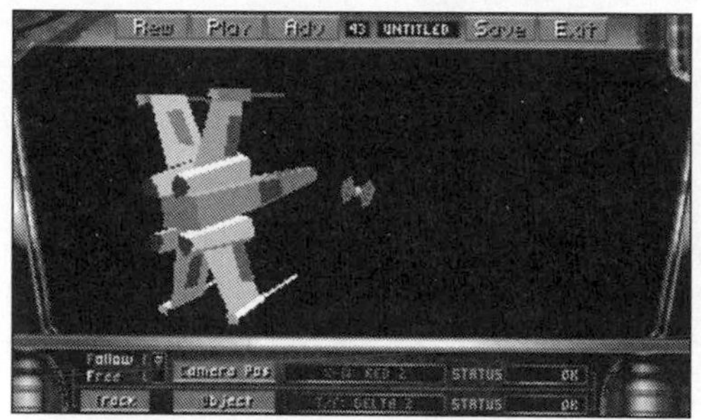
Following your ship, tracking the enemy.

Following the enemy, tracking your ship.

Free Mode

Free mode gives you a great deal of control over what you see. Use the controller direction controls and buttons to activate Pan and Zoom. Using the Pan and Zoom controls, you can position your view as far away or as close to the action as you want. Sometimes you want to get in tight to watch your enemies maneuver and learn their tendencies. Other times, you want to pull back to see more of the melee. It may turn out that you missed a particularly good opportunity or that you were hit by an unseen enemy. Using Free mode, you should be able to see everything in as much detail as you want.

If you lose sight of your starfighter while you're viewing in Free mode, press [F] quickly to enter Follow mode, and then press [F] again to return to Free mode.

Follow and Track

Use Follow mode in combination with object Tracking to obtain revealing views of the action. Here are some suggestions:

- Follow your fighter and select your current target as the Object. Press [O] until you find the craft you want to track. The target always stays in view.

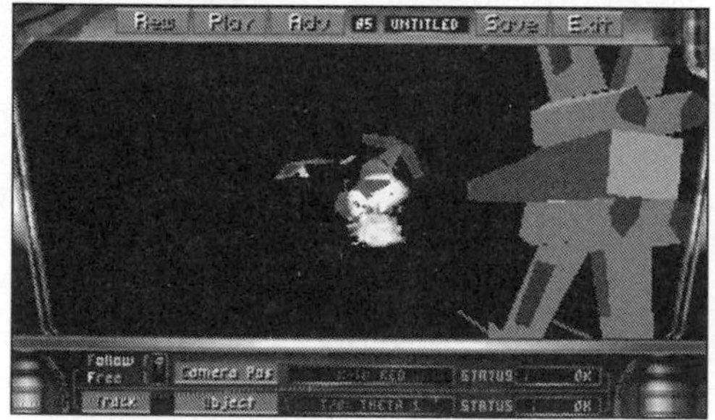
Catching a dramatic moment . . .

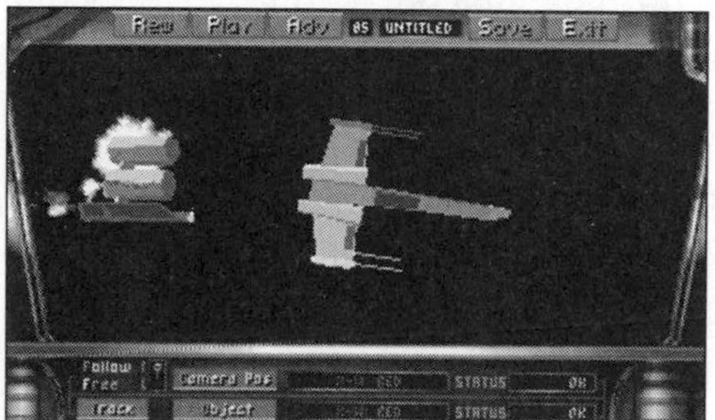
. . . from different positions.

- Follow your current target and Track your own starfighter. This dramatic view shows your craft maneuvering and attacking the target, from the target's perspective. This view is useful not only to see how accurate your shooting is (because you can see the weapon blasts as they either hit or miss the target), but also to see behind your own fighter if you are being pursued by other enemies. Suppose that you are targeting a TIE Bomber and several TIE Interceptors are on your tail. You can see how effective your evasive maneuvers are. Or watch yourself in a Wotan Weave to see whether you are performing it correctly.

It's a good idea to watch an engagement several times. First, watch in Follow mode to relive your mission from the original perspective — yours. You might also log the mission by notating the camera counter number (to the right of the Adv button) that shows when particular events occur — you get a kill, for instance, or you get hit, or even if someone else gets a kill. Press the Play [P] button to pause the display whenever you want.

Next, watch again in Free mode to get the overall picture. Finally, dissect the mission by using combinations of Free, Follow, and Track to understand in more detail what happens around you.

Remember that you can use the Advance [A] button to move quickly through parts of the holo film, although you do not hear any sound cues while the holo film is advancing. Watch the counter number to find a particular event in the clip.

When new friendly or enemy ships jump into the engagement, you might want to press Play [P] to pause the clip and then switch the Camera Pos. [C] to that new object. Now switch to Free [F] and use Pan and Zoom to observe how this new ship may have affected the situation and where it is relative to your current position. Finally, return to the view you were in earlier, and resume the clip (or resume in Free mode).

Taking a Snapshot

Some pilots like to use the camera in place of the map screen. Here's how: During a mission, if you want to see the relative positions of friendly and enemy craft, you can switch to the map screen [M] at any time. But the map is a two-dimensional image. A better way to get a picture of what's going on is to press [C] to start the camera and then press [V] to view the clip. Doing this quickly is similar to taking a snapshot of the action in 3-D space! You can use this method in the middle of a mission.

Study the Holo Film

If you're having problems with one or more missions, *study the film*, *study the film*, and *study the film*!

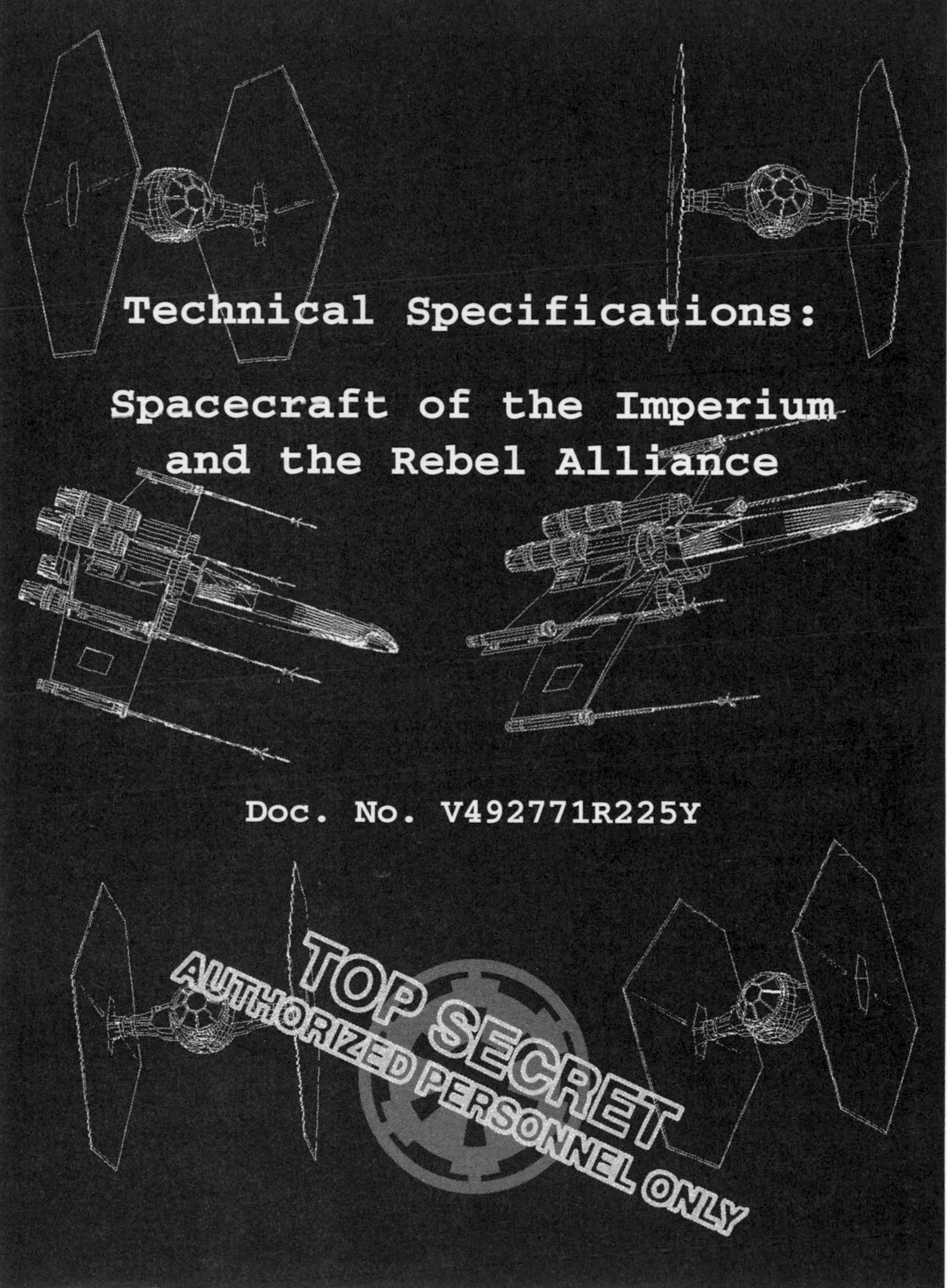
Technical Specifications:
Spacecraft of the Imperium and the Rebel Alliance
Doc. No. V492771R225Y
TOP SECRET
AUTHORIZED PERSONNEL ONLY

Doc. No. V492771R225Y

Lord Darth Vader
Imperial Headquarters

Preliminary report (in progress) on the military vehicles of the Imperium and the Rebel Alliance.

To Lord Vader:

This report is still preliminary. It will take several months more to complete. You requested an update, so we are sending it to you now. The files are pretty mixed, but we've put all the Rebel craft at the beginning, the Imperial craft in the middle, and some miscellaneous vessels are mentioned at the end.

We trust you will understand that much of the data we have gathered is incomplete and we cannot include it until we have verified it. Also, our work would be more productive if certain Imperial Navy officers would allow us access to their records and files. To date, they have not. We have requested this information on numerous occasions, so it does no good to repeat the request.

Regarding the Death Star project. Should we expect to receive technical specifications of this new weapon in the near future? Or is it to be left out of this document?

We humbly regret the incompleteness of this document and ask your lordship's indulgence in giving us more time.

Captain Mordaph Clafdatha
Lieutenant Jord Kraas

Starfighters of the Alliance

As the former senatorial malcontents and dissidents continue to sway the weak-minded to their side, the puny forces of the Rebellion have been able to attract some supporters who should know better. Not counting the alien scum of Mon Calamari who are reportedly refitting their considerable starfleet to aid the Alliance, there are several key firms who at one time worked legitimately with the Empire. Among them are the traitors at several important starfighter design facilities. The most notorious of these are the Rebel sympathizers at Incom Corporation who stole the X-wing prototypes and handed them over to the Alliance.

Given their shortage of supplies and skilled workers, we had previously doubted that the Rebel trash could, in fact, produce any viable starfighters, but they have far exceeded our expectations. There are certainly several squadrons of X-wings in operation, and more are being built at secret facilities not yet known to our sources. In addition to the X-wing, we have obtained preliminary information regarding two other Alliance starfighters—the Y-wing, and the A-wing.

Of course, the Y-wing is no secret. Before the hated X-wings began to show up, the Y-wing was the basic Rebel starfighter. In fact, it may be that the dogs at Koensayr had something to do with the defection of the Incom turncoats. Whatever the truth may be, Y-wings have been turned out in large numbers, and most of the pre-Rebellion Y-wings have somehow turned up in Alliance hands.

The A-wing is something new, and our information about it is sketchy. We have heard reports from our TIE pilots about a very fast spacecraft that swooped in on them, took some quick shots, and flew away before they could pursue. Many of them swear (before being reprimanded) that these new craft were faster than the TIE Interceptor. More on these reports later.

The only information we can rely on is that the A-wing is a new design. Everything else is conjecture. One unconfirmed rumor has it that the A-wing uses the powerful Novaldex J-77 "Event Horizon" engines. Other evidence suggests it has a new sensor jamming array. We continue to investigate this mysterious new starfighter.

X-WING

The X-wing fighter is the most versatile and well-balanced of the Rebel fighters. Its combination of speed, maneuverability, and firepower make it an ideal attack craft for dogfighting TIE fighters or for fast-paced torpedo runs against larger targets. Many of our pilots have complained about the emergence of the X-wing and the traitorous defection of the senior design team at Incom who now oversee the production of these rebel craft.

It is not known how the Alliance rabble have been able to scrape together the materiel necessary to produce these sophisticated spacecraft, particularly the rare alloys and advanced control systems integral to their construction. Many of our TIE pilots joke that the X-wings will surely rattle themselves apart without needing to be shot at, but this, regrettably, seems to be mere battlefield humor and is without confirmation in the field. In fact Imperial losses to the X-wing have mounted as that craft has become more numerous.

One significant advantage of the X-wing is its ability to travel through hyperspace. With an R2 droid unit mounted behind the pilot, the X-wing is able to make jumps into Imperial space, carry out its mission, and jump back out without fear of being followed by our TIE fighters, which lack hyperspace capabilities.

In our favor, the newest of the TIE fighters is more than a match for the X-wing and our craft generally outnumber the rebels when they meet. We only lack highly trained pilots. Many of our TIE pilots are ill-trained and it is these pilots who most frequently fail when confronted by rebel X-wings.

Imperial Technical Starship Report

Name/Model#	T-65C A2 X-wing
Designer/Manufacturer:	Incom
Combat Designation:	Space Superiority Fighter
Crew:	1 pilot plus 1 Astromech Droid
Power System:	Novaldex O4-Z cryogenic power cells and ionization reactor
Propulsion System:	Four Incom 4j.4 fusial thrust engines (rated at 300 KTU)
Speed Rating:	100 MGLT
Flight Control System:	Torplex Rq8.Y flight control avionics package
Maneuverability Rating:	75 DPF
Navigation:	Astromech Droid, usually R2 unit
Hyperdrive:	Incom GBk-585 motivator drive unit
Sensor Systems:	Fabritech ANS-5d unit with a long range Phased Tachyon Detection Array model# PA-9r and one short range Primary Threat Analysis Grid model# PG-7u
Targeting Computer:	Fabritech ANq 3.6 tracking computer and IN-344-B "Sightline" holographic imaging system
Weapons:	Four Taim & Bak IX4 Laser Cannons (single fire or fire-linked) Two Krupx MG7 Proton Torpedo Launchers (3 torpedoes each)
Shields/Armor:	Forward/Rear Projecting Chempat Shields (rated at 50 SBD) Titanium Alloy Hull (rated at 20 RU)
Special Design Features:	S Foil Wings, adjustable for atmospheric flight

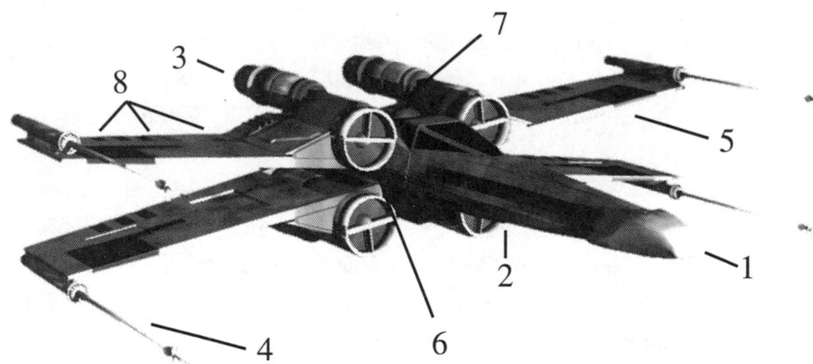

1. Sensor Systems
2. Proton Torpedo Launchers
3. Fusial Thrust Engine Assembly
4. Laser Cannon
5. S Foil Wing
6. Shield Projector
7. R2 Unit
8. Thrustor Control Jets (trailing edge of wing)

Y-WING

The Rebel Y-wing starfighter is a rugged, versatile spacecraft. Although it lacks the speed and maneuverability of more modern fighters, it is nothing to trifle with. Its combination of weapons—including both laser and ion cannons as well as proton torpedoes—can deliver a deadly attack on small and medium craft, especially when the Y-wings attack in formation. And what it lacks in speed and maneuverability, it makes up for in toughness. Its shields are quite effective, and its pilots are adept at focusing shield strength where necessary. After the shields are breached, however, the Y-wing is easily crippled if it's hit in the engine spars.

Imperial spies have identified two types of Y-wing starfighters. One, designated the BTL-S3, is a standard two-seat attack fighter designed for a variety of missions. The other, the BTL-A4, seems to be a single-seat model. Imperial military analysts suspect that the A4 is equipped with extensive hyperspace capability. The BTL-S3 is rarely seen anymore, and it is suspected that the Rebels have begun to favor the A4.

Pilots report that the A4 model seems to have somewhat reduced shields, but the hull is reinforced. In combat, the A4's ion cannons seem to fire in a fixed position only. We know that the Y-wings' ion cannons are used to disable our freighters and even some light military ships and, furthermore, that the Rebels are in the habit of stealing these vehicles and their cargo to supply their hopeless, ragtag resistance.

Pilots still report encountering more Y-wings than any other Rebel starfighter, although X-wings are gradually becoming more common. Despite their strong shields, Y-wings are no match for our TIE fighters, especially when our TIEs are attacking in large numbers. Our new TIE Interceptors should be able to carve up Y-wings with ease.

The only disadvantage we suffer is the lack of hyperspace capability in our starfighters. When the Y-wing can 'space in, launch a raid, and then 'space out again before encountering any starfighter resistance, it can be very effective. Recently, as more X-wings seem to be available, the Rebels have taken to sending these more effective craft to provide close cover support for the Y-wings.

Imperial Technical Starship Report

Name/Model#	BTL-A4 Y-wing Starfighter
Designer/Manufacturer:	Koensayr
Combat Designation:	Long Range Fighter/Bomber
Crew:	1 pilot plus 1 Astromech Droid
Power Systems:	Thiodyne O3-R cryogenic power cells and ionization reactor
Propulsion System:	Two Koensayr R200 ion fission engines (rated at 250 KTU)
Speed Rating:	80 MGLT
Flight Control System:	Subpro NH-7 flight control avionics package
Maneuverability Rating:	50 DPF
Navigation:	Astromech Droid, usually R2 unit
Hyperdrive:	Koensayr R300-H motivator drive unit
Sensor Systems:	Fabritech ANs-5d unit with one long range Phased Tachyon Detection Array model# PA-9r and one short range Primary Threat Analysis Grid model# PG-7u
Targeting Computer:	Fabritech ANc-2.7 tracking computer and SI 5g7 "Quickscan" vector imaging system
Weapons:	Two Taim & Bak KX5 Laser Cannons (single fire or fire-linked) Two ArMek SW-4 Ion Cannons (single fire or fire-linked) Two Arakyd Flex Tube Proton Torpedo Launchers (4 torpedoes each)
Shields/Armor:	Forward/Rear Projecting Chempat Shields (rated at 75 SBD) Titanium reinforced Alusteel® Alloy Hull (rated at 40 RU)

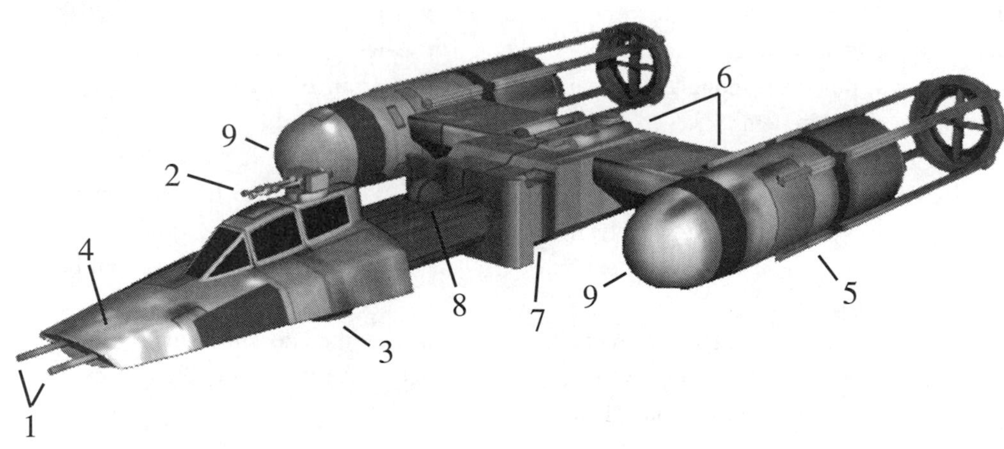

1. Laser Cannons
2. Ion Cannons
3. Proton Torpedo Launcher
4. Computer Targeting System
5. Ion Fission Engines
6. Thrustor Control Jets
7. Thiodyne Power System
8. R2 Unit
9. Sensor System

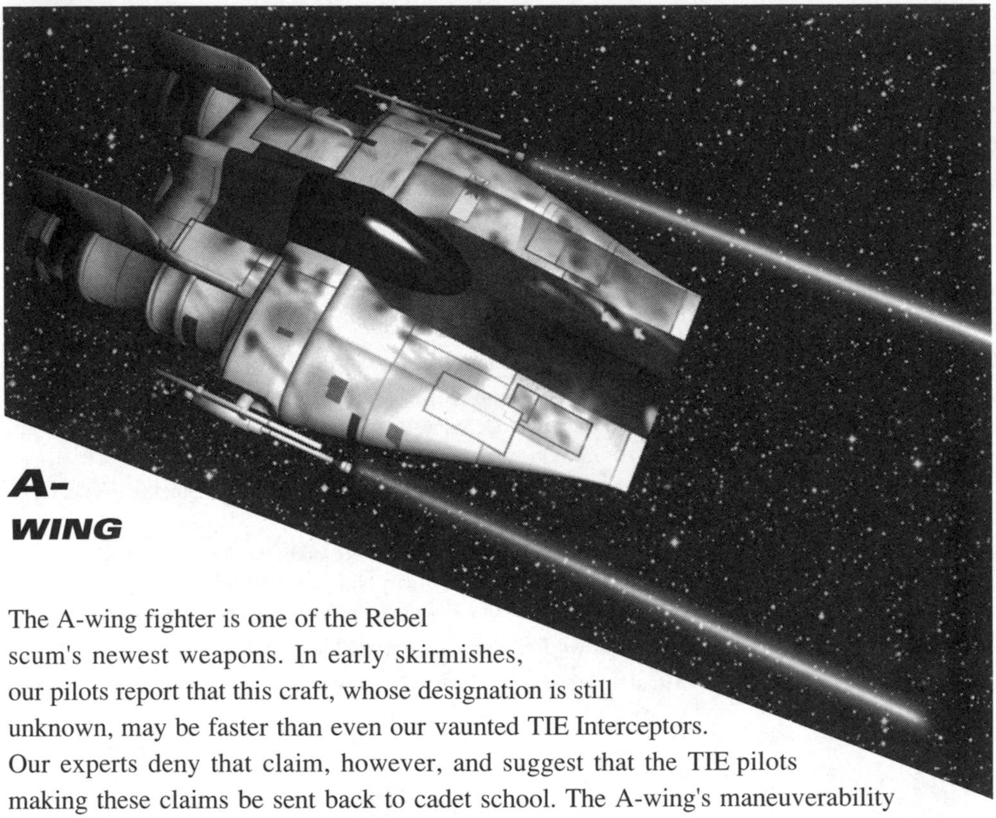

A-WING

The A-wing fighter is one of the Rebel scum's newest weapons. In early skirmishes, our pilots report that this craft, whose designation is still unknown, may be faster than even our vaunted TIE Interceptors. Our experts deny that claim, however, and suggest that the TIE pilots making these claims be sent back to cadet school. The A-wing's maneuverability is very good, however, though it appears to carry only a pair of laser cannons and no auxiliary weapons systems.

The A-wing appears to have a strong sensor array. None of our ships has been able to surprise one. We have noticed on two occasions that A-wings seemed to cease operation suddenly. Unfortunately, overzealous TIE pilots blasted the crippled spacecraft into rubble without thinking once of salvaging them intact. To date, we have not be able to get our hands on one of these fighters.

One pilot reports that the A-wing laser cannons seemed to shoot at odd angles, indicating a maneuverable firing system. He also stated that the A-wing fired backward, though we doubt the veracity of that claim.

Imperial Technical Starship Report

Name/Model#	RZ-1 A-wing Starfighter
Designer/Manufacturer:	Dodonna/Blissex
Combat Designation:	Long Range Fighter/Interceptor
Crew:	1 pilot
Power System:	MPS BPr-99 power convertor and fusion reactor
Propulsion Engines:	Twin Novaldex J-77 "Event Horizon" engines (rated at 400 KTU)*
Speed Rating:	120 MGLT*
Flight Control System:	Torplex Rq9.Z advanced flight control avionics package
Maneuverability Rating:	100 DPF*
Navigation:	Microaxial LpL-449 computer system
Hyperdrive:	Incom GBk-785 motivator drive unit
Sensor Systems:	Fabritech ANs-7e unit with one Phased Tachyon Detection Array model# PA-9r and one short range Primary Threat Analysis Grid model# PG-7u
Targeting Computer:	Fabritech ANq 3.6 tracking computer and IN-344-B "Sightline" holographic imaging system
Weapons:	Two Borstel RG9 Laser Cannons (single fire or fire-linked) Two Dymek HM-6 Concussion Missile Launchers (6 missiles each)
Shields/Armor:	Forward/Rear Projecting Sirplex Z-9 Shields (rated at 50 SBD) Titanium alloy hull (rated at 15 RU)

** This information is highly suspect. Other information is best guess based on remote telemetry, pilot debriefings, and incomplete field operative reports.*

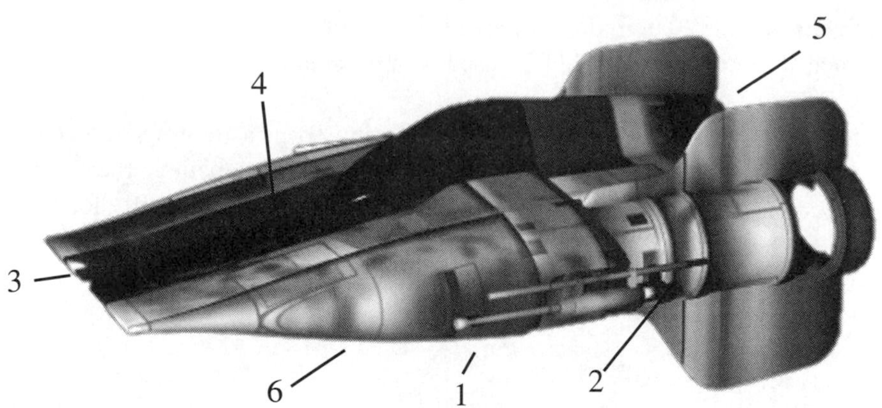

1. Laser Cannon
2. Novaldex Engine
3. Sensor System (?)
4. Fabritech Targeting Computer
5. Thrustor Control Jets
6. Concussion Missile Launcher (ventral mounting)

B-WING

What we know about the B-wing starfighter is that it was designed to be a heavy, mobile assault vehicle. It remains in the starfighter class, but is heavily armed—so much so, that it could conceiveably be used to attack and destroy a Frigate or other medium-sized capital ship.

The B-wing is designed with "wings" projecting from a rotating hub. The hub stays in a basic orientation and the wings rotate around it. We believe the wings can be set in one of four positions, at 90 degree increments. We are currently looking for weaknesses in this unusual fighter. Our engineers believe that the rotating hub may be subject to jamming, but the fighter is well shielded, so it will take a lot of damage before any attack is effective.

Name/Model#	B-wing
Designer/Manufacturer:	Slayn & Korpil
Combat Designation:	Heavy assault starfighter
Crew:	1 pilot
Power System:	Vinop O2 K cryogenic power cells and ionization reactor
Propulsion Engines:	Four Slayn & Korpil JZ-5 fusial thrust engines (rated at 290 KTU)
Speed Rating:	90 MGLT
Flight Control System:	Narmox HG.6w flight control avionics package
Maneuverability Rating:	65 DPF
Navigation:	Microaxial LpM-549 computer system
Hyperdrive:	Slayn & Korpil HYd-997 motivator drive unit
Sensor Systems:	Fabritech ANv-9q unit with one Phased Tachyon Detection Array model# PH-5s and one short range Primary Threat Analysis Grid model# PK-8f
Targeting Computer:	Fabritech ANq 3.6 tracking computer and IN-344-B "Sightline" holographic imaging system
Weapons:	Three Gyrhil R-9X Laser Cannons (single fire or fire-linked) Three ArMek SW-7a Ion Cannons (single fire or fire-linked) Two Krupx MG9 Proton Torpedo Launchers (6 torpedoes each)
Shields/Armor:	Forward/Rear Projecting Sirplex Zr-41 Shields (rated at 125 SBD) Titanium alloy hull (rated at 60 RU)
Special Design Features:	S Foil wings, adjustable for atmospheric flight

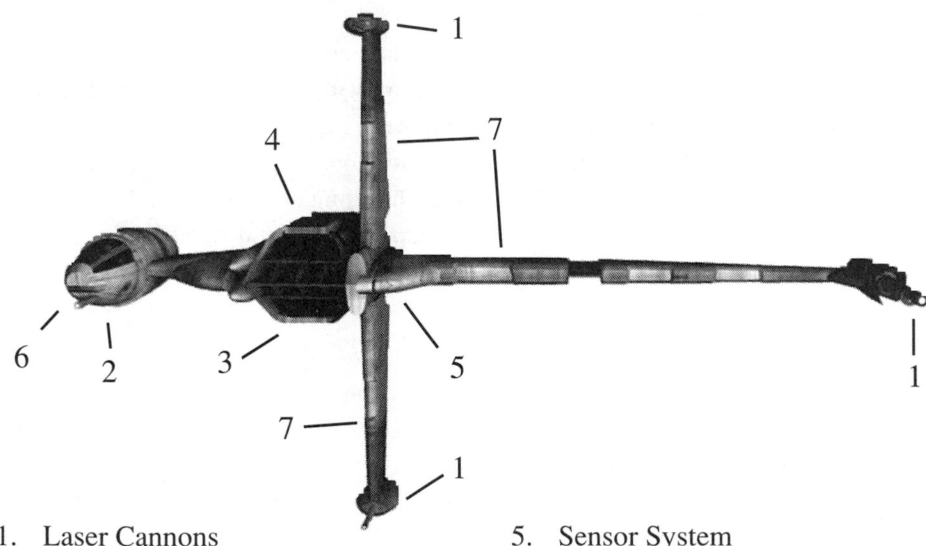

1. Laser Cannons
2. Ion Cannons
3. Proton Torpedo Launcher
4. Engine
5. Sensor System
6. Computer Targeting System
7. S Foil Wing

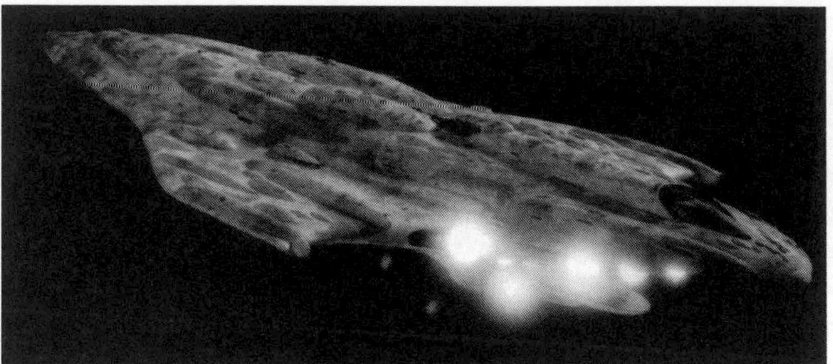

Mon Calamari Cruiser

Those vile-smelling creatures of that drenched planet Mon Calamari have turned their eccentric talents to the other side. How they can build effective starships when they appear to have no plans or specifications is beyond the scope of this document to answer. However, it remains true that they have refitted many of their decadent luxury vehicles to the purposes of the enemy.

Their largest vehicle, designated the MC80 Star Cruiser, is an organically shaped monstrosity, something like a pickle to our observers. Unfortunately the laughter stops when the MC80 opens fire with its 48 turbolaser batteries and 20 ion cannons. This is a spacecraft that can actually challenge a Star Destroyer! Not that it would defeat our mighty craft, but it could do significant damage.

Mon Calamari vehicles are difficult to defeat. They are made with many redundant systems, so they do not cripple easily. They can also carry with them a large crew of soldiers and serve as a base for several squadrons of starfighters. Finally, they are crewed by the bizarre combination of Calamarians and Quarren, whom our Imperial Navy experts must reluctantly acknowledge as superior spacefarers. Their handling of the ships of their fleet has added significantly to the Rebels' cause. We recommend the total annihilation of Mon Calamari as soon as operations permit such an endeavor.

Name/Model#	MC80a
Designer/Manufacturer:	Mon Calamari
Combat Designation:	Capital Starship
Length:	1200 meters
Crew:	5,402 (668 officers, 4734 enlisted)
Weapons:	48 Taim & Bak XV9 Turbolasers (computer assisted targeting) 20 ArMek SW-7 Ion Batteries Six Phylon-Q7 Tractor Beam Projectors
Starfighter Squadrons:	2 X-wing, 3 Y-wing, 1 A-wing

NEBULON B ESCORT FRIGATE

Although the Nebulon B still sees service as an Imperial convoy escort craft, reports have been reaching military HQ regarding its increasing use with the Rebel dogs. It is not clear where the rabble are obtaining such powerful ships, but the reports are too numerous to doubt. We have, therefore, included the Nebulon B among the Rebel ships, even though it is still technically one of ours.

The addition of the Nebulon B frigate to the side of the enemy represents a disturbing trend. This is a powerful ship. Certainly not a Star Destroyer, but still a capital ship of immense capability. In the service of the Empire, it holds a complement of two squadrons of TIE fighters (24 in all). With its powerful turbolasers and other weapons and shields, this is a formidable escort vehicle that has made the enemy think twice about attacking our convoys.

However, in enemy hands, this represents a dangerous opponent, as there are few ships outside of the Star Destroyers and the older Victory class destroyers, that out-gun the Nebulon B. With a squadron or two of X-wing fighters, this can become the platform for dangerous Rebel missions. We recommend that all efforts be taken to search out and destroy any Nebulon B frigates that have found their way into enemy hands, and further, that stringent means be undertaken to tighten security and to prevent more of these ships from being used against us.

Name/Model#	EF76-B
Designer/Manufacturer:	KDY
Combat Designation:	Escort Starship
Length:	300 meters
Crew:	920 (77 officers, 843 enlisted)
Weapons:	12 Taim & Bak XI 7 Turbolasers (computer assisted targeting) 12 Borstel RH8 Laser Cannons Two Phylon-Q7 Tractor Beam Projectors
Starfighter Squadrons:	One X-wing or A-wing plus one Y-wing

Corellian Corvette (Blockade Runner)

The Corellian Engineering Corporation builds multi-purpose ships of all kinds. While most shipyards are building specialized spacecraft, Corellians still produce models that cover a wide range of purposes. The Corellian Corvette is a good example of such versatility. This mid-range vessel can function equally well as a troop transport, light escort, cargo or passenger carrier. Although the Corvette may be unable to compete with more specialized vehicles, it is to be found throughout the galaxy.

Many older Corellian Corvettes find their way into the hands of smugglers and other criminals, and not a few of them have been enlisted by the Rebel traitors. Because the Corellians like very fast sublight ships with quick turnaround into hyperspace, these vehicles can prove troublesome to many of our Imperial picket lines and patrol ships.

Name/Model#	CR90 Blockade Runner
Designer/Manufacturer:	Corellian Engineering Corporation
Combat Designation:	Multi-purpose starship and transport vessel
Length:	150 meters
Crew:	46 (8 officers, 38 enlisted)
Weapons:	Six Taim & Bak H9 Dual Turbolasers

Imperial Vessels

TIE Fighters

The Twin Ion Engine (TIE) fighter is the primary starfighter of the Empire. There are several models of TIE starfighter currently in service throughout the Imperium. No single starfighter is as well represented throughout the galaxy, and our TIE fighters perform well against all opposition.

All TIE fighters are manufactured by Sienar Fleet Systems (SFS), formerly known as Republic Sienar Systems. SFS has produced TIE fighters in enormous quantities, though their output has recently fallen off as resources are diverted to top secret projects outside the scope of this document.

Propulsion

Propulsion systems in all TIE fighters are the same, using twin ion engines. Using microparticle accelerators, ionized gasses are excited to near lightspeed. When released through the adjustable rear vents of the TIE fighter, the resultant thrust produces a fast-moving, highly maneuverable craft. Extremely efficient mass-to-energy conversion and the addition of the distinctive solar panels allow the TIE fighter to carry limited fuel supplies. Since TIE fighters do not have hyperspace capability, they rarely venture far from their mother craft. Hyperdrives would affect the performance of the TIE fighter as well as cost the Imperial treasury a considerable sum due to the vast numbers of TIE fighters in service.

Maneuverability

Ion streams can be directed in almost any direction, making the TIE fighter highly maneuverable. Once a pilot has mastered the craft, he can perform complex rolls and spins as well as slip-and-drift maneuvers that can lose all but the most determined of pursuers. Some maneuvers place great strain on the spacecraft, however, and it is not advisable to come to a 180-degree, full-thrust stop as severe damage may result.

Weapons Systems

Standard armament on the TIE fighter consists of twin laser cannons mounted in the spherical shell of the spacecraft. Originally these cannons were powered by the ion engines, but during battle, the starfighter's performance would suffer, so separate power batteries were later installed, making the lasers even more powerful without substantially reducing the performance of the TIE fighter. Some models of the TIE fighter have different armament configurations.

Shields

One dangerous weakness of the TIE series of fighters is its lack of deflector shields. When going up against the shielded Rebel craft such as the X-wing and Y-wing fighters, an individual TIE fighter can be at a disadvantage. Although we make up for this problem with sheer numbers and superior tactics, our armored solar panels and main hull rarely provide much protection against a direct laser hit, let alone a proton torpedo.

TIE Starfighter Models

There are several TIE fighters in service. Some are only specialized variants of the most common model, the TIE Starfighter. Others are redesigned and rebuilt for specific purposes. For instance, the TIE/rc is a lightly-armed version used for reconnaissance missions. The TIE/fc is used as a long-range fire control and target acquisition craft to help direct more accurate long-range bombardment missions. The TIE/gt is a retrofitted TIE Starfighter used for carrying missiles and bombs, but is largely giving way to the new TIE Bomber which features a secondary hull used for carrying armaments. Finally, the TIE Interceptor is arguably the fastest fighter in galactic space, though some have suggested that the Rebel A-wing is as fast or faster.

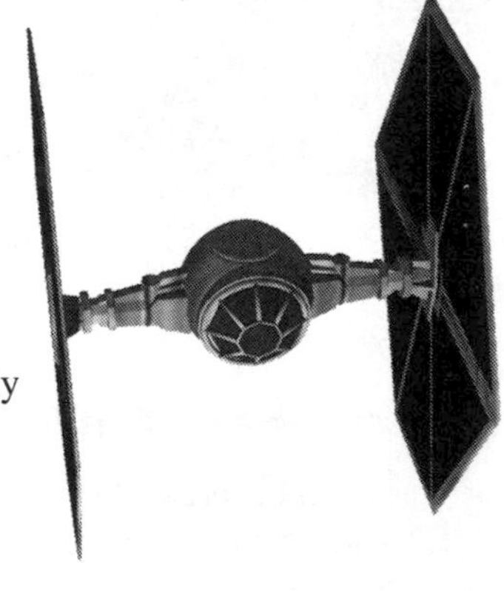

TIE Starfighter

The backbone of the Imperial starfighter fleet is the TIE Starfighter. This versatile craft performs all operations including fleet escort, reconnaissance, space patrol, planetary guard, and hunter/destroyer. Pilots of the TIE Starfighter enjoy a speed and maneuverability advantage over almost any spacecraft currently in operation, although recent advances by the Rebels have brought them close, or even superior to, the TIE.

The TIE Starfighter matches well with the Rebel X-wing and shows some superiority to the Y-wing. However, Rebel starfighters support more weaponry and have deflector shields, making them dangerous foes in one-on-one combat. Fortunately, our TIEs generally enjoy superiority of numbers, making even the most talented and stubborn of Rebel pilots run away and jump to hyperspace to escape.

Name/Model#	TIE Starfighter
Designer/Manufacturer:	Sienar Fleet Systems
Combat Designation:	Space Superiority Fighter
Crew:	1 pilot
Power System:	SFS I-a2b solar ionization reactor
Propulsion System:	SFS P-s4 Twin ion engines (rated at 150 KTU)
Speed Rating:	100 MGLT
Flight Control System:	SFS F-s3.2 flight avionics system
Maneuverability Rating:	100 DPF
Navigation:	SFS N-s6 Navcon computer system
Hyperdrive:	none
Weapons:	Two SFS L-s1 Laser Cannons (single or fire-linked)
Shields/Armor:	No shields; Titanium hull with Quadanium® Steel armored Solar Panels (rated 15 RU)

TIE Interceptor

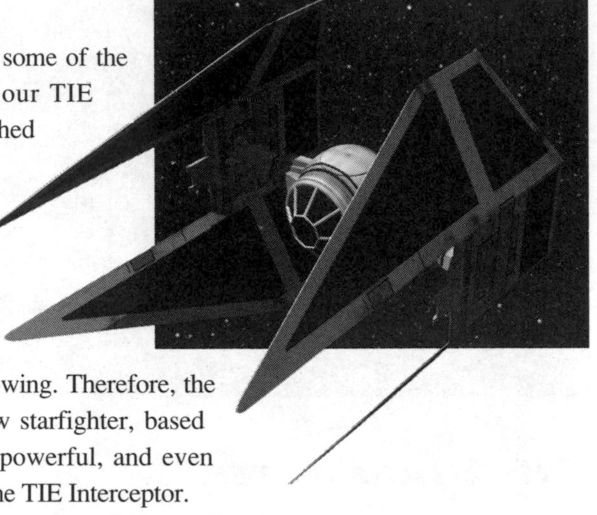

There has been concern on the part of some of the leaders of our Imperial forces that our TIE Starfighters were no longer distinguished as the most advanced starfighter in the galaxy. The rabble of the Alliance have managed, with the help of the Incom traitors and other sympathizers, to create a highly versatile and dangerous series of starfighters, led most notably by the X-wing. Therefore, the Imperial leaders have conceived a new starfighter, based on the TIE designs, but faster, more powerful, and even more maneuverable. This new craft is the TIE Interceptor.

The TIE Interceptor is based on the custom bent-wing TIE fighter designed by Lord Darth Vader. Its twin ion engines have been enlarged with added power coming from the greater surface area of the solar panels. At this time, the TIE Interceptor is the fastest starfighter in existence. Some claim that the Rebel A-wing is faster, but no evidence exists to confirm or deny that claim.

Visibility problems with the oversized solar panels are solved by the dagger shape of the front panels, and firepower has been increased by the addition of four laser cannons mounted in the fronts of the solar panels, at the points of the "daggers." The twin chin-mounted cannons have been removed from the fuselage. To improve accuracy, the targeting software for the weapons guidance systems has also been updated.

Name/Model#	TIE Interceptor
Designer/Manufacturer:	Sienar Fleet Systems
Combat Designation:	Space Superiority Fighter
Crew:	1 pilot
Power System:	SFS I-s3a solar ionization reactor
Propulsion System:	SFS P-s5.6 Twin ion engines (rated at 175 KTU)
Speed Rating:	110 MGLT
Flight Control System:	SFS F-s4 flight avionics system
Maneuverability Rating:	125 DPF
Navigation:	SFS N-s6 Navcon computer system
Hyperdrive:	none
Weapons:	Four SFS L-s9.3 Laser Cannons (single or fire-linked)
Shields/Armor:	No shields; Titanium hull with Quadanium® Steel armored Solar Panels (rated 20 RU)

TIE Bomber

The TIE Bomber is one of the newest of the TIE series. Featuring a double-hull, this fighter/bomber can carry a lethal load of proton torpedoes, guided missiles, orbital mines, or free-falling thermal detonators.

The TIE Bomber excels at surgical placement of ordinance, picking out small targets on planetary surfaces or on enemy ships. In contrast with full-scale naval bombardment which leaves only rubble behind, the TIE Bomber can selectively destroy military targets while leaving commercial or military assets untouched. With its small size and high speed, the TIE Bomber can often slip past defense systems set up to watch for larger craft.

Name/Model#	TIE Bomber
Designer/Manufacturer:	Sienar Fleet Systems
Combat Designation:	Space Bomber
Crew:	1 pilot
Power System:	SFS I-a2b solar ionization reactor
Propulsion System:	SFS P-s4 Twin ion engines (rated at 125 KTU)
Speed Rating:	80 MGLT
Flight Control System:	SFS F-s3.2 flight avionics system
Maneuverability Rating:	75 DPF
Navigation:	SFS N-s4 Navcon computer system
Hyperdrive:	none
Weapons:	Two SFS L-s1 Laser Cannons (single or fire-linked) Two SFS M-s3 Concussion Missile Launchers (4 missiles each) Two SFS T-s5 Proton Torpedo Launchers (2 torpedoes each)
Shields/Armor:	No shields; Titanium hull with Quadanium® Steel armored Solar Panels (rated 50 RU)

TIE Advanced

The most deadly fighter we have produced to date, the TIE Advanced is based on a design from Lord Vader. Equipped with fast-recharging shields and an extended Twin Ion Engine capacity, this new ship should out-speed the Rebel X-wing and will provide safety for its pilot within the shield array.

TIE Advanced are still in limited production, but they should see service in greater numbers in the months ahead.

Name/Model#	TIE/Ad
Designer/Manufacturer:	Sienar Fleet Systems
Combat Designation:	Space Superiority Fighter/Interceptor
Crew:	1 pilot
Power System:	SFS I-s3a solar ionization reactor
Propulsion System:	SFS P-sx7.4 Twin ion engines (rated at 230 KTU)
Speed Rating:	145 MGLT
Flight Control System:	SFS F-s5x flight avionics system
Maneuverability Rating:	150 DPF
Navigation:	SFS N-s6 Navcon computer system
Hyperdrive:	none
Weapons:	Two SFS L-s9.3 Laser Cannons (single or fire-linked)
Shields/Armor:	Forward/Rear projecting Novaldex Shields (rated at 100 SBD) Titanium hull with Quadanium® Steel armored Solar Panels (rated 20 RU)

Imperial Shuttle

The Imperial Shuttle was designed for transporting very important personnel from one base to another. It can be used in both vacuum and atmospheric conditions and can carry as many as 14 passengers, although it often carries only one or two in more luxurious conditions.

The Imperial Shuttle has some hyperspace capability and carries strong shields. Some models are heavily armed, while others may be almost stripped of armament and shields.

Name/Model#	*Lamda* Class T-4a "Imperial Shuttle"
Designer/Manufacturer:	Cygnus Spaceworks
Combat Designation:	Armed Government Transport Shuttle
Length:	20 meters
Crew:	4
Passengers:	1-14
Weapons:	10 Taim & Bak KX5 Laser Cannons (8 fwd and 2 aft)

Stormtrooper Transport

The Stormtrooper Transport is an assault vehicle designed to take over enemy ships. With only five crewmembers, it can ferry up to 30 stormtroopers, or 10 elite Imperial Zero-G stormtroopers—highly trained assault and boarding units of the Imperial Navy.

Stormtrooper Transports feature very strong shielding, particularly in the front of the craft. It also carries a variety of weapons. Using a universal docking mechanism, it can attach itself to most ships, or it can bore its own hole in the hulls of most enemy vessels.

Name/Model#	Delta Class Dx-9
Designer/Manufacturer:	Telgorn Corporation
Combat Designation:	Assault Fighter/Gunboat
Length:	25 meters
Crew:	5
Weapons:	Eight Taim & Bak KT4 Laser Cannons Four AirMek SW-2 Ion Cannons Two Krupx MG7 Proton Torpedo Launchers (5 torpedoes each)
Shields/Armor:	Forward/Rear Projecting Novaldex Shields (rated at 125 SBD) Quadanium® Steel armored titanium hull (rated at 80 RU)

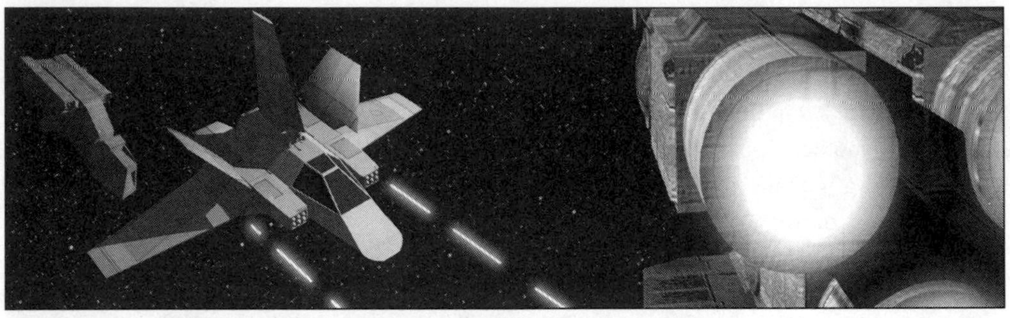

Assault Gunboat

The Imperial Navy's newest spacecraft is the Cygnus Alpha Class Xg-1. After developing the beautiful Imperial Shuttle, Cygnus was awarded the contract to develop an assault vehicle, and the Xg-1 is the result. Due to its unique five-wing design, the Xg-1 is commonly known as the Star Wing. Equally at home in vacuum or atmosphere, the unique wing design can adjust to conditions, thanks in part to a revolutionary computer system from Miradyne.

The Star Wing is designed for offensive strike missions against enemy convoys and fleet craft. Its fire power and heavy shielding make it ideal for escort roles as well, and as an assault vehicle in combination with the Stormtrooper Transport, it is unmatched.

Name/Model#	Alpha Class Xg-1 Star Wing
Designer/Manufacturer:	Cygnus Spaceworks
Combat Designation:	Assault Fighter/Gunboat
Crew:	1 pilot
Power System:	Iotek 9j ion power cells and ionization reactor
Propulsion Engines:	Cygnus 4K7 Dual Line ion engines (rated at 300 KTU)
Speed Rating:	90 MGLT
Flight Control System:	Miradyne RCS-6 flight avionics system
Maneuverability Rating:	90 DPF
Navigation:	SFS N-s8.6 Navcon computer system
Weapons:	Two Taim & Bak KX5 Laser Cannons (single fire or fire-linked) Two Borstel NK-3 Ion Cannons (single fire or fire-linked) Two SFS M-s-3 Concussion Missile Launchers (8 missiles each)
Shields/Armor:	Forward/Rear Projecting Novaldex Shields (rated at 100 SBD) Quadanium® Steel armored titanium hull (rated at 50 RU)

Interdictor Cruiser

Our esteemed engineers have come up with yet anothert way to dedeat the Rebel Alliance fools who boast of the hyperspace capabilities of their starfighters. With the development of the gravity well projector, we were just single step away from cre-ating a new weapon in the fight against the rabble.

Using the gravity well technology, Sienar Fleet Systems had created the Interdictor Cruiser whose primary purpose is to set up an artificial gravity well in battle zones and high security areas. The gravity well serves two purposes.

First, it appears as a large gravitational body to any hyperdrive system. This prevents a ship from jumping into the vicinity of the gravity well. The Interdictor Cruiser is designed to be placed near engagement areas or areas of potential conflict. It will stay outside the battle zones and set up the gravity well as required by circumstances.

Second, any ships already in hyperspace that pass within the gravity well's field will be drawn immediately into realspace. Thus, the Interdictor Cruiser can help set up ambush zones by locating in known hyperspace corridors, forcing Rebel craft to reenter realspace where our battle fleets can destroy them.

Name/Model#	Interdictor Im-418
Designer/Manufacturer:	Sienar Fleet Systems
Combat Designation:	Heavy Cruiser/Immobilizer
Length:	600 meters
Crew:	2,807 (427 officers, 2,380 enlisted)
Weapons:	20 Taim & Bak GX-7 Laser Cannons (computer assisted firing) Four SFS G7-x Gravity Well Projectors
Starfighter Squadrons:	1 TIE Fighter squadron 1 TIE Interceptor squadron
Other Onboard Craft:	1 Lambda Class Imperial Shuttle 3 Stormtrooper Transports

Imperial Class Star Destroyer

Imperial Class Star Destroyer

We look back to the various budgetary arguments with a certain sense of amusement. We remember when the bureaucrats of the former government fought so hard against the Imperial Class project. Their arguments about costs and feasibility studies and the like ring hollow in the face of the reality of a single Star Destroyer.

The Star Destroyer is an awesome achievement. Capable of reducing whole civilizations to ruin, it carries a full complement of AT-AT and AT-ST walkers along with assault craft, a full Storm Trooper division, and many squadrons of TIE fighters. Its 60 Turbolaser and 60 Ion Cannon batteries make it the most formidable weapons platform currently operating in galactic space.

Imperial Class Star Destroyers are expensive to produce, but their value in maintaining order and control throughout the inhabited worlds is immense. Their planetary assault capabilities are sufficient to subdue most underdeveloped worlds without additional support. Larger, more advanced civilizations may require several Star Destroyers working together. And in open space, nothing can truly challenge the Star Destroyer, though the ugly Calamarian monstrosity, the MC80, can cause trouble for a Star Destroyer, and two such ships could perhaps defeat it.

Name/Model#	Imperial-1 Class
Designer/Manufacturer:	KDY
Combat Designation:	Capital Starship
Length:	1600 meters
Crew:	37,085 (4,520 officers; 32,565 enlisted)
Power System:	SFS I-a2b solar ionization reactor
Weapons:	60 Taim & Bak XX-9 Heavy Turbolasers (computer assisted targeting) 60 Borstel NK-7 Ion Cannons (computer assisted targeting) 10 Phylon Q7 Tractor Beam Projectors
Starfighter Squadrons:	Three TIE Starfighter squadrons Two TIE Interceptor squadrons One TIE Bomber squadron
Planetary Assault Troops:	Full Standard Stormtrooper division 12 Landing Barges 20 AT-AT Walkers 30 AT-ST Walkers
Other Onboard Craft:	Eight *Lambda*-Class Imperial Shuttles 15 Stormtrooper Transports 5 Assault Gunboats

Bulk Freighter

Bulk Freighters are the mainstay of galactic commerce. These huge spacecraft contain powerful, but slow, hyperspace and sublight engines (although many captains have refitted their engines for greater speed). A cargo vehicle of this size and capacity is simply not expected to outclass other vehicles, particularly not those of the Imperial Navy.

Bulk Freighters are tough, reliable spacecraft. Though they generally lack luxury and a lot of state-of-the-art components and weapons, they serve their purpose well, and often travel in convoys with more military ships to protect their cargo.

Space Tug

Space Tugs are small utility vehicles whose sole task is to move Space Containers from one location to another. Though small, Space Tugs contain very powerful (but slow) engines and tractor beams. We have found no military uses for Space Tugs, but they are obviously critical to the continued movement of materiel throughout the Empire.

Space Container

Space Containers are the basic modules of galactic commerce. These huge containers are packed with important goods and then loaded onto Bulk Freighters for transport to other systems. Space Containers are simple boxes, durable and rugged, and have no engines or other significant systems, other than those designed for special storage conditions.

APPENDIX D

Mission Statistics Tables

How to read Flight Groups:

#1 1 X-W Red 1 [1]	**Start:** Always, 0, No	**Waves:** 0	**Mother:** No	**Win:** 0
	Orders: Attack All	**Form:** Vic	**AI:** Novice	**Val:** 5

#1 1 X-W Red 1 [1]
First is the Flight Group #. This number affects the order in which targets appear on the CMD. An asterisk indicates that the player is in this group. Next is the number of the craft, the type of craft, and the name. A bracketed number indicates the player's position in the group.

Start: Always, 0, No
The starting conditions are circumstance, time delay, and the number of the FG the circumstance depends on (if any). Some flight groups may start in one of two or three positions. These positions, selected at random, are sometimes used to create easy, medium, or hard versions of the same mission.

Waves: 0
Next is the number of waves. Waves are created when the last ship of the current wave is destroyed, returns to its mother ship, or hyperspaces away.

Win Condition Variables

0: Ignore this flight group
1: All craft destroyed
2: All craft survived
3: All craft captured
4: All craft docked
5: Special craft destroyed
6: Special craft survived
7: Special craft captured
8: Special craft docked
9: At least 50 percent of craft destroyed
10: At least 50 percent of craft survived
11: At least 50 percent of craft captured
12: At least 50 percent of craft docked
13: All craft identified
14: Special craft identified
15: At least 50 percent of craft identified
16: Flight group created

- "Special" craft is one ship in the flight group. A second number indicates position within the flight group. (for example, 8-4 indicates the fourth ship in this flight group must be docked with).
- When a flight group appears in waves, the win condition applies across all waves.
- "Survival" usually means the craft has to make it into hyperspace.

Mother: 0

Next is the mother ship's FG# (0 means none).

Win: 0

Win is the win condition variable (see accompanying chart).

Orders: Attack All

Orders are the flight group's activity. For orders followed by a P # and S #, (Primary and Secondary), these numbers refer to priority FGs. Note that the specific orders are meaningless if the player's FG has only one craft (his).

Form: Vic

Form is the FG's formation.

AI: Novice

AI is the skill level of the nonplayer craft. These range from Novice to Officer to Veteran to Ace to Top Ace.

Val: 5

Val times 10 is the percentage of top speed the FG starts at. For example, 4 means that the FG is set at 40 percent of its top speed. (Zero is 100 percent.)

In the case of FGs with escort orders, Val is the number that sets the escort's position relative to the FG being escorted. The escorts match speed with the FG they are escorting.

In the case of FGs with boarding orders, Val is the number of minutes the boarding takes.

Starship Orders

Stationary: Flight group does nothing.
Go Home: Flight group goes to hyperspace jump point or to mother ship. If unable to jump (no hyperdrive) and/or mother ship not present, flight group circles last waypoint.
Circle & Ignore: Flight group circles through waypoints and ignores enemy actions.
Fly Once & Ignore: Flight group flies once through waypoints and ignores enemy actions. Then hyperspaces away if it's able.
Circle & Evade: Flight group circles through waypoints and evades enemy attacks.
Fly Once & Evade: Flight group flies once through waypoints and evades enemy attacks. Then hyperspaces away if it's able.
Close Escort: Flight group maintains escort position for designated flight group (or groups) until enemy craft come within 1 km. Enemy craft approaching within 1 km are intercepted.
Loose Escort: Flight group maintains escort position for designated flight group (or groups) until enemy craft come within 4 km. Enemy craft approaching within 4 km are intercepted.
Attack Escorters: Attack flight groups with "escort" orders.
Attack Pri & Sec: Attack designated primary and secondary flight groups.
Rendezvous: Fly to waypoint and wait to be boarded.
Disabled: Flight group does nothing and is disabled.
Board & Deliver: Flight group docks with designated flight group to deliver cargo or passengers.
Board & Take: Flight group docks with designated flight group to take cargo or passengers.
Board & Exchange: Flight group docks with designated flight group to exchange cargo or passengers.
Board & Capture: Flight group docks with designated flight group and captures ships.
Board & Destroy: Flight group docks with designated flight group to destroy ships.
Disable Pri & Sec: Disable designated primary and secondary flight groups.
Disable All: Disable any enemy craft.
Attack Transports: Attack transports.
Attack Freighters: Attack freighters. Corvettes are considered freighters for this purpose.
Attack Starships: Attack Starships.
Attack Sat & Mines: Attack satellites and mines.
Disable Freighters: Disable freighters. Corvettes are considered freighters for this purpose.
Disable Starships: Disable Starships.
Starship Sit & Fire: Starship remains stationary while firing (if targets are available).
Starship Fly Once: Starship flies once through waypoints while firing (if targets are available).
Starship Circle: Starship circles through waypoints while firing (if targets are available).
Starship Wait Return: Starship remains stationary while waiting for all ships (and waves) of all flight groups that have this ship designated as the mother ship.
Starship Wait Create: Starship remains stationary until all ships (and waves) of all designated flight groups have been created.
Starship Wait Board: Starship remains stationary until all ships (and waves) of all designated flight groups have boarded this ship.

Ships

X-W = X-wing
Y-W = Y-wing
A-W = A-wing
T/F = TIE Fighter
T/I = TIE Interceptor
T/B = TIE Bomber
T/A = TIE Advanced (Vader-type)
GUN = Assault Gunboat
SHU = shuttle
TRN = transport
CON = container
FRT = freighter
CRV = corvette
FRG = Nebulon B Frigate
CRS = Calamarian Cruiser
STD = Star Destroyer

Note that certain objects, (satellites, mines, asteroids, and planets) are not really flight groups, but are listed here for completeness.

Historical Missions

X-wing Mission 1: Dev's Sidestep

Flight groups:

#1	1 X-W Red 1 [1]	**Start:** Always, 0, No **Orders:** Attack All	**Waves:** 0 **Form:** Vic	**Mother:** 0 **AI:** Novice	**Win:** 0 **Val:** 5
#2	1 T/F Alpha	**Start:** Always, 0, No **Orders:** Stationary	**Waves:** 0 **Form:** Echelon Right	**Mother:** 0 **AI:**Novice	**Win:** 1 **Val:** 0
#3	1 T/F Beta	**Start:** Always, 0, No **Orders:** Stationary	**Waves:** 0 **Form:** Echelon Left	**Mother:** 0 **AI:** Novice	**Win:** 1 **Val:** 0
#4	3 T/F Gamma	**Start:** Always, 0, No **Orders:** Stationary	**Waves:** 0 **Form:** Echelon Right	**Mother:** 0 **AI:** Novice	**Win:** 1 **Val:** 0
#5	3 T/I Delta	**Start:** Always, 0, No **Orders:** Circle & Ignore	**Waves:** 0 **Form:** Line Astern	**Mother:** 0 **AI:** Novice	**Win:** 1 **Val:** 6
#6	2 T/F Zeta	**Start:** Destroy, 0, 8 **Orders:** Attack P 1	**Waves:** 0 **Form:** Vic	**Mother:** 0 **AI:** Novice	**Win:** 1 **Val:** 6
#7	3 TRN Omega	**Start:** Always, 0, No **Orders:** Stationary	**Waves:** 0 **Form:** Diamond	**Mother:** 0 **AI:** Novice	**Win:** 1 **Val:** 0
#8	2 CON Phi	**Start:** Always, 0, No **Orders:** Stationary	**Waves:** 0 **Form:** Vic	**Mother:** 0 **AI:** Novice	**Win:** 1 **Val:** 0
#9	1 FRT Rouh	**Start:** Always, 0, No **Orders:** Stationary	**Waves:** 0 **Form:** Vic	**Mother:** 0 **AI:** Novice	**Win:** 1 **Val:** 0

#10 2 T/B Theta	**Start:** Always, 0, No **Orders:** Circle & Evade	**Waves:** 0 **Form:** Vic	**Mother:** 0 **AI:** Novice	**Win:** 0 **Val:** 7
#11 2 T/I Eta	**Start:** Always, 0, No **Orders:** Circle & Ignore	**Waves:** 0 **Form:** Line Astern	**Mother:** 0 **AI:** Novice	**Win:** 1 **Val:** 3
#12 2 T/B Kappa	**Start:** Always, 0, No **Orders:** Circle & Evade	**Waves:** 0 **Form:** Echelon Left	**Mother:** 0 **AI:** Novice	**Win:** 1 **Val:** 4
#13 2 T/B Lambda	**Start:** Always, 0, No **Orders:** Circle & Evade	**Waves:** 0 **Form:** Line Astern	**Mother:** 0 **AI:** Novice	**Win:** 1 **Val:** 5

X-wing Mission 2: Wingmen are Important

Flight groups:

*#1 1 X-W Red [2]	**Start:** Always, 0, No **Orders:** Attack P 2 & S 3	**Waves:** 0 **Form:** Vic	**Mother:** 0 **AI:** Veteran	**Win:** 0 **Val:** 9
#2 2 T/F Alpha	**Start:** Always, 0, No **Orders:** Attack All	**Waves:** 0 **Form:** Vic	**Mother:** 0 **AI:** Veteran	**Win:** 1 **Val:** 8
#3 2 T/F Beta	**Start:** Always, 0, No **Orders:** Attack All	**Waves:** 0 **Form:** Vic	**Mother:** 0 **AI:** Veteran	**Win:** 1 **Val:** 6
#4 2 T/F Gamma	**Start:** Always, 0, No **Orders:** Attack All	**Waves:** 0 **Form:** Vic	**Mother:** 0 **AI:** Veteran	**Win:** 1 **Val:** 5
#5 1 Planet 3	(Tatooine)			

X-wing Mission 3: Satellites Near Coruscant

Flight groups:

*#1 1 X-W Red [1]	**Start:** Always, 0, No **Orders:** Stationary	**Waves:** 0 **Form:** Vic	**Mother:** 0 **AI:** Novice	**Win:** 0 **Val:** 2
#2–5 2 by 2 array of Mine 1				
#6–10 1 Comm Sat				
#11 1 FRG Sentinel	**Start:** Always, 4, No **Orders:** Starship Circle	**Waves:** 0 **Form:** Vic	**Mother:** 0 **AI:** Top Ace	**Win:** 0 **Val:** 9
#12 1 Planet 7 (Coruscant)				
#13 2 TRN Epsilon	**Start:** Always, 0, No **Orders:** Fly Once & Evade	**Waves:** 0 **Form:** Vic	**Mother:** 0 **AI:** Top Ace	**Win:** 1 **Val:** 2

X-wing Mission 4: Beat the Odds

Flight groups:

*#1 3 X-W Red [2]	**Start:** Always, 0, No **Orders:** Attack All	**Waves:** 0 **Form:** Vic	**Mother:** 0 **AI:** Officer	**Win:** 0 **Val:** 9
#2 3 T/F Alpha	**Start:** Always, 0, No **Orders:** Attack All	**Waves:** 0 **Form:** Vic	**Mother:** 0 **AI:** Novice	**Win:** 1 **Val:** 8
#3 3 T/F Beta	**Start:** Always, 0, No **Orders:** Attack All	**Waves:** 0 **Form:** Vic	**Mother:** 0 **AI:** Officer	**Win:** 1 **Val:** 7

#4	3 T/F Gamma	**Start:** Always, 0, No **Orders:** Attack All	**Waves:** 0 **Form:** Vic	**Mother:** 0 **AI:** Veteran	**Win:** 1 **Val:** 7
#5	1 Planet 7 (Circarpous IV)				

X-wing Mission 5: Rescue at Mon Calamari

Flight groups:

*#1	2 X-W Red [2]	**Start:** Always, 0, No **Orders:** Attack All	**Waves:** 0 **Form:** Vic	**Mother:** 0 **AI:** Veteran	**Win:** 0 **Val:** 9
#2	2 Y-W Gold	**Start:** Always, 0:24, No **Orders:** Disable P 8 & S 9	**Waves:** 0 **Form:** Vic	**Mother:** 0 **AI:** Ace	**Win:** 2 **Val:** 9
#3	2 T/F Alpha	**Start:** Always, 0, No **Orders:** Close Escort P 8 & S 6	**Waves:** 0 **Form:** Echelon Right	**Mother:** 14 **AI:** Veteran	**Win:** 0 **Val:** 5
#4	2 T/F Beta	**Start:** Always, 0, No **Orders:** Attack All P 2 & S 1	**Waves:** 0 **Form:** Vic	**Mother:** 14 **AI:** Ace	**Win:** 0 **Val:** 0
#5	2 T/F Gamma	**Start:** Always, 0, No **Orders:** Close Escort P 9 & S 7	**Waves:** 0 **Form:** Echelon Left	**Mother:** 14 **AI:** Officer	**Win:** 0 **Val:** 1
#6	2 CON Xi	**Start:** Always, 0, No **Orders:** Stationary	**Waves:** 0 **Form:** Line Abreast	**Mother:** 0 **AI:** Novice	**Win:** 8-1 **Val:** 0
#7	2 CON Psi	**Start:** Always, 0, No **Orders:** Stationary	**Waves:** 0 **Form:** Vic	**Mother:** 0 **AI:** Novice	**Win:** 1 **Val:** 0
#8	1 FRT Wiggins	**Start:** Always, 0, No **Orders:** Stationary	**Waves:** 0 **Form:** Vic	**Mother:** 0 **AI:** Novice	**Win:** 4 **Val:** 0
#9	1 FRT Betar	**Start:** Always, 0, No **Orders:** Stationary	**Waves:** 0 **Form:** Vic	**Mother:** 0 **AI:** Novice	**Win:** 1 **Val:** 0
#10	1 TUG T-87	**Start:** Always, 0, No **Orders:** Circle & Evade	**Waves:** 0 **Form:** Vic	**Mother:** 0 **AI:** Novice	**Win:** 0 **Val:** 9
#11	1 TUG T-85	**Start:** Always, 0, No **Orders:** Circle & Evade	**Waves:** 0 **Form:** Vic	**Mother:** 0 **AI:** Top Ace	**Win:** 0 **Val:** 9
#12	1 FRT Citadel 2	**Start:** ID, 0:30, 8 **Orders:** Board & Take P 8	**Waves:** 0 **Form:** Vic	**Mother:** 0 **AI:** Top Ace	**Win:** 2 **Val:** 6
#13	1 FRT Citadel 1	**Start:** ID, 0:30, 6 **Orders:** Board & Take P 6	**Waves:** 0 **Form:** Vic	**Mother:** 0 **AI:** Top Ace	**Win:** 2 **Val:** 6
#14	1 STD Warrior	**Start:** Attack, 2:54, 8 **Orders:** Starship Sit & Fire	**Waves:** 0 **Form:** Vic	**Mother:** 0 **AI:** Top Ace	**Win:** 0 **Val:** 0
#15	3 T/B Theta	**Start:** Attack, 3:12, 8 **Orders:** Attack FRTs Pri 6 & Sec 8	**Waves:** 5 **Form:** Diamond	**Mother:** 14 **AI:** Officer	**Win:** 0 **Val:** 9
#16	3 T/F Delta	**Start:** Attack, 3:06, 8 **Orders:** Attack FRTs Pri 8 & Sec 6	**Waves:** 5 **Form:** Diamond	**Mother:** 14 **AI:** Veteran	**Win:** 0 **Val:** 9
#17	1 Planet 9 (Mon Calamari)				

X-wing Mission 6: Farlander's First Mission

Flight groups:

*#1	2 X-W Red [2]	**Start:** Always, 0, No **Orders:** Close Escort P 13 & S 11	**Waves:** 0 **Form:** Vic	**Mother:** 0 **AI:** Novice	**Win:** 0 **Val:** 2
#2	1 X-W Red 3	**Start:** Always, 0:06, No **Orders:** Close Escort P 13 & S 12	**Waves:** 0 **Form:** Vic	**Mother:** 0 **AI:** Novice	**Win:** 0 **Val:** 0
#3	1 X-W Red 4	**Start:** Always, 0:12, No **Orders:** Close Escort P 13 & S 12	**Waves:** 0 **Form:** Vic	**Mother:** 0 **AI:** Novice	**Win:** 0 **Val:** 9
#4	4 X-W Blue	**Start:** Always, 0:12, No **Orders:** Attack All P 8 & S 7	**Waves:** 0 **Form:** Vic	**Mother:** 5 **AI:** Novice	**Win:** 0 **Val:** 9
#5	1 FRG Liberator	**Start:** Always, 0, No **Orders:** Starship Sit & Fire	**Waves:** 0 **Form:** Vic	**Mother:** 0 **AI:** Novice	**Win:** 0 **Val:** 0
#6	1 CRV Talon	**Start:** Always, 0, No **Orders:** Starship Fly Once	**Waves:** 0 **Form:** Vic	**Mother:** 0 **AI:** Veteran	**Win:** 4 **Val:** 4
#7	4 T/F Alpha	**Start:** Always, 0, No **Orders:** Attack Starships P 5	**Waves:** 0 **Form:** Diamond	**Mother:** 0 **AI:** Top Ace	**Win:** 0 **Val:** 9
#8	4 T/B Beta	**Start:** Always, 0, No **Orders:** Attack All P 5 & S 4	**Waves:** 0 **Form:** Diamond	**Mother:** 0 **AI:** Top Ace	**Win:** 0 **Val:** 9
#9	2 T/F Gamma	**Start:** Always, 0, No **Orders:** Close Escort P 6	**Waves:** 0 **Form:** Vic	**Mother:** 6 **AI:** Top Ace	**Win:** 1 **Val:** 4
#10	2 T/F Delta	**Start:** Always, 0, No **Orders:** Loose Escort P 6	**Waves:** 0 **Form:** Vic	**Mother:** 6 **AI:** Top Ace	**Win:** 1 **Val:** 6
#11	1 Y-W Gold 1	**Start:** Always, 0, No **Orders:** Disable FRTs P 6	**Waves:** 0 **Form:** Echelon Right	**Mother:** 5 **AI:** Ace	**Win:** 0 **Val:** 9
#12	1 Y-W Gold 2	**Start:** Always, 0:06, No **Orders:** Disable FRTs P 6	**Waves:** 0 **Form:** Vic	**Mother:** 5 **AI:** Ace	**Win:** 0 **Val:** 9
#13	1 TRN Storm Unit	**Start:** Disable, 1, 6 **Orders:** Board & Take Pri 6	**Waves:** 0 **Form:** Vic	**Mother:** 5 **AI:** Top Ace	**Win:** 2 **Val:** 4
#14	1 Planet 4 (Turkana)				

Y-wing Mission 1: Commerce Raid

Flight groups:

*#1	2 Y-W Red [2]	**Start:** Always, 0, No **Orders:** Attack All	**Waves:** 0 **Form:** Vic	**Mother:** 0 **AI:** Veteran	**Win:** 0 **Val:** 8
#2	1 Planet 8 (Bonadan)				
#3	1 SHU Krayt	**Start:** Always, 2:54, No **Orders:** Fly Once & Evade	**Waves:** 0 **Form:** Vic	**Mother:** 0 **AI:** Novice	**Win:** 1 **Val:** 4
#4	1 TUG T-54	**Start:** Always, 0, No **Orders:** Circle & Evade	**Waves:** 0 **Form:** Vic	**Mother:** 0 **AI:** Officer	**Win:** 0 **Val:** 0
#5	1 TUG T-55	**Start:** Always, 0, No **Orders:** Board & Deliver P 8	**Waves:** 0 **Form:** Vic	**Mother:** 0 **AI:** Officer	**Win:** 0 **Val:** 9

#6	2 CON Lambda	**Start:** Always, 0, No **Orders:** Stationary	**Waves:** 0 **Form:** Line Astern	**Mother:** 0 **AI:** Novice	**Win:** 9 **Val:** 0
#7	1 CON Lambda 3	**Start:** Always, 0, No **Orders:** Stationary	**Waves:** 0 **Form:** Vic	**Mother:** 0 **AI:** Novice	**Win:** 1 **Val:** 0
#8	2 CON Kappa	**Start:** Always, 0, No **Orders:** Stationary	**Waves:** 0 **Form:** Line Abreast	**Mother:** 0 **AI:** Novice	**Win:** 9 **Val:** 0
#9	2 CON Iota	**Start:** Always, 0, No **Orders:** Stationary	**Waves:** 0 **Form:** Vic	**Mother:** 0 **AI:** Novice	**Win:** 9 **Val:** 0
#10	1 FRT Banthar	**Start:** Always, 0, No **Orders:** Board & Take P 9 & S 8	**Waves:** 0 **Form:** Vic	**Mother:** 0 **AI:** Veteran	**Win:** 1 **Val:** 5
#11	1 FRT Deddite	**Start:** Always, 1:42, No **Orders:** Board & Take P 6 & S 7	**Waves:** 0 **Form:** Vic	**Mother:** 0 **AI:** Veteran	**Win:** 1 **Val:** 5
#12	1 FRT Birkby	**Start:** Always, 3:42, No **Orders:** Board & Take P 7 & S 6	**Waves:** 0 **Form:** Vic	**Mother:** 0 **AI:** Officer	**Win:** 0 **Val:** 5
#13	1 FRG Enforcer	**Start:** Destroy, 3:36, 10 **Orders:** Starship Circle	**Waves:** 0 **Form:** Vic	**Mother:** 0 **AI:** Top Ace	**Win:** 0 **Val:** 9
#14	3 T/F Alpha	**Start:** Destroy, 3:48, 10 **Orders:** Attack All P 1	**Waves:** 1 **Form:** Vic	**Mother:** 13 **AI:** Officer	**Win:** 0 **Val:** 9
#15	3 T/F Beta	**Start:** Destroy, 4, 10 **Orders:** Attack All P 1	**Waves:** 1 **Form:** Vic	**Mother:** 13 **AI:** Officer	**Win:** 0 **Val:** 9

Y-wing Mission 2: Y-wing Gunnery Practice

Flight groups:

*#1	1 Y-W Red 2 [1]	**Start:** Always, 0, No **Orders:** Attack All	**Waves:** 0 **Form:** Vic	**Mother:** 0 **AI:** Novice	**Win:** 0 **Val:** 8
#2	2 T/F Alpha	**Start:** Always, 0, No **Orders:** Stationary	**Waves:** 0 **Form:** Line Abreast	**Mother:** 0 **AI:** Novice	**Win:** 1 **Val:** 0
#3	2 T/B Beta	**Start:** Always, 0, No **Orders:** Stationary	**Waves:** 0 **Form:** Line Abreast	**Mother:** 0 **AI:** Novice	**Win:** 1 **Val:** 0
#4	2 T/F Gamma	**Start:** Always, 0, No **Orders:** Stationary	**Waves:** 0 **Form:** Line Abreast	**Mother:** 0 **AI:** Novice	**Win:** 1 **Val:** 0
#5	2 T/B Delta	**Start:** Always, 0, No **Orders:** Board & Deliver P 12	**Waves:** 0 **Form:** Line Abreast	**Mother:** 12 **AI:** Officer	**Win:** 1 **Val:** 2
#6	2 T/F Zeta	**Start:** Always, 0, No **Orders:** Board & Deliver P 12	**Waves:** 0 **Form:** Line Abreast	**Mother:** 12 **AI:** Officer	**Win:** 1 **Val:** 2
#7	2 T/B Eta	**Start:** Always, 0, No **Orders:** Board & Deliver P 12	**Waves:** 0 **Form:** Line Abreast	**Mother:** 12 **AI:** Officer	**Win:** 1 **Val:** 2
#8	2 T/F Theta	**Start:** Always, 0, No **Orders:** Circle & Evade	**Waves:** 0 **Form:** Echelon Left	**Mother:** 0 **AI:** Veteran	**Win:** 1 **Val:** 4
#9	2 T/I Iota	**Start:** Always, 0, No **Orders:** Circle & Evade	**Waves:** 0 **Form:** Echelon Left	**Mother:** 0 **AI:** Veteran	**Win:** 1 **Val:** 4

#10	1 CON Phi 1	**Start:** Always, 0, No **Orders:** Stationary	**Waves:** 0 **Form:** Vic	**Mother:** 0 **AI:** Novice	**Win:** 0 **Val:** 0
#11	1 CON Phi 2	**Start:** Always, 0, No **Orders:** Stationary	**Waves:** 0 **Form:** Vic	**Mother:** 0 **AI:** Novice	**Win:** 0 **Val:** 0
#12	1 FRT Bofor	**Start:** Always, 0, No **Orders:** Stationary	**Waves:** 0 **Form:** Vic	**Mother:** 0 **AI:** Officer	**Win:** 0 **Val:** 0
#13	1 FRG Red Wind	**Start:** Always, 12, No **Orders:** Starship Circle	**Waves:** 0 **Form:** Vic	**Mother:** 0 **AI:** Novice	**Win:** 0 **Val:** 0
#14	3 T/I Alpha	**Start:** Always, 13, No **Orders:** Attack All P 1	**Waves:** 1 **Form:** Vic	**Mother:** 13 **AI:** Top Ace	**Win:** 0 **Val:** 9
#15	3 T/B Beta	**Start:** Always, 14, No **Orders:** Attack All P 1	**Waves:** 1 **Form:** Vic	**Mother:** 13 **AI:** Top Ace	**Win:** 0 **Val:** 9
#16	1 Planet 6				

Y-wing Mission 3: S.O.S. from Corvette Karinne

Flight groups:

*#1	2 Y-W Red [2]	**Start:** Always, 0, No **Orders:** Attack All	**Waves:** 0 **Form:** Echelon Right	**Mother:** 0 **AI:** Ace	**Win:** 0 **Val:** 9
#2	3 T/B Alpha	**Start:** Always, 0, No **Orders:** Attack Starships P 5	**Waves:** 0 **Form:** Finger Four	**Mother:** 6 **AI:** Officer	**Win:** 1 **Val:** 6
#3	3 T/B Beta	**Start:** Always, 0, No **Orders:** Attack Starships P 1 & S 5	**Waves:** 0 **Form:** Finger Four	**Mother:** 6 **AI:** Officer	**Win:** 1 **Val:** 6
#4	3 T/B Gamma	**Start:** Always, 0, No **Orders:** Attack All	**Waves:** 0 **Form:** Vic	**Mother:** 6 **AI:** Novice	**Win:** 1 **Val:** 5
#5	1 CRV Karinne	**Start:** Always, 0, No **Orders:** Fly Once & Evade	**Waves:** 0 **Form:** Vic	**Mother:** 0 **AI:** Veteran	**Win:** 2 **Val:** 0
#6	1 STD Avenger	**Start:** Always, 0, No **Orders:** Starship Fly Once	**Waves:** 0 **Form:** Vic	**Mother:** 0 **AI:** Veteran	**Win:** 0 **Val:** 2
#7	1 Planet 7 (Twi'lek)				

Y-wing Mission 4: Prisoners from Kessel

Flight groups:

*#1	3 Y-W Red [2]	**Start:** Always, 0, No **Orders:** Disable All	**Waves:** 0 **Form:** Vic	**Mother:** 0 **AI:** Top Ace	**Win:** **Val:** 9
#2	1 SHU 224	**Start:** Always, 0, No **Orders:** Go Home	**Waves:** 0 **Form:** Vic	**Mother:** 15 **AI:** Top Ace	**Win:** 4 **Val:** 3
#3	1 SHU 227	**Start:** Always, 0, No **Orders:** Go Home	**Waves:** 0 **Form:** Vic	**Mother:** 15 **AI:** Top Ace	**Win:** 4 **Val:** 3
#4	1 SHU 249	**Start:** Always, 0, No **Orders:** Go Home	**Waves:** 0 **Form:** Vic	**Mother:** 15 **AI:** Top Ace	**Win:** 4 **Val:** 3

#	Flight Group	Start / Orders	Waves / Form	Mother / AI	Win / Val
#5	1 SHU 247	**Start:** Always, 0, No **Orders:** Go Home	**Waves:** 0 **Form:** Vic	**Mother:** 15 **AI:** Top Ace	**Win:** 4 **Val:** 3
#6	1 SHU 213	**Start:** Always, 0, No **Orders:** Go Home	**Waves:** 0 **Form:** Vic	**Mother:** 15 **AI:** Top Ace	**Win:** 4 **Val:** 3
#7	1 T/F Alpha 1	**Start:** Always, 0, No **Orders:** Attack All	**Waves:** 0 **Form:** Vic	**Mother:** 15 **AI:** Ace	**Win:** 0 **Val:** 4
#8	1 SHU Rescue 1	**Start:** Always, 3, No **Orders:** Board & Take P 4	**Waves:** 0 **Form:** Vic	**Mother:** 0 **AI:** Top Ace	**Win:** 2 **Val:** 1
#9	1 SHU Rescue 2	**Start:** Always, 3, No **Orders:** Board & Take P 3	**Waves:** 0 **Form:** Vic	**Mother:** 0 **AI:** Top Ace	**Win:** 2 **Val:** 1
#10	1 SHU Rescue 3	**Start:** Always, 3, No **Orders:** Board & Take P 5	**Waves:** 0 **Form:** Vic	**Mother:** 0 **AI:** Top Ace	**Win:** 2 **Val:** 1
#11	1 SHU Rescue 4	**Start:** Always, 3, No **Orders:** Board & Take P 2	**Waves:** 0 **Form:** Vic	**Mother:** 0 **AI:** Top Ace	**Win:** 2 **Val:** 1
#12	1 SHU Rescue 5	**Start:** Always, 3, No **Orders:** Board & Take P 6	**Waves:** 0 **Form:** Vic	**Mother:** 0 **AI:** Top Ace	**Win:** 2 **Val:** 1
#13	3 T/I Beta	**Start:** Always, 1, No **Orders:** Attack All	**Waves:** 2 **Form:** Vic	**Mother:** 15 **AI:** Veteran	**Win:** 0 **Val:** 7
#14	1 T/F Alpha 2	**Start:** Always, 0, No **Orders:** Attack All	**Waves:** 0 **Form:** Vic	**Mother:** 15 **AI:** Ace	**Win:** 0 **Val:** 9
#15	1 STD Tiger	**Start:** Always, 0, No **Orders:** Starship Wait Return	**Waves:** 0 **Form:** Vic	**Mother:** 0 **AI:** Ace	**Win:** 0 **Val:** 0
#16	1 Planet 5 (Kessel)				

Y-wing Mission 5: Escape from Mytus VII

Flight groups:

#	Flight Group	Start / Orders	Waves / Form	Mother / AI	Win / Val
*#1	1 Y-W Red [1]	**Start:** Always, 0, No **Orders:** Disable FRTs P 8 & S 9	**Waves:** 0 **Form:** Vic	**Mother:** 0 **AI:** Top Ace	**Win:** 0 **Val:** 9
#2	1 FRT Hampton	**Start:** Always, 0, No **Orders:** Disabled	**Waves:** 0 **Form:** Vic	**Mother:** 0 **AI:** Novice	**Win:** 4 **Val:** 5
#3	1 TRN Omicron 1	**Start:** Always, 0, No **Orders:** Board & Exchange P 2	**Waves:** 0 **Form:** Vic	**Mother:** 10 **AI:** Top Ace	**Win:** 1 **Val:** 3
#4	1 TRN Omicron 2	**Start:** Attack, 4, 3 **Orders:** Disable All P 11	**Waves:** 1 **Form:** Vic	**Mother:** 10 **AI:** Top Ace	**Win:** 1 **Val:** 9
#5	1 TRN Omicron 3	**Start:** Attack, 4, 3 **Orders:** Board & Capture P 11	**Waves:** 0 **Form:** Vic	**Mother:** 10 **AI:** Top Ace	**Win:** 1 **Val:** 2
#6	2 T/F Alpha	**Start:** Always, 0, No **Orders:** Close Escort P 3	**Waves:** 0 **Form:** Line Abreast	**Mother:** 10 **AI:** Top Ace	**Win:** 0 **Val:** 9
#7	2 T/F Beta	**Start:** Always, 0, No **Orders:** Close Escort P 3	**Waves:** 0 **Form:** Vic	**Mother:** 10 **AI:** Veteran	**Win:** 0 **Val:** 2

#8	3 T/F Gamma	**Start:** Attack, 5, 3 **Orders:** Attack All P 11	**Waves:** 1 **Form:** Vic	**Mother:** 10 **AI:** Veteran	**Win:** 0 **Val:** 7
#9	3 T/F Delta	**Start:** Attack, 3, 3 **Orders:** Attack All P 11	**Waves:** 1 **Form:** Vic	**Mother:** 10 **AI:** Officer	**Win:** 0 **Val:** 8
#10	1 FRG Furious	**Start:** Attack, 2, 3 **Orders:** Starship Circle P 11	**Waves:** 0 **Form:** Vic	**Mother:** 0 **AI:** Novice	**Win:** 0 **Val:** 9
#11	1 SHU Mercy	**Start:** Always, 0, No **Orders:** Board & Take P 2	**Waves:** 0 **Form:** Vic	**Mother:** 0 **AI:** Top Ace	**Win:** 2 **Val:** 3
#12	1 Y-W Red 2	**Start:** Always, 0, No **Orders:** Attack All P 9 & S 8	**Waves:** 0 **Form:** Vic	**Mother:** 0 **AI:** Top Ace	**Win:** 0 **Val:** 9
#13	1 Planet 3 (Star's End)				

Y-wing Mission 6: Interception and Capture

Flight groups:

*#1	1 Y-W Red 3 [1]	**Start:** Always, 0, No **Orders:** Disable P 4	**Waves:** 0 **Form:** Echelon Right	**Mother:** 0 **AI:** Ace	**Win:** 0 **Val:** 9
#2	2 Y-W Red	**Start:** Always, 0, No **Orders:** Attack Escorters	**Waves:** 0 **Form:** Finger Four	**Mother:** 0 **AI:** Ace	**Win:** 0 **Val:** 9
#3	2 Y-W Blue	**Start:** Create, 0, 8 **Orders:** Close Escort P 8	**Waves:** 0 **Form:** Vic	**Mother:** 0 **AI:** Ace	**Win:** 0 **Val:** 0
#4	5 SHU Epsilon	**Start:** Always, 0, No **Orders:** Go Home	**Waves:** 0 **Form:** Diamond	**Mother:** 7 **AI:** Veteran	**Win:** 8 **Val:** 3
#5	3 T/F Alpha	**Start:** Always, 0, No **Orders:** Close Escort P 4	**Waves:** 0 **Form:** Line Abreast	**Mother:** 7 **AI:** Officer	**Win:** 0 **Val:** 1
#6	1 Planet 2 (Mon Calamari)				
#7	1 FRG Vehemence	**Start:** Always, 0, No **Orders:** Starship Wait Return	**Waves:** 0 **Form:** Vic	**Mother:** 0 **AI:** Top Ace	**Win:** 0 **Val:** 0
#8	1 SHU Hasti	**Start:** ID, 0:30, 4 **Orders:** Board & Take P 4	**Waves:** 0 **Form:** Vic	**Mother:** 0 **AI:** Top Ace	**Win:** 2 **Val:** 1
#9	3 T/F Beta	**Start:** Always, 0, No **Orders:** Loose Escort P 4	**Waves:** 1 **Form:** Line Abreast	**Mother:** 7 **AI:** Novice	**Win:** 0 **Val:** 9
#10	3 T/F Gamma	**Start:** Always, 2:24, No **Orders:** Attack All P 2 & S 1	**Waves:** 2 **Form:** Vic	**Mother:** 7 **AI:** Veteran	**Win:** 0 **Val:** 9
#11	3 T/F Gamma	**Start:** Always, 2:24, No **Orders:** Attack All P 8	**Waves:** 2 **Form:** Vic	**Mother:** 7 **AI:** Officer	**Win:** 0 **Val:** 9

A-wing Mission 1: Repair Depot Raid

Flight groups:

*#1	1 A-W Red Leader [1]	**Start:** Always, 0, No * **Orders:** Attack All	**Waves:** 0 **Form:** Vic	**Mother:** No **AI:** Novice	**Win:** 0 **Val:** 9

#2	4 TRN Omega	**Start:** Always, 0, No **Orders:** Disabled	**Waves:** 0 **Form:** Line Abreast	**Mother:** No **AI:** Novice	**Win:** 1 **Val:** 0
#3	3 SHU Kappa	**Start:** Always, 0, No **Orders:** Stationary	**Waves:** 0 **Form:** Line Abreast	**Mother:** No **AI:** Novice	**Win:** 1 **Val:** 0
#4	1 TUG T-34	**Start:** Always, 0, No **Orders:** Circle & Ignore	**Waves:** 0 **Form:** Vic	**Mother:** No **AI:** Officer	**Win:** 0 **Val:** 0
#5	1 TUG T-35	**Start:** Always, 0, No **Orders:** Stationary	**Waves:** 0 **Form:** Vic	**Mother:** No **AI:** Novice	**Win:** 1 **Val:** 0
#6	1 FRT Repair Dock	**Start:** Always, 0, No **Orders:** Stationary	**Waves:** 0 **Form:** Line Abreast	**Mother:** No **AI:** Veteran	**Win:** 1 **Val:** 0
#7	1 FRT Repair Dock	**Start:** Always, 0, No **Orders:** Stationary	**Waves:** 0 **Form:** Line Abreast	**Mother:** No **AI:** Novice	**Win:** 1 **Val:** 9
#8	1 TRN Sigma	**Start:** Always, 0, No **Orders:** Disabled	**Waves:** 0 **Form:** Vic	**Mother:** No **AI:** Novice	**Win:** 1 **Val:** 0
#9	2 T/B Alpha	**Start:** Always, 0, No **Orders:** Stationary	**Waves:** 0 **Form:** Line Abreast	**Mother:** No **AI:** Novice	**Win:** 1 **Val:** 0
#10	2 T/B Beta	**Start:** Always, 0, No **Orders:** Disabled	**Waves:** 0 **Form:** Line Abreast	**Mother:** No **AI:** Novice	**Win:** 1 **Val:** 0
#11	3 T/B Gamma	**Start:** Always, 0, No **Orders:** Disabled	**Waves:** 0 **Form:** Line Abreast	**Mother:** No **AI:** Novice	**Win:** 1 **Val:** 0
#12	2 T/F Delta	**Start:** Always, 0, No **Orders:** Circle & Evade	**Waves:** 0 **Form:** Echelon Left	**Mother:** No **AI:** Novice	**Win:** 1 **Val:** 4
#13	3 T/F Eta	**Start:** Always, 0, No **Orders:** Stationary	**Waves:** 0 **Form:** Line Abreast	**Mother:** No **AI:** Novice	**Win:** 1 **Val:** 0
#14	2 T/I Zeta	**Start:** Create, 0:24, 15 **Orders:** Attack All Pri 2	**Waves:** 5 **Form:** Vic	**Mother:** 15 **AI:** Top Ace	**Win:** 0 **Val:** 0
#15	1 FRG Virulence	**Start:** Attack, 7:00, 6 **Orders:** Starship Circle	**Waves:** 0 **Form:** Vic	**Mother:** No **AI:** Top Ace	**Win:** 0 **Val:** 9
#16	1 Planet 10 (No name)				

A-wing Mission 2: Aggressor Squadron Training

Flight groups:

*#1	1 A-W Red [1]	**Start:** Always, 0, No **Orders:** Attack All	**Waves:** 0 **Form:** Vic	**Mother:** No **AI:** Novice	**Win:** 0 **Val:** 9
#2	1 X-W Novice	**Start:** Always, 0, No **Orders:** Attack All	**Waves:** 0 **Form:** Vic	**Mother:** No **AI:** Novice	**Win:** 0 **Val:** 9
#3	1 X-W Officer	**Start:** Destroy, 1:00, 2 **Orders:** Attack All	**Waves:** 0 **Form:** Vic	**Mother:** No **AI:** Officer	**Win:** 0 **Val:** 9
#4	1 X-W Veteran	**Start:** Destroy, 1:00, 3 **Orders:** Attack All	**Waves:** 0 **Form:** Vic	**Mother:** No **AI:** Veteran	**Win:** 1 **Val:** 9

#5	1 X-W Ace	**Start:** Destroy, 1:00, 4 **Orders:** Attack All	**Waves:** 0 **Form:** Vic	**Mother:** No **AI:** Ace	**Win:** 1 **Val:** 9
#6	1 X-W Top Ace	**Start:** Destroy, 1:00, 5 **Orders:** Attack All	**Waves:** 0 **Form:** Vic	**Mother:** No **AI:** Top Ace	**Win:** 1 **Val:** 9
#7	1 Y-W Novice	**Start:** Always, 1:00, No **Orders:** Attack All	**Waves:** 0 **Form:** Vic	**Mother:** No **AI:** Novice	**Win:** 0 **Val:** 9
#8	1 Y-W Officer	**Start:** Destroy, 1:00, 7 **Orders:** Attack All	**Waves:** 0 **Form:** Vic	**Mother:** No **AI:** Officer	**Win:** 0 **Val:** 9
#9	1 Y-W Veteran	**Start:** Destroy, 1:00, 8 **Orders:** Attack All	**Waves:** 0 **Form:** Vic	**Mother:** No **AI:** Veteran	**Win:** 1 **Val:** 9
#10	1 Y-W Ace	**Start:** Destroy, 1:00, 9 **Orders:** Attack All	**Waves:** 0 **Form:** Vic	**Mother:** No **AI:** Ace	**Win:** 1 **Val:** 9
#11	1 Y-W Top Ace	**Start:** Destroy, 1:00, 10 **Orders:** Attack All	**Waves:** 0 **Form:** Vic	**Mother:** No **AI:** Top Ace	**Win:** 1 **Val:** 9
#12	1 A-W Novice	**Start:** Always, 2:00, No **Orders:** Attack All	**Waves:** 0 **Form:** Vic	**Mother:** No **AI:** Novice	**Win:** 0 **Val:** 9
#13	1 A-W Officer	**Start:** Destroy, 1:00, 12 **Orders:** Attack All	**Waves:** 0 **Form:** Vic	**Mother:** No **AI:** Officer	**Win:** 0 **Val:** 9
#14	1 A-W Veteran	**Start:** Destroy, 1:00, 13 **Orders:** Attack All	**Waves:** 0 **Form:** Vic	**Mother:** No **AI:** Veteran	**Win:** 1 **Val:** 9
#15	1 A-W Ace	**Start:** Destroy, 1:00, 14 **Orders:** Attack All	**Waves:** 0 **Form:** Vic	**Mother:** No **AI:** Ace	**Win:** 1 **Val:** 9
#16	1 A-W Top Ace	**Start:** Destroy, 1:00, 15 **Orders:** Attack All	**Waves:** 0 **Form:** Vic	**Mother:** No **AI:** Top Ace	**Win:** 1 **Val:** 9

A-wing Mission 3: Intercept TIE Bomber Run

Flight groups:

#1	2 T/F Alpha	**Start:** Always, 0, No **Orders:** Attack Pri 8	**Waves:** 0 **Form:** Line Abreast	**Mother:** 10 **AI:** Novice	**Win:** 0 **Val:** 7
#2	1 T/F Alpha 3	**Start:** Always, 0, No **Orders:** Close Escort Pri 3	**Waves:** 0 **Form:** Vic	**Mother:** 10 **AI:** Top Ace	**Win:** 0 **Val:** 7
#3	3 T/B Mu	**Start:** Always, 0, No **Orders:** Attack Pri 9	**Waves:** 0 **Form:** Vic	**Mother:** 10 **AI:** Top Ace	**Win:** 1 **Val:** 9
#4	2 T/F Beta	**Start:** Always, 0, No **Orders:** Attack All	**Waves:** 0 **Form:** Line Abreast	**Mother:** 10 **AI:** Novice	**Win:** 0 **Val:** 7
#5	2 T/F Gamma	**Start:** Always, 0, No **Orders:** Attack All	**Waves:** 0 **Form:** Line Abreast	**Mother:** 10 **AI:** Novice	**Win:** 0 **Val:** 7
#6	1 X-W Red 1	**Start:** Always, 0, No **Orders:** Loose Escort Pri 9	**Waves:** 0 **Form:** Vic	**Mother:** No **AI:** Top Ace	**Win:** 0 **Val:** 8

#7	1 Y-W Red 3	**Start:** Always, 0, No **Orders:** Close Escort Pri 9	**Waves:** 0 **Form:** Vic	**Mother:** No **AI:** Top Ace	**Win:** 0 **Val:** 3
*#8	1 A-W Red 2 [1]	**Start:** Always, 0, No **Orders:** Attack All	**Waves:** 0 **Form:** Vic	**Mother:** No **AI:** Novice	**Win:** 0 **Val:** 8
#9	1 SHU Maria	**Start:** Always, 0, No **Orders:** Go Home	**Waves:** 0 **Form:** Vic	**Mother:** No **AI:** Top Ace	**Win:** 2 **Val:** 0
#10	1 STD Malice	**Start:** Always, 0, No **Orders:** Go Home	**Waves:** 0 **Form:** Vic	**Mother:** No **AI:** Novice	**Win:** 0 **Val:** 9

A-wing Mission 4: Attack Run on Freighters

Flight groups:

*#1	1 A-W Red 2 [1]	**Start:** Always, 0, No * **Orders:** Loose Escort	**Waves:** 0 **Form:** Vic	**Mother:** No **AI:** Ace	**Win:** 0 **Val:** 9
#2	1 FRT Century 1	**Start:** Always, 0, No **Orders:** Fly Once & Evade	**Waves:** 0 **Form:** Vic	**Mother:** No **AI:** Officer	**Win:** 1 **Val:** 9
#3	1 FRT Century 2	**Start:** Always, 0, No **Orders:** Fly Once & Evade	**Waves:** 0 **Form:** Vic	**Mother:** No **AI:** Officer	**Win:** 1 **Val:** 9
#4	1 FRT Century 3	**Start:** Always, 0, No **Orders:** Fly Once & Evade	**Waves:** 0 **Form:** Vic	**Mother:** No **AI:** Officer	**Win:** 1 **Val:** 9
#5	2 T/F Alpha	**Start:** Always, 0, No **Orders:** Attack Pri 9 & Sec 1	**Waves:** 0 **Form:** Vic	**Mother:** 3 **AI:** Veteran	**Win:** 0 **Val:** 9
#6	2 T/F Beta	**Start:** Always, 0, No **Orders:** Loose Escort Pri 2 & Sec 4	**Waves:** 0 **Form:** Line Astern	**Mother:** 2 **AI:** Novice	**Win:** 0 **Val:** 9
#7	2 T/F Gamma	**Start:** Always, 0, No **Orders:** Loose Escort Pri 4 & Sec 2	**Waves:** 0 **Form:** Vic	**Mother:** 2 **AI:** Officer	**Win:** 0 **Val:** 9
#8	2 T/F Delta	**Start:** Always, 0, No **Orders:** Close Escort Pri 3 & Sec 4	**Waves:** 0 **Form:** Vic	**Mother:** 3 **AI:** Novice	**Win:** 0 **Val:** 8
#9	1 Y-W Red 1	**Start:** Always, 0, No * **Orders:** Attack freighters	**Waves:** 0 **Form:** Vic	**Mother:** No **AI:** Veteran	**Win:** 2 **Val:** 9
#10	1 Planet 7 (Ghorman)				

A-wing Mission 5: Protect Returning Starfighters

Flight groups:

#1	2 X-W Red	**Start:** Always, 0, No **Orders:** Attack All	**Waves:** 0 **Form:** Vic	**Mother:** 0 **AI:** Ace	**Win:** 0 **Val:** 7
#2	1 X-W Gold 4	**Start:** Always, 4, No **Orders:** Go Home	**Waves:** 0 **Form:** Vic	**Mother:** 10 **AI:** Top Ace	**Win:** 2 **Val:** 1
#3	1 X-W Gold 2	**Start:** Always, 0, No **Orders:** Go Home	**Waves:** 0 **Form:** Vic	**Mother:** 10 **AI:** Top Ace	**Win:** 2 **Val:** 1
#4	1 X-W Gold 1	**Start:** Always, 0, No **Orders:** Go Home	**Waves:** 0 **Form:** Vic	**Mother:** 10 **AI:** Top Ace	**Win:** 2 **Val:** 1

#5	1 X-W Gold 3	**Start:** Always, 3, No **Orders:** Go Home	**Waves:** 0 **Form:** Vic	**Mother:** 10 **AI:** Top Ace	**Win:** 2 **Val:** 1
*#6	2 A-W Red [1]	**Start:** Always, 0, No **Orders:** Attack All	**Waves:** 0 **Form:** Vic	**Mother:** 0 **AI:** Top Ace	**Win:** 0 **Val:** 6
#7	1 X-W Blue 5	**Start:** Always, 0, No **Orders:** Go Home	**Waves:** 0 **Form:** Vic	**Mother:** 10 **AI:** Top Ace	**Win:** 2 **Val:** 1
#8	1 X-W Blue 9	**Start:** Always, 0, No **Orders:** Go Home	**Waves:** 0 **Form:** Vic	**Mother:** 10 **AI:** Top Ace	**Win:** 2 **Val:** 0
#9	1 X-W Blue 8	**Start:** Always, 0, No **Orders:** Go Home	**Waves:** 0 **Form:** Vic	**Mother:** 10 **AI:** Top Ace	**Win:** 2 **Val:** 1
#10	1 CRS Cathleen	**Start:** Always, 0, No **Orders:** Wait for Return	**Waves:** 0 **Form:** Vic	**Mother:** No **AI:** Top Ace	**Win:** 0 **Val:** 2
#11	1 FRG Terminator	**Start:** Always, 5, No **Orders:** Go Home	**Waves:** 0 **Form:** Vic	**Mother:** 0 **AI:** Top Ace	**Win:** 0 **Val:** 7
#12	1 SHU Blue 1	**Start:** Always, 4, No **Orders:** Go Home	**Waves:** 0 **Form:** Vic	**Mother:** 10 **AI:** Top Ace	**Win:** 2 **Val:** 8
#13	1 SHU Blue 2	**Start:** Always, 5, No **Orders:** Go Home	**Waves:** 0 **Form:** Vic	**Mother:** 10 **AI:** Top Ace	**Win:** 2 **Val:** 4
#14	6 T/B Alpha	**Start:** Always, 5:18, No **Orders:** Attack Pri 2 & Sec 6	**Waves:** 0 **Form:** Vic	**Mother:** 11 **AI:** Top Ace	**Win:** 0 **Val:** 9
#15	6 T/B Beta	**Start:** Always, 2:18, No **Orders:** Attack Pri 2 & Sec 11	**Waves:** 0 **Form:** Vic	**Mother:** 16 **AI:** Top Ace	**Win:** 0 **Val:** 9
#16	1 FRG Terminator	**Start:** Always, 2, No **Orders:** Fly Once	**Waves:** 0 **Form:** Vic	**Mother:** 0 **AI:** Top Ace	**Win:** 0 **Val:** 7

A-wing Mission 6: Deep Space Reconnaissance

Flight groups:

*#1	1 A-W Red [1]	**Start:** Always, 0, No **Orders:** Attack All	**Waves:** 0 **Form:** Vic	**Mother:** 0 **AI:** Top Ace	**Win:** 0 **Val:** 9
#2	3 T/F Alpha	**Start:** ID, 0, 12 **Orders:** Attack Pri 1	**Waves:** 0 **Form:** Vic	**Mother:** 12 **AI:** Ace	**Win:** 9 **Val:** 9
#3	3 T/F Beta	**Start:** ID, 0, 13 **Orders:** Attack Pri 1	**Waves:** 0 **Form:** Vic	**Mother:** 13 **AI:** Top Ace	**Win:** 9 **Val:** 0
#4	3 T/F Gamma	**Start:** ID, 1:00, 12 **Orders:** Attack Pri 1	**Waves:** 2 **Form:** Echelon Right	**Mother:** 14 **AI:** Top Ace	**Win:** 0 **Val:** 9
#5	3 T/F Delta	**Start:** ID, 2:00, 12 **Orders:** Attack Pri 1	**Waves:** 2 **Form:** Echelon Left	**Mother:** 14 **AI:** Veteran	**Win:** 0 **Val:** 9
#6	2 CON Lambda	**Start:** Always, 0, No **Orders:** Stationary	**Waves:** 0 **Form:** Line Astern	**Mother:** 0 **AI:** Novice	**Win:** 13 **Val:** 0

#7	1 CON Delta	**Start:** Always, 0, No **Orders:** Stationary	**Waves:** 0 **Form:** Vic	**Mother:** 0 **AI:** Novice	**Win:** 13 **Val:** 0
#8	2 CON Sigma	**Start:** Always, 0, No **Orders:** Stationary	**Waves:** 0 **Form:** Line Abreast	**Mother:** 0 **AI:** Novice	**Win:** 13 **Val:** 0
#9	2 CON Mu	**Start:** Always, 0, No **Orders:** Stationary	**Waves:** 0 **Form:** Vic	**Mother:** 0 **AI:** Novice	**Win:** 13 **Val:** 0
#10	1 CON Delta	**Start:** Always, 0, No **Orders:** Stationary	**Waves:** 0 **Form:** Vic	**Mother:** 0 **AI:** Novice	**Win:** 13 **Val:** 0
#11	3 CON Tau	**Start:** Always, 0, No **Orders:** Stationary	**Waves:** 0 **Form:** Diamond	**Mother:** 0 **AI:** Novice	**Win:** 13 **Val:** 0
#12	1 CON Dodek	**Start:** Always, 0, No **Orders:** Stationary	**Waves:** 0 **Form:** Vic	**Mother:** 0 **AI:** Novice	**Win:** 13 **Val:** 0
#13	1 CON Penta	**Start:** Always, 0, No **Orders:** Stationary	**Waves:** 0 **Form:** Vic	**Mother:** 0 **AI:** Novice	**Win:** 13 **Val:** 0
#14	1 FRG Merciless	**Start:** ID, 0, 12 * **Orders:** Starship Circle	**Waves:** 0 **Form:** Vic	**Mother:** 0 **AI:** Novice	**Win:** 0 **Val:** 9
#15	3 T/I Rho	**Start:** Destroy, 1:00, 2 **Orders:** Attack Pri 1	**Waves:** 1 **Form:** Vic	**Mother:** 14 **AI:** Top Ace	**Win:** 0 **Val:** 9
#16	3 T/I Sigma	**Start:** Destroy, 1:00, 3 **Orders:** Attack Pri 1	**Waves:** 1 **Form:** Vic	**Mother:** 9 **AI:** Top Ace	**Win:** 0 **Val:** 9

Tour of Duty 1

OP 1: Destroy Imperial Convoy [defect] {X-wing}

Flight Groups:

*#1	2 X-W Red 1 [2]	**Start:** Always, 0, No **Orders:** Attack P 6+Sec 7	**Waves:** 0 **Form:** Vic	**Mother:** 0 **AI:** Veteran	**Win:** 0 **Val:** 8

* you can start out in one of three positions, randomly determined

#2	1 planet 8				
#3	1 Y-W Blue 1	**Start:** Always, 0, No **Orders:** Close Escort P 11	**Waves:** 0 **Form:** Vic	**Mother:** 0 **AI:** Novice	**Win:** 0 **Val:** 7
#4	1 Y-W Blue 2	**Start:** Always, 0, No **Orders:** Close Escort P 11	**Waves:** 0 **Form:** Vic	**Mother:** 0 **AI:** Novice	**Win:** 0 **Val:** 8
#5	1 CRV Dagger (commandos)	**Start:** Always, 1:06, No **Orders:** Board & Capture P 11	**Waves:** 0 **Form:** Vic	**Mother:** 0 **AI:** Top Ace	**Win:** 0 **Val:** 1
#6	1 FRT Orcim (munitions)	**Start:** Always, 0, No **Orders:** Fly Once + Evade	**Waves:** 0 **Form:** Vic	**Mother:** 0 **AI:** Top Ace	**Win:** 1 **Val:** 9

#7	1 FRT Esorp (mines)	Start: Always, 0, No **Orders:** Fly Once + Evade	**Waves:** 0 **Form:** Vic	**Mother:** 0 **AI:** Top Ace	**Win:** 1 **Val:** 4
#8	1 FRT Arreis (robo-haulers)	Start: Always, 0, No **Orders:** Fly Once + Evade	**Waves:** 0 **Form:** Vic	**Mother:** 0 **AI:** Top Ace	**Win:** 1 **Val:** 9
#9	1 FRT Nigiro (munitions)	Start: Always, 0, No **Orders:** Fly Once + Evade	**Waves:** 0 **Form:** Vic	**Mother:** 0 **AI:** Top Ace	**Win:** 1 **Val:** 9
#10	1 FRT Murtceps (TIE fighters)	Start: Always, 0, No **Orders:** Fly Once + Evade	**Waves:** 0 **Form:** Vic	**Mother:** 0 **AI:** Top Ace	**Win:** 0 **Val:** 9
#11	1 CRV Bixby (defectors)	Start: Always, 0, No **Orders:** Stationary	**Waves:** 0 **Form:** Vic	**Mother:** 5 **AI:** Novice	**Win:** 3 **Val:** 5
#12	1 FRG Gorgon	Start: Destroy, 2:06, 10 **Orders:** Starship Circle	**Waves:** 0 **Form:** Vic	**Mother:** 0 **AI:** Top Ace	**Win:** 0 **Val:** 9
#13	3 T/F Alpha	Start: Destroy, 3:00, 10 **Orders:** Attack All P 1	**Waves:** 1 **Form:** Vic	**Mother:** 12 **AI:** Officer	**Win:** 0 **Val:** 9
#14	3 T/F Beta	Start: Destroy, 2:42, 10 **Orders:** Attack All P 1	**Waves:** 9 **Form:** Vic	**Mother:** 12 **AI:** Veteran	**Win:** 0 **Val:** 9

OP 2: Reconnaissance Mission [id-recon] {A-wing}

Flight groups:

*#1	1 A-W Red [1]	Start: Always, 0, No **Orders:** Attack P 6+Sec 7	**Waves:** 0 **Form:** Vic	**Mother:** 0 **AI:** Top Ace	**Win:** 0 **Val:** 9
#2	1 FRG Warspite	Start: Always, 0, No **Orders:** Starship Sit + Fire	**Waves:** 0 **Form:** Vic	**Mother:** 0 **AI:** Officer	**Win:** 13 **Val:** 0
#3	2 FRG Harasser	Start: Always, 9:00, No **Orders:** Starship Fly Once	**Waves:** 0 **Form:** Vic	**Mother:** 0 **AI:** Officer	**Win:** 13 **Val:** 0
#4	3 CRV 758 (base eqpt.)	Start: Always, 3:00, No **Orders:** Starship Fly Once	**Waves:** 0 **Form:** Vic	**Mother:** 0 **AI:** Officer	**Win:** 13 **Val:** 9
#5	3 CRV 427 (military eqpt.)	Start: Always, 6:00, No **Orders:** Starship Fly Once	**Waves:** 0 **Form:** Vic	**Mother:** 0 **AI:** Veteran	**Win:** 13 **Val:** 9
#6	2 CRV 327 (TIE parts)	Start: Always, 1:00, No **Orders:** Starship Fly Once	**Waves:** 0 **Form:** Vic	**Mother:** 0 **AI:** Novice	**Win:** 13 **Val:** 9
#7	2 CRV 524 (power units)	Start: Always, 8:00, No **Orders:** Starship Fly Once	**Waves:** 0 **Form:** Vic	**Mother:** 0 **AI:** Ace	**Win:** 13 **Val:** 9
#8	1 FRT Ruggert (military eqpt.)	Start: Always, 2:00, No **Orders:** Fly Once + Ignore	**Waves:** 0 **Form:** Line Astern	**Mother:** 0 **AI:** Top Ace	**Win:** 13 **Val:** 0
#9	1 FRT Eichler (military eqpt.)	Start: Always, 7:00, No **Orders:** Fly Once + Ignore	**Waves:** 0 **Form:** Line Astern	**Mother:** 0 **AI:** Top Ace	**Win:** 13 **Val:** 0
#10	1 STD Invincible	Start: ID, 0:06, 3 **Orders:** Starship Fly Once	**Waves:** 0 **Form:** Vic	**Mother:** 0 **AI:** Top Ace	**Win:** 0 **Val:** 0

#11	6 T/B theta	**Start:** Attack, 0, 10 **Orders:** Attack All P 1	**Waves:** 9 **Form:** Vic	**Mother:** 10 **AI:** Top Ace	**Win:** 0 **Val:** 6
#12	6 T/I Beta	**Start:** ID, 0:09, 3 **Orders:** Attack All P 1	**Waves:** 9 **Form:** Vic	**Mother:** 10 **AI:** Top Ace	**Win:** 0 **Val:** 0
#13	2 T/F Gamma	**Start:** Always, 0, No **Orders:** Attack All	**Waves:** 9 **Form:** Vic	**Mother:** 2 **AI:** Novice	**Win:** 0 **Val:** 4
#14	3 T/F Delta	**Start:** Always, 10:00, No **Orders:** Attack All P 1	**Waves:** 9 **Form:** Vic	**Mother:** 3 **AI:** Top Ace	**Win:** 0 **Val:** 5
#15	1 SHU Kappa (officers)	**Start:** Always, 14:00, No **Orders:** Go Home	**Waves:** 0 **Form:** Vic	**Mother:** 10 **AI:** Top Ace	**Win:** 0 **Val:** 2
#16	1 TRN Omega (military eqpt.)	**Start:** Always, 14:00, No **Orders:** Go Home	**Waves:** 0 **Form:** Vic	**Mother:** 2 **AI:** Top Ace	**Win:** 0 **Val:** 5
#17	1 Planet 8				
#18	1 Nav Sat				

OP 3: Fly Point During Evacuation [wxrgard1] {X-wing}

*#1	2 X-W Red 1 [2]	**Start:** Always, 0, No **Orders:** Attack All	**Waves:** 0 **Form:** Vic	**Mother:** 0 **AI:** Novice	**Win:** 0 **Val:** 4
#2	1 Y-W Gold 3	**Start:** Always, 0, No **Orders:** Close Escort P 4	**Waves:** 0 **Form:** Vic	**Mother:** 3 **AI:** Officer	**Win:** 0 **Val:** 3
#3	1 FRG Fugazi (base supplies)	**Start:** Always, 0, No **Orders:** Starship Fly Once	**Waves:** 0 **Form:** Vic	**Mother:** 0 **AI:** Ace	**Win:** 2 **Val:** 9
#4	3 SHU Arroyo (high command)	**Start:** Always, 0, No **Orders:** Fly Once + Evade	**Waves:** 0 **Form:** Vic	**Mother:** 0 **AI:** Novice	**Win:** 2 **Val:** 5
#5	1 TRN Rhoon (base eqpt.)	**Start:** Always, 0, No **Orders:** Fly Once + Evade	**Waves:** 0 **Form:** Vic	**Mother:** 0 **AI:** Top Ace	**Win:** 0 **Val:** 1
#6	1 CRV Sonnel (troops)	**Start:** Always, 0, No **Orders:** Starship Fly Once	**Waves:** 0 **Form:** Vic	**Mother:** 0 **AI:** Novice	**Win:** 0 **Val:** 4
#7	1 CRV Mahan (troops)	**Start:** Always, 0, No **Orders:** Fly Once + Evade	**Waves:** 0 **Form:** Vic	**Mother:** 0 **AI:** Top Ace	**Win:** 0 **Val:** 4
#8	1 STD Invincible	**Start:** Always, 0:54, No **Orders:** Starship Circle	**Waves:** 0 **Form:** Vic	**Mother:** 0 **AI:** Top Ace	**Win:** 0 **Val:** 9
#9	1 Planet 1				
#10	2 T/F Alpha	**Start:** Always, 1:06, No **Orders:** Attack All P 4	**Waves:** 2 **Form:** Vic	**Mother:** 8 **AI:** Veteran	**Win:** 0 **Val:** 9
#11	2 T/F Beta	**Start:** Always, 2:42, No **Orders:** Attack All P 4	**Waves:** 9 **Form:** Vic	**Mother:** 8 **AI:** Ace	**Win:** 0 **Val:** 9

#12 6 T/I Eta	**Start:** Always, 18:00, No **Orders:** Attack All P 1	**Waves:** 9 **Form:** Vic	**Mother:** 8 **AI:** Top Ace	**Win:** 0 **Val:** 0
#13 6 T/B Theta	**Start:** Always, 19:00, No **Orders:** Attack All P 1	**Waves:** 9 **Form:** Vic	**Mother:** 8 **AI:** Top Ace	**Win:** 0 **Val:** 0
#14 3 T/B Gamma	**Start:** Always, 1:42, No **Orders:** Attack Starships P 6	**Waves:** 0 **Form:** Vic	**Mother:** 8 **AI:** Veteran	**Win:** 0 **Val:** 9
#15 3 T/F Delta	**Start:** Always, 5:00, No **Orders:** Attack Starships P 6	**Waves:** 0 **Form:** Vic	**Mother:** 8 **AI:** Ace	**Win:** 0 **Val:** 9

OP 4: Protect Medical Frigate [wxprot2] {X-wing}

Flight groups:

*#1 1 X-W Red 2 [1]	**Start:** Always, 0, No **Orders:** Attack All	**Waves:** 0 **Form:** Line Abreast	**Mother:** 5 **AI:** Veteran	**Win:** 0 **Val:** 2
#2 1 X-W Red 1	**Start:** Always, 0, No **Orders:** Attack All	**Waves:** 0 **Form:** Vic	**Mother:** 5 **AI:** Novice	**Win:** 0 **Val:** 9
#3 1 X-W Red 3	**Start:** Always, 0, No **Orders:** Attack All	**Waves:** 0 **Form:** Vic	**Mother:** 5 **AI:** Novice	**Win:** 0 **Val:** 9
#4 1 X-W Red 4	**Start:** Always, 0, No **Orders:** Attack All	**Waves:** 0 **Form:** Vic	**Mother:** 0 **AI:** Novice	**Win:** 0 **Val:** 9
#5 1 FRG Redemption	**Start:** Always, 0, No **Orders:** Stationary P 6 S 7	**Waves:** 0 **Form:** Diamond	**Mother:** 0 **AI:** Top Ace	**Win:** 0 **Val:** 0
#6 3 SHU Medevac	**Start:** Always, 0:06, No **Orders:** Board + Deliver P 5	**Waves:** 0 **Form:** Vic	**Mother:** 5 **AI:** Top Ace	**Win:** 2 **Val:** 1
#7 1 CRV Korolev	**Start:** Always, 0:18, No **Orders:** Board + Deliver P 5	**Waves:** 0 **Form:** Vic	**Mother:** 5 **AI:** Top Ace	**Win:** 2 **Val:** 2
#8 1 Planet 15				
#9 1 FRG Warspite	**Start:** Always, 1:18, No **Orders:** Starship Fly Once P 5	**Waves:** 0 **Form:** Vic	**Mother:** 0 **AI:** Top Ace	**Win:** 0 **Val:** 9
#10 1 FRG Warspite	**Start:** Always, 2:48, No **Orders:** Starship Fly Once	**Waves:** 0 **Form:** Vic	**Mother:** 0 **AI:** Top Ace	**Win:** 0 **Val:** 9
#11 3 T/B Alpha	**Start:** Always, 1:24, No **Orders:** Attack All P 7 S 6	**Waves:** 0 **Form:** Line Abreast	**Mother:** 9 **AI:** Officer	**Win:** 0 **Val:** 9
#12 2 T/F Beta	**Start:** Always, 1:30, No **Orders:** Attack All P 1 S 6	**Waves:** 0 **Form:** Vic	**Mother:** 9 **AI:** Novice	**Win:** 0 **Val:** 9
#13 3 T/B Gamma	**Start:** Always, 4:00, No **Orders:** Attack All P 7 S 6	**Waves:** 0 **Form:** Line Abreast	**Mother:** 10 **AI:** Veteran	**Win:** 0 **Val:** 9
#14 2 T/F Delta	**Start:** Always, 3:06, No **Orders:** Attack All P 1	**Waves:** 9 **Form:** Vic	**Mother:** 10 **AI:** Veteran	**Win:** 0 **Val:** 9

OP 5: Ambush Imperial Supply Convoy [attackxy]

*#1	2 X-W Red [1]	**Start:** Always, 0, No **Orders:** Attack All	**Waves:** 0 **Form:** Vic	**Mother:** 0 **AI:** Top Ace	**Win:** 0 **Val:** 9
#2	2 Y-W Blue	**Start:** Always, 1:00, No **Orders:** Attack freighters P 3 S 4	**Waves:** 0 **Form:** Vic	**Mother:** 0 **AI:** Novice	**Win:** 0 **Val:** 9
#3	1 FRT Juno 1 (droids)	**Start:** Always, 0, No **Orders:** Fly Once + Ignore	**Waves:** 0 **Form:** Vic	**Mother:** 0 **AI:** Top Ace	**Win:** 1 **Val:** 9
#4	1 FRT Juno 2 (foodstuffs)	**Start:** Always, 0, No **Orders:** Fly Once + Ignore	**Waves:** 0 **Form:** Vic	**Mother:** 0 **AI:** Top Ace	**Win:** 1 **Val:** 9
#5	1 FRT Juno 3 (machinery)	**Start:** Always, 0, No **Orders:** Fly Once + Ignore	**Waves:** 0 **Form:** Vic	**Mother:** 0 **AI:** Top Ace	**Win:** 1 **Val:** 9
#6	2 T/F Alpha	**Start:** Always, 0, No **Orders:** Loose Escort S 3	**Waves:** 0 **Form:** Vic	**Mother:** 9 **AI:** Ace	**Win:** 0 **Val:** 1
#7	3 T/F Beta	**Start:** Always, 0, No **Orders:** Attack P1+ S 2	**Waves:** 0 **Form:** Vic	**Mother:** 9 **AI:** Ace	**Win:** 0 **Val:** 7
#8	2 T/F Delta	**Start:** Always, 0, No **Orders:** Loose Escort P 5 S 4	**Waves:** 0 **Form:** Vic	**Mother:** 9 **AI:** Ace	**Win:** 0 **Val:** 3
#9	1 STD Invincible	**Start:** Always, 0, No **Orders:** Starship Sit + Fire	**Waves:** 0 **Form:** Vic	**Mother:** 0 **AI:** Top Ace	**Win:** 0 **Val:** 9
#10	3 T/I Eta	**Start:** Always, 0:12, No **Orders:** Attack P 2 S1	**Waves:** 9 **Form:** Vic	**Mother:** 9 **AI:** Top Ace	**Win:** 0 **Val:** 9
#11	6 T/I Zeta	**Start:** Attack, 0, 9 **Orders:** Attack All	**Waves:** 9 **Form:** Vic	**Mother:** 9 **AI:** Top Ace	**Win:** 0 **Val:** 0
#12	3 T/I Theta	**Start:** Always, 3:00, No **Orders:** Attack P 2 S 1	**Waves:** 0 **Form:** Vic	**Mother:** 9 **AI:** Ace	**Win:** 0 **Val:** 9
#13	1 CRV Ranger	**Start:** Always, 0, No **Orders:** Starship Fly Once	**Waves:** 0 **Form:** Vic	**Mother:** 0 **AI:** Top Ace	**Win:** 0 **Val:** 8

OP 6: Raid for R2 Units [max13]

*#1	3 A-W Red [1]	**Start:** Always, 0, No **Orders:** Close Escort P 2	**Waves:** 0 **Form:** Vic	**Mother:** 0 **AI:** Veteran	**Win:** 0 **Val:** 9
#2	1 FRT Ars Opus	**Start:** Always, 0, No **Orders:** Disabled	**Waves:** 0 **Form:** Vic	**Mother:** 0 **AI:** Top Ace	**Win:** 3 **Val:** 1
#3	2 Y-W Alpha	**Start:** Always, 0:30, No **Orders:** Attack P 1 S 1	**Waves:** 0 **Form:** Vic	**Mother:** 0 **AI:** Top Ace	**Win:** 0 **Val:** 9

*** These Y-wings may appear in one of several places thirty seconds after the mission begins.

#4	2 Y-W Beta	**Start:** Always, 1:00, No **Orders:** Attack P 1 S 1	**Waves:** 0 **Form:** Vic	**Mother:** 0 **AI:** Top Ace	**Win:** 0 **Val:** 9

*** These Y-wings may appear in one of several places one minute after the mission begins.

#5 4 TRN Epsilon **Start:** Always, 2:00, No **Waves:** 1 **Mother:** 0 **Win:** 0
Orders: Disable P2 **Form:** Vic **AI:** Top Ace **Val:** 9

*** These transports may appear in onc of two places two minutes after the mission begins.

#6 2 Y-W Gamma **Start:** Always, 3:30, No **Waves:** 1 **Mother:** 0 **Win:** 0
Orders: Attack P 1 S 1 **Form:** Vic **AI:** Top Ace **Val:** 9

*** These Y-wings may appear in one of several places three and a half minutes after the mission begins.

#7 2 Y-W Delta **Start:** Always, 4:00, No **Waves:** 1 **Mother:** 0 **Win:** 0
Orders: Attack P 1 S 1 **Form:** Vic **AI:** Top Ace **Val:** 9

*** These Y-wings may appear in one of several places four minutes after the mission begins.

#8 1 SHU Kappa **Start:** Always, 4:00, No **Waves:** 3 **Mother:** 0 **Win:** 0
Orders: Board + Capture P 2 S 2 **Form:** Vic **AI:** Top Ace **Val:** 1

* The raiding party shuttle will appear randomly in one of several locations four minutes into the mission.

#9 2 A-W Blue **Start:** Capture, 0, 2 **Waves:** 0 **Mother:** 0 **Win:** 16
Orders: Close Escort **Form:** Vic **AI:** Ace **Val:** 3

*** These A-wings may appear in one of several places when the mission begins.

#10 1 SHU Rescue Riker **Start:** Always, 0, No **Waves:** 3 **Mother:** 0 **Win:** 0
Orders: Board + Capture P 2 **Form:** Vic **AI:** Top Ace **Val:** 1

*** The rescue shuttle may appear in one of several places when the mission begins.

#11 1 Planet 7

OP 7: Recover Stolen X-wings [max10]

*#1 1 Y-W Red 2 [1] **Start:** Always, 0, No **Waves:** 0 **Mother:** 0 **Win:** 0
Orders: Disable All P 5 **Form:** Vic **AI:** Top Ace **Val:** 9

#2 1 Y-W Red 1 **Start:** Always, 0, No **Waves:** 0 **Mother:** 0 **Win:** 0
Orders: Disable P 4 S 6 **Form:** Vic **AI:** Officer **Val:** 9

#3 1 Y-W Red 3 **Start:** Always, 0, No **Waves:** 0 **Mother:** 0 **Win:** 0
Orders: Disable P 6 S 4 **Form:** Vic **AI:** Officer **Val:** 9

#4 1 X-W Blue 1 **Start:** Always, 0, No **Waves:** 0 **Mother:** 12 **Win:** 3
Orders: Circle + Evade **Form:** Vic **AI:** Veteran **Val:** 6

#5 1 X-W Blue 2 **Start:** Always, 0, No **Waves:** 0 **Mother:** 12 **Win:** 3
Orders: Fly Once + Evade **Form:** Vic **AI:** Veteran **Val:** 6

#6 1 X-W Blue 3 **Start:** Always, 0, No **Waves:** 0 **Mother:** 12 **Win:** 3
Orders: Fly Once + Evade **Form:** Vic **AI:** Top Ace **Val:** 6

#7 1 SHU Rescue 1 **Start:** Disable, 0:12, 4 **Waves:** 0 **Mother:** 10 **Win:** 2
(new R2 unit) **Orders:** Board + Capture P 4 **Form:** Vic **AI:** Top Ace **Val:** 1

#8 1 SHU Rescue 2 **Start:** Disable, 0:12, 5 **Waves:** 0 **Mother:** 10 **Win:** 2
(new R2 unit) **Orders:** Board + Capture P 5 **Form:** Vic **AI:** Top Ace **Val:** 1

#9 1 SHU Rescue 3 **Start:** Disable, 0:12, 6 **Waves:** 0 **Mother:** 10 **Win:** 2
(new R2 unit) **Orders:** Board + Capture P 6 **Form:** Vic **AI:** Top Ace **Val:** 1

#	Craft	Start / Orders	Waves / Form	Mother / AI	Win / Val
#10	1 CRS Maximus	**Start:** Capture, 0:18, 4	**Waves:** 0	**Mother:** 0	**Win:** 0
		Orders: Starship Wait Return	**Form:** Vic	**AI:** Top Ace	**Val:** 9

* The Cruiser Maximus may warp in at different positions, which are randomly determined.

#	Craft	Start / Orders	Waves / Form	Mother / AI	Win / Val
#11	1 planet 7				
#12	1 STD Invincible	**Start:** Always, 0, No	**Waves:** 0	**Mother:** 0	**Win:** 0
		Orders: Starship Fly Once	**Form:** Vic	**AI:** Top Ace	**Val:** 3
#13	2 T/I Alpha	**Start:** Always, 0:12, No	**Waves:** 9	**Mother:** 12	**Win:** 0
		Orders: Attack All P 2 S 3	**Form:** Vic	**AI:** Officer	**Val:** 9
#14	2 T/I Beta	**Start:** Always, 0:24, No	**Waves:** 2	**Mother:** 12	**Win:** 0
		Orders: Attack All P 7 S 8	**Form:** Vic	**AI:** Officer	**Val:** 9
#15	2 T/I Gamma	**Start:** Always, 1:06, No	**Waves:** 2	**Mother:** 12	**Win:** 0
		Orders: Attack All P 8 S 9	**Form:** Vic	**AI:** Officer	**Val:** 9
#16	2 T/I Delta	**Start:** Always, 2:00, No	**Waves:** 9	**Mother:** 12	**Win:** 0
		Orders: Attack All P 1 S 7	**Form:** Vic	**AI:** Officer	**Val:** 9
#17	6 T/I Zeta	**Start:** Always, 0, No	**Waves:** 9	**Mother:** 0	**Win:** 0
		Orders: Attack All P 1	**Form:** Vic	**AI:** Top Ace	**Val:** 0

OP 8: Rescue Sullustan Tech Staff [attack3]

#	Craft	Start / Orders	Waves / Form	Mother / AI	Win / Val
*#1	1 Y-W Red 1 [1]	**Start:** Always, 0, No	**Waves:** 0	**Mother:** 0	**Win:** 0
		Orders: Attack Transports	**Form:** Vic	**AI:** Novice	**Val:** 9
#2	6 TRN Lambda	**Start:** Always, 0, No	**Waves:** 0	**Mother:** 5	**Win:** 8
	(troopers/prisoners (3))	**Orders:** Fly Once + Evade	**Form:** Finger Four	**AI:** Top Ace	**Val:** 3
#3	6 TRN Omicron	**Start:** Always, 0, No	**Waves:** 0	**Mother:** 4	**Win:** 8
	(troopers/prisoners (4))	**Orders:** Fly Once + Evade	**Form:** Echelon Right	**AI:** Top Ace	**Val:** 3
#4	1 FRG Warspite	**Start:** Always, 0, No	**Waves:** 0	**Mother:** 0	**Win:** 0
		Orders: Starship Wait Return	**Form:** Vic	**AI:** Ace	**Val:** 0
#5	FRG Negra Star	**Start:** Always, 0, No	**Waves:** 0	**Mother:** 0	**Win:** 0
		Orders: Starship Wait Return	**Form:** Vic	**AI:** Ace	**Val:** 0
#6	1 Planet 2				
#7	1 TRN Rescue 2	**Start:** Disable, 0, 2	**Waves:** 0	**Mother:** 0	**Win:** 2
	(rescue team)	**Orders:** Board + Take P 2	**Form:** Vic	**AI:** Top Ace	**Val:** 1
#8	1 TRN Rescue 1	**Start:** Disable, 0, 3	**Waves:** 0	**Mother:** 0	**Win:** 2
	(rescue team)	**Orders:** Board + Take P 3	**Form:** Vic	**AI:** Top Ace	**Val:** 1
#9	2 T/I Alpha	**Start:** Create, 0, 8	**Waves:** 1	**Mother:** 5	**Win:** 0
		Orders: Attack P 8	**Form:** Vic	**AI:** Officer	**Val:** 5
#10	2 T/I Beta	**Start:** Create, 0, 7	**Waves:** 1	**Mother:** 4	**Win:** 0
		Orders: Attack P 7	**Form:** Vic	**AI:** Officer	**Val:** 5
#11	4 T/I Gamma	**Start:** Attack, 0, 4	**Waves:** 9	**Mother:** 4	**Win:** 0
		Orders: Attack All P 1	**Form:** Vic	**AI:** Top Ace	**Val:** 0

#12	4 T/I Delta	**Start:** Attack, 0, 5 **Orders:** Attack All P 1	**Waves:** 9 **Form:** Vic	**Mother:** 5 **AI:** Top Ace	**Win:** 0 **Val:** 0
#13	2 T/F Zeta	**Start:** Always, 0:24, No **Orders:** Attack All	**Waves:** 9 **Form:** Vic	**Mother:** 4 **AI:** Novice	**Win:** 0 **Val:** 4

OP 9: Diplomatic Summit at Sullust [sullust]

*#1	2 A-W Red [2]	**Start:** Always, 0, No **Orders:** Attack All	**Waves:** 0 **Form:** Double Astern	**Mother:** 0 **AI:** Veteran	**Win:** 0 **Val:** 1
#2	2 CRV D5 (Alliance delegation)	**Start:** Always, 0:12, No **Orders:** Starship Wait Return	**Waves:** 0 **Form:** Form 9	**Mother:** 0 **AI:** Top Ace	**Win:** 0 **Val:** 0
#3	1 FRG Sor-Sull II (Sullust delegation)	**Start:** Always, 0:30, No **Orders:** Starship Wait Return P 6 S 5	**Waves:** 0 **Form:** Vic	**Mother:** 0 **AI:** Top Ace	**Win:** 2 **Val:** 0
#4	1 SHU Freedom 1 (Alliance Ambassador)	**Start:** Create, 0:30, 2 **Orders:** Board + Exchange P 5	**Waves:** 0 **Form:** Line Abreast	**Mother:** 2 **AI:** Top Ace	**Win:** 2 **Val:** 8
#5	1 SHU Sor X (Sullust ambassador)	**Start:** Create, 0:12, 3 **Orders:** Rendezvous	**Waves:** 0 **Form:** Line Abreast	**Mother:** 3 **AI:** Top Ace	**Win:** 2 **Val:** 0
#6	2 TRN CoSof (Sullust diplomats)	**Start:** Always, 0:36, No **Orders:** Rendezvous	**Waves:** 0 **Form:** Double Astern	**Mother:** 3 **AI:** Top Ace	**Win:** 2 **Val:** 0

* The transports of CoSof group may initially appear in one of two positions

#7	2 TRN Tector (tech staff)	**Start:** Always, 0:12, No **Orders:** Board + Deliver P 6	**Waves:** 0 **Form:** Double Astern	**Mother:** 3 **AI:** Top Ace	**Win:** 2 **Val:** 7
#8	1 STD Invincible	**Start:** Always, 3:06, No **Orders:** Starship Fly Once	**Waves:** 0 **Form:** Vic	**Mother:** 0 **AI:** Ace	**Win:** 0 **Val:** 1
#9	3 T/I Alpha	**Start:** Create, 0:12, 8 **Orders:** Attack All P 2	**Waves:** 0 **Form:** Vic	**Mother:** 8 **AI:** Novice	**Win:** 0 **Val:** 0
#10	3 T/I Beta	**Start:** Destroy, 0, 13 **Orders:** Attack All P 4 S 5	**Waves:** 0 **Form:** Vic	**Mother:** 8 **AI:** Novice	**Win:** 0 **Val:** 0
#11	3 T/I Gamma	**Start:** Destroy, 0, 14 **Orders:** Attack All P 7 S 6	**Waves:** 0 **Form:** Vic	**Mother:** 8 **AI:** Novice	**Win:** 0 **Val:** 0
#12	3 T/I Delta	**Start:** Destroy, 0, 15 **Orders:** Attack All P 3	**Waves:** 0 **Form:** Vic	**Mother:** 8 **AI:** Novice	**Win:** 0 **Val:** 0
#13	3 T/B Zeta	**Start:** Create, 0:18, 9 **Orders:** Attack All P 2	**Waves:** 0 **Form:** Vic	**Mother:** 8 **AI:** Novice	**Win:** 0 **Val:** 0
#14	3 T/F Theta	**Start:** Create, 0:36, 10 **Orders:** Attack All P 4 S 5	**Waves:** 0 **Form:** Vic	**Mother:** 8 **AI:** Novice	**Win:** 0 **Val:** 0
#15	3 T/F Eta	**Start:** Create, 0:36, 11 **Orders:** Attack All P 7 S 6	**Waves:** 0 **Form:** Vic	**Mother:** 8 **AI:** Novice	**Win:** 0 **Val:** 0
#16	3 T/B Iota	**Start:** Create, 0:18, 12 **Orders:** Attack All P 3	**Waves:** 0 **Form:** Vic	**Mother:** 8 **AI:** Novice	**Win:** 0 **Val:** 0

OP 10: Rescue Sullustan Leader [ack-hard]

*#1	1 Y-W Red 2 [1]	**Start:** Always, 0, No **Orders:** Disable All S 3	**Waves:** 0 **Form:** Echelon Right	**Mother:** 0 **AI:** Ace	**Win:** 0 **Val:** 9
#2	2 X-W Gold	**Start:** Always, 0, No **Orders:** Attack P 5 S 6	**Waves:** 0 **Form:** Echelon Left	**Mother:** 0 **AI:** Veteran	**Win:** 0 **Val:** 9
#3	4 SHU Kappa (officers)	**Start:** Always, 0, No **Orders:** Close Escort P 4	**Waves:** 0 **Form:** Line Abreast	**Mother:** 8 **AI:** Top Ace	**Win:** 0 **Val:** 3
#4	1 SHU Kappa 5 (Sullustan)	**Start:** Always, 0, No **Orders:** Go Home	**Waves:** 0 **Form:** Vic	**Mother:** 8 **AI:** Top Ace	**Win:** 4 **Val:** 3
#5	3 T/F Alpha	**Start:** Always, 0, No **Orders:** Attack P1	**Waves:** 0 **Form:** Line Abreast	**Mother:** 8 **AI:** Officer	**Win:** 0 **Val:** 1
#6	3 T/I Beta	**Start:** Always, 0, No **Orders:** Attack P 1 S 9	**Waves:** 0 **Form:** Finger Four	**Mother:** 8 **AI:** Officcr	**Win:** 0 **Val:** 9
#7	1 Planet Sullust				
#8	1 STD Invincible	**Start:** Always, 0, No **Orders:** Starship Sit + Fire	**Waves:** 0 **Form:** Vic	**Mother:** 0 **AI:** Top Ace	**Win:** 0 **Val:** 0
#9	1 SHU Rescue 1 (rescue team)	**Start:** Disable, 0, 4 **Orders:** Board + Take P 4	**Waves:** 0 **Form:** Vic	**Mother:** 0 **AI:** Top Ace	**Win:** 2 **Val:** 2
#10	3 T/F Gamma	**Start:** Always, 0, No **Orders:** Close Escort P3	**Waves:** 0 **Form:** Line Abreast	**Mother:** 8 **AI:** Officer	**Win:** 0 **Val:** 3
#11	3 T/I Delta	**Start:** Create, 0, 9 **Orders:** Attack P 9 S 1	**Waves:** 9 **Form:** Echelon Right	**Mother:** 8 **AI:** Officer	**Win:** 0 **Val:** 9
#12	3 T/I Zeta	**Start:** Attack, 0:18, 8 **Orders:** Attack All P 1	**Waves:** 9 **Form:** Vic	**Mother:** 8 **AI:** Top Ace	**Win:** 0 **Val:** 0
#13	2 T/B Theta	**Start:** Attack, 0:42, 8 **Orders:** Attack All P 1	**Waves:** 9 **Form:** Vic	**Mother:** 8 **AI:** Top Ace	**Win:** 0 **Val:** 8

OP 11: Capture Staff from Cygnus [cygnus]

*#1	2 A-W Red [1]	**Start:** Always, 0, No **Orders:** Attack P 7 S 6	**Waves:** 0 **Form:** Vic	**Mother:** 0 **AI:** Officer	**Win:** 0 **Val:** 5
#2	2 TRN Lambda (personnel)	**Start:** Always, 0, No **Orders:** Board + Deliver P 4 S 5	**Waves:** 0 **Form:** Echelon Right	**Mother:** 0 **AI:** Top Ace	**Win:** 0 **Val:** 5
#3	1 TRN Kappa (tech staff)	**Start:** Always, 0, No **Orders:** Stationary	**Waves:** 0 **Form:** Echelon Left	**Mother:** 0 **AI:** Top Ace	**Win:** 4 **Val:** 0
#4	1 FRT Dock 1 (TIE Interceptors)	**Start:** Always, 0, No **Orders:** Stationary	**Waves:** 0 **Form:** Line Abreast	**Mother:** 0 **AI:** Veteran	**Win:** 0 **Val:** 0
#5	1 FRT Dock 2 (TIEs)	**Start:** Always, 0, No **Orders:** Stationary	**Waves:** 0 **Form:** Vic	**Mother:** 0 **AI:** Novice	**Win:** 0 **Val:** 0
#6	3 T/B Alpha	**Start:** Always, 0, No **Orders:** Stationary	**Waves:** 0 **Form:** Line Abreast	**Mother:** 0 **AI:** Novice	**Win:** 0 **Val:** 0

#7 3 T/F Beta — **Start:** Always, 0, No — **Orders:** Stationary — **Waves:** 0 — **Form:** Line Abreast — **Mother:** 0 — **AI:** Novice — **Win:** 0 — **Val:** 0

#8 1 T/I Alpha — **Start:** Always, 0, No — **Orders:** Stationary P 1 — **Waves:** 0 — **Form:** Vic — **Mother:** 0 — **AI:** Novice — **Win:** 0 — **Val:** 0

#9 1 Planet Ralltiir

#10 1 GUN Mu — **Start:** Always, 0, No — **Orders:** Attack P 8 — **Waves:** 0 — **Form:** Vic — **Mother:** 0 — **AI:** Top Ace — **Win:** 0 — **Val:** 0

#11 2 T/I Delta — **Start:** Attack 0:06, 5 — **Orders:** Attack P1 — **Waves:** 1 — **Form:** Vic — **Mother:** 4 — **AI:** Veteran — **Win:** 0 — **Val:** 0

#12 2 T/F Zeta — **Start:** ID, 0:12, 3 — **Orders:** Attack P 13 — **Waves:** 2 — **Form:** Vic — **Mother:** 5 — **AI:** Novice — **Win:** 0 — **Val:** 0

#13 1 TRN Lightning (strike team) — **Start:** ID, 0, 3 — **Orders:** Board + Take P 3 — **Waves:** 0 — **Form:** Vic — **Mother:** 0 — **AI:** Top Ace — **Win:** 2 — **Val:** 2

#14 2 T/F Theta — **Start:** Create, 0:12, 3 — **Orders:** Attack P 1 — **Waves:** 1 — **Form:** Vic — **Mother:** 4 — **AI:** Veteran — **Win:** 0 — **Val:** 0

#15 4 T/I Iota — **Start:** Always, 0, No — **Orders:** Stationary — **Waves:** 0 — **Form:** Line Astern — **Mother:** 0 — **AI:** Novice — **Win:** 0 — **Val:** 0

OP 12: Recover Explosive Warhead [max20]

Note: Several of the ship groups in this mission have randomly determined starting points. There are, in fact, three different beginnings to this mission. Some are more difficult than others. If you find the mission impossible, try restarting and you may get an easier starting position.

*#1 1 Y-W Red [1] — **Start:** Always, 0, No — **Orders:** Attack Sat + Mines — **Waves:** 0 — **Form:** Vic — **Mother:** 0 — **AI:** Top Ace — **Win:** 0 — **Val:** 9

* You may begin this mission in one of three spots.

#2 1 SHU Herald — **Start:** Disable, 1:00, 3 — **Orders:** Board + Capture P 3 — **Waves:** 0 — **Form:** Vic — **Mother:** 0 — **AI:** Top Ace — **Win:** 0 — **Val:** 1

* This shuttle may appear in one of three positions.

#3 1 FRT Gafra (warheads) — **Start:** Always, 0, No — **Orders:** Stationary — **Waves:** 0 — **Form:** Vic — **Mother:** 0 — **AI:** Top Ace — **Win:** 3 — **Val:** 0

#4–5 3 Mines

#6 2 SHU Psi — **Start:** Capture, 0, 3 — **Orders:** Attack P 1 S 3 — **Waves:** 0 — **Form:** Vic — **Mother:** 0 — **AI:** Ace — **Win:** 0 — **Val:** 9

* These shuttles may appear in one of three positions.

#7 2 TRN Lambda — **Start:** Capture, 0, 3 — **Orders:** Attack P 3 S 1 — **Waves:** 0 — **Form:** Vic — **Mother:** 0 — **AI:** Ace — **Win:** 0 — **Val:** 9

* These transports may appear in one of three positions.

Tour of Duty 2

OP 1: Rescue from Star's End [starsndb]

*#1	2 A-W Red [1]	**Start:** Always, 0, No **Orders:** Attack P 6 S 10	**Waves:** 0 **Form:** Vic	**Mother:** 0 **AI:** Officer	**Win:** 0 **Val:** 9
#2	1 FRT Genue (rebels)	**Start:** Always, 0, No **Orders:** Disabled	**Waves:** 0 **Form:** Vic	**Mother:** 0 **AI:** Top Ace	**Win:** 3 **Val:** 0
#3	1 TRN Lambda (troopers)	**Start:** Always, 0, No **Orders:** Board + Capture P 2	**Waves:** 0 **Form:** Vic	**Mother:** 4 **AI:** Veteran	**Win:** 1 **Val:** 2
#4	1 STD Intrepid	**Start:** Always, 0, No **Orders:** Starship Sit + Fire	**Waves:** 0 **Form:** Vic	**Mother:** 0 **AI:** Top Ace	**Win:** 0 **Val:** 0
#5	3 T/I Gamma	**Start:** Destroy, 1:00, 9 **Orders:** Attack All P 8 S 2	**Waves:** 1 **Form:** Vic	**Mother:** 4 **AI:** Ace	**Win:** 0 **Val:** 9
#6	2 T/F Beta	**Start:** Attack 0, No **Orders:** Close Escort P 3 S 4	**Waves:** 9 **Form:** Vic	**Mother:** 4 **AI:** Ace	**Win:** 0 **Val:** 9
#7	4 T/F Delta	**Start:** Always, 1:00, No **Orders:** Attack All	**Waves:** 3 **Form:** Diamond	**Mother:** 4 **AI:** Officer	**Win:** 0 **Val:** 9
#8	1 SHU Drago (rescue team)	**Start:** Destroy, 4:00, 3 **Orders:** Board + Capture P 2	**Waves:** 0 **Form:** Vic	**Mother:** 0 **AI:** Top Ace	**Win:** 2 **Val:** 2
#9	3 T/B Eta	**Start:** Destroy, 3:00, 3 **Orders:** Attack P 2 S 8	**Waves:** 1 **Form:** Vic	**Mother:** 4 **AI:** Veteran	**Win:** 0 **Val:** 9
#10	2 T/I Alpha	**Start:** Always, 0, No **Orders:** Loose Escort P 3 S 4	**Waves:** 0 **Form:** Vic	**Mother:** 4 **AI:** Officer	**Win:** 0 **Val:** 9
#11	3 T/I Iota	**Start:** Attack 0:18, 4 **Orders:** Attack P1	**Waves:** 9 **Form:** Vic	**Mother:** 4 **AI:** Top Ace	**Win:** 0 **Val:** 0
#12	3 T/B Theta	**Start:** Attack, 0:42, 4 **Orders:** Attack All P 1	**Waves:** 9 **Form:** Vic	**Mother:** 4 **AI:** Top Ace	**Win:** 0 **Val:** 0

OP 2: Rescue Wookiee Slaves [rescue1]

*#1	3 A-W Red [3]	**Start:** Always, 0, 1 **Orders:** Attack All	**Waves:** 0 **Form:** Finger Four	**Mother:** 0 **AI:** Veteran	**Win:** 0 **Val:** 9
#2	1 TRN Rescue 1 (rescue team)	**Start:** Disable, 0, 7 **Orders:** Board + Take P 7	**Waves:** 0 **Form:** Vic	**Mother:** 0 **AI:** Top Ace	**Win:** 0 **Val:** 1
#3	2 GUN Mu	**Start:** Always, 0, 1 **Orders:** Attack S 1	**Waves:** 0 **Form:** Vic	**Mother:** 6 **AI:** Veteran	**Win:** 0 **Val:** 9
#4	2 GUN Nu	**Start:** Always, 0, 1 **Orders:** Attack S 1	**Waves:** 0 **Form:** Vic	**Mother:** 6 **AI:** Veteran	**Win:** 0 **Val:** 9
#5	2 GUN Tru	**Start:** Always, 0, 1 **Orders:** Attack P 1	**Waves:** 0 **Form:** Vic	**Mother:** 6 **AI:** Ace	**Win:** 0 **Val:** 9

#6	1 STD Intrepid	**Start:** Always, 0, 1 **Orders:** Starship Sit + Fire	**Waves:** 0 **Form:** Vic	**Mother:** 0 **AI:** Veteran	**Win:** 0 **Val:** 1
#7	1 FRT Toral (Wookiees)	**Start:** Always, 0, 1 **Orders:** Go Home	**Waves:** 0 **Form:** Vic	**Mother:** 6 **AI:** Veteran	**Win:** 4 **Val:** 1
#8	3 T/F Alpha	**Start:** Always, 0, No **Orders:** Loose Escort P 7	**Waves:** 0 **Form:** Vic	**Mother:** 6 **AI:** Veteran	**Win:** 0 **Val:** 1
#9	3 T/F Beta	**Start:** Always, 0, No **Orders:** Close Escort P 7	**Waves:** 0 **Form:** Vic	**Mother:** 6 **AI:** Officer	**Win:** 0 **Val:** 3
#10	3 T/F Gamma	**Start:** Always, 0, No **Orders:** Loose Escort P 7	**Waves:** 0 **Form:** Vic	**Mother:** 6 **AI:** Veteran	**Win:** 0 **Val:** 4
#11	3 T/F Delta	**Start:** Always, 0, No **Orders:** Close Escort P 7	**Waves:** 0 **Form:** Vic	**Mother:** 6 **AI:** Veteran	**Win:** 0 **Val:** 1
#12	3 T/F Zeta	**Start:** Disable, 1:00, 7 **Orders:** Attack P 2 S 7	**Waves:** 3 **Form:** Vic	**Mother:** 6 **AI:** Veteran	**Win:** 0 **Val:** 9
#13	3 T/F Theta	**Start:** Create, 0, 16 **Orders:** Attack All	**Waves:** 9 **Form:** Vic	**Mother:** 6 **AI:** Veteran	**Win:** 0 **Val:** 9
#14	3 T/I Iota	**Start:** Attack, 0:18, 6 **Orders:** Attack All P 1	**Waves:** 9 **Form:** Vic	**Mother:** 6 **AI:** Top Ace	**Win:** 0 **Val:** 0
#15	3 T/B Theta	**Start:** Attack, 0:42, 6 **Orders:** Attack All P 1	**Waves:** 9 **Form:** Vic	**Mother:** 6 **AI:** Top Ace	**Win:** 0 **Val:** 0
#16	2 Y-W Gold	**Start:** ID, 0, 7 **Orders:** Disable P 7	**Waves:** 0 **Form:** Vic	**Mother:** 0 **AI:** Top Ace	**Win:** 0 **Val:** 9

OP 3: Attack Weapons Convoy [ystrike5]

*#1	3 Y-W Red [2]	**Start:** Always, 0, No **Orders:** Attack All P 7 S 6	**Waves:** 0 **Form:** Finger Four	**Mother:** 0 **AI:** Officer	**Win:** 0 **Val:** 9
#2	3 Y/W Gold	**Start:** Always, 0, No **Orders:** Attack All P 8 S 9	**Waves:** 0 **Form:** Finger Four	**Mother:** 0 **AI:** Novice	**Win:** 0 **Val:** 9
#3	3 Comm-Sats				
#4	1 X-W Blue	**Start:** Always, 0, No **Orders:** Loose Escort P 1 S 2	**Waves:** 0 **Form:** Vic	**Mother:** 0 **AI:** Veteran	**Win:** 0 **Val:** 3
#5	2 GUN Mu	**Start:** Create, 1:00, 12 **Orders:** Attack All	**Waves:** 1 **Form:** Vic	**Mother:** 0 **AI:** Ace	**Win:** 0 **Val:** 9
#6	2 SHU Kappa (officers)	**Start:** Create, 0, 8 **Orders:** Fly Once + Evade	**Waves:** 0 **Form:** Vic	**Mother:** 0 **AI:** Novice	**Win:** 1 **Val:** 3
#7	2 CRV Hyko	**Start:** Always, 1:00, No **Orders:** Starship Fly Once	**Waves:** 0 **Form:** Vic	**Mother:** 0 **AI:** Novice	**Win:** 1 **Val:** 4
#8	3 TRN Epsilon (troopers)	**Start:** Create, 0, 7 **Orders:** Fly Once + Ignore	**Waves:** 0 **Form:** Line Astern	**Mother:** 0 **AI:** Novice	**Win:** 1 **Val:** 4

#9	2 TRN Lambda (troopers)	**Start:** Create, 0, 6 **Orders:** Fly Once + Ignore	**Waves:** 0 **Form:** Vic	**Mother:** 0 **AI:** Novice	**Win:** 1 **Val:** 4
#10	1 FRT Uhuru (supplies)	**Start:** Create, 0, 9 **Orders:** Fly Once + Ignore	**Waves:** 0 **Form:** Vic	**Mother:** 0 **AI:** Novice	**Win:** 1 **Val:** 9
#11	1 FRT The Tone (supplies)	**Start:** Create, 0, 9 **Orders:** Fly Once + Ignore	**Waves:** 0 **Form:** Vic	**Mother:** 0 **AI:** Novice	**Win:** 1 **Val:** 9
#12	2 GUN Tru	**Start:** Create, 0, 6 **Orders:** Close Escort P 6	**Waves:** 0 **Form:** Vic	**Mother:** 0 **AI:** Veteran	**Win:** 0 **Val:** 9
#13	2 GUN Rho	**Start:** Create, 1:00, 5 **Orders:** Attack All	**Waves:** 1 **Form:** Vic	**Mother:** 0 **AI:** Ace	**Win:** 0 **Val:** 9
#14	1 Planet Orron III				

OP 4: Capture Stolen Freighter [wycapt2]

*#1	1 Y-W Red [1]	**Start:** Always, 0, 1 **Orders:** Attack All	**Waves:** 0 **Form:** Vic	**Mother:** 0 **AI:** Top Ace	**Win:** 0 **Val:** 9

* You may start this mission in one of three fixed locations, randomly selected.

#2	1 SHU Wilsey (boarding party)	**Start:** Disable, 0, 3 **Orders:** Board + Capture P 3	**Waves:** 0 **Form:** Vic	**Mother:** 0 **AI:** Top Ace	**Win:** 2 **Val:** 2

* The Wilsey starts the mission in one of three positions; some better, some worse.

#3	1 FRT Phoenix (comm sats)	**Start:** Always, 0, 1 **Orders:** Go Home	**Waves:** 0 **Form:** Vic	**Mother:** 0 **AI:** Top Ace	**Win:** 3 **Val:** 9
#4	1 TRN Epsilon (troopers)	**Start:** Always, 0, No **Orders:** Board + Capture P 3	**Waves:** 1 **Form:** Vic	**Mother:** 0 **AI:** Veteran	**Win:** 0 **Val:** 2
#5	1 TRN Kappa (troopers)	**Start:** Always, 0, No **Orders:** Disable freighters P 3	**Waves:** 1 **Form:** Vic	**Mother:** 0 **AI:** Top Ace	**Win:** 0 **Val:** 9
#6	2 SHU Lambda	**Start:** Always, 0, No **Orders:** Disable P 1 S 2	**Waves:** 0 **Form:** Vic	**Mother:** 0 **AI:** Top Ace	**Win:** 0 **Val:** 9
#7	2 SHU Omicron	**Start:** Always, 0, No **Orders:** Attack P 2 S 1	**Waves:** 0 **Form:** Vic	**Mother:** 0 **AI:** Top Ace	**Win:** 0 **Val:** 9
#8	1 STD Intrepid	**Start:** Capture, 1:00, 3 **Orders:** Starship Circle	**Waves:** 0 **Form:** Vic	**Mother:** 0 **AI:** Top Ace	**Win:** 0 **Val:** 9

* The Intrepid enters the mission in one of three positions.

#9	3 T/F Alpha	**Start:** Capture, 1:18, 3 **Orders:** Attack All P 1	**Waves:** 0 **Form:** Echelon Right	**Mother:** 8 **AI:** Officer	**Win:** 0 **Val:** 9
#10	3 T/F Beta	**Start:** Capture, 3:00, 3 **Orders:** Attack All P 1	**Waves:** 3 **Form:** Echelon Left	**Mother:** 8 **AI:** Veteran	**Win:** 0 **Val:** 9
#11	3 T/B Gamma	**Start:** Capture, 1:24, 3 **Orders:** Attack All P 3 S 1	**Waves:** 3 **Form:** Line Abreast	**Mother:** 8 **AI:** Veteran	**Win:** 0 **Val:** 9

#12 6 T/I Iota	**Start:** Attack, 0, 8 **Orders:** Attack All P 1	**Waves:** 9 **Form:** Vic	**Mother:** 8 **AI:** Top Ace	**Win:** 0 **Val:** 0
#13 6 T/B Theta	**Start:** Attack, 0, 8 **Orders:** Attack All P 1	**Waves:** 9 **Form:** Vic	**Mother:** 8 **AI:** Top Ace	**Win:** 0 **Val:** 0
#14 1 Planet Orron III				

OP 5: Protect Captured Satellites [max9]

#1 2 T/I Alpha	**Start:** Always, 0, No **Orders:** Attack P 12 S 13	**Waves:** 0 **Form:** Vic	**Mother:** 3 **AI:** Top Ace	**Win:** 0 **Val:** 9

* These TIE Interceptors start out in one of two positions, randomly determined.

#2 2 T/B Beta	**Start:** Always, 0, No **Orders:** Attack P 12 S 13	**Waves:** 1 **Form:** Vic	**Mother:** 3 **AI:** Top Ace	**Win:** 0 **Val:** 9

* These TIE Bombers start out in one of two positions, randomly determined.

#3 1 STD Intrepid	**Start:** Always, 0, No **Orders:** Starship Fly Once	**Waves:** 0 **Form:** Vic	**Mother:** 0 **AI:** Top Ace	**Win:** 0 **Val:** 4
#4 1 T/I Delta	**Start:** Always, 1:00, No **Orders:** Attack P 12 S 13	**Waves:** 2 **Form:** Vic	**Mother:** 3 **AI:** Top Ace	**Win:** 0 **Val:** 9
#5 1 T/I Zeta	**Start:** Always, 2:00, No **Orders:** Attack P 12 S 13	**Waves:** 0 **Form:** Vic	**Mother:** 3 **AI:** Top Ace	**Win:** 0 **Val:** 9
#6 1 T/F Theta	**Start:** Always, 3:00, No **Orders:** Attack P 12 S 13	**Waves:** 0 **Form:** Vic	**Mother:** 3 **AI:** Top Ace	**Win:** 0 **Val:** 9
#7 1 T/F Iota	**Start:** Always, 4:00, No **Orders:** Attack P 12 S 13	**Waves:** 0 **Form:** Vic	**Mother:** 3 **AI:** Top Ace	**Win:** 0 **Val:** 9
#8 1 T/B Gamma	**Start:** Always, 5:00, No **Orders:** Attack All P 12 S 13	**Waves:** 0 **Form:** Vic	**Mother:** 3 **AI:** Top Ace	**Win:** 0 **Val:** 9
#9 1 T/B Eta	**Start:** Always, 6:00, No **Orders:** Attack All	**Waves:** 0 **Form:** Vic	**Mother:** 3 **AI:** Top Ace	**Win:** 0 **Val:** 9
#10 1 T/I Alpha	**Start:** Always, 7:00, No **Orders:** Attack All	**Waves:** 0 **Form:** Vic	**Mother:** 3 **AI:** Top Ace	**Win:** 0 **Val:** 9
#11 1 T/F Beta	**Start:** Always, 8:00, No **Orders:** Attack All	**Waves:** 0 **Form:** Vic	**Mother:** 3 **AI:** Top Ace	**Win:** 0 **Val:** 9
*#12 1 A-W Red [1]	**Start:** Always, 0, No **Orders:** Attack All	**Waves:** 0 **Form:** Vic	**Mother:** 0 **AI:** Top Ace	**Win:** 0 **Val:** 9
#13 1 FRT Phoenix (comm sats)	**Start:** Always, 0, No **Orders:** Stationary	**Waves:** 0 **Form:** Vic	**Mother:** 0 **AI:** Top Ace	**Win:** 4 **Val:** 0
#14 1 FRT Ojai	**Start:** Always, 9:00, No **Orders:** Board + Take P 13	**Waves:** 0 **Form:** Vic	**Mother:** 0 **AI:** Top Ace	**Win:** 2 **Val:** 2

#15 1 CRS Maximus	**Start:** Always, 9:00, 1 **Orders:** Starship Fly Once	**Waves:** 0 **Form:** Vic	**Mother:** 0 **AI:** Top Ace	**Win:** 16 **Val:** 1
#16 4 X-W Blue	**Start:** Always, 10:00, No **Orders:** Attack All	**Waves:** 4 **Form:** Vic	**Mother:** 15 **AI:** Ace	**Win:** 0 **Val:** 3

OP 6: Ambush in the Cron Drift [crndrft1]

*#1 2 X-W Red [1]	**Start:** Always, 0, No **Orders:** Attack All	**Waves:** 0 **Form:** Vic	**Mother:** 0 **AI:** Veteran	**Win:** 0 **Val:** 2
#2 2 GUN Mu	**Start:** Always, 0:48, No **Orders:** Attack All P 5	**Waves:** 2 **Form:** Vic	**Mother:** 0 **AI:** Veteran	**Win:** 0 **Val:** 8
#3 1 FRT Ojai	**Start:** Always, 0:12, No **Orders:** Board + Deliver P 4	**Waves:** 0 **Form:** Line Astern	**Mother:** 0 **AI:** Top Ace	**Win:** 0 **Val:** 2
#4 1 CRV Jeffrey	**Start:** Always, 0, No **Orders:** Starship Wait Board P 5 S 3	**Waves:** 0 **Form:** Vic	**Mother:** 0 **AI:** Top Ace	**Win:** 2 **Val:** 0
#5 1 TRN Magnus (supplies)	**Start:** Always, 0:06, No **Orders:** Board + Deliver P 4	**Waves:** 0 **Form:** Vic	**Mother:** 0 **AI:** Top Ace	**Win:** 0 **Val:** 1
#6–14 1 asteroid				
#15 2 GUN Nu	**Start:** Always, 1:24, No **Orders:** Attack All P 1	**Waves:** 2 **Form:** Vic	**Mother:** 0 **AI:** Officer	**Win:** 0 **Val:** 9
#16 1 TRN Lambda	**Start:** Always, 1:12, No **Orders:** Attack freighters P 3	**Waves:** 0 **Form:** Vic	**Mother:** 0 **AI:** Ace	**Win:** **Val:** 7
#17 1 TRN Kappa	**Start:** Destroy, 0:30, 16 **Orders:** Attack freighters P 4	**Waves:** 0 **Form:** Vic	**Mother:** 0 **AI:** Veteran	**Win:** 0 **Val:** 7
#18 1 TRN Omicron	**Start:** Destroy, 0:30, 17 **Orders:** Attack freighters	**Waves:** 0 **Form:** Vic	**Mother:** 0 **AI:** Veteran	**Win:** 0 **Val:** 7
#19 1 TRN Sigma	**Start:** Destroy, 0:30, 18 **Orders:** Attack freighters	**Waves:** 0 **Form:** Vic	**Mother:** 0 **AI:** Veteran	**Win:** 0 **Val:** 0
#20 1 GUN Tru	**Start:** Destroy, 1:00, 2 **Orders:** Attack freighters	**Waves:** 2 **Form:** Vic	**Mother:** 0 **AI:** Veteran	**Win:** 0 **Val:** 9

OP 7: Protect a Disabled X-wing [max18]

This mission has three possible starting places for several ships. You may find it very difficult to complete, depending on which configuration is randomly chosen. If the mission seems impossible, try again and hope for easier starting positions.

#1 1 X-W Blue	**Start:** Always, 0, No **Orders:** Disabled	**Waves:** 0 **Form:** Vic	**Mother:** 0 **AI:** Top Ace	**Win:** 2 **Val:** 0
*#2 3 A-W Red [1]	**Start:** Always, 0, No **Orders:** Close Escort P 1	**Waves:** 0 **Form:** Vic	**Mother:** 0 **AI:** Top Ace	**Win:** 0 **Val:** 9

#3	1 SHU ATK 253	**Start:** Always, 2:00, No **Orders:** Board + Capture P 1	**Waves:** 0 **Form:** Vic	**Mother:** 10 **AI:** Top Ace	**Win:** 0 **Val:** 2

* This shuttle craft may begin the mission in one of three possible places.

#4	3 GUN Mu	**Start:** Always, 1:00, No **Orders:** Attack P 1	**Waves:** 0 **Form:** Vic	**Mother:** 0 **AI:** Top Ace	**Win:** 0 **Val:** 9

* These gunboats may begin the mission in one of three possible places, one of them very close to the corvettes.

#5	3 GUN Nu	**Start:** Always, 1:00, No **Orders:** Attack P 2	**Waves:** 0 **Form:** Vic	**Mother:** 0 **AI:** Top Ace	**Win:** 0 **Val:** 9

* These gunboats may begin the mission in one of three possible places, one of them very close to the corvettes.

#6	3 GUN Tau	**Start:** Destroy, 1:00, 5 **Orders:** Attack P 2	**Waves:** 0 **Form:** Vic	**Mother:** 0 **AI:** Top Ace	**Win:** 0 **Val:** 9

* These gunboats may begin the mission in one of three possible places, one of them very close to the corvettes.

#7	3 GUN Rho	**Start:** Destroy, 1:00, 4 **Orders:** Attack P 2	**Waves:** 0 **Form:** Vic	**Mother:** 0 **AI:** Top Ace	**Win:** 0 **Val:** 9

* These gunboats may begin the mission in one of three possible places.

#8	1 SHU ATK 592 (troopers)	**Start:** Destroy, 0, 3 **Orders:** Board + Capture P 1	**Waves:** 0 **Form:** Vic	**Mother:** 10 **AI:** Top Ace	**Win:** 0 **Val:** 1

* This shuttle craft may begin the mission in one of three possible places.

#9	1 SHU ATK 664 (troopers)	**Start:** Destroy, 0, 8 **Orders:** Board + Capture P 1	**Waves:** 0 **Form:** Vic	**Mother:** 10 **AI:** Top Ace	**Win:** 0 **Val:** 2

* This shuttle craft may begin the mission in one of three possible places.

#10	1 STD Intrepid	**Start:** Capture, 0, 1 **Orders:** Starship Fly Once	**Waves:** 0 **Form:** Vic	**Mother:** 0 **AI:** Top Ace	**Win:** 0 **Val:** 4
#11	1 CRV Tantive II	**Start:** Destroy, 0, 9 **Orders:** Starship Fly Once	**Waves:** 0 **Form:** Vic	**Mother:** 0 **AI:** Top Ace	**Win:** 0 **Val:** 5
#12	1 CRV Tantive III	**Start:** Destroy, 0, 9 **Orders:** Starship Fly Once	**Waves:** 0 **Form:** Vic	**Mother:** 0 **AI:** Top Ace	**Win:** 0 **Val:** 5
#13	1 CRV Tantive I	**Start:** Destroy, 0, 9 **Orders:** Starship Fly Once	**Waves:** 0 **Form:** Vic	**Mother:** 0 **AI:** Top Ace	**Win:** 0 **Val:** 5
#14	1 SHU Rescue (power generator)	**Start:** Destroy, 0, 9 **Orders:** Board + Deliver P 1 S 1	**Waves:** 0 **Form:** Vic	**Mother:** 0 **AI:** Top Ace	**Win:** 2 **Val:** 1

* This shuttle craft may begin the mission in one of three possible places.

#15	1 SHU Rescue 2 (power generator)	**Start:** Always, 18:00, No **Orders:** Board + Deliver P 1	**Waves:** 0 **Form:** Vic	**Mother:** 0 **AI:** Top Ace	**Win:** 0 **Val:** 9

* This shuttle craft may begin the mission in one of three possible places.

#16	4 T/B Iota	**Start:** Attack, 0:18, 10 **Orders:** Attack All P 2	**Waves:** 9 **Form:** Vic	**Mother:** 10 **AI:** Top Ace	**Win:** 0 **Val:** 0

OP 8: Stop Hyperdrive Replacement [max1]

#1	1 FRT Kiam I (sensors)	**Start:** Always, 0, 1 **Orders:** Board + Deliver P 11 S 11	**Waves:** 0 **Form:** Vic	**Mother:** 0 **AI:** Novice	**Win:** 0 **Val:** 7
#2	1 FRT Kiam II (supplies)	**Start:** Always, 0, 1 **Orders:** Board + Deliver P11 S11	**Waves:** 0 **Form:** Vic	**Mother:** 0 **AI:** Top Ace	**Win:** 0 **Val:** 7
*#3	1 X-W Red [1]	**Start:** Always, 0, 1 **Orders:** Attack All	**Waves:** 0 **Form:** Vic	**Mother:** 0 **AI:** Novice	**Win:** 0 **Val:** 9
#4	2 A-W Blue	**Start:** Always, 0, 1 **Orders:** Close Escort P 3	**Waves:** 0 **Form:** Line Astern	**Mother:** 0 **AI:** Top Ace	**Win:** 0 **Val:** 1
#5	2 T/F Alpha	**Start:** Always, 0, 1 **Orders:** Attack All P 3 S 4	**Waves:** 0 **Form:** Vic	**Mother:** 11 **AI:** Top Ace	**Win:** 0 **Val:** 9

* These TIE Fighters may begin the mission in one of two possible places, one very close to your position.

#6	2 T/F Beta	**Start:** Always, 0, 1 **Orders:** Attack All P 4 S 3	**Waves:** 0 **Form:** Vic	**Mother:** 11 **AI:** Top Ace	**Win:** 0 **Val:** 9

* These TIE Fighters may begin the mission in one of two possible places, one very close to your position.

#7	2 T/I Delta	**Start:** Always, 2:00, 1 **Orders:** Attack All P 4	**Waves:** 2 **Form:** Line Astern	**Mother:** 11 **AI:** Officer	**Win:** 0 **Val:** 7
#8	2 T/I Gamma	**Start:** ID, 0, 12 **Orders:** Attack All P 3	**Waves:** 3 **Form:** Vic	**Mother:** 11 **AI:** Top Ace	**Win:** 0 **Val:** 9
#9	2 T/I Zeta	**Start:** ID, 0, 13 **Orders:** Attack All P 3	**Waves:** 3 **Form:** Vic	**Mother:** 11 **AI:** Top Ace	**Win:** 0 **Val:** 9
#10	2 T/I Theta	**Start:** Always, 3:00, 1 **Orders:** Attack All P 3	**Waves:** 9 **Form:** Vic	**Mother:** 11 **AI:** Top Ace	**Win:** 0 **Val:** 9
#11	1 STD Intrepid	**Start:** Always, 0, 1 **Orders:** Starship Sit + Fire	**Waves:** 0 **Form:** Vic	**Mother:** 0 **AI:** Novice	**Win:** 0 **Val:** 0
#12	1 FRT Kiam III (hyperdrive)	**Start:** Always, 0, 1 **Orders:** Board + Deliver P 11 S 11	**Waves:** 0 **Form:** Vic	**Mother:** 0 **AI:** Novice	**Win:** 1 **Val:** 7

* This freighter, which is one of the main objects of this mission, may start in one of three places. All are equally distant from the Star Destroyer, but some are much farther away from your starting position.

#13	1 FRT Kiam IV (machinery)	**Start:** Always, 0, 1 **Orders:** Board + Deliver P 11 S 11	**Waves:** 0 **Form:** Vic	**Mother:** 0 **AI:** Novice	**Win:** 0 **Val:** 7

* This freighter may start from one of three positions, but they have meaning only in that it makes this serve as a decoy for Kiam III or Kiam V, which are your targets.

#14	1 FRT Kiam V (hyperdrive)	**Start:** Always, 0, 1 **Orders:** Board + Deliver P 11 S 11	**Waves:** 0 **Form:** Vic	**Mother:** 0 **AI:** Novice	**Win:** 1 **Val:** 7

* This freighter, which is one of the main objects of this mission, may start in one of three places. Some are much farther away from your starting position.

#15	6 T/I Iota	**Start:** Attack, 0,11 **Orders:** Attack All P 3 S 4	**Waves:** 9 **Form:** Vic	**Mother:** 11 **AI:** Top Ace	**Win:** 0 **Val:** 0
#16	1 Planet				

OP 9: Take Out Intrepid's Escort [std1]

*#1	3 Y-W Red [1]	**Start:** Always, 0, No **Orders:** Attack All	**Waves:** 0 **Form:** Line Abreast	**Mother:** 0 **AI:** Ace	**Win:** 0 **Val:** 0
#2	1 X-W Blue	**Start:** Always, 0:06, No **Orders:** Close Escort P 1	**Waves:** 0 **Form:** Vic	**Mother:** 0 **AI:** Ace	**Win:** 0 **Val:** 1
#3	1 STD Intrepid	**Start:** Always, 0, No **Orders:** Starship Sit + Fire	**Waves:** 0 **Form:** Vic	**Mother:** 0 **AI:** Top Ace	**Win:** 0 **Val:** 0
#4	1 CRV Viper 1 (stormtroopers)	**Start:** Always, 0, No **Orders:** Starship Fly Once	**Waves:** 0 **Form:** Vic	**Mother:** 0 **AI:** Top Ace	**Win:** 1 **Val:** 0
#5	1 CRV Viper 2 (stormtroopers)	**Start:** Always, 0, No **Orders:** Starship Fly Once	**Waves:** 0 **Form:** Vic	**Mother:** 0 **AI:** Top Ace	**Win:** 1 **Val:** 0
#6	1 CRV Viper 3 (stormtroopers)	**Start:** Always, 0, No **Orders:** Starship Fly Once	**Waves:** 0 **Form:** Vic	**Mother:** 0 **AI:** Top Ace	**Win:** 1 **Val:** 0
#7	3 GUN Mu	**Start:** Always, 0, No **Orders:** Close Escort P 6	**Waves:** 0 **Form:** Vic	**Mother:** 0 **AI:** Top Ace	**Win:** 1 **Val:** 0
#8	3 GUN Rho	**Start:** Always, 0, No **Orders:** Close Escort P 5	**Waves:** 0 **Form:** Vic	**Mother:** 0 **AI:** Top Ace	**Win:** 1 **Val:** 0
#9	3 GUN Tru	**Start:** Always, 0, No **Orders:** Attack P 1	**Waves:** 0 **Form:** Vic	**Mother:** 0 **AI:** Top Ace	**Win:** 1 **Val:** 0
#10	6 GUN Nu	**Start:** Attack, 0, 3 **Orders:** Attack All P 1	**Waves:** 9 **Form:** Vic	**Mother:** 3 **AI:** Top Ace	**Win:** 0 **Val:** 0
#11	6 T/B Nu	**Start:** Attack, 0, 3 **Orders:** Attack All P 1	**Waves:** 9 **Form:** Vic	**Mother:** 3 **AI:** Top Ace	**Win:** 0 **Val:** 0

OP 10: Destroy the Intrepid [std2]

*#1	2 X-W Red [1]	**Start:** Always, 0, No **Orders:** Attack All	**Waves:** 0 **Form:** Vic	**Mother:** 0 **AI:** Top Ace	**Win:** 0 **Val:** 0
#2	4 Y-W Blue	**Start:** Always, 0, No **Orders:** Attack Starships P 9	**Waves:** 6 **Form:** Vic	**Mother:** 0 **AI:** Ace	**Win:** 0 **Val:** 0
#3	2 A-W Gold	**Start:** Always, 0:06, No **Orders:** Close Escort P 1	**Waves:** 0 **Form:** Vic	**Mother:** 0 **AI:** Top Ace	**Win:** 0 **Val:** 1
#4	4 T/F Alpha	**Start:** Always, 0, No **Orders:** Attack All P 2 S 3	**Waves:** 0 **Form:** Line Abreast	**Mother:** 9 **AI:** Top Ace	**Win:** 0 **Val:** 0
#5	2 T/F Beta	**Start:** Always, 0, No **Orders:** Attack All P 3 S 2	**Waves:** 9 **Form:** Finger Four	**Mother:** 9 **AI:** Top Ace	**Win:** 0 **Val:** 0

#6	2 T/B Gamma	**Start:** Always, 0, No **Orders:** Attack All P 1 S 2	**Waves:** 9 **Form:** Echelon Right	**Mother:** 9 **AI:** Top Ace	**Win:** 0 **Val:** 0
#7	2 T/I Zeta	**Start:** Always, 0, 9 **Orders:** Attack All P 1 S 3	**Waves:** 9 **Form:** Vic	**Mother:** 9 **AI:** Top Ace	**Win:** 0 **Val:** 0
#8	4 GUN Rho	**Start:** Always, 10:00, No **Orders:** Attack All P 1 S 3	**Waves:** 9 **Form:** Double Astern	**Mother:** 9 **AI:** Top Ace	**Win:** 0 **Val:** 0

* These Gunboats may appear in one of three positions. Two are very close to the Intrepid. One is farther away.

#9	1 STD Intrepid	**Start:** Always, 0, No **Orders:** Starship Sit + Fire	**Waves:** 0 **Form:** Vic	**Mother:** 0 **AI:** Top Ace	**Win:** 1 **Val:** 0

OP 11: Deliver Plans to Princess Leia [leia]

In this mission, flight groups 5, 7, 8, and 9 may each appear in one of three positions, so it is difficult to determine where each will be at the beginning of the mission. For this reason, the corvette carrying the princess is not always found in the same starting position.

*#1	1 X-W Red 2 [1]	**Start:** Always, 0, No **Orders:** Attack All	**Waves:** 0 **Form:** Vic	**Mother:** 0 **AI:** Top Ace	**Win:** 0 **Val:** 0
#2	2 X-W Gold	**Start:** Always, 0, No **Orders:** Attack All	**Waves:** 0 **Form:** Vic	**Mother:** 0 **AI:** Ace	**Win:** 0 **Val:** 0
#3	1 STD Immortal (Vader)	**Start:** Disable, 0, 7 **Orders:** Starship Wait Return P 7	**Waves:** 0 **Form:** Vic	**Mother:** 0 **AI:** Top Ace	**Win:** 0 **Val:** 0
#4	1 CRV T-Force 1 (power generator)	**Start:** Always, 0, No **Orders:** Wait Until Ship P 13	**Waves:** 0 **Form:** Vic	**Mother:** 0 **AI:** Top Ace	**Win:** 0 **Val:** 9
#5	1 CRV T-Force 2 (supplies)	**Start:** Always, 0, No **Orders:** Starship Sit + Fire P 14 S 12	**Waves:** 0 **Form:** Vic	**Mother:** 0 **AI:** Top Ace	**Win:** 0 **Val:** 0
#6	1 CRV T-Force 3 (base equipment)	**Start:** Always, 0, No **Orders:** Wait Until Ship P 13	**Waves:** 0 **Form:** Vic	**Mother:** 0 **AI:** Top Ace	**Win:** 0 **Val:** 3
#7	1 CRV Tantive IV (Princess Leia)	**Start:** Always, 0, No **Orders:** Starship Wait Board P 9	**Waves:** 0 **Form:** Vic	**Mother:** 0 **AI:** Top Ace	**Win:** 2 **Val:** 9
#8	1 CRV T-Force 4 (supplies)	**Start:** Always, 0, No **Orders:** Starship Sit + Fire P 14 S 12	**Waves:** 0 **Form:** Vic	**Mother:** 0 **AI:** Top Ace	**Win:** 0 **Val:** 0
#9	1 SHU Maria (DS plans)	**Start:** ID, 0, 7 **Orders:** Board + Deliver P 7	**Waves:** 0 **Form:** Vic	**Mother:** 0 **AI:** Top Ace	**Win:** 16 **Val:** 1
#10	1 SHU Epsilon (stormtroopers)	**Start:** Disable, 0:18, 7 **Orders:** Board + Capture P 7	**Waves:** 9 **Form:** Vic	**Mother:** 3 **AI:** Top Ace	**Win:** 0 **Val:** 1
#11	4 GUN Mu	**Start:** ID, 1:12, 7 **Orders:** Disable P 7	**Waves:** 0 **Form:** Vic	**Mother:** 13 **AI:** Top Ace	**Win:** 0 **Val:** 0
#12	4 GUN Tau	**Start:** ID, 1:06, 7 **Orders:** Attack All	**Waves:** 0 **Form:** Vic	**Mother:** 13 **AI:** Top Ace	**Win:** 0 **Val:** 0

#13	1 STD Immortal (Vader)	**Start:** ID, 1:00, 7 **Orders:** Starship Fly Once	**Waves:** 0 **Form:** Vic	**Mother:** 0 **AI:** Top Ace	**Win:** 0 **Val:** 9
#14	2 T/I Zeta	**Start:** Disable, 0:12, 7 **Orders:** Attack All P 1	**Waves:** 9 **Form:** Vic	**Mother:** 3 **AI:** Top Ace	**Win:** 0 **Val:** 0
#15	2 Y-W Blue	**Start:** Capture, 0, 7 **Orders:** Disable P 7	**Waves:** 2 **Form:** Vic	**Mother:** 0 **AI:** Top Ace	**Win:** 0 **Val:** 0
#16	1 SHU Fate	**Start:** Capture, 1:00, 7 **Orders:** Board + Capture P 7	**Waves:** 2 **Form:** Vic	**Mother:** 0 **AI:** Top Ace	**Win:** 0 **Val:** 1

OP 12: Protect Princess Leia [intcep1]

#1	2 X-W Gold	**Start:** Always, 0, No **Orders:** Close Escort P 4 S 3	**Waves:** 0 **Form:** Line Astern	**Mother:** 0 **AI:** Novice	**Win:** 0 **Val:** 1
*#2	2 A-W Red [2]	**Start:** Always, 0, No **Orders:** Attack All	**Waves:** 0 **Form:** Finger Four	**Mother:** 0 **AI:** Veteran	**Win:** 0 **Val:** 9
#3	1 CRS Liberty	**Start:** Always, 0, No **Orders:** Starship Fly Once	**Waves:** 0 **Form:** Vic	**Mother:** 0 **AI:** Top Ace	**Win:** 0 **Val:** 9
#4	1 CRV Tantive IV (Princess Leia)	**Start:** Always, 0, No **Orders:** Go Home	**Waves:** 0 **Form:** Vic	**Mother:** 0 **AI:** Top Ace	**Win:** 2 **Val:** 9
#5	1 STD Immortal	**Start:** Always, 0, No **Orders:** Starship Fly Once	**Waves:** 0 **Form:** Vic	**Mother:** 0 **AI:** Top Ace	**Win:** 0 **Val:** 0
#6	3 T/I Alpha	**Start:** Always, 0, No **Orders:** Attack All P 1 S 2	**Waves:** 0 **Form:** Echelon Right	**Mother:** 5 **AI:** Officer	**Win:** 0 **Val:** 9
#7	3 T/I Beta	**Start:** Always, 0, No **Orders:** Attack All P 2 S 1	**Waves:** 0 **Form:** Line Abreast	**Mother:** 5 **AI:** Officer	**Win:** 0 **Val:** 9
#8	3 T/B Gamma	**Start:** Always, 0, No **Orders:** Attack All P 4 S 2	**Waves:** 2 **Form:** Double Astern	**Mother:** 5 **AI:** Officer	**Win:** 0 **Val:** 9
#9	3 GUN Tau	**Start:** Always, 2:00, No **Orders:** Attack All P 2 S 1	**Waves:** 1 **Form:** Vic	**Mother:** 0 **AI:** Veteran	**Win:** 0 **Val:** 0
#10	4 T/B Delta	**Start:** Always, 0, No **Orders:** Attack All P 4	**Waves:** 2 **Form:** Echelon Left	**Mother:** 5 **AI:** Veteran	**Win:** 0 **Val:** 9
#11	4 T/B Zeta	**Start:** Attack, 0, 5 **Orders:** Attack All P 2	**Waves:** 9 **Form:** Vic	**Mother:** 5 **AI:** Top Ace	**Win:** 0 **Val:** 0

Tour of Duty 3

OP 1: Guard Weapons Transfer [defend2]

*#1	2 A-W Red [1]	**Start:** Always, 0, No **Orders:** Attack P 2 S 3	**Waves:** 0 **Form:** Vic	**Mother:** 0 **AI:** Officer	**Win:** 0 **Val:** 9

#	Craft	Start / Orders	Waves / Form	Mother / AI	Win / Val
#2	3 T/F Alpha	**Start:** Always, 0, No **Orders:** Attack P 1	**Waves:** 2 **Form:** Line Astern	**Mother:** 10 **AI:** Ace	**Win:** 0 **Val:** 9
#3	3 T/F Beta	**Start:** Always, 0, No **Orders:** Attack P 6 S 8	**Waves:** 0 **Form:** Line Astern	**Mother:** 10 **AI:** Ace	**Win:** 0 **Val:** 9
#4	3 T/B Gamma	**Start:** Always, 0, No **Orders:** Attack freighters P 8 S 9	**Waves:** 0 **Form:** Echelon Left	**Mother:** 10 **AI:** Ace	**Win:** 0 **Val:** 7
#5	3 T/B Delta	**Start:** Always, 0, No **Orders:** Attack freighters P 9 S 8	**Waves:** 0 **Form:** Echelon Right	**Mother:** 10 **AI:** Ace	**Win:** 0 **Val:** 7
#6	1 CON Dara 2 (military equip.)	**Start:** Always, 0, No **Orders:** Stationary	**Waves:** 0 **Form:** Vic	**Mother:** 0 **AI:** Veteran	**Win:** 0 **Val:** 0
#7	1 CON Dara 1 (military equip.)	**Start:** Always, 0, No **Orders:** Stationary	**Waves:** 0 **Form:** Vic	**Mother:** 0 **AI:** Veteran	**Win:** 0 **Val:** 0
#8	1 FRT Sidral II (military equip.)	**Start:** Always, 0, No **Orders:** Rendezvous	**Waves:** 0 **Form:** Vic	**Mother:** 0 **AI:** Top Ace	**Win:** 2 **Val:** 0
#9	1 CRV Frazier	**Start:** Always, 0:24, No **Orders:** Board + Deliver P 8	**Waves:** 0 **Form:** Vic	**Mother:** 0 **AI:** Top Ace	**Win:** 2 **Val:** 5
#10	1 STD Immortal	**Start:** Always, 0, No **Orders:** Starship Sit + Fire	**Waves:** 0 **Form:** Vic	**Mother:** 0 **AI:** Top Ace	**Win:** 0 **Val:** 0
#11	6 T/I Zeta	**Start:** Attack, 0, 11 **Orders:** Attack All P 1	**Waves:** 9 **Form:** Vic	**Mother:** 0 **AI:** Top Ace	**Win:** 0 **Val:** 0

OP 2: Destroy Repair Dock [yraid]

#	Craft	Start / Orders	Waves / Form	Mother / AI	Win / Val
*#1	2 Y-W Red [2]	**Start:** Always, 0, No **Orders:** Attack freighters	**Waves:** 0 **Form:** Line Abreast	**Mother:** 0 **AI:** Top Ace	**Win:** 0 **Val:** 9
#2	4 TRN Lambda	**Start:** Always, 0, No **Orders:** Disabled	**Waves:** 0 **Form:** Double Astern	**Mother:** 0 **AI:** Novice	**Win:** 1 **Val:** 0
#3	3 SHU Omega	**Start:** Always, 0, No **Orders:** Stationary	**Waves:** 0 **Form:** Double Astern	**Mother:** 0 **AI:** Novice	**Win:** 1 **Val:** 0
#4	1 FRT Repair Dock	**Start:** Always, 0, No **Orders:** Stationary	**Waves:** 0 **Form:** Vic	**Mother:** 0 **AI:** Veteran	**Win:** 1 **Val:** 0
#5	2 Mines				
#6	1 CRV Falcon	**Start:** Always, 0, No **Orders:** Starship Sit + Fire P 4	**Waves:** 0 **Form:** Line Abreast	**Mother:** 0 **AI:** Top Ace	**Win:** 0 **Val:** 9
#7	1 Mine				
#8	6 T/B Zeta	**Start:** Always, 0, No **Orders:** Stationary	**Waves:** 0 **Form:** Double Astern	**Mother:** 0 **AI:** Novice	**Win:** 1 **Val:** 0
#9	2 Mines				
#10	2 T/B Gamma	**Start:** Always, 0, No **Orders:** Attack All	**Waves:** 0 **Form:** Line Abreast	**Mother:** 0 **AI:** Officer	**Win:** 1 **Val:** 0

#11	2 T/F Beta	**Start:** Always, 0, No **Orders:** Attack All	**Waves:** 0 **Form:** Echelon Left	**Mother:** 0 **AI:** Officer	**Win:** 1 **Val:** 4
#12	3 T/F Delta	**Start:** Always, 0, No **Orders:** Stationary	**Waves:** 0 **Form:** Double Astern	**Mother:** 0 **AI:** Novice	**Win:** 1 **Val:** 0
#13	2 T/I Alpha	**Start:** Attack, 2:18, 4 **Orders:** Attack All P 1	**Waves:** 9 **Form:** Vic	**Mother:** 15 **AI:** Top Ace	**Win:** 0 **Val:** 9
#14	2 T/B Eta	**Start:** Attack, 2:24, 4 **Orders:** Attack All	**Waves:** 1 **Form:** Line Astern	**Mother:** 15 **AI:** Officer	**Win:** 0 **Val:** 0
#15	1 FRG Vulture	**Start:** Attack, 2:00, 4 **Orders:** Starship Fly Once P 1	**Waves:** 0 **Form:** Vic	**Mother:** 0 **AI:** Top Ace	**Win:** 0 **Val:** 9

* The Vulture may appear in one of three places.

#16 1 Planet

OP 3: Capture Military Transport [max14]

#1	3 X-W Blue	**Start:** Always, 0, No **Orders:** Loose Escort P 5	**Waves:** 0 **Form:** Line Abreast	**Mother:** 0 **AI:** Officer	**Win:** 0 **Val:** 9
*#2	3 Y-W Red [1]	**Start:** Always, 0, No **Orders:** Close Escort P 5	**Waves:** 0 **Form:** Line Abreast	**Mother:** 0 **AI:** Top Ace	**Win:** 0 **Val:** 9
#3	1 SHU Hunter (boarding party)	**Start:** Always, 0, No **Orders:** Board + Capture P 5	**Waves:** 0 **Form:** Vic	**Mother:** 13 **AI:** Top Ace	**Win:** 0 **Val:** 2
#4	1 SHU Hunter 2 (boarding party)	**Start:** Disable, 0, 5 **Orders:** Board + Capture	**Waves:** 1 **Form:** Vic	**Mother:** 13 **AI:** Top Ace	**Win:** 0 **Val:** 1
#5	1 TRN Omicron (military advisors)	**Start:** Always, 0, No **Orders:** Disabled	**Waves:** 0 **Form:** Vic	**Mother:** 9 **AI:** Top Ace	**Win:** 3 **Val:** 6
#6	3 GUN Mu	**Start:** Always, 1:00, No **Orders:** Attack P 1 S 2	**Waves:** 1 **Form:** Vic	**Mother:** 0 **AI:** Top Ace	**Win:** 0 **Val:** 9

* These Gunboats may enter the mission at one of three positions.

#7	1 TRN Lambda (boarding party)	**Start:** Always, 4:00, No **Orders:** Attack P 5	**Waves:** 2 **Form:** Vic	**Mother:** 0 **AI:** Ace	**Win:** 0 **Val:** 2
#8	3 GUN Rho	**Start:** Always, 1:00, No **Orders:** Attack P 1 S 2	**Waves:** 9 **Form:** Vic	**Mother:** 0 **AI:** Veteran	**Win:** 0 **Val:** 9

* These Gunboats may enter the mission at one of three positions.

#9	1 STD Immortal	**Start:** Capture, 1:00, 5 **Orders:** Starship Fly Once	**Waves:** 0 **Form:** Vic	**Mother:** 0 **AI:** Top Ace	**Win:** 0 **Val:** 3
#10	6 T/I Alpha	**Start:** Attack, 0, 9 **Orders:** Attack All S 2	**Waves:** 9 **Form:** Double Astern	**Mother:** 9 **AI:** Top Ace	**Win:** 0 **Val:** 0
#11	6 T/B Theta	**Start:** Attack, 0, 9 **Orders:** Attack All P 2	**Waves:** 9 **Form:** Vic	**Mother:** 9 **AI:** Top Ace	**Win:** 0 **Val:** 0

#12	6 T/F Beta	**Start:** Capture, 2:00, 5 **Orders:** Attack P 1 S 2	**Waves:** 9 **Form:** Vic	**Mother:** 9 **AI:** Top Ace	**Win:** 0 **Val:** 0
#13	1 FRG Inad	**Start:** Capture, 0, 5 **Orders:** Starship Wait Return	**Waves:** 0 **Form:** Vic	**Mother:** 0 **AI:** Top Ace	**Win:** 0 **Val:** 0

OP 4: Scramble! [max17]

*#1	3 X-W Red [3]	**Start:** Always, 0, No **Orders:** Attack All P 6 S 7	**Waves:** 0 **Form:** Echelon Right	**Mother:** 9 **AI:** Veteran	**Win:** 0 **Val:** 1
#2	2 A-W Blue	**Start:** Always, 0, No **Orders:** Attack All	**Waves:** 2 **Form:** Vic	**Mother:** 9 **AI:** Veteran	**Win:** 0 **Val:** 9
#3	1 STD Immortal	**Start:** Always, 0, No **Orders:** Go Home	**Waves:** 0 **Form:** Vic	**Mother:** 0 **AI:** Top Ace	**Win:** 0 **Val:** 9
#4	1 STD Immortal	**Start:** Always, 0, No **Orders:** Starship Fly Once	**Waves:** 0 **Form:** Vic	**Mother:** 0 **AI:** Top Ace	**Win:** 0 **Val:** 0

* When the *Immortal* returns to the scene of this mission after six minutes, it appears in one of two positions. One is much closer to the action than the other!

#5	6 T/B Alpha	**Start:** Always, 0:18, No **Orders:** Attack Starships P 9	**Waves:** 0 **Form:** Vic	**Mother:** 3 **AI:** Top Ace	**Win:** 0 **Val:** 9
#6	6 T/I Alpha	**Start:** Always, 0, No **Orders:** Attack All P 1 S 2	**Waves:** 0 **Form:** Vic	**Mother:** 3 **AI:** Top Ace	**Win:** 0 **Val:** 9
#7	6 T/B Gamma	**Start:** Always, 0, No **Orders:** Attack Starships P 9	**Waves:** 0 **Form:** Echelon Left	**Mother:** 3 **AI:** Top Ace	**Win:** 0 **Val:** 9
#8	6 T/B Delta	**Start:** Always, 0, No **Orders:** Attack Starships P 9	**Waves:** 0 **Form:** Vic	**Mother:** 3 **AI:** Top Ace	**Win:** 0 **Val:** 9
#9	1 CRS Defiance	**Start:** Always, 0, No **Orders:** Starship Fly Once	**Waves:** 0 **Form:** Vic	**Mother:** 0 **AI:** Top Ace	**Win:** 2 **Val:** 9
#10	4 T/I Zeta	**Start:** Always, 7:00, No **Orders:** Attack All S 1	**Waves:** 0 **Form:** Line Abreast	**Mother:** 4 **AI:** Top Ace	**Win:** 0 **Val:** 9
#11	4 T/B Beta	**Start:** Always, 8:00, No **Orders:** Attack All P 1	**Waves:** 9 **Form:** Line Abreast	**Mother:** 4 **AI:** Veteran	**Win:** 0 **Val:** 0
#12	6 T/I Iota	**Start:** Attack, 0, 4 **Orders:** Attack Starships P 9	**Waves:** 9 **Form:** Vic	**Mother:** 4 **AI:** Top Ace	**Win:** 0 **Val:** 9
#13	3 T/I Zeta	**Start:** Always, 7:00, No **Orders:** Attack All P 1 S 2	**Waves:** 1 **Form:** Vic	**Mother:** 4 **AI:** Veteran	**Win:** 0 **Val:** 0
#14	6 T/I Eta	**Start:** Attack, 0, 4 **Orders:** Attack All P 1	**Waves:** 9 **Form:** Vic	**Mother:** 4 **AI:** Top Ace	**Win:** 0 **Val:** 0
#15	6 T/I Iota	**Start:** Attack, 9:00, 4 **Orders:** Attack All P 1	**Waves:** 9 **Form:** Line Abreast	**Mother:** 4 **AI:** Top Ace	**Win:** 0 **Val:** 0
#16	1 Planet Bestine				

OP 5: Intercept and Capture [wyresc3]

*#1	1 Y-W Red [1]	**Start:** Always, 0, No **Orders:** Disable All	**Waves:** 0 **Form:** Vic	**Mother:** 0 **AI:** Top Ace	**Win:** 0 **Val:** 9
#2	1 SHU Rescue 1 (attack team)	**Start:** Disable, 1:00, 5 **Orders:** Board + Take P 5	**Waves:** 0 **Form:** Vic	**Mother:** 0 **AI:** Top Ace	**Win:** 2 **Val:** 1
#3	2 X-W Blue	**Start:** Always, 0, No **Orders:** Go Home	**Waves:** 0 **Form:** Vic	**Mother:** 0 **AI:** Top Ace	**Win:** 0 **Val:** 9

* These X-wings may appear in one of three positions.

#4	2 GUN Rho	**Start:** Always, 0, No **Orders:** Close Escort P 5	**Waves:** 0 **Form:** Echelon Right	**Mother:** 7 **AI:** Veteran	**Win:** 0 **Val:** 6
#5	1 CRV Godar (design team)	**Start:** Always, 0 No **Orders:** Starship Fly Once	**Waves:** 0 **Form:** Vic	**Mother:** 0 **AI:** Top Ace	**Win:** 4 **Val:** 4
#6	2 GUN Tau	**Start:** Always, 0, No **Orders:** Close Escort P 5	**Waves:** 0 **Form:** Vic	**Mother:** 7 **AI:** Veteran	**Win:** 0 **Val:** 4
#7	1 STD Immortal	**Start:** Always, 0, No **Orders:** Starship Fly Once	**Waves:** 0 **Form:** Vic	**Mother:** 0 **AI:** Ace	**Win:** 0 **Val:** 9
#8	2 T/F Alpha	**Start:** Always, 0, No **Orders:** Close Escort P 4 S 5	**Waves:** 0 **Form:** Line Abreast	**Mother:** 7 **AI:** Veteran	**Win:** 0 **Val:** 6
#9	2 T/F Beta	**Start:** Always, 0, No **Orders:** Close Escort P 5 S 6	**Waves:** 0 **Form:** Vic	**Mother:** 7 **AI:** Ace	**Win:** 0 **Val:** 5
#10	2 T/F Gamma	**Start:** Always, 0, No **Orders:** Close Escort P 6 S 4	**Waves:** 0 **Form:** Vic	**Mother:** 7 **AI:** Top Ace	**Win:** 0 **Val:** 3
#11	3 T/I Delta	**Start:** Attack, 1:00, 5 **Orders:** Attack All	**Waves:** 9 **Form:** Finger Four	**Mother:** 7 **AI:** Veteran	**Win:** 0 **Val:** 9
#12	3 T/I Zeta	**Start:** Attack, 2:00, 5 **Orders:** Attack All P 1 S 3	**Waves:** 1 **Form:** Echelon Right	**Mother:** 7 **AI:** Veteran	**Win:** 0 **Val:** 9
#13	3 T/I Eta	**Start:** Disable, 1:00, 5 **Orders:** Attack All	**Waves:** 1 **Form:** Echelon Right	**Mother:** 7 **AI:** Officer	**Win:** 0 **Val:** 9
#14	3 T/I Iota	**Start:** Disable, 2:00, 5 **Orders:** Attack All P 3	**Waves:** 1 **Form:** Vic	**Mother:** 7 **AI:** Ace	**Win:** 0 **Val:** 9
#15	6 T/I Theta	**Start:** Attack, 0, 7 **Orders:** Attack All P 1 S 2	**Waves:** 9 **Form:** Vic	**Mother:** 7 **AI:** Top Ace	**Win:** 0 **Val:** 0
#16	1 Planet Coruscant				

OP 6: Destroy Imperial Base [larry1]

#1	4 CON Yar (equip. - power supply)	**Start:** Always, 0, No **Orders:** Stationary	**Waves:** 0 **Form:** Echelon Right	**Mother:** 0 **AI:** Novice	**Win:** 1 **Val:** 0
#2	3 CON Enna (weapons - launchers)	**Start:** Always, 0, No **Orders:** Stationary	**Waves:** 0 **Form:** Line Abreast	**Mother:** 0 **AI:** Novice	**Win:** 1 **Val:** 0

#	Craft	Start / Orders	Waves / Form	Mother / AI	Win / Val
#3	3 T/B Beta	**Start:** Always, 8:00, No	**Waves:** 2	**Mother:** 7	**Win:** 0
		Orders: Attack All	**Form:** Echelon Right	**AI:** Top Ace	**Val:** 0
#4	4 CON Evad	**Start:** Always, 0, No	**Waves:** 0	**Mother:** 0	**Win:** 1
	(machinery - tools)	**Orders:** Stationary	**Form:** Echelon Left	**AI:** Novice	**Val:** 0
#5	2 mines				
#6	2 FRT diputs	**Start:** Always, 4:00 No	**Waves:** 0	**Mother:** 0	**Win:** 1
	(repair equip. - techs)	**Orders:** Fly Once + Ignore	**Form:** Line Astern	**AI:** Top Ace	**Val:** 9

* These freighters appear in one of three positions when they enter the scene.

#	Craft	Start / Orders	Waves / Form	Mother / AI	Win / Val
#7	1 FRG Priam	**Start:** Always, 7:00, No	**Waves:** 0	**Mother:** 0	**Win:** 0
		Orders: Starship Fly Once	**Form:** Vic	**AI:** Top Ace	**Val:** 9
#8	3 T/F Alpha	**Start:** Always, 7:18, No	**Waves:** 0	**Mother:** 7	**Win:** 0
		Orders: Attack All	**Form:** Vic	**AI:** Top Ace	**Val:** 9
*#9	3 X-W Red [1]	**Start:** Always, 0, No	**Waves:** 0	**Mother:** 0	**Win:** 0
		Orders: Attack All	**Form:** Vic	**AI:** Top Ace	**Val:** 9
#10–16	2 Mines				

OP 7: Destroy Priam's Escort [larry2]

#	Craft	Start / Orders	Waves / Form	Mother / AI	Win / Val
*#1	2 Y-W Red [1]	**Start:** Always, 0, No	**Waves:** 0	**Mother:** 0	**Win:** 0
		Orders: Attack All P 7 S 8	**Form:** Vic	**AI:** Top Ace	**Val:** 9
#2	2 A-W Blue	**Start:** Always, 0, No	**Waves:** 0	**Mother:** 0	**Win:** 0
		Orders: Attack All	**Form:** Vic	**AI:** Top Ace	**Val:** 0
#3	1 FRG Priam	**Start:** Always, 0, No	**Waves:** 0	**Mother:** 0	**Win:** 0
		Orders: Starship Sit + Fire	**Form:** Vic	**AI:** Top Ace	**Val:** 0
#4	3 T/F Alpha	**Start:** Always, 0, No	**Waves:** 2	**Mother:** 3	**Win:** 0
		Orders: Attack All	**Form:** Vic	**AI:** Ace	**Val:** 0
#5	3 T/B Beta	**Start:** Always, 10:00, No	**Waves:** 3	**Mother:** 3	**Win:** 0
		Orders: Attack All	**Form:** Vic	**AI:** Top Ace	**Val:** 0
#6	3 T/F Gamma	**Start:** Always, 1:00, No	**Waves:** 1	**Mother:** 3	**Win:** 0
		Orders: Attack All	**Form:** Vic	**AI:** Ace	**Val:** 0
#7	1 CRV Dar Es I	**Start:** Always, 0, No	**Waves:** 0	**Mother:** 0	**Win:** 1
		Orders: Starship Circle	**Form:** Vic	**AI:** Ace	**Val:** 5
#8	1 CRV Dar Es II	**Start:** Always, 0, No	**Waves:** 0	**Mother:** 0	**Win:** 1
		Orders: Starship Circle	**Form:** Vic	**AI:** Ace	**Val:** 5
#9	1 CRV Dar Es III	**Start:** Always, 3:00, No	**Waves:** 0	**Mother:** 0	**Win:** 1
		Orders: Starship Circle	**Form:** Vic	**AI:** Top Ace	**Val:** 9
#10	1 TRN Omega	**Start:** Always, 3:00, No	**Waves:** 0	**Mother:** 3	**Win:** 1
	(supplies - personnel)	**Orders:** Go Home	**Form:** Vic	**AI:** Top Ace	**Val:** 6
#11–12	3 Mines				

OP 8: Capture the Frigate Priam [larry3]

#	Craft	Start / Orders	Waves / Form	Mother / AI	Win / Val
*#1	1 A-W Red [1]	**Start:** Always, 0, No	**Waves:** 0	**Mother:** 0	**Win:** 0
		Orders: Attack All	**Form:** Vic	**AI:** Top Ace	**Val:** 6
#2	6 Y-W Gold	**Start:** Always, 0, No	**Waves:** 1	**Mother:** 0	**Win:** 0
		Orders: Disable P 9	**Form:** Double Astern	**AI:** Top Ace	**Val:** 0
#3	1 TRN Jordi 1	**Start:** Disable, 1:00, 9	**Waves:** 0	**Mother:** 9	**Win:** 0
		Orders: Go Home P 9	**Form:** Vic	**AI:** Top Ace	**Val:** 9
#4	1 TRN Jordi 2	**Start:** Disable, 1:00, 9	**Waves:** 0	**Mother:** 9	**Win:** 0
		Orders: Go Home P 9	**Form:** Vic	**AI:** Top Ace	**Val:** 9
#5	1 SHU Panda 1	**Start:** Disable, 1:00, 9	**Waves:** 0	**Mother:** 9	**Win:** 0
	(crew - officers)	**Orders:** Go Home P 9	**Form:** Vic	**AI:** Top Ace	**Val:** 9
#6	1 SHU Panda 2	**Start:** Disable, 1:00, 9	**Waves:** 0	**Mother:** 9	**Win:** 0
	(crew - officers)	**Orders:** Go Home P 9	**Form:** Vic	**AI:** Top Ace	**Val:** 9
#7	1 TRN Assault 1	**Start:** Disable, 0, 9	**Waves:** 0	**Mother:** 9	**Win:** 0
	(commandos)	**Orders:** Board + Capture P 9	**Form:** Vic	**AI:** Top Ace	**Val:** 3
#8	1 TRN Assault 2	**Start:** Disable, 0, 9	**Waves:** 0	**Mother:** 9	**Win:** 0
	(commandos)	**Orders:** Go Home	**Form:** Vic	**AI:** Top Ace	**Val:** 9
#9	1 FRG Priam	**Start:** Always, 0, No	**Waves:** 0	**Mother:** 0	**Win:** 4
		Orders: Starship Sit + Fire	**Form:** Vic	**AI:** Top Ace	**Val:** 0
#10	3 T/F Alpha	**Start:** Always, 0:12, No	**Waves:** 0	**Mother:** 9	**Win:** 0
		Orders: Attack All	**Form:** Vic	**AI:** Top Ace	**Val:** 9
#11	1 T/B Beta	**Start:** Always, 2:00, No	**Waves:** 1	**Mother:** 9	**Win:** 0
		Orders: Attack All	**Form:** Vic	**AI:** Top Ace	**Val:** 9
#12–13	2 Mines				

OP 9: Capture Ethar I and II [assault2]

#	Craft	Start / Orders	Waves / Form	Mother / AI	Win / Val
*#1	3 X-W Red [2]	**Start:** Always, 0, No	**Waves:** 0	**Mother:** 0	**Win:** 0
		Orders: Attack All	**Form:** Vic	**AI:** Veteran	**Val:** 9

* Your group of X-wings begin the mission in one of three randomly determined positions; however, the difference shouldn't affect the mission much.

#	Craft	Start / Orders	Waves / Form	Mother / AI	Win / Val
#2	1 CRV Ethar 1	**Start:** Always, 0 No	**Waves:** 0	**Mother:** 0	**Win:** 3
	(senator)	**Orders:** Disabled	**Form:** Vic	**AI:** Ace	**Val:** 5
#3	1 CRV Ethar 2	**Start:** Always, 0 No	**Waves:** 0	**Mother:** 0	**Win:** 3
	(admiral)	**Orders:** Disabled	**Form:** Vic	**AI:** Ace	**Val:** 5
#4	1 SHU Ceptor 1	**Start:** Always, 0, No	**Waves:** 0	**Mother:** 0	**Win:** 0
	(repair team)	**Orders:** Board + Deliver P 2	**Form:** Vic	**AI:** Veteran	**Val:** 1
#5	1 SHU Ceptor 2	**Start:** Always, 0, No	**Waves:** 0	**Mother:** 0	**Win:** 0
	(repair team)	**Orders:** Board + Deliver P 3	**Form:** Vic	**AI:** Veteran	**Val:** 1
#6	2 GUN Mu	**Start:** Create, 1:06, 9	**Waves:** 0	**Mother:** 0	**Win:** 0
		Orders: Attack All P 9 S 10	**Form:** Echelon Right	**AI:** Officer	**Val:** 5

#7	3 GUN Rho	**Start:** Always, 0, No **Orders:** Attack All P 1 S 11	**Waves:** 1 **Form:** Line Abreast	**Mother:** 0 **AI:** Veteran	**Win:** 0 **Val:** 9
#8	3 GUN Tau	**Start:** Always, 0, No **Orders:** Attack All P 12 S 1	**Waves:** 2 **Form:** Echelon Left	**Mother:** 0 **AI:** Veteran	**Win:** 0 **Val:** 9
#9	1 SHU Rogue 2 (rescue team)	**Start:** Create, 6:00, 11 **Orders:** Board + Capture P 3 S 2	**Waves:** 0 **Form:** Vic	**Mother:** 0 **AI:** Top Ace	**Win:** 2 **Val:** 1
#10	1 SHU Rogue 1 (rescue team)	**Start:** Create, 6:00, 12 **Orders:** Board + Capture P 2 S 3	**Waves:** 0 **Form:** Vic	**Mother:** 0 **AI:** Top Ace	**Win:** 2 **Val:** 1
#11	3 Y-W Gold	**Start:** Always, 3:00, No **Orders:** Disable freighters P 2 S 3	**Waves:** 0 **Form:** Echelon Left	**Mother:** 0 **AI:** Top Ace	**Win:** 0 **Val:** 9
#12	3 Y-W Blue	**Start:** Always, 3:00, No **Orders:** Disable freighters P 3 S 2	**Waves:** 0 **Form:** Echelon Right	**Mother:** 0 **AI:** Top Ace	**Win:** 0 **Val:** 0
#13	2 GUN Nu	**Start:** Create, 2:00, 10 **Orders:** Attack All P 10 S 9	**Waves:** 0 **Form:** Echelon Left	**Mother:** 0 **AI:** Novice	**Win:** 0 **Val:** 5
#14	2 GUN Tau	**Start:** Capture, 2:00, 2 **Orders:** Attack All P 1 S 1	**Waves:** 0 **Form:** Echelon Left	**Mother:** 0 **AI:** Novice	**Win:** 0 **Val:** 5
#15	2 GUN Mu	**Start:** Capture, 3:00, 3 **Orders:** Attack All P 1	**Waves:** 3 **Form:** Echelon Right	**Mother:** 0 **AI:** Veteran	**Win:** 0 **Val:** 5

OP 10: Guard Vital Supply Depot [max19]

*#1	3 A-W Red [1]	**Start:** Always, 0, No **Orders:** Close Escort P 2	**Waves:** 0 **Form:** Vic	**Mother:** 0 **AI:** Top Ace	**Win:** 0 **Val:** 9
#2	4 CON ZL (power supply)	**Start:** Always, 0 No **Orders:** Stationary	**Waves:** 0 **Form:** Vic	**Mother:** 0 **AI:** Novice	**Win:** 10 **Val:** 0
#3	4 CON LT (weapons)	**Start:** Always, 0 No **Orders:** Stationary	**Waves:** 0 **Form:** Vic	**Mother:** 0 **AI:** Novice	**Win:** 10 **Val:** 0
#4	4 CON XZ (food supplies)	**Start:** Always, 0 No **Orders:** Stationary	**Waves:** 0 **Form:** Vic	**Mother:** 0 **AI:** Novice	**Win:** 10 **Val:** 0
#5	4 T/B Alpha	**Start:** Always, 2:00, 8 **Orders:** Attack P 1 S 2	**Waves:** 1 **Form:** Vic	**Mother:** 8 **AI:** Novice	**Win:** 0 **Val:** 9
#6	4 T/B Beta	**Start:** Always, 6:00, No **Orders:** Attack P 1 S 4	**Waves:** 3 **Form:** Vic	**Mother:** 8 **AI:** Top Ace	**Win:** 0 **Val:** 9
#7	4 T/B Gamma	**Start:** Always, 4:00, No **Orders:** Attack P 1 S 1	**Waves:** 1 **Form:** Vic	**Mother:** 8 **AI:** Veteran	**Win:** 0 **Val:** 9
#8	1 FRG Retsub	**Start:** Always, 1:30, No **Orders:** Starship Fly Once	**Waves:** 0 **Form:** Vic	**Mother:** 0 **AI:** Ace	**Win:** 0 **Val:** 9

* This Nebulon B Frigate may appear in the mission in one of three positions, randomly determined.

#9	3 A-W Blue	**Start:** Always, 13:00, No **Orders:** Attack All	**Waves:** 0 **Form:** Vic	**Mother:** 0 **AI:** Top Ace	**Win:** 16 **Val:** 9

* A-wing group Blue may appear in one of two positions 13 minutes into the mission.

#10	2 FRT Zep	**Start:** Always, 7:00, No **Orders:** Fly Once + Ignore	**Waves:** 0 **Form:** Vic	**Mother:** 0 **AI:** Top Ace	**Win:** 0 **Val:** 0

OP 11: Defend the Independence [defend1]

*#1	2 X-W Red [1]	**Start:** Always, 0, No **Orders:** Attack All P 9 S 12	**Waves:** 0 **Form:** Vic	**Mother:** 0 **AI:** Ace	**Win:** 0 **Val:** 9
#2	2 A-W Blue	**Start:** Always, 0 No **Orders:** Attack All P 10 S 5	**Waves:** 4 **Form:** Vic	**Mother:** 3 **AI:** Veteran	**Win:** 0 **Val:** 9
#3	1 CRV Ethar 2 (admiral)	**Start:** Always, 0 No **Orders:** Disabled	**Waves:** 0 **Form:** Vic	**Mother:** 0 **AI:** Ace	**Win:** 3 **Val:** 5
#4	1 CRS Independence (Mon Mothma)	**Start:** Always, 0, No **Orders:** Starship Fly Once	**Waves:** 0 **Form:** Vic	**Mother:** 0 **AI:** Novice	**Win:** 2 **Val:** 9
#5	2 GUN Mu	**Start:** Always, 0, No **Orders:** Attack All P 2 S 1	**Waves:** 2 **Form:** Vic	**Mother:** 0 **AI:** Ace	**Win:** 0 **Val:** 9
#6	6 T/B Alpha	**Start:** Always, 0, No **Orders:** Attack All P 3	**Waves:** 9 **Form:** Line Abreast	**Mother:** 11 **AI:** Top Ace	**Win:** 0 **Val:** 9
#7	6 T/B Eta	**Start:** Attack, 0, 11 **Orders:** Attack All P 1	**Waves:** 9 **Form:** Line Abreast	**Mother:** 11 **AI:** Top Ace	**Win:** 0 **Val:** 0
#8	6 T/I Zeta	**Start:** Attack, 0, 11 **Orders:** Attack All P 1 S 2	**Waves:** 9 **Form:** Vic	**Mother:** 11 **AI:** Top Ace	**Win:** 0 **Val:** 0
#9	4 T/B Beta	**Start:** Always, 0, No **Orders:** Attack All P 3 S 3	**Waves:** 5 **Form:** Line Abreast	**Mother:** 11 **AI:** Ace	**Win:** 0 **Val:** 9
#10	4 T/B Gamma	**Start:** Always, 0, No **Orders:** Attack All P 3 S 3	**Waves:** 6 **Form:** Line Abreast	**Mother:** 11 **AI:** Ace	**Win:** 0 **Val:** 9
#11	1 STD Immortal	**Start:** Always, 3:00, No **Orders:** Starship Circle P 3	**Waves:** 0 **Form:** Vic	**Mother:** 0 **AI:** Top Ace	**Win:** 0 **Val:** 9
#12	2 GUN Nu	**Start:** Always, 0, No **Orders:** Attack All P 2 S 1	**Waves:** 2 **Form:** Vic	**Mother:** 0 **AI:** Ace	**Win:** 0 **Val:** 9

OP 12: Begin Death Star Assault [dstar1]

*#1	3 X-W Red [2]	**Start:** Always, 0, No **Orders:** Attack All	**Waves:** 0 **Form:** Vic	**Mother:** 0 **AI:** Veteran	**Win:** 0 **Val:** 9
#2	3 T/F Alpha	**Start:** Always, 0 No **Orders:** Attack All P 1 S 13	**Waves:** 9 **Form:** Vic	**Mother:** 9 **AI:** Top Ace	**Win:** 0 **Val:** 0
#3	2 T/B Beta	**Start:** Always, 0 No **Orders:** Attack All P 1 S 13	**Waves:** 9 **Form:** Vic	**Mother:** 9 **AI:** Top Ace	**Win:** 0 **Val:** 0
#4	3 T/I Gamma	**Start:** Always, 0 No **Orders:** Attack All P 1 S 13	**Waves:** 9 **Form:** Vic	**Mother:** 9 **AI:** Top Ace	**Win:** 0 **Val:** 0

#5	2 GUN Mu	**Start:** Always, 0 No **Orders:** Attack All P 1 S 13	**Waves:** 9 **Form:** Vic	**Mother:** 0 **AI:** Top Ace	**Win:** 0 **Val:** 0
#6	1 CRV BB 45	**Start:** Always, 0, No **Orders:** Starship Circle P 1 S 13	**Waves:** 0 **Form:** Vic	**Mother:** 0 **AI:** Top Ace	**Win:** 0 **Val:** 0
#7	1 CRV SB 35	**Start:** Always, 0, No **Orders:** Starship Circle P 1 S 13	**Waves:** 0 **Form:** Vic	**Mother:** 0 **AI:** Top Ace	**Win:** 0 **Val:** 0
#8	4 T/A Delta	**Start:** Always, 0 No **Orders:** Attack All P 1 S 13	**Waves:** 9 **Form:** Line Abreast	**Mother:** 9 **AI:** Top Ace	**Win:** 0 **Val:** 0
#9	1 FRG Divad	**Start:** Always, 0, No **Orders:** Starship Sit + Fire	**Waves:** 0 **Form:** Vic	**Mother:** 0 **AI:** Top Ace	**Win:** 0 **Val:** 0
#10	1 Comm-sat				
#11	Death Star				
#12	1 Planet Yavin				
#13	2 A-W Blue	**Start:** Always, 0, No **Orders:** Close Escort P 1	**Waves:** 0 **Form:** Vic	**Mother:** 0 **AI:** Ace	**Win:** 0 **Val:** 3

OP 13: Attack Death Star Surface [dstar2]

*#1	2 X-W Red [2]	**Start:** Always, 0, No **Orders:** Attack All	**Waves:** 0 **Form:** Vic	**Mother:** 0 **AI:** Veteran	**Win:** 0 **Val:** 0
#2	3 T/F Alpha	**Start:** Always, 0, No **Orders:** Attack All P 1	**Waves:** 0 **Form:** Vic	**Mother:** 0 **AI:** Veteran	**Win:** 0 **Val:** 0
#3	3 T/F Beta	**Start:** Always, 17:00, No **Orders:** Attack All P 1	**Waves:** 9 **Form:** Vic	**Mother:** 15 **AI:** Top Ace	**Win:** 0 **Val:** 0
#4	2 T/F Gamma	**Start:** Destroy, 0:18, 2 **Orders:** Attack All P 1	**Waves:** 3 **Form:** Vic	**Mother:** 16 **AI:** Ace	**Win:** 0 **Val:** 0
#5	3 T/F Gamma	**Start:** Destroy, 0, 13 **Orders:** Attack All P 1	**Waves:** 0 **Form:** Vic	**Mother:** 0 **AI:** Top Ace	**Win:** 0 **Val:** 0
#6	2 T/B Delta	**Start:** Destroy, 0:12, 11 **Orders:** Attack All P 1	**Waves:** 3 **Form:** Vic	**Mother:** 14 **AI:** Ace	**Win:** 0 **Val:** 0
#7	3 T/F Zeta	**Start:** Always, 15:00, No **Orders:** Attack All P 1	**Waves:** 9 **Form:** Vic	**Mother:** 14 **AI:** Top Ace	**Win:** 0 **Val:** 0
#8	2 T/F Eta	**Start:** Destroy, 1:18, 2 **Orders:** Attack All P 1	**Waves:** 3 **Form:** Vic	**Mother:** 13 **AI:** Ace	**Win:** 0 **Val:** 0
#9	2 T/F Eta	**Start:** Destroy, 0, 16 **Orders:** Attack All P 1	**Waves:** 0 **Form:** Vic	**Mother:** 13 **AI:** Top Ace	**Win:** 0 **Val:** 0
#10	3 T/F Theta	**Start:** Always, 3:00, No **Orders:** Attack All P 1	**Waves:** 2 **Form:** Vic	**Mother:** 15 **AI:** Top Ace	**Win:** 0 **Val:** 0

#11	2 T/B Iota	**Start:** Always, 0, No **Orders:** Attack All P 1	**Waves:** 0 **Form:** Vic	**Mother:** 0 **AI:** Ace	**Win:** 0 **Val:** 0
#12	1 Nav-Sat				
#13	1 CON Hangar Port (TIE Squadrons)	**Start:** Always, 0, No **Orders:** Stationary	**Waves:** 0 **Form:** Vic	**Mother:** 0 **AI:** Novice	**Win:** 1 **Val:** 0
#14	1 CON Hangar Port (TIE Squadrons)	**Start:** Always, 0, No **Orders:** Stationary	**Waves:** 0 **Form:** Vic	**Mother:** 0 **AI:** Novice	**Win:** 1 **Val:** 0
#15	1 CON Hangar Port (TIE Squadrons)	**Start:** Always, 0, No **Orders:** Stationary	**Waves:** 0 **Form:** Vic	**Mother:** 0 **AI:** Novice	**Win:** 1 **Val:** 0
#16	1 CON Hangar Port (TIE Squadrons)	**Start:** Always, 0, No **Orders:** Stationary	**Waves:** 0 **Form:** Vic	**Mother:** 15 **AI:** Novice	**Win:** 1 **Val:** 0

OP 14: Death Star Trench Run [dstar3]

*#1	1 X-W Red [1]	**Start:** Always, 0, No **Orders:** Stationary	**Waves:** 0 **Form:** Vic	**Mother:** 0 **AI:** Novice	**Win:** 0 **Val:** 0
#2–3	1 Nav-Sat				
#4	2 T/F Alpha	**Start:** Always, 0, No **Orders:** Attack All P 1	**Waves:** 0 **Form:** Vic	**Mother:** 0 **AI:** Top Ace	**Win:** 0 **Val:** 0
#5	3 T/A Omega	**Start:** Always, 0, No **Orders:** Attack All P 1	**Waves:** 0 **Form:** Vic	**Mother:** 0 **AI:** Top Ace	**Win:** 0 **Val:** 0

(Note: Mission Statistics other than those for the original tours of duty and historical missions are currently classified Top-Secret.)

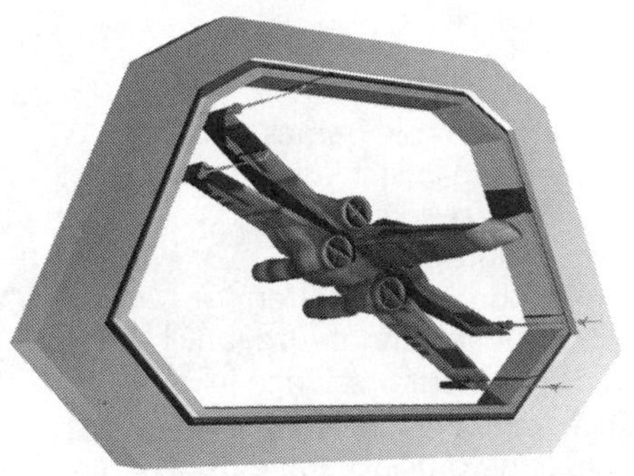

APPENDIX E

About the X-Wing Team

Larry Holland

Larry "Dutch" Holland is the brains behind the X-Wing game, spending most of his time sleeping on the couch. Larry began his career intending to be an anthropologist; he studied at Cornell University and went on digs in France, Africa, and India. He's fond of saying how he started out studying man's early evolution and his most primitive stone tools before turning his attention to the world of microcomputers.

Larry began programming out of a sense of curiosity and found himself almost accidentally involved in writing games. His early works included Project Space Station and Super Zaxxon.

Later, Larry began developing projects for Lucasfilm's Games Division, where he has gained a reputation as one of the best simulator developers in the business. His games include HMS Pegasus, Strike Fleet, and the critically acclaimed World War II series of flight simulators: Secret Weapons of the Luftwaffe; Battlehawks: 1942 and; Their Finest Hour: The Battle of Britain.

X-wing represents a culmination of the work that went before it, blending the *Star Wars* adventure with a spaceborne flight simulator.

Edward Kilham

Ed "Killer" Kilham began creating simple games and graphics systems on the Apple II while still in high school. He moved on to the Amiga in 1985 and wrote a color font-editing utility called The Calligrapher.

Ed's next big project was RoboSport, written for Maxis while he was still attending the University of Oregon. He graduated magna cum laude in computer science in 1990.

Ed then joined LucasArts and began work on his cinematic engine. In late 1991, he officially joined Larry Holland's simulator team and began incorporating his cinematic approach with Larry's simulator technology.

An Interview with Larry and Ed

LARRY: Ed and I took distinctly different parts of the game and both designed and programmed them as well as performed the project leadership—carried the vision of what the project was. Also, hand-holding people through parts of the project, cheerleading—wearing all kinds of hats.

The project was a long time coming. I think it was originally conceived of—the idea of doing a space combat simulator—back at the conclusion of Battlehawks. So that was back in, I guess, 1988, when Battlehawks was done. At that time Broderbund had the *Star Wars* rights. So the (Lucasfilm) Games Division couldn't even do it at that point. We had to wait.

Anyway, when that license ran out, then we started thinking of doing it again. But I'm glad we waited until now because I think the technology finally reached the point where we could make it pay off. Back in 1989, I was just interested in carrying on my World War II stuff with Their Finest Hour and Secret Weapons. I had a lot I wanted to do on that topic. No one else could do *Star Wars* at that point. It was a property that we had taken control of, and we weren't worried that we were going to have to compete with another *Star Wars* game, whereas when you're doing simulators you always worry that someone else might also come up with the same idea as you. It's an open playing field.

DEMARIA: *So you were planning this game while you were finishing Secret Weapons?*

LARRY: Yes. Certainly. Actually, Ed started getting involved before Secret Weapons was done.

ED: In February of 1991 I was approached to start doing X-Wing by someone I was doing some work for at Lucasfilm. So I began to develop the simulation, the front-end cinematics, the animation system, in order to pull off a lot of the testing that we wanted to do. But I knew I wasn't really going to be able to come up with a simulator of the kind the project needed. They originally thought that I would do it all, but I knew that I would need to work with Larry, and when he came off of Swotl, thank goodness I had the opportunity to join him and become part of his group. So the best part of it was that I was developing the whole front-end system during that entire time. I had an engine and a technology that could join with what Larry would do.

LARRY: There's a kitchen sink of possibilities, and I always longed to have time to add a lot of things like guys sitting in the barracks looking out the back window and seeing planes coming in and landing and taking off and the battles take place—to start building an environment where a lot of things were happening. So it was natural, then, that the progression in the way we went was to Ed's technology. It blended perfectly, and it also provided a way to really differentiate our roles on the product. Whatever we did was synergistic. And Peter Lindcroff, the programmer, spent his time building the 3-D technology, extending the 3-D polygon engine that we had from Secret Weapons. So the three of us started programming. We were able to break up the project into various coherent pieces that worked out quite well.

ED: That's what really made the whole thing possible. We knew when we started the project that we wanted to get it done very quickly, and there was a lot that had to go into it. We started out with extremely elaborate designs and we then trimmed down to something we really felt we could accomplish.

LARRY: Yeah, we started out with a Secret Weapons kind of approach. You know, actually, I learned my lessons in Secret Weapons because the project took longer than I would have liked. Ed and I started working on the design, looking to combine simulator elements with other types of game play. We wanted it to be a flexible game system that allowed people to do different parts, not be forced to go always along the path. We also wanted to have some storytelling and some of the Wing Commander-like elements that were proving themselves to be what people wanted.

ED: There are some people who I know would love to see a Swotl-type approach to *Star Wars*, where you had a larger universe to work with and maybe more freedom of choice and a more complex story—

LARRY:—a strategic approach, campaigns . . . well, all those elements we thought valuable as well, but we didn't want ourselves to try to build too much at once.

***DEMARIA:** You might expand this?*

LARRY: Yes. Absolutely.

ED: We came into a situation with kind of two clashing metaphors. A metaphor of Wing Commander, which is a cinematic experience, and the metaphor of Secret Weapons of the Luftwaffe, which is a grand campaign experience. They didn't really work that well together. In fact, what we came to was a whole new kind of game that had we had never done before—so we had to learn how to make it.

***DEMARIA:** Did you see Wing Commander before you were on this project?*

ED: Oh yeah, it was a very highly popular product that we had all seen and experienced it and knew that it was a new kind of genre that was really fascinating to work on. The whole idea of interactive movies is an interesting approach. We kind of tried to back away from that because, again, we wanted to get into a game. We were making a game; we weren't making a movie, and we weren't planning on doing that.

The author with Ed and Larry.

LARRY: To focus on it, I think one of the weaknesses of Wing Commander is the actual flight experience. It's a kind of two-dimensional arcade-like experience. What we wanted to draw on were the strengths of our simulation background to create a world that people believe that they are in, flying around and doing a lot of little, dynamic things. Also, it has always been our intention with the evolution of the display, the graphics, to move to polygons. I always saw bit maps as an interim step until the performance capabilities of the machines allowed us to start creating polygon images that were detailed.

X-Wing is a true polygon game, but also it's hybrid technology. One of those great sort of breakthroughs we had when we were working on the 3-D technology was to integrate the pulley (the bit map) with the 3-D technology. So moving forward now, we've got a really good foundation. The bit maps are integrated at the lowest level into the polygon technology in a way that allows explosions or (stuff) or whatever we choose. So we have a real sort of war chest of different approaches to use.

ED: And hopefully, even as our technology becomes more sophisticated and the machines become better, my system and their system will become fully integrated. We're already seeing that out in the industry—2-D and 3-D systems very tightly integrating—and that's really where all this is going . . . to the point where the actors, so to speak, that are in 2-D—the people we have talking can be integrated with views of ships flying by . . . or even three-dimensionally done personalities.

DEMARIA: *You used 3-D modeling for images in the cut scenes as well as in the documentation. Were the models used in the simulation built in 3D Studio and then trimmed down?*

LARRY: They were built by a separate method. They were actually created in AutoCAD first, because they're very simple and we had to keep control of the exact number of polygons. Something like 100 polygons would be considered a lot for our flight engine models. So we had a special guy do that using AutoCAD, and then Peter Lincroft wrote a utility that we call Twiddle, which allowed us to twiddle the models and tweak them. I wanted to call it Tweak, but he wanted to call it Twiddle, so it ended up Twiddle.

Taking those AutoCAD files, we wrote conversions, utilities that would allow us to analyze the model, because it wasn't just the point definition of the models that was important. There was a lot of rendering information about how to sort all the polygons, break them up into components . . . One of the elements we wanted to stress was like when you hit an X-wing, a wing would blow off. Or when you hit the TIEs, there's a hierarchy of pieces and components within the models. So those were sort of handcrafted by AutoCAD and into Twiddle and into the game, and I think Rod has produced some really neat things that I think come off pretty well, considering the small number of polygons that are on them.

The best comment I've heard so far is that people got images of something from the movies; something popped into their head—an X-wing battling a TIE fighter, for instance.

Originally we were going to try to use bit maps for medium distances and then do a transition to a polygon version of a spacecraft or object. But the polygon versions were looking so good and the problem with the bit maps was [that] they took a lot of space. Like in Swotl. They restricted the number of different aircraft that we could have at once in a particular mission. There would be like a limitation of like four. Going to polygons, they took a lot less storage. We didn't have the same limitations.

DEMARIA: *In Swotl, you already had to face the challenge of taking a situation where there were an ungodly number of planes in the air and reduce it down to the scope that the game could handle. You had some similar challenges in X-Wing. For instance, in some* Star Wars *battles, there might be 30 or 40 starfighters, several capital ships. . . .*

LARRY: We made some real advances in the way we built missions. For me, personally, the way we designed and built missions was one of the things I was most proud of: coming up with a new way to create missions that were more story-oriented—the way the different craft triggered events, interacted and worked with each other. In Swotl, typically you had to create all the craft that were going to be in the mission at the beginning. Because we wanted the missions to be short, so the American craft would suddenly show up, only they really had to be flown from England.

DEMARIA: *We didn't have hyperspace then.*

LARRY: Right—they didn't have hyperspace and they didn't just pop out from essentially aircraft carriers in space, which is what all these starships are. So designing X-Wing, we came up with a new idea on how to build missions that, among other things, would let us have a lot more craft simultaneously in the air—I mean space—like about 28, where Secret Weapons had about 15.

And then we could spread those craft out more over time. During the missions, some of the craft that would get triggered were created, sent out by a Star Destroyer based upon a particular event. So it became very cool the way stuff would show up more in response to what the player did. The events that took place were less random and more consistent with the actions taking place.

It was a kind of simple idea, but in the implementation it suddenly opened all kinds of things, like hyperspace in when someone docks or gets captured. All of a sudden you start triggering these advances to the mission development. You really feel like you're impacting something because of the way everything interacts.

The scale of the story we're telling is localized in the sense that we're looking at a particular event or engagement, whereas in something like Swotl, you're talking more about thousand-bomber missions, all going and trying to bomb oil refineries here or there. You're just like one bomber in a massive group. It's a different scale.

You look at the movie, Luke Skywalker, a man in one spacecraft—an X-wing—actually went down to destroy this monstrous manmade Death Star. So we operate on the heroic scale of a single guy having an impact on larger-than-life events, but still you wanted the sense of the larger story going on around the hero.

The hardest thing to balance actually is the skill level. For a while, while we were tuning, the player sometimes didn't have to do anything, and there'd still be a Rebel victory. We really wanted the player to be central, though. His efforts primarily determine victory or defeat.

DEMARIA: *I'm interested in the role of wingmen in X-Wing. Sometimes I wish they'd be more effective. Other times I wish they'd just go away.*

LARRY: You can't have the wingmen be too active—get too many kills. Most players will just tell them to stop. Or go home. But they do fulfill a role. We're constantly trying to find the right balance between effectiveness and interference. The trouble is, it's almost impossible to please everybody. Some people want the missions to be harder. Many others think they're too hard. In the end, the more you learn to use the weapons and energy systems, the wingmen, and the other capabilities of your starfighter, the more you'll succeed. We tried to design a lot of different challenges in the game. Sometimes you'll go head-to-head against another starfighter. Other times you may have to penetrate a minefield or even attack a Star Destroyer. In the end, you get to destroy the Death Star, but you have to earn the opportunity.

DEMARIA: *How many times did you see the* Star Wars *movies?*

LARRY: Not that many. I wasn't the guy that went back and saw this 25 times. I probably saw it 4 or 5 times. Probably only about twice in the movies, but then I probably watched it 5 times. I've paused a lot of parts of the movies and looked through them, but I'd say, just a few.

ED: When I was young, I watched *Star Wars* five times, and I watched all the others a couple of times. During the course of the project, I watched each of the movies, not that much, four or five times. The thing was, I was hanging around with the artists, and they were watching it almost continuously. If I hang around with them at all, they always have *Jedi* or *Empire* on.

LARRY: There are parts that you watch a lot of times, like the descent on the Death Star at the end of *Star Wars*, and I personally watch all the combat sequences—to look at the lasers and the weaponry and all that stuff—more than the plot.

ED: You get the musical themes to figure out all the really powerful moments, like how did Darth come into situations, that kind of thing.

LARRY: We watched all three of them. Even though the story line in the game is sort of like pre-*Star Wars* and then *Star Wars* itself, we actually watched all three of the movies early intentionally to look for style, any situations.

ED: One thing I enjoyed a lot was reading all the books, reading all the literature out there. Timothy Zahn, a lot of the old Han Solo books, and the comic books. Finding out the whole history and story of the universe and trying to figure out what had really gone on during the period of time we chose to depict was really very enjoyable. And to find out what really worked and what didn't work in all of those—trying to tie them all together and make it seem possible.

LARRY: I think the challenge for us was all these different avenues that the *Star Wars* stuff (has taken) . . . the West End books, Timothy Zahn, and all that. It certainly wasn't necessarily consistent or thought out in a way to try to fit in with other people, but we stayed consistent within our group.

DEMARIA: *What about a sequel to X-Wing?*

LARRY AND ED: Sequel? Well, don't tell anybody, but we've been looking into the dark side.

David Maxwell

"Max" originally signed on with LucasArts as a technician in the Quality Assurance department, where he tested games like Indiana Jones Graphic Adventure, Star Wars, The Empire Strikes Back, Defenders of Dynatron City, Swotl and more. Eventually, he joined Larry's team and began building missions for X-Wing. An ace simulator pilot, Max was afraid that X-Wing would be too easy.

"One of my favorite missions used to be the one where you have to save the weapons cache, but then it was really hard and I had to tone it down. There's still a hard version. It has three different versions. One where the Frigate comes right into the middle of all the containers and just starts ripping on them. People say you can't win that one, but you can. You just play around the Frigate and make them shoot at you instead. It's a matter of trying to draw off the fire. And there's just unlimited TIE Bombers that come out, and you just sit there and blow up TIE Bombers in your A-wing. The A-wing's my favorite fighter. I like it for the speed and because it's an interceptor and has concussion missiles.

"Another really fun one is Larry 1. That's the one I built where there's a bunch of containers and mines around them, and you have to take out the containers and the mines before the Frigate shows up, so it can eventually be captured. You have to be quick to destroy all the mines. You destroy the mines so your wingmen don't get blown up. You only have to destroy the containers and Freighters that fly through to complete the mission. But it's a good one because you only have a limited amount of time to do it. There's a lot to blow up. I like shooting mines because it requires more accuracy—more like shooting targets.

"What I do is shoot the mines and tell my wingmen to blow up the containers. I take out the mines to save them, tackling the mines in sections. I'll tell my wingmen to wait and take out the bottom three first. When I get the mines cleared out, I tell my wingmen to attack the containers while I finish off the mines. And as soon as the Freighters come in, I tell them to attack the Freighters. Because you're in X-wings, they'll fire torpedoes. That way, I get to save my torpedoes. In the meantime, I can still take out the rest of the mines. After they're finished with that, I tell them to come back and finish off the containers.

Dave Maxwell and Dave Wessman.

"We also tried to put variations in the way the missions unfolded. If you approach the mission differently, something will happen differently. So if you play, like, five times, you might see something new and have to change your approach—like maybe by attacking a container could bring in a wave of Gunboats. If attacking that container is not part of the win condition, you normally wouldn't do that; you'd only be doing it for points. We did a lot of that, so hopefully each mission every once in a while will be different. There are a couple of missions that have up to three different endings. Depends on what you do. For instance, in Tour of Duty 2, Mission 7, if you lose it one way, a Star Destroyer might come in, and the captured X-wing will go up into it. If you win it one way, corvettes will come in formation and save your tail and rescue it. If your timing is right, both will come in at the same time and have a major battle."

David Wessman

"Wotan" is an avid amateur military historian and a totally avid computer game player. He and Max are longtime buddies and worked together to build missions for X-Wing. Wotan did all the research and wrote up the mission descriptions. He also added strategic ideas based on his studies of military history and *Star Wars* lore.

"Larry and Ed came up with the plot line. Actually, a lot of the way the whole story came together was this kind of . . . everybody put something into it. The artists had their ideas of what would make a good cut scene, and that influenced what kind of missions we built because we wanted them to go with the art and vice versa. Generally, Larry set down the overall structure, and occasionally he'd give us specific missions that he would want designed. Other than that, he let us be creative, and then we took the best of what we had. We actually built about two or three times as many missions as we used. We ended up using the ones that worked the best. The limitations with the technology made it difficult to be really realistic because, for instance, if the Star Destroyer shows up to launch TIE fighters at you, it's not going to "piecemeal" them out three at a time. It'll swamp you with a few squadrons. From the individual starfighter pilot's point of view, though, I think they came out pretty well.

"Every mission can be beaten, and you don't have to know a secret to beat them. You can figure it out. That was an important consideration in design—that you can always figure it out even if you fail the mission the first time. The debriefing tells you exactly what you failed to do, and if you took a film of the missions, then you can go find those groups and see what they were doing and why you missed them. A lot of things happen very quickly and all at once, and your only notification is on the message line, that some new ship is being created or detected or destroyed, and you tend to miss those a lot. So you really have to keep cycling through the CMD to see what's out there or go to the map and survey the situation."

Jim McLeod

Jim created 95 percent of the 3-D models used to create the game. Most of the models were built by using plans from plastic models because the Industrial Light and Magic archives were being reorganized and the original models weren't available.

Martin Cameron

Martin created much of the two-dimensional artwork, including the medals, menu screens, and some of the animations as well as helping with the 3-D work. His favorite mission so far (he was still on the first Tour of Duty) was Mission 8.

Most Commonly Asked Questions About X-Wing

These questions and answers were provided by the kindly folks at LucasArts' Customer Support. They are the most commonly asked technical questions about playing the X-Wing game. (Any strategic questions have already been answered, of course, within the pages of this book!)

Q: There's snow (little white dots) on my screen! What's causing it?

A: Engine glow from the Imperial Frigates sometimes causes snow. You can turn off the engine glow by going to the in-flight detail screen (press D and then the left or right arrow at the top of the screen) and turn the engine glow to the Off setting.

Q: When I fire my lasers, the game gets really choppy!

A: With SoundBlaster and SoundBlaster Pro, the lasers firing along with the iMUSE score and other ships flying by is sometimes simply too much digitized sound for some machines to handle. To solve any freezing or slowing problems, try setting "digitized sound" to the Off setting. (Press D while in flight, and go to the configuration screen.)

Q: My game is slowing down and looking as though it's starting and stopping.

A: Check to make sure that your joystick is firmly plugged in. Many people experience this problem when their joystick is loose.

Q: My music stops and cuts out while I'm in flight!

A: This random anomaly may occur every 10 or 15 hours of game play. Generally, if you press D while in flight and then return to the simulator, the music returns. If you're having this problem every 10 or 15 *minutes* of game play, be sure to check that your sound card and its accompanying software are installed correctly, and that there are no DMA or IRQ conflicts within your system. (See the README file on your X-Wing disk for more information.)

Q: Sometimes, when something's exploding, my game freezes cold and I have to reboot!

A: This is also a random and relatively rare anomaly. If it occurs more frequently than every 10 to 20 hours of game play, check the computer configuration as mentioned in the preceding question.

Q: Tour of Duty #3 has 14 missions, but I get only 12 ribbons!

A: This is correct. The additional missions are considered to be rewards in themselves.

Q: My Tour of Duty score always says "zero" in the "captured" section!

A: This is correct. In X-Wing, things are never captured [md] only disabled.

Q: Gee, those cut-scene voices have low volume!

A: Because cut-scene voices are sampled, they tend to have lower volume than the music does. If the voices are too low for your taste, you can turn up the volume.

Q: My X-Wing fires only on every other shot!

A: If you have a Roland card and your X-wing is set to single-fire mode, it shoots from only every other S foil.

Q: Any tips for flying the defensive missions?

A: When you first play a mission, find out the names of the flight group or groups that are targeting what you're protecting. Retry the mission and immediately go after that group or groups. Or see *Appendix D*, refer to the mission in question, and see which flight groups are targeting which.

GLOSSARY

Ackbar, Admiral Mon Calamari leader and principal tactician of all the Rebel Alliance's most important missions.

Agamar Keyan Farlander's home world. Located in the Lahara sectior.

Ahsmar A Rebel pilot. He gets killed on a mission with Keyan Farlander.

Alderaan Princess Leia's home planet. It is destroyed by the Death Star.

Antilles, Wedge One of the heroes of the battle of Yavin. He flies as one of Luke's wingmen. Wedge survives the battle.

ASC Alliance Starfighter Corps

Banthas Large, wooly, elephant-like beasts found on many planets in the galaxy and domesticated by a variety of beings.

Basic Common language used throughout the galaxy.

Bestine A planet used by the Empire for a secret military base.

Binka trees Native to Agamar. The grow in a regular spacing, and Keyan used them to practice maneuvers in his T-16 skyhopper.

Bitz bugs Particularly tiny, annoying insectoids found on many planets. There are several varieties.

Blaster A generic term for weapons using packets or beams of intense light energy. Blasters come in all shapes and sizes and are the most commonly employed weapons in the galaxy.

Blastwell, Hamo Ace pilot and Keyan's first orientation officer. Little is known about Hamo's past, but he admits to having met Princess Leia. He's frequently away on mysterious assignments. MIA after Yavin.

Briggia Rebel base before Yavin.

C-3PO A protocol droid in the service of Princess Leia who becomes involved in the plot to destroy the Death Star.

Calamari A water planet, home world of the Calamarians and the Quarren.

Calamarian One of the two dominant races that inhabit Calamari; also, anything to do with Calamari.

Calna Muun A large city on Agamar.

Cardacs Transfer pilot from rogue squadrons to Rebel flagship *Independence*. KIA when acting as Keyan's wingman.

Celanon A planet with two resources: agriculture and Celanon City.

Celanon City Hub of commerce in the Outer Rim of the galaxy.

Chatham House Bail Organa's home in Imperial City, where Mon Mothma and Organa forged the Alliance.

Chewbacca Han Solo's friend; co-pilot of the *Millennium Falcon*.

Chiithii'n Name of the Sullustan navigator on the *Independence*.

Chintassa grass Delicacy grown in specialized farms on various worlds. Features a vaguely spicy flavor and is renowned for its nutritional properties. Usually marinated and steamed.

Combat Multi-view Display (CMD) The sensor readout on a starfighter.

Comm Communication lines, either on-board ship or ship to ship.

Corellian A native to the Corellian system. Notorious spacefarers.

Cron drift An asteroid belt in the Outer Rim.

CRV Abbreviation for Corvette.

Dafid, Wex "TIE Die" Chief tactical training officer for Rebel Starfighter Command.

Darklighter, Biggs Luke's friend on Tatooine who enlists in the Imperial Navy, then defects to the Alliance. KIA at Yavin.

Dellalt A planetary system in the Outer Rim.

Delline, Lynia Half-human aide to Mon Mothma who becomes Keyan's friend.

Dodonna, General Head of Starfighter Command. A member of the Alliance High Command.

Dogfighting Fighting one-on-one in starfighters or atmospheric fighters.

Dontal A Rebel pilot (KIA).

Droid artificially intelligent machine. A robot.

Drutash grubs Edible delicacy of the Sullustan. Offered to Keyan as a reward if he ever visits Sullust.

ELS Engine-Laser-Shield energy array.

Ewok Natives of a moon of the planet Endor.

Farlander, Keyan Young Agamarian who enlists in the Rebel Alliance and becomes a hero flying various starfighters.

Farlander, Kitha Keyan's sister, disfigured during an Imperial attack on her home town. Status unknown.

Fragged Fragmented; ASC slang for destroyed.

FRG Abbreviation for Frigate.

FRT Abbreviation for freighter.

Gamorrean Short, porcine creatures from Gamorr. Belligerent by nature.

Gart, Breth Young Agamarian who becomes a starfighter pilot. KIA during the attack on the Imperial base at Kalla VII.

Ghorman Scene of an infamous massacre credited to the young Tarkin.

Hatcher, B'ante Leader of the Rebellion on Agamar.

Holos 3D imaging system. Refers to the individual holo disks as well as the decks used to view them.

Homeworld A person's planet of origin.

Horansi A particularly competitive card game popular among Rebel pilots.

Horodi A Rebel pilot. KIA during the mission to capture the corvettes *Ethar I* and *II*.

Hoska An animal most often used as a food source; easy to hunt and tasty.

Hyperdrive Complex technology designed to push spacecraft out of realspace and into hyperspace.

Hypered Slang for going into hyperspace.

Hyperspace A dimension of space/time that can be entered at faster-than-light speeds. Although time as we know it is not exactly adhered to in hyperspace, there is a corresponding point-to-point relationship between hyperspace and realspace, thus making it possible to move from one location to another very quickly. Hyperspace jumps require extensive calculations, however, which must be performed by an on-board computer or droid.

Inflight map Pilot's navigational map which shows nearby objects.

ISP Imperial Secret Police.

Jan-lo, Sunnar Agamarian who joins the Alliance with Keyan and becomes a starfighter pilot, then transfers to Intelligence. Current whereabouts classified.

Jedi A mysterious group of highly-trained warriors who helped bring an end to the Clone Wars and established the subsequent peace. Few Jedi survive, as the Emperor has had them killed whenever possible.

Jinking Quick maneuvers used to throw off an enemy's aim during a dogfight.

Kadorto, Halley An early hero of the Alliance; veteran of the Clone Wars. Currently ASC-retired.

Kenobi, Ben The name taken by Obi-Wan Kenobi when he lived as a hermit in the desert on Tatooine.

Kenobi, Obi-Wan Famous Jedi Knight of the Clone Wars. Thought by most to be dead or missing. He becomes Luke Skywalker's mentor.

Kitel Phard An ancient dynasty, predating the Republic.

Klick Military slang for kilometer.

Commander Lagrane Keyan's debriefing officer.

Lahara A sector in the Outer Rim.

Madine, General Crix Commander of Alliance Special Forces.

Marskan, Casal Younger brother of Captain Ernek Marskan. KIA during the operation to recapture *Ethar I* and *II*.

Marskan, Captain Ernek A senior flight leader for Blue Squadron.

Medevac Medical evacuation shuttle craft.

MGLT Unit of sub-light speed.

Mimya Keyan Farlander's aunt on Oort Tchis.

Misch'an A popular pilot sometimes assigned to Red Squadron on the *Independence*.

Moff An uber-governor.

Mothership The "home" ship for a fighter or other smaller craft.

Mon Mothma Elected leader of the Rebel Alliance, and co-founder of the Rebellion with Bail Organa.

Mugruebe stew A special Agamarian dish, not too popular throughout the galaxy. It is usually prepared with roots and a particular tree bark indigenous to Agamar, with chunks of a small mammal about twice the size of a womp rat.

Musti Small, intensely loyal, domesticated creatures used as pets in urban areas. Can be trained to fulfill a variety of roles.

Mutandan porf A pasty blend of grain, meat and spices, generally served with flat bread and eaten with the hands. An acquired taste, but very filling. One of the ingredients seems to contain a slight stimulant.

Mytus VII A notorious prison planet, also known as Stars' End.

Naeco A pilot in Red Squadron who is known for his practical jokes and accurate deflection shooting.

Namrhe A rookie pilot, KIA during a mission to capture Imperial military advisors.

Nebulon-B Frigate A capital ship used by both the Rebels and the Imperial fleet.

Nogdra, Captain Former captain of the captured corvette *Talon*.

Nova The violent end of a star; ASC slang when used as a verb to describe what happens when a ship explodes in battle.

Omin-Oreh Bestinian pilot severely injured during mission to capture Imperial military advisors.

Oorn Tchis A small, rural world where Keyan Farlander's aunt and uncle live. Oorn Tchis is best known for exporting colorful fabrics and a rare ore used in guidance system design.

Organa, Bail Foster father of Princess Leia Organa and a hero of the Clone Wars, he served as Viceroy and First Chairman of the Alderaan system. Founded the Rebellion with Mon Mothma.

Organa, Princess Leia Former senator of the Republic, now a principle member of the Alliance.

Orron III A small world located along a prime Imperial convoy route. Scene of a Rebel attack on an Imperial shipment.

Palpatine, Emperor Former senator of the Republic who declares himself Emperor, disbands the senate, and unleashes a reign of terror and oppression throughout the galaxy. A powerful being in league with the dark side.

Piringiisi A resort spot on Sullust, famous for its caustic green mud baths.

Porkins A former trader and independent pilot who joins the Alliance and flies for a time with Red Squadron. KIA at Yavin.

Poussan, N'dranth Agamarian native who joins the Rebels at the same time as Keyan. KIA in his first mission.

Quarren Natives of the seas of Calamari.

R2 unit An utility droid used for a variety of purposes, including acting as the computer unit for starfighters.

Repulsors Special lifting units designed for work close to surfaces with gravitational pull (i.e. planets, moons, or large capital ships).

Rodian A native of the planet Rodia. Notorious bounty hunters. Greedo is a Rodian bounty hunter killed by Han Solo in the Cantina in Mos Eisley spaceport.

S'man, Commander One of the chief planning officers on board the *Independence*.

Scarns An unusual part of the Sullustan anatomy. You have to be a Sullustan to understand.

Sern Sector An area of the galaxy close to the Core where the famous massacre of Ghorman took place.

SHU Abbreviation for Shuttle.

Skywalker, Luke Hero of Yavin. A native of Tatooine, natural starfighter pilot, and, as it turns out, Princess Leia's brother and Darth Vader's son.

Starfighter A small, mobile, armed spacecraft.

Starship Basically any space-going vehicle. Usually refers to larger craft.

Stormtroopers Intensely loyal Imperial troops.

Sullust Home planet of the Sullustan.

Sullustan Creatures with highly-developed navigational senses.

T-16 Skyhopper Pleasure and sport craft often flown on rural planets. The controls are very similar to those on an X-wing.

Tan'tro Pilot KIA during attack on Imperial weapons convoy.

Tarkin, Grand Moff Chief architect of the Imperial doctrine of "rule by fear," and chief officer in charge of the Death Star project.

Tatooine Small desert planet known more for smuggling and its wild spaceport at Mos Eisley than anything else.

TIE Twin Ion Engine, designation for the Imperial fighter series.

Toalagar Former prisoner from Stars' End, friend of Sam Raider, KIA in mission to rescue Wookiee slaves near Kashyyyk.

Tondatha Home town of Keyan Farlander, destroyed by Imperial forces in retribution for alleged Rebel activities.

Trinn Keyan's uncle on Oort Tchis.

TRN Abbreviation for Transport.

Turbolaser High-powered, quick-firing laser battery.

Tuz A Calamarian pirate working undercover reluctantly for the Alliance.

Vader, Darth, Dark Lord of the Sith Formerly Anakin Skywalker, Luke Skywalker's father, who is now aligned with the dark side of the Force. Left for dead by his Master, Obi-Wan Kenobi, Darth survives in a special outfit with breathing gear and other life support.

Veronian berry wine One of the finest vintages in the galaxy, though many imitations are sold.

Wingman A pilot who flies in a formation with one or more other pilots. The designation of wingman usually implies that this pilot should consider the protection of his flight leader as the highest priority.

Womp Rat Small, quick-moving mammal found on Tatooine and some other systems.

Wookiee Native of the world Kashyyyk.

Wotan Developer of the famous weave technique used by starfighter pilots to avoid enemy fire.

Yavin Large gaseous planet. One of its moons is used temporarily by the Rebels as a military base.

INDEX

D

E

F

G

J

K

L

M

S